Learning Digital Media

Emergent Learning

Pearson

Boston • Columbus • Indianapolis • New York • San Francisco • Upper Saddle River
Amsterdam • Cape Town • Dubai • London • Madrid • Milan • Munich • Paris • Montréal • Toronto
Delhi • Mexico City • São Paulo • Sydney • Hong Kong • Seoul • Singapore • Taipei • Tokyo

330 Hudson Street, New York, NY 10013

Hardcover ISBN 10: 0-13-442743-2
Hardcover ISBN 13: 978-0-13-442743-0

Pearson

1 16

Introduction

Learning Digital Media gives you an introduction to careers in the Web and Digital Communications pathway of the Information Technology career cluster. In addition to exploring the careers available in this pathway, it provides practical experience with the technology applications you will need to pursue these careers, including Adobe Illustrator for graphic design and illustration, Photoshop for photo editing, Premiere Pro for video and audio editing, Flash (renamed Animate in 2016) for animation and game design, and Dreamweaver for design of high-quality Web sites complete with graphics, animation, and more. This book supports the Adobe Creative Cloud versions of these applications. Adobe Creative Cloud gives you access to the most up-to-date tools and features for all Adobe applications.

How the Book is Organized

Learning Digital Media starts with an overview of the Web and Digital Communications career pathway, titled Getting Started. This section explores the careers available in the pathway as well as the businesses and industries that provide employment in these fields. It helps you identify the education and skill requirements necessary for careers in this pathway, as well as employment trends.

After Getting Started, the book includes seven chapters. Chapters 1 and 2 focus on how to use Illustrator for graphic design and illustration. Chapters 3 and 4 cover commercial photography and printing using Photoshop. Chapter 5 explores animation using Flash. Chapter 6 covers audio/video production with Premiere Pro. Finally, Chapter 7 focuses on Dreamweaver for Web site design. Each chapter's lessons introduce a number of application features. You will learn and practice these features as you complete real-world projects such as preparing advertising and marketing materials, designing a Web site, or readying files for various types of output.

Chapters are structured to make the learning process simple and enjoyable. Each lesson begins with a listing of the topics that will be covered in the chapter's lessons, followed by an overview of why those topics are important.

Lesson 7 Overview

In this lesson, you will learn about:

- Starting Photoshop and Opening a File
- Using the Photoshop Tools
- Working with Color in Photoshop
- Working with Tools and Tool Properties
- Exploring Photoshop Panels
- Creating Career Search Documents

Adobe® Photoshop® is a software program used for editing and manipulating digital photographs and other raster images. Recall that raster, or bitmap, images are created by colored pixels arranged side by side in a regular grid. The Adobe Photoshop work area includes menus, toolbars, and panels that give you quick access to a variety of tools and options for editing and adding elements to your image. You can also add commands and filters to the menus by installing third-party software known as plug-ins.

In Photoshop, you primarily work with bitmapped, digitized images but you can also work with vector graphics. You can create original artwork in Photoshop, or you can import images from many sources. These include:

- Photographs from a digital camera or mobile phone
- Stock photography
- Scans of photographs, transparencies, negatives, graphics, or other documents
- Captured video images
- Artwork created in drawing programs

Almost all design and print-related careers require the use of Adobe Photoshop or another similar program. For example, graphic designers, video game designers, and desktop publishers can create and edit artwork, and Web designers can design page layouts or visual elements for a Web site. Artists, designers, and photographers may be self-employed, or they may work in a variety of businesses that employ people who know how to use Adobe Photoshop. Some such businesses include those in advertising, manufacturing, Web development, and publishing.

The lesson's Try It! exercises allow you to practice what you learn about each feature. Each exercise is introduced so you know what you are going to accomplish in the following steps. Numbered steps make it easy for you to complete each part of the project. Frequent illustrations show you how to select settings, as well as show you results you can use to check your progress.

Making Basic Photo Corrections | Lesson 8

Applying a Content Aware Patch

Use the Patch tool to remove unwanted elements from an image. You'll use a content-aware patch to remove an unrelated person from the right side of the photo. In Content-Aware mode, the Patch tool creates nearly seamless blending with the nearby content.

Learn what you're going to do.

Try It!

1. In the Tools panel, select the Patch tool, hidden beneath the Spot Healing Brush tool.
2. In the Options bar, choose Content-Aware from the Patch mode menu. Type 4 into the Structure slider.

   The Structure menu determines how closely the patch reflects the existing image patterns. You can choose from 1 to 7, with 1 allowing the loosest adherence to the source structure and 7 requiring the strictest.

Steps are short and clear.

3. Drag the Patch tool around the boy and his shadow, as closely as possible. You may want to zoom in to see him more clearly.
4. Click within the area you've just selected, and drag it to the left. Photoshop displays a preview of the content that will replace the boy. Keep dragging to the left until the preview area no longer overlaps the area occupied by the boy, but without overlapping the woman or the girl she's holding. Release the mouse button when the patch is positioned where you want it.

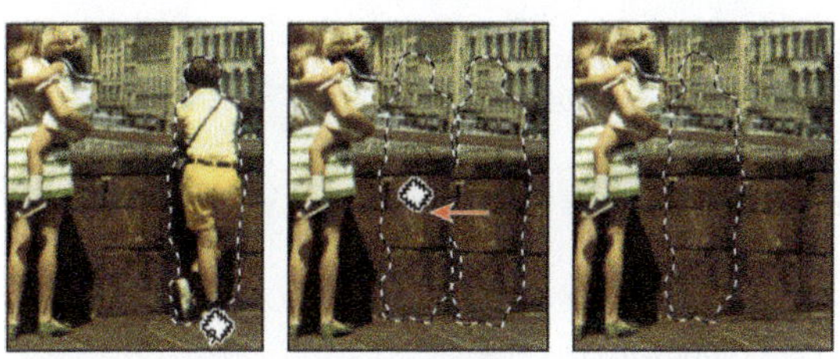

Illustrations help you choose the right settings and check your work.

The selection changes to match the area around it. The boy is gone, and where he stood is a section of the bridge wall and of a building.

Additional text explains the last step and introduces the next step.

5. Choose Select > Deselect.

   The effect was pretty impressive, but not quite perfect. You'll touch up the results next.
6. Save the changes to **L8_start_xx.psd**, and leave it open.

LEARNING DIGITAL MEDIA 233

Exercises include numerous notes that provide helpful tips or alternate methods of performing tasks and definitions of important terms. Feature boxes include more in-depth information on design topics, tools, shortcuts, and professional methodology.

Note:

To apply style sheets to all pages in the Web site, or site root, your site must have a valid http:// address. For this course, you will apply CSS formatting to the current page only.

Named anchor

A named location in a Web page that is used for links on the same page.

Softskills features cover a variety of subjects related to the study of digital communications, audio/video technology, and Web design, such as career preparation, and the skills and qualities a person needs to be a successful employee. Many of these features include review projects that allow you to explore the feature through further research, writing, and designing. Softskills topics include employability skills; legal and ethical issues; communication, teamwork, and leadership; and how to prepare career search materials.

Developing Employability Skills

Employability means having and using skills and abilities to be hired and stay hired, and even advance to higher-level jobs. Once you recognize the skills that make you employable, you can practice and develop them in school and at home, so you are ready to use them on the job.

Transferable Skills

Employability skills can generally be placed into two groups: hard skills and transferable skills. Employers often look for people with hard skills to fill specific jobs. For example, a software development company looks to hire people skilled at writing code.

Transferable skills can be used on almost any job. They are called transferable skills because you can transfer them from one situation or career to another.

Time management is an important transferable skill for succeeding at work. Employers want you to make the most of your time–to them, time is money. That means showing up on time, taking breaks at scheduled times, meeting deadlines, and taking care of personal business on your own time. Making the most of your time demonstrates to your employer that you take your responsibilities seriously.

Planning is an equally important transferable skill. Developing a plan or strategy will help you successfully complete projects and meet goals. Successful planning requires organization and setting priorities for tasks and responsibilities.

Each chapter concludes with review questions designed to remind you of the most important skills and features you have learned and to test your knowledge of the chapter's key points.

Hands-on projects at the end of each chapter give you another chance to practice the skills you have learned. The chapter's Portfolio Builder provides step-by-step instructions on how to complete a project that uses the skills and features covered in the chapter. The Critical Thinking project challenges you to complete a project on your own or with minimal instruction.

Chapter 1 – Portfolio Builder

Selecting and Aligning Practice

As you have learned, selecting objects is an important part of working with Illustrator. In this activity, you will use techniques discussed in this chapter to practice selecting and aligning objects.

1. Choose File > Open, and open the **PB1_start.ai** file from the data files for this lesson. Save the file as **PB1_start_xx.ai** in the location where your teacher instructs you to store the files for this lesson.
2. Click OK in the Illustrator Options dialog box. Choose View > Fit Artboard In Window to fit the artboard in the Document window.
3. Choose View > Smart Guides to temporarily deselect the Smart Guides.
4. With the Selection tool drag the steering wheel shape in the upper-right corner into place. Drag the black rounded rectangle in the upper-left corner of the artboard to the front of the bus.
5. With the Selection tool, select the headlight shapes (the circles) in the lower-right corner of the art-board by dragging a marquee across them. Choose Object > Group.
6. Drag the center of the headlight group to slide it to its new location to the right of the rounded rectangle.
7. Double-click the center of the headlight group to enter Isolation mode. Click to select the white shape and drag it so that it's visually centered on the other shapes. Choose Select > Deselect. Press the Escape key to exit Isolation mode.
8. Click the headlight group to select it, press Alt (Windows) or Option (Mac OS) and drag the head-light group to the left to duplicate it. Release the mouse button, and then the modifier key.
9. Shift-click the rounded rectangle and the headlight group to the right to select all three objects.
10. In the Control panel, choose Align to Selection from the Align To button menu, and then click the Horizontal Distribute Center button. Choose Object > Group.
11. Shift-click the orange shape behind the selected group. Click the orange shape again to make it the key object. Click the Horizontal Align Center button and then the Vertical Align Center button to align the rounded rectangle group to the orange shape.
12. With the Selection tool, Shift-click the orange shape to deselect it. With the group of objects that contains the headlights selected, choose Object > Lock > Selection to keep them in position. You cannot select the shapes until you choose Object > Unlock All.
13. Select the Zoom tool in the Tools panel, and click three times, slowly, on the dome at the top of the bus, above the text, "SCHOOL BUS."

Working with Data and Solution Files

As you work through the projects in this book, you'll be creating, opening, and saving files. Keep the following instructions in mind:

- Most projects will require you to open a data file to begin the project. These files are named with the lesson number and the word "Start"; i.e., **L12_Start.psd**. Additional files may be required to complete some steps; they are generally given a name that relates to their content, such as **terrace.jpg**. Data files for the end-of-chapter projects include the project type and the chapter number; i.e., **PB6.psd**.
- Usually the Start files are saved with a new name. Saving the Start file with a new name preserves the original file in case you want to go back and start over or repeat steps as a review.
- You will be directed to include the initials of your first and last name so you can easily locate your files if you have to share a computer. Solution file names will appear in the text with two xx's to stand for your initials; i.e., **L12_Start_xx.psd**.
- Follow your instructor's directions for where to access and save the files on a network, local computer hard drive, or portable storage device such as a USB drive.

Getting Started

Getting Started

Exploring Careers in Web and Digital Communications

Identifying the Types of Businesses in Web and Digital Communications

Identifying Educational Requirements

Identifying Employment Trends

Exploring Emerging Technologies

Getting Started Overview

In this lesson, you will learn about:

- Explore Careers in Web and Digital Communications
- Identify the Types of Businesses in Web and Digital Communications
- Identify Educational Requirements
- Identify Employment Trends
- Explore Emerging Technologies

Learning Digital Media introduces you to the knowledge, skills, and education requirements for careers in the Web and Digital Communications pathway of the Information Technology career cluster. You will explore the wide range of career areas in this pathway while you develop your skill with the following technology applications:

- Adobe Illustrator® for Graphic Design and Illustration
- Adobe Photoshop® for Photography Editing
- Adobe Flash® for Animation and Game Design
- Adobe Audition® for Audio Editing
- Adobe Premiere Pro® for Video Editing

Exploring Careers in Web and Digital Communications

The career you choose has a major impact on the kind of life you will lead. It determines the type of training and education you will need. It might impact where you live, and the type of lifestyle you achieve.

Career

A chosen field of work in which you try to advance over time by gaining responsibility and earning more money.

Career Cluster

Categories used to identify occupations in a similar area or industry.

Pathway

A group of jobs within a career cluster.

The Web and Digital Communications **pathway** prepares you for a career that involves creating, designing, and producing interactive multimedia products and services used in business, training, entertainment, communications, and marketing. The U.S. Department of Education organizes careers into 16 **career clusters**. Career clusters help you sort career possibilities into 16 manageable groups. (You can find information on all the career clusters at the careertech.org Web site.) The Web and Digital Communications pathway falls under the Information Technology career cluster. This pathway prepares you for careers in developing and creating digitally generated or computer-enhanced media that is used to communicate with existing and potential customers, provide information and training, and collaborate with others.

The courses you can take now that will help prepare you for a career in Web and digital communications include computer programming, computer graphics, graphic design, Web page design, Internet marketing, interactive media, animation, digital video production, and game design and authoring.

People who find satisfaction working in Web and digital communications careers are generally interested in providing entertaining and thought-provoking information in creative ways. Individuals in this profession must have effective communication skills, a willingness to learn new software applications and systems, and the ability to recognize and critique creative work. Those who work in programming careers, such as Web developers and video game designers, must also possess strong mathematical and scientific skills. Some personal qualities that are helpful for success in these careers include:

- Creativity
- Confidence
- Detail-oriented
- Resourcefulness

Many careers in this pathway require both technical and artistic skills. A Web designer, for example, creates the look, layout, and features of a Web site. An individual in this job must have design skills to create an attractive product that engages visitors to the Web site, but he or she should also be familiar with Web programming languages. Other careers in Web and digital communications are listed in the following table.

Career	Description and Duties/Tasks
Animator	Uses computer programs to create graphics, animation, and visual effects for television, movies, video games, and other forms of media
Audio/Video Engineer	Operates, maintains, and repairs equipment, such as microphones, video recorders, projectors, lighting, and sound mixing equipment
Digital Media Designer	Uses computer programs to develop visual design and animation for computers, Web pages, mobile devices, and digital videos
Instructional Technologist	Develops computer training materials and often assists in teaching computer applications
Media Specialist	Coordinates audio-visual equipment and materials; sets up and operates requested software and equipment; inventory and maintain supplies, equipment, and available material
Multimedia Author	Creates content such as educational tools, advertising materials, and video games, for the Internet, computers, mobile devices, and video game systems
Producer	Supervises creation of digital content, such as blogs, Web-based publications, DVDs, training materials, marketing presentations, podcasts, and video games. Responsible for hiring artists and technicians, overseeing idea development and execution, and managing budgets.
Programmer	Uses programming languages to combine multimedia assets, such as text, sound, graphics, digital photography, animation, and video, to create online and interactive products and services
Web Designer	Creates the look, layout, and features of a Web site.
Web Developer	Writes code using Web-specific programming languages to build functionally sound Web sites
Webmaster	Maintains a Web site by examining traffic through the site, reviewing search engine optimization, generating and revising Web pages, and interacting with users/visitors to the site
Social Networking Specialist	Builds and executes social media strategy; generates, edits, publishes, and shares daily content; moderates all user-generated content; and creates editorial calendars and syndication schedules
Search Engine Marketing Specialist	Manages search engine optimization (SEO) activities such as content strategy, link building, and keyword strategy to increase rankings on all major search networks

Identifying the Types of Businesses in Web and Digital Communications

If you pursue a career in Web and digital communications, you could end up working for just about any type of business or employer in any type of industry. That's because these days, most organizations use online technology and electronic communications to reach a target market or desired audience, whether it's the local coffee shop wanting to attract customers or the regional medical center providing healthy living tips or the national corporation advertising a new product.

Many jobs in Web and digital communications are based in the information and communications technology industry at businesses such as the following:

- computer manufacturers
- software development companies
- video gaming companies
- telecommunications firms
- Internet service providers

Other opportunities can be found in any of the following industries:

- Advertising and marketing
- Finance and insurance
- Retail
- Engineering
- Manufacturing
- Health care
- Recreation and leisure
- Transportation
- Internet and traditional publishing
- Broadcasting
- Motion picture and video recording
- Education and academia

In addition, jobs can be found with charitable and nonprofit organizations, and in the technical and communications departments of local, state, and federal government agencies.

Identifying Educational Requirements

The educational requirements for careers in Web and digital communications vary, depending on the area in which you are interested. Most jobs in this pathway require a two- or four-year college degree. Employers in this industry are often looking for workers who can bring a combination of technical, creative, and business skills to the job. For this reason, areas of study often include a combination of both design- and technology related courses in the following areas:

- Business information systems
- Computing and computer science
- Filmmaking and digital photography
- Fine art
- Graphic design
- Multimedia design
- Software development
- Web development and design

In addition, some occupations may require certification in a commonly used computer software program. Adobe, for example, offers certification on many of its software applications such as Adobe Flash or Photoshop. To obtain certification, you typically must complete a course on the program.

Identifying Employment Trends

Will there be jobs for graphic designers when I get out of school? Are there more jobs in Texas for animators or authors? Is the salary for Web designers increasing or decreasing? One way to learn the answers to these questions is to look at **employment trends**. Sometimes trends in a specific field or industry are called the **job outlook**, which means it is a forecast or prediction about trends affecting that job. Analyzing employment trends can help you compare and evaluate job opportunities.

Employment trend
One way the job market changes over time.

Job outlook
A forecast or prediction about trends affecting that job.

Employment trends include things such as the number of jobs in a certain industry. For example, experts see a growing number of jobs in the software development industry, but a shrinking need for workers in the manufacture of audio and video equipment. Other employment trends include where the jobs are. For example, are businesses opening offices in Texas and closing them in the Northeast?

Salaries and job outlook for careers in Web and digital communications vary. According to the U.S. Bureau of Labor Statistics (BLS), the median annual pay for computer programmers is about $77,500; Web designers earn roughly $63,500; and multimedia artists and animators can expect to make about $63,300 a year. Employment prospects for those in digital media careers is good. According to the BLS, employment in computer and information technology occupations is expected to grow 12 percent between 2014 and 2024. This is due in part to an increasing demand for multimedia artwork, advanced special effects in video, more sophisticated video games, and expanding mobile technologies.

Exploring Emerging Technologies

You will encounter new trends when you start your career, in the workplace in general and in the field of digital media. Typically, new technologies are used in the workplace when they save time and money compared with traditional ways of working. Just as USB flash drives have replaced burnable CD-ROMs, so new technology trends have begun to replace more time-consuming or inefficient ways of working in many areas of business. Consider some of these cutting-edge and emerging technologies and how they speed up our work.

- *Videoconferencing* enables people to meet "face-to-face" without having to travel any distance at all. By setting up two video cameras and establishing an Internet link, employees at distant offices are able to see and speak to each other without spending time and money on traveling.
- *Collaborative software* allows more than one person to work on a document at one time. For example, more than one person at a time, working at different computers in different locations, can work on the same word processing document, spreadsheet, or presentation. Collaboration software increases productivity. It also saves time, money, and trees (paper).
- Cloud computing and virtualization make computers more efficient by using centralized storage, memory, and processing. *Cloud computing* uses the Internet and central remote servers to host data and applications. *Virtualization* is when physical storage is pooled from multiple network storage devices into what seems to be one single storage device managed from a central console.
- Not all repetitive tasks must be done by people anymore, thanks to automation software. Skilled programmers can create scripts that use the power of a computer to complete tasks that are repetitive, time-consuming, and boring. For instance, most computers can now perform data backups, software updates, and virus scans automatically. Another example is software that lets a computer calculate large data-sets using only a few bits of user input.
- *Software as a Service* makes computer applications available for use online; for example, Microsoft Office suite online and Adobe Creative Cloud. For free or a subscription fee, users can access the applications using an Internet connection instead of installing the program on their own computer or mobile device.
- Now that so many objects have embedded computer chips, *pervasive computing* applications are emerging that let users interact with their things. For example, applications make it possible for you to use voice activated telephone calling in your car and to program your dishwasher to alert you when it is full. Also referred to as the *Internet of Things*, pervasive computing is basically a network between devices (both tech and non-tech) that allow them to send and receive data.
- An emerging category of virtual reality is called *augmented reality*. Cameras in mobile devices are used to layer virtual information onto real information. One example is a smart phone app for translation. When you point your phone at foreign language text, the English translation displays on the screen. Head-mounted displays (HMDs) that allow for images to be superimposed over real-world images allow a computer to interact with the physical world. These HMDs have lenses that use optical mixers to display digital images without blocking real-world images. Google Glasses are an HMD that allows for mixed reality, or the combination of the real world and digital information.

Comprehension Check

1. Define the Web and Digital Communications pathway.
2. What are some of the courses you can take now to prepare for a career in Web and digital communications?
3. Why does a career in Web and digital communications often require both technical and artistic or creative skills?
4. What is an employment trend?
5. List at least two emerging technologies and the software that would be required to implement them to develop projects in a Web and digital communications career.

Review Project

Select and research a career that interests you in the Web and Digital Communications pathway. The careertech.org Web site is a good source of information on the pathways in each career cluster. Make a column chart that lists the types of businesses that employ professionals in your selected career, as well as the experience, education requirements, training opportunities, and available certifications for that career. Use the information to write a help wanted advertisement or job posting for your selected career. Include the education requirements, training, and skills an employer might be looking for and a starting salary. Share your ad with a partner or with the class.

Chapter 1

Introduction to Digital Design & Illustration

Lesson 1 | Getting to Know the Illustrator Work Area

Lesson 2 | Techniques for Selecting Artwork in Illustrator

Lesson 3 | Using Shapes to Create Artwork for a Postcard in Illustrator

End-of-Chapter Activities

Lesson 1 Overview

In this lesson, you will learn about:

- Working with Graphics
- Identifing Graphics Programs
- Exploring the Elements of Layout and Design
- Exploring the Principles of Design
- Starting Illustrator and Opening a File
- Exploring the Workspace
- Changing the View of Artwork
- Navigating Multiple Artboards
- Using the Navigator Panel
- Finding Information Online
- Examining Intellectual Property Laws
- Evaluating Information for Accuracy and Validity

This lesson introduces you to digital graphics and the Adobe® Illustrator® software program, which is used to create and edit graphics and other artwork. In Illustrator, you primarily create and work with vector graphics (sometimes called vector shapes or vector objects). Vector graphics (below, left) are made up of lines and curves defined by mathematical objects called Bezier curves. You can freely move or modify vector graphics without losing detail or clarity because they are resolution-independent. In other words, vector graphics maintain crisp edges when resized, printed to a PostScript printer, saved in a PDF file, or imported into a vector-based graphics application. As a result, vector graphics are the best choice for artwork, such as logos, that will be used at various sizes and in various output media.

Illustrator also allows you to incorporate raster images—also called bitmaps—that use a rectangular grid of picture elements (pixels) to represent the visual (below, right). Each pixel is assigned a specific location and color value. Raster images can be created in a program like Adobe® Photoshop®.

The ability to use a program such as Illustrator is a valuable skill for many careers in many businesses. Digital media designers, for example, might use Illustrator to create images for animation, artwork for a Web page, or an entire publication. They may work at advertising and marketing agencies, or they may work in the communications or design department of a business that produces its own publications and online content. They may be self-employed, and take work from many different types of companies. Examples of some things they may do include illustrating books, designing Web pages, and creating two-and three-dimensional models.

Working with Graphics

In day-to-day speech, people use the word **graphic** to refer to any visual image or object. A family photo, a road map, and a stick figure drawn on a chalkboard are all examples of graphics. When people talk about a computer graphic, they usually are referring to a digital image. Images include drawings, painted backgrounds, and photographs. Computer graphics can be displayed in a variety of ways. They can appear on the screen as a background, or they can be placed into a document to add color and information. Thus, in the broadest sense of the term, **computer graphic** could refer to anything that can be seen on the computer or device screen.

Graphic

Refers to any visual image or object.

Computer Graphic

Anything that can be seen on the computer and device screen.

Types of Digital Graphics

The most common ways to create digital graphics are using a graphics program, by scanning printed content, or by using a digital camera. The digital images can be transferred and saved as files on a storage device, such as a hard drive, a network drive, or a flash drive. Graphics may stand on their own, or be inserted into a different application file using the Insert Picture or Insert Clip Art command. In the application, you can usually modify them to suit your needs. For example, you can crop unwanted areas, change the height, width or scale, and position them on the page.

There are hundreds of different uses for computer graphics. However, graphics fall into only two categories: raster graphics and vector graphics.

A **raster graphic** or bitmap, is an image formed by a pattern of dots. Imagine a sheet of graph paper with each of its squares filled in with a certain color to make a picture. If seen from far enough away, the picture will look clear, and the squares won't be noticed. But up close, you can see the individual squares of the graph paper.

Raster Graphic

An image formed by a pattern of dots called pixels. Also called a bitmap.

Raster graphics are composed of tiny dots of different colors. Each single point in the image is a pixel, short for "picture element." The smaller the pixels in the image, the smoother it will look. The more colors in the image, the brighter and sharper the image will look.

Some common raster file formats include:

- Graphics Interchange Format (GIF)
- Joint Photographic Experts Group (JPG)
- Portable Network Graphics (PNG)
- Windows Bitmap (BMP)
- Tagged Image File Format (TIF)

Some formats are used for images on Web pages, while others are used for icons and images in the operating system. In Windows, these same abbreviations are used as the file extensions. A file ending in .gif, for example, is in the GIF file format.

Raster graphics are preferred for some types of images. They often are used for photos or images that require backgrounds. They use **layers**, or stacks of information, to create a graphic. Imagine three or four sheets of wax paper, each with a different part of a drawing. When all of them are stacked, the complete picture is visible. You can edit each layer separately. Changes only affect the layer you are working on. The default layer is the background. You can add or delete layers as needed. The layer you're working with is usually highlighted in a color. You can hide a layer you're not using to see other parts of the image.

Layers

Stacks of information placed on top of each other to create a graphic.

Vector Graphic

An image that is created using paths or lines defined by mathematical objects called Bezier curves.

A **vector graphic** is an image that is created using paths or lines called Bezier curves. A vector image tells the computer where a line starts and where it ends. It allows the computer to figure out how to connect the two points. The lines can form shapes, which may be filled with a color or pattern.

Encapsulated PostScript, or EPS, is one of several formats commonly used for vector art. EPS files contain the information that a printer needs in order to print a graphic correctly. The information is combined with a small sketch of what the graphic should look like. The sketch inside an EPS file allows you to preview an image on-screen. This way, you can be sure the image is correct before printing it.

Importing and Exporting

Importing

Bringing information, such as a graphic, from one file into another file.

Exporting

When data is saved in a format that can be used in another application.

Bringing information, such as a graphic, into a file from another file is called **importing**. Once imported, the image can then be modified or expanded.

Exporting is when data is saved in a format that can be used in another application. When you export a graphic, you must consider how it will be used, and select an appropriate format that balances quality and file size.

Image Quality

Two basic qualities affect how every raster image will appear. Size, the height and width of the graphic, is normally measured either in pixels or in inches. Resolution tells how many pixels are in a certain piece of an image. Resolution also determines the quality of the computer image. Resolution is usually measured in dots per inch, or dpi. An image that is 1 inch square at 72 dpi will contain a total of 5,184 pixels (72 × 72). Generally, the higher the resolution, the sharper the image will look.

Vector graphics are created using lines or paths rather than pixels. Thus, the number of dots per inch is not a concern when changing the size of vector graphics. If a raster image is enlarged to twice its normal size, it will look fuzzy and jagged. A vector image can be enlarged to any size and keep its quality.

Converting Graphics

If you want to use a graphic that is in a format your program does not support, you may have to convert it. You can use a file conversion program, or open the file and use the Save As command to save it in a different file format. File conversion is also required if you want to change a vector graphic to a raster graphic, or vice versa.

Vector-to-Raster Graphics

Vector graphics must be changed to pixels before the image can be edited in a paint program.

Raster-to-Vector Graphics

Tracing

A process used to convert raster graphics to vector graphics.

Converting raster graphics to vectors requires a special process called **tracing**. Tracing requires special software and can be complicated when an image has a lot of color and detail.

Working with Clip Art

It is not always necessary to create an image from scratch. Instead, you can start with clip art (graphics files that come with a program) or stock image services that you download from the Internet.

- Clip art in a raster format (such as GIF, JPG, or PNG) can be imported into a paint document. The art then can be edited like any other raster graphic.
- Vector art can be imported in a draw program and modified. If the image is complex, it can be ungrouped. Its individual parts can then be edited or moved.

Identifying Graphics Programs

Different programs allow you to create, edit, and view different graphic file types. Choosing the right program depends on which type of graphic you are working with and what your project needs are. Many application programs including Microsoft Word and PowerPoint come with built-in basic tools for creating and editing drawings and photos. However, professionals will almost certainly need a full-featured program with advanced drawing and editing tools.

A **paint program**, such as Adobe® Photoshop® allows you to create a new raster image. Paint programs also allow you to open a raster image, view it on-screen, and make changes to it. Microsoft Windows comes with a basic paint program called Paint. An advanced paint program is called an **image editor**. Image editors are designed for editing raster images and are used for adding special effects to photographs. Photoshop and Adobe® Photoshop® Elements are image editors.

Draw programs, such as Adobe® Illustrator,® let you to create and edit vector images. Since draw programs focus on vector images, they make editing easy. You can change the size of an image or add color to it.

Paint Programs

Programs used to create, open, view, and edit raster images.

Image Editors

An advanced paint program designed for editing raster images.

Draw Programs

Programs used to create and edit vector images.

Interacting with the Program

A variety of different input tools allow you to work easily with a graphics program. Use a mouse to select part of an image or to activate tools on the toolbar. You can perform other functions by dragging, releasing, or double-clicking the mouse.

A graphics tablet is a piece of hardware used for drawing or inking. The user moves a stylus or pointing device over the drawing surface. The tablet senses the movement of the stylus and moves the cursor on-screen. As the cursor moves, it creates on the screen the image that is being drawn on the tablet. The skills for writing with a stylus on a tablet are quite different than writing with a pen and will take some time to master. Some tablet computers combine the features of a graphics tablet with the functions of a personal computer.

Pixar Animation Studios

You may have never heard the name *Pixar*, but you've probably heard of their animated films. *Toy Story* and *Monsters, Inc*. are just two examples of their work. These films were created using computers. Pixar films are known for their realistic cartoon characters. Some aspects of creating these characters involved technology similar to the draw and paint programs and image editors discussed in this lesson.

After final drawings or clay models of the characters were approved, 3-D models were designed on computers. Next, designers considered movements and expressions. They looked at photos of live actors in various positions and with different expressions to get an idea of how each figure should move. Animators then used Pixar's animation software to make the images come to life with movements and expressions.

Exploring the Elements of Layout and Design

The elements of layout and design are qualities or basic units that help define visual communications. They apply to any kind of design, from illustrations to photography to the layout of a printed or digital page or publication. Understanding the elements of layout and design and how they work together is important to creating effective and engaging digital media products. The elements of layout and design include the following:

- **Color**— Property of an image that depends on the light it reflects. Each individual color has its own hue, value, and saturation. Hue is the base color, like blue or red. Value is the color's brightness; adding black or white to the color changes the value. Saturation is the colors intensity. Colors are also related to each other. If they are complementary color's they are on opposite sides of the color wheel.
- **Line**–Path between two points. Considered the most basic of design elements, line can be used to express many concepts and emotions. The direction of a line suggests movement; the weight of a line suggests strength vs. weakness; and the character of a line (squiggly, elongated curves, or simply straight up and down) can suggest emotions such as frustration, contentment, or division.
- **Shape**— Form of something, or perceivable area. Graphics are made up of many shapes, such as triangles and circles.
- **Size**–How big or small something is. Size plays an important role in a layout's functionality, organization, and ability to attract attention.
- **Space**–The placement of lines and shapes on a two-dimensional surface. The illusion of three-dimensional space and depth is achieved through perspective, such as backgrounds, light, shades, shadow, and linear effects.
- **Texture**–Actual or simulated tactile quality or feel of a surface.
- **Type**–Text placed in a graphic. Like line, type is a fundamental design element that is useful in conveying emotions and moods.

The elements are the building blocks that define the composition of a graphic or image. The way they relate to each other – whether it is on canvas, a computer monitor, fabric, or in print is an important consideration for every designer.

Color

Property of an image that depends on the light it reflects.

Line

Path between two points.

Shape

The form of something, or perceivable area.

Space

The placement of lines and shapes on a two-dimensional surface.

Texture

Actual or simulated tactile quality or feel of a surface.

Type

Text placed in a graphic.

Exploring the Principles of Design

The principles of design are the qualities that describe the way the elements of layout and design work together. These include the following:

- **Balance**—The relationship between elements in the graphic; are arranged or distributed. Symmetrical balance is when elements are arranged evenly on both sides; asymmetrical balance is when elements are arranged unevenly.
- **Contrast**—The differences between objects or elements in the graphic.
- **Emphasis**–Focal point(s) within a graphic, usually defined through the use of perspective elements, such as light, shades, shadows, size, and linear effects.
- **Harmony**–Unified arrangement of elements, such as colors, textures, and lines.
- **Proportion**—The size and location of one object in relation to other objects.
- **Repetition**–Using the same color, shape, size, or other element repeatedly within the graphic.
- **Unity**–Connection of objects or elements through style, shape, color, etc.
- **Variety**–Combination of visual elements to establish relationships and achieve interest.

Balance

The relationship between elements in the graphic; or the way elements are arranged or distributed.

Contrast

Differences between objects or elements in a graphic.

Emphasis

Focal point(s) within a graphic.

Harmony

Unified arrangement of elements, such as colors, textures, and lines.

Proportion

The size and location of one object in relation to other objects

Repetition

Using the same color, shape, or other element repeatedly within the graphic.

Unity

Connection of objects or elements through style, shape, color, etc.

Variety

Combination of visual elements to establish relationships and achieve interest.

Graphic Artist

A graphic artist creates the design and layout of different products, such as advertisements, brochures, Web sites, CD-ROMs/DVDs, and apps used on and mobile devices. They design or acquire images and choose and edit text features to communicate a message.

An art degree, courses in graphic arts or design, and recent experience using related software are important qualifications for this career.

Starting Illustrator and Opening a File

Try It!

To Launch Illustrator on a Macintosh:

Do one of the following:

- On the startup drive, open the Applications > Adobe Illustrator CC 2015 folder, then double-click the Adobe Illustrator CC 2015 application icon.
- To launch Illustrator by opening a file, double-click an Illustrator file icon or drag an Illustrator file icon over the application icon in the Dock.
- Press F4 on the keyboard to start apple Launchpad, then click the Illustrator application icon.

To Launch Illustrator in Windows:

Do one of the following:

- In Windows 8, display the Start screen, then click the tile for Adobe Illustrator CC 2015.

- In Windows 10, click the Start button, choose All Programs, then click Adobe Illustrator CC 2015.
- Double-click an Illustrator file icon (the file will open and Illustrator will launch).

1. Choose Window > Workspace > Reset Essentials to ensure that the workspace is set to the default settings.
2. Choose File > Open, to open the L1_start1.ai file from the data files for this lesson.

   This file contains a fictitious business name, address, and website address made up for the purposes of the project.
3. Click Disable Sync Settings if the sync dialog window appears.
4. Choose View > Fit Artboard In Window.

   This fits the active artboard into the Document window so that you can see the entire artboard. As you'll soon learn, an artboard is the area that contains your printable artwork.
5. If the Libraries panel is displayed, click the word "Libraries" in the panel tab on the right to collapse it.

When the file is open and Illustrator is fully launched, the Application bar, menus, Tools panel, Control panel, and panel groups appear on the screen. Docked on the right side of the screen, you will see that default panels appear as icons. Illustrator also consolidates many of your most frequently accessed options in the Control panel below the menu bar. This lets you work with fewer visible panels and gives you a larger area in which to work.

You will use the **L1_start1.ai** file to practice navigating, zooming, and investigating an Illustrator document and the workspace.

6. Choose File > Save As.
7. Save the file as **L1_start1_xx.ai** in the location where your teacher instructs you to store the files for this lesson.

8. Leave the Format option (Mac) and the Save as type option (Windows) set to Adobe Illustrator.

9. Click Save. In the Illustrator Options dialog box, leave the options at their default settings and click OK.

   The Illustrator Options dialog box contains options that control how the file is saved, in which version of Illustrator it's saved, and more.

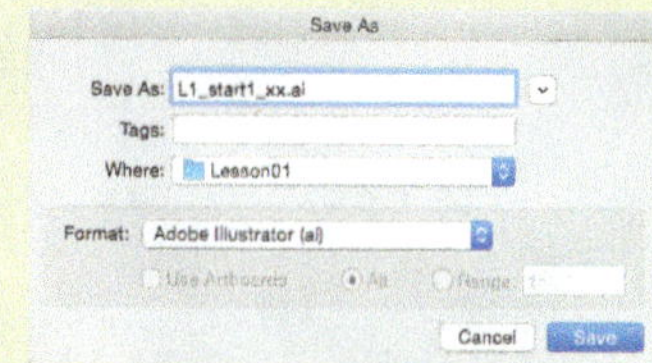

Replace xx with your initials or full name, as instructed by your teacher.

Exploring the Workspace

You create and manipulate your documents and files using various elements, such as panels, bars, and windows. Any arrangement of these elements is called a **workspace**. When you first start Illustrator, you see the default workspace called Essentials, which you can customize for the tasks you perform. You can create and save multiple workspaces—one for editing and another for viewing, for example—and switch among them as you work.

Workspace

Any arrangement of panels, bars and windows in an Adobe application.

The areas of the default workspace are described below.

Note:

The figures in this lesson are taken using the Mac operating system and may look slightly different from what you see if you are using a Windows system.

Note:

The Tools panel shown here has one column. You may see a two-columns Tools panel, depending on your screen resolution and workspace.

A. The **Application bar** across the top contains a workspace switcher, a menu bar (Windows only, depending on screen resolution), and application controls.

B. The **Control panel** displays options for the currently selected object.

C. **Panels** help you monitor and modify your work. Certain panels are displayed by default, and you can display any panel by choosing it from the Window menu. Many panels have menus with panel-specific options. Panels can be grouped, stacked, docked, or free-floating.

D. The **Tools panel** contains tools for creating and editing images, artwork, page elements, and more. Related tools are grouped together.

E. The **Document window** displays the file you're working on.

F. The **Status bar** appears at the lower-left edge of the Document window. It displays information, zooming, and navigation controls.

Working with the Tools Panel

The Tools panel contains selection tools, drawing and painting tools, editing tools, viewing tools, the Fill and Stroke boxes, drawing modes, and screen modes. As you work through the lessons, you'll learn about the specific function of each tool.

Tip:

You can turn the tool tips on or off by choosing Illustrator > Preferences > General (Mac) or Edit > Preferences > General (Windows) and deselecting Show Tool Tips.

1. Position the pointer over the Selection tool in the Tools panel. Notice that the name (Selection tool) and keyboard shortcut (V) are displayed.

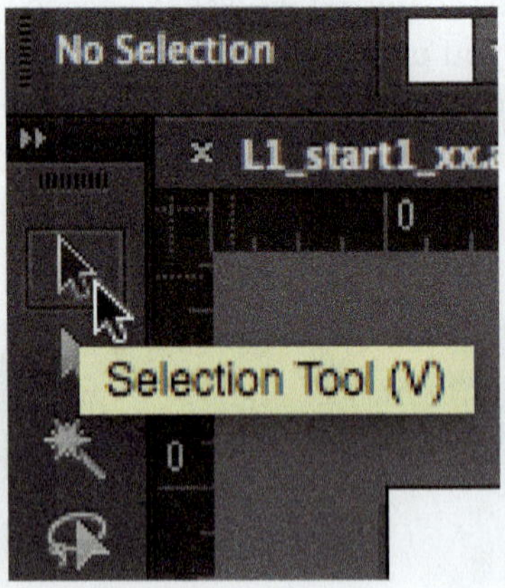

Tip:

You can also select hidden tools by pressing the Option key (Mac) or Alt key (Windows) and clicking the tool in the Tools panel. Each click selects the next hidden tool in the hidden tool sequence.

2. Position the pointer over the Direct Selection tool, and click and hold down the mouse button. You'll see additional selection tools appear in a menu. Click the Group Selection tool to select it.

Any tool in the Tools panel that displays a small triangle contains additional tools that can be selected in this way.

3. Click and hold down the mouse button on the Rectangle tool to reveal more tools. Click the arrow at the right edge of the hidden tools panel to separate the tools from the Tools panel so that you can access them at all times.

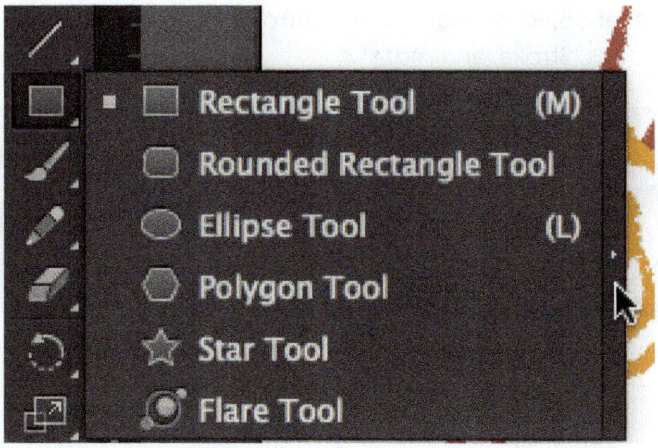

4. Click the Close button (X) in the upper-left corner (Mac) or upper-right corner (Windows) on the floating tool panel's title bar to close it. The tools return to the Tools panel.

   Next, you'll learn how to resize and float the Tools panel. In the figures in this lesson, the Tools panel is a double column by default. You may see a single-column Tools panel to start with, depending on your screen resolution and workspace, and that's okay.

5. Click the double arrow in the upper-left corner of the Tools panel to either expand the one column into two columns or collapse the two columns into one (depending on your screen resolution). Click the double arrow again to expand or collapse the Tools panel.

6. Click the dark-gray title bar at the top of the Tools panel or the dashed line beneath the title bar, and drag the panel into the workspace. The Tools panel is now floating in the workspace.

7. To dock the Tools panel again, drag its title bar or the dashed line below it to the left side of the screen (Mac) or Application window (Win). When the pointer reaches the left edge, a translucent blue border, called the drop zone, appears. Release the mouse button to dock the Tools panel neatly into the side of the workspace.

8. Save **start1_xx.ai** and leave it open.

> **Tip:**
>
> You can click the double arrow at the top of the Tools panel or double-click the title bar at the top of the Tools panel to switch between two columns and one column. Just be careful not to click the X.

Exploring the Control Panel

The Control panel is the panel that's docked at the top of the workspace, just above the docked Tools panel. It offers quick access to options, commands, and other panels relevant to the currently selected content. You can click the underlined text like "Stroke" or "Opacity" to display its panel.

Try It!

1. Select the Selection tool in the Tools panel, and click the letter "f" in the word "fiber" in the artwork on the artboard.

   Notice that options for that object appear in the Control panel, including the word "Group," color options, Stroke, and more.

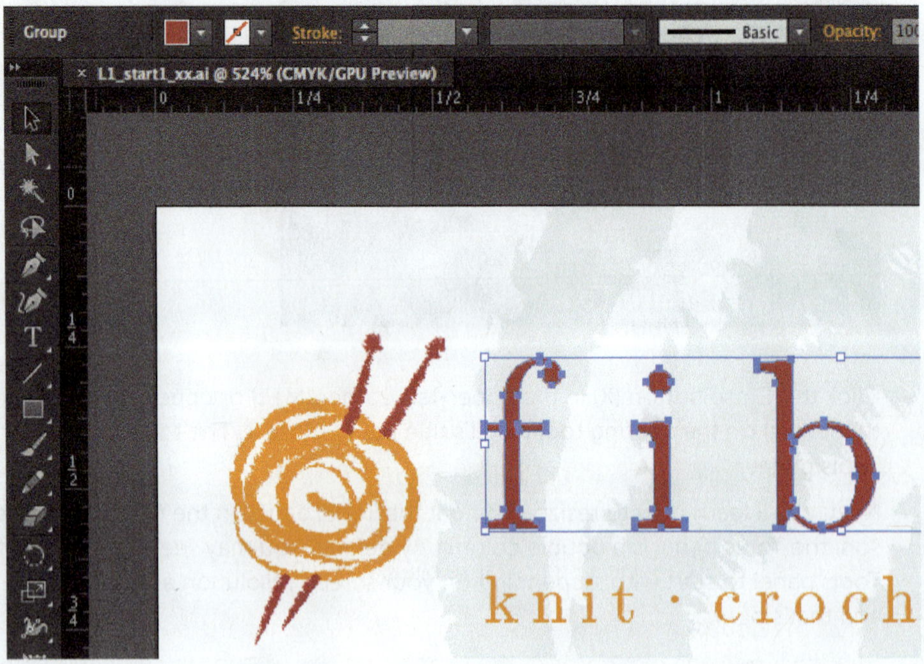

2. Click on and drag the gripper bar (the dashed line along the left edge) of the Control panel into the workspace.

   Once the Control panel is free-floating, you can drag the dark-gray gripper bar that appears on the left edge of the Control panel to move it to the top or bottom of the workspace.

3. Drag the Control panel by the gripper bar on the left edge of the panel. When the pointer reaches the bottom of the Application bar, to the right of the Tools panel, a blue line appears indicating the drop zone. When you release the mouse button, the panel is docked.

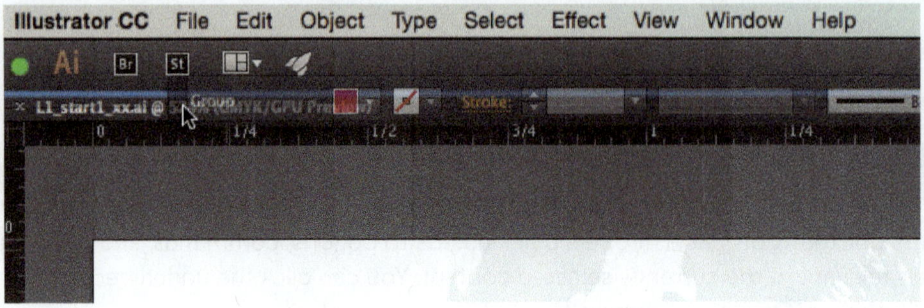

4. Choose Select > Deselect so that the content on the artboard is no longer selected.

5. Save the **L1_start1_xx.ai** file and leave it open.

Tip:

The Control panel can be dragged by the dark-gray gripper bar on the left edge to the bottom of the screen (Mac) or Application window (Windows). When the pointer (not the panel) reaches the bottom of the screen (Mac) or Application window (Windows), a blue line appears, indicating the drop zone in which it will be docked. You can then release the mouse button to dock it.

Working with Panels

Panels, which are listed alphabetically on the Window menu, give you quick access to many tools that make modifying artwork easier. By default, some panels are docked and appear as icons on the right side of the workspace.

Next, you'll experiment with hiding, closing, and opening panels.

Try It!

1. First, choose Reset Essentials from the workspace switcher in the upper-right corner of the Application bar to reset the panels to their original location.
2. Click the Swatches panel icon on the right side of the workspace to expand the panel, or choose Window > Swatches.

   Notice that the Swatches panel appears with two other panels—the Brushes panel and the Symbols panel. They are all part of the same panel group.
3. Click the Symbols panel tab to view the Symbols panel.
4. Now click the Color panel icon in the dock. Notice that a new panel group appears and that the panel group that contained the Swatches panel collapses.
5. Click and drag the gripper bar at the bottom of the Color panel down to resize the panel, showing more of the color spectrum.
6. Click the Color panel icon to collapse the panel group.
7. Click the double arrow at the top of the dock to expand the panels. Click the double arrow again to collapse the panels. Use this method to show more than one panel group at a time. Your panels may look different when expanded, and that's okay.

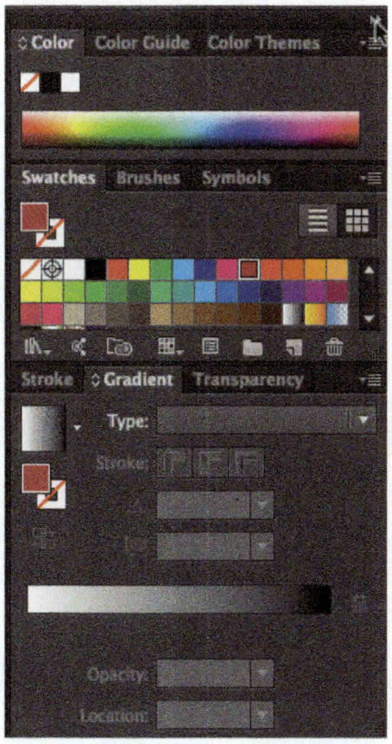

Tip:

To find a hidden panel, choose the panel name from the Window menu. A check mark to the left of the panel name indicates that the panel is already open and in front of other panels in its panel group. If you choose a panel name that is already selected in the Window menu, the panel and its group collapse.

8. To increase the width of all the panels in the dock, drag the left edge of the docked panels to the left until text appears. To decrease the width, click and drag the left edge of the docked panels to the right until the text disappears.

9. Choose Window > Workspace > Reset Essentials to reset the workspace.
10. Drag the Swatches panel icon away from the dock to remove the panel from the dock and make it a free-floating panel. Notice that the panel stays collapsed as an icon when it is free-floating.
11. Click the double arrow in the Swatches panel title bar to expand the panel so you can see its contents.

    You can also move panels from one panel group to another. In this way, you can create custom panel groups that contain the panels you use most often.

12. Drag the Swatches panel by the panel tab, the panel title bar, or the area behind the panel tab onto the Brushes and Symbols panel icons. Release the mouse button when you see a blue line between the panel icons and an outline around the Brushes panel group.

Tip:

To close a panel, drag the panel away from the dock and click the X in the panel title bar. You can also right-click a docked panel tab or panel icon and choose Close from the menu.

Next, you'll organize the panels to create more room in your workspace.

13. Choose Reset Essentials from the workspace switcher in the Application bar to make sure that the panels are reset to their default state.
14. Click the double arrow at the top of the dock to expand the panels.

Note:

Many panels only require that you double-click the panel tab twice to return to the full-size view of the panel. If you double-click one more time, the panel fully expands.

15. Click the Color Guide panel tab to make sure it's selected. Double-click the panel tab to reduce the size of the panel. Double-click the tab again to minimize the panel. This can also be done when a panel is free-floating (not docked).

16. Save the **L1_start1_xx.ai** file and leave it open.

Using Panel Menus

Most panels have more options that are available in a panel menu. Clicking the panel menu icon in the upper-right corner gives you access to additional options for the selected panel, including changing the panel display in some cases.

Next, you will change the display of the Symbols panel using its panel menu.

> **Tip:**
>
> To reduce and expand the panel size, instead of double-clicking the panel tab, you can click the small arrow icon to the left of the panel name in the panel tab, if present.

Try It!

1. Click the Symbols panel icon on the right side of the workspace. You can also choose Window > Symbols to display this panel.

2. Click the panel menu icon in the upper-right corner of the Symbols panel.

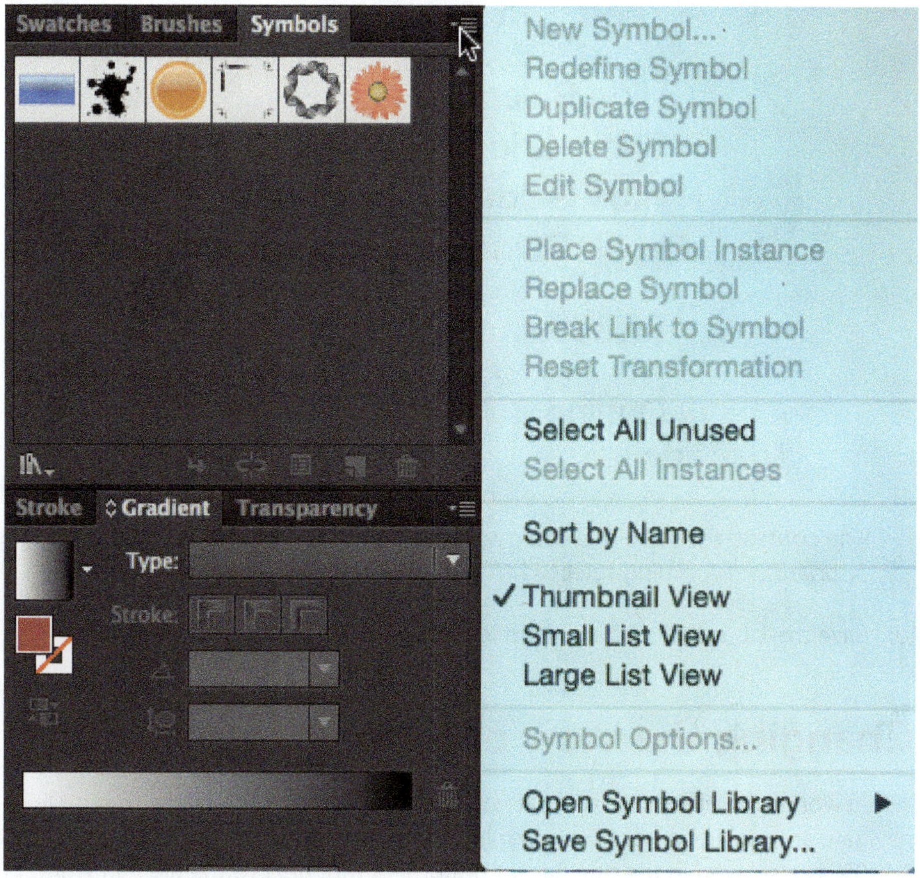

3. Choose Small List View from the panel menu.

   This displays the symbol names, together with thumbnails. Because the options in the panel menu apply only to the active panel, only the Symbols panel view is affected.

4. Click the Symbols panel menu icon and choose Thumbnail View to return the symbols to their original view. Click the Symbols panel tab to hide the panel again.

   In addition to the panel menus, context-sensitive menus display commands relevant to the active tool, selection, or panel. Usually the commands in a context menu are available in another part of the workspace, but using a context menu can save you time.

5. Position the pointer over the Document window or the contents of a panel. Then, right-click to show a context menu with specific options.

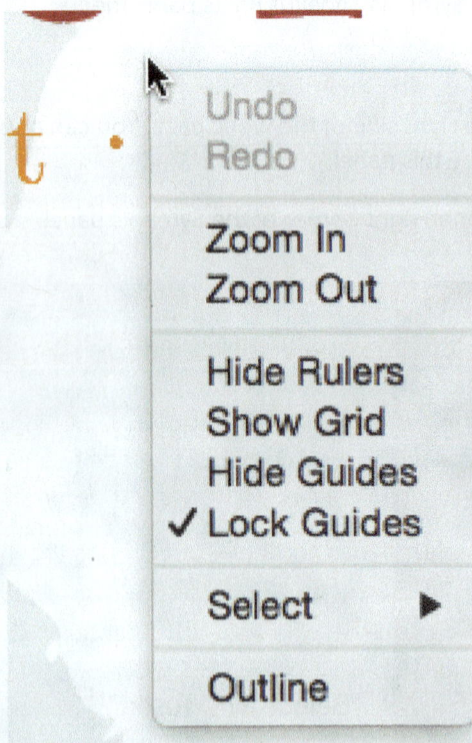

The context-sensitive menu shown here is displayed when you right-click the artboard with nothing selected.

6. Save the **L1_start1_xx.ai** file and leave it open.

Changing the View of Artwork

When working in files, it's likely that you'll need to change the magnification level and navigate among artboards. The magnification level, which can range from 3.13% to 6400%, is displayed in the title bar (or document tab) next to the file name and in the lower-left corner of the Document window. Using any of the viewing tools and commands affects only the display of the artwork, not the actual size of the artwork.

Using View Commands

To enlarge or reduce the view of artwork using the View menu, do one of the following:

- Choose View > Zoom In to enlarge the display of the artwork.
- Choose View > Zoom Out to reduce the view of the artwork.

Each time you choose a Zoom option, the view of the artwork is resized to the closest preset zoom level. The preset zoom levels appear in a menu in the lower-left corner of the Document window, identified by a down arrow next to a percentage.

You can also use the View menu to fit the artwork for the active artboard to your screen, to fit all artboards into the view area, or to view artwork at actual size.

Try It!

1. Choose View > Fit Artboard In Window.
2. Choose View > Actual Size (or Command+1 for Mac or Ctrl+1 for Windows), to display the artwork at actual size.

   The artwork is displayed at 100%. The actual size of your artwork determines how much of it can be viewed onscreen at 100%.
3. Choose View > Fit Artboard In Window before continuing to the next section.

Using the Zoom Tool

In addition to the View menu options, you can use the Zoom tool to magnify and reduce the view of artwork to predefined magnification levels.

1. Select the Zoom tool in the Tools panel, and then move the pointer into the Document window.

   Notice that a plus sign (+) appears at the center of the Zoom tool pointer.
2. Position the Zoom tool over the text "Jane Mitchell," and click once. The artwork is displayed at a higher magnification.

   Notice that where you clicked is now in the center of the Document window.
3. Click two more times on the "Jane Mitchell" text. The view is increased again, and you'll notice that the area you clicked is magnified.

Tip:

You can also zoom in using the keyboard shortcut Command++ (Mac) or Ctrl++ (Windows). That's Command *and* + (Mac) or Ctrl and + (Windows). You can also zoom out using the keyboard shortcut Command+– (Mac) or Ctrl+– (Windows). That's Command *and* – (Mac) or Ctrl *and* – (Windows).

Tip:

You can also double-click the Hand tool in the Tools panel to fit the active artboard in the Document window.

Note:

Because the canvas (the area outside the artboards) extends to 227", you can easily lose sight of your illustration. By choosing View > Fit Artboard In Window or by using the keyboard shortcuts Command+0 (Mac) or Ctrl+0 (Windows), artwork is centered in the viewing area.

Tip:

You can also double-click the Zoom tool in the Tools panel to display artwork at 100%.

4. With the Zoom tool still selected, position the pointer over the text "Jane Mitchell" and hold down the Option (Mac) or Alt (Windows) key. A minus sign (–) appears at the center of the Zoom tool pointer. With the Option or Alt key pressed, click the artwork twice to reduce the view of the artwork.

   For a more controlled zoom, you can drag a marquee around a specific area of your artwork. This magnifies only the selected area.

5. Choose View > Fit Artboard in Window.

6. With the Zoom tool still selected, click and drag a marquee around the fiber logo in the upper-left corner of the artboard. When you see the marquee around the area you are dragging, release the mouse button. The marquee area is now enlarged to fit the size of the Document window (as best it can).

Note:

The percent of the magnification is determined by the size of the marquee you draw with the Zoom tool —the smaller the marquee, the higher the level of magnification.

7. Double-click the Hand tool in the Tools panel to fit the artboard in the Document window.

   The Zoom tool is used frequently during the editing process to enlarge and reduce the view of artwork. Because of this, Illustrator allows you to select it using the keyboard at any time without first deselecting any other tool you may be using.

8. Select any other tool in the Tools panel, and move the pointer into the Document window.

9. Press spacebar+Command (Mac) or Ctrl+spacebar (Windows) to use the Zoom tool. Click or drag to zoom in on any area of the artwork, and then release the keys.

10. To zoom out using the keyboard, hold down Spacebar+Command+Option

    (Mac) or Ctrl+Alt+spacebar (Windows). Click the desired area to reduce the view of the artwork, and then release the keys.

11. Double-click the Hand tool in the Tools panel to fit the artboard in the Document window.

12. Save the **L1_start1_xx.ai** file and leave it open.

Scrolling Through a Document

You can use the Hand tool to pan to different areas of a document. Using the Hand tool allows you to push the document around much like you would a piece of paper on your desk.

Try It!

1. With the Hand tool selected in the Tools panel, drag down in the Document window. As you drag, the artwork moves with the hand.

   As with the Zoom tool, you can select the Hand tool with a keyboard shortcut without first deselecting the active tool.

2. Click any other tool except the Type tool in the Tools panel, and move the pointer into the Document window.
3. Hold down the spacebar on the keyboard to temporarily select the Hand tool, and then drag to bring the artwork back into the center of your view.
4. Double-click the Hand tool to fit the active artboard in the Document window.
5. Save the **L1_start1.ai_xx** file and leave it open for the next exercise.

> **Note:**
>
> The spacebar shortcut for the Hand tool does not work when the Type tool is active and the cursor is in text. To access the Hand tool when the cursor is in text, press the Option (Mac) or Alt (Windows) key.

Viewing Artwork

To save time when working with large or complex documents, you can create your own custom views within a document so that you can quickly jump to specific areas and zoom levels. Set up the view that you want to save, and then choose View >New View. Name the view, and click OK. The view is saved with the document.

Try It!

1. Choose View > Email (at the very bottom of the View menu), to display a saved view of the image. (This custom view was saved with the document by the author.)
2. Choose View > Fit Artboard In Window.

   When you open a file, it is automatically displayed in Preview mode, which shows how the artwork will print. When you're working with large or complex illustrations, you may want to view only the outlines, or wireframes, of objects in your artwork so that the screen doesn't have to redraw the artwork each time you make a change. This is called Outline mode. Outline mode can be helpful when selecting objects.

3. Choose View > Outline.

   Only the outlines of the objects are displayed. Use this view to find objects that might not be visible in Preview mode.

4. Choose View > GPU Preview to see all the attributes of the artwork.
5. Choose View > Overprint Preview to view any lines or shapes that are set to overprint.

   This view is helpful for those in the print industry who need to see how inks interact when set to overprint. You may not actually see much of a change in the content when you change to this view.

> **Note:**
>
> Depending on the resolution of your screen, the bottom of the View menu and the menu options may be cut off. You may need to click the black arrow at the bottom of the View menu several times to see more options.

> **Tip:**
>
> Press Command+Y (Mac OS) or Ctrl+Y (Windows) to toggle between Preview and Outline modes.

> **Note:**
>
> When switching between viewing modes, visual changes may not be readily apparent. Zooming in and out (View > Zoom In and View > Zoom Out) may help you see the differences more easily.

6. Choose View > Pixel Preview to see how the artwork will look when it is rasterized and viewed onscreen in a Web browser. Choose View > Pixel Preview to deselect pixel preview.

7. Choose View > Fit Artboard In Window to view the entire active artboard.

8. Save the **L1_start1_xx.ai** file and leave it open.

Navigating Multiple Artboards

Illustrator allows for multiple artboards within a single file. This is a great way to create a document so that you can have collateral pieces, like a brochure, a postcard, and a business card, in the same document. You can easily share content among designs, create multi page PDFs, and print multiple pages by creating more than one artboard. For more information on artboards, check out the sidebar titled "Artboard Overview" at the end of this section.

Multiple artboards can be added when you initially create an Illustrator document by choosing File > New. You can also add or remove artboards after the document is created by using the Artboard tool in the Tools panel.

Next, you will learn how to efficiently navigate a document that contains multiple artboards.

Try It!

1. Choose File > Open, open the **L1_start2.ai** file from the data files for this lesson, and save the file as **L1_start2_xx.ai**. If necessary, click OK in the Illustrator Options dialog box.

2. Choose View > Fit All In Window to fit all artboards in the Document window. Notice that there are two artboards in the document.

The artboards in a document can be arranged in any order, orientation, or artboard size—they can even overlap. Suppose that you want to create a four-page brochure. You can create different artboards for every page of the brochure, all with the same size and orientation. They can be arranged horizontally or vertically or in whatever way you like.

3. The **L1_start2.ai** document has two artboards that contain the designs for the front of a postcard and a business flyer.

   Press Command+– (Mac OS) or Ctrl+– (Windows) until you can see the logo in the upper-left corner of the canvas, which is outside the artboards.

4. Choose View > Fit Artboard In Window.

   This command fits the currently active artboard in the window. The active artboard is identified in the Artboard Navigation menu in the lower-left corner of the Document window.

5. Choose 2 Artboard 2 from the Artboard Navigation menu in the lower-left corner. The postcard appears in the Document window.

6. Choose View > Zoom Out. Notice that zooming occurs on the currently active artboard.

   Notice the arrows to the right and left of the Artboard Navigation menu. You can use these to navigate to the first, previous, next, and last artboards.

7. Click the Previous navigation button to view the previous artboard (Artboard 1) in the Document window.

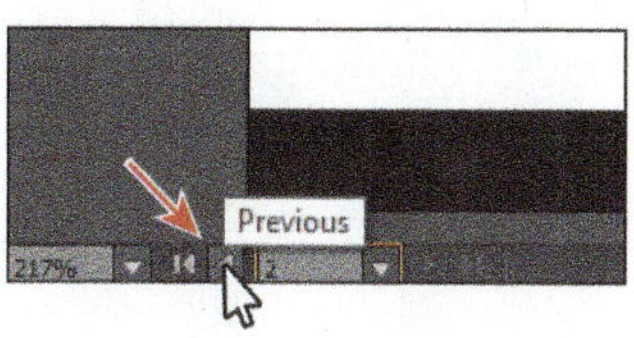

8. Choose View > Fit Artboard In Window to make sure that the first artboard (Artboard 1) fits in the Document window.

   Another method for navigating multiple artboards is to use the Artboards panel. Next, you will open the Artboards panel and navigate the document.

9. Choose Window > Artboards to expand the Artboards panel on the right side of the workspace.

   The Artboards panel lists all artboards in the document. This panel allows you to navigate between artboards, rename artboards, add or delete artboards, edit artboard settings, and more.

   Next, you will focus on navigating the document using this panel.

10. Double-click the number 2 in the Artboards panel. This fits Artboard 2 in the Document window.

Note:

Double- clicking the artboard name in the Artboards panel allows you to change the name of the artboard. Clicking the artboard icon to the right of the artboard name in the panel allows you to edit artboard options.

11. Double-click the number 1 to the left of Artboard 1 in the Artboards panel to show the first artboard in the Document window.

    Notice that when you double-click to navigate to an artboard, that artboard fits in the Document window.

12. Click the Artboards panel icon in the dock to collapse the Artboards panel.

13. Save the **L1_start2_xx.ai** file and leave it open.

Artboard Overview

Artboards represent the regions that can contain printable artwork (similar to pages in a program like Adobe InDesign). You can use artboards to crop areas for printing or placement purposes. Multiple artboards are useful for creating a variety of things, such as multipage PDFs, printed pages with different sizes or different elements, independent elements for Web sites, video storyboards, or individual items for animation in Adobe Flash® or Adobe After Effects.

A. **Printable area** is bounded by the innermost dotted lines and represents the portion of the page on which the selected printer can print.

B. **Nonprintable area** is between the two sets of dotted lines representing any nonprintable margin of the page. This example shows the nonprintable area of an 8.5" x 11" page for a printer that cannot print to the edge of the page.

C. **Artboard** is bounded by solid lines and represents the entire region that can contain printable artwork.

D. **Bleed area** is the amount of artwork that falls outside of the printing bounding box, or outside the crop area and trim marks.

E. **Canvas** is the area outside the artboard that extends to the edge of the 227" square window. Objects placed on the canvas are visible on-screen, but they do not print.

Using the Navigator Panel

The Navigator panel is another way to navigate a document with a single artboard or multiple artboards. This is useful when you need to see all artboards in the document in one window and to edit content in any of those artboards in a zoomed-in view.

Try It!

1. Choose Window > Navigator to open the Navigator panel. It is in a free-floating group of two panels in the workspace.
2. In the Navigator panel, type **50%** in the Zoom box in the lower-left corner of the panel and press Enter or Return to decrease the level of magnification.

   The red box in the Navigator panel, called the proxy view area, becomes larger, indicating the area of the document that is being shown. Depending on the zoom percentage, you may or may not see the proxy view area yet, but you will in the next few steps.
3. Click the larger mountain icon in the lower-right corner of the Navigator panel several times to zoom in to the brochure until the percentage in the Navigator panel shows approximately 150%.
4. Position the pointer inside the proxy view area of the Navigator panel. When the pointer becomes a hand, drag to pan to different parts of the artwork. Try dragging the proxy view area over the postcard in the Navigator panel preview.

5. In the Navigator panel preview area at the top of the panel, move the pointer outside of the proxy view area (red box) and click. This moves the box and displays a different area of the artwork in the Document window.
6. Choose View > Fit Artboard In Window.
7. Click the Navigator panel menu icon and deselect View Artboard Contents Only so that you see any artwork that is on the canvas, as well. Notice the logo on the canvas in the panel.

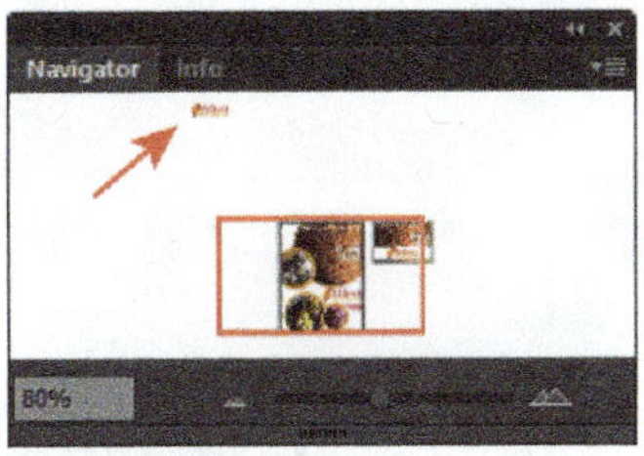

Note: You can also drag the slider in the Navigator panel to change the view of your artwork. Pause for a moment after dragging to allow the panel to catch up.

Note: The percentage and proxy view area in your Navigator panel may appear differently in this section. That's okay.

Note: You may need to adjust the slider in the Navigator panel to see the logo in the proxy view area.

8. Close the Navigator panel group by clicking the Close button (X) in the upper-left corner (Mac OS) or the upper-right corner (Windows).

9. Save the **L1_start2_xx.ai** file and leave it open.

Arranging Multiple Documents

> **Note:**
>
> Be careful to drag directly to the right. Otherwise, you could undock the Document window and create a new group. If that happens, choose Window > Arrange > Consolidate All Windows.
>
> **Tip:**
>
> You can cycle between open documents by pressing Command+~ (next document), Command+Shift+~ (previous document) (Mac OS) or Ctrl+F6 (next document), Ctrl+Shift+F6 (previous document) (Windows).

When you open more than one Illustrator file, the Document windows are tabbed. You can arrange the open documents in other ways, such as side by side, so that you can easily compare or drag items from one document to another. You can also use the Arrange Documents window to quickly display your open documents in a variety of configurations.

You should currently have two Illustrator files open: **L1_start1_xx.ai** and **L1_start2_xx.ai**. Each file has its own tab at the top of the Document window. These documents are considered a group of Document windows. You can create document groups to loosely associate files while they are open.

Try It!

1. Click the **L1_start1_xx.ai** document tab to show the business card in the Document window.

2. Click and drag the **L1_start1_xx.ai** document tab to the right of the **L1_start2_xx.ai** document tab.

   Dragging the document tabs allows you to change the order of the documents. This can be very useful if you use the document shortcuts to navigate to the next or previous document.

   These two documents are marketing pieces for the same company. To see both of them at one time, you can arrange the Document windows by cascading the windows or tiling them. **Cascading** allows you to cascade (stack) different document groups. **Tiling** shows multiple Document windows at one time, in various arrangements.

   Next, you will tile the open documents so that you can see them both at one time.

> **Cascading**
>
> Allows you to stack different document groups.
>
> **Tiling**
>
> Shows multiple Document windows at one time.

3. *Windows users skip to the next step.* On the Mac OS, choose Window > Application Frame. Then, click the green button (green by default) in the upper-left corner of Mac OS users can use the Application frame to group all the workspace elements in a single, integrated window, similar to working in Windows. If you move or resize the Application frame, the elements respond to each other so that they don't overlap.

4. Choose Window > Arrange > Tile.

   This shows both Document windows arranged overlapped side by side.

5. Click in each of the Document windows to activate the documents and choose View > Fit Artboard In Window for each of the documents. Also, make sure that Artboard 1 is showing for each document in the Document window.

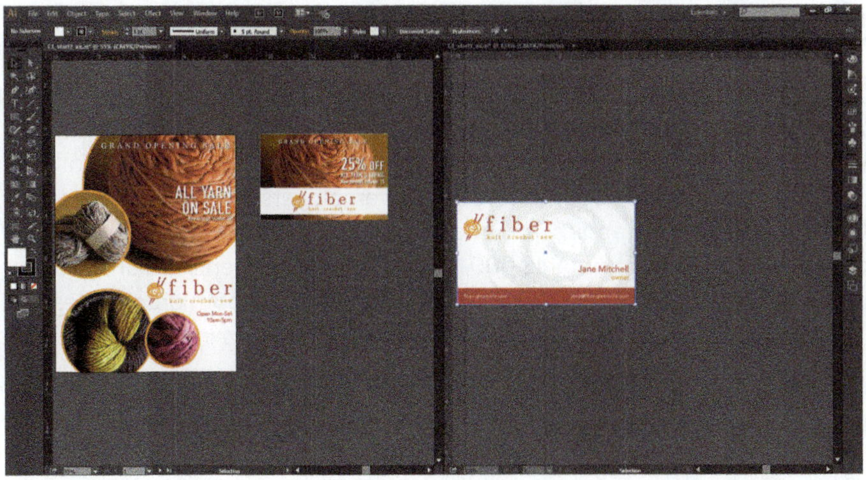

With documents tiled, you can drag the dividing line between each of the Document windows to reveal more or less of a particular document. You can also drag objects between documents, which copies them from one document to another.

To change the arrangement of the tiled windows, it's possible to drag document tabs to new positions. However, it's easier to use the Arrange Documents window to quickly arrange open documents in a variety of configurations.

Note:

On the Mac OS, the menu bar is above the Application bar. Also, depending on the resolution of your screen, the Windows menus may appear in the Application bar.

6. Click the Arrange Documents button in the Application bar to display the Arrange Documents window. Click the Consolidate All button to bring the documents back together.

7. Click the Arrange Documents button in the Application bar to display the Arrange Documents window again. Click the 2-Up vertical button in the Arrange Documents window.

8. Click to select the **L1_start1_xx** tab, if it is not already selected. Then, click the Close button (X) on the **L1_start1_xx** document tab to close the document. If a dialog box appears asking you to save the document, click Don't Save (Mac) or No (Win).

   Choose File > Close to close the **L1_start2_xx.ai** document without saving.

Tip:

You can also choose Window > Arrange > Consolidate All Windows to return the two documents to tabs in the same group.

Digital Design and Illustration Careers

Various careers within the Web and Digital Communications pathway require skills and expertise in graphic design and illustration. The look and feel of a Web site, video game, or other multimedia product are often the primary elements that engage the end user.

Careers in these areas include 2D/3D artist, animator, and Web designer. According to the Bureau of Labor Statistics, the average annual salary for an artist or animator is about $63,500. Most employers require a bachelor's degree in computer graphics, art, or a related field. The average annual salary for a Web designer is about $45,000. Education requirements are an associate's or bachelor's degree in Web design. Strong skills in both graphic design and Web programming languages are a plus for all careers in this field.

Finding Information Online

The Web is an amazing tool for acquiring information, but because it is so vast, it can be hard to locate the information you need. Subject guides and search engines can help.

- Subject guides group pages together under headings like Careers, News, or Travel. These guides include links only to articles and pages that provide useful information about a specific subject.
- A knowledge base is a searchable collection or database of information related to a specific subject. For example, a law library might have a knowledge base of law articles, cases, and other relevant information. Companies often maintain a knowledge base of help information that customers can use to solve problems on their own.
- A search engine is a program or Web site designed to search the Web looking for documents that match specified criteria, such as keywords. In a matter of moments, the search engine displays a list of links to pages that match. General search engines, such as Google, Yahoo, or Bing, search throughout the Web to find matches. Some search engines are customized for a certain topic. For example, the Web site fedworld.gov, maintained by the U.S. Department of Commerce, lets you search U.S. government documents. Some search engines support advanced searches that let you search for files based on file type, size, category, and other properties. For example, you can search for picture files, videos, or music.

Examining Intellectual Property Laws

Intellectual property laws are designed to protect individuals and companies from the theft or misuse of their intellectual property, including copyrights, trademarks, and patents. Copyrights are geared toward creative, literary, and artistic work. This includes music, lyrics, literature, scripts, choreography, graphics, pictures, sculpture, videos, films, and architecture. The protection extends to online content and productions and performances that use these copyrighted materials. Copyright exists as soon as a work is created, but the creator can register it with the U.S. Copyright Office. It is a crime to copy this kind of work without the permission of the person who owns the copyright to it. Penalties include paying a large fine and possibly jail time.

If the content is protected by copyright, you must have permission from the copyright holder to use the work. However, part of copyright law called the Fair Use Doctrine allows you to use a limited amount of copyrighted material without permission for educational purposes. For example, you can quote a few lines of a song or a passage from a book for a school report or presentation.

Avoiding the Problem

If you want to quote someone, or use content created by someone else, such as a song, or picture, or article you find online make sure that you identify the owner of the content and contact that person or entity to request permission. Placing a quote in a school assignment is usually considered fair use, or acceptable with the correct citation. Written permission may be required for long quotes or if you use content for commercial use, such as advertising. You may also quote or use content that is in the public domain, meaning the copyright has expired, or is no longer valid.

Cite Your Source

If you use information you find on the Web in your work, you must give credit to the source. You do this by inserting a reference to the source, called a citation, in a footnote, endnote, or bibliography. A proper citation gives credit to the source, and provides the tools a reader needs to locate the source on his or her own. Some Web sites have features that automatically generate the citation information for you.

Plagiarism

If you do not cite your sources you are guilty of plagiarism, which is the unauthorized use of another person's idea's or creative work without giving that person credit. Plagiarism is equivalent to stealing another person's work and passing it off as your own. The consequences of plagiarism can be quite significant. If you plagiarize work in school, you may have to redo the assignment or lose credit all together. Your school may also take disciplinarian actions, like detention. In the professional world, the consequences of plagiarism are even more significant. A professional who plagiarizes work suffers a loss to his or her reputation and may face legal ramifications, such as a lawsuit. He may be liable for fines and other punishments.

To avoid plagiarism you need to properly cite your source. You should insert a citation when you quote, summarize, or paraphrase someone else, use someone else's idea, or reference someone else's work. In a works cited section or footnote, you tell the reader the source of the information.

Trademarks and Patents

Some intellectual property is protected by trademark or patent. A trademark protects items that help define a company brand, such as a symbol, name, or terms that are used to identify it. A patent is the exclusive right to make, use, or sell a device or process. Many types of inventions can be patented. Using trademarked or patented property without permission is called infringement. The penalty is usually a large fine and a court order to stop.

Other Tools for Protecting Intellectual Property

A content owner, such as an author, artist, or software developer may provide a creative commons license so others may share, use, or even modify the work. The owner may set limitations on the usage, such as allowing students or teachers unlimited use, but restricting commercial use. Some software developers create open-source software, which means they make the source code for their programs available to the public so users can change the way it works.

Owners of intellectual property might also enter into an intellectual property agreement. This is a legal contract between or among various parties for the purchase and sale of intellectual property rights. For example, if you create a piece of artwork that you have agreed to sell to a specified buyer for a specified purpose, an intellectual property agreement with the buyer will ensure that it's used as intended.

Many business owners opt for nondisclosure agreements with employees to protect their intellectual property. With this type of agreement, employees are legally restricted from sharing certain types of information, even if they leave the company. These types of agreements are common in the information technology field. Many software development companies require their programmers to sign nondisclosure agreements to bar them from sharing or re-using proprietary computer code outside of the company.

Evaluating Information for Accuracy and Validity

Whether you're doing schoolwork, work for an employer, or pursuing your own interests, it is important to use critical thinking to evaluate printed, spoken, and digital information for accuracy before you believe it, or incorporate it into your own work. One example is news. Before the Internet, most news was covered by news organizations such as newspapers and television. With the Internet's easy access and global reach, citizen journalists have emerged.

Citizen journalists are not professional journalists, but instead they are just everyday people who take the time to post articles online on sites other than those run by major media outlets, or to upload photos and videos. These "journalists" can often give accurate reports of world events and fact-check the news at newspapers. However, they can also make things up. Unofficial reporting must be evaluated by the accuracy of the information given.

When evaluating information consider these criteria:

- **Author or Artist:** The author or artist should be identified. If you can't locate this information, there may be a reason the author chooses to remain anonymous, or the work may be used without permission. If you do locate a name, conduct a search to find out more about the person or organization responsible for the content.
- **Purpose:** Evaluate whether the information is objective or designed for a purpose. Objective information is balanced and fair. Information designed for a purpose is presented to achieve a desired result, such as to promote a particular viewpoint, to mislead, or to support preconceived assumptions. An **assumption** is something that is accepted as being true even if there is no factual proof. Many people try to twist information or use it out of context in order to influence

Assumption

Something that is accepted as being true even if there is no factual proof.

thinking. This type of misleading information is called **propaganda**. Always evaluate the content to determine if it is presented in a balanced, factual manner and is supported by facts, or if it is biased or argumentative.

- **Content Validity:** Does the author or artist indicate the sources of the work? Do those sources appear to be respected, valid, and authoritative? Run a search on the references or other sources to see what you can learn. Determine if the information given is fact or just opinion. Also check for spelling and grammatical errors, which can indicate that the creator is not a professional.
- **Relevancy:** Evaluate the work to make sure it is relevant to your purpose before you choose to believe it, or to use it. Online, most search engines list results in the order of hits received. Thus, search engines sometimes place popular sites before relevant sites. Don't be fooled into thinking that a page is relevant simply because it appears at the top of a list of results. Also, commercial search engines allow advertising and sponsored links, which are paid for by companies hoping to get your business. Don't assume the first link on a results page is the best. It might just be for the company that pays the most.

Propaganda

Information used out of context to try to mislead and influence thinking.

Comprehension Check

1. Identify and describe the computer programs you would use to create, view, and edit raster images and vector images.
2. How do you select a tool in Illustrator?
3. Describe three ways to navigate among artboards in Illustrator.
4. How do you save panel locations and visibility preferences?
5. Describe how arranging document windows can be helpful.
6. Explain search strategies you would use to find information about careers on the Internet.
7. What is propaganda, and how is it used?
8. Define copyrights, trademarks, and patents, and explain the differences between them. What are the consequences for violating intellectual property laws?
9. Describe the function of a non-disclosure agreement and an intellectual property agreement. How would these apply to businesses and employees in the information technology field?

Review Project 1

Use the Internet to research the scope of career opportunities in the Web and Digital Communications pathway. Use appropriate search strategies to locate information and resources on the types of businesses in the industry, trends affecting them, and the outlook for growth and new jobs. Evaluate the content you find for accuracy and validity. Summarize your findings in a one-page report that you can share with a partner or with the class. Be sure to properly cite your sources.

Review Project 2

With a partner, review the elements and principles of design described in this lesson. Using the Internet and/or library resources, find two samples of printed or digital communications, one of which, in your opinion, demonstrates the appropriate use of design and layout principles and the other of which does not. Be sure to address each of the eight principles of design that were discussed in the lesson, noting how the elements of layout and design were used to achieve each. Create a poster that compares and contrasts the two pieces and share it with the class.

Lesson 2 Overview

In this lesson, you will learn about:

- Selecting Objects
- Aligning Objects
- Working with Groups
- Exploring Object Arrangement
- Exploring Selection and Anchor Point Preferences
- Developing Employability Skills
- Using Technology Ethically

Selecting content in Adobe Illustrator is an important function to master. When changing colors or size and adding effects or attributes, you must first select the object to which you are applying the changes. In this lesson, you learn how to locate and select objects using the Selection tools; protect other objects by grouping, hiding, and locking them; and align objects to each other and the artboard.

Selecting Objects

Whether you are creating artwork from scratch or editing existing artwork in Illustrator, you will need to become familiar with selecting objects. There are many methods and tools for doing this. In this section, you'll explore the Selection and Direct Selection tools.

Using the Selection Tool

The Selection tool in the Tools panel lets you select, move, and resize entire objects. In this section, you'll become familiar with the tool.

Try It!

1. Choose File > Open, and open **L2_start.ai** from the data files for this lesson.
2. Save the file as **L2_start_xx.ai**. If necessary, click OK in the Illustrator Options dialog box to close it.
3. Select the Selection tool in the Tools panel, if it's not already selected. Move the pointer over different shapes on the artboards, without clicking.

   The small black square that appears at the corner of the Selection tool as you pass over objects indicates there is an object that can be selected under the pointer. When you hover over an object, that object is also outlined in a color (blue in this instance).
4. Select the Zoom tool in the Tools panel, and drag a marquee around the two red circles on the artboard on the right to zoom in.
5. Select the Selection tool in the Tools panel, and then position the pointer over the black edge of the red circle on the left. A word such as "path" or "anchor" may appear, because Smart Guides are turned on by default.
6. Click anywhere in the red circle on the left to select it. A bounding box with eight handles appears.

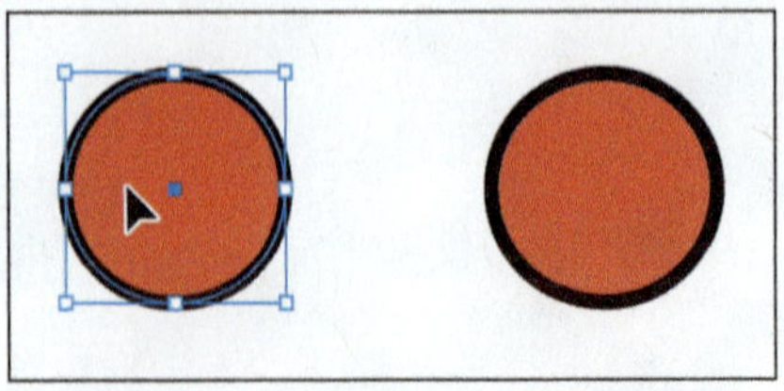

   The bounding box is used when making changes to objects, such as resizing or rotating them. The bounding box also indicates that an item is selected and ready to be modified, and the color of the bounding box indicates which layer the object is on.
7. Using the Selection tool, click in the red circle on the right. Notice that the left red circle is now deselected and only the right circle is selected.

Smart Guides are temporary snap-to guides that help you align, edit, and transform objects or artboards. You'll learn more about Smart Guides in Lesson 3, "Using Shapes to Create Artwork for a Postcard."

Note:

To select an item without a fill, you can click the stroke (the edge), or drag a selection marquee across the object.

8. Hold down the Shift key, and click the left red circle to add it to the selection. Both red circles are now selected, and a larger bounding box surrounds them.

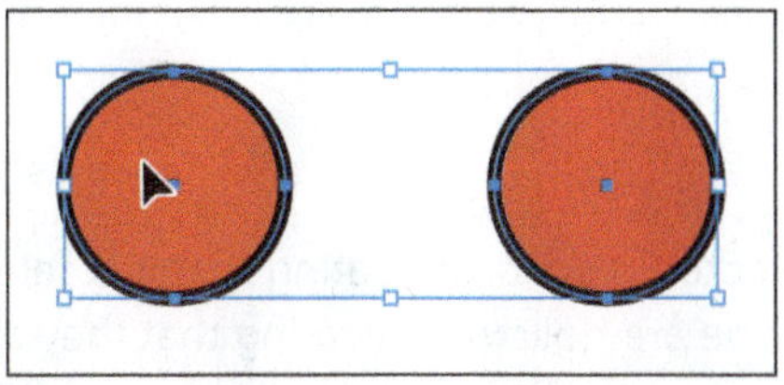

9. Reposition the circles anywhere in the document by clicking inside either selected circle (in the red area) and dragging. Because both circles are selected, they move together.

   As you drag, you may notice the green lines that appear. These are called **alignment guides** and are visible because Smart Guides are turned on (View > Smart Guides). As you drag, the objects are aligned to other objects on the artboard. Also notice the measurement label (gray box) next to the pointer that shows the object's distance from its original position. Measurement labels also appear because Smart Guides are turned on.

> **Alignment guides**
>
> Green lines which appear when moving objects on the artboard to show alignment in relation to the artboard or other objects.

10. Deselect the circles by clicking the artboard where there are no objects or by choosing Select > Deselect.

11. Revert to the last saved version of the document by choosing File > Revert. In the dialog box that appears, click Revert.

Using the Direct Selection Tool

In Illustrator, as you draw, you create paths that are made up of anchor points and paths. Anchor points are used to control the shape of the path. The Direct Selection tool selects anchor points or path segments within an object so that it can be reshaped. Next, you will become familiar with selecting anchor points and path segments using the Direct Selection tool.

Try It!

1. Choose View > Fit All In Window.

2. Select the Zoom tool in the Tools panel, and drag a marquee around the series of orange shapes below the red circles you selected previously to zoom in.

3. Select the Direct Selection tool in the Tools panel. Without clicking, position the pointer over the top edge of one of the orange shapes. Move the pointer along the top edge of the shape until the word "anchor" appears by the pointer.

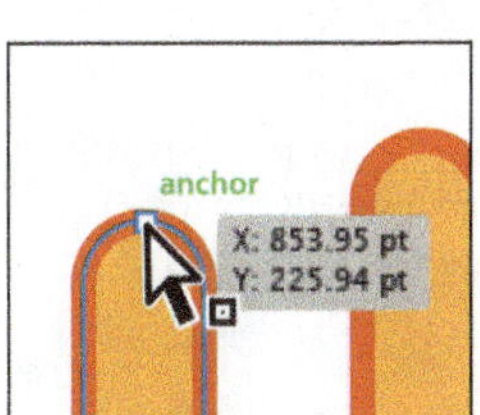

> **Tip:**
>
> You can also click in the middle of a shape to select it and to see the anchor points around its edge. This can be an easy way to see where the points are, and then you can click a point to select it.

When the Direct Selection tool is over an anchor point of a path or object, the word "anchor" appears. The "anchor" label is showing because Smart Guides are turned on (View > Smart Guides). Also notice the little white box to the right of the pointer. The small dot that appears in the center of the white box indicates that the cursor is positioned over an anchor point.

4. Click to select that anchor point.

   Notice that only the anchor point you selected is solid, indicating that it is selected, and the other anchor points in the shape are hollow, indicating that they are not selected. Also notice the small blue lines extending from the selected anchor point. These are called direction lines. At the end of the direction lines are direction points. The angle and length of the direction lines determine the shape and size of the curved segments. Moving the direction points can reshape the path.

5. With the Direct Selection tool still selected, drag the selected anchor point up to edit the shape of the object.

6. Try clicking another point on the edge of the shape, and notice that the previous point is deselected.

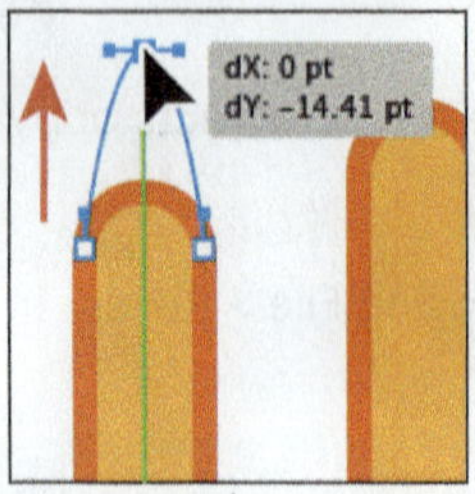

7. Revert to the last saved version of the file by choosing File > Revert. In the Revert dialog box, click Revert.

8. Save the **L2_start_xx.ai** file and leave it open.

Exploring Selection and Anchor Point Preferences

To display selection and anchor point preferences, choose Illustrator > Preferences > Selection & Anchor Display (Mac) or Edit > Preferences > Selection & Anchor Display (Win). You can change the size of anchor points (called anchors in the dialog box) or the display of the direction lines (called handles in the dialog box).

As you move the pointer over anchor points in your artwork, they are highlighted. You can also turn off the highlighting of anchor points as the pointer hovers over them. Highlighting anchor points makes it easier to determine which point you are about to select.

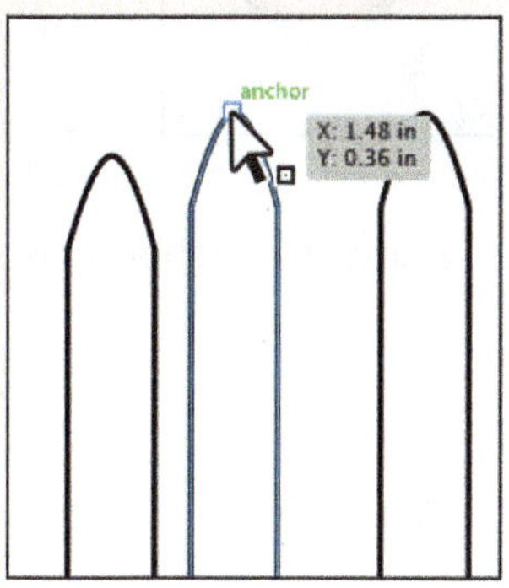

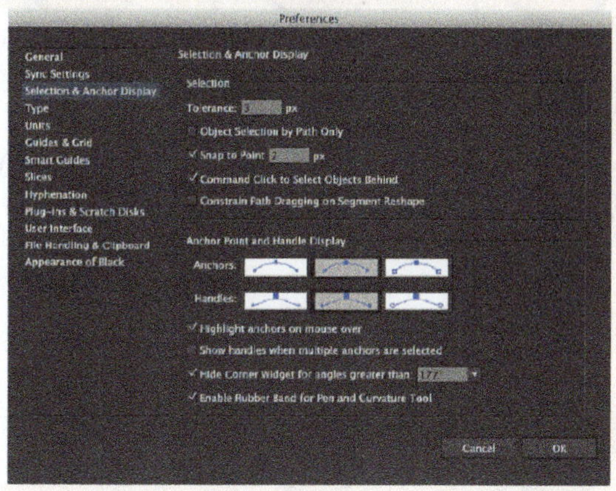

Creating Selections with a Marquee

Another way to select content is by dragging a marquee around the objects that you want to select, which is what you'll do next.

Try It!

1. Choose View > Fit All In Window.
2. Select the Zoom tool in the Tools panel, and click three times, slowly, on the red circles.
3. Select the Selection tool in the Tools panel. Position the pointer above and to the left of the leftmost red circle, and then drag downward and to the right to create a marquee that overlaps just the tops of the circles.

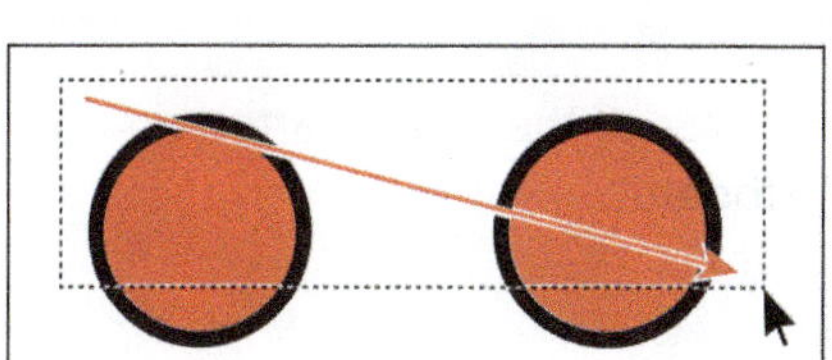

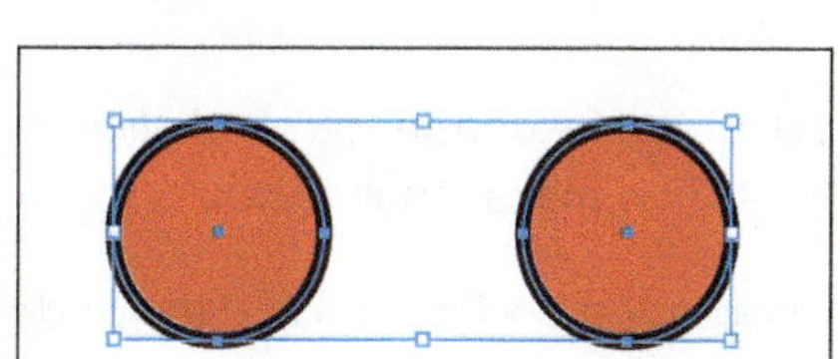

Tip:

When dragging with the Selection tool, you need to encompass only a small part of an object to select it.

4. Choose Select > Deselect, or click where there are no objects.

   Now you'll use the Direct Selection tool to select multiple anchor points in the red circles by dragging a marquee around anchor points.

5. Select the Direct Selection tool in the Tools panel. Starting off the top, left of the leftmost red circle (see the figure), drag across the top edges of the two circles. Only the top anchor points become selected.

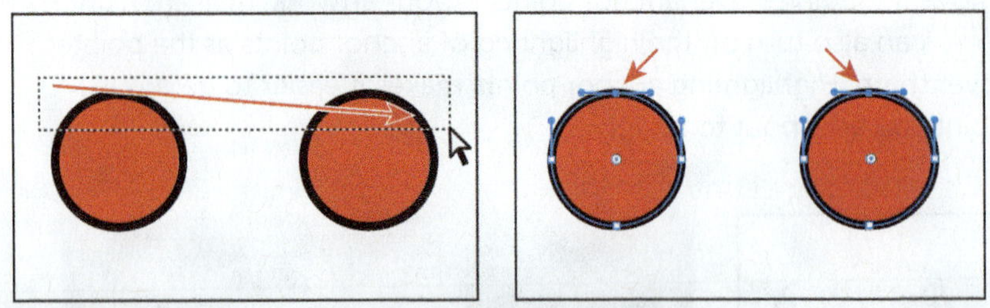

6. Click one of the selected anchor points, and drag to see how the anchor points reposition together.

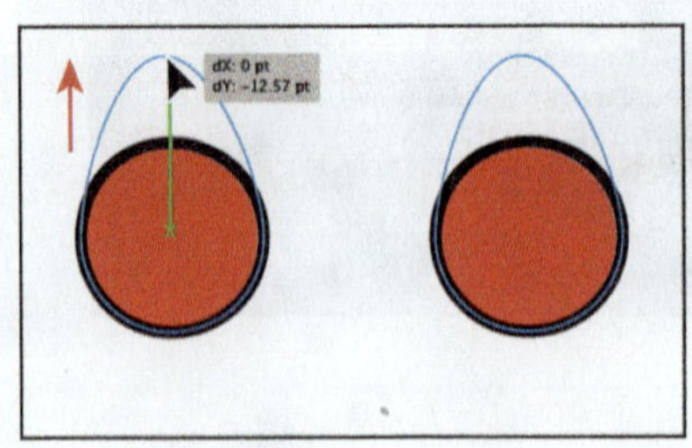

7. You can use this method when selecting points so that you don't have to click exactly on the anchor point that you want to select.

8. Revert to the last saved version of the file by choosing File > Revert. In the dialog box that appears, click Revert.

Creating Selections with the Magic Wand Tool

You can use the Magic Wand tool to select all objects in a document that have the same attributes, like a color fill. The fill is a color applied to the inside of an object. You can customize the Magic Wand tool to select objects based on options–such as stroke weight and stroke color–by double-clicking the Magic Wand tool in the Tools panel. You can also change the tolerances (range) used to identify similar objects.

Try It!

1. Select the Selection tool and click in a blank area of the smaller artboard on the right. This makes that artboard the active artboard.

2. Choose View > Fit Artboard In Window.

3. Select the Magic Wand tool in the Tools panel. Click one of the red circles on the right artboard, and notice that the other red circle becomes selected as well. No bounding box (a box surrounding the two shapes) appears, because the Magic Wand tool is still selected.

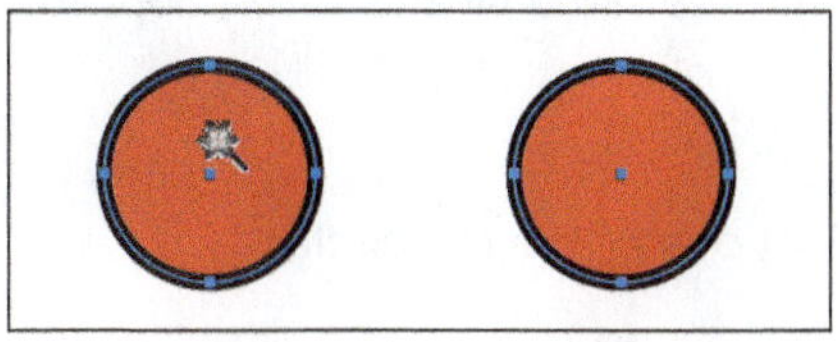

4. Holding down the Shift key, notice that the pointer has a plus sign (+) next to it. Click one of the orange shapes (below the red shapes) with the Magic Wand tool, and then release the key.

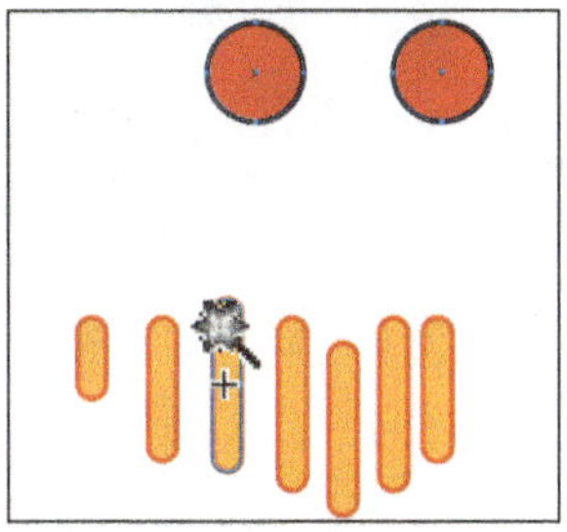

   This adds all of the shapes filled with that same orange color to the selection.

5. With the Magic Wand tool still selected, hold down the Option key (Mac) or Alt key (Win) and notice that a minus sign appears next to the pointer. Click one of the orange shapes to deselect all of the shapes with that same fill, and then release the key. The red circles should still be selected.
6. Choose Select > Deselect, or click where there are no objects.
7. Save the **L2_start_xx.ai** file and leave it open.

Selecting Similar Objects

You can also select objects based on similar fill color, stroke color, stroke weight, and so forth, using the Select Similar Objects button or the Select > Same command. The stroke of an object is the outline (border), and the stroke weight is the width of the stroke. Next, you will select several objects with the same fill and stroke applied.

Try It!

1. Select the Selection tool and click to select one of the red circles.
2. Click the arrow to the right of the Select Similar Objects button in the Control panel to show a menu. Choose Fill Color to select all objects on any artboard with the same fill color (red) as the selected object.

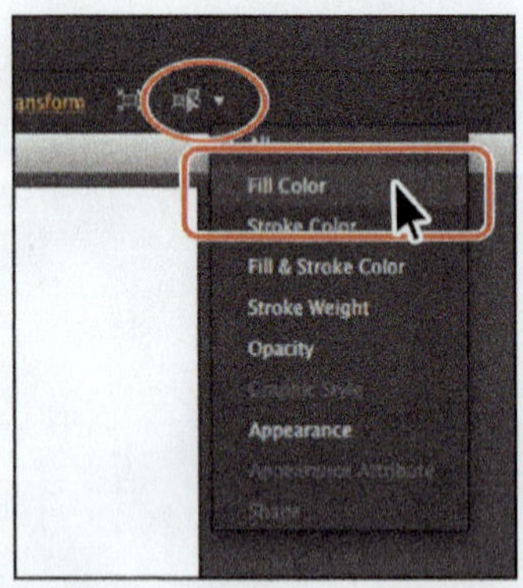

Notice that the circles with the same red-colored fill are selected.

3. Click to select one of the orange shapes, and then choose Select > Same > Fill & Stroke.

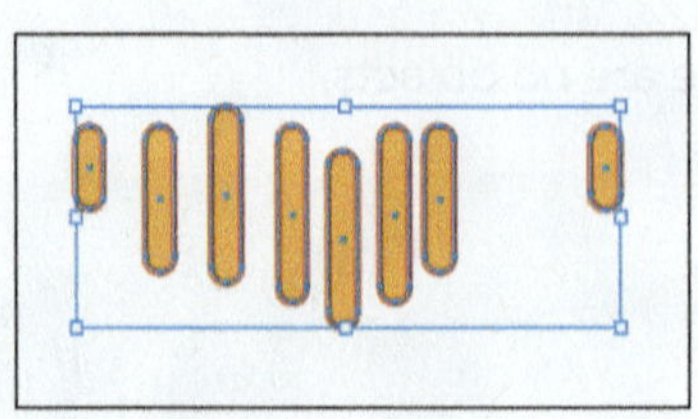

All of the orange-filled shapes with the same stroke and fill and are now selected.

4. With the orange shapes still selected, choose Select > Save Selection. Name the selection RobotMouth in the Save Selection dialog box, and click OK so that you'll be able to choose this selection at a later time.
5. Choose Select > Deselect, save the **L2_start_xx.ai** file and leave it open.

Selecting in Outline Mode

By default, Adobe Illustrator displays all artwork with their paint attributes, like fill and stroke, showing. However, you can choose to display artwork so that only its outlines (or paths) are visible. The next method for selecting involves viewing artwork in Outline mode and can be very useful if you want to select objects within a series of stacked objects.

Try It!

1. Choose View > Fit Artboard In Window to fit the artboard with the orange shapes into the Document window.
2. With the Selection tool, click within the gray half-circle shape at the bottom of the artboard to select it. This will become the body of the robot.

   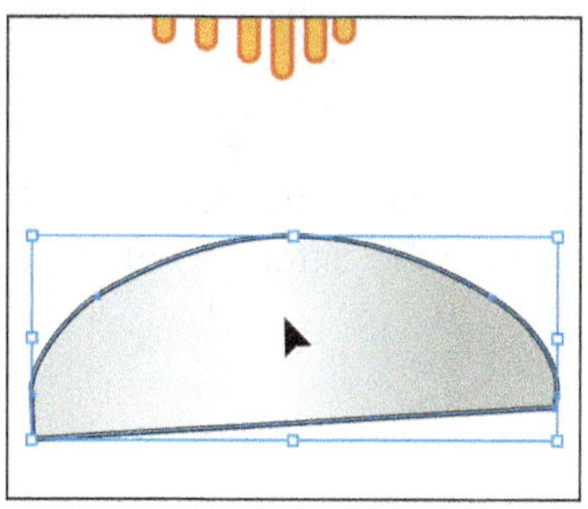

   Since the shape has a fill (a color, pattern, or gradient filling the inside of an object), you can click anywhere within the bounds of the object to select it.
3. Choose Select > Deselect, to deselect the shape.
4. Choose View > Outline to view the artwork as outlines.
5. With the Selection tool, click inside that same half-circle shape.

   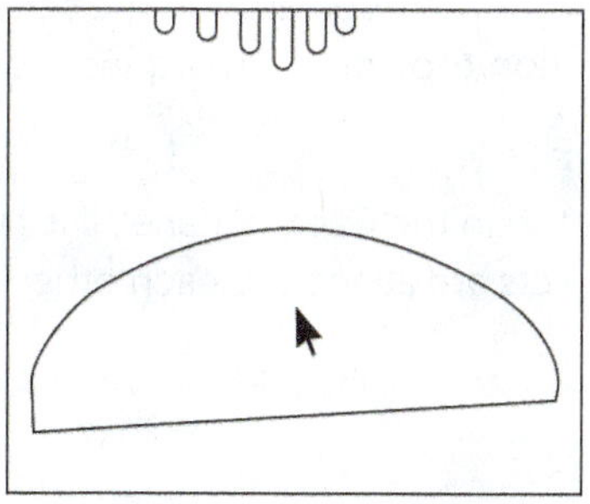

   Notice that you cannot select the object using this method. Outline mode displays artwork as outlines with no fill. To select in Outline mode, you can click the edge of the object or drag a marquee across the shape to select it.
6. Click the Previous artboard button in the lower-left corner of the Document window to fit the first artboard in the window.

7. On the left artboard, with the Selection tool selected, drag a marquee across the right (smaller) ellipse that makes the robot's eye. Press the Left Arrow key several times to move the ellipse so that it almost touches the ellipse to the left.

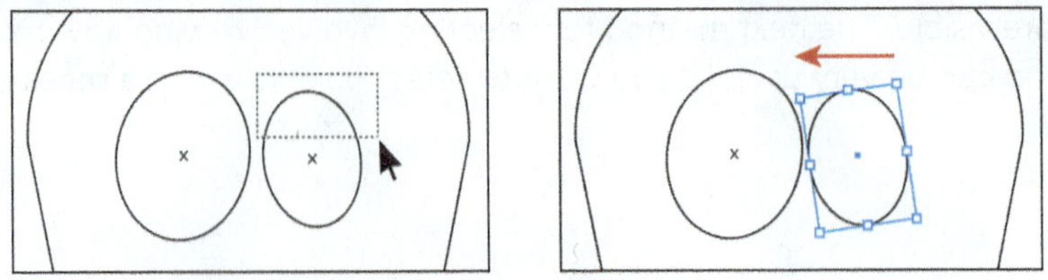

8. Choose View > Preview to see the artwork.

9. Save the **L2_start_xx.ai** file and leave it open.

Aligning Objects

Illustrator makes it easy to align or distribute multiple objects relative to each other, the artboard, or a key object. In this section, you'll explore the different options for aligning objects.

Aligning Objects to Each Other

The simplest type of alignment is aligning objects to each other, and that's what you'll do next.

Try It!

1. Choose Select > RobotMouth to reselect the orange shapes.

2. Click the Next artboard button in the lower-left corner of the Document window to fit the artboard with the orange and red shapes in the window.

3. Select the Zoom tool in the Tools panel, and drag a marquee around the series of orange-filled shapes to zoom in. With the Selection tool, drag a marquee around the shapes to select them.

4. Choose Align To Selection from the Align To button in the Control panel, if it's not already selected, to ensure that the selected objects are aligned to each other.

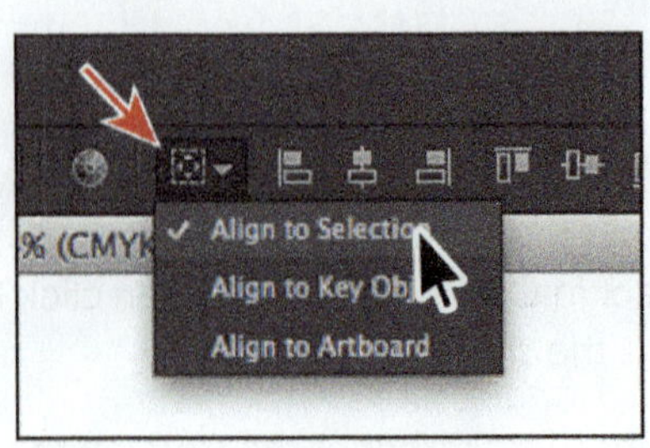

5. Click the Vertical Align Bottom button in the Control panel.

   Notice that the bottom edges of all the orange objects move to align with the lowest orange object.

6. Choose Edit > Undo Align to return the objects to their original positions. Leave the objects selected for the next section.

7. Save the **L2_start_xx.ai** file and leave it open.

Aligning to a Key Object

A **key object** is an object that you want other objects to align to. You specify a key object by selecting all the objects you want to align, including the key object, and then clicking the key object again. When selected, the key object has a thick outline, and the Align To Key Object icon appears in the Control panel and the Align panel. Next, you will align the orange shapes.

Key Object

An object that you want to align other objects to.

Try It!

1. With the orange shapes still selected, click the leftmost shape with the Selection tool.

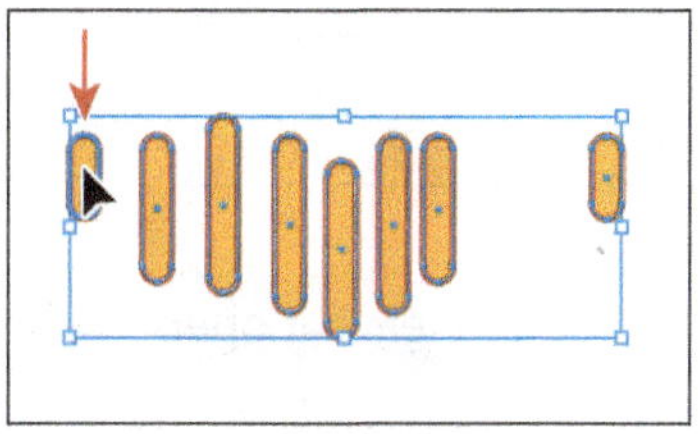

   The thick blue outline indicates that the leftmost shape is the key object that other objects will align to.

2. Click the Vertical Align Top button in the Align options in the Control panel. Notice that all of the orange shapes move to align to the top edge of the key object.

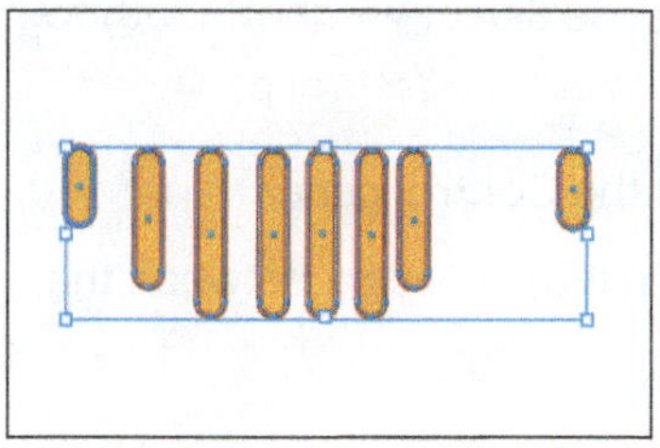

3. Choose Select > Deselect, save the **L2_start_xx.ai** file and leave it open.

Aligning Anchor Points

Next, you'll align two anchor points to each other using the Align options. Like setting a key object in the previous section, you can also set a key anchor point that other anchor points will align to.

Try It!

1. Choose View > Fit Artboard In Window.
2. Select the Direct Selection tool, and click the lower-left point of the gray half-circle at the bottom of the artboard. Shift-click to select the lower-right point of the same gray half-circle.

   You select the points in a specific order because the last selected anchor point is the key anchor point. Other points align to this point.
3. Click the Vertical Align Top button in the Control panel. The first anchor point selected aligns to the second anchor point selected.

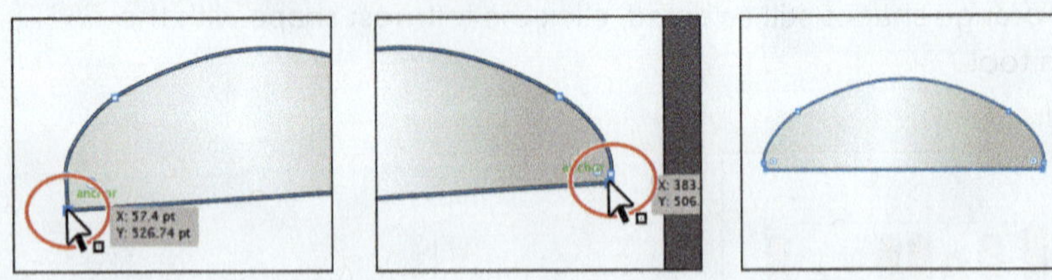

4. Choose Select > Deselect, save the **L2_start_xx.ai** file and leave it open.

Distributing Objects

Distributing objects using the Align panel enables you to select multiple objects and to distribute the spacing between those objects equally. Next, you will make the spacing between the orange shapes even, using a distribution method.

Try It!

1. Select the Selection tool in the Tools panel. Choose Select > RobotMouth to reselect all of the orange shapes.
2. Click the Horizontal Distribute Center button in the Control panel.

   Distributing moves all of the orange shapes so that the spacing between the center of each of them is equal.
3. Choose Edit > Undo Align.
4. Choose Select > Deselect.
5. Choose View > Zoom In, twice, to zoom in to the orange shapes. With the Selection tool selected, hold down the Shift key and click/drag the rightmost orange shape slightly to the left. Stop dragging just before the shape touches the orange shape to its left. Release the mouse button and then the key.

   The Shift key keeps the shape aligned vertically with the other shapes.

6. Choose Select > RobotMouth to select all of the orange shapes again, and then click the Horizontal Distribute Center button again. Notice that, with the right-most shape repositioned, the objects move to redistribute the spacing between the centers.

7. Choose Select > Deselect, save the **L2_start_xx.ai** file, and leave it open.

Aligning to the Artboard

You can also align content to the artboard rather than to a selection or a key object. Aligning to the artboard aligns each selected object separately to the artboard. Next, you'll get the gray half-circle shape on the artboard with the rest of the robot and align it to the bottom, center of the artboard.

Try It!

1. With the Selection tool, click the gray half-circle shape at the bottom of the artboard to select it. Choose Edit > Cut.

2. Click the Previous artboard button in the lower-left corner of the Document window to navigate to the first (left) artboard in the document, which contains the robot head.

3. Choose Edit > Paste to paste the gray half-circle.

4. Click the Align To Selection button in the Control panel, and choose Align To Artboard in the menu that appears. Selected content will now align to the artboard.

5. Click the Horizontal Align Center button (just in case), and then click the Vertical Align Bottom button to align the selection to the horizontal center and vertical bottom of the artboard.

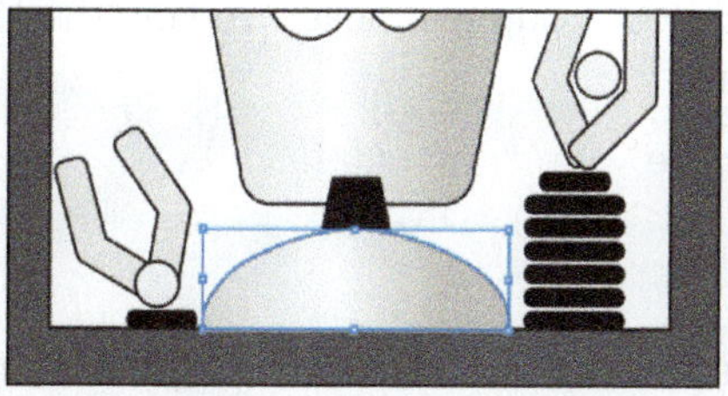

6. Choose Select > Deselect, save the **L2_start_xx.ai** file, and leave it open.

Working with Groups

You can combine objects into a group so that the objects are treated as a single unit. This way, you can move or transform a number of objects without affecting their individual attributes or relative positions.

Grouping Items

Next, you will select multiple objects and create a group from them.

Try It!

1. Choose View > Fit All In Window to see both artboards.
2. Choose Select > RobotMouth to reselect the series of orange shapes.
3. Choose Object > Group, and notice that the word "Group" appears in the Selection Indicator on the left side of the Control panel.

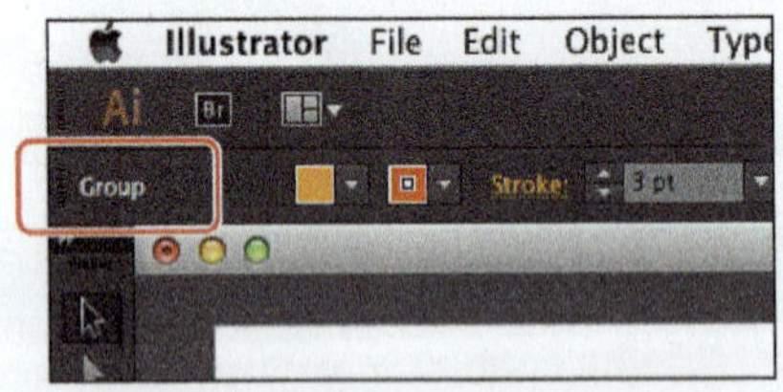

4. Choose Select > Deselect.
5. With the Selection tool, click one of the orange shapes in the group. Because they are grouped together, all are now selected.
6. Drag the group of orange shapes onto the robot head (below the eyes).
7. Choose Select > Deselect, save the **L2_start_xx.ai** file, and leave it open.

Working in Isolation Mode

Isolation mode isolates groups or sublayers so that you can easily select and edit specific objects or parts of objects without having to ungroup the objects. When in Isolation mode, all objects outside of the isolated group are locked and dimmed so that they aren't affected by the edits you make.

Next, you will edit a group using Isolation mode.

Try It!

1. With the Selection tool, click the robot's hand at the end of the longer arm. You will see a group of shapes that make up the hand is selected.
2. Double-click a shape in the hand to enter Isolation mode.

> **Tip:**
>
> To enter Isolation mode, you can also select a group with the Selection tool, and then click the Isolate Selected Object button in the Control panel.

3. Choose View > Fit Artboard In Window, and notice that the rest of the content in the document appears dimmed.

   At the top of the Document window, a gray bar appears with the words "Layer 1" and "<Group>." This indicates that you have isolated a group of objects that is on Layer 1.
4. Choose View > Smart Guides to turn them off. This way, when you drag content, it won't snap to other content.

5. Drag the light-gray circle down to approximately match the position of the circle shape in the other hand.

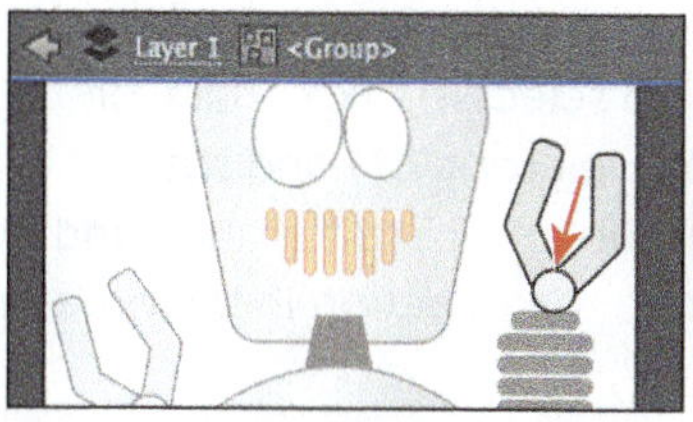

When you enter Isolation mode, groups are temporarily ungrouped. This enables you to edit objects in the group or to add new content without having to ungroup.

6. Double-click outside the shapes within the group to exit Isolation mode.

7. Click to select the circle shape. Notice that it is once again grouped with the rest of the shapes in the hand, and you can also select other objects.

8. Choose Select > Deselect, save the **L2_start_xx.ai** file, and leave it open.

Tip:

To exit Isolation mode, you can also click the gray arrow in the upper-left corner of the Document window, or deselect all content and click the Exit Isolation Mode button in the Control panel. You can also press the Escape key when in Isolation mode or double-click a blank area of the Document window to exit Isolation mode.

Creating a Nested Group

Groups can also be **nested**—grouped within other objects or grouped to form larger groups. Nesting is a common technique used when designing artwork. It's a great way to keep associated content together.

In this section, you will explore how to create a nested group.

Nested Group

A group that is combined with other objects or groups to form a larger group.

Try It!

1. With the Selection tool, drag a marquee across the series of black shapes below the hand that make up the longer arm of the robot.

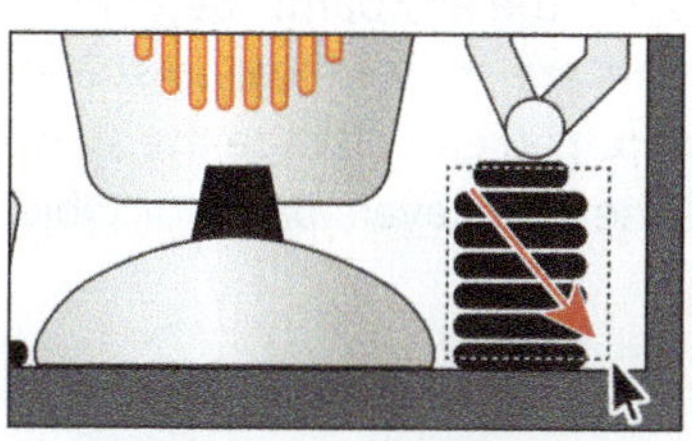

2. Choose Object > Group.

3. With the Selection tool, Shift-click the hand above the arm to select that group as well. Choose Object > Group.

   You have created a nested group.

4. Choose Select > Deselect.

5. With the Selection tool, click one of the grouped objects in that same arm.

   All objects in the nested group become selected.

6. Click a blank area on the artboard to deselect the objects.

   Next, you will explore the Group Selection tool.

7. Hold down the Direct Selection tool in the Tools panel to reveal more tools. Click the Group Selection tool to select it. The Group Selection tool adds the object's parent group(s) to the current selection.
8. Click one of the shapes in the same robot hand to select it. Click again, on the same shape, to select the object's parent group (the group of hand shapes). Click once more, on that same shape, to select the group composed of the hand and arm. The Group Selection tool adds each group to the selection in the order in which it was grouped.

   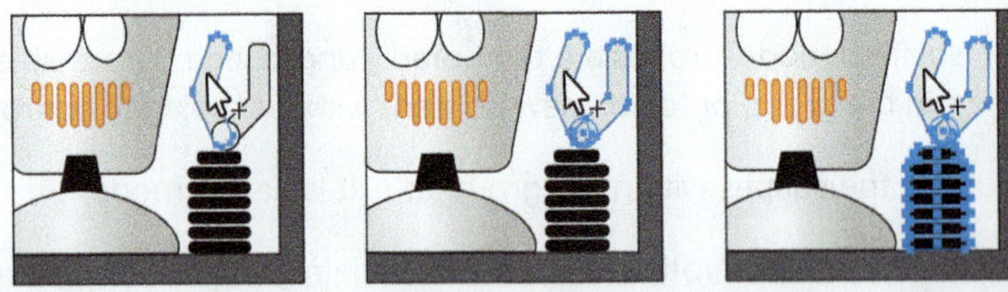

   Choose Select > Deselect.
9. With the Selection tool, click any of the objects in the nested group to select the group. Choose Object > Ungroup to ungroup the objects.
10. Choose Select > Deselect.
11. Click to select the hand. Notice that it is still a group of objects.
12. Save the **L2_start_xx.ai** file and leave it open.

Exploring Object Arrangement

> **Stacking order**
>
> The order in which objects are stacked, which determines how they display when they overlap.

As you create objects, Illustrator stacks them in order on the artboards, beginning with the first object created. The order in which objects are stacked (called **stacking order**) determines how they display when they overlap. You can change the stacking order of objects in your artwork at any time, using either the Layers panel or Object > Arrange commands.

Arranging Objects

Next, you will work with the Arrange commands to change how objects are stacked.

Try It!

1. Choose View > Fit All In Window to see both artboards in the document.
2. With the Selection tool, click to select the black shape below the robot's head (the robot's "neck").

   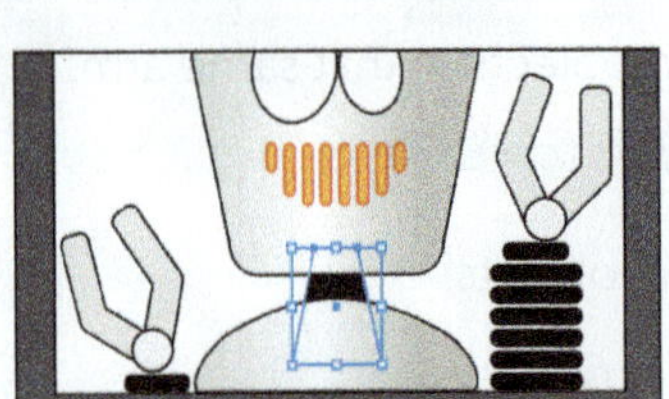

3. Choose Object > Arrange > Send To Back to send the shape behind the robot's head.

4. Click to select either of the red circles on the right artboard.

5. Drag the selected circle on top of the robot's smaller eye. Release the mouse, and notice that the red circle disappears, but it's still selected.

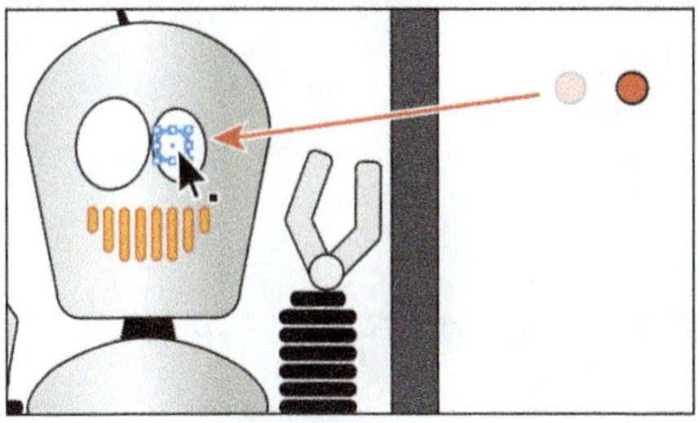

It went behind the ellipse (the eye) because it was probably created before the eye shape, which means it is lower in the stacking order.

6. With the red circle still selected, choose Object > Arrange > Bring to Front. This brings the red circle to the front of the stack, making it the topmost object.

7. Save the **L2_start_xx.ai** file and leave it open.

Selecting Objects Behind

When you stack objects on top of each other, sometimes it becomes difficult to select objects that are underneath other objects. Next, you will learn how to select an object through a stack of objects.

Try It!

1. With the Selection tool, select the other red circle on the right artboard, drag it onto the larger robot eye on the left artboard, and then release the mouse.

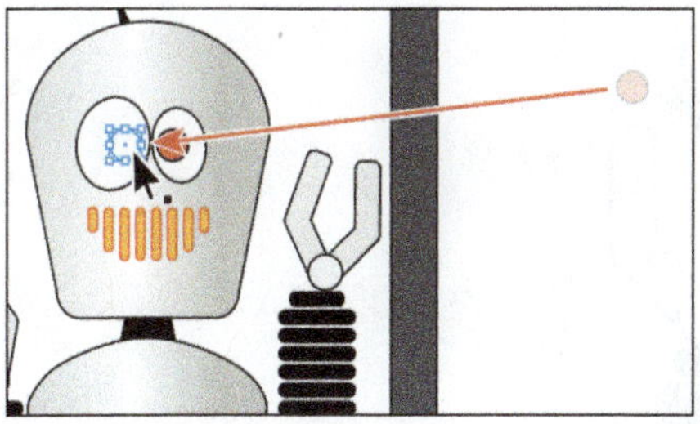

2. Notice that this circle disappears like the other, but is still selected. This time, you will deselect the circle and then reselect it using another method.

3. Choose Select > Deselect, and the red circle is no longer selected.

Note:

You may see an angle bracket displayed with the pointer.

Note:

To select the hidden red circle, make sure that you click where the circle and the eye overlap. Otherwise, you won't be able to select the red circle.

4. With the pointer positioned over the location of the second red circle you just deselected, the one behind the eye shape, hold down the Command (Mac) or Ctrl (Windows) key and click until the circle is selected again (this may take several clicks).

5. Choose Object > Arrange > Bring To Front to bring the circle on top of the eye.
6. Choose Select > Deselect.

Hiding and Locking Objects

When working on complex artwork, it may become more difficult to make selections. In this section, you'll learn how to lock and hide content to make selecting objects easier.

Try It!

1. Choose View > Fit Artboard In Window.
2. Choose Object > Show All to reveal a mask over the robot's eyes. Choose Object > Arrange > Bring To Front to bring the mask to the front.
3. With the Selection tool, click to attempt to select one of the eyes.

Notice that you can't, since the mask is on top of them. In order to access the eyes, you could use one of the methods we previously discussed or use one of two other methods: hide or lock.

4. With the mask still selected, choose Object > Hide > Selection, or press Command+3 (Mac) or Ctrl+3 (Windows). The mask is hidden so that you can more easily select other objects. (This is how we hid the mask when we set up the file.)

5. Click to select one of the red circles in the eyes, and move it.
6. Choose Object > Show All to show the mask again.
7. With the mask selected, choose Object > Lock > Selection, or press Command+2 (Mac) or Ctrl+2 (Windows).

   The mask is still visible, but you cannot select it.
8. With the Selection tool, click to select one of the eye shapes.
9. Choose Object > Unlock All, and then choose Object > Hide > Selection to hide the mask again.
10. Choose View > Smart Guides to turn them on.
11. Save the **L2_start_xx.ai** file and then choose File > Close.

Developing Employability Skills

Employability means having and using skills and abilities to be hired and stay hired, and even advance to higher-level jobs. Once you recognize the skills that make you employable, you can practice and develop them in school and at home, so you are ready to use them on the job.

Transferable Skills

Employability skills can generally be placed into two groups: hard skills and transferable skills. Employers often look for people with hard skills to fill specific jobs. For example, a software development company looks to hire people skilled at writing code.

Transferable skills can be used on almost any job. They are called transferable skills because you can transfer them from one situation or career to another.

Time management is an important transferable skill for succeeding at work. Employers want you to make the most of your time–to them, time is money. That means showing up on time, taking breaks at scheduled times, meeting deadlines, and taking care of personal business on your own time. Making the most of your time demonstrates to your employer that you take your responsibilities seriously.

Planning is an equally important transferable skill. Developing a plan or strategy will help you successfully complete projects and meet goals. Successful planning requires organization and setting priorities for tasks and responsibilities.

The foundation skills you use to succeed in other areas of your life, such as decision-making and problem-solving, are also transferable skills. You can practice and develop these skills in school and at home.

Some computer skills are also transferable. There are very few jobs today that do not require basic computer use. If you have these basic skills, you can take them wherever you go:

- Turn a computer on and start a program.
- Type on a computer keyboard without making many mistakes.
- Access the Internet and navigate from one location to another.

- Use a search engine to do basic Internet research.
- Write and send e-mail.

Professional Qualities

Professionalism, or work ethic, is the ability to show respect to everyone around you while you perform your responsibilities as best you can. It includes a basic set of personal qualities that make an employee successful. These qualities include:

- Integrity
- Courtesy
- Honesty
- Dependability
- Punctuality
- Responsibility
- Cooperative
- Positive
- Open-minded
- Flexibility

Professionalism also means you demonstrate professional standards and positive work behaviors, such as regular attendance. A professional also maintains a clean and safe work environment, performs tasks effectively, shows initiative, and takes pride in his or her work accomplishments. These behaviors lead to advancement at work, in school, and in everyday life.

Professional Appearance

Dress standards vary depending on the career that you choose. For example, you wouldn't expect a prepress technician to be wearing a suit and tie, and you wouldn't want a business manager to be wearing grease-covered clothing. However, good grooming habits are required in all professions. The following are recommendations for maintaining a well-groomed, professional appearance:

- Wear clothes that are clean, neat, and in good repair.
- Wear clean and appropriate shoes.
- Keep your hair neat and clean.
- Brush your teeth at least twice a day.
- Floss daily.
- Use mouthwash or breath mints.
- Bathe daily.
- Use unscented deodorant.
- Keep makeup light and neutral.
- Keep jewelry to a minimum.
- Do not use perfume or cologne.
- Keep nails clean.

Part of your responsibility as a worker is to make sure that you keep your work environment safe for yourself and for others. You can practice this at school and at home. You have to take some responsibility for your own safety. That means using equipment properly, according to instructions, and being aware of safety hazards.

Ethics at Work

Ethics are a set of beliefs about what is right and what is wrong. Work ethics are beliefs and behaviors about what is right and wrong in a work environment. Ethical behavior includes treating people with respect and also following the law. For example, taking credit for someone else's ideas is not ethical, and taking home office supplies is not ethical—it's stealing. Ethical employees respect confidentiality. They do not share client information or sensitive company content with unauthorized individuals. Employers value employees who behave ethically at work. It shows that you are honest and respectful, so others will trust and respect you in return.

Behaving ethically at work also means following the company rules, regulations, and processes. Usually, when you start a new job you are given an employee handbook. An employee handbook describes company policies and procedures, such as how to request vacation time, and the different benefits that are available. It should also list all rules and policies that you are expected to obey. These might include:

- Maintaining confidentiality of information.
- Respecting copyrights and patents.
- Respecting co-workers' and customers' rights.

Ethics extends beyond the actions and behaviors of individual workers. It also applies to companies and organizations as a whole. A company that ignores the safety of workers, or hides information customers need to make an informed purchasing decision, is not behaving ethically.

Communication Standards

E-mail and other forms of digital communication sometimes feel anonymous, which might make you think you do not have to be polite and respectful. Personal communication with family and friends may be more informal than communicating for school or business, but in both cases it is important to follow basic rules of netiquette, or online behavior.

- Use correct spelling. Proofread before sending to make sure there are no errors.
- Using all capital letters is considered to be shouting. Be sure to use proper capitalization.
- Don't forward or send unwanted messages or spam.
- Don't flame, or insult, anyone, even as a joke. Sometimes written communication is misinterpreted as being serious, even when if you said it out loud it might be considered funny.
- Don't be a cyberbully. Using electronic communication to hurt, scare, intimidate, or otherwise bully others is a crime.
- Don't make false statements that might hurt someone's reputation. It's called libel, or slander, and it's illegal.

Using Technology Ethically

How people use technology, including computers, smartphones, networks, and e-mail, can affect other people. People who practice ethics behave morally. Ethical computer users respect others, and make sure their actions do not harm anyone.

Using Software Legally

Buying proprietary, copyrighted software comes with a software license, which allows the buyer to use and install the program, and sometimes entitles the buyer to receive free or reduced cost technical support and updates. Individuals might buy a single-user license for one copy of the program, or a single-seat license to install the program on a single computer. Organizations such as schools or businesses usually buy a volume or site license, which lets them install on multiple systems or a network for multiple users. Network licensing generally costs less per user and allows users to share resources.

Software Piracy

People who copy copyrighted software to install on other computers, give away, or sell are guilty of violating federal copyright laws and stealing, called software piracy. Violating a copyright and pirating software are both morally wrong and illegal. These activities discourage the authors of good software from writing new and better programs because they may not get paid for their work. Pirated software cannot be registered, so users do not get the support services they may need.

Acceptable Use Policies

AUP

Acceptable use policy provides guidelines for the use of computers, network, and Internet access.

One way you can act ethically is to follow an acceptable use policy, or AUP. Schools and businesses use AUPs, to govern the way students and workers use technology. The goal of an AUP is to clearly inform students or workers of the rules for appropriate use of technology, and the consequences of breaking those rules. Inappropriate technology use includes online bullying and harassment; hacking (using a computer to gain unauthorized access to data); data vandalism, such as intentionally setting viruses; invading others' privacy; piracy of software, music, video, and other media; and the unauthorized capture and use of photos and video. An AUP may include the following guidelines:

- Do not visit Web sites that contain content that does not meet community standards.
- Do not use language that is profane, abusive, or impolite.
- Do not copy copyrighted material or damage computer equipment.
- Do respect the privacy of other people.

Schools and businesses may restrict the content that users can access from internal computers. For example, they may censor, or block, specific sites that they determine are inappropriate.

They may also use a filter to block access to sites. Disabling the filters or otherwise accessing blocked sites is considered breaking the AUP, and may result in punishment.

More and more, AUPs also include rules and guidelines for digital photography and video. The ease with which we can capture these images, digitally alter them, and then share and distribute them, has raised important ethical issues and lead many organizations to address them in their AUPs. Many schools, for example, prohibit students from using technology to take a photo or record video or audio of other students, faculty, and staff without their knowledge and consent.

People who do not follow these rules may face consequences. They might lose privileges or be suspended from school activities; employees may lose their job. Very serious violations, such as using a school or company computer to threaten someone, may require police involvement.

Practicing Netiquette

Electronic communications have an informal set of rules for expected behavior called netiquette. As an ethical user of technology, you have a responsibility to use netiquette at all times. Some ways to practice netiquette include:

- Send e-mails only to people who really need to see a message.
- Keep e-mail messages short.
- Avoid sending extremely large files via e-mail.
- Do not use impolite or rude language when communicating online.
- Do not pretend to be someone else when communicating online.
- Do not use someone else's work without citing the source.
- Do not share files illegally.

The rules of netiquette are similar to general standards for good behavior. If you go to a search engine and type "netiquette," you will find many Web sites on the topic.

Personal Security Guidelines

In addition to being an ethical user of technology, it is important that you protect your personal security online. Following are some guidelines for maintaining your security and privacy:

- Set your Internet browser to the highest level for security and privacy.
- Delete e-mail from unknown senders without opening it.
- Do business online only with established companies that you know and trust.
- Never send your user name, password, account information, or social security number over the Internet.
- Never reveal financial or other personal information over the Internet.

Managing Your Online Identity

Online, people learn about you by what you post and what sites you frequent. You can use your online profile to both promote a positive image, or brand, of yourself, and to protect your identity. Building your brand means making sure everything you post or display online supports the reputation and character you want people to associate with you.

You can protect your identity by making sure you effectively manage all of your online profiles, including on gaming sites and on social networking sites such as Twitter, LinkedIn, and Face-book. Be sure to set privacy settings and to never give out your personal information in your profiles. You might also maintain both a professional and a personal identity. For example, you might have two e-mail accounts: one for professional and business communication such as with co-workers and clients, and one for personal communication with your friends and family.

Comprehension Check

1. How can you select an object that has no fill?
2. Explain two ways you can select an item in a group without choosing Object > Ungroup.
3. Of the two Selection tools, Selection and Direct Selection, which allows you to edit the individual anchor points of an object?
4. What should you do after creating a selection that you are going to use repeatedly?
5. Sometimes you are unable to select an object because it is underneath another object. Explain two ways to get around this issue.
6. To align objects to the artboard, what do you need to first select in the Align panel or Control panel before you choose an alignment option?

Review Project 1

In groups of three to four, identify and define at least five examples of unethical uses of technology. Then, obtain a copy of your school's AUP or print a sample one from the Internet. Using the AUP as a guide, create a new AUP for a small Web design and development business. The AUP should clearly explain the following:

- The appropriate uses of technology
- The inappropriate or unethical uses of technology
- The consequences for breaking the rules

Share your AUP with the class.

Review Project 2

With a partner, prepare a short skit of a job candidate in an interview with a potential employer. The focus of the interview should be on work behaviors, work qualities, and transferable skills that enhance employability and lead to advancement. Practice your skit and then perform it for the class.

Lesson 3 Overview

In this lesson, you will learn about:

- Creating a New Document
- Working with Basic Shapes
- Editing and Combining Paths and Shapes
- Working with the Pathfinder Panel
- Working with Drawing Modes

In this lesson, you'll use the shape, color, alignment, and other tools to create artwork for a postcard.

Creating a New Document

In this section, you will create a document for a postcard that will have two artboards, each with content that you will later combine.

Try It!

1. Choose File > New to open a new, untitled document. In the New Document dialog box, change the following options:
   - Name: L3_start_xx, replacing xx with your initials or full name, as instructed by your teacher.
   - Profile: Print (the default setting).
   - Number Of Artboards: 2. When you change the number of artboards, the Profile changes to [Custom].
   - Click the Arrange By Row button.
   - Make sure that the Left–To–Right Layout arrow is showing.
   - Units: Inches
   - Spacing: 1 in. (The spacing value is the distance between each artboard.)
   - Width: 6 in. (You don't need to type the "in" for inches, since the units are set to inches.)
   - Height: 4 in.
2. Click OK in the New Document dialog box.
3. Choose File > Save. In the Save dialog box, ensure that the name of the file is: **L3_start1_xx.ai**, and that you are saving to in the location where your teacher instructs you to store the files for this lesson.

   Leave the Format option (Mac) and the Save as type option (Windows) and click Save.

   In the Illustrator Options dialog box, accept the default settings and click OK.
4. Click the Document Setup button in the Control panel.

   The Document Setup dialog box is where you can change the artboard size (by clicking the Edit Artboards button), units, bleeds, and more, after a document is created.
5. In the Bleed section of the Document Setup dialog box, change the value in the Top field to 0.125 in, either by clicking the Up Arrow to the left of the field once or by typing the value in the box. Notice that the values in the Bottom, Left, and Right fields also change. Click OK.

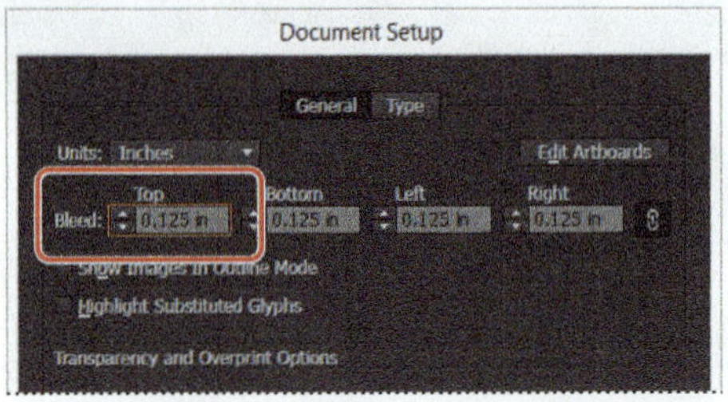

Note:

You can set up a document for different kinds of output, such as print, Web, video, and more, by choosing a Profile. For example, if you are designing a Web-page mockup, you can use a Web document profile, which automatically displays the page size and units in pixels, changes the color mode to RGB, and changes the raster effects to Screen (72 ppi).

Notice the red line that appears around both artboards. The red line indicates the bleed area. Typical bleeds for printing are about 1/8 of an inch, but it can depend on the printing vendor.

6. Save the changes to **L3_start1_xx.ai** and leave it open.

> **Note:**
> You could have set up the bleeds when you first set up the document in the New Document dialog box by choosing File > New.

Working with Basic Shapes

In the first part of this lesson, you'll create some lamps for the postcard using basic shapes, like rectangles, ellipses, rounded rectangles, and polygons. You'll begin this exercise by setting up the workspace.

Try It!

1. Choose Window > Workspace > Essentials (if it's not already selected), and then choose Window > Workspace > Reset Essentials.

2. Choose View > Rulers > Show Rulers to display rulers along the top and left side of the Document window (if they are not already showing).

   The ruler units are inches because you specified them in the New Document dialog box. You can change the ruler units for all documents or for the current document only. The ruler unit shows when measuring objects, moving and transforming objects, setting grid and guide spacing, and creating shapes. It does not affect the units used in the Character, Paragraph, and Stroke panels. The units used in these panels can be changed by choosing (Illustrator > Preferences > Units [Mac OS] or Edit > Preferences > Units [Windows]).

3. Save the changes to **L3_start1_xx.ai** and leave it open.

> **Tip:**
> You can also show/hide rulers by pressing Command+R (Mac) or Ctrl+R (Windows).

Creating Rectangles

First, you'll create a series of rectangles that will be the start of a lamp on the postcard. Rectangles and rounded rectangles are considered Live Shapes. This means that attributes like width, height, rotation, corner radius, and corner style are still editable later and are retained even if you scale or rotate the shape.

Try It!

1. Make sure that the number 1 is showing in the Artboard Navigation area in the lower-left corner of the Document window, which indicates that the first artboard is showing. Choose View > Fit Artboard In Window.

2. Select the Rectangle tool in the Tools panel. Position the pointer anywhere in the artboard, and click and drag down and to the right. As you drag, notice the gray tool tip that appears indicating width and height. Drag until the rectangle is approximately 1.5 in wide and has a height of 1 in, as seen in the tool tip next to the cursor.

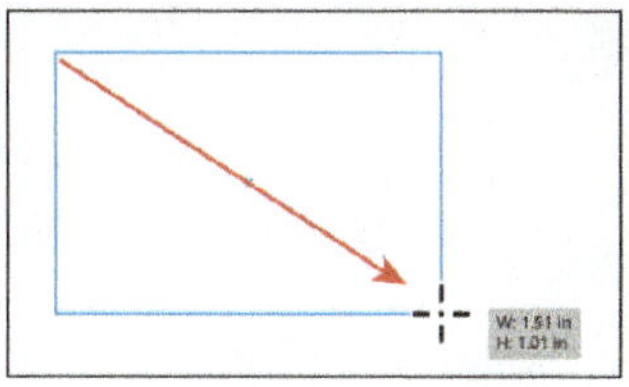

Measurement Label

The tooltip that appears next to the pointer when drawing a shape.

As you drag to create shapes, the tool tip that appears next to the pointer is called the **measurement label** and is a part of the Smart Guides (View > Smart Guides), which will be discussed later in this lesson. When you release the mouse button, the rectangle is selected. Also, by default, shapes are filled with a white color and have a black stroke (border). A shape with a fill can be selected and moved by first positioning the pointer anywhere inside the shape and then clicking and dragging.

After drawing a shape, you can easily edit its size, position, and more using any number of methods.

Tip:

Holding down the Option (Mac) or Alt (Windows) key as you drag with the Rectangle, Rounded Rectangle, or Ellipse tool draws a shape from its center point rather than from its upper-left corner. Holding down the Shift key as you draw with the Rectangle, Rounded Rectangle, or Ellipse tool draws a shape in perfect proportion (a square, rounded corner square, or circle).

3. Choose Window > Transform. In the Transform panel that appears, click the Constrain Width and Height Proportions icon, then change the size of the selected object by typing 0.9 for the width (W:) and 0.35 for the height (H:). Typing the in for inches isn't necessary; it is added automatically.

From the Transform panel, you can change the appearance of your Live Rectangle, including its dimensions, rotation, and corner properties. The center point of the rectangle lets you drag to align the object with other elements in your artwork.

4. Change the X value to 4.9 and the Y value to 3.6 to move the rectangle *relative to* the upper-left corner of the artboard. Press Enter or Return after typing in the Y value to accept it.

5. With the new rectangle still selected, click the Fill color in the Control panel to open the Swatches panel. When you position the pointer over colors in the panel, a tool tip with the color name appears. Choose the yellow/green swatch with the tool tip that shows "C=20 M=0 Y=100 K=0."

Tip:

If you would like the Transform panel to open every time you create a rectangle or rounded rectangle, you can choose Show On Rectangle Creation in the Transform panel menu to toggle it on and off.

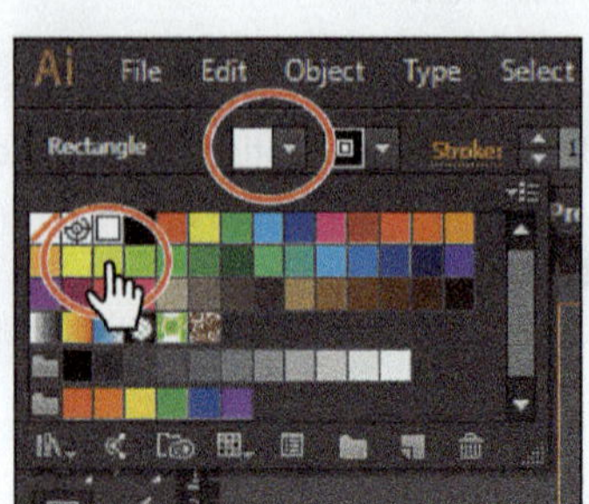

6. Press the Escape key to hide the Swatches panel.

   Next, you will create another rectangle by entering values rather than by drawing it. Using any of the shape tools, you can either draw a shape or click on the artboard with a shape tool selected to enter values in a dialog box. This rectangle will become another part of the lamp.

7. With the Rectangle tool selected, position the pointer above the rectangle you drew on the artboard and click.

   The Rectangle dialog box appears. In the Rectangle dialog box, the width and height values that you see match the last shape drawn.

8. In the Rectangle dialog box, change the Width to 0.6 in, press the Tab key, and change the Height to 0.1. Click OK.

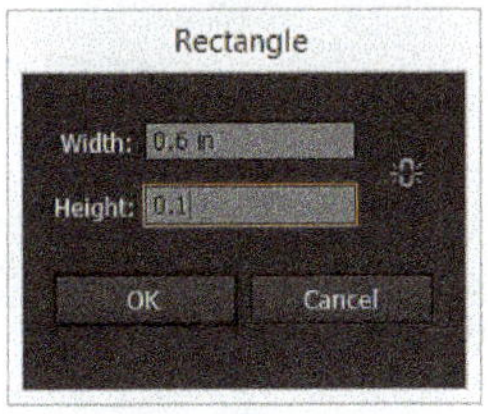

   Notice that the new rectangle has the same fill color and stroke as the previous shape you drew.

9. Select the Selection tool in the Tools panel. Drag the new rectangle about halfway up the artboard, above the first rectangle you drew.

   This is to get the shape out of the way of some new shapes you will be creating.

10. With the new rectangle still selected, click the Fill color in the Control panel to open the Swatches panel. Choose the yellow swatch with the tool tip that shows "C=5 M=0 Y=90 K=0." Press the Escape key to hide the Swatches panel.

11. Save the changes to **L3_start1_xx.ai** and leave open.

Tip:

You also could have simply copied and pasted the original rectangle and changed its size and position. You can also Option-drag (Mac) or Alt-drag (Windows) a shape to create a copy.

Working with the Document Grid

The grid allows you to work more precisely by creating a series of non-printing horizontal and vertical guides behind your artwork in the Document window that objects can snap to.

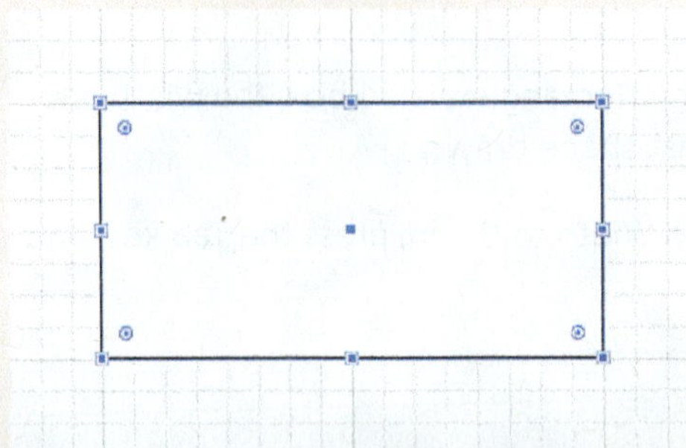

To turn the grid on and use its features, do the following:

- To show the grid, choose View > Show Grid. To hide the grid, choose View > Hide Grid.
- To snap objects to the gridlines, choose View > Snap To Grid, select the object you want to move, and drag it to the desired location. When the object's boundaries come within two pixels of a gridline, it snaps to it.
- To specify grid properties such as the spacing between gridlines, grid style (lines or dots), grid color, or whether grids appear in the front or back of artwork, choose Illustrator > Preferences > Guides & Grid (Mac) or Edit > Preferences > Guides & Grid (Windows).

Creating a Rounded Rectangle

Next, you'll create a rectangle with rounded corners for another part of the illustration. You'll also round the corners of one of the existing rectangles. This involves working with Live Corners.

Try It!

1. Select the Zoom tool in the Tools panel, and click once, on the smaller rectangle you created.
2. Click and hold down the mouse button on the Rectangle tool, and select the Rounded Rectangle tool in the Tools panel.
3. Position the pointer below the smaller rectangle. Click and drag down and to the right until the rectangle has an approximate width of 0.45 inches and a height of 0.2 inches, but *do not release the mouse button yet*. With the mouse button still held down, press the down arrow key a few times to see the corner radius become less rounded (the R value in the tool tip). Press the up arrow key to see the corner become more rounded. Release the mouse button.

4. With the new rectangle still selected, click the Fill color in the Control panel to open the Swatches panel. Choose the yellow swatch with the tool tip that shows "C=20 M=0 Y=100 K=0." Press the Escape key to hide the Swatches panel.

5. With the rounded rectangle selected, change the upper-left corner radius to 0.05 in by typing the value into the field in the Transform panel. Click in another field, or press the Tab key to see the other corners change as well. The Link Corner Radius Values button is on by default.

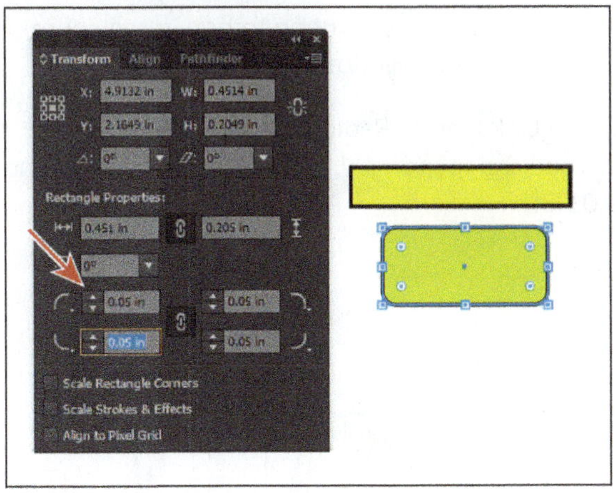

By default, the corners are rounded, but you will see shortly that you can choose from three corner types.

Next, you'll use Smart Guides to help you align the rounded rectangle to the smaller rectangle.

6. Select the Selection tool in the Tools panel. Drag the rounded rectangle up so that it's centered horizontally with the rectangle above it and so that its top edge snaps to the bottom of that same rectangle, as shown in the figure. When the word "intersect" and the green line(s) appear (Smart Guides), release the mouse button.

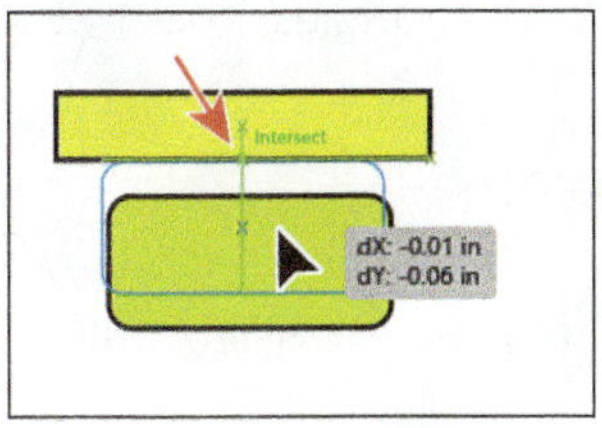

7. With the rounded rectangle selected, click and drag the right, middle bounding point to the right. As you drag, press the Option (Mac) or Alt (Windows) key. This allows you to resize from the center of the shape. Drag until the width is approximately 0.5 in, release the mouse button, and then release the modifier key.

8. Save the changes to **L3_start1_xx.ai** and leave it open.

Editing the Corners of a Live Shape

After creating a rectangle or rounded rectangle, you can later easily edit the corner radius and the corner type. Next, you will edit the corner radius and type of the larger rectangle you drew.

Try It!

1. With the Selection tool, click to select the larger rectangle beneath the other two shapes, and notice that the shape has four corner widgets that you can drag to edit all of the corners at one time (an arrow is pointing to one in the figure). You may need to scroll down in the Document window to see it.

> **Tip:**
>
> In the Transform panel, with a Live Shape selected, you will see the Scale Rectangle Corners option. With this option selected, if you were to scale the Live Shape larger or smaller, the corner radius would scale as well. Otherwise, without the option selected, the corner radius would stay the same.

2. In the Transform panel, click the Link Corner Radius Values button to turn it off. That way you can edit the corners independently. Change the lower-left and lower-right radius values to 0.1 in.

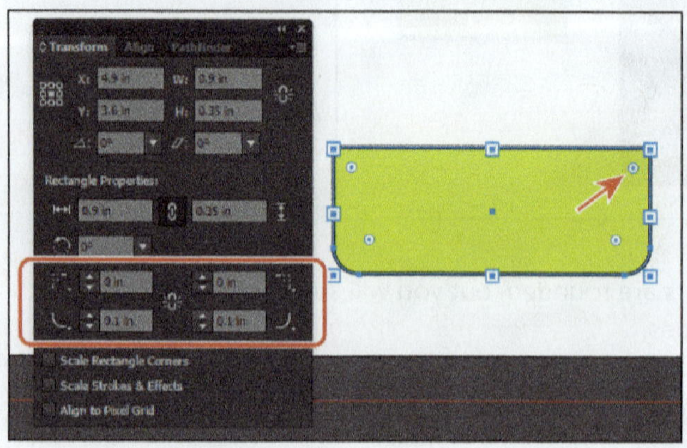

3. In the Transform panel, click the lower-left Corner Type button and select the Chamfer option to edit the type of corner. Do the same for the lower-right corner type (shown in the figure).

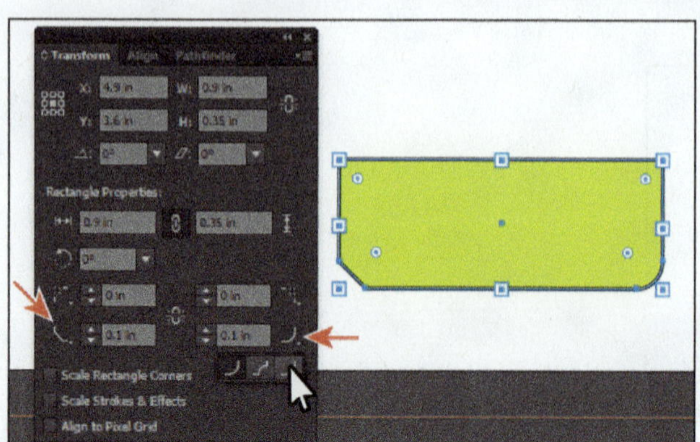

Another method for editing the corners of a Live Shape involves editing the corner widgets directly on the selected shape(s), which is what you'll do next. You may want to zoom in further to the selected rectangle.

4. Choose Select > Deselect.
5. Select the Direct Selection tool and drag a marquee across the top half of the rectangle to select the top two corner points.

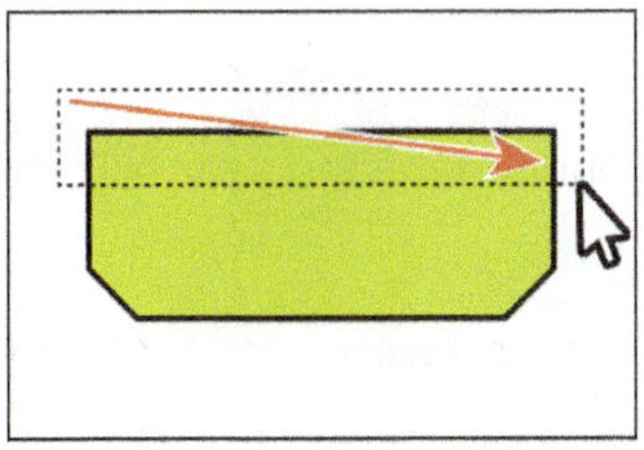

Notice that there are now two corner widgets showing, one for each of the selected anchor points. Using the following method allows you to edit the corner radius and type for only the selected anchor points in one shape or across multiple shapes.

6. Click either corner widget and drag it toward the center of the shape without worrying about how much right now. The corners of a drawn shape are referred to as Live Corners.

If you drag too far, you would see a bold red line appear, indicating that you can drag no further.

7. Double-click either corner widget to open the Corners dialog box. In the dialog box, change the Radius value to 0.15 in and click OK.

The Corners dialog box allows you to edit the corner type and radius, but it also has an extra option called Rounding for setting absolute versus relative rounding. Absolute means the rounded corner is exactly the radius value. Relative makes the radius value based on the angle of the corner point.

8. Click the word *Corners* in the Control panel to show the same Corners options as a menu. Change the Corner Radius value to 0 (zero) and click away from the shape to deselect it.

Setting the radius to 0 (zero) for the selected anchor points is one way of removing the corner radius from the selected anchor points.

9. Choose View > Fit Artboard In Window.
10. Save the changes to **L3_start1_xx.ai** and leave it open.

Tip:

You can Option-click (Mac) or Alt-click (Windows) a corner widget in a shape to cycle through the different corner types.

Creating an Ellipse

Next, you'll draw an ellipse using the Ellipse tool to make up the next part of the lamp. You can draw perfect circles by holding down the Shift key as you drag the Ellipse tool.

Try It!

1. Click and hold down the mouse button on the Rounded Rectangle tool in the Tools panel, and select the Ellipse tool.
2. Choose View > Smart Guides to turn them off. Next, you will create a shape with no Smart Guides turned on to see the difference.
3. Position the pointer over a blank area of the artboard. Begin dragging down and to the right to draw a circle that isn't very large (see the figure).

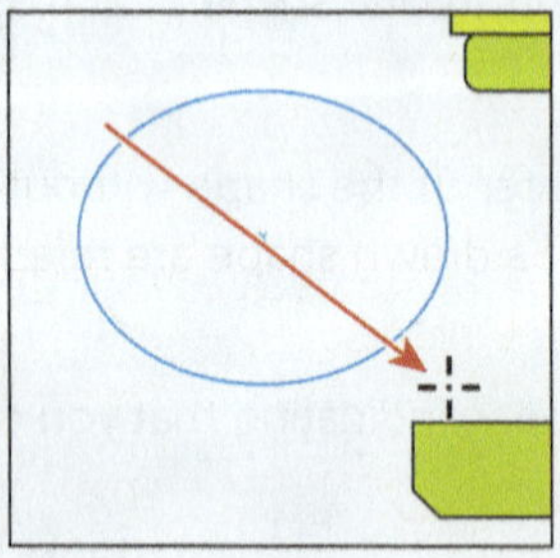

   Notice that you cannot see the size of the circle in the measurement tool tip, since the tool tip is part of the Smart Guides that were turned off. The green alignment guides are also not showing, since the shape is not snapping to other content on the artboard. Smart Guides can be useful in certain situations, such as when more precision is necessary, and can be toggled on and off when needed.

4. Select the Selection tool, and in the Transform panel, ensure that the Constrain Width and Height Proportions is turned off. Change the Width to 1.35 in and the Height to 1.2 in.
5. Choose View > Hide Bounding Box.

   The bounding box, as you saw in previous lessons, allows you to transform the shape. With the bounding box not showing, you can drag the shape by an edge or an anchor point without transforming it.

6. Choose View > Smart Guides to turn them back on.

7. Click and drag the ellipse by the anchor point at the very top of the shape to the center, bottom of the smaller rounded rectangle. Release the mouse button when the ellipse snaps. Don't worry about the position of your larger rectangle toward the bottom of the artboard. You'll position that later on.

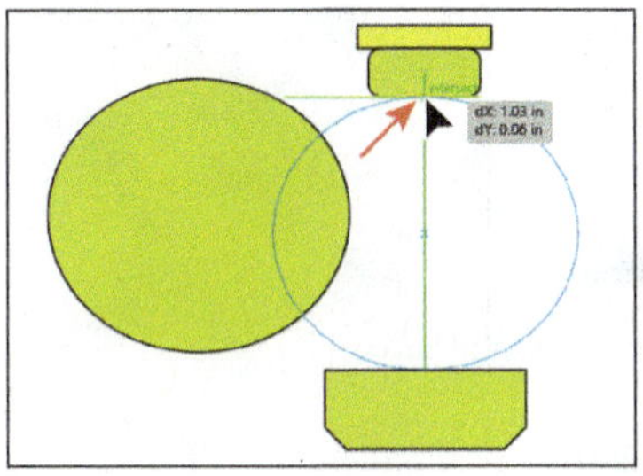

8. Choose View > Show Bounding Box.

9. Choose Select > Deselect. Save the changes to **L3_start1_xx.ai** and leave it open.

Creating Polygons

Now you'll create a triangle using the Polygon tool to finish the lamp. Polygons are drawn from the center by default, which is different than the other tools you've worked with so far.

Try It!

1. Click and hold down the mouse button on the Ellipse tool in the Tools panel, and select the Polygon tool.

2. Click the Fill color in the Control panel, and select the yellow color with the tool tip values "C=5 M=0 Y=90 K=0." Press the Escape key to hide the Swatches panel.

   Next, you'll draw a triangle with the Polygon tool. By default, the Polygon tool draws a six-sided shape, but we need a three-sided shape. As you draw, you will press arrow keys to increase or decrease the number of sides on the shape.

3. Position the pointer above the top yellow rectangle. Drag to the right to begin drawing a polygon, but **don't release the mouse button yet**. Press the Down Arrow key three times to reduce the number of sides on the polygon to three (a triangle), and don't release the mouse yet. Hold down the Shift key to straighten the triangle. Without releasing the Shift key, drag left or right until the Smart Guides measurement label displays a width of approximately 0.5 in. Release the mouse, and then release the modifier key.

4. Select the Selection tool in the Tools panel, and drag the triangle from its center until the bottom of the triangle snaps to the top of the yellow rectangle beneath it. The word "intersect" appears when it is snapped.

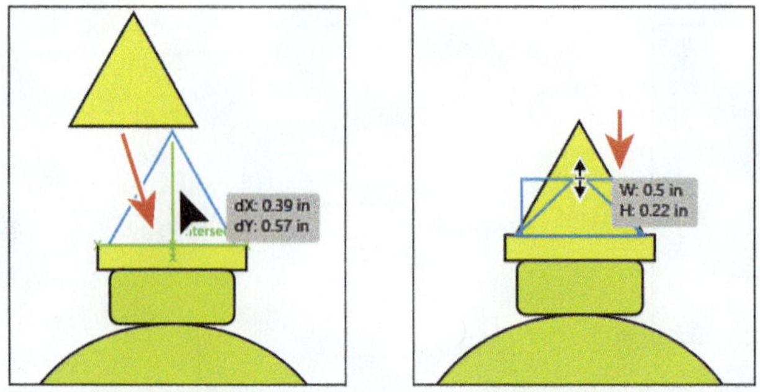

5. With the Selection tool, drag the top point of the triangle down until the measurement label shows a height of approximately 0.22 in.

6. In the Transform panel, change the Width (W) to 0.6 in to match the rectangle beneath it.

7. Choose Select > Deselect.

8. Save the changes to **L3_start1_xx.ai** and leave it open.

Creating Stars

Next, you'll use the Star tool to create a few stars to decorate the lampshade you'll create later. When drawing with the Star tool, you'll use keyboard modifiers to get the number of points you want and to change the radius, or length, of the arms of the star. Here are the keyboard modifiers you will use when drawing the star, and what each does:

- **Arrow keys:** Pressing the up arrow and down arrow adds and removes points from the star as you draw it.
- **Shift:** Straightens the star (constrains it).
- **Command (Mac) or Ctrl (Windows):** Pressing the key and dragging while creating a star allows you to change the radius of the arms of the star (make them longer or shorter).

Try It!

1. Click and hold down the mouse button on the Polygon tool in the Tools panel, and select the Star tool. Position the pointer above the shapes already on the artboard.

   Next, you will create a few stars to get the hang of how it works.

2. Click and drag slowly to the right to create a star shape. Notice that as you move the pointer, the star changes size and rotates freely. Without releasing the mouse button, stop dragging and press the down arrow key once (to decrease the number of points on the star to four). Drag the mouse until you see a width of approximately 0.5 in and stop dragging. Release the mouse button.

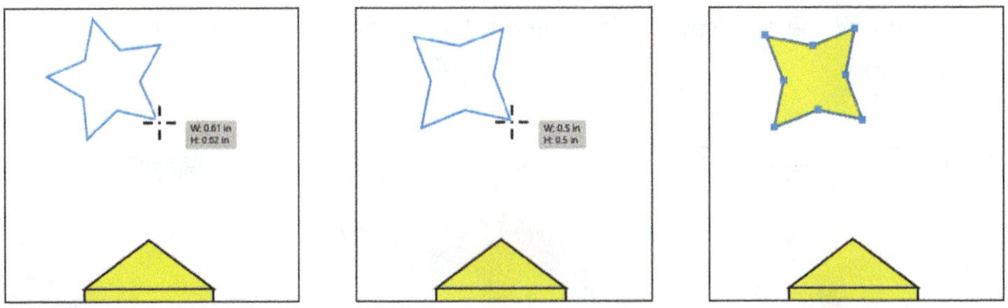

3. Delete the star you just created.

   Next, you will create a star that is straight (constrained), and has arms that are a little longer. This requires that you edit the star you create using two keyboard modifiers.

4. Click and drag slowly to the right to create a star shape. Notice that it has the same number of points as the last star you created (four). Drag until you see a width of approximately 0.5 in, then press the Command (Mac) or Ctrl (Windows) key, and continue dragging to the right. This keeps the inner radius constant, making the arms longer. Drag until you see a width of approximately 0.65 in and stop dragging, *without releasing the mouse button*. Release the Ctrl or Command key, but not the mouse. Hold down the Shift key, and ensure that the star has a width of about 0.8 in. Release the mouse button, and then release the Shift key.

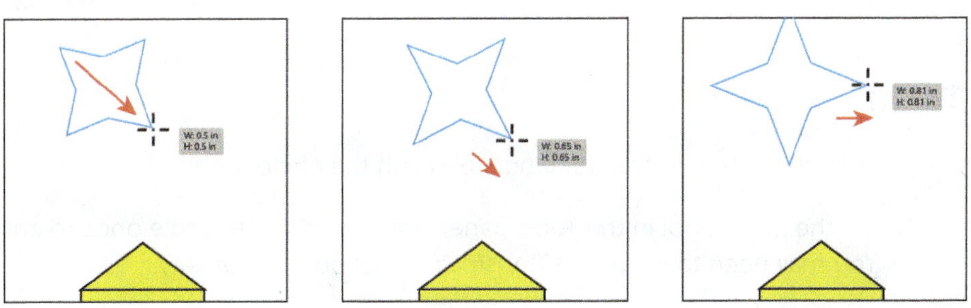

   The next time you draw a star, it will have the same settings. If you want to practice creating another star, try using the keyboard modifiers you've explored. Remember, do not release the mouse button until you are sure you are finished drawing the star. If you do try a few more, delete them and then select the star you made in this step before moving on. Your star doesn't have to exactly match the stars in the figures.

5. Change the Stroke weight of the selected star by entering 0 in the box to the right of the word "Stroke" in the Control panel.
6. Change the Fill color in the Control panel to the orange color with the tool tip "C=0 M=80 Y=95 K=0." Press the Escape key to hide the Swatches panel.
7. Select the Selection tool and Option-drag (Mac) or Alt-drag (Windows) to create a copy of the star (see the following figure). Release the mouse button and then the key.

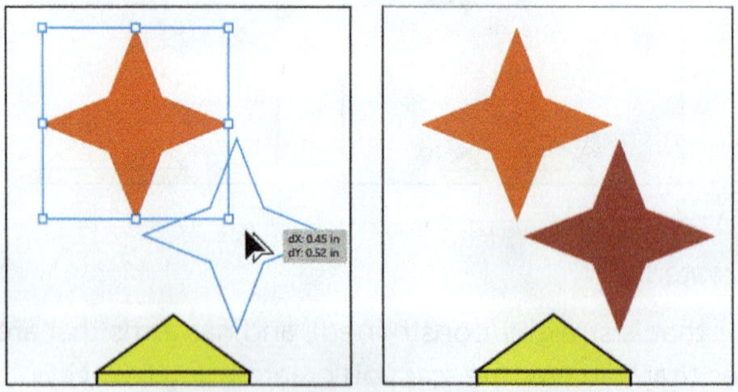

8. Change the Fill color of the copy in the Control panel to the red color with the tool tip "C=15 M=100 Y=90 K=10."
9. Choose Select > Deselect.
10. Save the changes to **L3_start1_xx.ai** and leave it open.

Changing Stroke Width and Alignment

Every shape and path, by default, is created with a 1-point black stroke. You can easily change the color or weight of a stroke to make it thinner or thicker. Strokes are also aligned to the center of a path edge by default, but you can change the alignment as well using the Stroke panel.

Try It!

1. Click to select the bottom rectangle beneath the circle.
2. Select the Zoom tool in the Tools panel, and click that rectangle once to zoom in. You may need to move the Transform panel out of your way.
3. Click the word "Stroke" in the Control panel to open the Stroke panel. In the Stroke panel, change the Stroke weight to 5 pt. Notice that the stroke of the rectangle is centered on the edge of the shape by default.

4. Click the Align Stroke to Inside button in the Stroke panel. This aligns the stroke to the inside edge of the rectangle.

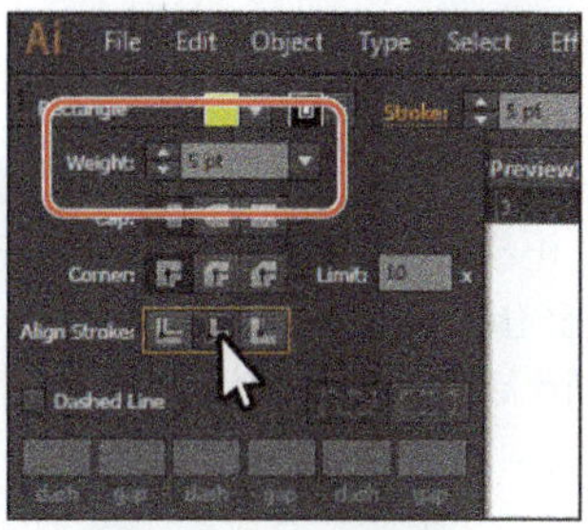

5. With the rectangle still selected, click the Stroke color in the Control panel (to the left of the word "Stroke"), and change the stroke color to yellow "C=5 M=0 Y=90 K=0." Press the Escape key to hide the panel.
6. Press Shift+X to swap the stroke and fill colors.
7. Choose Select > Deselect.

Note:

If pressing Shift+X doesn't work, you can also click the Swap Fill And Stroke arrow toward the bottom of the Tools panel.

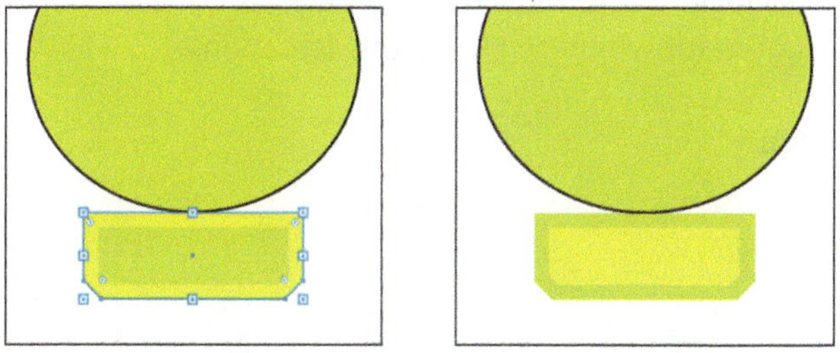

8. Save the changes to **L3_start1_xx.ai** and leave it open.

About Aligning Strokes

If an object is a closed path (such as a square), you can select an option in the Stroke panel to align the stroke along the path to the center (default), inside, or outside.

Working with Lines

Next, you'll work with straight lines and line segments, known as open paths, to create another lamp. Shapes can be created in many ways in Illustrator, and the simpler way is usually better.

Try It!

1. Choose View > Fit Artboard In Window.
2. Select the Zoom tool in the Tools panel, and click once in the empty area near the upper-left corner of the artboard to zoom in.

3. Choose Reset Essentials from the workspace switcher in the Application bar.

   So far, you've been working in the default Preview mode, which lets you see how objects are painted with fill and stroke colors. If paint attributes seem distracting, you can work in Outline mode, which you'll do next.

> **Note:**
>
> Outline mode temporarily removes all paint attributes, such as colored fills and strokes, to speed up selecting and redrawing artwork. You can't select or drag shapes by clicking in the middle of a shape, because the fill temporarily disappears.

4. Choose View > Outline to switch from Preview to Outline mode.

5. Click and hold down the mouse button on the Star tool in the Tools panel, and select the Ellipse tool. In a blank area near the top of the artboard, draw an ellipse that has a width of 1.5 in and a height of 0.1 in, as shown in the measurement label that appears.

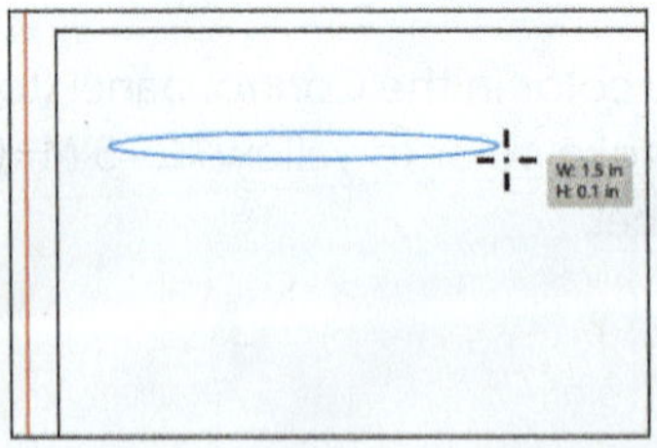

6. Select the Direct Selection tool in the Tools panel. Drag across the top anchor point to select it. See the figure for where to create the selection.

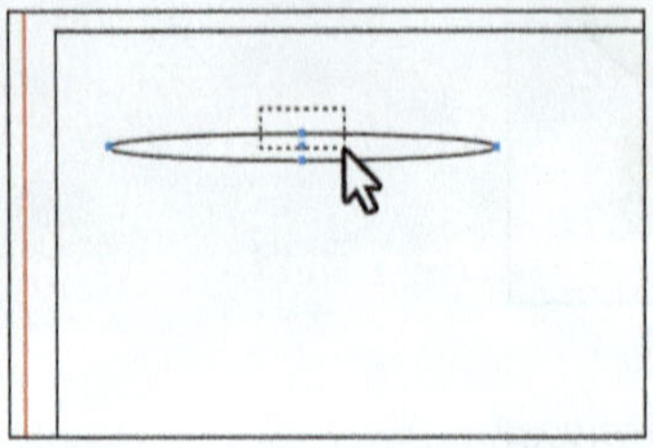

   Dragging across a path will select the line segment and anchor points associated with it. If you drag across an anchor point in a path, you also select the line segments on either side of the anchor point.

7. Choose Edit > Cut, and then choose Edit > Paste In Front to create a new path that is directly on top of the original.

   This copies and pastes only the top half of the ellipse as a single path, because that is what you selected with the Direct Selection tool.

8. Select the Selection tool, and select the bottom half of the shape. Press Shift+Down Arrow five times to move the line down.

   Pressing an arrow key will move a selected object 1 pt, by default. Pressing Shift+arrow will move an object 10 pts per arrow keypress.

9. Choose View > Fit Artboard In Window.

10. Select the Line Segment tool in the Tools panel. Position the point over the center of the path you just moved down (see the red X in the figure). When the word "anchor" appears, press the Shift key and drag down until you see roughly D: 2.5 in. The "D:" in the measurement label is Distance. Release the mouse button and then the Shift key.

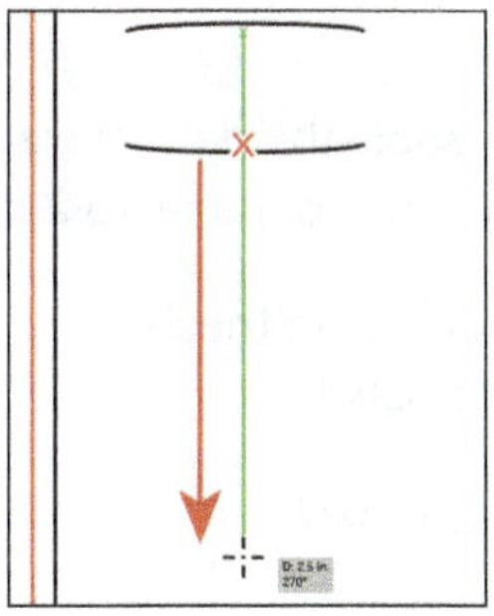

11. With the line selected, change the Stroke weight to 9 pt and change the Stroke color to Black in the Control panel.

12. Choose Select > Deselect. Save the changes to **L3_start1_xx.ai** and leave it open.

Joining Paths

Suppose you draw a "U" shape and later decide you want to close the shape, essentially joining the ends of the "U" with a straight path. If you select the path, you can use the Join command to create a line segment between the end points, closing the path. When more than one open path is selected, you can join them together to create a closed path. You can also join the end points of two separate paths. Next, you will join the two paths to create a single closed path.

Try It!

1. Select the Selection tool in the Tools panel. Drag a selection marquee across the two paths. Make sure not to select the line you just drew.

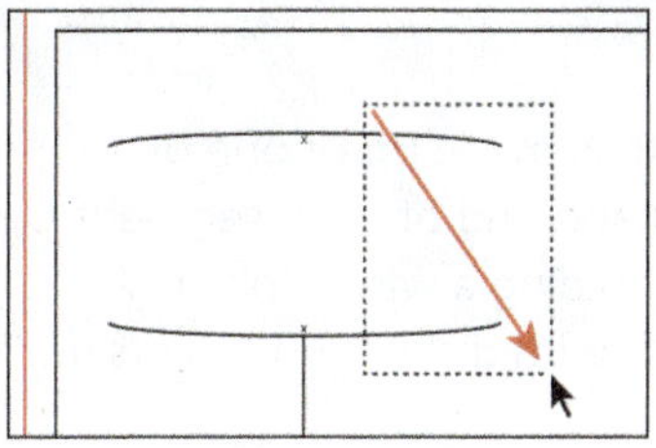

2. Choose Object > Path > Join. Notice that the anchor points on the left side of the paths are now joined with a path.

3. Choose Object > Path > Join once more.

Tip:

If you want to join specific anchor points from separate paths, select the anchor points and press Command+J (Mac) or Ctrl+J (Windows).

Note:

If you only want to fill the shape with a color, it is not necessary to join the path to make a closed path. An open path can have a color fill. It is, however, necessary to join a path if you want a stroke to appear around the entire fill area.

4. Choose Select > Deselect to see the closed path.

   When you apply the Join command to two or more open paths, Illustrator first looks for and joins the paths that have end points stationed closest to each other. This process is repeated every time you apply the Join command until all paths are joined.

5. Choose View > Preview.
6. Click the joined path to select it and press the letter D to apply the default black 1 pt stroke and white fill. Change the Stroke weight in the Control panel to 2 pt.
7. Select the Ellipse tool in the Tools panel and click the artboard. In the Ellipse dialog box, change the Width to 1.1 and the Height to 0.35. Click OK.
8. Change the Fill color to Black and change the Stroke weight to 0 in the Control panel.
9. Press the letter V to select the Selection tool. Drag the ellipse from the center to the bottom of the vertical path. Snap the center to the bottom of the path.

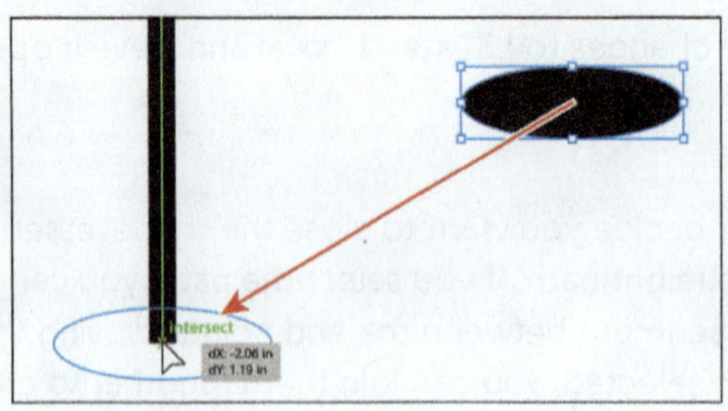

   Don't worry if the bottom of the lamp is off the bottom of the artboard. Later, you will align all of the lamps to each other.

10. Save the changes to **L3_start1_xx.ai** and leave it open.

Path

As you draw you create a path which is made up of one or more straight or curved segments.

Open Path vs. Closed Path

As you draw, you create a line called a **path**. A path is made up of one or more straight or curved segments. The beginning and end of each segment is marked by anchor points, which work like pins holding a wire in place. A path can be closed (for example, a circle), or open, with distinct endpoints (for example, a wavy line).

Both open and closed paths can have fills applied to them.

Editing and Combining Paths and Shapes

In Illustrator, you can edit and combine paths and shapes in different ways to achieve what you want.

Using the Width Tool

Not only can you adjust the stroke weight and the alignment of the stroke, but you can also alter regular stroke widths either by using the Width tool or by applying width profiles to the stroke. This allows you to create a variable width along the stroke of a path.

Next, you will use the Width tool to create the base for another new lamp.

Try It!

1. Select the Line Segment tool in the Tools panel, and click roughly in the center of the artboard. In the Line Segment Tool Options dialog box, change the length to 1.5 and leave the rest of the settings at their defaults. Click OK to create a line.

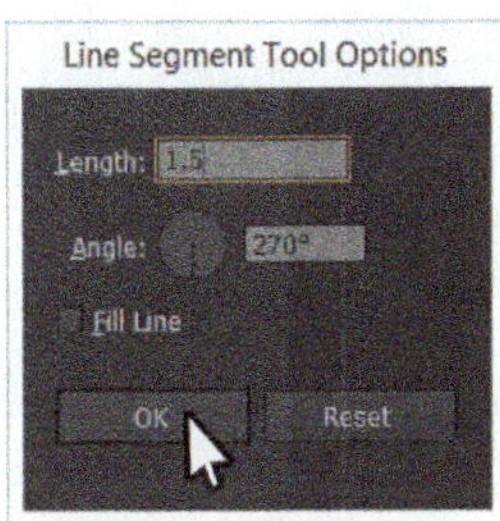

2. Make sure that the Stroke color of the line is Black, the Fill color is None (important), and that the Stroke weight is 1 pt in the Control panel.
3. Select the Zoom tool in the Tools panel and click twice, slowly, on the line to zoom in.
4. Select the Width tool in the Tools panel. Position the pointer over the middle of the line, and notice that the pointer has a plus symbol next to it, indicating that if you click and drag, you can edit the stroke. Click and drag to the right, away from the line. Notice that, as you drag, you are stretching the stroke to the left and right equally. Release the mouse when the measurement label shows Side 1 and Side 2 at approximately 0.29 in.

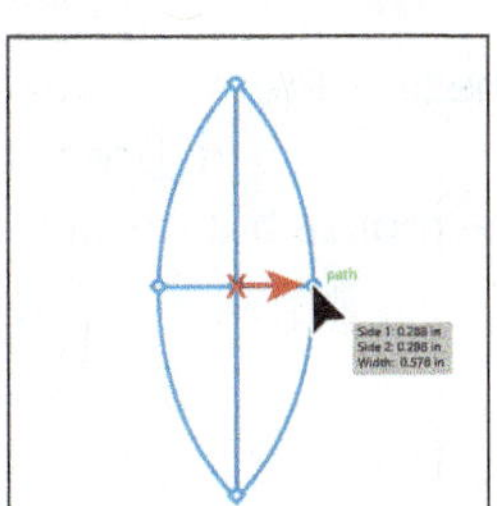

The new point that is filled with blue on the original line is called the width point. The lines extending from the width point are the handles. Width points created at a corner or at a direct-selected anchor point stick to the anchor point during basic editing of the path.

5. Click in a blank area of the artboard to deselect the path. Position the pointer over the path again and the new width point you just created will appear (an arrow is pointing to it in the figure). The width point you see in line with the pointer is where a new point would be created if you were to click. Position the pointer over the original width point and when you see lines extending from it and the pointer has a wavy line next to it, drag it up a bit.

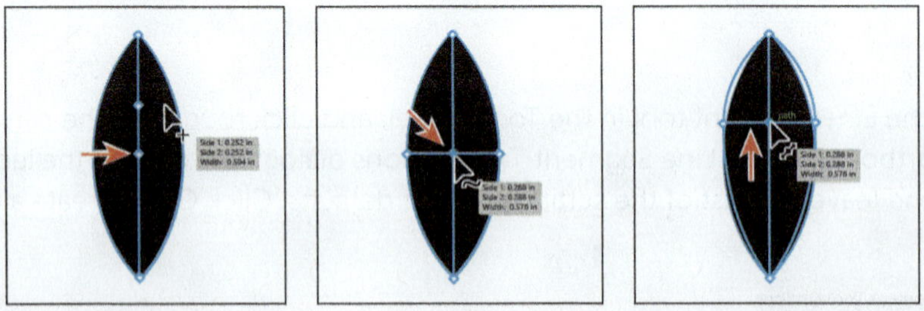

Aside from clicking and dragging to add a width point to a path, you can also double-click and enter values in a dialog box. That's what you'll do next.

6. Position the pointer over the top anchor point of the line, and notice that the pointer has a wavy line next to it and the word "anchor" appears. Double-click on the point to create a new width point and to open the Width Point Edit dialog box.
7. Change the Side 1 width to 0.2 in and change Side 2 to 0.2 in as well, and click OK.

   The Width Point Edit dialog box allows you to adjust the sides together or separately, using more precision. Clicking the Adjust Widths Proportionately button would link Side 1 with Side 2 so that they adjust together, in proportion. Also, if you select the Adjust Adjoining Width Points option, any changes you make to the selected width point affect neighboring width points as well.
8. Double-click the bottom anchor point of the path and repeat step 7 above to make the stroke width the same at the top and bottom of the path.

   You can also duplicate a width point if you like, which is what you'll do next.
9. Position the pointer over the bottom anchor point of the line. Press the Option (Mac) or Alt (Windows) key, and drag up to duplicate the width point. Use the figure below to see roughly how far to drag. Release the mouse button, and then release the modifier key.

10. Position the pointer over the right end of the width point handle and drag to the right until you see a Side 1 and Side 2 of roughly 0.42 in.

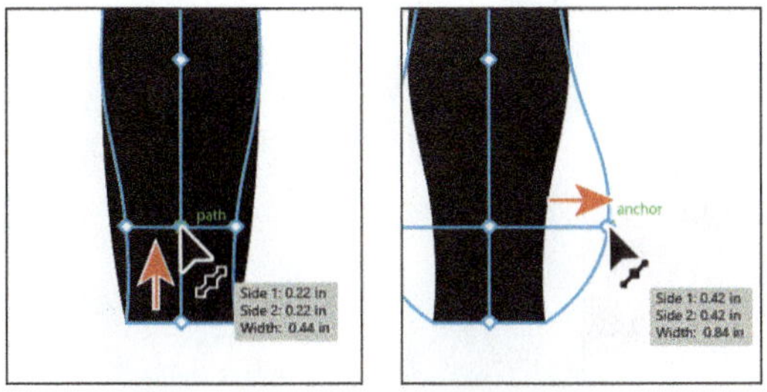

Tip:

If you Option-drag (Mac) or Alt-drag (Windows) a width point handle, you will adjust only the side you are dragging.

11. Position the pointer over the edge of the stroke above the last point (indicated by the red X in the figure). Click and drag to the left until you see a Side 1 width of approximately 0.24 in.

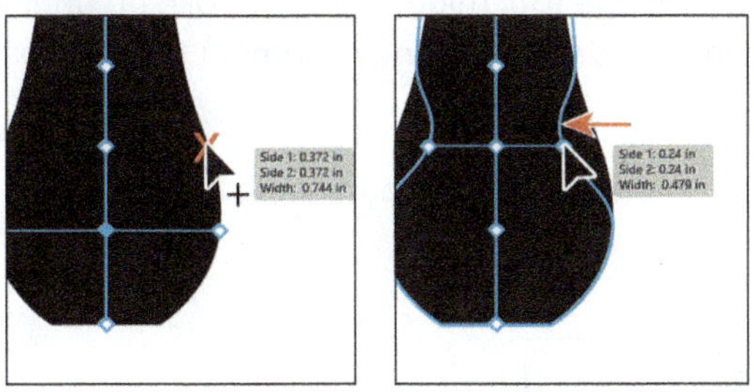

12. Position the pointer between the top width point and the second width point from the top. See the red X in the figure for help. Click and drag to the left until you see a Side 1 width of approximately 0.14 in.

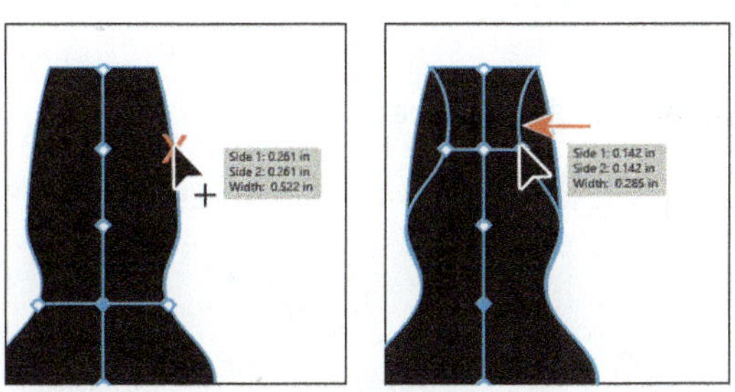

Tip:

In the Control panel you may need to change the Variable Width Profile to Uniform (drop down menu to the right of the Stroke Weight).

13. Select the Rectangle tool in the Tools panel. In the blank area above the lamp you just created, click to open the Rectangle dialog box. Change the Width to 1.5 in and the Height to 0.8 in. Click OK.

14. Change the Fill color to an orange with a tool tip of "C=0 M=80 Y=95 K=0" in the Control panel. Change the Stroke color to the same orange with a Stroke weight of 1 pt.

15. Select the Selection tool and drag the rectangle so that it is centered with the lamp body and covers the very top. See the figure for placement help.

    Next, you will use the Width tool to edit one side of the stroke, rather than both, as you've been doing.

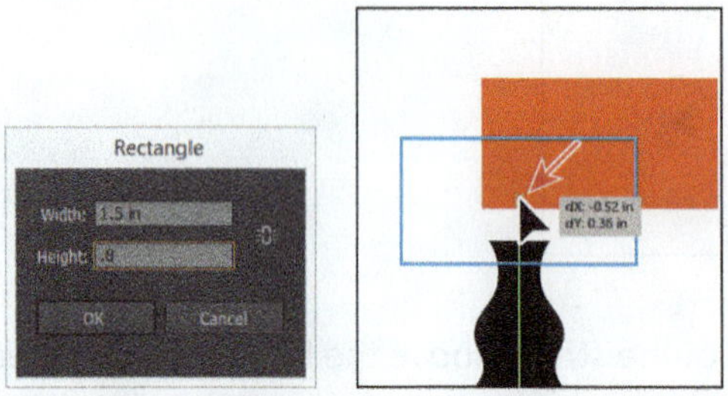

16. With the rectangle still selected, select the Width tool in the Tools panel. Option-drag (Mac) or Alt-drag (Windows) the top, middle of the stroke up until you see a value of approximately 0.1 in for Side 1 in the measurement label. Release the mouse button and then the key.

17. Do the same for the bottom of the rectangle—but dragging down with the Option (Mac) or Alt (Windows) key held down.

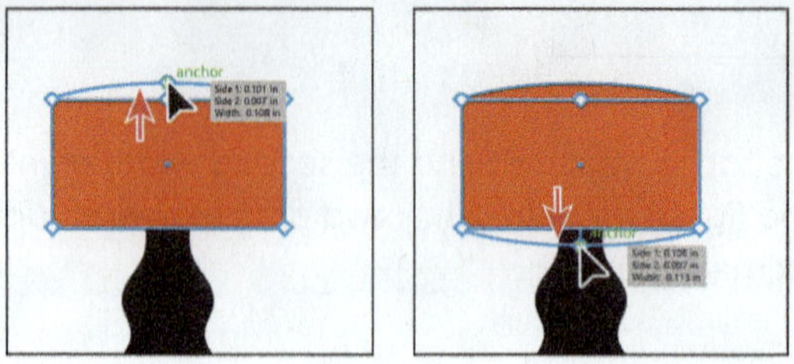

18. Save the changes to **L3_start1_xx.ai** and leave it open.

Saving Width Profiles

After defining the stroke width, you can save the variable width profile from the Stroke panel or the Control panel by selecting a modified stroke and then clicking the Add To Profiles button at the bottom of the Variable Width Profiles menu in the Control panel, or the Profile menu at the bottom of the Stroke panel.

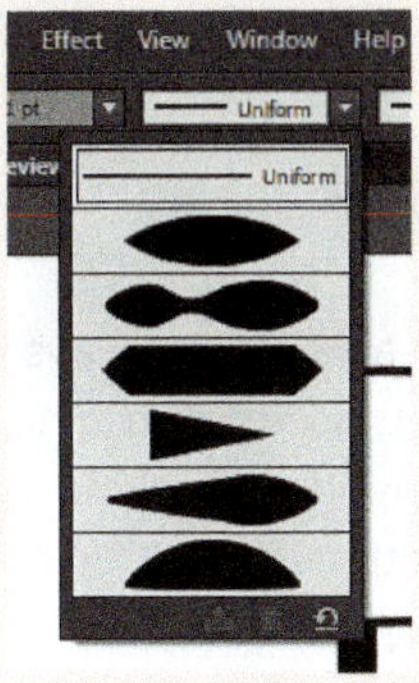

Width profiles can be applied to selected paths by choosing them from the Variable Width Profile menu in the Control panel or the Profile menu in the Stroke panel. When a stroke with no variable width is selected, the list displays the Uniform option. You can also select the Uniform option to remove a variable width profile from an object. To restore the default width profile set, click the Reset Profiles button at the bottom of the Profile menu.

If you apply a variable width profile to a stroke, it is indicated with an asterisk (*) in the Appearance panel.

—From Illustrator Help

Outlining Strokes

Paths, such as a line, can show a stroke color but not a fill color by default. If you create a line in Illustrator and want to apply both a stroke and a fill, you can outline the stroke, which converts the line into a closed shape (or compound path). By outlining the stroke, you can no longer edit the path using the Width tool.

Next, you will outline the stroke of the lamp you just created with the Width tool.

Try It!

1. With the Selection tool, select the black path you edited with the Width tool and choose Object > Path > Outline Stroke.
2. This creates a filled shape that is a closed path.
3. With the new shape selected, click the Fill color in the Control panel and change the color to the yellow/green that shows "C=20 M=0 Y=100 K=0" in the tool tip.
4. Shift-click the orange lampshade and choose Object > Group.

5. Choose View > Fit Artboard In Window.

6. Choose Select > Deselect. Save the changes to **L3_start1_xx.ai** and leave it open.

Working with the Shape Builder Tool

In Illustrator, you can combine vector objects to create shapes in a variety of ways. The resulting paths or shapes differ depending on the method you use to combine the paths. The first method you will learn for combining shapes involves working with the Shape Builder tool. This tool allows you to visually and intuitively merge, delete, fill, and edit overlapping shapes and paths directly in the artwork. Using the Shape Builder tool, you'll create a lampshade for the lamp on the right.

Try It!

1. With the Selection tool, Shift-click both star shapes. Choose Object > Hide > Selection to temporarily hide them.

2. Select the Rectangle tool in the Tools panel. Near the top edge of the artboard on the right, above the yellow/green lamp shapes, click to open the Rectangle dialog box. Change the Width to 2 in and the Height to 1.2 in. Click OK.

3. Change the Fill color of the rectangle to an orange with a tool tip of "C=0 M=80 Y=95 K=0" in the Control panel, if necessary.

4. Click the artboard again to open the Rectangle dialog box. Ensure that the Width is still 2 in and change the Height to 0.15 in. Click OK. Change the fill of the smaller rectangle to Black in the Control panel.

5. With the Selection tool, drag the smaller rectangle so that its top edge snaps to the bottom of the first rectangle and aligns to its center.

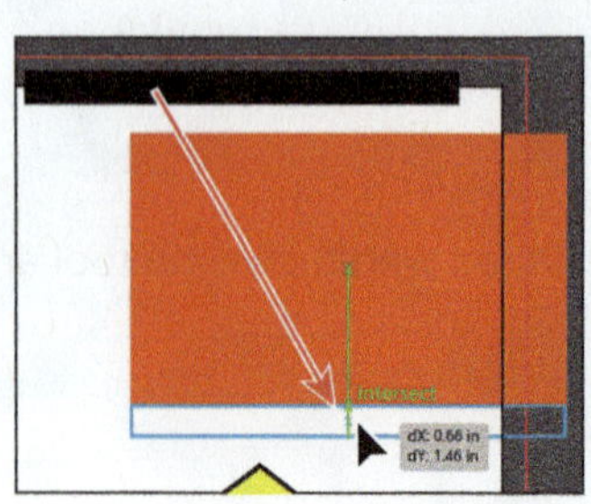

6. Click to select the yellow triangle at the top of the lamp shapes on the right. Choose Edit > Copy and then Edit > Paste.

7. In the Transform panel (Window > Transform), change the Width to 2 in and the Height to 2 in.
8. With the Selection tool, drag the triangle so that its bottom edge aligns with the bottom of the larger rectangle and is centered vertically with it.

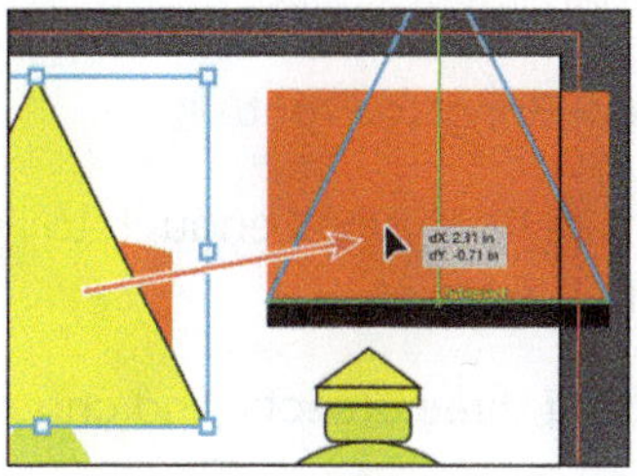

9. Drag across all three shapes to select them.

   In order to edit shapes with the Shape Builder tool, they need to be selected.

   Using the Shape Builder tool, you will now combine, delete, and paint these shapes.

10. Select the Shape Builder tool in the Tools panel. Position the pointer below the shapes, and drag from the red X in the figure up into the larger rectangle. Release the mouse button to combine the shapes.

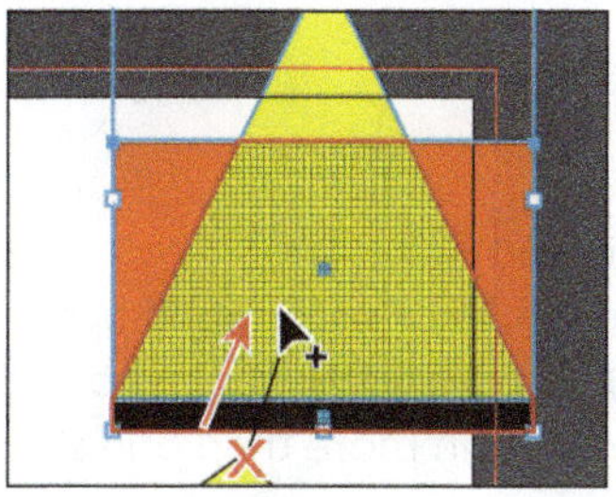

When you select the Shape Builder tool, the overlapping shapes are divided into separate objects temporarily. As you drag from one part to another, a red outline appears, showing you what the final shape outline will look like when it merges the shapes together.

11. With the shapes still selected, hold down the Option (Mac) or Alt (Windows) key. Notice that, with the modifier key held down, the pointer shows a minus sign. Click each shape indicated in the figure with a red X to delete them.

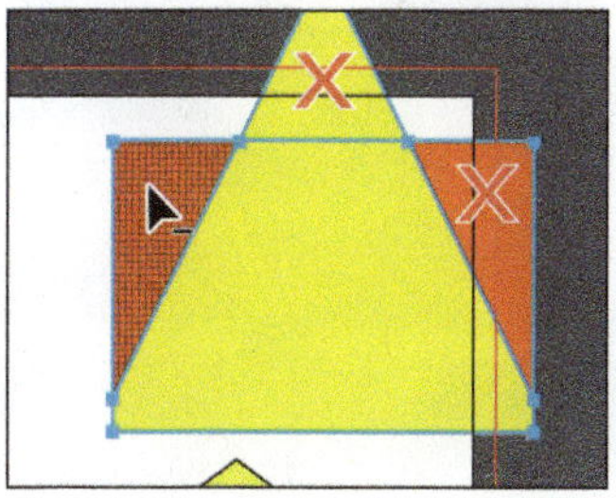

Tip:

You can also press the Shift key and drag a marquee across a series of shapes to combine them. Pressing Shift+Option (Mac) or Shift+Alt (Windows) and dragging a marquee across selected shapes with the Shape Builder tool selected allows you to delete a series of shapes within the marquee.

12. With the shape still selected, select the Selection tool. Change the Fill color in the Control panel to a light gray with the tool tip showing "C=0 M=0 Y=0 K=10." Press the Escape key to hide the panel. Change the Stroke weight to **0**.
13. Choose Select > Deselect.
14. Choose Object > Show All to redisplay the star shapes.
15. With the stars selected, choose Object > Arrange > Bring To Front.
16. With the Selection tool, Shift-drag a corner to make them small enough to fit on the gray lampshade. Position them like you see in the figure.
17. Shift-click the gray lampshade and stars to select all three objects, and choose Object > Group.

18. Choose Select > Deselect. Save the changes to **L3_start1_xx.ai** and leave it open.

Working with the Pathfinder Panel

The bottom row of buttons in the Pathfinder panel, called *Pathfinder effects*, lets you combine shapes in many different ways to create paths or compound paths by default. When a Pathfinder effect (such as Merge) is applied, the original objects selected are permanently transformed. If the effect results in more than one shape, they are grouped automatically.

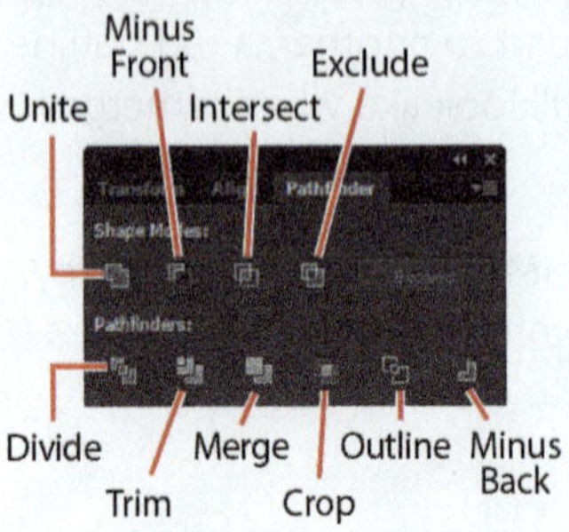

Pathfinder Effects in the Pathfinder Pane

Next, you will finish the yellow/green lamp using Pathfinder effects.

Try It!

1. Choose Window > Pathfinder to open the Pathfinder panel group.
2. With the Selection tool, hold down the Shift key and click the small yellow triangle and the small rectangle beneath the lampshade to select both objects.
3. With the shapes selected, in the Pathfinder panel, click the Merge button to combine the shapes into one.

4. With the new shape selected, notice the word "Path" on the left side of the Control panel.
5. Choose Select > Deselect. Save the changes to **L3_start1_xx.ai** and leave it open.

Shape Modes in the Pathfinder Panel

The buttons in the top row of the Pathfinder panel, called *shape modes*, create paths just like the Pathfinder effects, but they can also be used to create compound shapes. When several shapes are selected, clicking a shape mode while pressing the Option (Mac) or Alt (Windows) key creates a compound shape rather than a path. The original underlying objects of compound shapes are preserved. As a result, you can still select each original object within a compound shape. Using a shape mode to create a compound shape can be useful if you think that you may want to retrieve the original shapes at a later time.

Next, you will use shape modes to finish the yellow/green lamp.

Try It!

1. Select the Zoom tool, and click several times on the rectangle at the bottom of the yellow/green lamp to zoom in.
2. Select the Rectangle tool in the Tools panel. Draw a rectangle that has an approximate width of 0.5 in and a height of 0.1 in.
3. With the Selection tool, Shift-click the bottom yellow/green rectangle with the chamfered corners to select both shapes. Release the Shift key. Click again on the larger shape to make it the key object for alignment.

4. Click the Horizontal Align Center button and the Vertical Align Bottom button in the Control panel to align the two shapes.

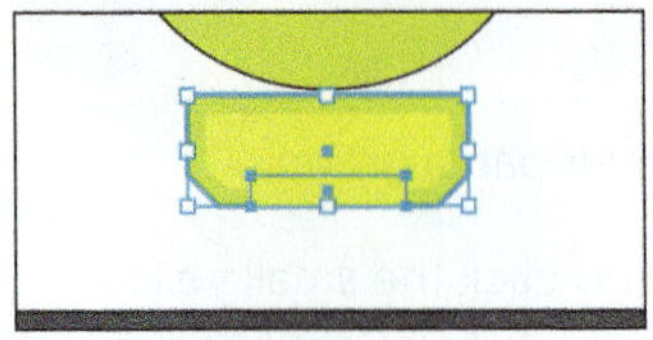

5. With the objects selected, click the Minus Front button in the Shape Modes section of the Pathfinder panel.

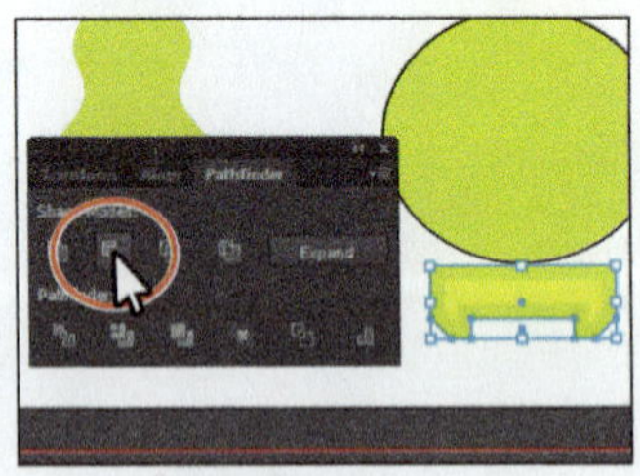

   This creates a compound shape that traces the outline where the two objects overlap. You will still be able to edit both shapes separately.

6. Choose Select > Deselect to see the final shape.
7. With the Selection tool, double-click the same shape to enter Isolation mode.
8. Choose View > Outline so that you can see the two shapes.
9. Click the edge of the smaller rectangle to select it. Option-drag (Mac) or Alt-drag (Windows) the right, middle bounding point of the smaller rectangle-bounding box to the left to make it a bit narrower. Drag until the measurement tool tip shows a width of approximately 0.4 in. Release the mouse button and then the key.

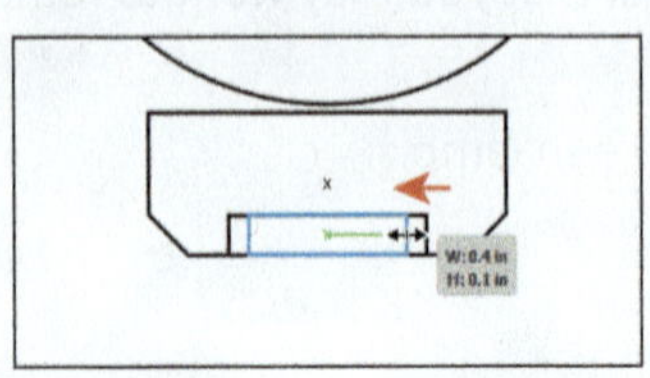

10. Press the Escape key to exit Isolation mode.

    Because you entered Outline mode while in Isolation mode, exiting Isolation mode switches back to Preview mode automatically.

    You will now expand the window shape. Expanding a compound shape maintains the shape of the compound object, but you can no longer select or edit the original objects. You will typically expand an object when you want to modify the appearance attributes and other properties of specific elements within it.

11. Click away from the shape to deselect it, and then click to select it again. Click the Expand button in the Pathfinder panel. Close the Pathfinder panel group.
12. Choose Select > Deselect.
13. Choose View > Fit Artboard In Window. Save the changes to **L3_start1_xx.ai** and leave it open.

Using the Eraser Tool

The Eraser tool lets you erase any area of your vector artwork, regardless of the structure. You can use the Eraser tool on paths, compound paths, paths inside Live Paint groups, and clipping content. Next, you'll use the Eraser tool to edit one of the lampshades.

Try It!

1. With the Selection tool, select the white lampshade on the left side of the artboard.

   By selecting the white lampshade, you'll erase only that shape and nothing else. If you leave all objects deselected, you can erase any object that the tool touches, across all layers.
2. Double-click the Eraser tool in the Tools panel to edit the tool properties. In the Eraser Tool Options dialog box, change the Size to 4 pt. Click OK.
3. Position the pointer off the upper-left corner of the white rectangle (where you see the red X in the figure). Click and drag diagonally across the rectangle. When you release the mouse button, the rectangle is cut in two and the two paths are closed shapes.

Note:

You cannot erase images, text, symbols, graphs, or gradient mesh objects.

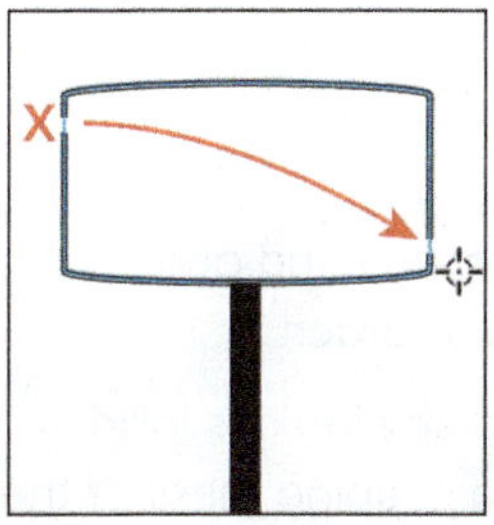

4. Try dragging across the lampshade some more to create an effect like you see in the figure below.
5. Choose Object > Group, and then choose Select > Deselect.

6. Select the Selection tool and drag across the lampshade you just created, the line, and the ellipse beneath it to select all *three* objects that make up that lamp. Choose Object > Group.

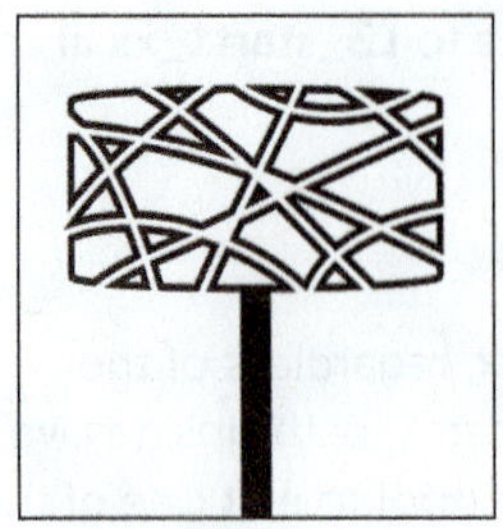

7. Choose Select > Deselect. Save the changes to **L3_start1_xx.ai** and leave it open.

Working with Drawing Modes

Illustrator has three different drawing modes available that are found at the bottom of the Tools panel: Draw Normal, Draw Behind, and Draw Inside. Drawing modes allow you to draw shapes in different ways. The three drawing modes are:

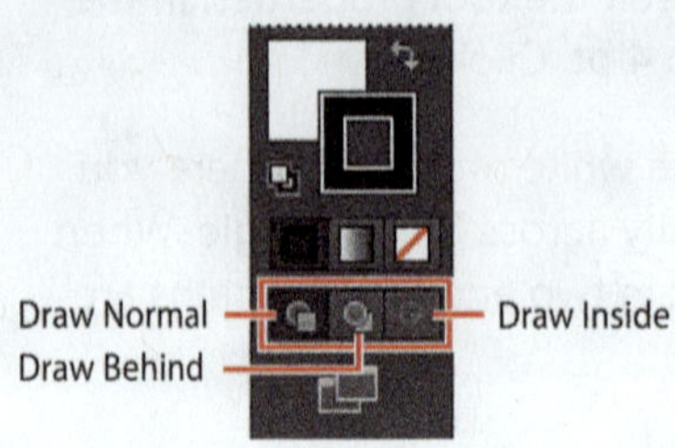

- **Draw Normal mode:** You start every document by drawing shapes in Normal mode, which stacks shapes on top of each other.
- **Draw Behind mode:** This mode allows you to draw objects behind other objects without choosing layers or paying attention to the stacking order.
- **Draw Inside mode:** This mode lets you draw objects or place images inside other objects, including live text, automatically creating a clipping mask of the selected object.

Working with Draw Behind Mode

Throughout this lesson, you've been working in the default Draw Normal mode. Next, you'll draw a rectangle that will cover the artboard and go behind the rest of the content using Draw Behind mode.

Try It!

1. Click the Draw Behind button at the bottom of the Tools panel.

   As long as this drawing mode is selected, every shape you create using the different methods you've learned will be created behind the other shapes on the page. The Draw Behind mode also affects placed content (File > Place).

2. Select the Rectangle tool in the Tools panel. Position the pointer off the upper-left corner of the artboard in the corner of the red bleed guides. Click and drag off the lower-right side of the artboard to the corner of the red bleed guides.

3. With the new rectangle selected, click the Fill color in the Control panel and change the fill color to a red with the tool tip values "C=15 M=100 Y=90 K=10." Press the Escape key to hide the Swatches panel.

4. Change the Stroke weight to 0 in the Control panel.

5. Choose Object > Lock Selection.

6. Click the Draw Normal button at the bottom of the Tools panel.

7. Save the changes to **L3_start1_xx.ai** and leave it open.

Using the Draw Inside Mode

Next, you will learn how to draw a shape inside of another using the Draw Inside drawing mode. This can be useful if you wanted to hide (mask) part of artwork.

Try It!

1. Select the Selection tool in the Tools panel. Click to select the yellow/green ellipse of the rightmost lamp.

2. Click the Draw Inside button, near the bottom of the Tools panel.

This button is active when a single object is selected (path, compound path, or text), and it allows you to draw within the selected object only. Every shape you create will now be drawn inside of the selected shape (the circle). Notice that the ellipse has a dotted open rectangle around it, indicating that, if you draw, paste, or place content, it will be inside of the circle, even if you were to choose Select > Deselect.

3. Select the Ellipse tool in the Tools panel. Position the pointer near the center of the yellow/green ellipse, press the Shift key, and draw a circle that has a width and height of 1.2 in. Release the mouse button and then the key.

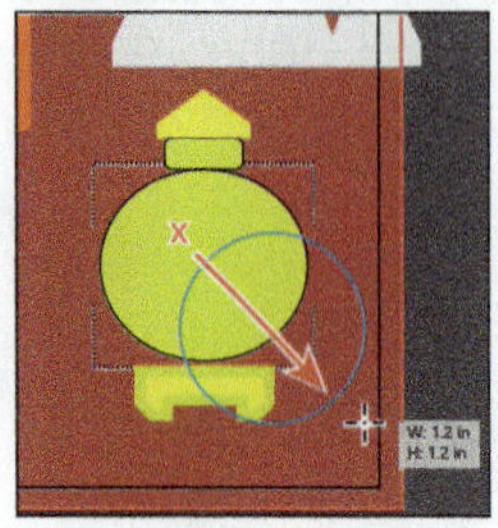

4. Change the Fill color of the new circle to the yellow with the tool tip that shows "C=5 M=0 Y=90 K=0."
5. Change the Stroke weight to 0 in the Control panel.
6. Choose Select > Deselect.

   Notice that the ellipse still has the dotted open rectangle around it, indicating that Draw Inside mode is still active.

When you are finished drawing content inside of a shape, you can click the Draw Normal button so that any new content you create will be drawn normally (stacked rather than drawn inside). Right now, if you were to attempt to select the ellipse or the circle inside of it, you would select the ellipse. If you move the ellipse, the shape inside goes with it. If you resize or reshape the yellow/green ellipse, the shape inside will resize or reshape.

7. Click the Draw Normal button at the bottom of the Tools panel.

   This ensures that any new content you create will not be drawn inside of the yellow/green ellipse.

8. Save the changes to **L3_start_xx.ai** and leave it open.

Editing Content Drawn Inside

Next, you will edit the circle inside of the yellow/green ellipse to see how you can later edit content drawn inside.

Try It!

1. Select the Selection tool, and click to select the yellow circle (that is inside of the yellow/green ellipse). Notice that it selects the yellow/green ellipse instead.

   The yellow/green ellipse is now a mask, also called a clipping path. The ellipse and the circle together make a clip group and are now treated as a single object. If you look on the left end of the Control panel, you will see "Clip Group" and two buttons that allow you to edit either the clipping path (the yellow/green ellipse) or the contents (the yellow circle).

2. Click the Edit Contents button on the left end of the Control panel to select the yellow circle.

Tip:

You can also double-click the yellow circle to enter Isolation mode and press the Escape key to exit.

3. Drag the yellow circle from within the yellow fill color up to match the figure as best you can.

4. Click the Edit Clipping Path button on the left end of the Control panel to select the yellow/green ellipse.

5. Change the Stroke weight to 0 in the Control panel.

   If you find it difficult to change the Stroke weight to 0 (zero), try changing it to another value first, and then 0.

6. Choose Select > Deselect.

   Next, you will assemble the yellow/green lamp by dragging shapes. Make sure that you keep the shapes aligned horizontally with each other using the Smart Guides for alignment.

7. Drag the shape below the clip group (circle) up to match the first part of the following figure (below).

8. Click to select the yellow/green rounded rectangle above the clip group (the circle).

9. Change the Stroke weight to 0 in the Control panel.

10. Drag that same rounded rectangle and the shape above it down to match the middle part of the circle, as shown in the following figure (you will need to select both).

11. Drag the lampshade over the top of the lamp to match the figure.

12. Drag across all of the shapes in the lamp to select them, and choose Object > Group.

13. Choose Select > Deselect. Save the changes to **L3_start_xx.ai** and leave it open.

Using Image Trace to Create Shapes

In this part of the lesson, you will learn how to work with the Image Trace command. Image Trace traces existing artwork, like a raster picture from Adobe Photoshop. You can then convert the drawing to vector paths or a Live Paint object. This can be useful for turning a drawing into vector art, tracing raster logos, tracing a pattern or texture, and much more.

Try It!

1. With the Selection tool selected, click the Next artboard button in the status bar in the lower-left corner of the Document window to navigate to the second artboard.

2. Choose File > Place. In the Place dialog box, select the Logo.png file from the data files for this lesson, and click Place (shown in the figure). Click on the left edge of the artboard to place the image. The image will be larger than the artboard, but that's okay.

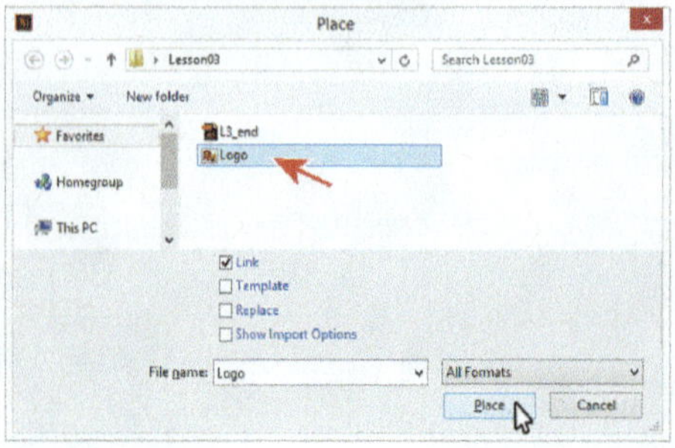

With the placed image selected, the Control panel options change. You can see the words "Linked File" on the left side of the Control panel, the name Logo.png and the resolution (PPI: 72), as well as other information.

3. Click the Image Trace button in the Control panel. The tracing results you see may differ slightly from the figure, and that's okay.

This converts the image into an image tracing object using the default tracing options. That means that you can't edit the vector content yet, but you can change the tracing settings or even the original placed image and then see the updates.

4. Choose 6 Colors from the Preset menu on the left end of the Control panel.

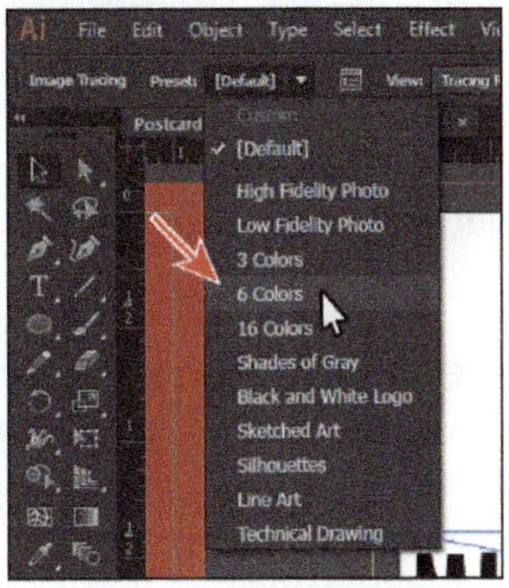

Illustrator comes with preset tracing options that you can apply to your image tracing object. You can then make changes to the tracing settings, if need be, using the default preset as a starting point.

5. Choose Outlines with Source Image from the View menu in the Control panel, and take a look at the image. Choose Tracing Result from that same menu.

   An image tracing object is made up of the original source image and the tracing result (which is the vector artwork). By default, only the tracing result is visible. However, you can change the display of both the original image and the tracing result to best suit your needs.

6. Choose Window > Image Trace to open the Image Trace panel. In the panel, click the Auto-Color button at the top of the panel.

   The buttons along the top of the Image Trace panel are saved settings for converting the image to grayscale, black and white, and more. Below the buttons at the top of the Image Trace panel, you will see the Preset and View options. These are the same as those in the Control panel. The Mode option allows you to change the color mode of resulting artwork (color, grayscale, or black and white). The Palette option is also useful for limiting the color palette or for assigning colors from a color group.

Tip:

Tracing a larger image or higher-resolution image will most likely result in better results.

Note:

You can also choose Object > Image Trace > Make, with raster content selected, or begin tracing from the Image Trace panel (Window > Image Trace).

Tip:

The Image Trace panel can also be opened with traced artwork selected, by clicking the Image Trace Panel button in the Control panel.

> **Note:**
>
> By selecting the Snap Curves To Lines option, the small yellow/green lamp pull cord no longer has rounded corners

7. Press and hold the eye icon to the right of the View menu in the Image Trace panel to see the source image on the artboard. Release the mouse button.
8. In the Image Trace panel, click the toggle arrow to the left of the Advanced options to reveal them. Change only the following options, using the values as a starting point:
   - Colors: **3**
   - Paths: **80%**
   - Corners: **90%**
   - Noise: **10 px**
   - Snap Curves To Lines: **Selected**
   - Ignore White: **Selected**

The type in the logo isn't perfect yet. You can clean up the type (see the sidebar "Cleaning Up Traced Artwork") or find out the original font used and replicate it.

9. Close the Image Trace panel.
10. With the logo image tracing object still selected, click the Expand button in the Control panel. The logo is no longer an image tracing object but is composed of shapes and paths that are grouped together.
11. With the Selection tool, double-click the logo to enter Isolation mode. Click one of the black letters to select it. Choose Select > Same > Fill Color to select all of the black letters. Change the Fill color to White in the Control panel. Press the Escape key to hide the Swatches panel.
12. Press the Escape key to exit isolation mode. Choose Select > Deselect, and then click to select the logo group.
13. Choose Object > Transform > Scale. In the Scale dialog box, change the Uniform value to 48 and click OK. This will scale the logo so you can place it into the previous artboard.
14. Choose View > Fit All In Window to see both artboards. Drag the logo into the upper-right corner of the first artboard (with the lamps on it). See the figure for placement.
15. Drag the lamps into position as shown in the figure.

16. Close **L3_start_xx.ai,** saving all changes, and exit Illustrator.

Cleaning Up Traced Artwork

After tracing, you may need to clean up the resulting vector artwork. Using the Object > Path > Simplify command, you can simplify selected paths.

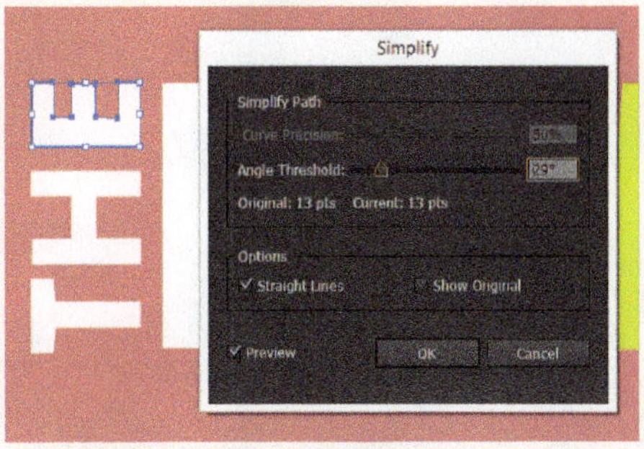

For instance, for the logo you traced, you could double-click the logo after it's been expanded and painted, and select a few of the letters. You can then choose Object > Path > Simplify to change the path settings in the Simplify dialog box. You can apply the Simplify command to other parts of the logo as well. By aligning points and editing paths using the drawing tools, you can turn the raster logo into a viable vector logo.

Comprehension Check

1. Describe two ways to draw a basic shape on the artboard.
2. Which panel on the Control panel allows you to apply a fill color to a shape?
3. How do you draw a perfect square with the Rectangle tool?
4. What is a stroke?
5. List and describe Illustrator's three drawing modes.

Review Project

Review the principles of layout and design that you learned about in Lesson 1. With a partner, write a brief critique of the postcard you created in Lesson 3. In your critique, you should comment on how well the principles of layout and design were applied to the graphic. Share your critique with another team.

End-of-Chapter Activities

Chapter Review

1. Analyze and summarize evidence of interdependence between the technical and the artistic sides of the Web and Digital Communications pathway.
2. What are two differences between a raster graphic and a vector graphic?
3. When editing graphics, why is it important to consider the file format in which an image is created?
4. Why are exporting and importing important functions for working with graphics?
5. Define resolution and explain why it is important when dealing with graphic images.

Multiple Choice

1. When drawing in Adobe Illustrator which kind of graphic are you creating?
   a. Bitmap
   b. Raster
   c. Vector
   d. JPEG
2. What is the default Illustrator workspace called?
   a. Workspace 1
   b. Essentials
   c. Toolbox
   d. Library
3. Which of the following tools do you use to change the magnification of artwork?
   a. Pen tool
   b. Magic Wand tool
   c. Zoom tool
   d. Selection tool
4. Which of the following tools allows you to select individual anchor points?
   a. Selection tool
   b. Direct Selection tool
   c. Group Selection tool
   d. Magic Wand tool
5. What is it called when you use trademarked or patented content without permission?
   a. infringement
   b. cheating
   c. plagiarism
   d. fair use

Chapter 1 – Portfolio Builder

Selecting and Aligning Practice

As you have learned, selecting objects is an important part of working with Illustrator. In this activity, you will use techniques discussed in this chapter to practice selecting and aligning objects.

1. Choose File > Open, and open the **PB1_start.ai** file from the data files for this lesson. Save the file as **PB1_start_xx.ai** in the location where your teacher instructs you to store the files for this lesson.
2. Click OK in the Illustrator Options dialog box. Choose View > Fit Artboard In Window to fit the artboard in the Document window.
3. Choose View > Smart Guides to temporarily deselect the Smart Guides.
4. With the Selection tool drag the steering wheel shape in the upper-right corner into place. Drag the black rounded rectangle in the upper-left corner of the artboard to the front of the bus.
5. With the Selection tool, select the headlight shapes (the circles) in the lower-right corner of the artboard by dragging a marquee across them. Choose Object > Group.
6. Drag the center of the headlight group to slide it to its new location to the right of the rounded rectangle.
7. Double-click the center of the headlight group to enter Isolation mode. Click to select the white shape and drag it so that it's visually centered on the other shapes. Choose Select > Deselect. Press the Escape key to exit Isolation mode.
8. Click the headlight group to select it, press Alt (Windows) or Option (Mac OS) and drag the headlight group to the left to duplicate it. Release the mouse button, and then the modifier key.
9. Shift-click the rounded rectangle and the headlight group to the right to select all three objects.
10. In the Control panel, choose Align to Selection from the Align To button menu, and then click the Horizontal Distribute Center button. Choose Object > Group.
11. Shift-click the orange shape behind the selected group. Click the orange shape again to make it the key object. Click the Horizontal Align Center button and then the Vertical Align Center button to align the rounded rectangle group to the orange shape.
12. With the Selection tool, Shift-click the orange shape to deselect it. With the group of objects that contains the headlights selected, choose Object > Lock > Selection to keep them in position. You cannot select the shapes until you choose Object > Unlock All.
13. Select the Zoom tool in the Tools panel, and click three times, slowly, on the dome at the top of the bus, above the text, "SCHOOL BUS."

14. Select the Direct Selection tool, select the top anchor point in the dome, and then begin dragging up to make the dome taller. As you drag, press the Shift key to constrain the movement. Release the mouse button and then the key.
15. Double-click the Hand tool to fit the artboard in the Document window.
16. Select the Zoom tool, and click three times on the four lines in the lower left corner to zoom in.
17. With the Selection tool, drag a marquee across the four lines to select them.
18. In the Control panel, click the Horizontal Align Left button.
19. Choose View > Smart Guides to turn them back on.
20. Deselect the vertical lines. With the Direct Selection tool click the right end of the top, shorter line to select the anchor point (the word "anchor" appears). Click and drag that point to the right until the anchor point aligns with the other lines.
21. With the Selection tool, drag a marquee around the lines to select them. Choose Object > Group to group them.
22. Double-click the Hand tool to fit the artboard in the Document window.
23. With the Selection tool, drag the line group to position it on the rounded rectangle between the headlights.
24. Notice that you need to drag one of the lines, not between the lines, to move the group. You could also align the lines group to the black rounded rectangle using the Align options in the Control panel.
25. Choose Select > Deselect.
26. Save the file and exit Illustrator.

Chapter 1 – Critical Thinking

Web and Digital Communications Poster

Working alone or in pairs, research the impact that businesses in the Web and Digital Communications field have on society. As you conduct your research, evaluate the information you find for accuracy and validity, and keep track of your sources. When your research is complete, analyze the information. Then, use the skills you have learned in this chapter to create a poster llustrating the impact you think is most interesting.

Directions

1. Create a new Illustrator document with the following settings:

   Name: CT1_start_xx.ai (saved to the location where your teacher instructs you to store the files for this chapter)

   Profile: Print

   Number of Artboards: 1

   Units: Inches

   Width: 18 in

   Height: 24 in
2. Using the skills you have learned in this chapter, design the poster. Consider the elements and principles of design and layout as you work. Be sure to obtain permission if you use any images or clip art, and to properly cite your sources.
3. Present your poster to a partner or to the class. Explain the topic, why you selected it, why you think it is important, and how you used the principles and elements of design.

Chapter 2

Creating and Enhancing Illustrations

Lesson 4 | Creating an Illustration with the Drawing Tools

Getting Started with the Pen Tool

Creating an Illustration with the Pen Tool

Drawing with the Curvature Tool

Editing Curves

Drawing and Editing with the Pencil Tool

Lesson 5 | Using Color and Patterns to Enhance Signage

Exploring Basic Color Theory

Getting Started with Color

Working with Color

Using Illustrator Swatch Libraries

Adjusting Colors

Working with Color in the Color Guide Panel

Editing Colors in Artwork

Lesson 6 | Adding Type to a Poster

Identifying the Concepts of Typography

Adding Type to a Poster

Working with Overflow Text and Text Reflow

Formatting Type

Creating and Applying Text Styles

Warping Text

Working with Type on a Path

End-of-Chapter Activities

Lesson 4 Overview

In this lesson, you will learn about:

- Getting Started with the Pen Tool
- Creating an Illustration with the Pen Tool
- Drawing with the Curvature Tool
- Editing Curves
- Drawing and Editing with the Pencil Tool

Although the Pencil tool is preferable for drawing and editing free-form lines, the Pen tool and Curvature tool are excellent for drawing precisely, including drawing straight lines, Bezier curves, and complex shapes. You'll practice using the Pen tool, and then use all of these tools to create an illustration of a dish of ice cream.

Getting Started with the Pen Tool

The Pen tool is one of the main drawing tools that is used to create both free-form and more precise artwork. It's also useful for editing existing vector artwork. Many users find that it takes a lot of practice to master and feel comfortable with the Pen tool. Once you do, though, you will possess a valuable and important skill that can be used in many careers in Web and digital communications.

In this section, you'll create illustrations using the Pen tool.

Try It!

1. Start Adobe Illustrator CC, and open **L4_practice.ai** from the data files for this lesson.

   The document is made up of six artboards, numbered 1 through 6 (you most likely won't see all six,). As you progress through the first part of this lesson, you will be asked to move to the next artboard.

2. Save the file as **L4_practice_xx.ai** in the location where your teacher instructs you to store the files for this lesson, and leave it open.

   Choose Adobe Illustrator (ai) from the Format menu (Mac), or choose Adobe Illustrator (*.AI) from the Save as type menu (Windows). Click Save. In the Illustrator Options dialog box, click OK to accept the default settings.

3. Choose 1 from the Artboard Navigation menu in the lower-left corner of the Document window. Choose View > Fit Artboard In Window.

4. Choose Window > Workspace > Reset Essentials.

5. Choose View > Smart Guides to turn off the Smart Guides. Smart Guides can be useful when you draw, but you won't need them now.

6. In the Control panel, click Fill color and choose None. Then, click the Stroke color and make sure that the Black swatch is selected.

7. Make sure the Stroke weight is 1 pt in the Control panel.

   When you begin drawing with the Pen tool, it's usually best to have no fill because the fill can cover the path you are trying to create. You can add a fill later, if necessary. Next, you'll draw a path in the work area of the artboard that looks like the zigzag path at the top of the artboard.

8. Select the Pen tool in the Tools panel. Position the pointer in the artboard area, and notice the asterisk (*) next to the Pen icon indicating that you are starting a path.

9. In the area labeled Work Area, click where the blue "start" square is, to set the first anchor point. Move the pointer to the right of the original point and you will see a line connecting the first point and the pointer, no matter where you move the pointer. This is called Pen tool preview (or Rubber Band). Later, as you create curved paths, it will make drawing them easier.

   The asterisk has disappeared, indicating that you are now drawing a path.

10. Position the pointer down and to the right of the original point, and click to create the next anchor point in the path.

> **Note:**
>
> The first segment you draw is not visible until you click to create a second anchor point. If the path looks curved, you have accidentally dragged with the Pen tool; choose Edit > Undo Pen, and then click again.

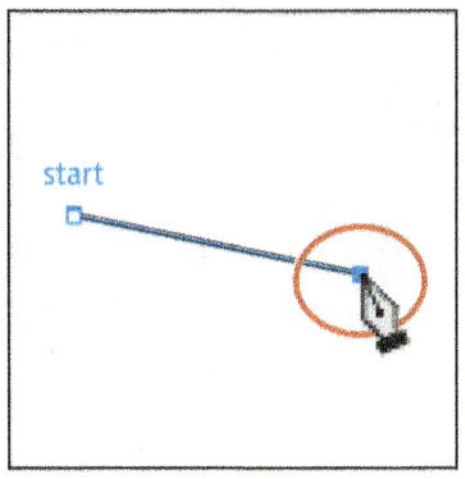

11. Click a third anchor point beneath the initial anchor point to create a zigzag pattern. Create a zigzag that has a total of six anchor points, which means you will click the artboard three more times.

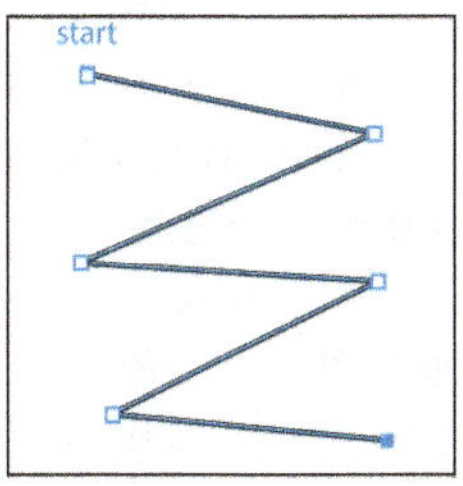

   One of the many benefits of using the Pen tool is that you can create custom paths and continue to edit the anchor points that make up the path. Notice that only the last anchor point is filled (not hollow like the rest of the anchor points), indicating that it is selected.

12. Choose Select > Deselect.

   The type of anchor points you just created are called corner points. Corner points are not smooth like a curve; rather, they create an angle where the anchor point is. Now you will learn a few more techniques for selecting paths.

13. Save the changes to **L4_practice_xx.ai**, and leave it open.

Selecting Paths

1. Select the Selection tool in the Tools panel, and position the pointer directly over a straight line in the zigzag path. When the pointer shows a solid black box next to it, click.

   This selects the path and all of the anchor points. You can tell the anchor points are selected because they become filled.

2. Drag from one of the straight lines in the path to a new location anywhere on the artboard. All the anchor points travel together, maintaining the zigzag path.

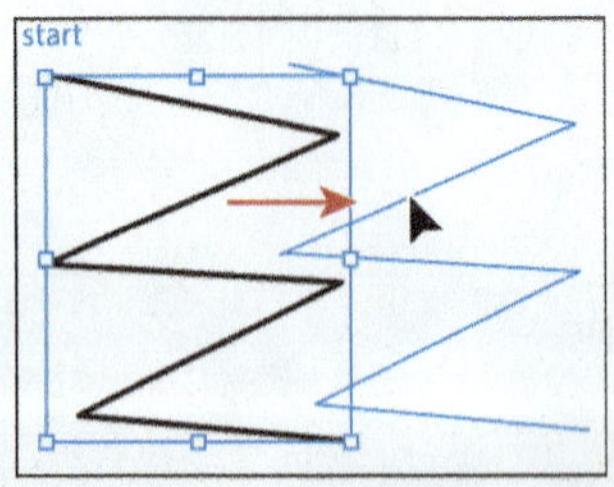

3. Deselect the zigzag path in one of the following ways:
   - With the Selection tool, click an empty area of the artboard.
   - Choose Select > Deselect.

4. In the Tools panel, select the Direct Selection tool and when the pointer changes, click the path to reveal all of the anchor points. Position the pointer over one of the anchor points. The anchor point will become larger than the others, and the pointer will show a small box with a dot in the center next to it (see the figure below). Both of these indicate that if you click, you will select the anchor point. Click to select the anchor point and the selected anchor point is filled (looks solid), whereas the deselected anchor points are still hollow.

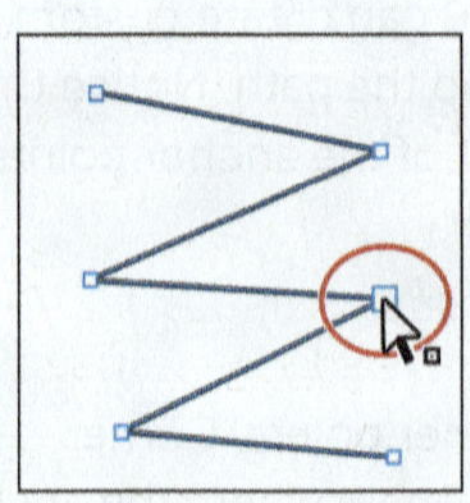

5. Drag the anchor point to the left a bit to reposition it.

   The anchor point moves, but the others remain stationary.

6. Click in a blank area of the artboard to deselect.

7. Position the Direct Selection pointer over a straight-line segment in the middle of the zigzag shape. When the pointer changes, click to select. Choose Edit > Cut. This cuts only the selected segment from the zigzag.

8. Select the Pen tool, and position the pointer over one of the end anchor points that was connected to the line segment that was cut. Notice that the Pen tool shows a forward slash, indicating that if you click, you will continue drawing from that anchor point. Click the point.

9. Position the pointer over the other anchor point that was connected to the cut line segment. The pointer now shows a merge symbol next to it, indicating that you are connecting to another path. Click the point to reconnect the paths.

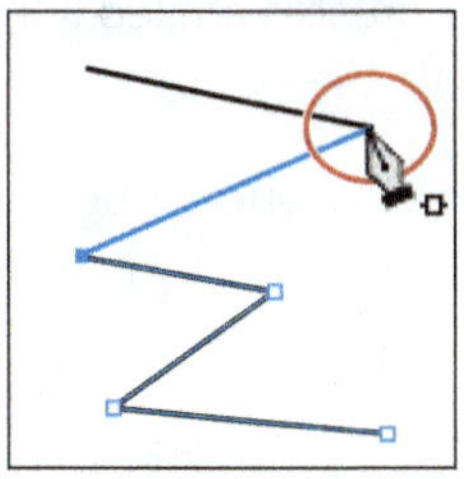

Constraining Lines

In previous lessons, you learned that using the Shift key and Smart Guides in combination with shape tools constrains the shape of objects. The Shift key and Smart Guides can also constrain paths drawn with the Pen tool to create paths in angles of 45°. Next, you will learn how to draw straight lines and constrain angles as you draw.

Try It!

1. Choose 2 from the Artboard Navigation menu in the lower-left corner of the Document window.

2. Choose View > Smart Guides to turn on the Smart Guides.

3. With the Pen tool selected, in the area labeled Work Area, click where the blue "start" square is to set the first anchor point.

   Don't worry if the Smart Guides are attempting to "snap" the anchor point you create to other content on the artboard, making it difficult to click directly on the "start" square. This is expected and is sometimes why we turn off the Smart Guides when drawing.

4. Move the pointer to the right of the original anchor point approximately 1.5 in, as indicated by the measurement label. It doesn't have to be exact. A green alignment guide appears when the pointer is vertically aligned with the previous anchor point. Click to set another anchor point.

   As you've learned in previous lessons, the measurement label and alignment guides are a part of the Smart Guides. When working with the Pen tool, you can achieve finer measurements in the measurement labels when you zoom in.

5. Click to set three more points, following the same generic shape as shown in the top half of the artboard.

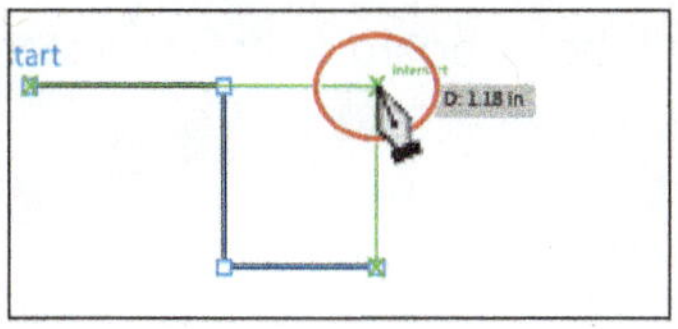

Notice the green alignment guides that appear as you draw. Sometimes they are helpful for aligning points, and sometimes they align to content that you don't necessarily want to align to.

6. Press the Shift key, and move the pointer to the right and down. When the measurement label shows 2 in, click to set an anchor point, and then release the modifier key.

   Notice that the new anchor point may not be where you clicked. That's because the line has been constrained to 45°. Pressing the Shift key creates angled lines constrained to 45°.

7. Position the pointer below the last point, and click to set the last anchor point for the shape.

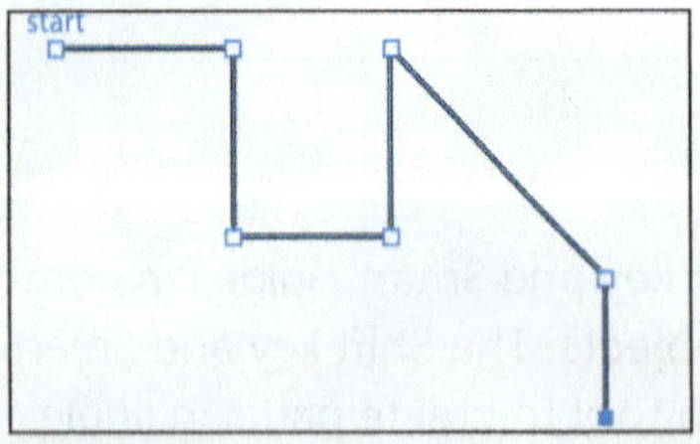

8. Choose Select > Deselect. Save the changes to **L4_practice_xx.ai**, and leave it open.

Introducing Curved Paths

In this part of the lesson, you'll learn how to draw smooth, curved lines with the Pen tool. In vector drawing applications such as Illustrator, you draw a curve, called a Bezier curve, with anchor points and direction handles. By setting anchor points and dragging direction handles, you can define the shape of the curve. This type of anchor point, with direction handles, is called a *smooth point*. Although drawing curves this way can take some time to learn, it gives you the greatest control and flexibility in creating paths.

First, you'll just get the feel for how to create a curved path. The goal for this exercise is not to create anything specific but to get accustomed to the feel of creating Bezier curves.

Try It!

1. Choose View > Smart Guides to deselect them.

2. Choose 3 from the Artboard Navigation menu in the lower-left corner of the Document window. You will draw in the area labeled Practice.

3. Press Z to switch to the Zoom tool (or select it in the Tools panel), and click twice in the bottom half of the artboard to zoom in.

4. With the Pen tool selected, click in a blank area of the artboard to create a starting anchor point.

5. Move the pointer away from the original point you created, and click and drag away from the point to create a curved path.

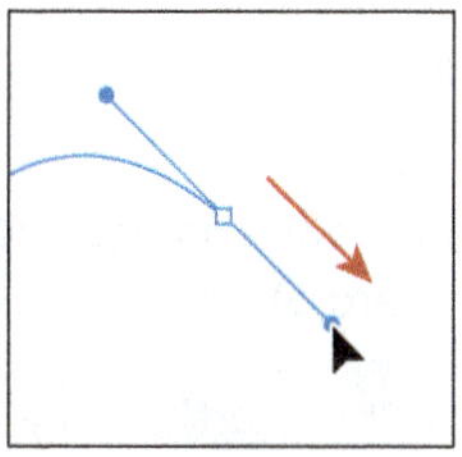

Notice that as you drag away from the point, direction handles appear. Direction handles consist of direction lines that end in round direction points. The angle and length of the direction handles determine the shape and size of the curve. Direction handles do not print and are not visible when the anchor point is inactive.

6. Move the pointer away from the anchor point you just created to see the Rubber Band (Pen tool preview). Move the pointer around a bit to see how it changes. Continue clicking and dragging in different areas to create a series of points.

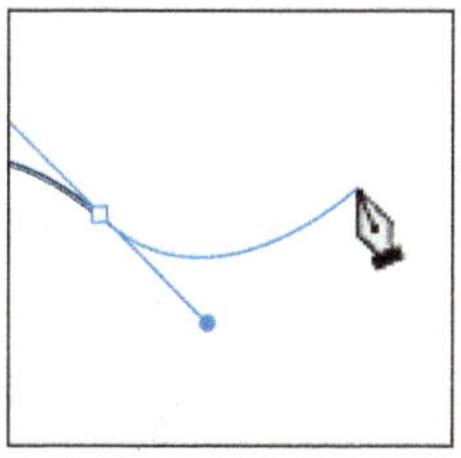

7. Choose Select > Deselect, then save the changes to **L4_practice_xx.ai**, and leave it open.

Components of a Path

As you draw, you create a line called a path. A path is made up of one or more straight or curved segments. The beginning and end of each segment are marked by anchor points, which work like pins holding a wire in place. A path can be closed (for example, a circle) or open, with distinct endpoints (for example, a wavy line). You change the shape of a path by dragging its anchor points, the direction points at the end of direction lines that appear at anchor points, or the path segment itself.

Paths can have two kinds of anchor points: corner points and smooth points. At a corner point, a path abruptly changes direction. At a smooth point, path segments are connected as a continuous curve.

You can draw a path using any combination of corner and smooth points. If you draw the wrong kind of point, you can always change it.

Drawing a Curve with the Pen Tool

In this part of the lesson, you'll use what you just learned to trace a curved shape with the Pen tool.

Try It!

1. Press and hold the spacebar to temporarily select the Hand tool, and drag down until you see the curve at the top of the artboard (on Artboard 3).

2. Select the Pen tool in the Tools panel. Click and drag from the "start" square, up to the gold dot, and then release the mouse button. This creates a direction line going in the same direction as the path.

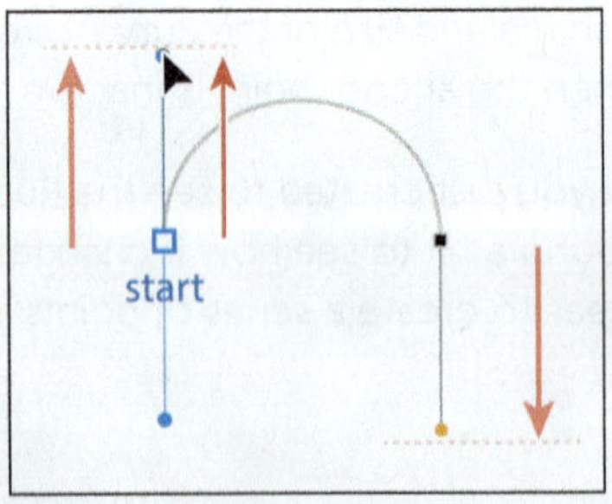

3. Click the black point on the right side of the arch and drag down. Release the mouse button when the pointer reaches the gold dot and the path you are creating follows the arch.

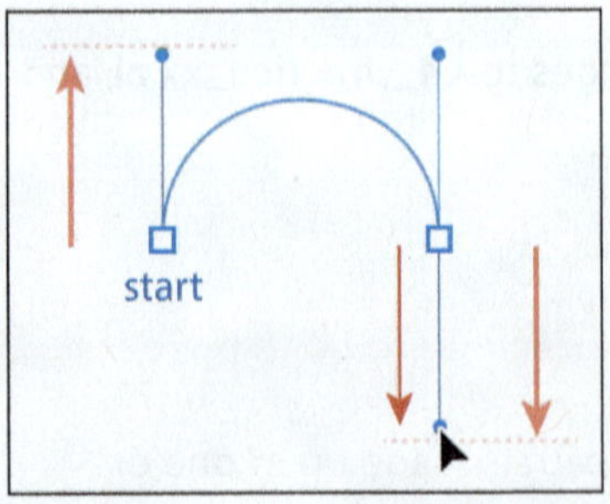

If the path you created is not aligned exactly with the template, select the Direct Selection tool and select the anchor points one at a time to show the direction handles. You can then adjust the direction handles using the Direct Selection tool until your path follows the template more accurately.

4. Select the Selection tool, and click the artboard in an area with no objects, or choose Select > Deselect.

Deselecting the first path allows you to create a new path. If you click somewhere on the artboard with the Pen tool while the path is still selected, the path connects to the next point you draw.

Note:

The artboard may scroll as you drag. If you lose visibility of the curve, choose View > Zoom Out until you see the curve and anchor point. Pressing the spacebar allows you to use the Hand tool to reposition the artwork.

5. Save the changes to **L4_practice_xx.ai**, and leave it open.

6. If you want to try drawing the curve for more practice, scroll down to the Practice area in the same artboard and trace the curve.

Drawing a Series of Curves with the Pen Tool

Now that you've experimented with drawing a few curves, you will draw a shape that contains several continuous curves.

Try It!

1. Choose 4 from the Artboard Navigation menu in the lower-left corner of the Document window. Select the Zoom tool, and click several times in the top half of the artboard to zoom in.

2. Select the Pen tool. Click the blue "start" square, and drag up in the direction of the arch, stopping at the gold dot.

3. Position the pointer over the black square point to the right, click and drag down to the gold dot, adjusting the first arch with the direction handle before you release the mouse button.

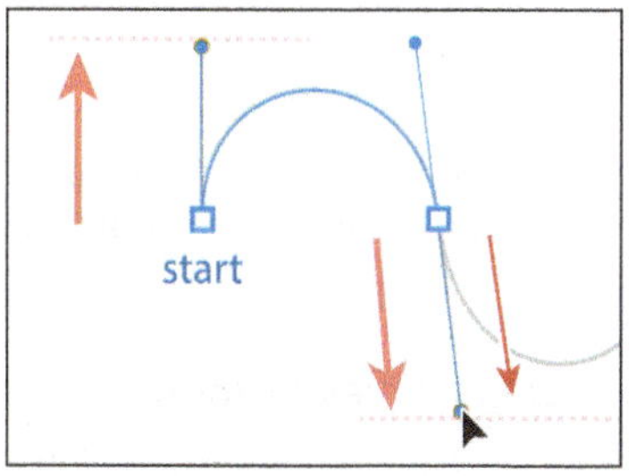

Note:

Don't worry if the path you draw is not exact. You can correct the line with the Direct Selection tool when the path is complete.

4. Continue along the path, alternating between dragging up and down. Put anchor points only where there are black squares (points).

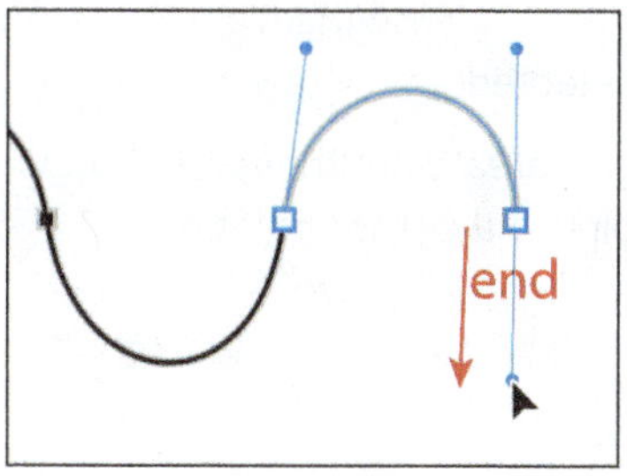

If you make a mistake as you draw, you can undo your work by choosing Edit > Undo Pen and then draw the last point again. Note that your direction lines may not match the figure at right, and that's okay.

5. When the path is complete, select the Direct Selection tool and click to select an anchor point.

   When the anchor point is selected, the direction handles appear and you can readjust the curve of the path if necessary. With a curve selected, you can also change the stroke and fill of the curve. When you do this, the next line you draw will have the same attributes.

   If you want to try drawing the shape again for more practice, scroll down to the bottom half of the same artboard (labeled Practice) and trace the shape down there.

6. Save the changes to **L4_practice_xx.ai** and leave it open.

Converting Smooth Points to Corner Points

When creating curves, the direction handles help to determine the shape and size of the curved segments, as you've already seen. Removing the direction lines from an anchor point can convert a smooth curve into a corner. In the next part of the lesson, you will practice converting between smooth points and corner points.

Try It!

1. Choose 5 from the Artboard Navigation menu in the lower-left corner of the Document window.

   On the top of the artboard, you can see the path that you will trace. You will use the top artboard as a template for the exercise, creating your paths directly on top of those. Use the Practice section at the bottom of the artboard for additional practice on your own.

2. In the top artboard, use the Zoom tool and click several times to zoom in.

3. Select the Pen tool, and pressing the Shift key, click the blue "start" square and drag up to the gold dot. Release the mouse button, and then release the Shift key.

4. Click the next black anchor point to the right, and pressing the Shift key, drag down to the red dot. When the curve looks correct, release the mouse button and then release the Shift key. Leave the path selected.

   Now you need the curve to switch directions and create another arch. You will split the direction lines to convert a smooth point to a corner point.

5. Press the Option (Mac) or Alt (Windows) key, and position the pointer over either the last anchor point created or the bottom direction point. When a convert-point icon appears next to the Pen tool pointer, click and drag a direction line up to the gold dot. Release the mouse button, and then release the modifier key. If you do not see the caret, you may create an additional loop.

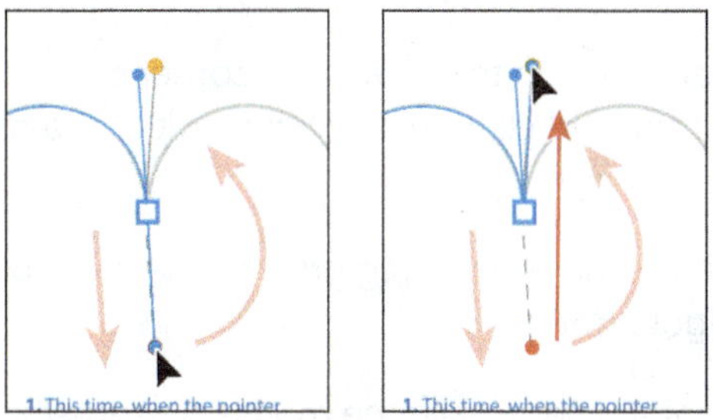

You can practice adjusting the direction handles with the Direct Selection tool when the path is completed.

6. Position the Pen tool pointer over the next (third) black square point on the template path, and drag down to the red dot. Release the mouse button when the path looks similar to the template path.

7. Press the Option (Mac) or Alt (Windows) key and after the convert-point icon appears, position the pointer over the anchor point or direction point and drag up to the gold dot. Release the mouse button, and then release the modifier key.

   For the next (fourth) point, you will not release the mouse button to split the direction handles, so pay close attention.

8. For the fourth anchor point, click the next black square on the template path and drag down to the red dot until the path looks correct. This time, *do not release the mouse button*. Press the Option (Mac) or Alt (Windows) key, and drag up to the gold dot for the next curve. Release the mouse button, and then release the modifier key.

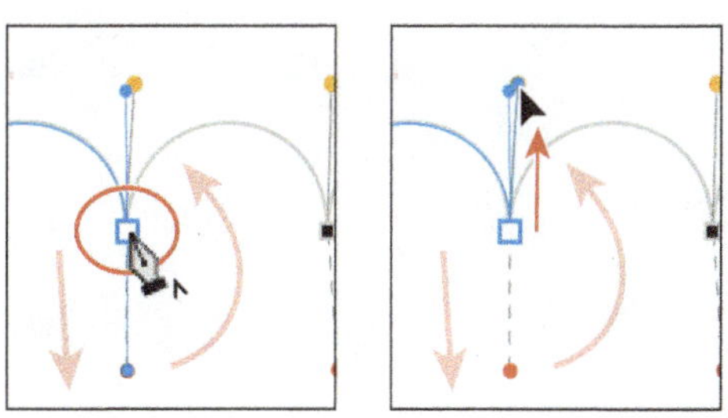

9. Continue this process using the Option (Mac) or Alt (Windows) key to create corner points until the path is completed.

10. Use the Direct Selection tool to fine-tune the path, and then deselect the path.

    If you want to try drawing the same shape for more practice, scroll down to the Practice area in the same artboard and trace the shape down there.

11. Save the changes to **L4_Start1_xx.ai** and leave it open.

Combining Curves and Straight Lines

Of course in the real world, when you draw with the Pen tool, you won't just create either curves or straight lines. In this next section, you'll learn how to go from curves to straight lines and from straight lines to curves.

Try It!

1. Choose 6 from the Artboard Navigation menu in the lower-left corner of the Document window. Select the Zoom tool, and click several times in the top half of the artboard to zoom in.
2. Select the Pen tool. Click the blue "start" square, and drag up. Release the mouse button when the pointer reaches the gold dot.
3. Drag down from the second anchor point, and release the mouse button when the pointer reaches the gold dot and the arch matches the template. This method of creating a curve should be familiar to you by now.

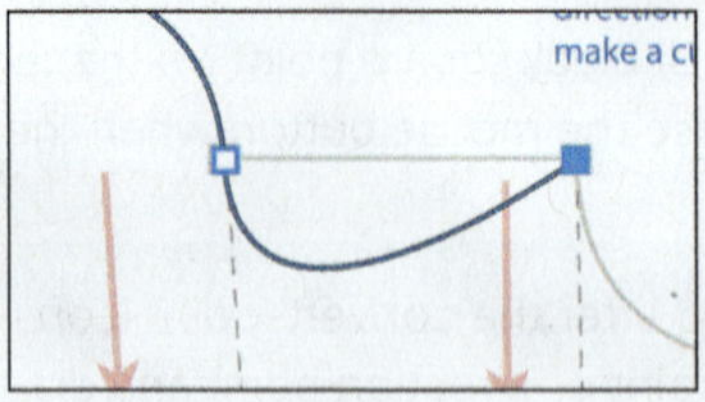

If you were to click on the next black anchor point (don't), even pressing the Shift key (to produce a straight line), the path would be curved. The last point you created is a smooth anchor point and has a direction line after the point.

You will now continue the path as a straight line.

4. Position the pointer over the last point created (notice that the convert-point icon appears), and click to delete the leading direction handle from the anchor point, as shown in the figure.

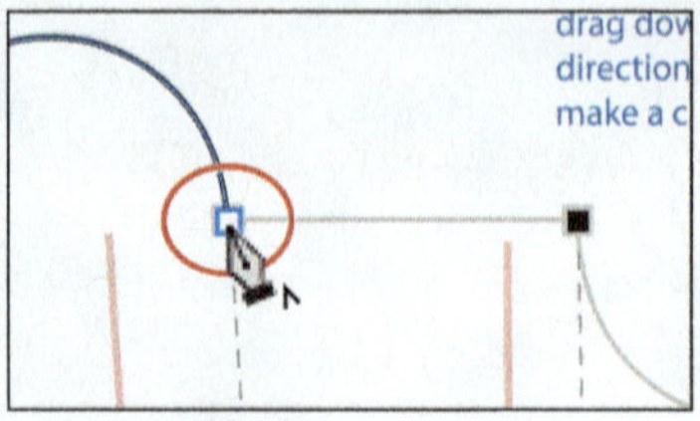

5. Press the Shift key, and click the next point in the template path to the right to set the next point, creating a straight segment.

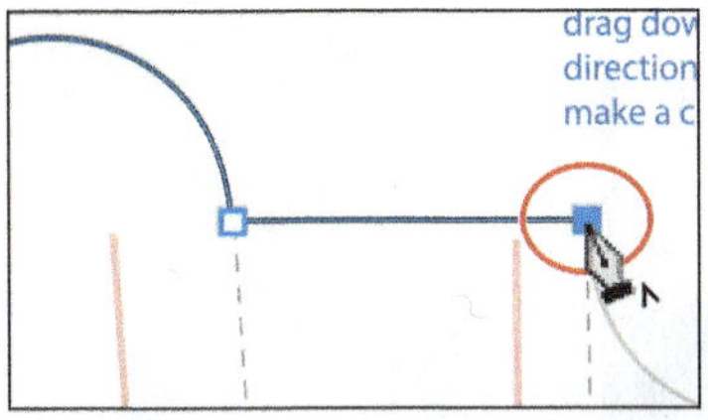

6. For the next arch, position the pointer over the last point created (notice that the convert-point icon appears), and then drag down from that point to the gold dot. This creates a new direction line.

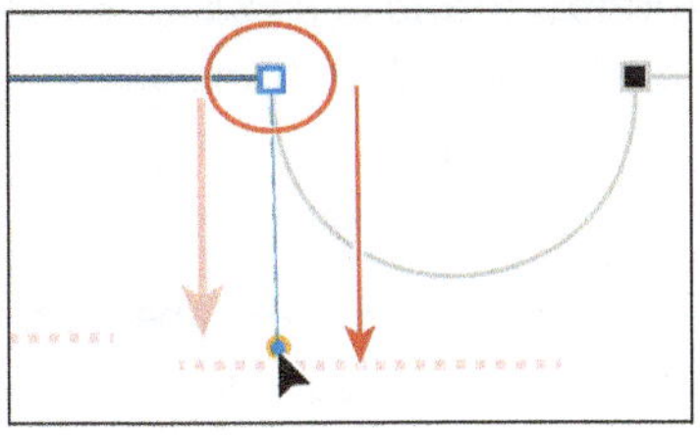

7. Click the next point, and drag up to complete the arch.
8. Click the last anchor point you just created to remove the direction line.
9. Shift-click the next point to create the second straight segment.
10. Click and drag up from the last point created to create a direction line, and then click and drag down on the end point to create the final arch.

    If you want to try drawing the same shape for more practice, scroll down to the Practice area in the same artboard and trace the shape down there.

11. Save the changes to **L4_practice_xx.ai** and close the file.

Creating an Illustration with the Pen Tool

With a bit of Pen tool practice behind you, in this next part of the lesson, you'll create an illustration of a dish of ice cream. You'll use the new skills you learned in the previous exercises, and you'll also learn some additional techniques and tools.

Try It!

1. Open **L4_start.ai** from the data files for this lesson.

2. Choose View > Fit All In Window.

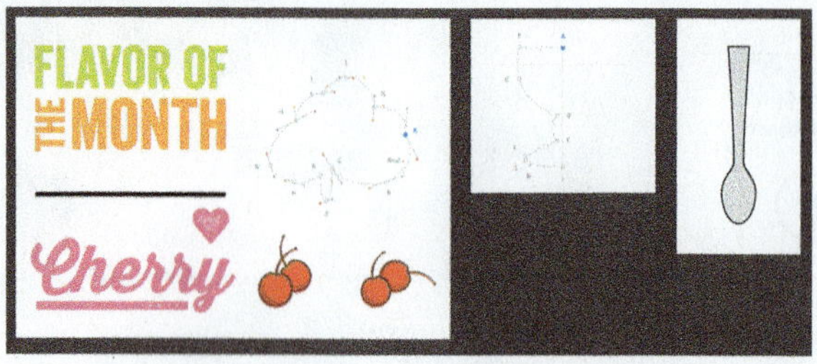

3. Save the file as **L4_start_xx.ai** in the location where your teacher instructs you to store the files for this lesson, and leave it open.

   Choose Adobe Illustrator (ai) from the Format menu (Mac) or choose Adobe Illustrator (*.AI) from the Save as type menu (Windows), and click Save. In the Illustrator Options dialog box, click OK to accept the default options.

Drawing with the Pen Tool

When using the Pen tool, pay attention to the stroke weight, or line thickness, of the lines and curves you are drawing. The treatment of lines and curves, and their repetition in a design, are important to creating balance and consistency. To start this section, you'll draw an ice cream shape, which combines curves and corners. Take your time as you practice with this shape, and use the guides provided to assist you in drawing it.

Try It!

1. Choose View > Ice Cream to zoom in to the ice cream path.
2. In the Control panel, make sure that the Fill color is None and the Stroke color is Black.
3. Make sure the Stroke weight is 1 pt in the Control panel.
4. With the Pen tool selected, drag from the blue square labeled A to the red dot beneath it to set the starting anchor point and direction of the first curve.

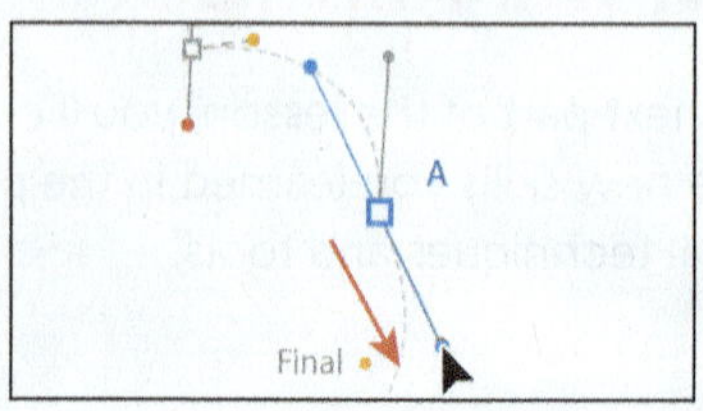

5. Continue on, dragging from point B to the red dot, to create the first curve.

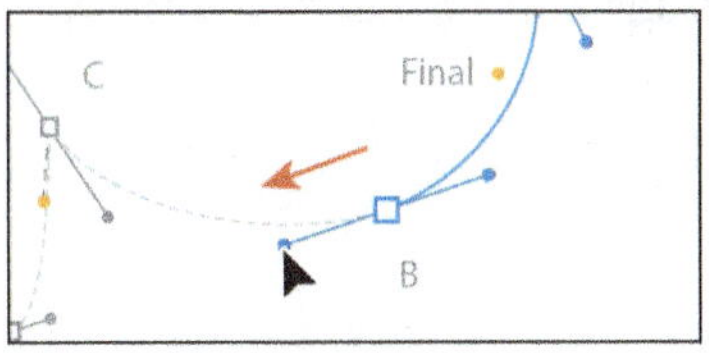

The next point you create will be converted from a smooth point to a corner point.

6. Drag from point C to the red dot, but don't release the mouse button yet. With the pointer over the red dot, hold down the Option (Mac) or Alt (Windows) key and continue dragging from the red dot to the gold dot below the point. Release the mouse button, and then release the modifier key. This splits the direction handles.

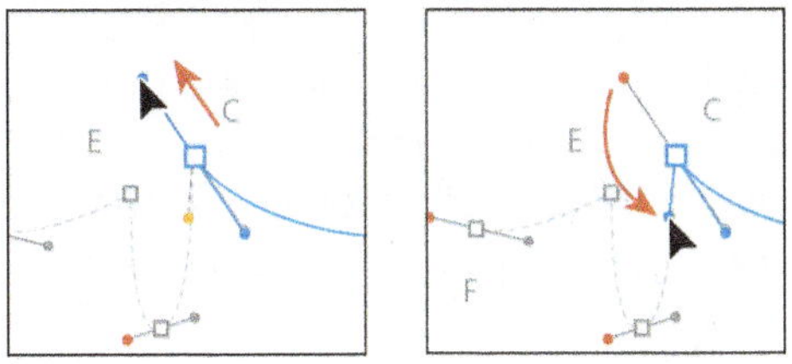

7. Drag from point D to the red dot. As you drag, pay attention to how the path looks between points C and D.
8. Click point E, without dragging, to create a corner point with no direction lines.

   You'll find that setting an anchor point without direction lines (a corner point) allows you to set a point with no curve.
9. For points F and G, drag from each point to the red dot to create curves.

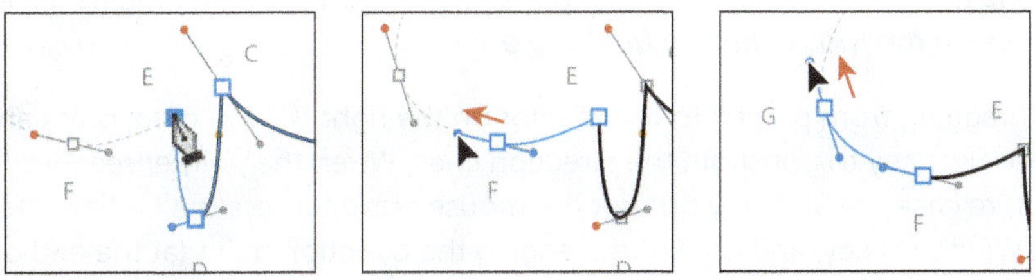

10. Drag from point H to the red dot, but don't release the mouse button yet. When the pointer reaches the red dot, hold down the Option (Mac) or Alt (Windows) key, and continue dragging from the red dot to the gold dot. Release the mouse button, and then release the modifier key.

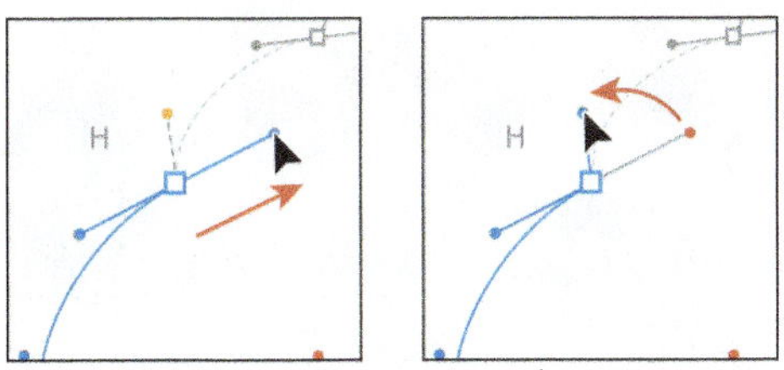

11. Drag from point I to the red dot, hold down the Option (Mac) or Alt (Windows) key, and continue dragging from the red dot to the gold dot. Release the mouse button, and then release the modifier key. This splits the direction handles.

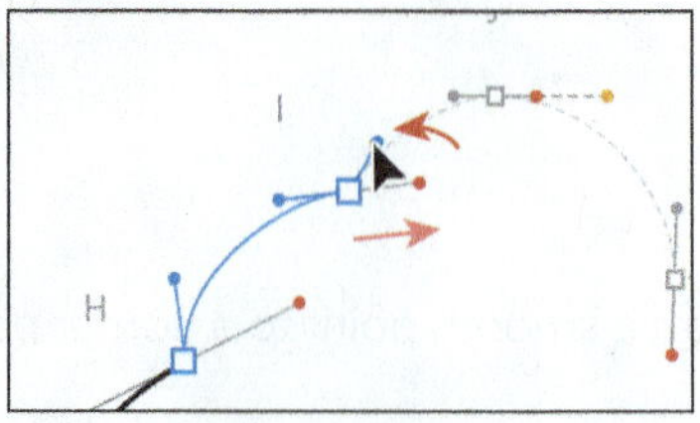

As you draw with the Pen tool, you may want to edit a curve you previously drew without ending the path you are drawing. Pressing a modifier key with the Pen tool selected, you can position the pointer over a previous path segment and drag to modify it, which is what you'll do next.

12. Position the pointer over the path between points H and I and press the Option (Mac) or Alt (Windows) key. The pointer changes appearance. Drag the path up and to the left to make the path have more curve, like you see in the figure. Release the mouse button and then the key. Now, you can continue drawing the path.

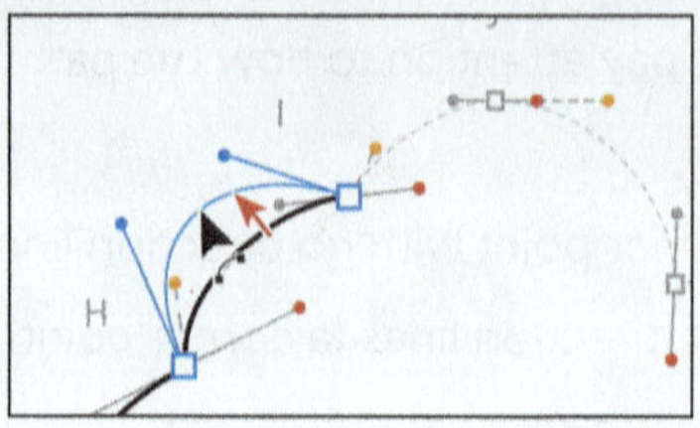

For the next point, J, you will create a smooth point, but you will edit the direction handles independently using a modifier key as you draw. For the next step, *don't release the mouse button until you are told*.

13. Begin dragging from point J to the red dot on the right. As you drag, press and hold the Shift key to constrain the direction lines. When the pointer reaches the red dot, release the Shift key but not the mouse button. Press the Option (Mac) or Alt (Windows) key, and continue dragging the direction point (at the end of the direction line) from the red dot to the gold dot to make just that one direction handle longer. When the pointer reaches the gold dot, release the mouse button, and then release the key.

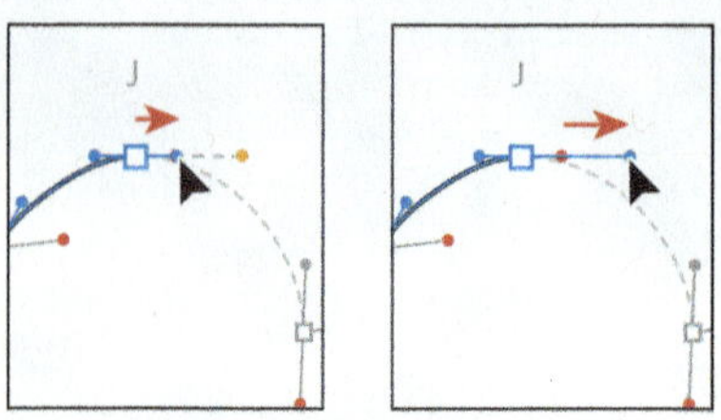

14. Continue drawing the point at K by first dragging from the anchor point to the red dot, and then pressing the Option (Mac) or Alt (Windows) key and dragging from the red dot to the gold dot.

    Next, you'll complete the drawing of the ice cream by closing the path.

15. Position the Pen tool over the starting point A without clicking.

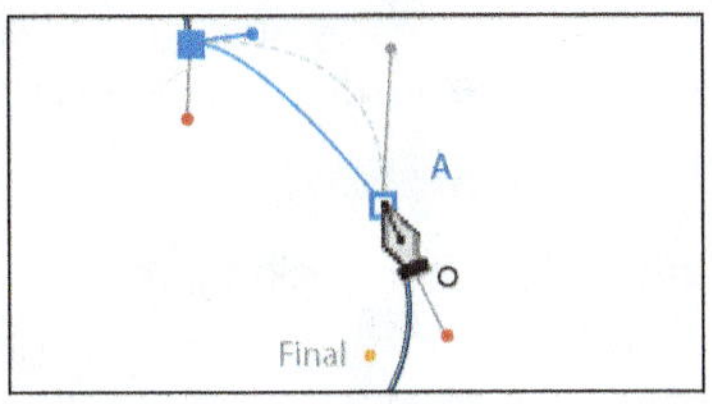

    Notice that an open circle appears next to the Pen tool pointer, indicating that the path will close if you were to click the anchor point (don't click yet). If you were to click and drag, the direction handles on either side of the point would move as a single straight line. We need to split the direction handles so the final point is a corner point.

16. Press the Option (Mac) or Alt (Windows) key with the pointer still over point A. Click and drag straight down and notice that a direction handle shows, but is going in the opposite direction (it's going up). Drag to the gold dot labeled "Final." Release the mouse button and then the key.

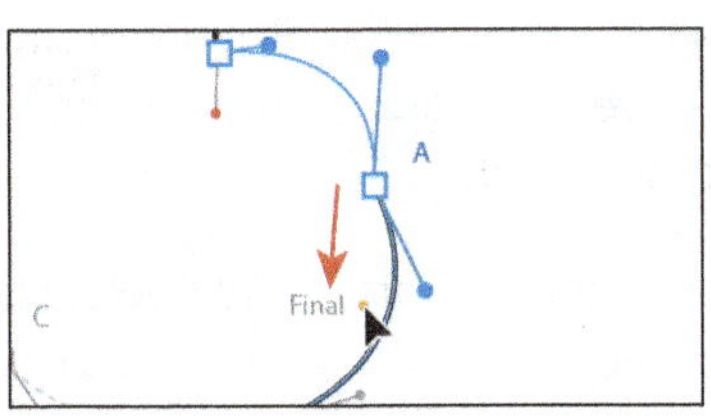

    As you drag down, another direction line appears above the point. Without the modifier key, as you drag away from closing point, you are reshaping the path before and after the anchor point. Pressing the Option/Alt modifier key on the closing point allows you to edit the previous direction handle independently.

17. Command-click (Mac) or Ctrl-click (Windows) away from the path to deselect it, and then save the **L4_start_xx.ai** file and leave it open.

    This is a shortcut method for deselecting a path while keeping the Pen tool selected. You could also choose Select > Deselect, among other methods.

Drawing with the Curvature Tool

With the Curvature tool, you can draw and edit paths quickly and visually to create paths with smooth refined curves and straight lines. Using the Curvature tool, you can also edit paths while drawing or after the path is complete using the same tool.

In this section, you'll explore the Curvature tool while creating a dish for the ice cream you already drew.

Try It!

1. Choose 2 Dish from the Artboard Navigation menu in the lower-left corner of the Document window. Choose View > Fit Artboard in Window.

   Looking at the template path, you will see a vertical red dotted line running through the A and I points. After you draw half of the ice cream dish, you will copy and reflect it around the red dotted line, then join the two halves together.

2. Select the Curvature tool in the Tools panel. Click the blue square at point A to set the starting anchor point.

3. Press the Shift key, and click on point B (to the left of A). After clicking, release the key.

4. Move the pointer away from point B and notice the preview of the curve before and after point B.

   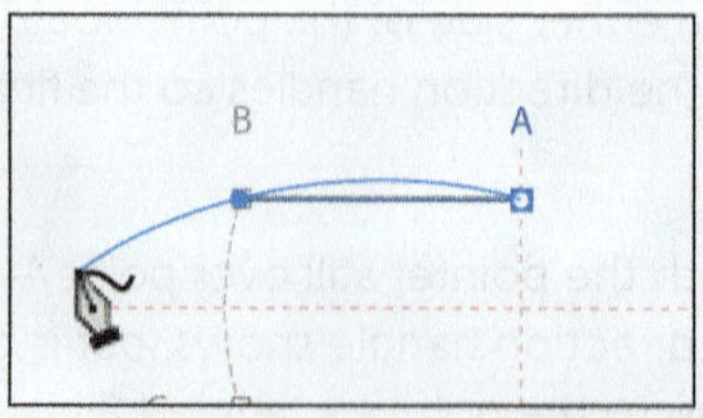

   The Curvature tool works by creating anchor points where you click. The drawing curve will "flex" around the points dynamically. Direction handles are created when necessary to curve the path for you. If you were to click in this instance, the curve preview you see would become the drawn path.

5. Press the Shift key, and click point C to align the anchor points B and C. Release the Shift key after clicking and notice the new curved path.

   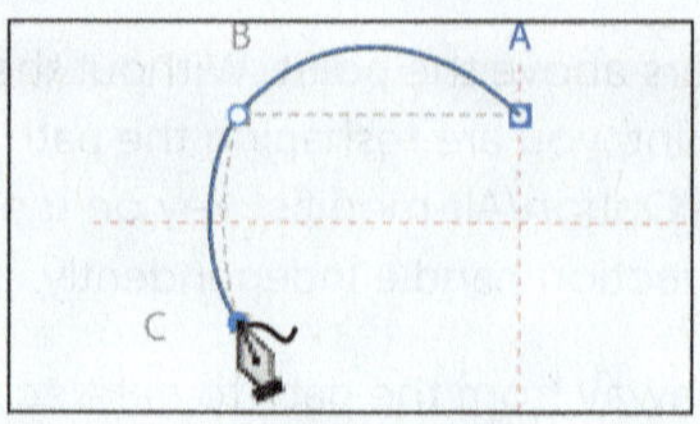

6. Hover the pointer over point B and the pointer will change. Double-click to convert the smooth point to a corner point.

   Double-clicking a point, which converts it to a corner point, has the effect of splitting the direction handles for the point.

7. Hover the pointer over point D and click to set the next point.

   Notice that the path segments before and after point C are curved.

8. Hover the pointer over the anchor point at D. When the pointer changes double-click to convert the point to a corner point.

9. Shift-click point E to create a point.

   Notice that the path doesn't follow the dotted line of the template path between points D and E. As you draw with the Curvature tool, you can easily go back and make corrections, even adding and deleting points, and then continue drawing.

10. Hover the pointer over the path segment between the D and E points. When a plus appears next to the pointer, click and drag to the left to create a point and curve the path. Drag to match the dotted template.

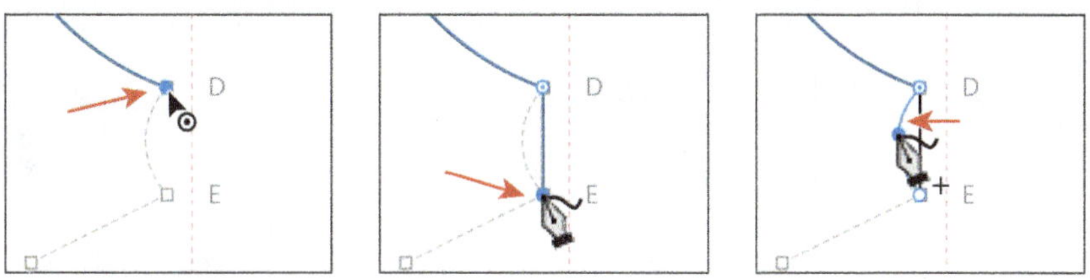

    Now you can just continue drawing the path with the Curvature tool.

11. Option-click (Mac) or Alt-click (Windows) point F and notice that the path at point E is curved.

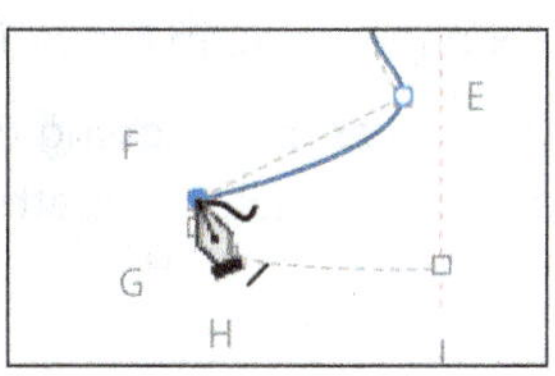

    By Option-clicking (Mac) or Alt-clicking (Windows) when you create a point with the Curvature tool, you create a corner point instead of the default smooth point.

12. Option-click (Mac) or Alt-click (Windows) point E to make it a corner point.

13. Shift-click point G.

14. Click point H and then click point I.

15. Press the Escape key to stop drawing and then choose Select > Deselect.

16. Save the **L4_start_xx.ai** file and leave it open.

Finishing the Illustration

With one-half of the shape created, you will now create a copy, reflect the copy, and then join the two halves together to make a perfectly symmetrical closed shape—the ice cream dish.

The first step is to make sure that the first and last anchor points are lined up vertically with each other.

Try It!

1. Select the Direct Selection tool, and click the last point you created (at point I). Shift-click the first point you created on the ice cream dish (at point A) to select both of the points at I and A.

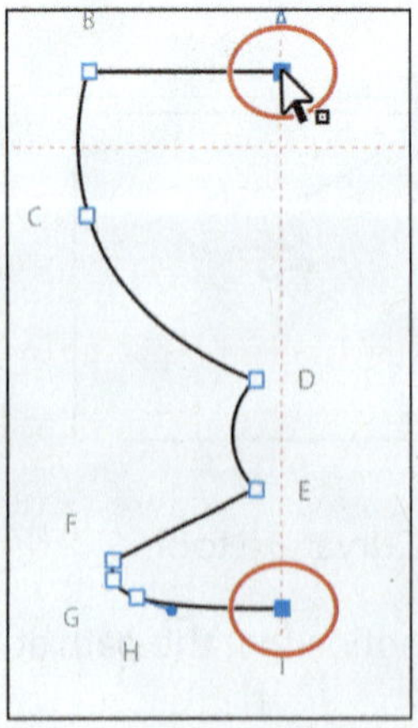

2. Click the Horizontal Align Center button in the Control panel to align the points.

   Aligning the points isn't necessary to copy and join two halves, but aligning them will ensure that extra points won't be added when you join the halves together.

> **Note:**
>
> The Align options may not appear in the Control panel. You can either click the word "Align" in the Control panel or choose Window > Align to see the align options.

3. Select the Selection tool.
4. Choose Select > Deselect, and then click to select the entire path.
5. Choose View > Smart Guides to turn on the Smart Guides.
6. Position the pointer over the Rotate tool, click and hold down the mouse button to reveal more tools. Select the Reflect tool.
7. Click the Layers panel icon to show the Layers panel. Click the eye icon to the left of the layer named "template" to hide its contents. Click the Layers panel tab to hide the panel.
8. Position the pointer over the last (bottom) anchor point (I). When the word "anchor" appears, Option-click (Mac) or Alt-click (Windows).

> **Note:**
>
> The modifier key sets the point that the shape will reflect around and opens the Reflect dialog box so you can copy the shape in one step.

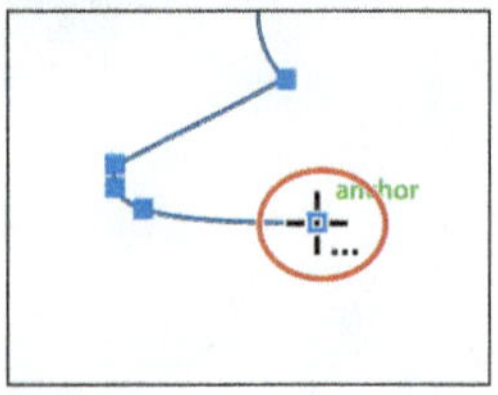

9. In the Reflect dialog box that opens, select Vertical, if it's not already selected, and then click Copy.
10. Select the Selection tool, and choose Select > All On Active Artboard to select both halves.

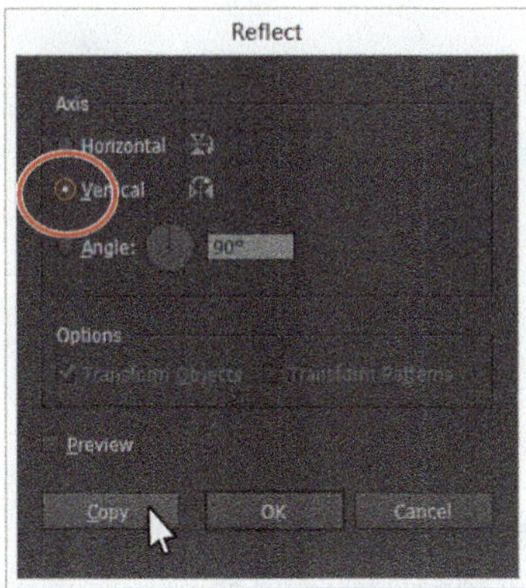

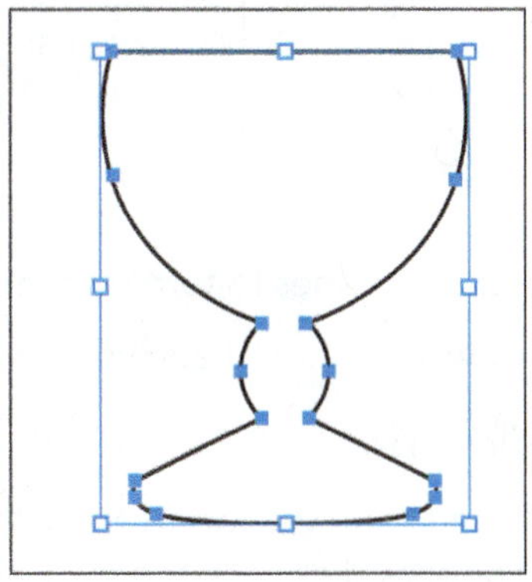

11. Press Command+J (Mac) or Ctrl+J (Windows) to join the two halves together into one closed path. Leave the path selected.

    After doing this, it may not look like much has changed, when in fact both halves are combined into a single, closed path.

12. Save the **L4_start_xx.ai** file and leave it open.

Editing Curves

For the remainder of this lesson, you will learn about tools you can use to edit lines and shapes to improve the appearance of an image. Next, you'll adjust curves you've drawn using different methods.

Try It!

1. Choose Select > Deselect.
2. Select the Direct Selection tool and drag across the two points shown in the following figure to select them.

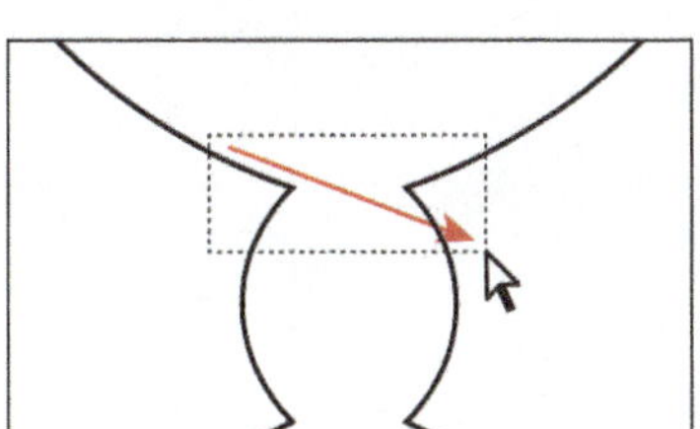

Notice that a Live Corners widget shows next to each of the anchor points. With both points selected, you can edit the radius of both by dragging one of the Live Corners widgets.

3. Drag the Live Corners widget on the right point to the right just a bit to make the path smoother. When the measurement label shows a radius of roughly 0.2 in, release the mouse button.

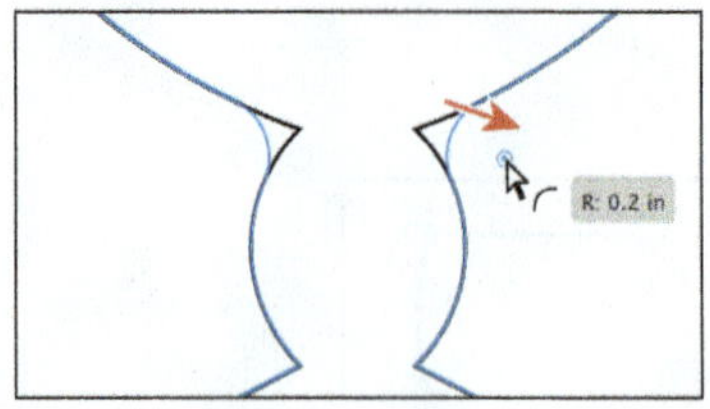

4. Choose View > Smart Guides to turn off the Smart Guides.

   Next, you'll edit the ice cream shape you created earlier.

5. Choose View > Ice Cream.

   Aside from zooming in on the ice cream path, the content from the template layer should be displayed as well, showing the guides you used to draw the path.

6. With the Direct Selection tool selected, click the ice cream path to select it. All of the anchor points will appear.

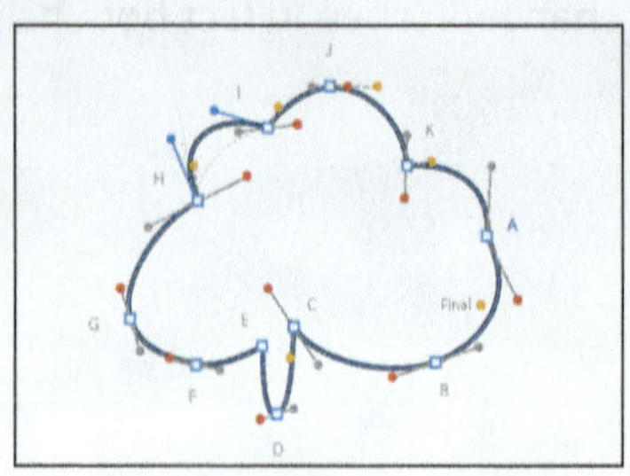

   Clicking with the Direct Selection tool displays the direction handles for the selected line segment and lets you adjust the shape of individual curved segments. Clicking with the Selection tool selects the entire path.

7. Click the anchor point (J) that is at the top of the ice cream path to select it. Drag the point down just a bit until it roughly matches the figure.

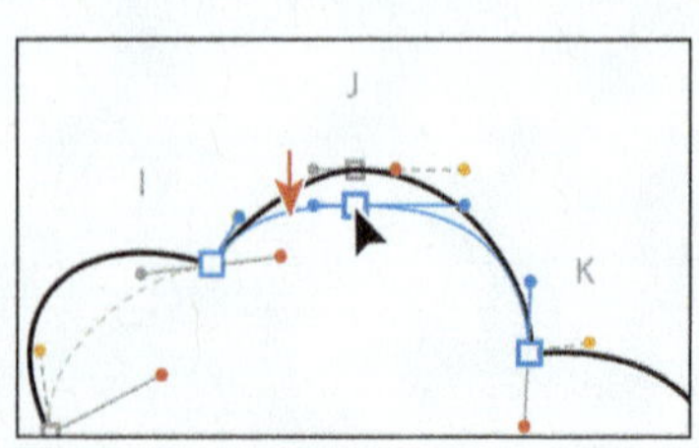

   The points will be filled (not hollow) when selected.

8. Click the Layers panel icon to show the Layers panel. Click the eye icon to the left of the layer named "template" to hide its contents. Click the Layers panel tab to hide the panel.

> **Tip:**
>
> You can also press the arrow keys to nudge an anchor point in a direction. Pressing and holding down the Shift key and then pressing an arrow key moves the point ten times farther than pressing the arrow key without the modifier key.

9. With the Direct Selection tool, position the pointer over the path, like you see in the figure. Notice that the pointer changes appearance. This indicates that you can drag the path, which will adjust the anchor points as you drag. Drag the path up and to the left to make the curve a little more rounded. As you drag the path, notice that the direction handles are changing as well. This is an easy way to make edits to a path.

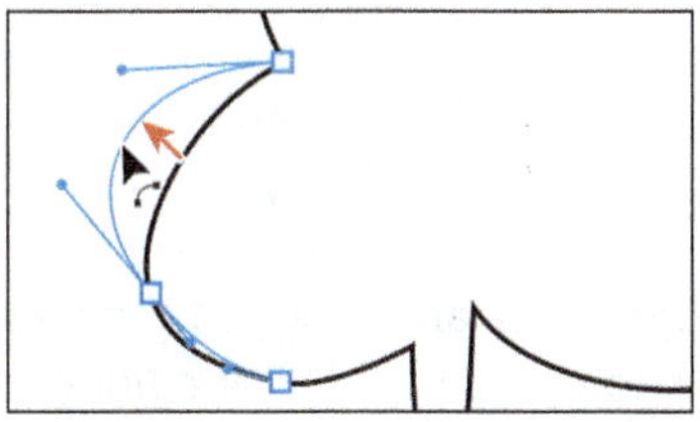

Tip:

If you wanted to adjust the direction handles instead of dragging the path, and wanted to see the direction handles for all of the selected points, you could click Show Handles For Multiple Selected Anchor Points in the Control panel.

10. Choose Select > Deselect. Save the **L4_start_xx.ai** file and leave it open.

Deleting and Adding Anchor Points

Most of the time, the goal of drawing paths with a tool like the Pen tool is to avoid adding more anchor points than necessary. You can, however, reduce a path's complexity or change its overall shape by deleting unnecessary points (and therefore gain more control over the shape), or you can extend a path by adding points to it. Next, you will delete and add anchor points to a path.

Try It!

1. Click the Layers panel icon to show the Layers panel. Click the eye icon to the left of the layer named "cherry" to show its contents (shown in the figure). Click the Layers panel tab to hide the panel.

2. With the Direct Selection tool selected, click the edge of the ice cream path.

3. Select the Zoom tool in the Tools panel, and click three times, slowly, on the cherry at the top of the ice cream path to zoom in.

4. Select the Pen tool in the Tools panel, and position the pointer over the ice cream path (see the figure). When a plus sign appears to the right of the Pen tool pointer, click to add another point to the path.

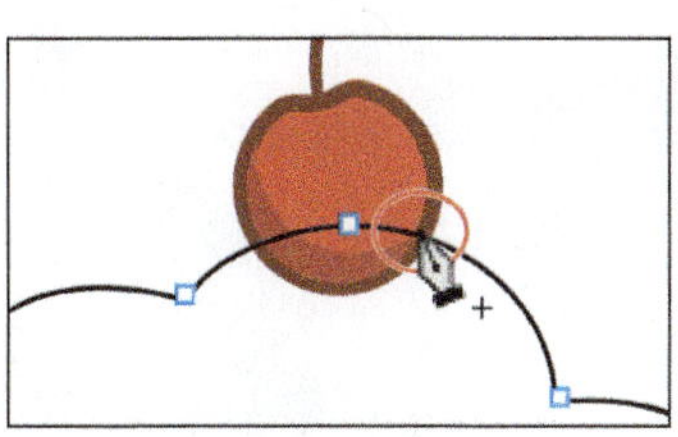

5. Select the Direct Selection tool, and drag the point up until it covers the cherry a bit. You're trying to make it look like the cherry was pushed into the ice cream.

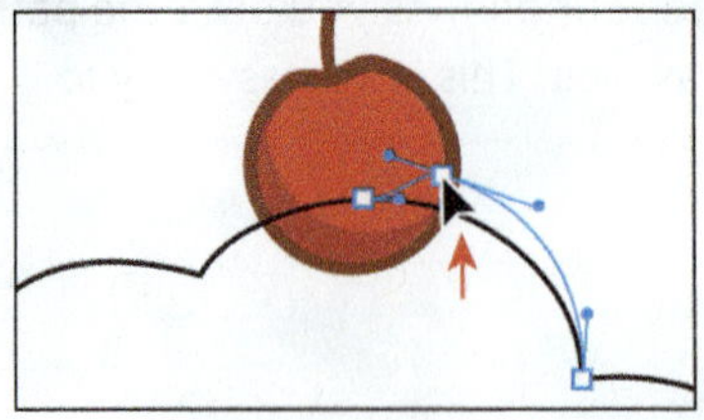

You could have simply selected the Direct Selection tool and dragged the path up, but we wanted to add specific anchor points to the path for later editing.

Next, you'll add another point and reposition it with the Pen tool.

6. Repeat steps 4 and 5 over the ice cream path on the left side of the cherry.
7. Choose Select > Deselect.

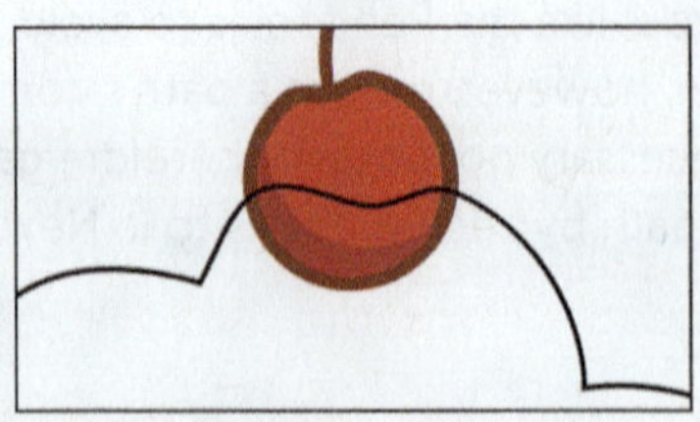

8. Press and hold down the spacebar to temporarily access the Hand tool. Drag up in the Document window until you see the bottom of the ice cream path, and then release the spacebar.
9. With the Selection tool, select the ice cream path.
10. Select the Pen tool in the Tools panel, and add points to the path on the right and left sides of the drip shape.

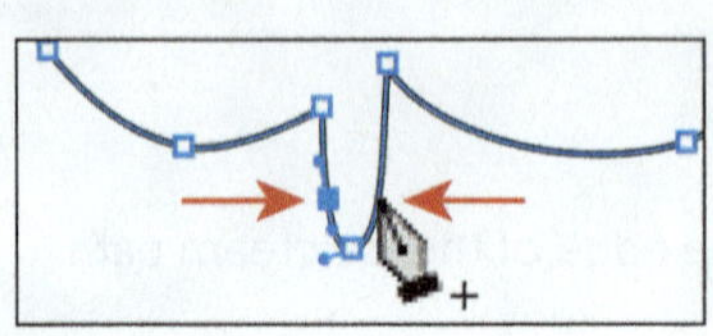

11. Position the Pen tool pointer over the bottom anchor point on that same drip. When a minus sign appears next to the pointer, click to delete the anchor point.

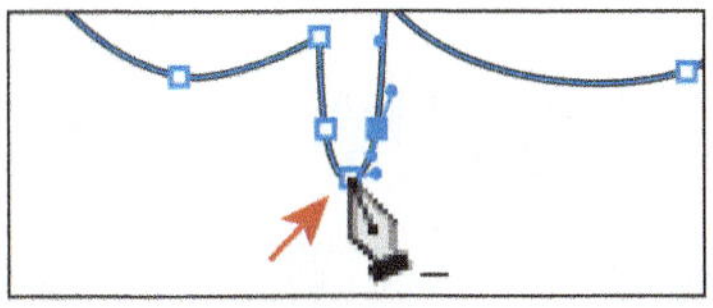

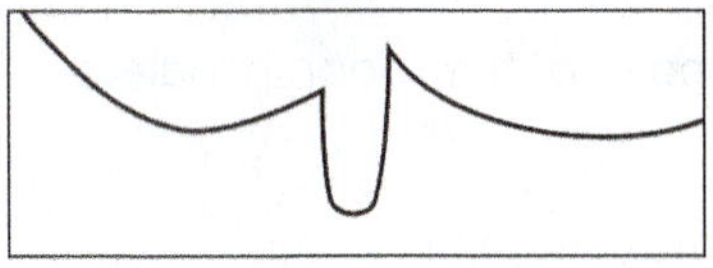

12. Choose Select > Deselect. Save the **L4_start_xx.ai** file and leave it open.

Converting Between Smooth Points and Corner Points

To more precisely control the path you create, you can convert points from smooth points to corner points and from corner points to smooth points, using several methods.

Try It!

1. Choose 3 Spoon from the Artboard Navigation menu in the lower-left corner of the Document window.
2. Select the Direct Selection tool, and position the pointer over the upper-left corner point on the spoon handle. When an open square with a dot in the center appears next to the pointer, click the anchor point to select it.

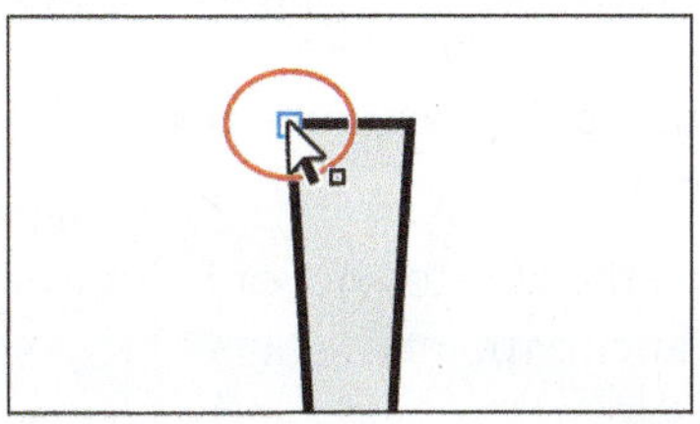

3. With the point selected, click the Convert Selected Anchor Points To Smooth button in the Control panel.

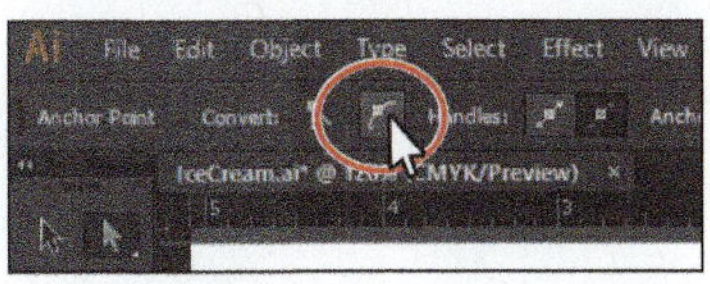

Tip:

You can also select multiple anchor points and convert them at the same time.

4. Drag the direction handle that's pointing down toward the center of the spoon. It doesn't have to match perfectly, but see the figure for roughly where to drag.

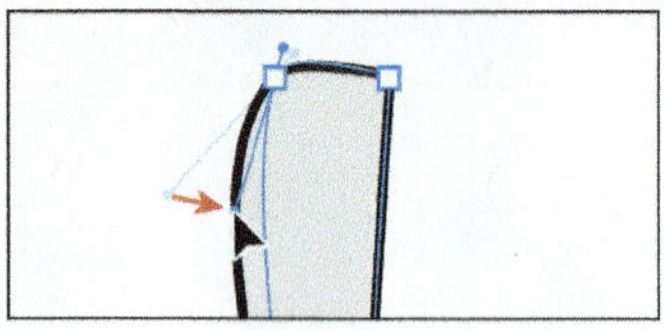

5. Repeat Steps 2–4 for the upper-right anchor point of the spoon handle.

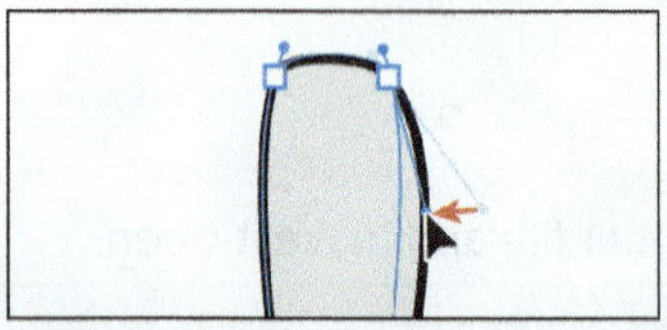

6. Save the **L4_start_xx.ai** file and leave it open.

Working with the Anchor Point Tool

Next, you'll convert anchor points using the Anchor Point tool.

Try It!

1. Choose 2 Dish from the Artboard Navigation menu in the lower-left corner of the Document window. Choose View > Fit Artboard In Window (if necessary).
2. Click the Layers panel icon to show the Layers panel. Click the visibility column to the left of the layer named "template" to show its contents.
3. Select the Selection tool in the Tools panel and click the dish path to select it.
4. Position the pointer over the Pen tool, click and hold down the mouse button to reveal more tools. Select the Anchor Point tool.

   You will also see the Add Anchor Point tool and the Delete Anchor Point tool , which are specifically for adding or removing anchor points.
5. Position the pointer over the C anchor point on the left side of the path. Hold down the Shift key, and click and drag down until the end of the opposite direction handle (that is pointing up) reaches point B (circled in red in the figure). Release the mouse button, and then release the key.

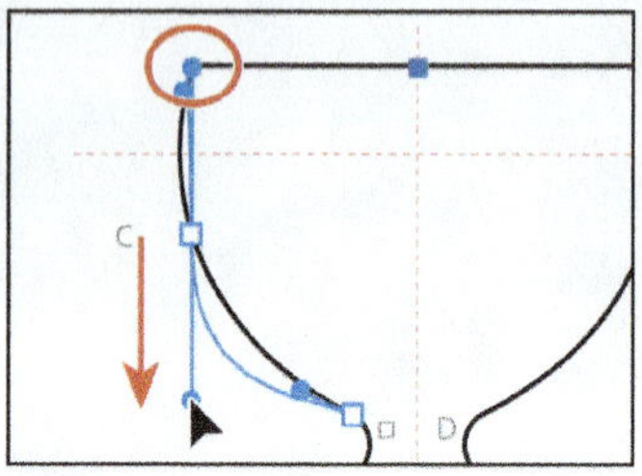

   With the Anchor Point tool, you can perform tasks like converting between smooth and corner points, edit direction handles, and more.

6. Click point B (left side) to convert the anchor point to a corner point.

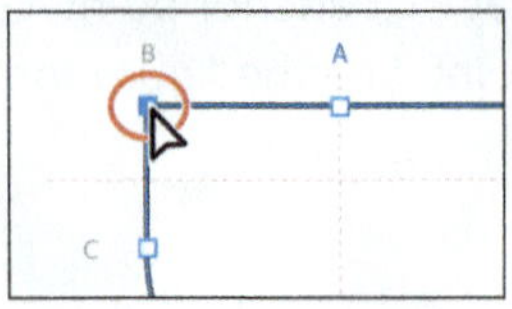

This is another way to convert an anchor point between smooth and corner. In order to convert an anchor point to a smooth point with the Anchor Point tool, you need to drag away from the point.

7. Position the pointer over the C anchor point on the right side of the dish path, and when the pointer looks like that shown in the figure below, press the Shift key, and click and drag up to snap to point B straight above it (on the right side). Release the mouse button and the release the Shift key.

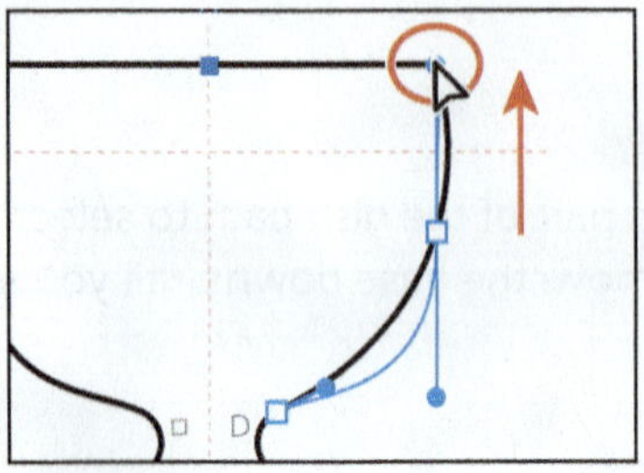

8. Click the upper-right corner point to convert it to a corner point.

9. Choose Select > Deselect. Save the **L4_start_xx.ai** file and leave it open.

Cutting with the Scissors Tool

There are several tools that allow you to cut and divide shapes. The Scissors tool splits a path at an anchor point or on a line segment, and the Knife tool allows you to cut objects that automatically become closed paths. Next, you'll cut the ice cream dish path with the Scissors tool to reshape it.

Try It!

1. Select the Selection tool in the Tools panel, and then choose Select > All On Active Artboard to select the dish path.

2. Choose View > Smart Guides to turn them on.

3. With the path selected, in the Tools panel, click and hold down the Eraser tool and select the Scissors tool . Position the pointer over point E (on the left), and when you see the word "anchor," click to cut the path at that anchor point. Go to the reflected side on the right, and click the same point. See the figure for where to click.

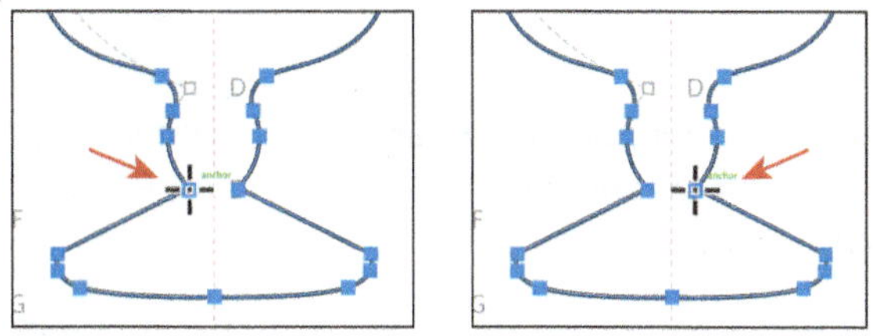

If you don't click directly on the path, you will see a warning dialog box. You can simply click OK and try again. Cuts made with the Scissors tool must be on a line or a curve rather than on an end point. When you click with the Scissors tool, a new anchor point appears and is selected.

4. Choose Select > Deselect.

5. Select the Selection tool, and click the bottom part of the dish path to select it. Press the Down Arrow key six times or so, to move the base down until you see a small gap between the two paths.

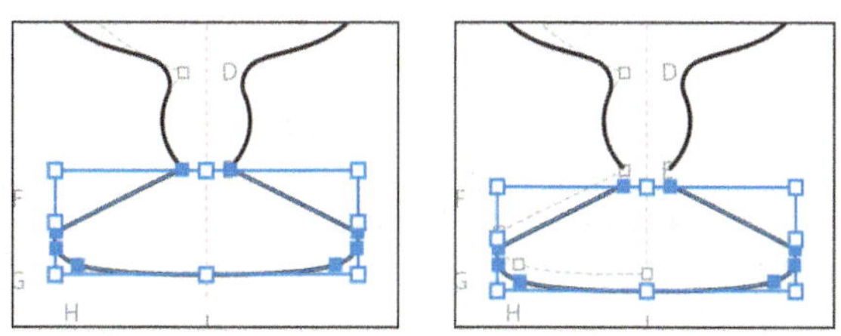

6. Choose Select > All On Active Artboard to select both paths.

7. Press Command+J (Mac) or Ctrl+J (Windows) once, and then press Command+J (Mac) or Ctrl+J (Windows) again to join the two open paths into one closed path. There should no longer be gaps between the cut paths.

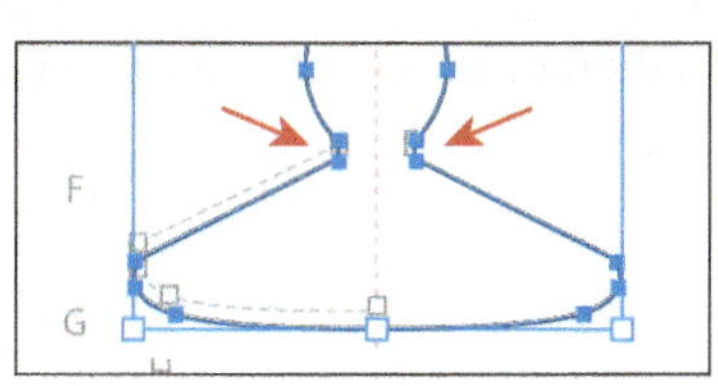

8. Save the **L4_start_xx.ai** file and leave it open.

Creating a Dashed Line

Dashed lines apply to the stroke of an object and can be added to a closed path or an open path. Dashes are created by specifying a sequence of dash lengths and the gaps between them. Next, you'll create a line and add a dash to it.

Try It!

1. Select the Zoom tool in the Tools panel, and click twice, slowly, on the top of the cup path to zoom in.
2. Select the Line Segment tool in the Tools panel, and then choose Select > Deselect.
3. Position the pointer over the left side of the cup path, where the red horizontal dashed line is (see the red X in the figure). Click, press Shift, and drag to the right. When the pointer reaches the other side of the shape and the word "intersect" displays, release the mouse, and then release the modifier key.

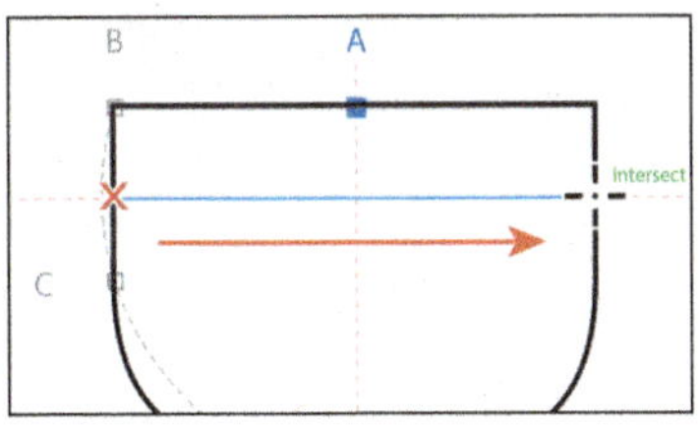

4. Choose View > Smart Guides to turn them off.
5. Click the word "Stroke" in the Control panel to show the Stroke panel. Change the following options in the Stroke panel:
   - Weight: **40 pt**
   - Dashed Line: **Selected**

     (By default, this creates a repeating dash pattern of 12 pt dash, 12 pt gap.)
   - First Dash value: **5 pt**

     (This creates a 5 pt dash, 5 pt gap repeating pattern.)
   - First Gap value: **3 pt**

     (This creates a 5 pt dash, 3 pt gap repeating pattern.)
   - Change the next Dash value to **2 pt**, and change the next Gap value to **4 pt**.
   - The values below Dashed Line should now be: 5 pt, 3 pt, 2 pt, 4 pt.
6. With the line still selected, change the Stroke color to the light-yellow swatch named "cup 65%" in the Control panel.

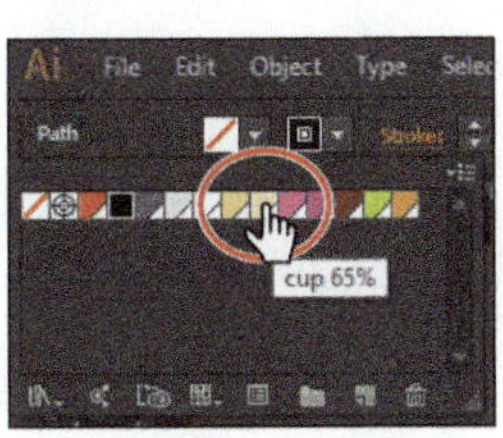

7. Select the Selection tool, and click to select the cup shape.

8. Change the Stroke weight to 6 pt in the Control panel. Change the fill color to the swatch named "cup" and the stroke color to the brown swatch named "cup stroke."

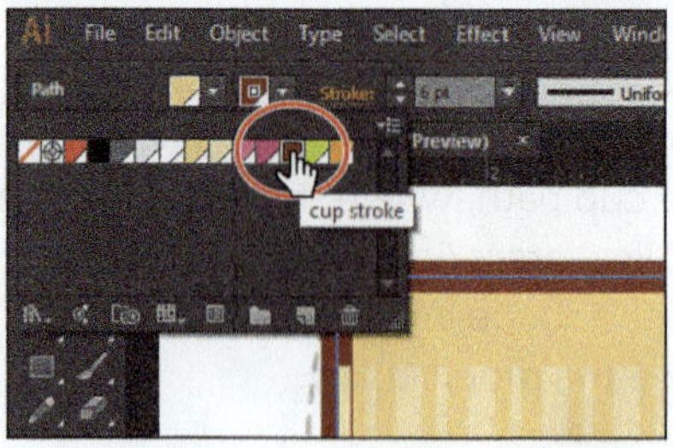

9. Click the word "Stroke" in the Control panel to display the Stroke panel.

   Click the Align Stroke To Outside button.

10. Choose Select > All On Active Artboard, and then choose Object > Group.

Cutting with the Knife Tool

Next, you'll cut the spoon in a straight line with the Knife tool to create two closed paths.

Try It!

1. Choose 3 Spoon from the Artboard Navigation menu in the lower-left corner of the Document window.

2. Choose Select > All On Active Artboard. The image needs to be selected to cut it with the Knife tool.

3. Click and hold down the mouse on the Scissors tool and select the Knife tool . Notice the Knife pointer in the Document window.

4. Position the pointer off the left side of the end of the spoon. Press and hold Option+Shift (Mac) or Alt+Shift (Windows), and drag all the way across the shape to cut in a straight line. See the figure for where to cut.

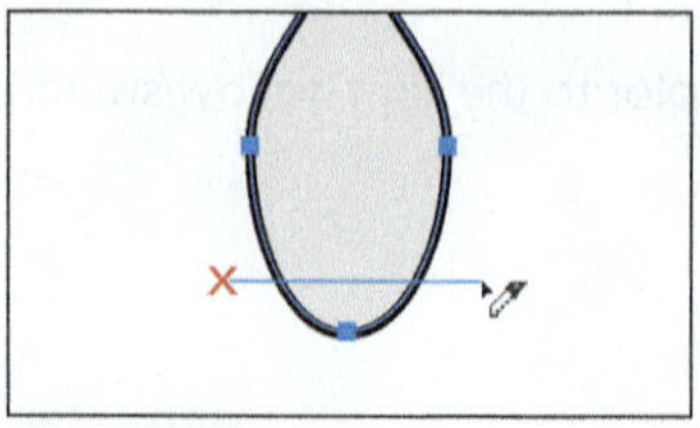

   Holding down the modifier keys ensures that your cut is straight.

5. Choose Select > Deselect.

6. Select the Selection tool, and drag the bottom part of the spoon path down a little bit to see that the spoon path is now cut into two closed paths.

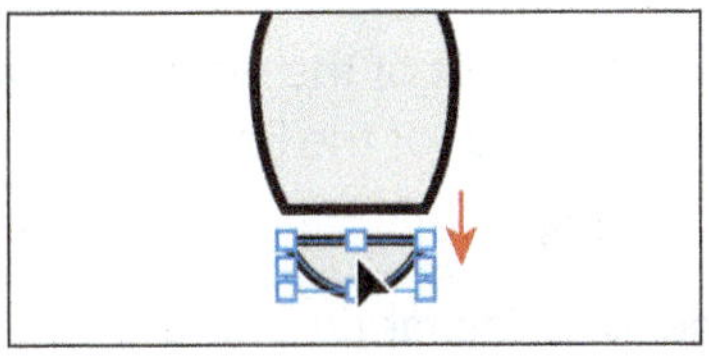

7. Choose Select > All On Active Artboard.
8. With the spoon shapes selected, choose Object > Transform > Rotate. In the Rotate dialog box, change the value to −45 and click OK.
9. Choose View > Fit All In Window.
10. With the Selection tool, drag the selected spoon shapes onto the ice cream path (see the figure), and choose Object > Arrange > Bring To Front.
11. Drag the cup group below the ice cream path and choose Object > Arrange > Send To Back. See the figure for position.

12. Click the Layers panel icon to show the Layers panel, if necessary. Click the eye icon to the left of the layer named "template" to hide its contents.
13. Choose Select > Deselect. Save the **L4_start_xx.ai** file and leave it open.

Adding Arrowheads

You can add arrowheads to both ends of a path using the Stroke panel. There are many different arrowhead styles to choose from in Illustrator, as well as arrowhead editing options. Next, you'll add different arrowheads to a path.

Try It!

1. Choose the 1 Ice Cream artboard from the Artboard Navigation menu in the lower-left corner of the Document window.
2. Choose View > Fit Artboard In Window, if necessary.
3. Select the Selection tool, and click the black line above the word "cherry."

4. Click the word "Stroke" in the Control panel to open the Stroke panel (or choose Window > Stroke). In the Stroke panel, change the following options:
    - Stroke Weight: **50 pt**
    - Choose **Arrow 20** from the menu directly to the right of the word "Arrowheads." This adds an arrowhead to the start (left end) of the line.
    - Scale (beneath where you chose Arrow 20): **30%**
    - Choose **Arrow 35** from the arrowheads menu to the far right of the word "Arrowheads." This adds an arrowhead to the end of the line.
    - Scale (beneath where you chose Arrow 35): **40%**
    - Make sure that the Place Arrow Tip At End Of Path button is selected. The Align options allow you to adjust the path to align to the tip or the end of the arrowhead.
5. Change the Stroke color of the selected path to the swatch named "cup stroke" in the Control panel.
6. Click the larger spoon shape on the ice cream, and choose Object > Arrange > Send To Back to send it behind all other shapes.
7. With the Selection tool selected, click the edge of the ice cream shape to select it.
8. Change the fill color to the pink swatch with the tool tip "ice cream," change the stroke color to the swatch with the tool tip "cup stroke" in the Control panel, and change the Stroke weight to 6 pt in the Control panel.

9. Choose Select > Deselect. Save the **L4_start_xx.ai** file and leave it open.

Drawing and Editing with the Pencil Tool

The Pencil tool lets you draw free-form open and closed paths that contain curves and straight lines. As you draw with the Pencil tool, anchor points are created on the path where necessary and according to the Pencil tool options you set. The path can easily be adjusted when the path is complete.

Next, you will draw and edit a few paths using the Pencil tool.

Try It!

1. Select the Zoom tool in the Tools panel and click several times, slowly, on the bottom of the pink ice cream shape to zoom in.

2. Double-click the Pencil tool in the Tools panel. In the Pencil Tool Options dialog box, set the following options, leaving the rest at their default settings:
   - Drag the Fidelity slider all the way to the right to Smooth. This will reduce the number of points on a path drawn with the Pencil tool and make the path smoother.
   - Fill New Pencil Strokes: **Selected** (Without this option selected, which is the default, paths you draw will have no fill.)
   - Alt Key (Option key on Mac) Toggles To Smooth Tool: **Selected**

     (The Smooth tool is used to smooth the path after it is drawn.)
   - Close path when ends are within: **Deselected**.
3. Click OK.
4. With the Pencil tool selected, position the pointer beneath the ice cream shape.

   The asterisk that appears next to the pointer indicates that you are about to create a new path. If you don't see the asterisk, it means that you are about to redraw a shape that the pointer is near.
5. Draw a "drip" shape beneath the ice cream shape (see the figure for what to draw). When the pointer gets close to the start of the path, a small circle displays next to it to indicate that if you release the mouse button, the path will close. When you see the circle, release the mouse button to close the path.

   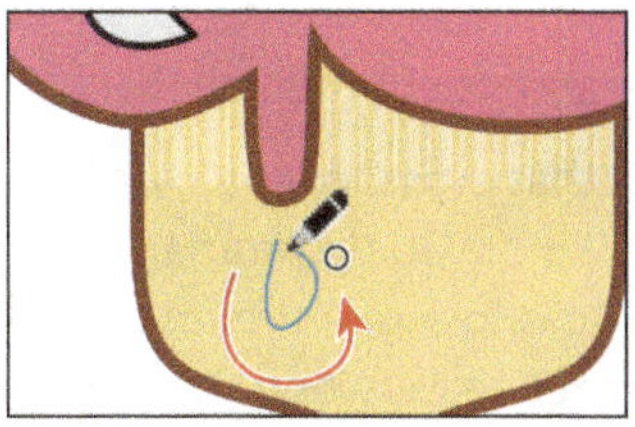

   Notice that as you are drawing, the path may not look perfectly smooth. After releasing the mouse button, the path is smoothed based on the Fidelity value that you set in the Pencil Tool Options dialog box.
6. With the new path still selected, position the Pencil tool over the bottom of the path and notice that the asterisk (*) disappears from the pointer, indicating that you are about to redraw the selected path. Try redrawing the drip. Make sure to start on the drip path and end on the drip path.

   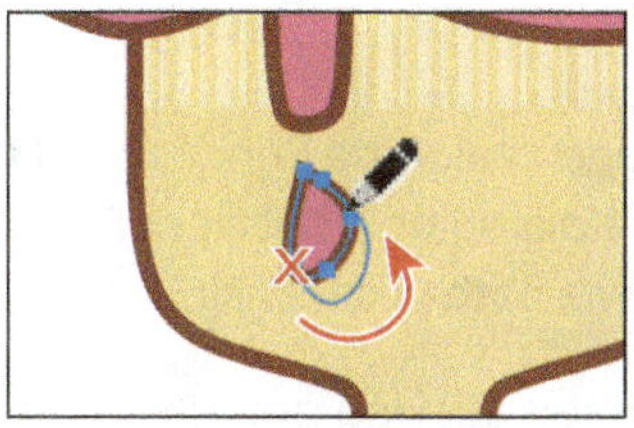

7. Press the Option (Mac) or Alt (Win) key and the pointer will change to a circle. With the key held down, drag across the bottom of the drip shape, following loosely along the path, to smooth it. Release the key when done smoothing. You can try this a few times.

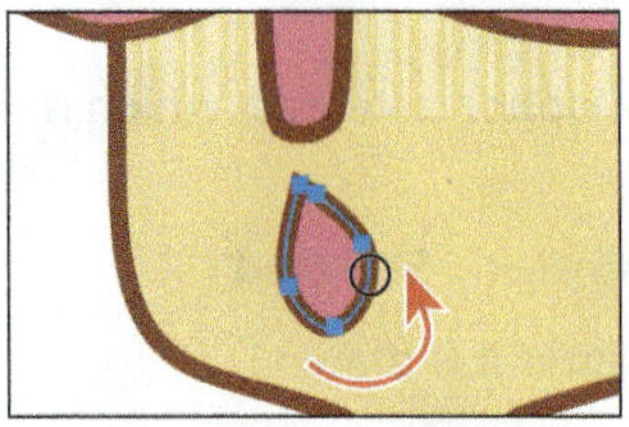

Since you selected the Alt Key (Option key on Mac) Toggles To Smooth Tool option in the Pencil Tool Options dialog box , you can smooth the path rather than redrawing it.

8. Draw a "U" shape beneath the first drip shape, without closing it.

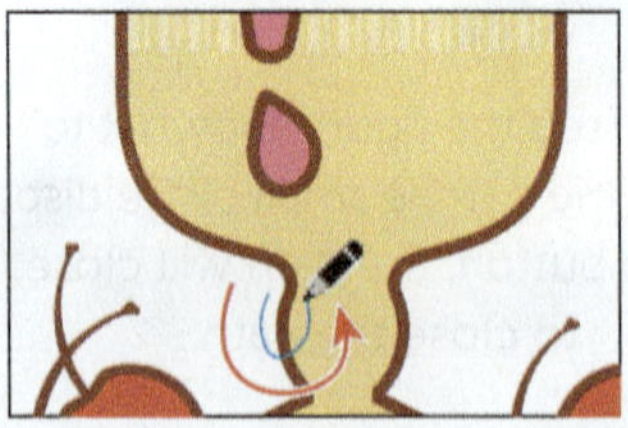

9. Click and hold down the mouse on the Pencil tool and select the Join tool.

   You can use the Join tool to intelligently join paths that cross, overlap, or have open ends without affecting the original paths. Unlike the Join command (Object > Path > Join), you learned previously, the Join tool can trim overlapping paths as it joins and it doesn't simply create a straight line between the anchor points you are joining. The angle created by the two paths to be joined are taken into account.

10. With the Join tool selected, drag across the two ends of the "U" shaped path you created to join them.

   When dragging (also called scrubbing) across paths, they will be either "extended and joined" or "trimmed and joined." In this example, the paths were extended and joined. The Join tool works on paths that are selected or not, but the result of joining is not selected, to continue working on more paths.

   Aside from drawing more free-form paths, you can also create straight lines with the Pencil tool.

11. Click and hold down the mouse on the Join tool and select the Pencil tool. Double-click the Pencil tool. In the Pencil Tool Options dialog box, deselect Fill New Pencil Strokes and click OK. This way you can draw a path with no fill.

12. Position the pointer above the end of the spoon that is sticking out of the ice cream shape (see red X in the following figure).

   You are going to draw a shape with a flat side. Don't forget, you can always choose Edit > Undo Pencil and try again.

13. Click and drag a small curve to the flat edge of the spoon shape. Without releasing the mouse button, press the Option (Mac) or Alt (Windows) key and drag a straight line that follows the flat edge of the spoon shape. Without releasing the mouse button, release the Option/Alt key and continue dragging to complete the shape as shown in the figure.

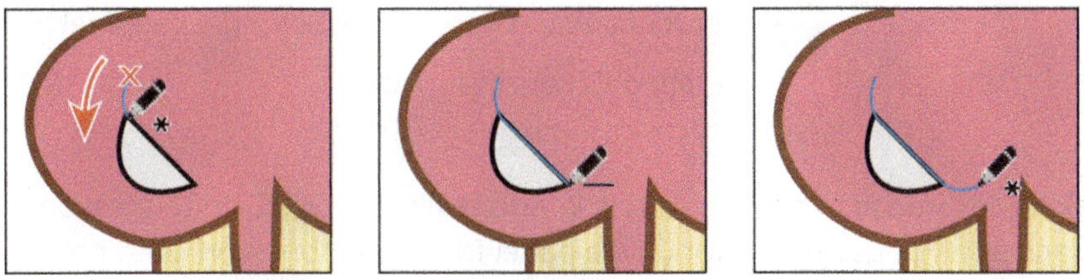

14. Choose View > Fit Artboard In Window.

15. Close **L4_start1_xx.ai**, saving all changes, and exit Illustrator.

Comprehension Check

1. Describe how to draw straight vertical, horizontal, or diagonal lines using the Pen tool.
2. How do you draw a curved line using the Pen tool?
3. What is the difference between a corner point and a smooth point?
4. Which tool would you use to edit a segment on a curved line?
5. How can you change the way the Pencil tool works?

Review Project

Open the **L4_start_xx.ai** file that you completed in this lesson and save it as **L4_review_xx.ai**. Using the skills you have learned so far, make adjustments to the layout and design of the illustration that you think improve the look. Be creative, but keep in mind the principles of layout and design as you make your changes. Exchange your illustration with a classmate and provide a critique of their modifications.

Lesson 5 Overview

In this lesson, you will learn about:

- Exploring Basic Color Theory
- Getting Started with Color
- Working with Color
- Using Illustrator Swatch Libraries
- Adjusting Colors
- Working with Color in the Color Guide Panel
- Editing Colors in Artwork

Spice up your illustrations with colors by taking advantage of color controls in Adobe Illustrator CC. In this lesson, you'll discover how to create and paint fills and strokes, use the Color Guide panel for inspiration, work with color groups, recolor artwork, create patterns, and more.

Exploring Basic Color Theory

Color is the way our eyes see light. Color theory defines the relationships between colors and provides insight into how to use and mix colors to create harmony and contrast. You can use a **color wheel** to explore the relationships among colors.

- **Primary colors** are red, yellow, and blue. You can mix the primary colors in different combinations and amounts to create all the other colors.
- **Secondary colors** are made by mixing equal amounts of two primary colors. Mix red and yellow to get orange, red and blue to get violet, and blue and yellow to get green.
- **Intermediate colors** are made by mixing a primary color and the secondary color that's next to it on the color wheel. Examples of intermediate colors are red-violet, blue-violet, blue-green, yellow-green, yellow-orange, and red-orange.
- **Complementary colors** are the colors opposite each other on the color wheel. Red and green are complementary. So are violet and yellow.
- **Analogous colors** are next to each other on the color wheel. For example green, blue-green, and blue are analogous.
- **Neutral colors** are black, white, and gray.

Describing Color

- Hue is the name of a color, such as blue or red. Hue describes the characteristics of a color that distinguish it from another color. For example, when you compare two orange scarves and notice that one is a more reddish orange and the other is more yellowish orange, you are seeing the difference in the hue.
- Color value refers to the lightness or darkness of a color. Lighter values are called tints and are made by adding white to a color. For example, adding white to red makes pink. Darker values are called shades and are made by adding black to a color. For example, adding black to blue makes navy blue. When you dress, you can make an outfit more interesting by using different—or contrasting—values. For example, wearing a pale blue shirt with gray pants and black shoes makes a very different statement from wearing a brown shirt, brown pants, and brown shoes.
- Intensity is the brightness or dullness of a color. Bright colors contain the most color and are the most vivid. Examples of bright colors are jewel tones such as emerald green and ruby red. Dull colors are softer and more subdued. Colors become duller if gray or their complement is added to them

Color

The way our eyes see light.

Color wheel

A visual representation of colors arranged in a circle according to their relationship.

Primary colors

Red, yellow, and blue.

Secondary colors

Made by mixing equal amounts of two primary colors.

Intermediate colors

Made by mixing a primary color and the secondary color that's next to it on the color wheel.

Complementary colors

The colors opposite each other on the color wheel.

Analogous colors

Next to each other on the color wheel.

Neutral colors

Black, white, and gray.

Color Harmony

A **color harmony** or **color scheme** is a combination of colors that look good together. You can use them as a guide-line for selecting colored clothing and accessories. The five most common color harmonies are described below.

Monochromatic: A color harmony that uses only one color. This harmony can include different values of one color or include neutrals.

Color harmony or color scheme

A combination of colors that look good together.

Monochromatic

A color harmony that uses only one color.

Analogous

A color harmony that includes two or more colors that are next to each other on the color wheel.

Complementary

A color harmony that uses two colors that are direct opposites on the color wheel.

Split-complementary

A color harmony that uses one color and the two colors on either side of its complement.

Triad

A color harmony that uses three colors that are an equal distance from each other on the color wheel.

Note:

In Mac OS, when opening lesson files, you may need to click the round, green button in the upper-left corner of the Document window to maximize the window's size.

Analogous: A color harmony that includes two or more colors that are next to each other on the color wheel. An example is orange, yellow-orange, and yellow.

Complementary: A color harmony that uses two colors that are direct opposites on the color wheel. An example is yellow and violet.

Split-complementary: A color harmony that uses one color and the two colors on either side of its complement. An example is red, blue-green, and yellow-green.

Triad: A color harmony that uses three colors that are an equal distance from each other on the color wheel. An example is the three primary colors, red, blue, and yellow.

Getting Started with Color

In this lesson, you will create and edit colors for a park sign and logo, using the Color panel, Swatches panel, and more.

Try It!

1. Start Adobe Illustrator CC.
2. Choose File > Open, and open the **L5_start.ai** from the data files for this lesson.

This file has all of the pieces already in it; they just need to be painted.

3. Save the file as **L5_start_xx.ai** in the location where your teacher instructs you to store the files for this lesson and leave it open.

4. Leave the Format option (Mac) and the Save as type option (Windows) set to Adobe Illustrator, and click Save.

5. In the Illustrator Options dialog box, click OK to accept the default settings.

6. Choose Window > Workspace > Reset Essentials.

Note:

If you don't see "Reset Essentials" on the menu, choose Window > Workspace > Essentials before choosing Window > Workspace > Reset Essentials.

Working with Color

There are many ways to experiment with and apply color to your artwork in Adobe Illustrator CC. As you work with color, it's important to keep in mind the medium in which the artwork will be published, such as a printed piece or on a Web site. The colors you create need to be described in the correct way for the medium. This usually requires that you use the correct color mode and color definitions for your colors.

Exploring Color Modes

Before starting a new illustration, you should decide which color mode to use CMYK or RGB.

- **CMYK**—Cyan, magenta, yellow, and black are the colors used in four-color process printing. These four colors are combined and overlapped in a screen pattern to create a multitude of other colors. Select this mode for printing (in the New Document dialog box or the File > Document Color Mode menu).
- **RGB**—Red, green, and blue light are added together in various ways to create an array of colors. Select this mode if you are using images for onscreen presentations or the Internet.

When creating a new document, you select a color mode by choosing File > New and picking the appropriate profile, such as Print, which uses CMYK for the color mode. You can change the color mode by clicking the arrow to the left of Advanced and making a selection in the Color Mode menu.

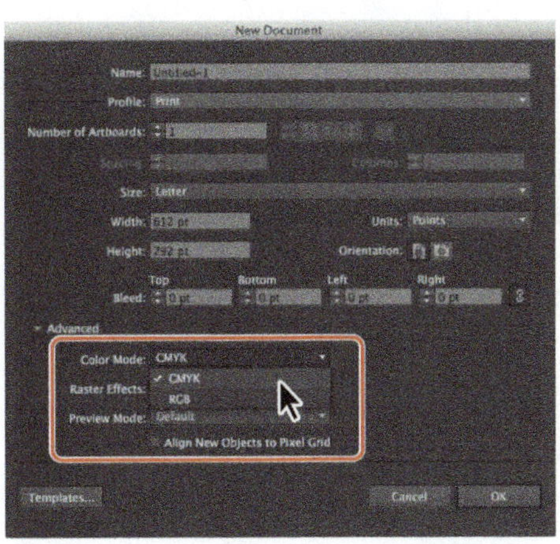

When a color mode is selected, the applicable panels open, displaying colors in the selected color mode. You can change the color mode of a document, after a file is created, by choosing File > Document Color Mode, and then selecting either CMYK Color or RGB Color in the menu.

Understanding the Main Color Controls

In this section, you will learn about the traditional methods of coloring (also called *painting*) objects in Illustrator. This includes painting objects with colors and patterns using a combination of panels and tools, such as the Control panel, Color panel, Swatches panel, Color Guide panel, Color Picker, and the paint options in the Tools panel.

You'll begin by exploring some of the more widely used options available for creating and applying color.

Try It!

1. Open the **L5_end.ai** document.
2. If necessary, choose 1 from the Artboard Navigation menu in the lower-left corner of the Document window.
3. Select the Selection tool, and click the large, light-brown shape in the sign behind the text "SHORELINE PARK."

   Objects in Illustrator can have a fill, a stroke, or both, as you've seen. At the bottom of the Tools panel, notice the Fill and Stroke boxes. The Fill box is brown for the selected object, and the Stroke box is None. Click the Stroke box, and then click the Fill box (making sure that the Fill box is the last selected). Notice that the box you click is brought to the front of the other. When a color is selected, it will apply to the fill or stroke of the selected object (whichever is in front).

   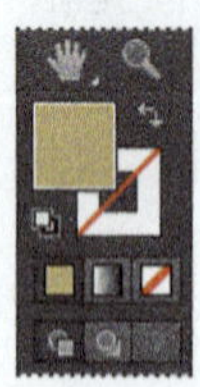

4. Click the Color panel icon on the right side of the workspace, if it isn't open already. Click the double arrow to the left of the word "Color" in the panel tab until the panel looks like the figure below.

   The Color panel displays the current fill and stroke of the selected content. The CMYK sliders in the Color panel show the percentages of cyan, magenta, yellow, and black used to create the selected color. The color spectrum bar at the bottom lets you quickly and visually select a fill or stroke color from a spectrum of colors.

   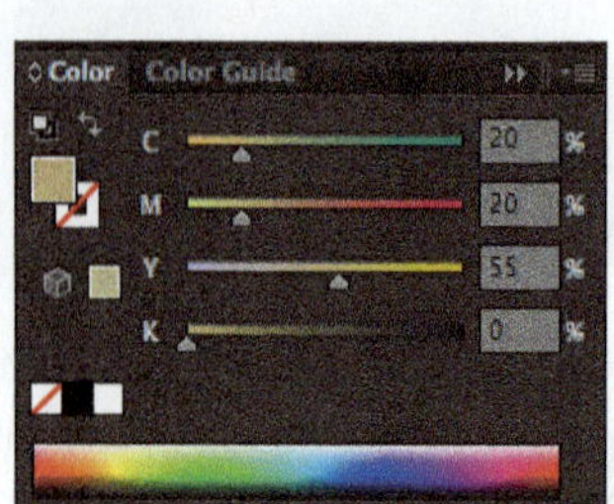

5. Click the Swatches panel icon on the right side of the workspace.

   You can name and save different types of colors, gradients, and patterns as swatches so that you can apply and edit them later. Swatches are listed in the Swatches panel in the order in which they were created, but you can reorder or organize the swatches into groups to suit your needs. All documents start with a set number of swatches, but any colors in the Swatches panel are available to the current document only (by default), since each document has its own defined swatches.

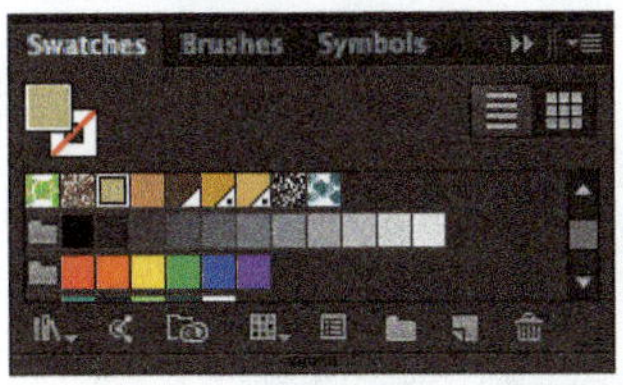

6. Click the Color Guide panel icon on the right side of the workspace. Click the brown swatch in the upper-left corner of the panel to set the base color.

   The Color Guide panel can provide color inspiration while you create your artwork. Either starting with the current color in the Fill box or by using an existing library of colors, it can help you pick color tints, analogous colors, and more. Those colors can then be applied directly to artwork using various methods, saved as swatches, or within groups, or edited using the Edit Colors feature.

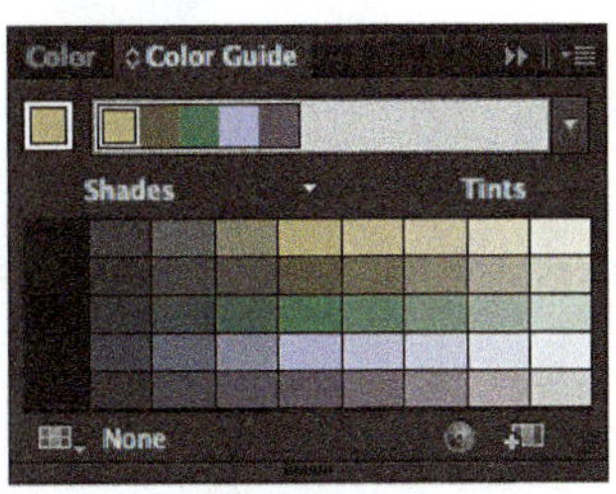

7. Click the Color panel icon. Using the Selection tool, click various shapes in the **L5_end.ai** file to see how their paint attributes are reflected in the Color panel and the Tools panel.

8. Choose File > Close to close the file without saving changes.

Applying an Existing Color

As was mentioned previously, every new document in Illustrator has a series of default colors available in the form of swatches in the Swatches panel. In the next section, you will paint a shape with an existing color.

Note:

Throughout this lesson, you'll be working on a document with a color mode that was set to CMYK when the document was created, which means that the majority of colors you create will, by default, be composed of cyan, magenta, yellow, and black.

Try It!

1. If necessary, choose from the Artboard Navigation menu in the lower-left corner of the Document window, and then choose View > Fit Artboard In Window.

2. Choose Window > Workspace > Reset Essentials.

3. With the Selection tool, click to select the large red shape.
4. Click the Fill color in the Control panel, and the Swatches panel appears. Hover the pointer over various swatches to display a tooltip with the swatch name. Click to apply the swatch named "Sign Bg." Press the Escape key to hide the Swatches panel.

5. Choose Select > Deselect to ensure that nothing is selected.
6. Save the changes to **L5_start_xx.ai** and leave it open.

Creating and Saving a Custom Color as a Swatch

At times, you may want to create a custom color and save it for later use. Repetition of colors is a design principle that helps achieve continuity and flow in visual communications. Next, you'll create a color using the Color panel, and then you'll save that color as a swatch in the Swatches panel.

Try It!

1. With the Selection tool, click to select the white bar above the green bar, in the middle of the artboard (on the sign).

   If the Color panel is not visible, click the Color panel icon. Click the Color panel menu icon, if necessary, and choose CMYK.

2. In the Color panel, click the white Fill box (if it's not selected) to apply the color to the fill of the selected shape. Drag the bottom of the Color panel down to reveal more of the color spectrum bar. Click in the light-green part of the color spectrum to sample a light-green color and apply it to the fill.

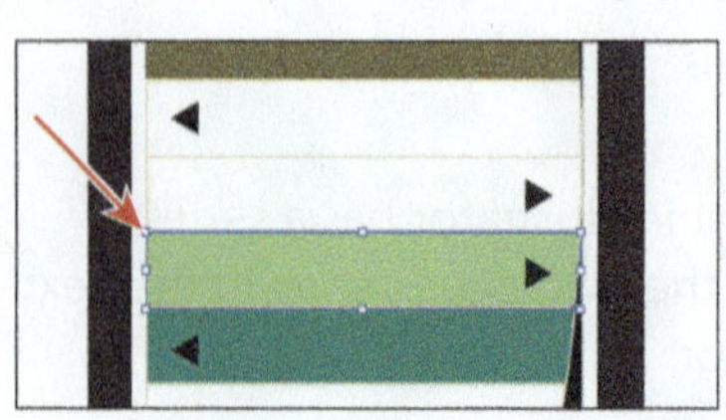

3. Type the following values in the CMYK text fields: C=42, M=0, Y=62, K=0.

   Now that you've created a color, you can save it as a swatch in the Swatches panel so that later you can edit or apply it elsewhere in this document.

4. Click the Swatches panel icon, and click the New Swatch button at the bottom of the panel.
5. In the New Swatch dialog box, name the color Light Green, leave the rest of the options as they are, and click OK.

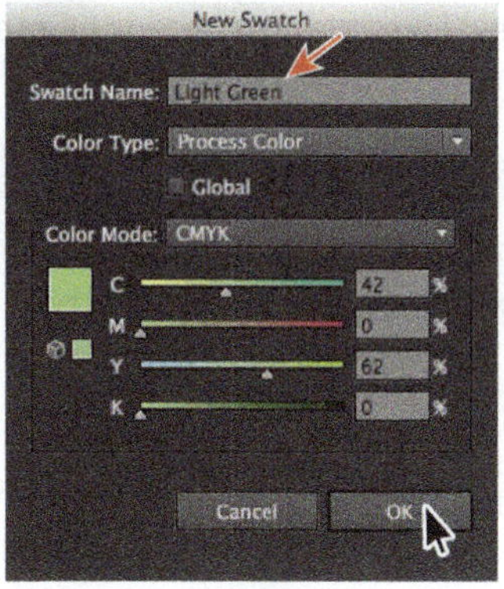

Notice that the new Light Green swatch is highlighted in the Swatches panel (it has a white border around it). That's because it is applied to the selected shape automatically. You may need to scroll in the Swatches panel to see it.

6. With the Selection tool, select the third white tree from the left, on the top of the sign.
7. In the Swatches panel on the right, drag the bottom of the panel down to see more swatches. Ensure that the Fill box at the top of the panel is selected to paint the fill of the shape, and select the swatch named "Light Green" to apply it.

   When applying a swatch from the Swatches panel, it's always important to select the stroke or the fill first so that it paints the right part.
8. Click the Stroke box at the top of the Swatches panel to paint the stroke of the selected shape. Select the None swatch in the Swatches panel to remove the stroke.

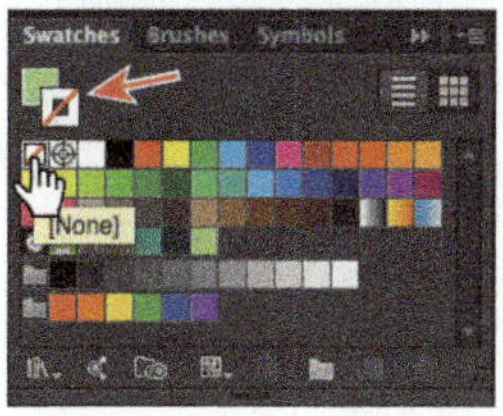

9. Choose Select > Deselect. Save the changes to **L5_start_xx.ai**, and leave it open.

Creating a Copy of a Swatch

Next, you will create another swatch by copying and editing the Light Green swatch you made.

Try It!

1. Click the Fill box at the top of the Swatches panel. This selects the Light Green swatch in the Swatches panel.
2. Click the New Swatch button at the bottom of the Swatches panel.

   Clicking the New Swatch button creates a swatch from the fill or stroke color (whichever is active at the top of the Swatches panel). If the None swatch is applied, the New Swatch button will be dimmed and you would not be able to select it.
3. In the New Swatch dialog box, change the name to Orange and change the values to C=15, M=45, Y=70, K=0. Click OK.
4. With the Selection tool, click the white bar above the Light Green-filled bar to select it. Click the Fill color in the Control panel, and click to select the color named "Orange."
5. Save the changes to **L5_start_xx.ai**, and leave it open.

> **Tip:**
>
> In the New Swatch dialog box, the Color Mode menu lets you change the color mode of a specific color to RGB, CMYK, Grayscale, or another mode, when you create it.

Editing a Swatch

You can edit a color that is saved in the Swatches panel. Next, you will edit the Orange swatch that you created.

Try It!

1. With the Selection tool selected, click to select the large brown sign shape you first applied a fill color to.
2. Make sure that the Fill box is selected in the Swatches panel, and then double-click the swatch named "Sign Bg" in the Swatches panel. In the Swatch Options dialog box, change the K value to 0, select Preview to see the change, and then click OK.

   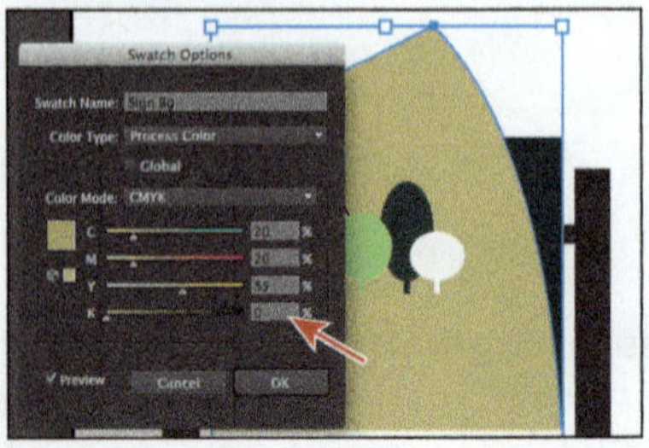

   If you want to apply the edited color to other objects with that swatch color, you must select them and then apply the new color. The color will not be updated automatically.
3. Save the changes to **L5_start_xx.ai**, and leave it open.

Creating and Editing a Global Swatch

Next, you will create a color and make it a global color. When you edit a global color, all objects to which that color has been applied will be updated automatically with the new color.

Try It!

1. With the Selection tool, click to select the white bar above the orange bar.
2. In the Swatches panel, click the New Swatch button at the bottom of the panel. In the New Swatch dialog box, change the following options:
    - Swatch Name: **Forest Green**
    - Global: **Selected**
    - Change the CMYK values to C=**91**, M=**49**, Y=**49**, K=**0**
    - Click OK.
3. In the Swatches panel, notice that the new swatch is in the top row of colors, to the right of the white swatch. When you selected the shape, it was filled with white, so the white swatch was selected in the panel. When you click the New Swatch button to make a new color, it duplicates the selected swatch and puts the new swatch next to the original.
4. Click and drag the Forest Green swatch to the right of the Orange swatch to keep the new colors together.

    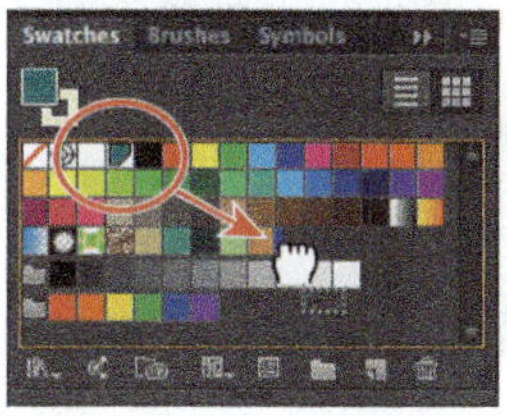

    Notice the little white triangle in the lower-right corner of the Forest Green swatch. This indicates that it's a global swatch.
5. With the Selection tool, click the second white tree from the left . Make sure the Fill box is selected (active) in the Swatches panel and apply the new "Forest Green" swatch to the fill.
6. Change the Stroke weight in the Control panel to 0 by either typing in the value or by clicking the down arrow to remove it.
7. Choose Select > Deselect.

    Now you'll see the power of a global swatch.
8. In the Swatches panel, double-click the "Forest Green" swatch. In the Swatch Options dialog box, change the K value to 24, select Preview to see the changes (you may need to click in another field to see the change), and then click OK.

    The two shapes with the Forest Green global swatch applied are updated, even though they weren't selected.
9. Save the changes to **L5_start_xx.ai**, and leave it open.

Note:

You can change an existing swatch into a global swatch, but it requires a bit more effort. You either need to select all of the shapes with that swatch applied before you edit the swatch and make it global, or you edit the swatch to make it global and then reapply the swatch to the objects.

Using the Color Picker to Create Color

Another method for creating color is to use the Color Picker. The Color Picker lets you select color in a color field and in a spectrum by either defining colors numerically or by clicking a swatch. (The Color Picker tool also is found in other Adobe applications like InDesign and Photoshop). Next, you will create a color using the Color Picker and then save the color as a swatch in the Swatches panel.

Try It!

1. With the Selection tool, click the bottom white bar on the sign.
2. Double-click the Fill box at the top of the Swatches panel to open the Color Picker.
3. In the Color Picker dialog box, the larger color field shows saturation (horizontally) and brightness (vertically). The color spectrum bar shows the hue.
4. In the Color Picker dialog box, click and drag in the color spectrum bar up and down to change the color range. Make sure that you wind up with the triangles in an orange/brown hue (it doesn't have to be exact).

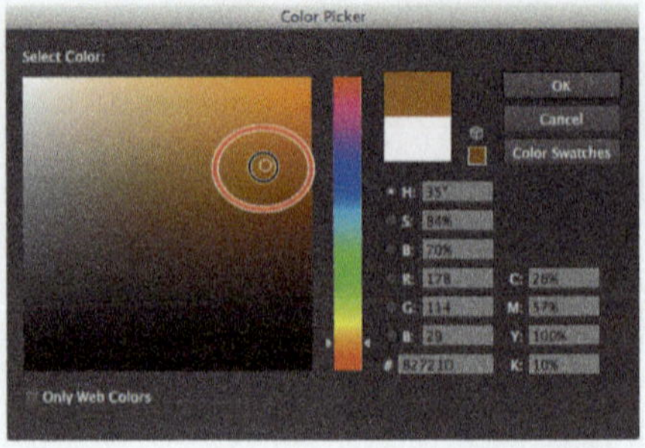

5. Click and drag in the color field. As you drag right and left, you adjust the saturation, and as you drag up and down, you adjust the brightness. The color you create when you click OK (don't yet) appears in the New color rectangle, labeled "C" in the figure. Don't worry about matching the color in the figure yet.
6. In the CMYK text fields, change the values to: C=40, M=65, Y=90, and K=33. Click OK.

   Next, you'll save the brown color that is applied to the bar as a swatch.
7. In the Swatches panel, click the New Swatch button at the bottom of the panel, and name the color **Dark Brown** in the New Swatch dialog box. Select Global, and then click OK to see the color appear as a swatch in the Swatches panel.
8. Choose Select > Deselect, and then choose File > Save.

Note:

The Color Swatches button in the Color Picker shows you the swatches in the Swatches panel and the default color books (the sets of swatches that come with Illustrator). It lets you select a color from one. You can return to the color spectrum by clicking the Color Models button and then editing the swatch color values, if necessary.

Using Illustrator Swatch Libraries

Swatch libraries are collections of preset colors, such as Pantone and TOYO, and thematic libraries, such as Earthtone and Ice Cream. Illustrator has default swatch libraries that appear as separate panels when you open them, and these cannot be edited. When you apply color from a library, the color in the library becomes a swatch that is saved in that document only and appears in the Swatches panel. Libraries are a great starting point for creating colors.

Next, you will create a spot color, using a Pantone Plus library. You will then apply that color to a logo. When color is defined in Illustrator and later printed, the appearance of the color could vary. This is why most printers and designers rely on a color-matching system, like the PANTONE system, to help maintain color consistency and, in some cases, to give a wider range of colors.

Creating a Spot Color

In this section, you will see how to load a color library, such as the PANTONE color system, and how to add a PANTONE MATCHING SYSTEM (PMS) color to the Swatches panel.

Try It!

1. In the Swatches panel, click the Swatch Libraries Menu button at the bottom of the panel. Choose Color Books > PANTONE+ Solid Coated.

   The PANTONE+ Solid Coated library appears in its own panel.

2. Type 755 in the Find field. As you type, the list is filtered, showing a smaller and smaller range of swatches. Type another 5 so that 7555 appears in the search field.
3. Click the swatch beneath the search field to add it to the Swatches panel. Click the X to the right of the search field to stop the filtering.
4. Close the PANTONE+ Solid Coated panel.

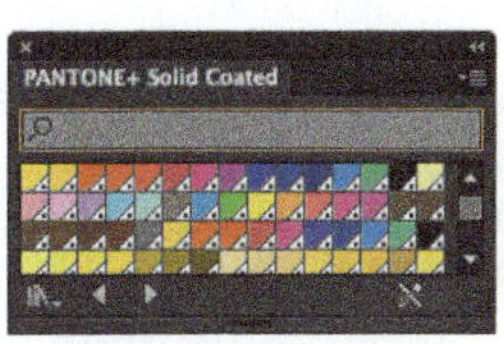

Note:

When you exit Illustrator with the PANTONE library panel still open and then relaunch Illustrator, the panel does not reopen. To automatically open the panel whenever Illustrator opens, choose Persistent from the PANTONE+ Solid Coated panel menu.

5. Choose 2 Artboard 2 from the Artboard Navigation menu in the lower-left corner of the Document window.
6. With the Selection tool, click the first white-filled tree shape on the left. Make sure the Fill box is selected (active) in the Swatches panel and select the "PANTONE 7555 C" swatch to fill the shape.

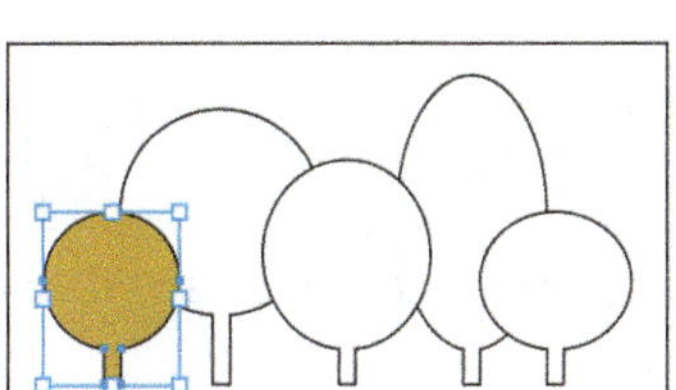
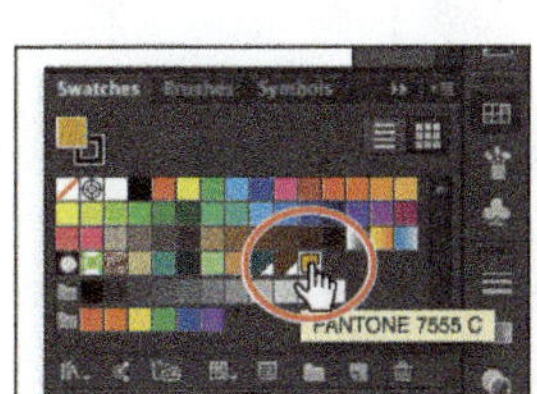

Tip:

Now that you know a number of ways to apply a fill and stroke (the Swatches panel and Control panel), you can use either of those methods to apply color swatches going forward.

7. Change the Stroke weight to 0 in the Control panel.

8. Choose Select > Deselect, save the changes to **L5_start_xx.ai**, and leave it open.

Creating and Saving a Tint of a Color

A tint is a mixture of a color with white to make the color lighter. You can create a tint from a global process color, like CMYK, or from a spot color.

Next, you will create a tint of the Pantone swatch.

Try It!

1. With the Selection tool, click the white tree shape just to the right of the tree shape filled with the Pantone color.

2. In the Swatches panel, apply the new Pantone color to the fill of the shape.

3. Click the Color panel icon to expand the Color panel. Make sure that the Fill box is selected in the Color panel, and then drag the tint slider to the left to change the tint value to 70%.

4. Click the Swatches panel icon on the right side of the workspace. Click the New Swatch button at the bottom of the panel to save the tint. Notice the tint swatch in the Swatches panel. Position the pointer over the swatch icon to see its name, PANTONE 7555 C 70%.

> **Note:**
>
> Don't forget, you need to make sure that the Fill box is selected in the Swatches panel to apply the color to the fill! Also, the Fill and Stroke boxes in the Tools panel, Color panel, and Swatches panel are linked together. When you change one, they all change.

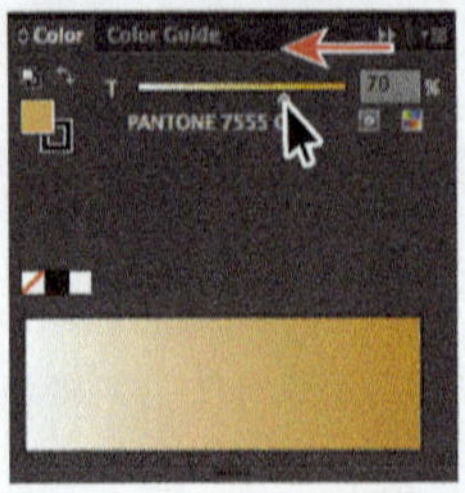

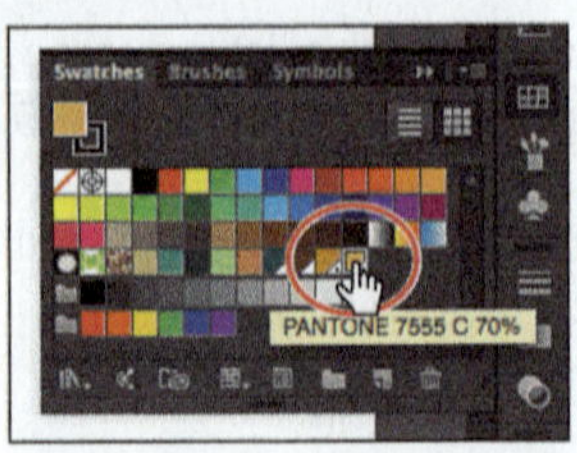

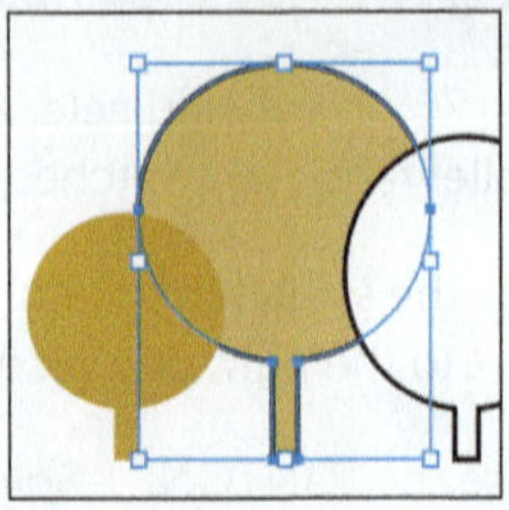

5. Change the Stroke weight to 0 in the Control panel for the selected tree shape.

6. For the remaining three tree shapes, apply the PANTONE 7555 C swatch, the tint swatch (PANTONE 7555 C 70%), and then the PANTONE 7555 C swatch to their fills, in that order.

7. Change the Stroke weight to 0 for each of the tree shapes.

8. Choose Select > Deselect, save the changes to **L5_start_xx.ai**, and leave it open.

Adjusting Colors

When working with colors, Illustrator offers an Edit Colors menu option that allows you to convert colors between color modes, blend colors, invert colors, and much more. Next, you will change the trees logo with the PANTONE 7555 C color applied to use CMYK colors instead.

1. While still on Artboard 2, choose Select > All On Active Artboard to select all of the shapes with the Pantone color and tint applied.
2. Choose Edit > Edit Colors > Convert To CMYK.

   The colors in the selected shapes are now composed of CMYK. Using this method for converting to CMYK does not affect the Pantone color swatches in the Swatches panel. It simply converts the selected *artwork* colors to CMYK. The swatches in the Swatches panel are no longer applied to the artwork.
3. Save the changes to **L5_start_xx.ai**, and leave it open.

Note:

Currently, Convert to RGB in the Edit Color menu is dimmed (you cannot select it). That's because the Document Color Mode is CMYK. To convert selected content color to RGB using this method, choose File > Document Color Mode > RGB Color.

Copying Appearance Attributes

At times you may want to copy object attributes, such as its fill or stroke color, to another object. This enables you to easily achieve repetition in your design and create connections among objects. You can do this with the Eyedropper tool.

Try It!

1. Choose 1 from the Artboard Navigation menu in the lower-left corner of the Document window to return to the artboard with the sign on it.
2. Using the Selection tool, select the first white tree on the left at the top of the sign.
3. Select the Eyedropper tool in the Tools panel. Click the green bar just above the bottom brown bar (see the figure).

   The tree has the attributes from the painted bar applied, including a cream-colored stroke.
4. Click the Stroke color in the Control panel, and change the color to None.
5. Choose Select > Deselect, save the changes to **L5_start_xx.ai**, and leave it open.

Creating a Color Group

In Illustrator, you can save colors in color groups, which consist of related color swatches in the Swatches panel. Organizing colors by their use, such as grouping all colors for a logo, can be helpful for organization and more, as you'll soon see. Color groups cannot contain patterns, gradients, the None color, or Registration color.

Next, you will create a color group of some of the swatches you've created for the logo to keep them organized.

Try It!

1. In the Swatches panel, click the swatch named Aqua to select it. Holding down the Shift key, click the swatch named Forest Green to the right to select five color swatches.
2. Command-click (Mac) or Ctrl-click (Windows) the orange swatch to remove it from the selection.

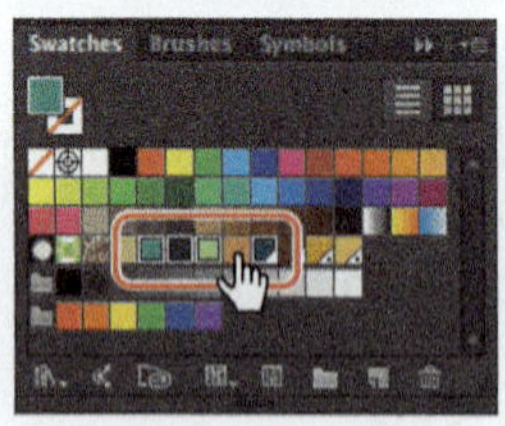

3. Click the New Color Group button at the bottom of the Swatches panel. Change the Name to **Tree Logo** in the New Color Group dialog box, and click OK to save the group.
4. With the Selection tool selected, click a blank area of the Swatches panel to deselect the color group you just created.

   Each swatch in a color group can still be edited independently by double-clicking a swatch in the group and editing the values in the Swatch Options dialog box.

   For the next step, you may want to drag the bottom of the Swatches panel down, so that you can see all of the swatches in the panel.
5. Click the white swatch in the top row of the Swatches panel, and drag it to the right of the Forest Green swatch in the tree logo color group.

   When dragging a color into a color group, make sure that you see a line appear on the right edge of the Forest Green swatch (see the figure). Otherwise, you may drag the white swatch to the wrong place. You can always choose Edit > Undo Move Swatches and try again. Aside from dragging colors in or out of a color group, you can rename a color group, reorder the colors in the group, and more.

6. Save the changes to **L5_start_xx.ai**, and leave it open.

Working with Color in the Color Guide Panel

The Color Guide panel can provide you with color inspiration as you create your artwork. You can use it to pick color tints, analogous colors, and much more, and then apply them directly to artwork, edit them, or save them as a group in the Swatches panel.

Next, you will use the Color Guide panel to select different colors for a version of a tree logo, and then you'll save those colors as a color group in the Swatches panel.

Try It!

1. Choose 3 Artboard 3 from the Artboard Navigation menu in the lower-left corner of the Document window.

2. With the Selection tool, click the first tree on the left (with the aqua color fill). Make sure that the Fill box is selected in the Tools panel or Swatches panel.

3. Click the Color Guide panel icon on the right side of the workspace to open the panel. Click the Set Base Color To The Current Color button (see the following figure).

   This allows the Color Guide panel to suggest colors based on the color showing in the Set Base Color To The Current Color button.

   Next, you'll experiment with colors using Harmony Rules.

4. Choose Analogous from the Harmony Rules menu (circled in the figure) in the Color Guide panel.

   A base group of colors is created to the right of the base color (aqua), and a series of tints and shades of those colors appears in the body of the panel.

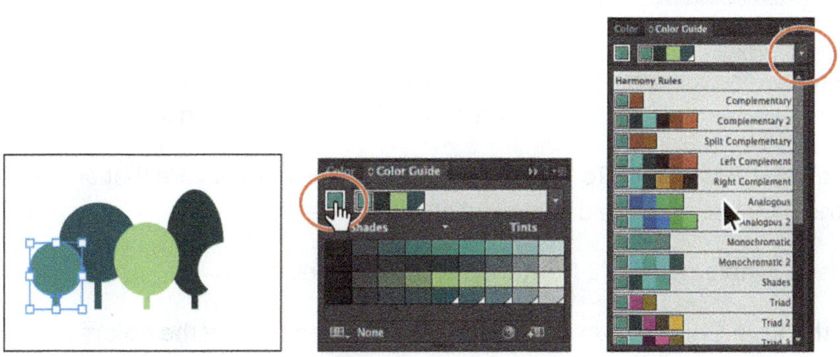

   There are lots of harmony rules to choose from, each instantly generating a color scheme based on any color you want. The base color you set (aqua) is the basis for generating the colors in the color scheme.

5. Click the Save Color Group To Swatch Panel button at the bottom of the Color Guide panel to save the base colors (the five colors at the top) in the Swatches panel as a group.

6. Click the Swatches panel icon. Scroll down to see the new group added.

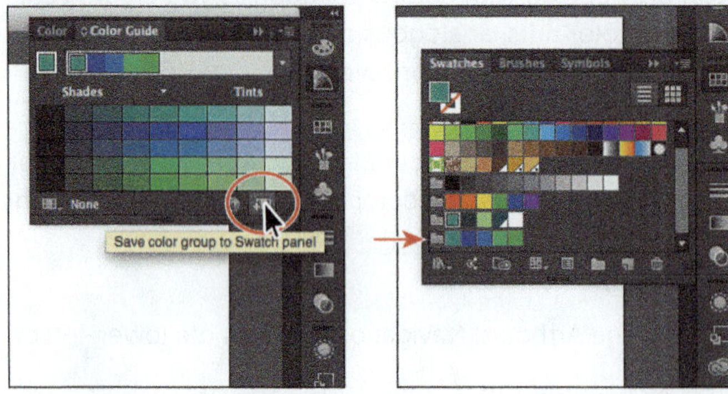

Next, you'll experiment with the colors in the color group that you just created to create an alternate group of colors.

7. Choose Select > Deselect.
8. Click the Color Guide panel icon to open the Color Guide panel.
9. In the list of swatches in the Color Guide panel, select the fifth color from the left, in the third row (see the figure).

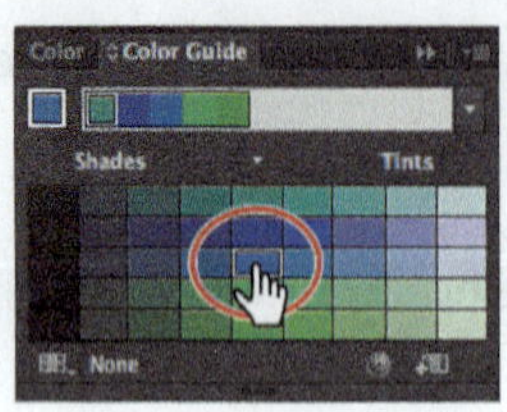

If the tree were still selected, it would have been filled with the blue. You can apply or save any of the colors in the Color Guide panel as an individual swatch.

10. Click the Set Base Color To The Current Color button to ensure that all colors that the panel creates are based on that same blue.
11. Choose Complementary 2 from the Harmony Rules menu.
12. Click the Save Color Group To Swatch Panel button to save the colors as a group in the Swatches panel.
13. Save the changes to **L5_start_xx.ai**, and leave it open.

Editing a Color Group in the Edit Colors Dialog Box

When you create color groups in the Swatches panel or in the Color Guide panel, you can edit the swatches in the group either individually from the Swatches panel, or together. In this section, you will learn how to edit the colors of a color group in the Swatches panel using the Edit Color dialog box. Later, you will apply those colors to a version of the logo.

Try It!

1. Choose Select > Deselect (if it's available), and then click the Swatches panel icon to show the panel.

   Deselecting right now is important! If artwork is selected when you edit the color group, the edits can apply to the selected artwork.

2. Click the Color Group icon to the left of the colors in the *bottom* color group (the one you just saved) to select the group.

3. Click the Edit Color Group button at the bottom of the Swatches panel to open the Edit Colors dialog box.

   The Edit Color Group button appears in multiple locations, like the Swatches and Color Guide panels. The Edit Colors dialog box allows you to edit a group of colors in various ways or even to create new color groups. On the right side of the Edit Colors dialog box, under the "Color Groups" section, all of the existing color groups in the Swatches panel are listed.

4. Select the name "Color Group 2" above the Color Groups if not already selected, on the right side of the dialog box (circled in the figure), and rename the group Logo 2. This is one way you can rename a color group.

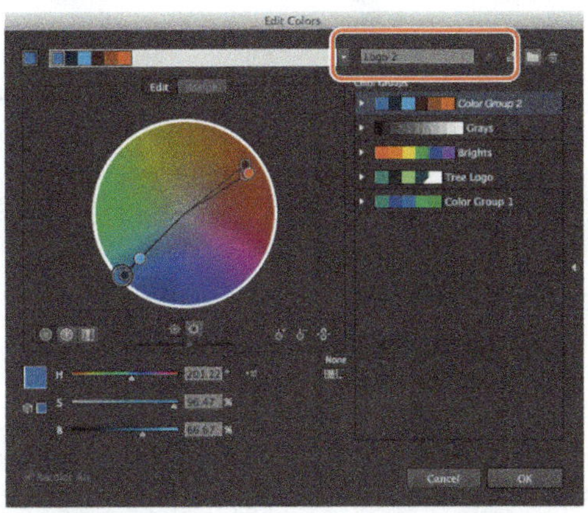

Next, you will make a few changes to the colors in the Logo 2 group. On the left side of the Edit Colors dialog box, you can edit the colors of each color group, either individually or together, and edit them visually or precisely using specific color values. In the color wheel, you'll see markers (circles) that represent each color in the selected group.

5. In the color wheel on the left side of the dialog box, drag the largest blue circle, called a marker, down and to the right just a little bit. The largest marker is the base color of the color group that you set in the Color Guide panel initially.

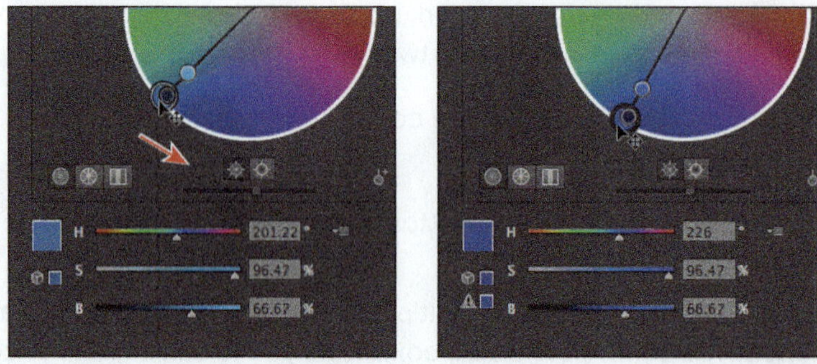

Moving the color markers away from the center of the color wheel increases saturation, and moving them toward the center decreases saturation. Moving a color marker around the color wheel (clockwise or counterclockwise) edits the hue.

6. Drag the Adjust Brightness slider below the color wheel to the right, to brighten all the colors at once.

   Next, you will edit the colors in the group independently, and then save the colors as a new named group.

7. Click the Unlink Harmony Colors button in the Edit Colors dialog box to edit the colors independently.

   The lines between the color markers (circles) and the center of the color wheel become dotted, indicating that you can edit the colors independently.

   Next, you will edit just one of the colors, since they are now unlinked, and you will edit that color by using specific color values rather than by dragging the color in the color wheel.

8. Click the Color Mode icon to the right of the H, S, B values below the color wheel, and choose CMYK from the menu, if the CMYK sliders are not already visible.

9. Click to select the lightest orange marker in the color wheel, as shown in the figure. Change the CMYK values to C=10, M=50, Y=100, and K=0. Notice that the marker has moved in the color wheel. Leave the dialog box open.

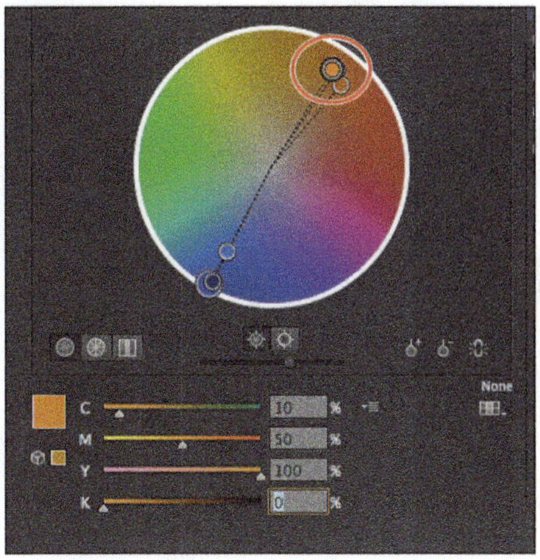

Note:

It's okay if the color markers in your Edit Colors dialog box are different from those shown in the figure.

10. Click the Save Changes To Color Group button in the upper-right corner of the Edit Colors dialog box to save the changes to the color group.

    If you decide to make changes to colors in another color group, you can select the color group you want to edit from the Color Groups list on the right side of the Edit Colors dialog box.

11. Click OK to close the Edit Colors dialog box.

    The subtle changes to the colors in the group should show in the Swatches panel.

12. Save the changes to **L5_start_xx.ai**, and leave it open.

Note:

If a dialog box appears after clicking OK, click Yes to save the changes to the color group in the Swatches panel.

Editing Colors in Artwork

You can also edit the colors in selected artwork using the Recolor Artwork command. It's useful when global swatches weren't used in the artwork.

Next, you will edit the colors for one of the logos that was created with colors that were not saved in the Swatches panel.

Try It!

1. Choose 4 Artboard 4 from the Artboard Navigation menu in the lower-left corner of the Document window.

2. Choose Select > All On Active Artboard to select all of the artwork.

3. Click the Recolor Artwork button in the Control panel to open the Recolor Artwork dialog box.

    The Recolor Artwork dialog box options allow you to edit, reassign, or reduce the colors in your selected artwork and to create and edit color groups. You'll probably notice that it looks similar to the Edit Colors dialog box. The big difference is that instead of editing color and creating color groups to apply later, you are dynamically editing colors in the selected artwork.

Like in the Edit Colors dialog box, all of the color groups in the Swatches panel appear on the right side of the Recolor Artwork dialog box (in the Color Groups storage area). In the Recolor Artwork dialog box, you can apply colors from these color groups to the selected artwork.

4. In the Recolor Artwork dialog box, click the Hide Color Group Storage icon on the right side of the dialog box.

5. Click the Edit tab to edit the colors in the artwork using the color wheel.

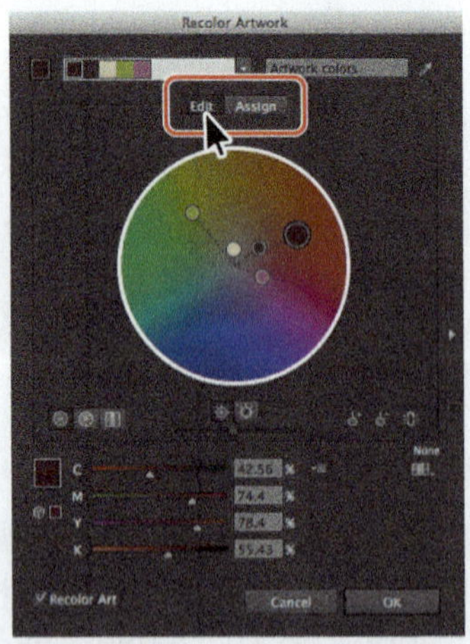

6. Make sure that the Link Harmony Colors icon is showing so that you can edit all of the colors independently.

   The lines between the color markers (circles) and the center of the color wheel should be dotted. If it looks like this, click it to unlink.

   When you created a color group, you worked with the color wheel and the CMYK sliders to edit color. This time, you will adjust color using a different method.

7. Click the Display Color Bars button to show the colors in the selected artwork as bars. Click the cream color bar to select it.

   At the bottom of the dialog box, change the CMYK values to C=5, M=10, Y=40, K=0. If the Recolor Artwork dialog box isn't in the way, you should see the artwork changing.

8. Click the green color bar to select it. With the pointer over the green color bar, right-click and choose Select Shade from the menu that appears. Click in the shade menu, and drag to change the color of the color bar to one of your choice.

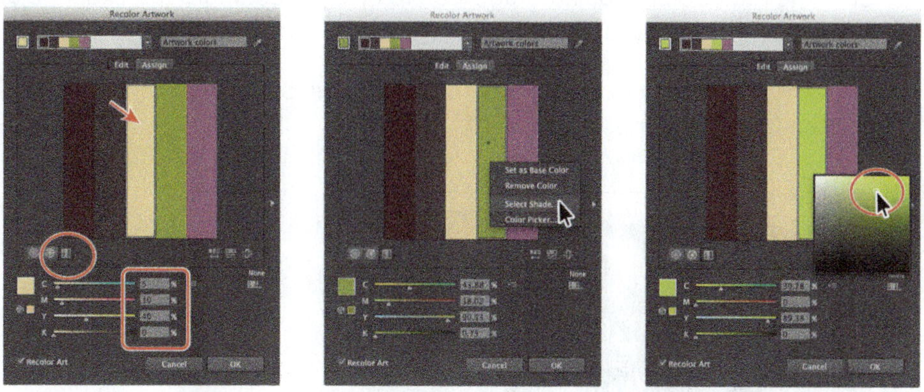

   Editing the colors as bars is another way to view and edit a color.

9. Click OK in the Recolor Artwork dialog box.

10. Choose Select Deselect, save the changes to **L5_start_xx.ai**, and leave it open.

Assigning Colors to Your Artwork

In the Recolor Artwork dialog box, you can edit colors in existing artwork. You can also "assign" colors from an existing color group to your artwork. Next, you will assign a color group to create a version of the logo.

Try It!

1. Choose 3 Artboard 3 from the Artboard Navigation menu in the lower-left corner of the Document window.

2. Choose Select > All On Active Artboard to select the logo trees.

3. Click the Recolor Artwork button in the Control panel.

4. Click the Show Color Group Storage icon (the small arrow) on the right side of the dialog box to show the color groups, if they aren't already showing. Make sure that, in the top left of the dialog box, the Assign button is selected.

   On the left side of the Recolor Artwork dialog box, notice that the five colors of the selected logo are listed in the Current Colors column, in what is called "hue-forward" sorting. That means they are arranged, from top to bottom, in the ordering of the color wheel: red, orange, yellow, green, blue, indigo, and violet

5. Under Color Groups in the Recolor Artwork dialog box, select the Logo 2 color group you created earlier. The selected artwork on the artboard should change in color.

   On the left side of the Recolor Artwork dialog box, notice that the colors of the color group named Logo 2 are assigned to the colors in the logo. The Current Colors column shows what the color was in the logo, and an arrow to the right of each of those colors points to the New column, which contains what the color has become (or has been reassigned to). Notice that the white color has not been modified and that there is no arrow pointing to a color in the New column. That's because white, black, and grays are typically *preserved*, or unchanged.

6. Click the Hide Color Group Storage icon to hide the color groups. Drag the dialog box by the title bar at the top so that you can see the artwork.
7. Click the small arrow to the right of the dark-green bar in the Current Colors column (see the figure).

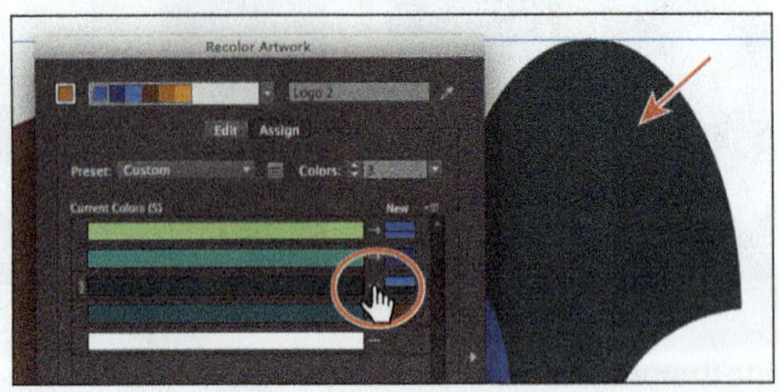

This tells Illustrator not to change that specific green color in the logo. You can see that reflected in the logo on the artboard.

Now suppose that you wanted to change the white color in the "Logo 2" color group. That's what you'll do next.

8. Click the line to the right of the white color in the Current Colors column and the line will change into an arrow that looks dimmed.

The arrow indicates to Illustrator that you want the white color to be different, but there currently is no color in the New column to change it to.

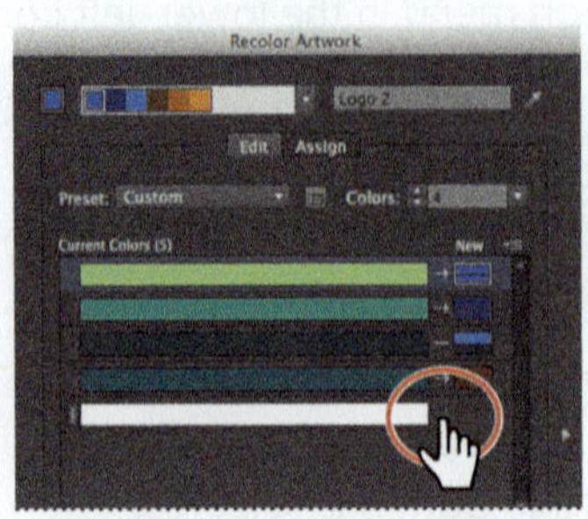

9. Click the Show Color Group Storage icon to show the color groups.
10. Click another color group in the Color Groups area on the right side of the panel, and then click to select the "Logo 2" color group again.

This is one of the easiest ways to reapply the color group colors, and it will fill in the missing color to the right of the white in the Current Colors column.

You might not like how it assigned the colors to your artwork, and that's what you'll edit next.

11. In the New column of the Recolor Artwork dialog box, drag the top blue color box in the column down on top of the brown color and release the mouse button.

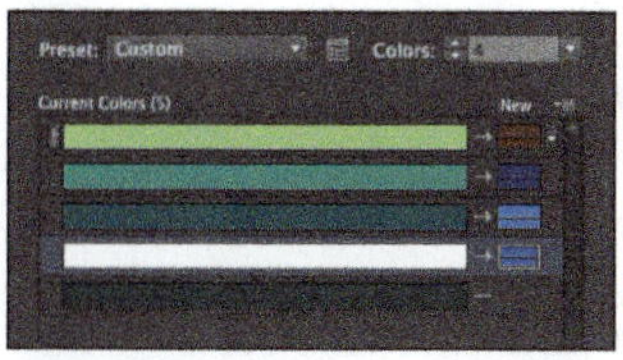

This is one way that you can reassign the "Logo 2" group colors to the colors in the logo. The colors in the New column show what you see in the artwork. If you click one of the colors in the New column, notice that the CMYK sliders at the bottom of the dialog box let you edit that one color.

12. Double-click the brown color box at the top of the New column. In the Color Picker dialog box, click the Color Swatches button (on the right side) and select the color named Light Green. You may need to scroll in the list of color swatches. Click OK to return to the Recolor Artwork dialog box.

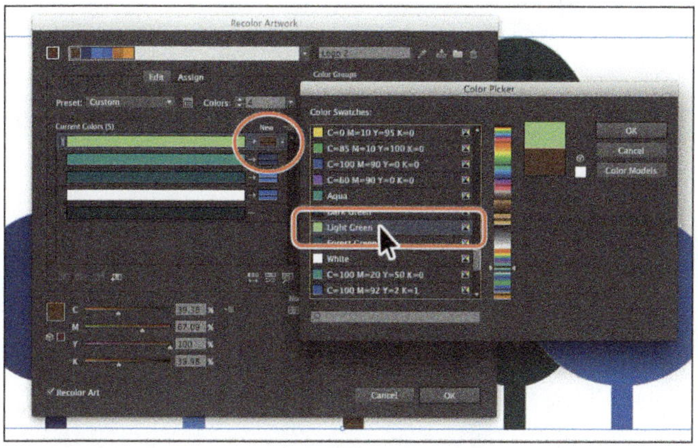

13. In the Recolor Artwork dialog box, click the Save Changes To Color Group button to save the changes to the color group without closing the dialog box. Click OK.

    The color changes that you made to the color group are saved in the Swatches panel.

14. Choose Select > Deselect, save the changes to **L5_start_xx.ai**, and close Illustrator.

Comprehension Check

1. What is color theory?
2. What is a color wheel?
3. What happens when you edit a global color in Illustrator?
4. How can you save a color in Illustrator?
5. Name two things that the Recolor Artwork dialog box allows you to do.

Review Project

Create a poster that explains color theory. Print a sample of a color wheel from the Internet or obtain a sample from your instructor or another resource. Using the sample as the focal point, create a poster that labels the colors (primary, secondary, and intermediate and explains the relationships among them. If desired, include complementary, analogous, and neutral colors as well. You can create the poster by hand or electronically.

Lesson 6 Overview

In this lesson, you will learn about:

- Exploring concepts of typography
- Adding Type to a Poster
- Working with Overflow Text and Text Reflow
- Formatting Type
- Creating and Applying Text Styles
- Warping Text
- Working with Type on a Path

Text as a design element plays a major role in your illustrations. Like other objects, type can be painted, scaled, rotated, and more. In this lesson, you'll discover how to create basic text and interesting text effects.

Exploring Concepts of Typography

Typography

The style, arrangement, and appearance of type.

Typography is the style, arrangement, and appearance of type. As you learned in Chapter 1, type is one of the elements of design. Your ability to make it work with other elements (lines, shapes, space, textures, and colors) is fundamental to creating effective and engaging visual communications. The basic concepts of typography include the following:

- Fonts: Also called typefaces. There are two categories of fonts--serif and sans serif. Serifs are the short lines at the end of characters in a font, such as Times New Roman. San serif fonts do not have the lines. Arial and Helvetica are widely used sans serif fonts. Most experts believe serif fonts are easier to read in printed pieces while sans serif fonts are easier for online reading.
- Font size: Fonts are sized in points; there are 72 points in an inch. Your choice of font size will depend largely on the use of the text. For example, use of a larger font size for headings and a smaller size for body text helps set a hierarchy for the content.
- Leading: The space between lines of text. The amount of leading used can have a significant impact on the legibility of type.
- Kerning and tracking: Kerning is the amount of space between a pair of characters of type. Tracking refers to the spacing of all characters in a line or block of type. When used appropriately, both can lend to the harmony of a visual piece.
- Alignment: Text can be aligned flush left (aligned to the left margin or edge); flush right (aligned to the right margin or edge); justified (aligned both to the left and right); and centered (center of the text area with an equal amount of space between the text and the left and right margins or edges).

Adding Type to a Poster

Type features are some of the most powerful tools in Illustrator. You can add a single line of type to your artwork, create columns and rows of text, flow text into a shape or along a path, and work with letterforms as graphic objects. In Illustrator, you can create text in three different ways: as point type, area type, and type on a path. You will learn about each in this lesson.

Restore the Default Preferences

You'll be adding type to a poster during this lesson, but before you begin, restore the default preferences for Adobe Illustrator CC.

Try It!

1. Start Adobe Illustrator CC.
2. Choose File > Open, and open **L6_start.ai** from the data files for this lesson.

   This file already has non-text components in it. You will add all of the text elements to complete the poster and card.

3. Save the files as **L6_start_xx.ai** in the location where your teacher instructs you to store the files for this lesson and leave it open.
4. Leave the Format option (Mac) and the Save as type option (Windows) set to Adobe Illustrator (ai), and click Save.
5. In the Illustrator Options dialog box, click OK to accept the default settings.
6. Choose View > Smart Guides to turn off the Smart Guides. Turning off the Smart Guides will make it easier to create text without snapping to existing content.
7. Choose Window > Workspace > Reset Essentials.
8. Save the changes to **L6_start_xx.ai**, and leave it open.

Adding Text at a Point

Point type is a horizontal or vertical line of text that begins where you click and expands as you enter characters. Each line of text is independent—the line expands or shrinks as you edit it but doesn't wrap to the next line unless you add a paragraph return or a soft return. Entering text this way is useful for adding a headline or a few words to your artwork. Next, you will enter some text in the poster as point type.

> **Note:**
>
> If you don't see "Reset Essentials" in the Workspace menu, choose Window > Workspace > Essentials before choosing Window > Workspace > Reset Essentials.

Try It!

1. If necessary, select 1 Flyer from the Artboard Navigation menu, and then choose View > Fit Artboard In Window.
2. Select the Zoom tool in the Tools panel, and click the upper-left corner of the artboard twice, slowly. Remember that where you click is centered in the Document window.

3. Choose Window > Layers to show the panel. Select the Text layer, if necessary to ensure that the content you create is on that layer. Click the Layers panel tab to collapse it.

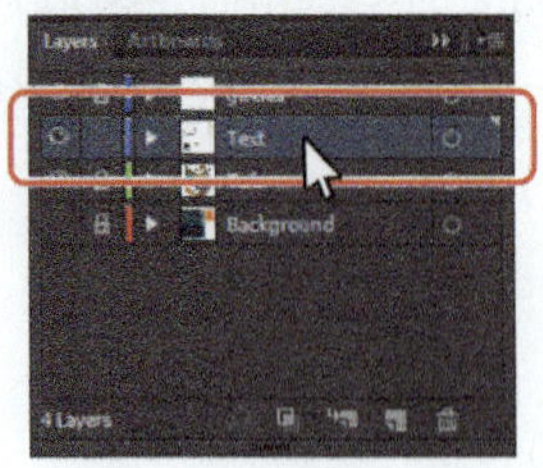

4. Select the Type tool, and click in the white area in the upper-left corner of the artboard. The cursor appears on the artboard. Type ZOO TALES (in uppercase). By simply clicking with the Type tool, you create a point type object.

5. Select the Selection tool in the Tools panel, and notice the bounding box that appears around the text. Drag the right, middle bounding point (NOT the circle), to the right. Notice that the text stretches as you drag any bounding point.

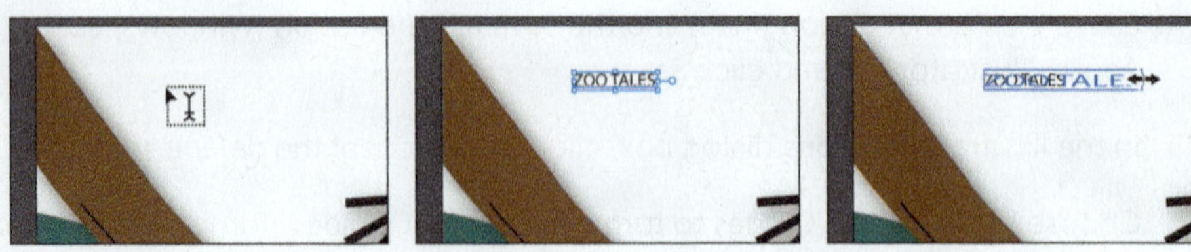

6. Choose Edit > Undo Scale, and then choose View > Fit Artboard In Window.

7. Save the changes to **L6_start_xx.ai**, and leave it open.

Adding Area Type

Area type uses the boundaries of an object (like a rectangle) to control the flow of characters, either horizontally or vertically. When the text reaches a boundary, it automatically wraps to fit inside the defined area. Entering text in this way is useful when you want to create one or more paragraphs, such as for a poster or a brochure.

To create area type, you click with the Type tool where you want the text and drag to create an area type object (also called a *text area*). You can also convert an existing shape or object to a type object by clicking the edge of an object (or inside the object) with the Type tool. When the cursor appears, you can type. An area type object has two extra boxes on the bounding box, called ports. Ports are used to thread (flow) text from one type area to another, which you will learn about later in this lesson.

Next, you will create an area type object and enter more text.

Try It!

1. Choose View > Smart Guides to turn on the Smart Guides.

2. Choose View > Zoo Sign to zoom in to the black shape at the bottom of the artboard.

3. Select the Type tool. Position the cursor to the left of the striped orange-and-black tail, in the white area (see the red X in the figure). Click and drag down and to the right to create a text area with an approximate width and height of 1 inch.

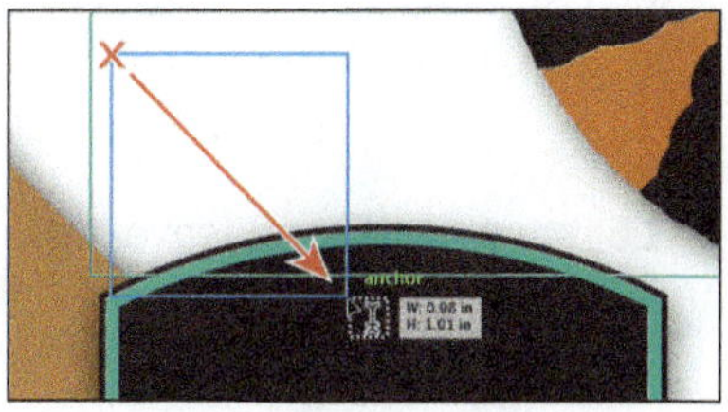

With the cursor in the new text area, type **Safari Zoo California**.

Notice how the text wraps horizontally to fit within the type area. By default, when you create area type by dragging with the Type tool, the type area will not resize to fit the text. If there is too much text, the text that doesn't fit will not be visible and will be considered overset.

4. Select the Selection tool, and looking at the bottom, middle bounding point you will see the Autosize widget indicating that the type area is not set to autosize. Hover the pointer over the box at the end of the widget, and double-click.

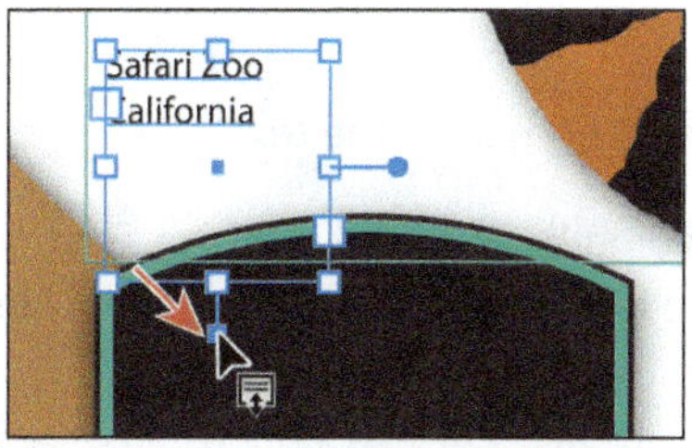

By double-clicking the widget, you turn Autosizing on. As the text is edited and re-edited, the frame shrinks and grows vertically to accommodate the changing amount of copy, and eliminates overset text without manually sizing and resizing frames.

5. Select the Type tool and insert the cursor after the word "California," press Enter or Return, and type **San Diego**. The type area will expand vertically to fit the new text.

6. Select the Selection tool and hover the pointer over the bottom, middle point again and the cursor will change.

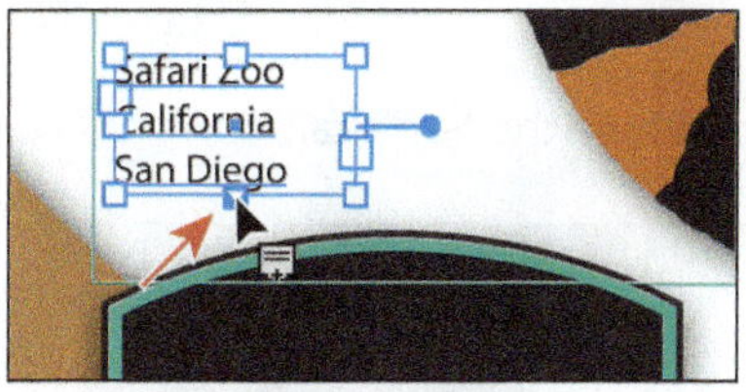

This annotator indicates that the type area is set to Autosize. If you were to double click, Autosizing would be turned off for the area type. The type area would remain the current size no matter how much text was added.

7. Select the Type tool and select all of the text, except for "Safari Zoo" and delete it.

   Notice that the type area shrank vertically to fit around the text.

8. Select the Selection tool and drag from within the "Safari Zoo" text down and to the left of the black sign shape. You need to drag directly from the text, not from a blank area in the type area.

9. Choose Select > Deselect, save the changes to **L6_start_xx.ai**, and leave it open.

Converting between Area and Point Type

You can easily convert between area and point type objects. This method can be useful if you type a headline by clicking (creating point type), but later decide to resize and add more text without stretching it.

Next, you will convert a text object from point type to area type.

Try It!

1. Choose View > Fit Artboard In Window.

2. Select the Type tool, and click to create a point type object in the white space to the right of the orange-and-black tail. Type **Thursdays at 6:30 pm** (without periods). You will move this text later, as well.

3. Select the Zoom tool, and click several times to zoom in to the text.

4. Select the Selection tool, and notice the bounding box around the text. Drag the right-center bounding point to the right. Since it's point type, the text stretches. Choose Edit > Undo Scale to reset the text.

   The text "6:30 pm" needs to wrap down below the text "Thursdays at..." An easy way to do that is to convert the point type to area type, which is what you'll do next. Of course, you could also insert a paragraph or soft return in the text, but later you may want to resize the type area.

5. Position the pointer over the annotator off the right edge of the type object. A hollow end on the annotator indicates point type. When the pointer changes, click once to see the message "Double-click to convert to Area Type." Double-click the annotator to convert the point type to area type. The annotator end should now be filled, indicating that it is an area type object.

6. Drag the lower-right bounding point down and to the left until the text "6:30 pm" wraps to the second line.

7. Drag the text area down on top of the brown end of the lion's tail.

8. Save the changes to **L6_start_xx.ai**, and leave it open.

Importing a Plain Text File

You can import text into artwork from a file that was created in another application. Illustrator supports the following formats for importing text:

- Microsoft Word (doc, docx)
- Microsoft RTF (rtf)
- Plain text (txt) (ASCII) with ANSI, Unicode, Shift JIS, GB2312, Chinese Big 5, Cyrillic, GB18030, Greek, Turkish, Baltic, and Central European encoding.

One of the advantages of importing text from a file, rather than copying and pasting it, is that imported text retains its character and paragraph formatting (by default). For example, text from an RTF file retains its font and style specifications in Illustrator, unless you choose to remove formatting when you import the text.

Try It!

1. Choose View > Fit Artboard In Window, and then choose Select > Deselect.
2. In the Layers panel (Window > Layers), click the visibility column of the Tails layer to temporarily hide some of the artwork.
3. Choose File > Place. Select the L6_text.txt file from the data files for this lesson, select Show Import Options, and click Place.
4. In the Text Import Options dialog box, you can set some options prior to importing text. Leave the default settings, and then click OK.

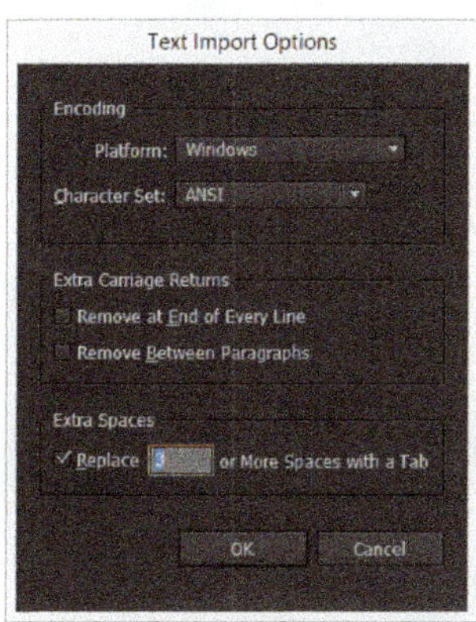

5. Position the loaded text pointer over the upper-left corner of the aqua guide box in the center of the artboard. When the word "anchor" appears, click and drag down and to the right. As you drag, notice that the width and height are constrained (always the same proportion). Drag until the pointer reaches the bottom of the aqua guide box, and then release the mouse button.

6. With the Selection tool, drag the corner bounding point of the text area up and to the right so that it snaps to the right edge of the aqua guide box and you see an overset text icon in the out port. Leave the text area selected.

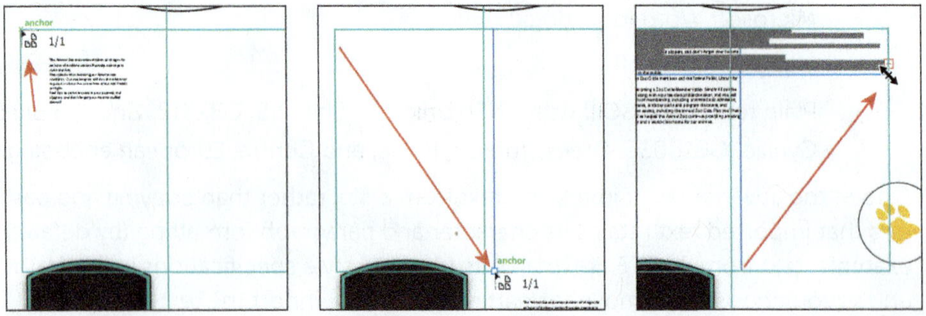

7. Save the changes to **L6_start_xx.ai**, and leave it open.

Working with Overflow Text and Text Reflow

Each area type object contains an in port and an out port. The ports enable you to link to other type objects and flow text between type objects. An empty out port indicates that all the text is visible and that the object isn't linked. An arrow in a port indicates that the type object is linked to another type object. A red plus sign in an out port indicates that the object contains additional text, which is called overflow text.

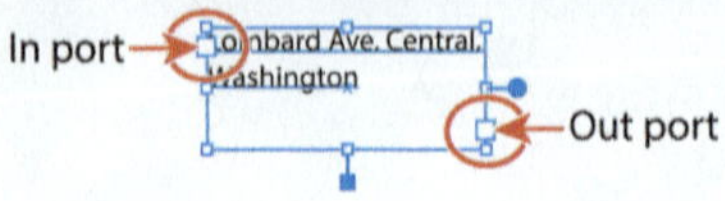

There are three main methods for remedying overflow text:

- Thread the text to another type object.
- Resize the type object.
- Adjust the text.

Threading Text

To thread, or continue, text from one object to the next, you have to link the objects. Linked type objects can be of any shape; however, the text must be entered in an object or along a path, not as point type (by simply clicking to create text).

Next, you will thread text from one type object to another by linking the type objects together.

Note:

If you double-click an out port, a new type object appears. If this happens, you can either drag the new object where you would like it to be positioned or choose Edit > Undo Link Threaded Text, and the loaded text icon reappears.

Try It!

1. Choose View > Smart Guides to turn them off so that you can more easily move objects without snapping.

2. With the Selection tool, click the out port (larger box) in the lower-right corner of the type object that has the red plus sign in it. The pointer changes to a loaded text icon when you move it away.

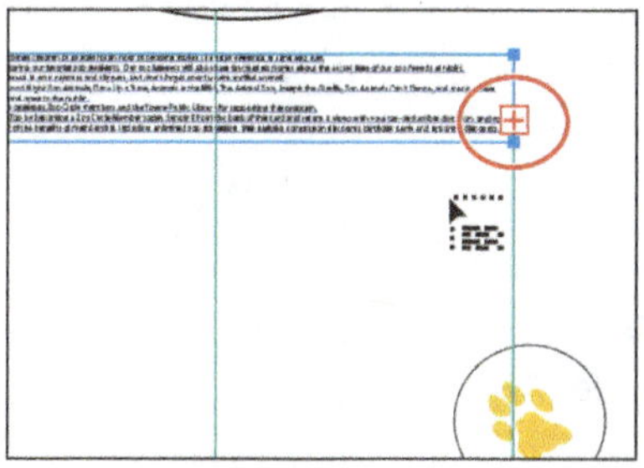

Next, you will flow the overflow text into an existing type object on the next artboard.

3. Click the Next Artboard button in the lower-left corner of the Document window to navigate to the postcard artboard.

4. Choose Select > All On Active Artboard to see the type object that's already there.

5. Position the pointer over the edge of the type object. When the pointer changes as shown in the figure below, click to thread the text areas.

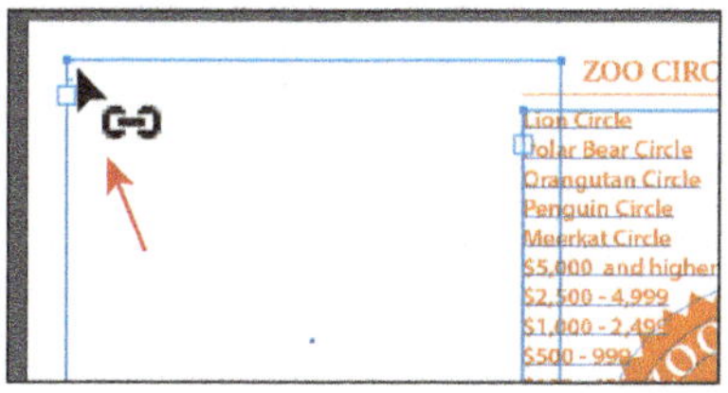

Notice the line between the two objects. This line is the thread that tells you that the two objects are connected. If you don't see this thread, choose View > Show Text Threads.

Notice the out port of the type object on the larger artboard and the in port of the type object on the smaller artboard (both circled in the figure below). The arrows in the ports indicate how the text is flowing from one to the other. If you delete the second type object, the text is pulled back into the original object as overflow text. Although not visible, the overflow text is not deleted.

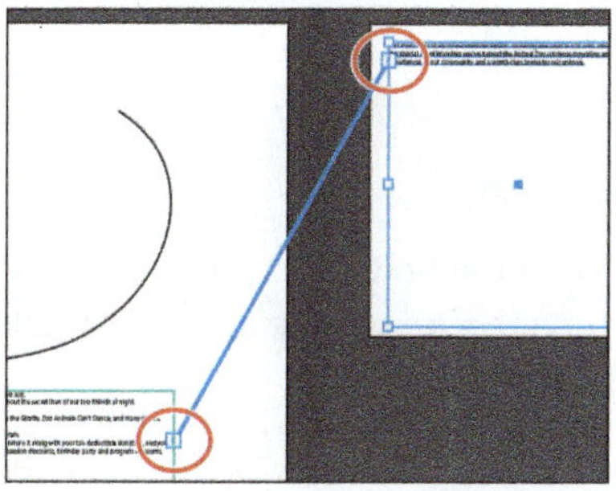

6. Choose Select > Deselect, and then save the changes to **L6_start_xx.ai**, and leave it open.

Note:

With the loaded text icon, you can also click the artboard instead of dragging to create a new type object.

Tip:

Another way to thread text between objects is to select an area type object, select the object (or objects) you want to link to, and then choose Type > Threaded Text > Create.

Creating Columns of Text

You can easily create columns and rows of text by using the Type > Area Type Options command. This can be useful for a single type object with multiple columns (instead of separate threaded text areas) or for organizing text, like a table or simple chart, for instance. Next, you'll add a few columns to the existing type object on the larger artboard.

Try It!

1. While still on the 2 Card artboard, with the Selection tool, click to select the text area that starts with the orange text "Lion Circle..."

> **Note:**
>
> If the cursor is still in the type object, you don't have to select the type object with the Selection tool to access the Area Type Options dialog box.

2. Choose Type > Area Type Options. In the Area Type Options dialog box, in the Columns section, change the Number to 2 and select Preview. Click OK. The text won't change in appearance, but you should see the column guides.

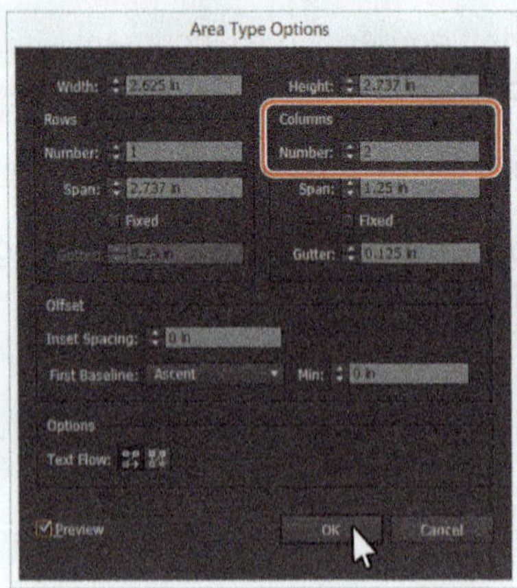

Next, you'll drag the bottom of the type object up to see the columns at work.

3. Drag the bottom, middle bounding point up until the text flows into the second column, like you see in the figure. Try to balance the text in the columns (make them even).

4. Choose Select > Deselect.

5. Save the changes to **L6_start_xx.ai**, and leave it open.

Formatting Type

You can format type by using character and paragraph formatting, apply fill and stroke attributes to it, and change its transparency. You can apply these changes to one character, a range of characters, or all characters in a type object that you select.

Selecting the type object, rather than selecting the text inside, allows you to apply global formatting options to all of the text in the object.

In this section, you'll discover how to change text attributes, such as size and **font**, and how to save that formatting as text styles.

Changing Font Size

By default, typeface size is measured in points (a **point** equals 1/72 of an inch). You can specify any typeface size from 0.1 point to 1296 points, in 0.001 point increments.

Font

A set of characters in a specific face, style, and size.

Point

A unit of measurement used in desktop publishing and graphic design.

Try It!

1. With the 1 Flyer artboard active, select the "Safari Zoo" text with the Selection tool.
2. Click the Type tool and choose 36 pt from the preset sizes on the Font Size menu in the Control panel.

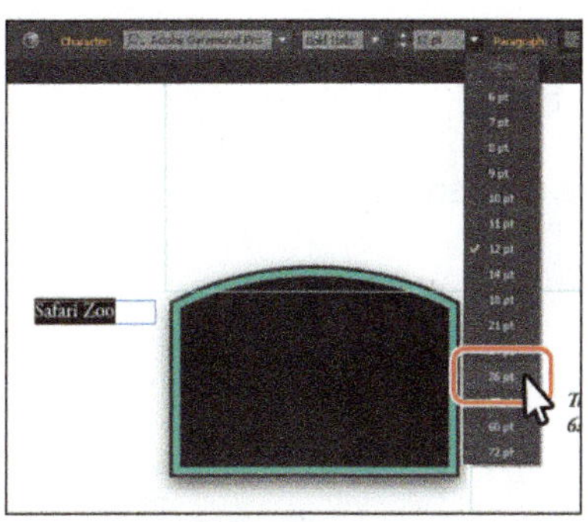

Note:

You may see the word "Character" instead of the Font Size field in the Control panel. Click the word "Character" to reveal the Character panel.

3. Select the 36 pt in the Font Size field in the Control panel and type 37. Press Enter or Return.

   The type area will resize to fit the text vertically, but the text may wrap horizontally. Remember, type objects don't resize by default when the text resizes unless you turn on Autosize (like we did earlier).

Tip:

You can dynamically change the font size of selected text using keyboard shortcuts. To increase the font size in increments of 2 points, press Command+Shift+> (Mac) or Ctrl+Shift+> (Windows). To reduce the font size, press Command+Shift+< (Mac) or Ctrl+Shift+< (Windows).

4. Select the Selection tool, and drag the middle-right point of the text object to the right until "Safari" is on one line and "Zoo" is on the next.

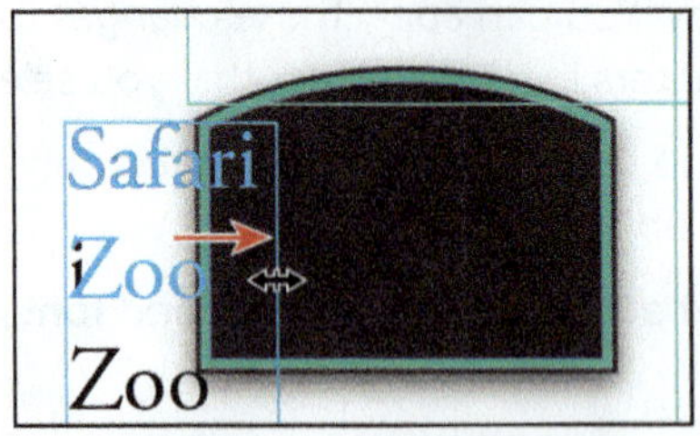

Make sure that the word "Zoo" is on its own line in the text object. You'll adjust the text later to make it look better. By dragging a bounding point, Autosize is turned off for the text area.

5. Choose View > Fit Artboard In Window.

6. With the Selection tool, click the "ZOO TALES" text at the top of the artboard.

7. Select the 12 pt font size in the Font Size field in the Control panel and type 74. Press Enter or Return.

8. Drag the text object down, if need be, so that it's still on the artboard. Leave the text object selected.

   Notice that the text object resizes to its point type.

9. Save the changes to **L6_start_xx.ai**, and leave it open.

Changing Font Color

You can change the appearance of text by applying fills, strokes, and more. In this example, you will change the stroke and then the fill of selected text.

Try It!

1. With the "ZOO TALES" text object still selected, click the Stroke color in the Control panel. In the Swatches panel, select White.

2. Change the Stroke weight of the text to 2 pt in the Control panel.

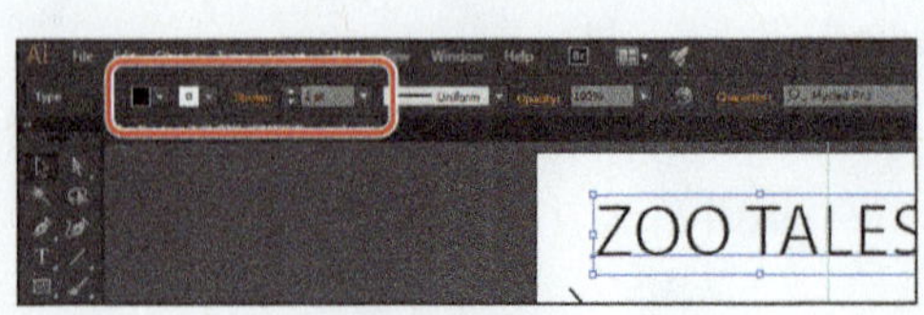

3. Select the Type tool in the Tools panel, and click on the text in the threaded text frames in the middle of the artboard. Press Command+A (Mac) or Ctrl+A (Windows) to select all of the text.

4. Click the Fill color in the Control panel. In the Swatches panel, select White. Change the Font Size by typing 15 in the Control panel and pressing Enter or Return.

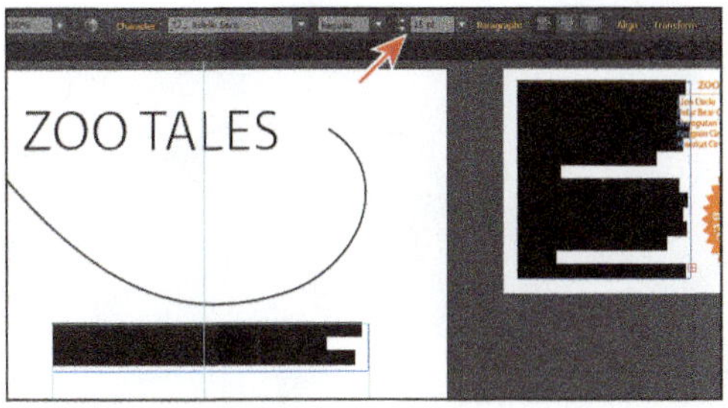

5. Choose Select > Deselect.
6. Select the Selection tool. Shift-click the two text objects, at the bottom of the artboard that contain the words "Safari Zoo" and "Thursdays at..."
7. Change the Fill color in the Control panel to White.

   The text will be white on the white artboard, which will make it difficult to see. In the next section, you will turn on layers to make it easier to see the text. You can either select the text or the text object to change most of the formatting, including fill and stroke.
8. Choose Select > Deselect, save the changes to **L6_start_xx.ai**, and leave it open.

Changing Additional Text Attributes

You can change many additional text attributes in the Character panel, which you can access by clicking the underlined word "Character" in the Control panel or by choosing Window > Type > Character. Below are the formatting options available in the Character panel when all options are showing.

Try It!

1. Open the Character panel by choosing Window > Type > Character. Click the double arrow on the left side of the Character panel tab to show more options.

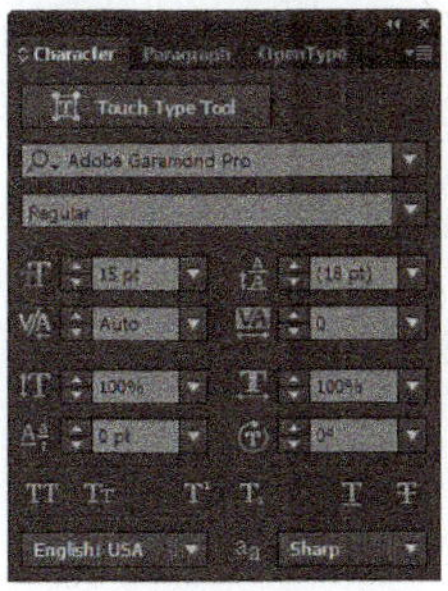

2. Close the Character panel. Click the Layers panel icon to expand the panel. Click the visibility column to the left of the layer named Background and the layer named Tails. Click the Layers panel tab to collapse it.

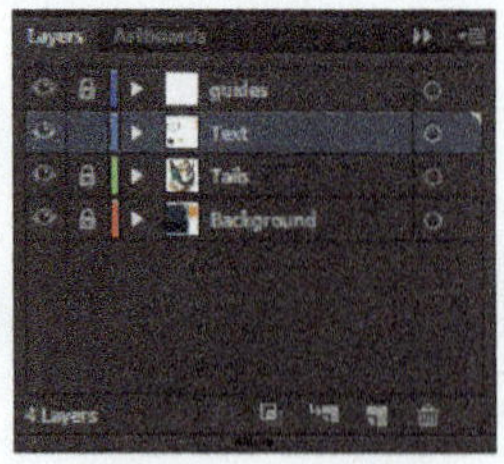

3. Select the Type tool, and click in either of the threaded text objects that contain the placed text. Choose Select > All.
4. Click the word "Character" in the Control panel, and click the down arrow to the left of the Leading field to change the value to 17 pt. Press the Escape key to hide the panel.

   Leading is the vertical space between lines. Notice the change in the vertical distance between the lines. Adjusting the leading can be useful for fitting text into a text area. Like other Character panel options, you can also type in a value for the Leading.
5. Insert the cursor in the text "Safari Zoo" in the lower-left corner of the artboard. With the cursor in the text, triple-click to select the entire paragraph.
6. With the text selected, click the Tracking icon in the Character panel to select the value in the Tracking field, and type −50. Press Enter or Return.

   Tracking changes the spacing between characters. A positive value pushes the letters apart horizontally; a negative value pulls the letters closer together.
7. Choose Type > Change Case > UPPERCASE. You might notice that the text wraps oddly in the type object.
8. With the Selection tool, drag the lower-right corner of the "SAFARI ZOO" text object to the right and up until the text fits again on two lines.
9. Double-click the text that begins with "Thursdays at..." to switch to the Type tool. With the cursor in the text, triple-click to select the entire paragraph.
10. In the Character panel, change the Font Size to 33 pt, Font Type to Adobe Garamond Pro, and the Font Style to Bold Italic. You'll need to either click the up arrow or type the value.
11. With the Selection tool, drag the lower-right corner of the "Thursdays at..." text object to the right and down until the text fits again on two lines.

Note:

If you choose to open the Character panel (Window > Type > Character), you may need to click the double arrow next to the word "Character" in the panel tab to reveal more options, like you learned earlier.

12. With the text object still selected, click the Vertical Scale icon in the Character panel to select the value and type 120. Press Enter or Return to accept the value. Leave the Character panel open.

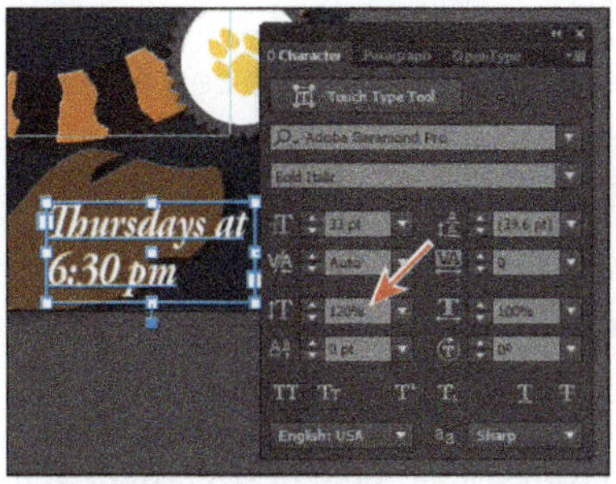

13. Choose View > Fit Artboard In Window.

14. Choose Select > Deselect, save the changes to **L6_start_xx.ai**, and leave it open.

Modifying Text with the Touch Type Tool

Using the Touch Type tool, you can modify the properties of a character, like size, scale, and rotation, using the mouse or touch controls. This is a highly visual way of applying the character formatting properties: baseline shift, horizontal and vertical scale, rotation, and kerning.

Next, you are going to use the Touch Type tool to alter the appearance of the "ZOO TALES" headline at the top of the artboard.

Try It!

1. Select the Zoom tool, and click the ZOO TALES several times. Make sure you can still see all of the ZOO TALES text.

2. With the Selection tool, click to select the ZOO TALES text object. Select whatever font is listed in the Font menu in the Control panel, and type Gar. In the menu that appears beneath where you are typing, click to select Adobe Garamond Pro Bold (or choose another font).

3. Click the Touch Type Tool button at the top of the Character panel.

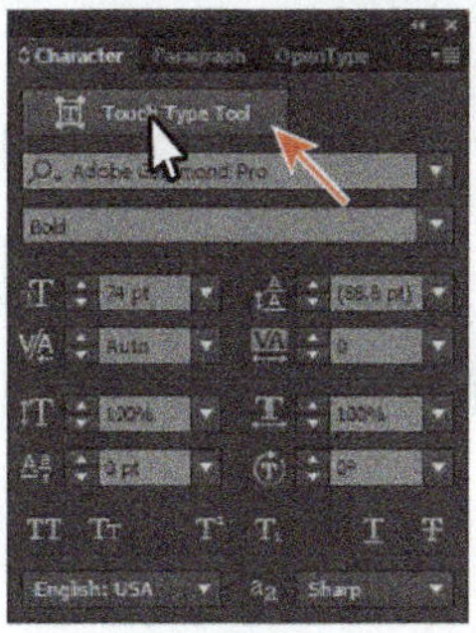

A message appears at the top of the Document window telling you to click on a character to select it.

4. Click the letter "Z" to select it. A box with a dot above it appears around the letter. The different points around the box allow you to adjust the character in different ways, as you'll see.

5. Choose View > Smart Guides to turn them on.

6. Click and drag the upper-right corner of the box away from the center, to make the letter larger. Stop dragging when you see roughly 190% for width (W:) and height (H:) in the measurement label.

   Notice that the movement is constrained—width and height change together proportionally. You just adjusted the horizontal scale and the vertical scale for the letter "Z" in the Character panel.

7. Look in the Character panel to see that the Horizontal Scale and Vertical Scale values are roughly 190%.

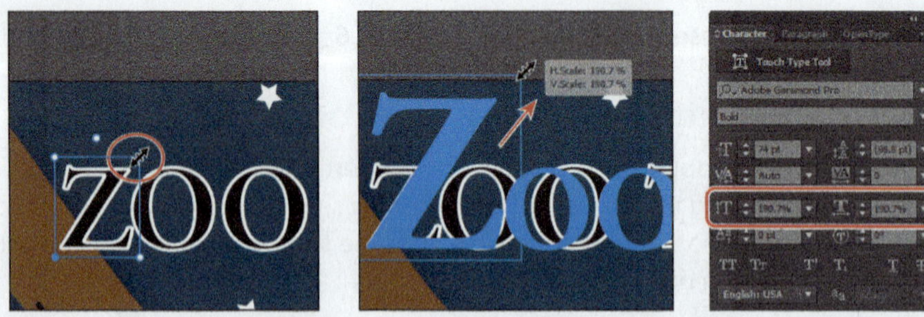

8. With the letter "Z" still selected, position the pointer in the center of the letter. Click and drag the letter down until the Baseline value shows approximately –24 pt in the gray measurement label.

   You just edited the baseline shift of the letter in the Character panel.

9. Click the "O" to the right of the "Z," and drag the rotate handle (the circle above the letter) counterclockwise until you see approximately 20° in the measurement label.

10. Click and drag the upper-right corner of the box around the selected "O," away from the center, to make the letter larger. Stop dragging when you see roughly 125% for width (W:) and height (H:) in the measurement label.

11. Drag the letter "O" from the center, to the left, until it looks something like the figure.

12. Click to select the second letter "O" in "ZOO," and change the following using the Touch Type tool:
    - Rotate the letter clockwise –35° (clockwise rotation shows a negative value).
    - Click and drag (what was) the upper-right corner of the box, away from the center, until you see roughly 105% for width (W:) and height (H:) in the measurement label.
    - Drag the letter from the center into the position you see in the figure.

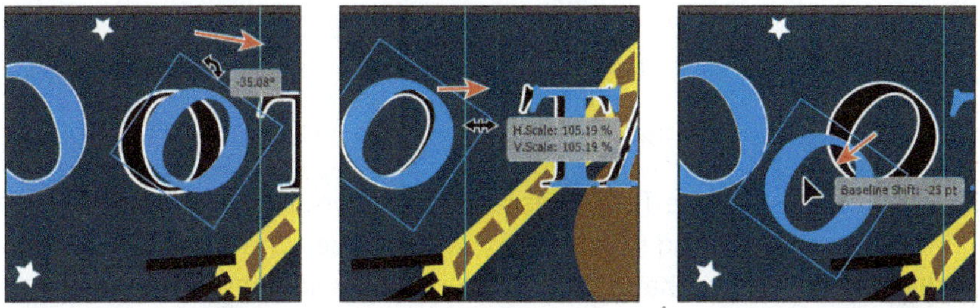

13. Click to select the letter "T" in "TALES," and change the following using the Touch Type tool:
    - Click and drag the upper-right corner of the box, away from the center, until you see roughly 150% for width (W:) and height (H:) in the measurement label.
    - Drag the letter "T" from the center down and to the left (a bit closer to the second "O" in "ZOO"), into the position you see in the figure.
    - Click and drag the upper-left point up until you see a Vertical Scale of 185%.

14. Click the letter "A" in "TALES." Drag the letter straight to the left to make it closer to the "T." See the figure for placement. Try not to drag up or down. The measurement label will show Baseline Shift: 0 pt.

15. Save the changes to **L6_start_xx.ai**, and leave it open.

Changing Paragraph Attributes

As with character attributes, you can set paragraph attributes, such as alignment or indenting, before you enter new type or to change the appearance of existing type. If you select several type paths and type containers, you can set attributes for them all at the same time. Most of this type of formatting is done in the Paragraph panel, which you can access by clicking the underlined word "Paragraph" in the Control panel or by choosing Window > Type > Paragraph.

Below are the formatting options available in the Paragraph panel.

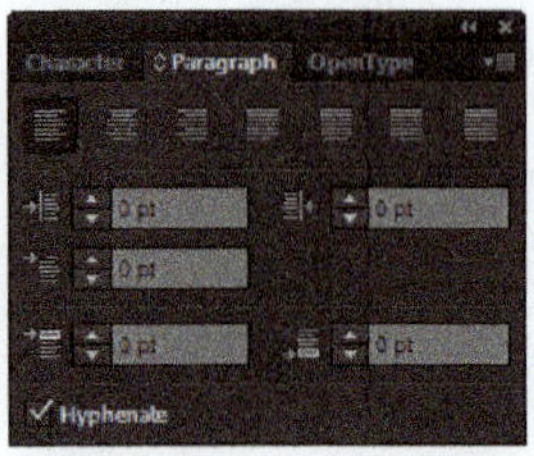

Next, you'll add more space after all the paragraphs in the main text.

Try It!

1. Choose View > Fit Artboard In Window.
2. Position the pointer over the Touch Type tool in the Tools panel, click and hold down the mouse button, and select the Type tool. Insert the cursor in the text in the middle of the artboard that begins with "The Animal Zoo welcomes..."
3. Click the word "Paragraph" in the Control panel to open the Paragraph panel.
4. Type 11 pt in the Space After Paragraph text field (in the lower-right corner), and press Enter or Return.

   Setting a spacing value after paragraphs, rather than pressing the Return key, is useful for maintaining consistency and ease of editing later.

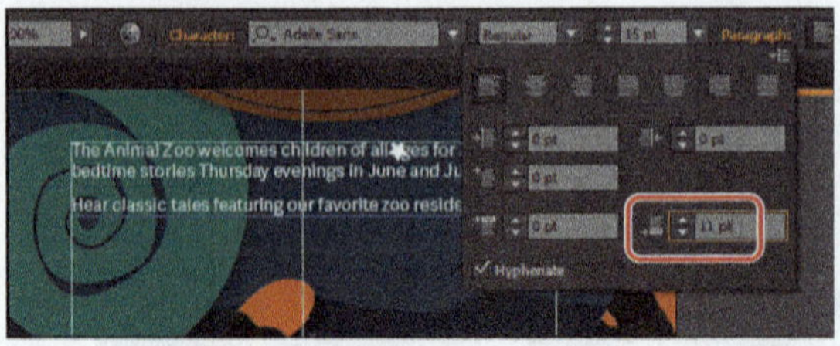

5. With the Selection tool, click the text "SAFARI ZOO" and then Shift-click the text "Thursdays at 6:30 pm" to select the two text objects only. Choose Window > Type > Paragraph to open the Paragraph panel. In the panel, click the Align Center button.

6. Close the Paragraph panel group.

7. Choose Select > Deselect, save the changes to **L6_start_xx.ai**, and leave it open.

Resizing and Reshaping Type Objects

You can create unique type object shapes by reshaping them using a variety of methods, including the Direct Selection tool. In this next section, you'll reshape and resize type objects to better fit text in them.

Try It!

1. Choose View > Fit All In Window.

   At times, you may need to reflow the text between text objects. Next, you will learn how to resize, unlink, relink, and reshape type objects.

2. With the Selection tool, click the text in the main type object on the larger artboard to select it. Drag the right, middle point to the vertical guide in the center of the artboard.

3. Double-click the out port in the lower-right corner of the text object (where the thread line is coming out).

   Because the two text objects were threaded, double-clicking the out port of the first text object (or the in port of the second type object) breaks the connection between them. Any text threaded between the type objects flows back into the first one. The other text object is still there, but it has no text.

4. Using the Selection tool, drag the bottom, middle handle of the bounding box down until the text "...favorite stuffed animal!" is the last text in the object. The text object changes in size vertically.

5. With the Selection tool, click the out port in the lower-right corner of the type object. The pointer changes to the loaded text icon.

6. Position the loaded text icon to the right of the existing type object and down from its top edge (see the figure). Click, and a new type object is created that should roughly fit into the aqua guide box. Leave the new type object selected.

When type objects are threaded, you can move them anywhere and still maintain the connection between them. When type objects are resized, especially those in the beginning of the thread, text can reflow. Now you will link the new type object to the type object on the Card artboard.

7. With the Selection tool, click the out port in the lower-right corner of the new type object. The pointer changes to the loaded text icon.

8. Choose View > Outline to see the artwork edges.

9. On the 2 Card artboard, position the loaded text icon on the edge (boundary) of the existing type object (see the figure), and click when the pointer changes as shown below.

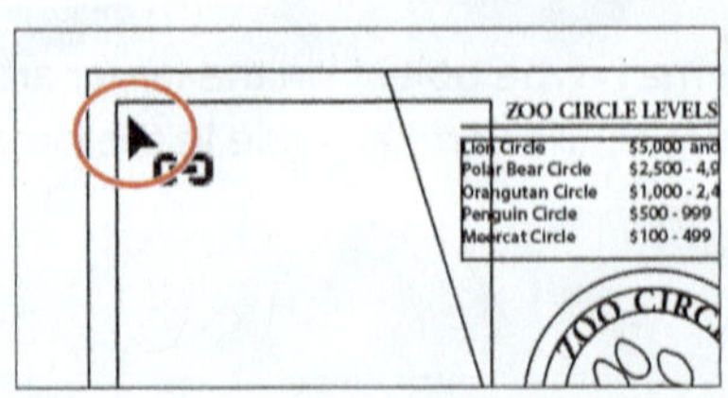

10. Choose View > Preview.

11. Using the Selection tool, on the 1 Flyer artboard, drag the bottom, middle handle of the right-hand type object up until the text "...for supporting this program." is the last text in the object. The text object changes in size vertically.

12. Select the Type tool and position the pointer over the threaded text on the 2 Card artboard. When the pointer changes shape, click three times to select the paragraph.

13. Change the Font Size to 10 pt in the Control panel. Click the word "Character" in the Control panel and, in the Character panel, change the Leading to 15 pt.

14. Select the Direct Selection tool. Click the upper-right corner of the type object to select the anchor point. Hold down the Shift key and drag that point to the left to adjust the shape of the path to fit the orange shape. Release the mouse button and then the Shift key when finished.

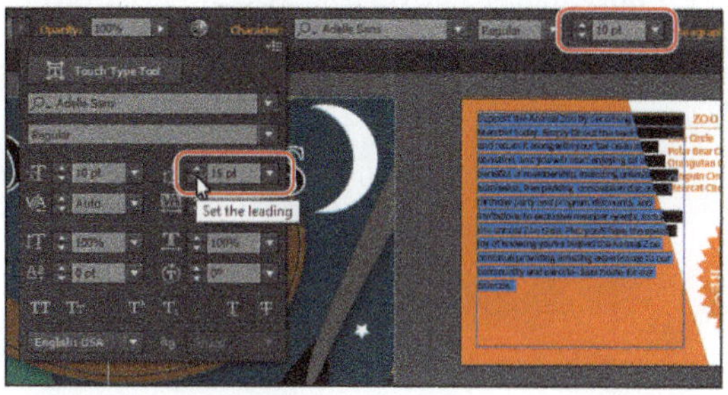

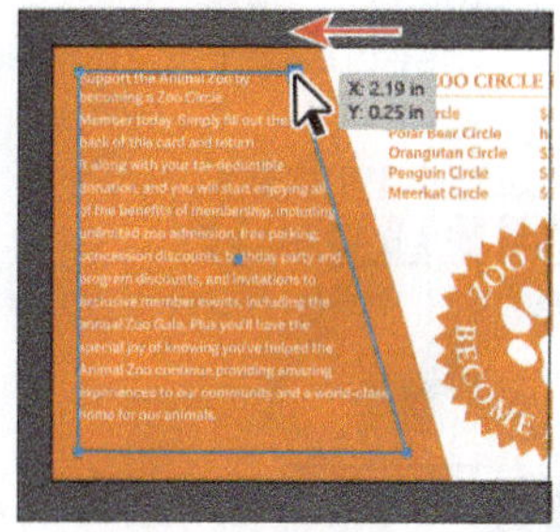

15. Save the changes to **L6_start_xx.ai**, and leave it open.

The Development of Type

Until the nineteenth century, printing was primarily limited to books. The Industrial Revolution brought a demand for printed brochures, product ads, and advertising posters. A variety of wooden display **typefaces** came into existence along with type-specimen catalogs. Up to that point, handbills looked similar to title pages of books, the book types merely enlarged.

Typeface

A set of one or more fonts each composed of glyphs that share common design features. Each font of a typeface has a specific weight, style, condensation, width, slant, italicization, and ornamentation.

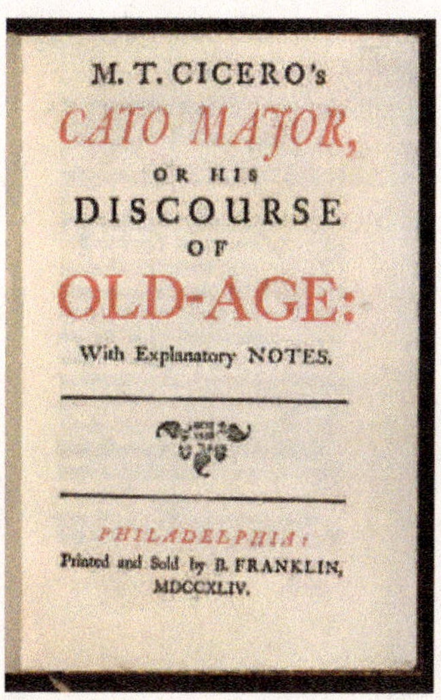
M. T. CICERO's
CATO MAJOR,
OR HIS
DISCOURSE
OF
OLD-AGE:
With Explanatory NOTES.

PHILADELPHIA:
Printed and Sold by B. FRANKLIN,
MDCCXLIV.

Two eighteenth century English founders of typefaces include William Caslon (1692–1766), whose typeface of 1724 was so distinct and legible it was used to set the Declaration of Independence, and the printer John Baskerville (1706–1775), whose typefaces were adopted by the U.S. government for its publishing.

In advertising, new display typefaces were being introduced. Slab Serif types from Britain were designed to help information stand out noticeably. These typefaces were used on pamphlets, posters, and anything that had short lengths of text. British type designer Robert Thorne (d. 1820) coined the term

Egyptian serifs to describe these thick Slab Serifs because the letterforms resembled the weight and bluntness of hieroglyphs. In 1803, Thorne developed what he called Fat Face typefaces, which had an even bolder look and weight than the Egyptians. Fat Faces appealed to advertisers because of the impact they created on the page.

Many variations of the Fat Faces soon followed, including forward and backward sloping italics, inline, shadow, and three-dimensional relief letters.

Book typesetting also kept pace with the growing demand as literacy increased, and in 1886, the German inventor Ottmar Mergenthaler (1854–1899) perfected what he called his "Linotype machine".

The mechanical process of composing type transformed the industry. The slow hand setting of type, letter by letter, was replaced with type composed from a keyboard and transmitted to a series of matrices that held brass letterforms, which cast slugs of raised lead lines of type ("line o' type").

Creating and Applying Text Styles

Repetition in type treatment is a design principal that helps you achieve consistency and continuity in visual communications. Styles are a tool that enable you to format text consistently. They are also helpful when text attributes need to be updated globally. Once a **style** is created, you only need to edit the saved style, and then all text formatted with that style is updated.

> **Style**
>
> A collection of formatting settings that can be applied all at once.

Illustrator provides two types of text styles:

- **Paragraph**—Retains character and paragraph attributes and applies them to an entire paragraph.
- **Character**—Retains character attributes and applies them to selected text.

Creating and Applying a Paragraph Style

First, you will create a paragraph style for the body copy.

Try It!

1. If necessary, choose 1 Flyer from the Artboard Navigation menu in the lower-left corner of the Document window.
2. With the Type tool selected, insert the cursor anywhere in the first paragraph in the first threaded type object that starts with "The Animal Zoo...".

   You do not need to select text to create a paragraph style, but you do have to place the text insertion point in the text that has the attributes you want to save.
3. Choose Window > Type > Paragraph Styles, and click the Create New Style button at the bottom of the Paragraph Styles panel.
4. In the New Paragraph Style dialog box, double-click directly on the style name "Paragraph Style 1" in the list of styles. Change the name of the style to Body, and press Enter or Return.

   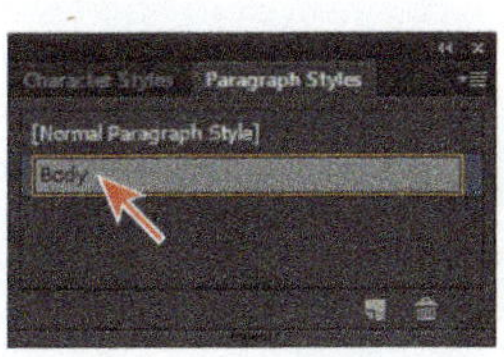

   By double-clicking the style to edit the name, you are also applying the new style to the paragraph (where the cursor is). This means that if you edit the Body paragraph style, this paragraph will update as well.

5. With the Type tool selected, click and drag from before the first word in the first paragraph that starts with the text "The Animal Zoo..." to after the last word "...for supporting this program." in the second "column" to select it.

6. Click the Body style in the Paragraph Styles panel.

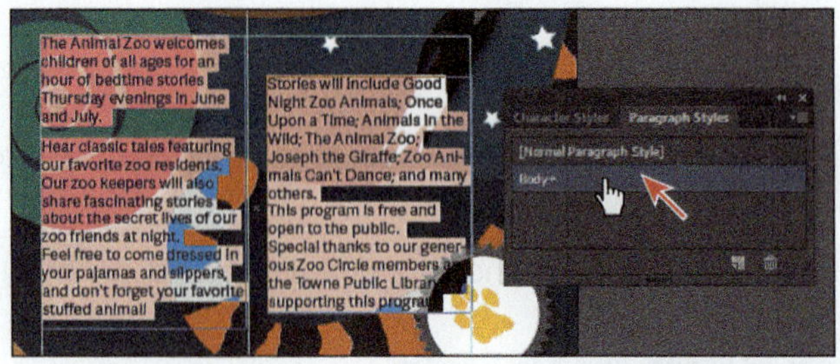

Notice that a plus sign appears to the right of the Body style name. The plus sign indicates that the style has an override. An override is any formatting that doesn't match the attributes defined by the style, for example, if you changed the font size for the selected paragraph.

7. Press the Option (Mac) or Alt (Win) key, and select the Body style again in the Paragraph Styles panel to overwrite existing attributes on the selected text.

   The text attributes of the Body style are applied to the selected text, including the Space After value, so the text may no longer all fit in the two columns.

8. Choose Select > Deselect.

9. Select the Selection tool, and click to select the type object on the right (the right column). Click and drag the bottom bounding point down until the text "supporting this program" is the last to appear in the column (if necessary).

10. Choose Select > Deselect, save the changes to **L6_start_xx.ai**, and leave it open.

Editing a Paragraph Style

After creating a paragraph style, you can easily edit the style formatting. Then anywhere the style has been applied, the formatting will be updated automatically.

Try It!

1. Double-click to the right of the Body style name in the Paragraph Styles panel list to open the Paragraph Style Options dialog box.

2. Select the Indents And Spacing category on the left side of the dialog box.

3. Change the Space After to 8 pt.

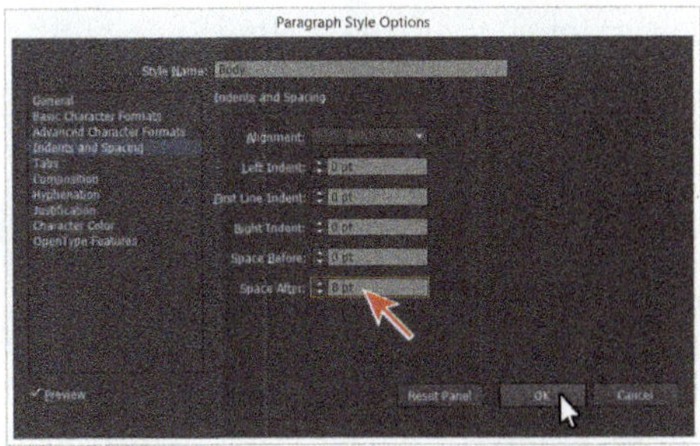

Since Preview is selected by default, you can move the dialog box out of the way to see the text change.

4. Click OK.

5. Save the changes to **L6_start_xx.ai**, and leave it open.

   There are many options for working with paragraph styles, most of which are found in the Paragraph Styles panel menu, including duplicating, deleting, and editing paragraph styles.

Creating and Applying a Character Style

Character styles, unlike paragraph styles, can only be applied to selected text and can only contain character formatting. Next, you will create a character style from text styling within the columns of text.

Try It!

1. Choose View > Zoom In twice to zoom in to the threaded text in the center.

2. Using the Type tool, in the first paragraph, select "The Animal Zoo."

3. Click the Fill color, and select the swatch named "gold" in the Control panel.

4. Click the word "Character" in the Control panel and choose Italic from the Font Style menu, and then click the Underline button to underline the text.

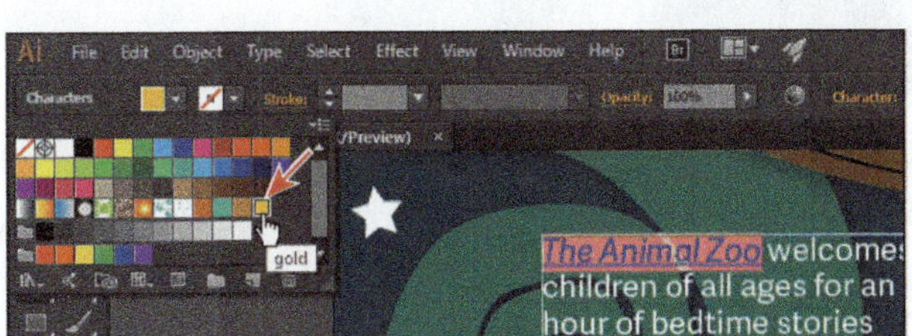

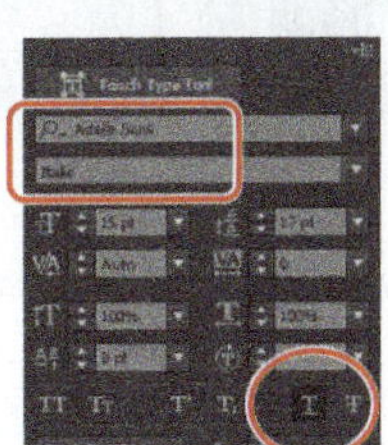

5. In the Paragraph Styles panel group, click the Character Styles panel tab.

6. In the Character Styles panel, Option-click (Mac) or Alt-click (Windows) the Create New Style button at the bottom of the Character Styles panel.

   Option-clicking (Mac) or Alt-clicking (Windows) the Create New Style button in the Character or Paragraph Styles panel allows you to edit the style options before it is added to the panel.

7. Name the style **Emphasis**, and click OK.

   The style records the attributes applied to your selected text.

8. With the text still selected, Option-click (Mac) or Alt-click (Win) the style named Emphasis in the Character Styles panel to assign the style to that text so that it will update if the style changes.

9. In the next column (text object), select the text "This program is free" and Option-click (Mac) or Alt-click (Win) the style named Emphasis in the Character Styles panel to apply it.

10. Choose Select > Deselect, save the changes to **L6_start_xx.ai,** and leave it open.

Editing a Character Style

After creating a character style, you can easily edit the style formatting. The formatting on any other text to which the style has been applied is automatically updated.

Try It!

1. Double-click to the right of the Emphasis style name in the Character Styles panel (not the style name itself). In the Character Style Options dialog box, make sure that Preview is selected. Click the Basic Character Formats category on the left side of the dialog box, and choose Regular from the Font Style menu. Click OK.

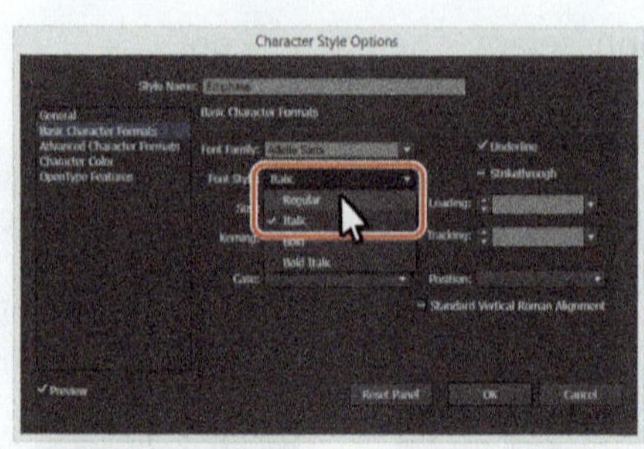

2. Save the changes to **L6_start_xx.ai**, and leave it open.

Sampling Text Formatting

Using the Eyedropper tool, you can quickly sample type attributes and copy them to text without creating a style.

1. Using the Type tool, select the text "dressed in your pajamas and slippers" in the first column of text.

2. Select the Eyedropper tool in the Tools panel, and click in the first text "The Animal Zoo." A letter "T" appears above the Eyedropper pointer.

The attributes are immediately applied to your selected text, along with the Emphasis character style.

3. Choose Select > Deselect, and then select the style named [Normal Character Style] in the Character Styles panel. Close the Character Styles panel group.

   Clicking [Normal Character Style] ensures that any new text you add to the document will not have the style named Emphasis applied.

4. Save the changes to **L6_start_xx.ai**, and leave it open.

Warping Text

You can create depth and other cool design effects by warping text into different shapes using envelopes. You can make an envelope out of an object on your artboard, or you can use a preset warp shape or a mesh grid as an envelope. As you explore warping with envelopes, you'll also discover that you can use envelopes on any object except graphs, guides, or linked objects.

Reshaping Text with a Preset Envelope Warp

Try It!

1. Choose View > Fit Artboard In Window. Select the Zoom tool and click the "SAFARI ZOO" text in the lower-left corner of the artboard several times.

2. With the Type tool, select the word "ZOO" and change the Font Size to 66 pt in the Control panel.

3. With the Selection tool, adjust the type object size so that it is just large enough to show all of the text.

4. With the Type tool, select the word "ZOO" again, and click the word "Character" in the Control panel to open the Character panel. Change the Leading value to 52 pt.

5. Select the Selection tool and make sure that the text object is selected. Click the Make Envelope button in the Control panel (not the arrow to the right). In the Warp Options dialog box, select Preview. The text appears as an arc.

6. Choose Arc Upper from the Style menu. Drag the Bend slider to the right to see it bend up further. You can experiment with many combinations to achieve depth and modify perspective. Drag the Horizontal and Vertical Distortion sliders to see the effect on the text. When you are finished experimenting, drag the Distortion sliders to 0%, make sure that the Bend is 20%, and then click OK.

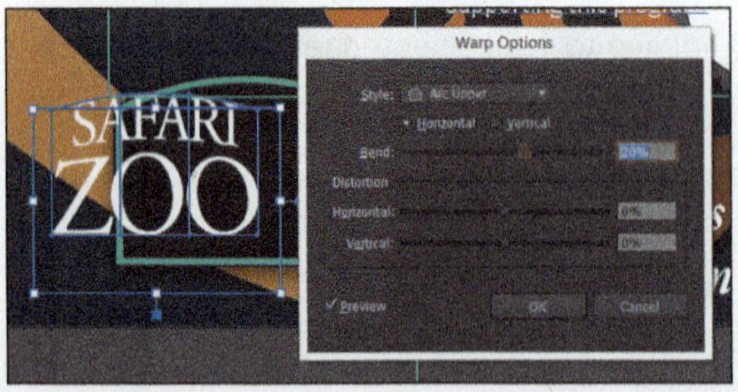

7. Drag the envelope object (warped text) into the approximate center of the black sign shape.

8. Save the changes to **L6_start_xx.ai**, and leave it open.

Editing a Text Warp

If you want to make any changes, you can edit the text and shape that make up the envelope warp object separately. Next, you will edit the text and then the warp shape.

Try It!

1. With the envelope object still selected, click the Edit Contents button in the Control panel. This is how you edit the text in the warped shape.

2. Make sure that Smart Guides are on (View > Smart Guides).

3. Using the Type tool, position the cursor over the warped text. Notice that another copy of the text appears in blue. The Smart Guides show you the original unwarped text in blue. Double-click to select the word "SAFARI."

Tip:

If you double-click with the Selection tool instead of with the Type tool, you enter Isolation mode. This is another way to edit the text within the envelope warp object. Press the Escape key to exit Isolation mode.

4. Type ANIMAL, and then press Shift+Enter or Shift+Return to add a soft return and wrap the word "ZOO" to the next line.

   Notice that the text automatically warps in the envelope shape.

   You can also edit the preset shape, which is what you'll do next.

5. Select the Selection tool, and make sure that the envelope object is still selected. Click the Edit Envelope button in the Control panel.

   Notice the options for the envelope warp object in the Control panel. You can choose another warp shape from the Style menu and then change the warp options, like Horizontal, Vertical, and Bend. These are the same options you saw in the Warp Options dialog box when you first created the envelope warp.

6. Change the Bend to 28% in the Control panel. Make sure that the H (horizontal) Distortion is 0 and the V (vertical) Distortion is 0.

7. Choose View > Smart Guides to turn them off.

8. Select the Selection tool, and Shift-drag the lower-right-corner bounding point away from the center to make the object a bit larger. Make sure that the text stays within the black sign shape.

9. Shift-click the black sign shape to select both objects, and then release the Shift key. Click the black sign shape once more to make it the key object. Click the Horizontal Align Center button, and then click the Vertical Align Center button to align the warped text to the black sign shape.

10. Save the changes to **L6_start_xx.ai** and leave it open.

Working with Type on a Path

In addition to having text in point and type areas, you can also have type along a path. You can place text to flow along the edge of an open or closed path.

Creating Type on a Path

First, you'll insert some text on an open path.

Try It!

1. Choose View > Fit Artboard In Window. You may wish to zoom in further to see the text you type.
2. With the Selection tool, select the black curved path on the brown monkey tail.

   When creating a new type object, this resets the formatting to default.
3. With the Type tool, position the cursor over the middle of the path to see an insertion point with an intersecting wavy path (see the figure). Click when this cursor appears.

   The text will start where you click the path. Also, the stroke attributes of the path change to None and a cursor appears.

4. Choose Window > Type > Paragraph Styles to open the panel. Option-click (Mac) or Alt-click (Windows) the [Normal Paragraph Style].
5. Type the text **Bedtime Stories With Your Wildest Friends**. Note that the new text follows the path.
6. With the Type tool, click three times on the new text to select it.
7. Select the Eyedropper tool in the Tools panel, and click in the text that begins, "Thursdays at..." A letter "T" appears above the Eyedropper pointer.

   The text formatting from the "Thursdays at..." text is applied to the text on the path. This causes the text to extend beyond the path, so the overset icon in the out port appears.
8. Click the word "Character" in the Control panel, and change the Vertical Scale to 100% in the Character panel. Press the Escape key to hide the panel.
9. Click the Align Left button in the Control panel.

   Next, you'll reposition the text on the path so that all of the text appears.

10. Select the Selection tool, and position the pointer over the line on the left edge of the text (just to the left of the "B"). When you see the cursor shown in the figure below, click and drag to the left end of the path.

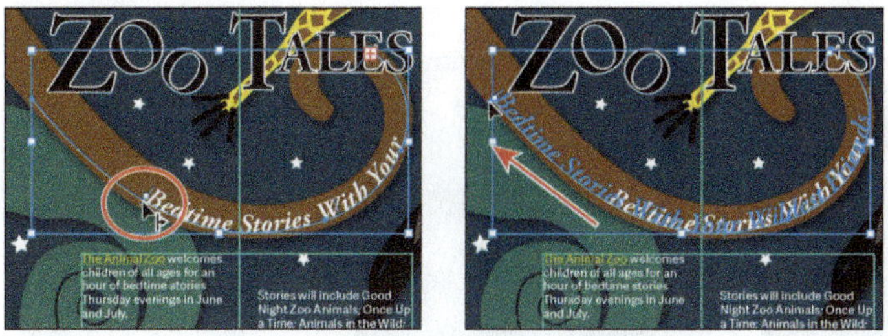

11. Choose Select > Deselect, save the changes to **L6_start_xx.ai** and leave it open.

Creating Type on a Closed Path

Next, you will add text around a circle.

Try It!

1. Select the Zoom tool in the Tools panel, and click the yellow paw print three times to zoom in.
2. With the Selection tool, Shift-click the threaded type object and the yellow paw print to select both and choose Object > Hide > Selection.
3. Select the Type tool, and position the pointer over the edge of the white circle. The pointer changes to a Type cursor with a circle. This indicates that, if you click (don't click), text will be placed inside of the circle, creating a type object in the shape of a circle.
4. While pressing the Option (Mac OS) or Alt (Windows) key, position the pointer over the left side of the circle. The insertion point with an intersecting wavy path appears. Click and type ZOO CIRCLE. The text flows on the circular path. Click three times on the text to select it.

5. With the text still selected, in the Control panel, change the font size to 16 pt, the Font Style to Bold (the Font Family should already be Adobe Garamond Pro), and the Fill color to the swatch named gold.

   Next, you will adjust the position of the text.

6. Select the Selection tool in the Tools panel. Position the pointer over the line (called a bracket) on the left end of the text (to the left of the word "ZOO"). When you see the cursor, with an arrow pointing to the right, drag up around the circle in a clockwise fashion. See the figure for position.

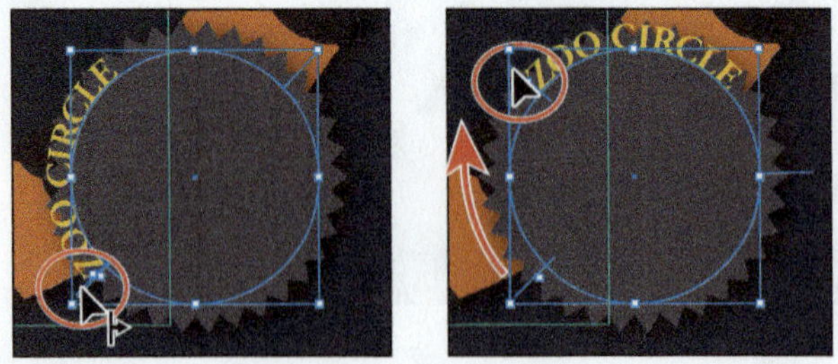

7. Save the changes to **L6_start_xx.ai** and leave it open.

Editing Type on a Path

When you create type on a path, you can set options to change the appearance of the text, including effects, alignment, and spacing. Next, you'll edit the type you placed on the circle.

Try It!

1. With the path type object selected with the Selection tool, choose Type > Type On A Path > Type On A Path Options.

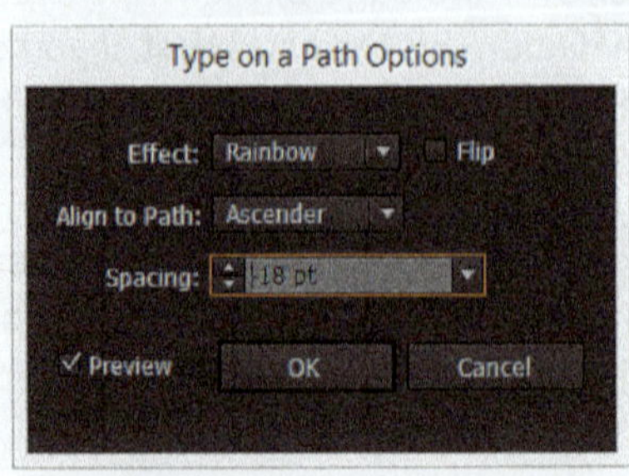

In the Type On A Path Options dialog box, select Preview and change the following options:

- Choose **Skew** from the Effect menu and notice how the text changes.
- Then choose **Rainbow**.
- Align To Path: **Ascender**
- Spacing: **–18 pt**

2. Click OK.

3. With the Selection tool, position the pointer over the line on the left end of the text (to the left of the word "ZOO").

   When the pointer changes to the black arrowhead, drag down around the circle in a counterclockwise fashion. See the figure.

4. Choose Object > Show All and then choose Select > Deselect.

5. Save the changes to **L6_start_xx.ai** and leave it open.

Wrapping Text Around an Object

In Illustrator, you can easily wrap text around objects, such as type objects, imported images, and vector artwork, to avoid text running over those objects or to create interesting design effects. Next, you will wrap text around the text on a path object.

Try It!

1. With the Selection tool selected, click directly on the "ZOO CIRCLE" text to select it. Choose Object > Arrange > Bring To Front.

2. Choose Object > Text Wrap > Make. Click OK if a dialog box appears. The text in the column wraps around the text on a path shape.

   If you move the object with the text wrap applied, the text responds and wraps differently.

3. Choose Object > Text Wrap > Text Wrap Options. In the Text Wrap Options dialog box, change Offset to 13 pt and select Preview to see the change.

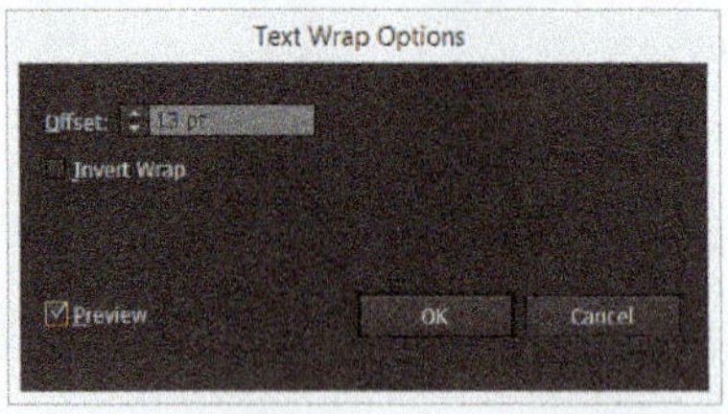

4. Click OK.

5. With the Selection tool selected, drag the bottom, middle point of the threaded text box down to make sure that the text "...for supporting this program" is the last showing.

6. Choose View > Fit Artboard In Window.

7. Choose Select > Deselect, save the changes to **L6_start_xx.ai,** and leave it open.

Creating Text Outlines

Converting text to outlines converts it into vector shapes that you can edit and manipulate as you would any other graphic object. Text outlines are useful for changing the look of large display type, but they are rarely useful for body text or other type at sizes of less than 10 points. The file recipient doesn't need to have your fonts installed to open and view the file correctly.

When you create outlines from text, you should consider that text as no longer editable. Also, bitmap fonts and outline protected fonts cannot be converted to outlines. When type is converted to outlines, the type loses its hints—instructions built into outline fonts to adjust their shape to display or print optimally at many sizes. You must also convert all type in a selection to outlines; you cannot convert a single letter within a type object.

Next, you will convert the main heading to outlines and position content.

Try It!

1. With the Selection tool selected, click the heading text "Zoo Tales" at the top of the artboard. Choose Type > Create Outlines. Drag it into position like you see in the figure (if it's not already there).

The text is no longer linked to a particular font. Instead, it is now artwork, much like any other vector art in your illustration.

2. With the Selection tool, drag the text "Thursdays at 6:30 pm" at the bottom of the artboard into position, like you see in the following figure.

3. Choose View > Guides > Hide Guides, and then choose Select > Deselect.

4. Save and close **L6_start_xx.ai**, and then close Illustrator.

Comprehension Check

1. What is the difference between point type and area type?
2. What does the Touch Type tool let you do?
3. What is overflow text?
4. What is text threading?
5. What is the difference between a character style and a paragraph style?

Review Project

At the beginning of this lesson, you learned about the concepts of typography and applied many of them as you worked on the Zoo Tales poster. In this project, you will create a document that defines and illustrates the concepts of typography. You can use the information presented in this lesson or do further research to find additional information on your own. You can type the content in a plain text file, Word document, or RTF file and import it to a new Illustrator document, or you can type the content directly in the Illustrator document. Be sure to apply the concepts of typography to effectively present the information. Draw shapes and use color and other elements of layout and design to enhance the appearance of your document.

End-of-Chapter Activities

Chapter Review

1. What is color theory?
2. What is the difference between an analogous color harmony and a complementary color harmony?
3. What three terms are used to describe color?
4. What are the components of a path?
5. What's the primary difference between the Pen tool and the Pencil tool?
6. What two tools would you use to cut and divide shapes?
7. List and define the concepts of typography.
8. Explain the difference between a serif font and a sans serif font. Provide an example of each.

Multiple Choice

1. What is the term for a visual representation of colors arranged according to their relationship?
   a. color theory
   b. color saturation
   c. color wheel
   d. color concept
2. Which of the following tools in NOT a drawing tool in Adobe Illustrator?
   a. Rectangle tool
   b. Pen tool
   c. Pencil tool
   d. Paintbrush tool
3. When working with color in Adobe Illustrator which of the following color modes should be used for print?
   a. CMYK
   b. HSB
   c. RGB
   d. Lab
4. Which of the following tools allows you to select individual anchor points?
   a. Selection tool
   b. Direct Selection tool
   c. Group Selection tool
   d. Magic Wand tool

Chapter 2 – Portfolio Builder

Creating Warped Text

In this activity, you will create warped text on a curve to develop a logo for a company named DreamPage. You will use both type-on-a-path and envelope techniques to create warped text on a curve. In addition, you will experiment with converting type into outlines.

1. Choose File > Open, and open the **PB2_start.ai** file from the data files for this lesson. Save it as **PB2_start_xx.ai** in the location where your teacher has instructed you to store files for this chapter.
2. Choose View > Fit Artboard In Window to fit the artboard in the Document window.
3. Select the Type tool.
4. Create point type for the company name, **DreamPage**, and place it in the center of the logo, just below the cloud.
5. Select the type.
6. Fill the type with the color blue.
7. Using the Selection tool, select all the shapes that create the cloud.
8. Choose Object > Group to group it.
9. Choose Edit > Copy, and then choose Edit > Paste in Place

   A duplicate of the clouds group is created in front of the other group.
10. Select the Group Selection tool.
11. Select the light blue part of the cloud.
12. Select the Type tool.
13. Click on the path and type **You dream...We search**.
14. Play with the position of the type.
15. Select the **DreamPage** type.
16. Choose Type > Create Outlines.
17. Select the letter D and enlarge it, then select the letter P and enlarge it.

    You made need to adjust the locations of the letters after resizing them.
18. Choose Object > Envelope Distort > Make with Warp.
19. Choose a style to match the curve at the bottom of the cloud.
20. Save and close the file, and then close Illustrator.

Chapter 2 – Critical Thinking

As you learned in this chapter, the treatment of type can be a powerful tool in visual communications. As you create more complex documents, you will need to carefully consider the principals of design as they relate to type. The principles of design are: proportion, balance, variety, contrast, emphasis, harmony, unity, and repetition (see Lesson 1 for a description of each principle).

Find two or three examples of visual communication pieces (either printed or online) with type treatments that you think illustrate these design principles. Create a presentation that explains how the design principles have been applied. Share your samples with the class.

Chapter 3

Understanding Digital Photography

Lesson 7 | Getting to Know the Photoshop Work Area

Starting Photoshop and Opening a File
Using the Photoshop Tools
Working with Color in Photoshop
Working with Tools and Tool Properties
Exploring Photoshop Panels
Creating Career Search Documents

Lesson 8 | Making Basic Photo Corrections

Developing a Strategy for Retouching
Straightening and Cropping an Image in Photoshop
Adjusting the Color and Tone
Removing Imperfections with the Spot Healing Brush Tool
Applying a Content-Aware Patch
Repairing Areas with the Clone Stamp Tool
Sharpening the Image

Lesson 9 | Exploring Digital Photography

Evaluating a Photograph
Measuring Light
Recognizing Camera Settings
Exploring Bracketing
Transferring Photos to a Computer
Understanding Safety Considerations
Using the Rule of Thirds
Explaining Fair Use and Appropriation

Lesson 10 | Understanding Repairs and Hoaxes

Making Digital Repairs
Creating a Hoax
Making Tonal Repairs with Dodge and Burn
Making a Layer Mask
Creating a Graphic Design Portfolio

End-of-Chapter Activities

Lesson 7 Overview

In this lesson, you will learn about:

- Starting Photoshop and Opening a File
- Using the Photoshop Tools
- Working with Color in Photoshop
- Working with Tools and Tool Properties
- Exploring Photoshop Panels
- Creating Career Search Documents

Adobe® Photoshop® is a software program used for editing and manipulating digital photographs and other raster images. Recall that raster, or bitmap, images are created by colored pixels arranged side by side in a regular grid. The Adobe Photoshop work area includes menus, toolbars, and panels that give you quick access to a variety of tools and options for editing and adding elements to your image. You can also add commands and filters to the menus by installing third-party software known as plug-ins.

In Photoshop, you primarily work with bitmapped, digitized images but you can also work with vector graphics. You can create original artwork in Photoshop, or you can import images from many sources. These include:

- Photographs from a digital camera or mobile phone
- Stock photography
- Scans of photographs, transparencies, negatives, graphics, or other documents
- Captured video images
- Artwork created in drawing programs

Almost all design and print-related careers require the use of Adobe Photoshop or another similar program. For example, graphic designers, video game designers, and desktop publishers can create and edit artwork, and Web designers can design page layouts or visual elements for a Web site. Artists, designers, and photographers may be self-employed, or they may work in a variety of businesses that employ people who know how to use Adobe Photoshop. Some such businesses include those in advertising, manufacturing, Web development, and publishing.

Starting Photoshop and Opening a File

To begin, you'll start Adobe Photoshop and reset the default preferences.

Try It!

1. Double-click the Adobe Photoshop icon on your taskbar (Windows) or dock (Mac), and then immediately hold down Ctrl+Alt+Shift (Windows) or Command+Option+Shift (Mac OS) to reset the default settings.

   If you don't see the Photoshop icon in your taskbar or dock, choose Start > All Programs > Adobe Photoshop CC (Windows) or look in the Applications folder (Mac).

2. When prompted, click Yes to confirm that you want to delete the Adobe Photoshop Settings file.

   The Photoshop work area appears similar to that shown in the following illustration.

> **Note:**
>
> On Mac OS, the application frame keeps the image, panels, and menu bar together.

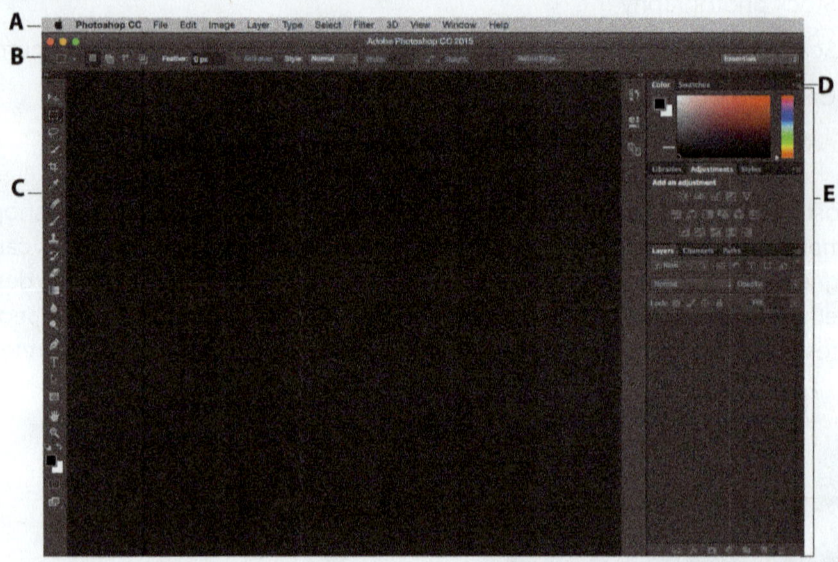

The default workspace in Photoshop consists of the menu bar (A) and Options bar (B) at the top of the screen, the Tools panel (C) on the left, and several open panels (D and E) in the panel dock on the right. When you have documents open, one or more image windows also appear, and you can display them at the same time using the tabbed interface. The Photoshop user interface is very similar to the one in Adobe Illustrator®, and Adobe Flash Professional®—so learning how to use the tools and panels in one application means that you'll be familiar with them when you work in the others.

There is one main difference between the Photoshop work area on a Windows-based system and that on Mac: In Windows, Photoshop is always in a contained window. On a Mac, you can choose to work with an application frame, which contains the Photoshop application's windows and panels, that is distinct from other applications you may have open; only the menu bar is outside the application frame. The application frame is enabled by default; to disable the application frame, choose Window > Application Frame.

Using the Photoshop Tools

Photoshop provides an integrated set of tools for producing sophisticated graphics for print, Web, and mobile viewing. We could easily fill the entire book with details on the wealth of Photoshop tools and tool configurations. While that would certainly be a useful reference, it's not the goal of this book. Instead, you'll start gaining experience by configuring and using a few tools on a sample project. Every lesson will introduce you to more tools and ways to use them. By the time you finish the lessons in this chapter, you'll have a solid foundation for further exploration of the Photoshop toolset.

Selecting and Using a Tool from the Tools Panel

The Tools panel is the long, narrow panel on the far left side of the work area. It contains selection tools, painting and editing tools, foreground- and background-color selection boxes, and viewing tools.

You'll start by using the Zoom tool, which is also available in many other Adobe applications, including Illustrator and Acrobat.

Try It!

1. Choose File > Open, navigate to the data files for this lesson, and open **L7_Start.psd**.

   The **L7_Start.psd** file contains the background image and a ribbon graphic that you'll use to create the birthday card shown on the first page of this lesson.

2. Click the double arrows just above the Tools panel to toggle to a double-column view. Click the double arrows again to return to a single-column Tools panel and use your screen space more efficiently.

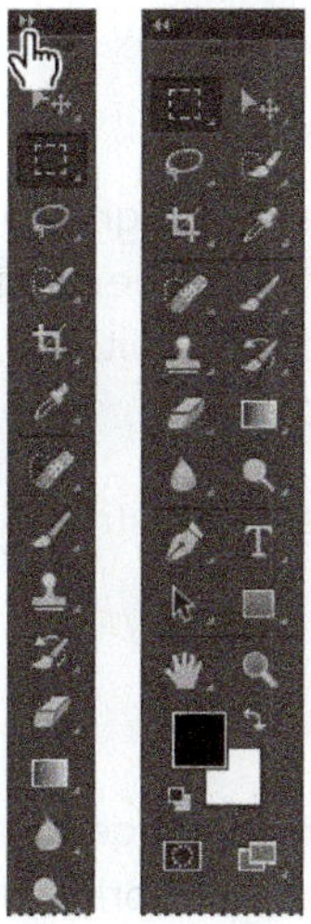

3. Examine the status bar at the bottom of the work area (Windows) or image window (Mac), and notice the percentage that appears on the far left.

   This represents the current enlargement view of the image, or zoom level.

4. Move the pointer over the Tools panel, and hover it over the magnifying-glass icon until a tool tip appears. The tool tip displays the tool's name (Zoom tool) and keyboard shortcut (Z).

5. Click the Zoom tool icon in the Tools panel, or press Z to select it.
6. Move the pointer over the image window. The pointer now looks like a tiny magnifying glass with a plus sign in the center of the glass.
7. Click anywhere in the image window.

   The image enlarges to a preset percentage level, which replaces the previous value in the status bar. If you click again, the zoom advances to the next preset level, up to a maximum of 3200%.
8. Hold down the Alt key (Windows) or Option key (Mac) so that the Zoom tool pointer appears with a minus sign in the center of the magnifying glass, and then click anywhere in the image. Then release the Alt or Option key.

   Now the view zooms out to a lower preset magnification, so that you can see more of the image, but in less detail.
9. Click Scrubby Zoom on the Options bar, click anywhere on the image, and drag the Zoom tool to the right. The image enlarges. Drag the Zoom tool to the left to zoom out.

   When Scrubby Zoom is selected, you can drag the Zoom tool across the image to zoom in and out.
10. Deselect Scrubby Zoom in the Options bar. Then, using the Zoom tool, drag a rectangle to enclose part of the rose blossom.

    The image enlarges so that the area you enclosed in your rectangle now fills the entire image window.
11. Click Fit Screen in the Options bar to see the entire image again.

    You have used the Zoom tool in four different ways to change the magnification in the image window. Many of the other tools in the Tools panel can be used with keyboard combinations and options as well. You'll have opportunities to use these techniques as you work through the lessons in this chapter.
12. Save the file as **L7_start_xx.psd** in the location where your teacher instructs you to store the files for this lesson, and leave it open

Brightening an Image

One of the most common edits you're likely to make is to brighten an image taken with a digital camera or phone. You'll brighten this image by changing its brightness and contrast values.

Try It!

1. In the Layers panel, on the right side of the workspace, make sure the Rose layer is selected.

2. In the Adjustments panel, which is above the Layers panel in the panel dock, click the Brightness/Contrast icon to add a Brightness/Contrast adjustment layer. The Properties panel opens, displaying the Brightness/Contrast settings.

3. In the Properties panel, move the Brightness slider to **98** and the Contrast slider to **18**.

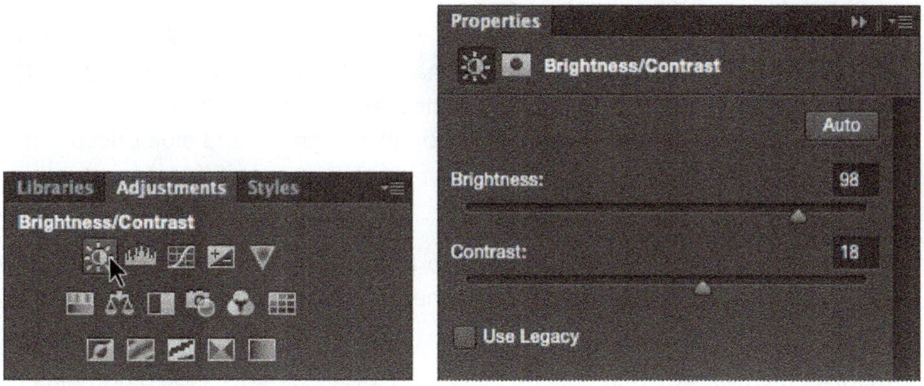

The image of the rose brightens.

In these lessons, you'll be instructed to enter specific numbers in panels and dialog boxes to achieve particular effects. When you're working on your own projects, experiment with different values to see how they affect your image. There is no right or wrong setting; the values you should use depend on the results you want.

4. In the Layers panel, examine the Brightness/Contrast adjustment layer.

   Adjustment layers let you make changes to your image, such as adjusting the brightness of the rose, without affecting the actual pixels. Because you've used an adjustment layer, you can always return to the original image by hiding or deleting the adjustment layer—and you can edit the adjustment layer at any time. You'll use adjustment layers in several lessons in this book.

   Layering is one of the fundamental and most powerful features in Photoshop. Photoshop includes many kinds of layers, some of which contain images, text, or solid colors, and others that simply interact with layers below them. You'll learn more about layers throughout this chapter.

5. Click the double arrows at the top of the Properties panel to close it.

6. Save **L7_start_xx.psd**, and leave it open.

7. If necessary, click OK in the Photoshop Format Options dialog box.

   You've just completed your first task in Photoshop. Your image is bright and punchy and ready for a birthday card.

Working with Color in Photoshop

RGB Model

A large percentage of the visible spectrum can be represented by mixing red, green, and blue (RGB) colored light in various proportions and intensities. Where the colors overlap, they create cyan, magenta, yellow, and white.

Because the RGB colors combine to create white, they are also called additive colors. Adding all colors together creates white—that is, all light is transmitted back to the eye. Additive colors are used for lighting, video, and monitors. Your monitor, for example, creates color by emitting light through red, green, and blue phosphors.

CMYK Model

The CMYK model is based on the light-absorbing quality of ink printed on paper. As white light strikes translucent inks, part of the spectrum is absorbed, while other parts are reflected back to your eyes.

In theory, pure cyan (C), magenta (M), and yellow (Y) pigments should combine to absorb all color and produce black. For this reason, these colors are called subtractive colors. But because all printing inks contain some impurities, these three inks actually produce a muddy brown, and must be combined with black (K) ink to produce a true black. (K is used instead of B to avoid confusion with blue.) Combining these inks to reproduce color is called four-color process printing.

Sampling a Color

By default, the foreground color in Photoshop is black and the background color is white. You can change the foreground and background colors in several ways. One way is to use the Eyedropper tool to sample a color from the image. You'll use the Eyedropper tool to sample the blue of one ribbon so that you can match that color when you create another ribbon.

First, you'll need to display the Ribbons layer so you can see the color you want to sample.

Try It!

1. In the Layers panel, click the Visibility column for the Ribbons layer to make the layer visible, if necessary. When a layer is visible, an eye icon appears in that column.

A ribbon with "Happy Birthday" written on it appears in the image window.

2. Select the Ribbons layer in the Layers panel so that it's the active layer.
3. Select the Eyedropper tool in the Tools panel.
4. Click the blue area in the Happy Birthday ribbon to sample a blue color.

   The foreground color changes in the Tools panel and the Color panel. Anything you draw will be this color until you change the foreground color again.
5. Save **L7_start_xx.ps**d and leave it open.

Working with Tools and Tool Properties

When you selected the Zoom tool in the previous exercise, you saw that the Options bar provided ways for you to change the view of the current image window. Now you'll learn more about setting tool properties using context menus, the Options bar, panels, and panel menus. You'll use all of these methods as you work with tools to add the second ribbon to your birthday card.

Using Context Menus

Context menus are short menus that contain commands and options appropriate to specific elements in the work area. They are sometimes referred to as "right-click" or "shortcut" menus. Usually, the commands on a context menu are also available in some other area of the user interface, but using the context menu can save time.

> **Context Menus**
>
> Short menus that contain commands appropriate to specific elements in the work area and which are displayed with a right click.

Try It!

1. Select the Zoom tool, and zoom in so you can clearly see the lower third of the card.
2. Select the Rectangular Marquee tool in the Tools panel.

   The Rectangular Marquee tool selects rectangular areas.
3. Drag the Rectangular Marquee tool to create a selection about 1/2 inch tall and 2 inches wide, ending at the right edge of the card.

   Selection areas are shown by moving dotted lines, sometimes referred to as **marching ants**.
4. Select the Brush tool in the Tools panel.
5. In the image window, right-click (Windows) or Control-click (Mac) anywhere in the image to open the Brush tool context menu.

   Context menus vary with their context, so you might see a menu of commands or a panel-like set of options, which is what happens in this case.

> **Marching Ants**
>
> The moving dotted lines that make up the selection.

6. Select the first brush (Soft Round), and change the size to 65 pixels.

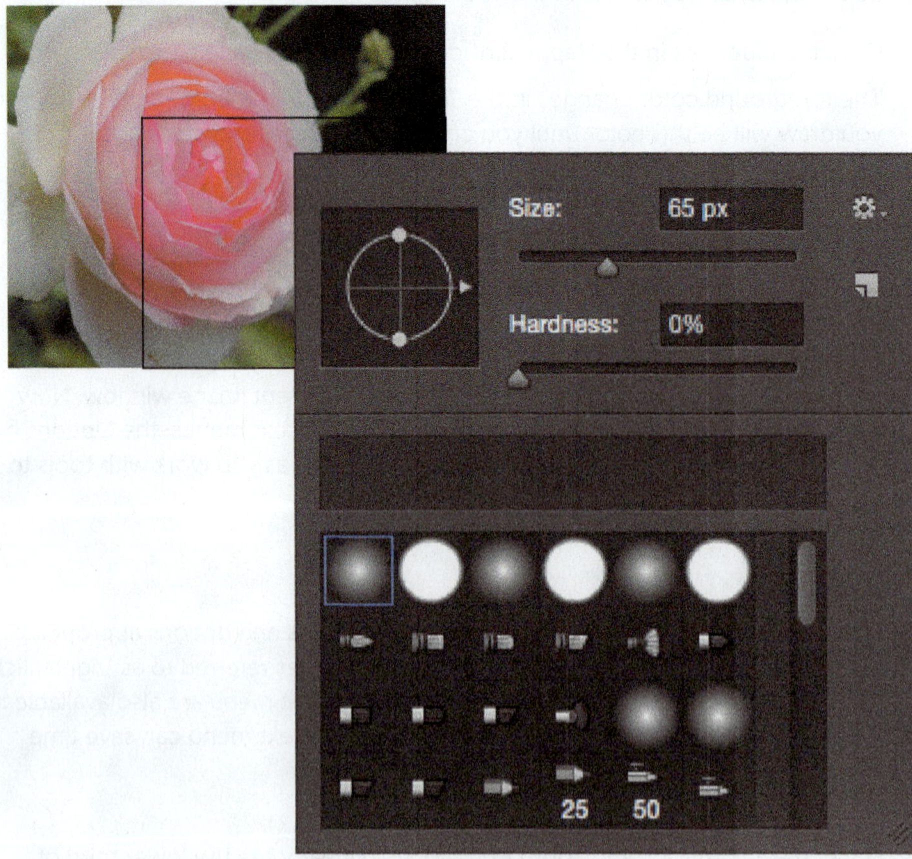

7. Click anywhere outside the selection to close the panel.
8. Drag the cursor across the selected area until it's fully painted blue. Don't worry about staying within the selection; you can't affect anything outside the selection as you paint.
9. When the bar is colored in, choose Select > Deselect so that nothing is selected.

   The selection is gone, but the blue bar remains.
10. Save **L7_start_xx.psd** and leave it open.

Selecting and Using a Hidden Tool

Photoshop has many tools you can use to edit image files, but you will probably work with only a few of them at a time. The Tools panel arranges some of the tools in groups, with only one tool shown for each group. The other tools in the group are hidden behind that tool. You'll use the Polygonal Lasso tool to remove a triangular notch from the color bar so that it matches the ribbon at the top of the card.

A small triangle in the lower right corner of a button is your clue that other tools are available but hidden under that tool.

Try It!

1. Position the pointer over the third tool from the top in the Tools panel until the tooltip appears. The tool-tip identifies the Lasso tool, and its keyboard shortcut of L. Select the Lasso tool.
2. Select the Polygonal Lasso tool, which is hidden behind the Lasso tool, using one of the following methods:
    - Press and hold the mouse button over the Lasso tool to open the pop-up list of hidden tools, and select the Polygonal Lasso tool.
    - Alt-click (Windows) or Option-click (Mac OS) the tool button in the Tools panel to cycle through the hidden lasso tools until the Polygonal Lasso tool is selected.
    - Press Shift+L, which cycles between the Lasso, Polygonal Lasso, and Magnetic Lasso tools tools.

    With the Lasso tool, you can draw free-form selections; the Polygonal Lasso tool makes it easier to draw straight-edged sections of a selection border.
3. Move the pointer over the left edge of the blue color bar that you just painted. Click just to the left of the upper left corner of the bar to start your selection. You should begin your selection just outside the colored area.
4. Move the cursor to the right about 1/4 inch, and click about halfway between the top and bottom of the bar. You're creating the first side of the triangle. It doesn't need to be perfect.
5. Click just to the left of the bottom left corner of the bar to create the second side of the triangle.
6. Click the point where you started to finish the triangle or double-click on the canvas with the tool.

7. Press the Delete key on your keyboard to delete the selected area from the colored bar, creating a notch for your ribbon.
8. Choose Select > Deselect to deselect the area you deleted.

    The ribbon is ready. Now you can add a name to your birthday card.
9. Save **L7_start_xx.psd** and leave it open.

Setting Text Formats in the Options Bar

Next you'll use the Options bar to select the text properties and add type to the image.

Try It!

1. In the Tools panel, select the Horizontal Type tool.

   The buttons and menus in the Options bar now relate to the Type tool.

2. In the Options bar, select a font of your choice from the first pop-up menu. (Minion Pro Italic is used in the data file).

3. Specify **32 pt** for the font size.

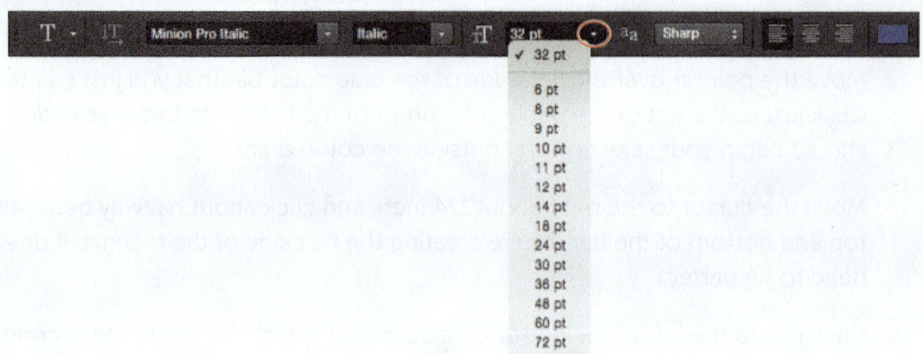

   You can specify 32 points by typing directly in the font size text box and pressing Enter or Return, or by scrubbing the font size menu label. You can also choose a standard font size from the font size pop-up menu.

4. Click once anywhere on the left side of the colored bar, and type **Elaine**. Or you can type a different name, if you like. Don't worry if the text isn't positioned well; you'll correct that later.

   The text is the same color as the bar you typed it on. You'll fix that next.

5. Save **L7_start_xx.psd** and leave it open.

Tip:

You can place the pointer over the labels of most numeric settings in the tool Options bar, in panels, and in dialog boxes in order to display a "scrubby slider." Dragging the pointing-finger slider to the right increases the value; dragging to the left decreases the value. Alt-dragging (Windows) or Option-dragging (Mac OS) changes the values in smaller increments; Shift-dragging changes them in larger increments.

Using Panels and Panel Menus

The text color is the same as the Foreground Color swatch in the Tools panel, which is the blue color you used to paint the bar. You'll select the text and choose another color from the Swatches panel.

Try It!

1. Make sure the Horizontal Type tool is selected in the Tools panel.

2. Drag the Horizontal Type tool across the text to select the full name or double-click.

3. Click the Swatches tab to bring that panel forward, if it's not already visible.
4. Select any light-colored swatch. (Pastel yellow is selected in the figure below.)

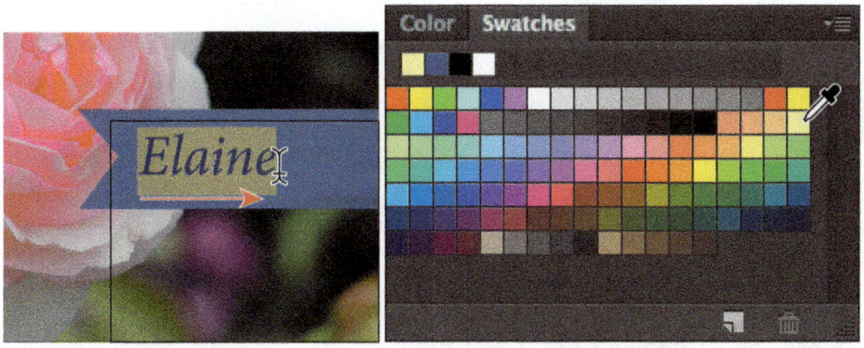

   The color you select appears in three places: as the Foreground Color in the Tools panel, in the text color swatch in the Options bar, and in the text you selected in the image window.

5. Select another tool in the Tools panel, such as the Move tool, to deselect the text so that you can see the text color.

   You might find it easier to select a color if you change the Swatches panel display.

6. Click the menu button on the Swatches panel to open the panel menu, and choose Small List.

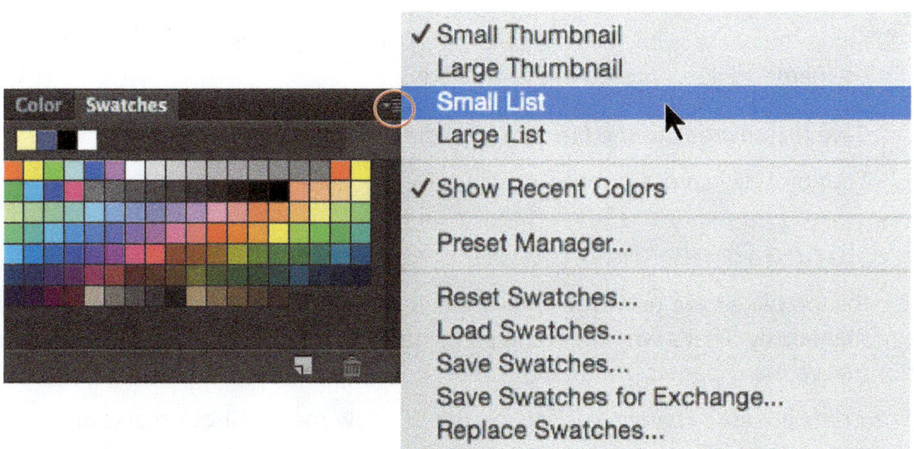

7. Select the Horizontal Type tool and reselect the text, as you did in steps 1 and 2.
8. In the Swatches panel, scroll about halfway down the list to find the Light Yellow Orange swatch, and then select it.
9. Select the Move tool again to deselect the text.

   Now the text appears in the orange color.

10. Save **L7_start_xx.psd** and leave it open.

Undoing Actions in Photoshop

In a perfect world, you'd never make a mistake. You'd never click the wrong object. You'd always correctly anticipate how specific actions would bring your design ideas to life exactly as you imagined them. You'd never have to backtrack.

For the real world, Photoshop gives you the power to step back and undo actions so that you can try other options. You can experiment freely, knowing that you can reverse the process.

Even beginning computer users quickly come to appreciate the familiar Undo command. You'll use it to move back one step, and then step further backward. In this case, you'll go back to the light color that you originally chose for the name.

> **Note:**
>
> When editing text don't select the Move tool using the V keyboard shortcut, because you're in text-entry mode. Typing V will add the letter to your text in the image window.
>
> **Note:**
>
> The Undo command isn't available if you've already saved your changes. However, you can still use the Step Backward command and the History panel, as long as you haven't closed the project since you made the changes.

Try It!

1. Choose Edit > Undo Edit Type Layer, or press Ctrl+Z (Windows) or Command+Z (Mac OS) to undo your last action.

   The name returns to its previous color.

2. Choose Edit > Redo Edit Type Layer, or press Ctrl+Z (Windows) or Command+Z (Mac OS) to reapply the orange color to the name.

   The Undo command in Photoshop reverses only one step. This is a practicality, because Photoshop files can be very large, and maintaining multiple Undo steps can tie up a lot of memory, which tends to degrade performance. If you press Ctrl+Z or Command+Z again, Photoshop restores the step you removed initially.

   However, you can often use the Step Backward and Step Forward commands (on the Edit menu) to move through multiple steps.

3. Once the name is back to the color you'd like it to be, use the Move tool to drag the name so it's centered in the blue bar.

4. Save the changes to the file, and then close it.

   Your birthday card is done!

Exploring Photoshop Panels

Photoshop panels are powerful and varied. Rarely would you need to see all panels simultaneously. That's why they're in panel groups, and why the default configurations leave many panels unopened.

The complete list of panels appears on the Window menu. Check marks appear next to the names of the panels that are open and active in their panel groups. You can open a closed panel or close an open one by selecting the panel name on the Window menu.

You can hide all panels at once—including the Options bar and Tools panel—by pressing the Tab key. To reopen them, press Tab again.

You already used panels in the panel dock when you used the Layers and Swatches panels. You can drag panels to or from the panel dock. This is convenient for bulky panels or ones that you use only occasionally but want to keep handy.

You can arrange panels in other ways, as well:

- To move an entire panel group, drag the title bar to another location in the work area.
- To move a panel to another group, drag the panel tab into that panel group so that a blue highlight appears inside the group, and then release the mouse button.

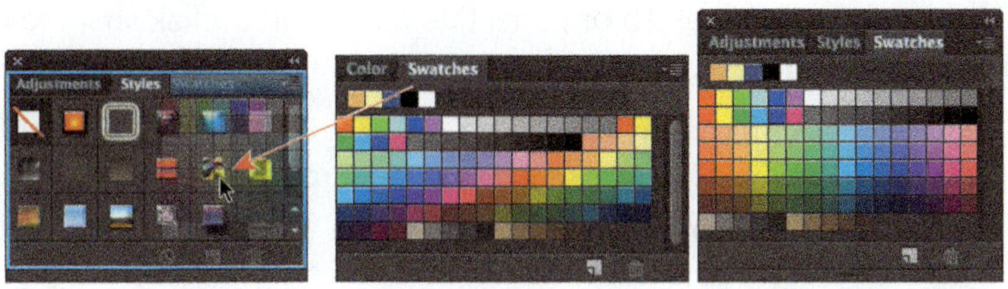

- To dock a panel or panel group, drag the title bar or panel tab onto the top of the dock.

- To undock a panel or panel group so that it becomes a floating panel or panel group, drag its title bar or panel tab away from the dock.

Expanding and Collapsing Panels

You can resize panels to use screen space more efficiently and to see fewer or more panel options, either by dragging or clicking to toggle between preset sizes:

- To collapse open panels to icons, click the double arrow in the title bar of the dock or panel group. To expand a panel, click its icon or the double arrow.

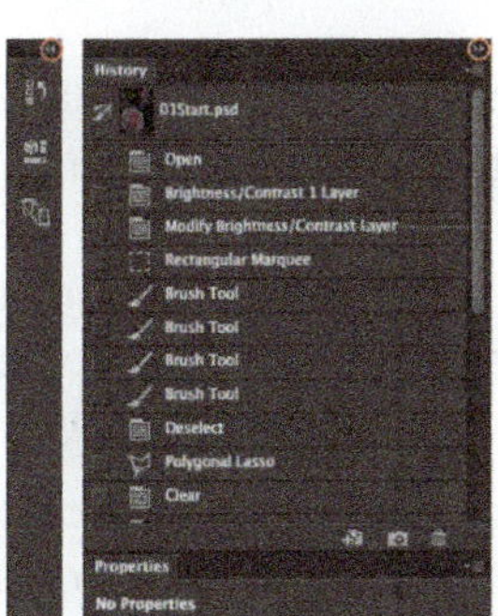

- To change the height of a panel, drag its lower right corner.

- To change the width of the dock, position the pointer on the left edge of the dock until it becomes a double-headed arrow, and then drag to the left to widen the dock, or to the right to narrow it.
- To resize a floating panel, move the pointer over the right, left, or bottom edge of the panel until it becomes a double-headed arrow, and then drag the edge in or out. You can also pull the lower right corner in or out.
- To collapse a panel group so that only the dock header bar and tabs are visible, double-click a panel tab or panel title bar. Double-click again to restore it to the expanded view. You can open the panel menu even when the panel is collapsed.

You will notice that the tabs for the panels in the panel group and the button for the panel menu remain visible after you collapse a panel.

Special Notes about the Tools Panel and Options Bar

The Tools panel and the Options bar share some characteristics with other panels:

- You can drag the Tools panel by its title bar to a different location in the work area. You can move the Options bar to another location by dragging the grab bar at the far left end of the panel.
- You can hide the Tools panel and Options bar.

However, some panel features are not available or don't apply to the Tools panel or options bar:

- You cannot group the Tools panel or Options bar with other panels.
- You cannot resize the Tools panel or Options bar.
- You cannot stack the Tools panel or Options bar in the panel dock.
- The Tools panel and Options bar do not have panel menus.

Creating Career Search Documents

Employers often consider tens or even hundreds of candidates for every job opening. Sometimes they shuffle through stacks of letters or field multiple phone calls. How can you make a positive impression and show you are serious and qualified for the job?

You can prepare professional, accurate job search materials, including a resume, cover letter, list of references, and thank-you note.

- A **resume** is a written summary of your work-related skills, experience, and education. It introduces you to the prospective employer by presenting a snapshot of your qualifications. It should be brief and to the point, printed on white paper, true and accurate, and be free of typographical, grammatical, or spelling errors. A good resume attracts the interest of the reader so he or she wants to learn more about you.
- A **cover letter**, or letter of interest, is sent a long with your resume. It introduces you to a potential employer and highlights the qualities that make you suitable for the position you want. It also helps convince employers to review your resume by focusing attention on specific resume information; for example, credentials, skills, or specific projects in your portfolio of design work.

Resume

A written summary of your work-related skills, experience, and education that you send to a potential employer

Cover Letter

A letter to a potential employer you send with a resume to introduce yourself, express interest in the position, and highlight key information.

- A list of **references** includes the names and contact information of people who know you and your qualifications and who are willing to speak about you to potential employers.
- A **thank-you note** reminds the interviewer that you are serious about the job. You send it to the employer after an interview to show your interest in the position.

References

People who know you and your personal and work-related qualities and will speak on your behalf to potential employers.

Thank-you Letter

A letter you write to thank a potential employer for considering you for the position.

What Do I Include on My Resume?

A typical resume has four main sections:

- Contact information: Include your full name, address, telephone number, and e-mail address at the top of the page.
- Objective: A statement that describes your career goal. It should be short and clear. You can have a general, long-term goal as your objective, or you can customize your resume for a specific position.
- Education: If you have little work experience, it is important to highlight your education. List the name, city, and state of every school where you earned a degree, starting with high school. Include the years you attended the school, the degree/diploma you earned, and any special courses or certificates that relate to your career. You might want to include your grade point average as well.
- Work experience: Include all full-time and part-time jobs, internships, apprenticeships, and volunteer experience, starting with the most recent experience first. Include employment dates, job titles, company names, city, and state. Briefly describe your main responsibility, and list your duties and accomplishments. Be specific. If you have work experience, you might want to put this section before Education.

You may also include a Skills section for listing job skills such as your ability to use computers or special equipment, such as a digital camera or video recording equipment. You might also want to include a Personal Information section that lists co-curricular activities, awards, and honors. You can include all clubs and organizations of which you are a member, and things you do in your school or community.

Here are some general best practice guidelines for a professional resume:

- Include a list of schools you attended, with dates and degrees you have earned.
- Include your work history, including internships and volunteer work. Emphasize jobs where you gained relevant experience, summarizing your responsibilities and skills with bullet lists.
- List all licenses and certifications you have earned.
- List relevant work samples, and/or provide links to an online portfolio where employers can view digital versions of your work.

Consider these tips when preparing a resume:

- Make it easy to read.
- Use one, easy-to-read font, and apply different font styles and sizes for emphasis.
- Bullets are effective for making lines of text stand out.
- Use proper spelling, punctuation, grammar, and use of any technical terms.

- Keep it to one page, if possible; two pages at the most. (If you use two pages, be sure to put your name in the header or footer on page 2, in case it becomes separated from page 1.)
- If you are printing the document, use plain white paper. Do not include a personal photograph.

For your reference list, select at least three people, and ask them for permission to use them as a reference. A good references knows your positive work qualities and values, understands your abilities and interests, and can describe how you behave in a work environment. People such as relatives and friends should not be used as references because they may not be objective about your and your strengths and weaknesses.

When applying for a job, some potential employers may ask you to fill out an application form—sometimes online and sometimes on paper. Application forms require you to enter specific information about your education and past employment, including dates and locations. As with your resume, it is important to be truthful and accurate.

If an employer thinks you have the qualifications for the job, you will be invited for a job interview. A preliminary interview may be by phone but almost all employers will expect a face-to-face meeting. The interview is an opportunity for you and the interviewer to ask questions and decide if the position is right for you. You should prepare for the interview by researching the company and the position and practicing the answers to questions you think the employer might ask. You should also prepare a few questions that you can ask the employer.

After the interview, you should write a thank-you note. A thank-you note reminds the interviewer that you are serious about wanting the job. You use a thank-you note to restate your interest in the job and your qualifications and to thank the interviewer for spending time with you. Refer to something specific that you discussed during the interview. Address the note to the person who interviewed you. It may be acceptable to send a thank-you note by e-mail, but mailing an actual printed letter will make a positive impression.

Creating a Portfolio

A portfolio is a collection of information, documents, and samples of current work. It is a tool to share with potential employers that shows the progress you make in school and in your career plan as well as your abilities and achievements. A portfolio typically contains your resume, cover letter, and list of references. If you are pursuing a career in design of any sort, your portfolio should also include samples of your current work.

While many people use physical paper portfolios, more and more job seekers opt for digital portfolios that are saved to a flash drive, CD, Web page, or other online location. A digital portfolio contains the same items as a paper portfolio, except they are in digital format. Resumes, cover letters, and reference lists can be saved as Word documents or as PDFs. You can scan samples of your current work to save in digital format, or take photos of pieces that you then transfer to your computer.

A digital portfolio provides many advantages--especially for those in the field of Web and digital communications:

- It is ideal for showcasing your work in various media formats, including photography, digital imaging, audio recording, videography, and animation.
- It allows you to demonstrate your technology skills and expertise with certain software applications.
- A portfolio that is saved to a flash drive or CD is fairly simple and inexpensive to reproduce, and easy to transport.
- A portfolio that is stored online can be accessed by multiple individuals in multiple locations at any time of the day.

The work in your portfolio reflects who you are, what you are interested in, and what you can do creatively and technically. Once you enter the professional field, your portfolio will be much more important to a potential employer or client than the schools you have attended or degrees you have received. It's a good idea to keep your portfolio updated with your latest work so you can respond to opportunities quickly.

If you plan to pursue a career in Web and digital communications, your portfolio should include analytic and metaphoric concepts in pieces ranging from print-based solutions to interactive and motion designs. The selection of the projects you present should represent just who you are and what you are capable of achieving, so make your selections wisely. Don't include every project you did in school.

Ideally, at least one project should cross over from one media to another. For example, to demonstrate a complete visual identity, you can show a crafted logo design plus its application to a printed item (a business card, brochure, or advertisement), a three-dimensional object (a package, truck, or piece of clothing), and a digital solution (a web page or motion design).

If there are gaps in your portfolio, fill them. Invent projects if necessary. Create a new logo, rework an existing website, or develop a new interactive element. The process of observing, identifying, and solving problems out in the world helps to validate your qualifications to an employer or client. If you are just finishing school, a potential employer will not assume that you have a vast amount of work experience, but he or she might be impressed by your initiative to pursue design projects on your own.

Creating a career portfolio requires careful effort in both its content and presentation, but in the end, it is your best opportunity to showcase your skills and professional qualities.

Portfolio Presentation Ideas

Here are a few things to remember as you prepare your portfolio:

- You should include 10 to 15 samples of your work.
- Begin with a few of your best samples and finish with what you consider to be your very best work.
- If you are using a paper portfolio and have pieces of various sizes, mount them on one of two board sizes—small or large—for easier handling.
- Don't turn pages for reviewers; let them look through the portfolio at their own pace.
- Don't defend your work. Allow them to stand on their own merits. However, be prepared to speak about them, and explain your motivation, goals, and feelings about each piece.
- After your interview, send an e-mail message or short note to the reviewer, thanking the person for his or her time. Include an image of your best piece to serve as a reminder of who you are.

Comprehension Check

1. Describe two types of images you can open in Photoshop.
2. How do you select tools in Photoshop?
3. Describe two ways to zoom in to or out from an image.
4. What is the purpose of a cover letter?
5. Why is it important to proofread and edit all documents that you send to a potential employer?

Review Project

In this project, you will create a digital portfolio that you can add to as you complete activities and projects in this course. Create a **Digital Portfolio_your name** folder on a flash drive or to a location specified by your instructor. In your word processor, create a resume, a cover letter, and a list of references. Review the information covered in this lesson on what to include in each. You might also explore the use of online templates to create these documents.

When you have completed the documents, exchange them with a partner. Review your partner's documents and make edits and suggestions on how they could be improved. Return the documents and update as necessary. Save them to your Digital Portfolio folder in both your word processing file format and as PDFs. By saving in both formats, you can update your word processing file as needed and then re-save it as a PDF. You will want to remove the word processing files from the portfolio before sharing it.

Create a folder within the Digital Portfolio folder named **Samples**. If you have samples of work that demonstrate your creative and/or technical skills, save them to the Samples folder now.

Lesson 8 Overview

In this lesson, you will learn about:

- Developing a Strategy for Retouching
- Straightening and Cropping an Image in Photoshop
- Adjusting the Color and Tone
- Removing Imperfections with the Spot Healing Brush Tool
- Applying a Content-Aware Patch
- Repairing Areas with the Clone Stamp Tool
- Sharpening the Image

Photoshop includes a variety of tools and commands for improving the quality of a photographic image. This lesson steps you through the process of resizing and retouching a vintage photograph.

Developing a Strategy for Retouching

How much retouching you do depends on the image you're working on and your goals for it. For many images, you may need only to change the resolution, lighten the image, or repair a minor blemish. For others, you may need to perform several tasks and employ more advanced filters.

Organizing an Efficient Sequence of Tasks

Most retouching procedures follow these general steps, though not every task may be necessary for all projects:

- Duplicating the original image or scan; working in a copy of the image file makes it easy to recover the original later if necessary.
- Ensuring that the resolution is appropriate for the way you'll use the image.
- Cropping the image to its final size and orientation.
- Removing any color casts.
- Adjusting the overall contrast or tonal range of the image.
- Repairing flaws in scans of damaged photographs (such as rips, dust, or stains).
- Adjusting the color and tone in specific parts of the image to bring out highlights, midtones, shadows, and desaturated colors.
- Sharpening the overall focus of the image.

The order of the tasks may vary depending on the project, though you should always start by duplicating the image and adjusting its resolution. Likewise, sharpening should usually be your final step. For the other tasks, consider your project and plan accordingly, so that the results of one process do not cause unintended changes to other aspects of the image, making it necessary for you to redo some of your work.

Adjusting Your Process for Different Intended Uses

The retouching techniques you apply to an image depend in part on how you'll use the image. Whether an image is intended for black-and-white publication on newsprint or for full-color online distribution affects everything from the resolution of the initial scan to the type of tonal range and color correction that the image requires. Photoshop supports the CMYK color mode for preparing an image to be printed using process colors, as well as RGB and other color modes for web and mobile authoring.

Resolution and Image Size

The first step in retouching a photograph in Photoshop is to make sure that the image has an appropriate resolution. The term **resolution** refers to the number of small squares, known as **pixels,** that describe an image and establish its detail. Resolution is determined by **pixel dimensions**, or the number of pixels along the width and height of an image.

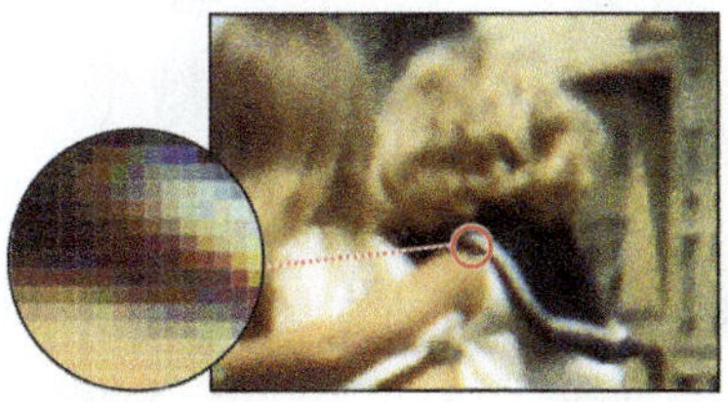

Resolution

The number of pixels in an image, determined by the number of pixels along the width and height of an image.

Pixels

The number of small squares that describe an image and establish its detail.

Pixel Dimensions

The number of pixels along the width and the height of an image.

Note:

To determine the necessary image resolution for a photograph you plan to print, follow the computer-graphics rule of thumb for color or grayscale images intended for print on large commercial printers: Scan at a resolution 1.5 to 2 times the screen frequency used by the printer. For example, if the image will be printed using a screen frequency of 133 lpi, scan the image at 200 ppi (133x1.5).

In computer graphics, there are different types of resolution:

The number of pixels per unit of length in an image is called the **image resolution**, usually measured in pixels per inch (ppi). An image with a high resolution has more pixels (and therefore a larger file size) than an image of the same dimensions with a low resolution. Images in Photoshop can vary from high resolution (300 ppi or higher) to low resolution (72 ppi or 96 ppi).

Image Resolution

The number of pixels per unit of length in an image, usually measured in pixels per inch (ppi).

Monitor Resolution

The number of pixels per unit of length on a monitor, usually measured in pixels per inch (ppi).

The number of pixels per unit of length on a monitor is the **monitor resolution**, also usually measured in pixels per inch (ppi). Image pixels are translated directly into monitor pixels. In Photoshop, if the image resolution is higher than the monitor resolution, the image appears larger onscreen than its specified print dimensions. For example, when you display a 1x1-inch, 144-ppi image on a 72-ppi monitor, the image fills a 2x2-inch area of the screen.

The number of ink dots per inch (dpi) produced by a platesetter or laser printer is the printer, or output, resolution. Higher resolution images output to higher resolution printers generally produce the best quality. The appropriate resolution for a printed image is determined both by the printer resolution and by the screen frequency, or lines per inch (lpi), of the halftone screens used to reproduce images.

Keep in mind that the higher the image resolution, the larger the file size, and the longer the file will take to print or to download from the Web.

Straightening and Cropping an Image in Photoshop

You'll use the Crop tool to straighten, trim, and scale the photograph. You can use either the Crop tool or the Crop command to crop an image. By default, cropping deletes the cropped pixels.

Try It!

1. Choose File > Open, to open the **L8_start.tif** file from the data files for this lesson. Click OK if you see the Embedded Profile Mismatch dialog box.

2. Save the file as **L8_start_xx.psd** (make sure you change the file type to Photoshop) in the location where your teacher instructs you to store the files for this lesson, and leave it open.

   Click OK if you see the Photoshop Format Options dialog box.

3. In the Tools panel, select the Crop tool.

   Crop handles appear, and a cropping shield covers the area outside the cropping selection.

4. In the Options bar, choose W x H x Resolution from the Preset Aspect Ratio menu. (Ratio is the default value.)

5. In the Options bar, type **7 in** for the width, **7 in** for the height, and **200** px/in for the resolution. A crop grid appears.

First, you'll straighten the image.

6. Click Straighten in the Options bar. The pointer changes to the Straighten tool.

7. Click at the top left corner of the photo and drag a straight line across the top edge.

   Photoshop straightens the image, so that the line you drew is parallel with the top of the image area. You drew a line across the top of the photo, but any line that defines either the vertical or horizontal axis of the image will work.

   Now, you'll trim the white border and scale the image.

8. Drag the corners of the crop grid inward to the corners of the photo itself to crop out the white border. If you need to adjust the position of the photo, click and drag it within the crop grid.

9. Press Enter or Return to accept the crop.

   The image is now cropped, and the cropped image fills the image window, straightened, sized, and positioned according to your specifications.

10. To see the image dimensions, choose Document Dimensions from the pop-up menu at the bottom of the application window.

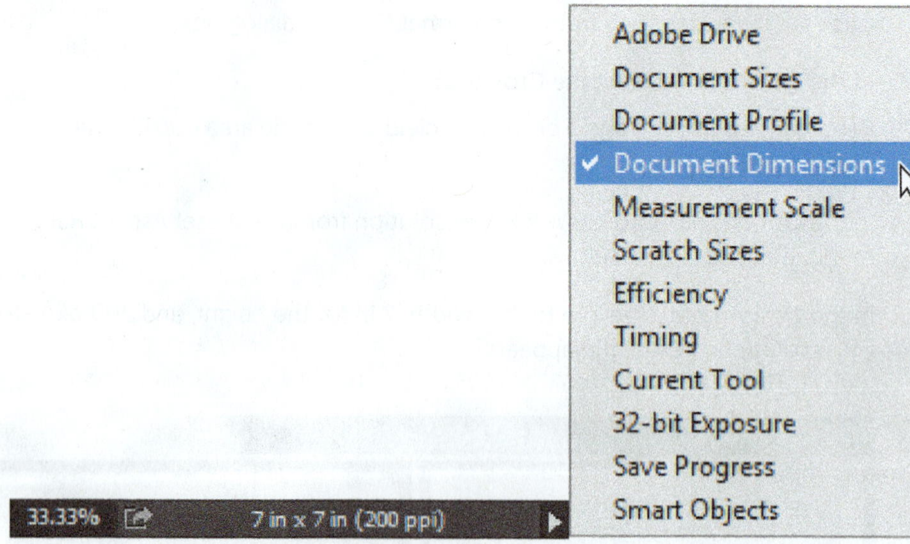

11. Choose File > Save to save your work.

Adjusting the Color and Tone

You'll use Curves and Levels adjustment layers to remove the color cast and adjust the color and tone in the image. Don't let the Curves or Levels options intimidate you. You'll work with them more in later lessons; for now, you'll take advantage of their tools to quickly brighten and adjust the tone of the image.

Try It!

1. Click Curves in the Adjustments panel to add a Curves adjustment layer.
2. Select the White Point tool on the left side of the Properties panel.

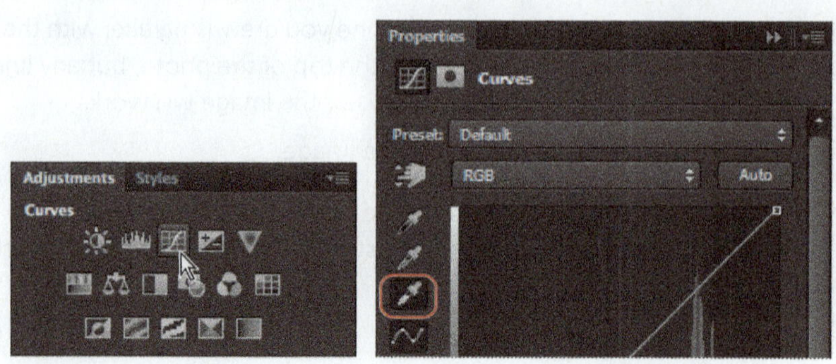

Specifying a white point changes all the colors in the image. The white point is the color that Photoshop defines as pure white, and it adjusts all other colors accordingly. To set an accurate white point, select a white area in the image.

3. Click a white stripe on the girl's dress.

   The color tone of the image changes dramatically. You can click different white areas, such as the child's sailor dress, a stripe on the woman's dress, or the girl's sock, to see how each selection changes the color.

   In some images, adjusting the white point is enough to remove a colorcast and correct the tone of the image. Here, selecting a white point is a good start. You'll use a Levels adjustment layer to fine-tune the tone.

4. Click Levels in the Adjustments panel to add a Levels adjustment layer.

   The Levels histogram in the Properties panel displays the range of dark and light values in the image. You'll learn more about working with levels in later lessons. Right now, you just need to know that the left triangle represents the black point (the point Photoshop defines as the darkest in the image), the right triangle represents the white point (the lightest in the image), and the middle triangle represents the midtones.

5. Drag the left triangle (blacks) under the histogram to the right, where the blacks are more pronounced. Our value was **15**.

6. Drag the middle triangle a little to the right to adjust the midtones. Our value was **.90**.

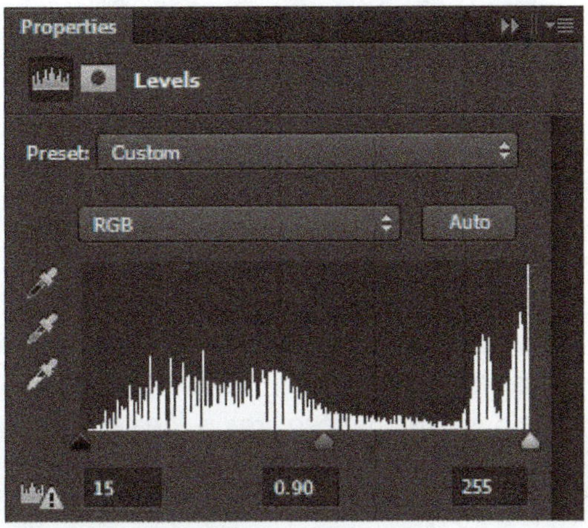

Now that you've adjusted the color, you'll flatten the image so it's easier to work with while you touch it up. Flattening an image merges its layers. After you flatten an image, you can no longer edit layers individually, but the file is smaller, and you can easily make changes to the entire image at once.

7. Choose Layer > Flatten Image.

   The adjustment layers merge with the Background layer.

8. Save the changes to **L8_start_xx.psd**, and leave it open.

Removing Imperfections with the Spot Healing Brush Tool

The next task is to remove the crease in the photo. You'll use the Spot Healing Brush tool to erase the crease. While you're at it, you'll use it to address a few other issues.

The Spot Healing Brush tool quickly removes blemishes and other imperfections. It samples pixels around the retouched area and matches the texture, lighting, transparency, and shading of the sampled pixels to the pixels being healed.

The Spot Healing Brush tool is excellent for retouching blemishes in portraits, but also works nicely wherever there's a uniform appearance near the areas you want to retouch.

Try It!

1. Zoom in to see the crease clearly.
2. In the Tools panel, select the Spot Healing Brush tool.
3. In the Options bar, open the Brush pop-up panel, and specify a size of about **25 px** in diameter and a **100%** hard brush. Make sure Content-Aware is selected in the Options bar.

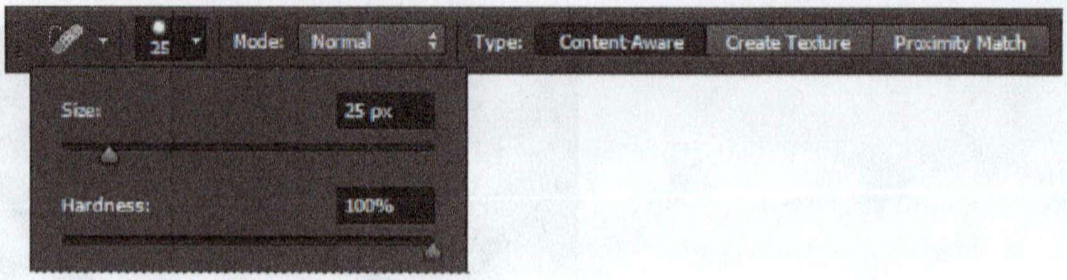

4. In the image window, drag the Spot Healing Brush down from the top of the crease. You can probably repair the entire crease with four to six neat downward strokes. As you drag, the stroke at first appears black, but when you release the mouse, the painted area is "healed."

5. Zoom in to see the white hair in the upper right area of the image. Then select the Spot Healing Brush tool again, and paint over the hair.
6. Zoom out, if necessary, to see the full sky. Then click the Spot Healing Brush tool wherever there are dark areas you want to heal.
7. Save the changes to **L8_start_xx.psd**, and leave it open.

Applying a Content Aware Patch

Use the Patch tool to remove unwanted elements from an image. You'll use a content-aware patch to remove an unrelated person from the right side of the photo. In Content-Aware mode, the Patch tool creates nearly seamless blending with the nearby content.

Try It!

1. In the Tools panel, select the Patch tool, hidden beneath the Spot Healing Brush tool.
2. In the Options bar, choose Content-Aware from the Patch mode menu. Type 4 into the Structure slider.

   The Structure menu determines how closely the patch reflects the existing image patterns. You can choose from 1 to 7, with 1 allowing the loosest adherence to the source structure and 7 requiring the strictest.

3. Drag the Patch tool around the boy and his shadow, as closely as possible. You may want to zoom in to see him more clearly.
4. Click within the area you've just selected, and drag it to the left. Photoshop displays a preview of the content that will replace the boy. Keep dragging to the left until the preview area no longer overlaps the area occupied by the boy, but without overlapping the woman or the girl she's holding. Release the mouse button when the patch is positioned where you want it.

   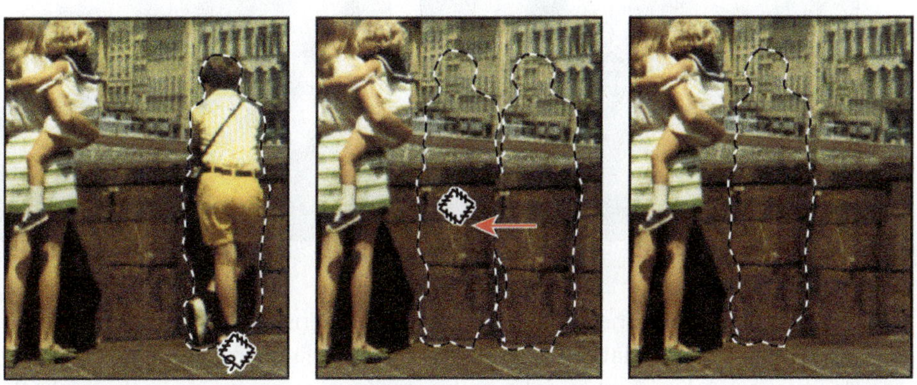

   The selection changes to match the area around it. The boy is gone, and where he stood is a section of the bridge wall and of a building.

5. Choose Select > Deselect.

   The effect was pretty impressive, but not quite perfect. You'll touch up the results next.

6. Save the changes to **L8_start_xx.psd**, and leave it open.

Repairing Areas with the Clone Stamp Tool

The Clone Stamp tool uses pixels from one area of an image to replace the pixels in another part of the image. Using this tool, you can not only remove unwanted objects from your images, but you can also fill in missing areas in photographs you scan from damaged originals.

You'll use the Clone Stamp tool to smooth out some irregularities in the height of the bridge wall and the windows on the building.

Try It!

1. Select the Clone Stamp tool in the Tools panel. From the Brush Preset Picker, select a **60** px brush with **30%** hardness. Make sure that the Aligned option is selected.

2. Move the Clone Stamp tool to an area where the top of the bridge wall is smooth. That's the area you want to copy to smooth out the area that was patched.
3. Alt-click (Windows) or Option-click (Mac), drag the Clone Stamp tool across the top of the bridge wall in the patched area to even it out, and then release the mouse button. (When you press Alt or Option, the pointer appears as target cross hairs.)

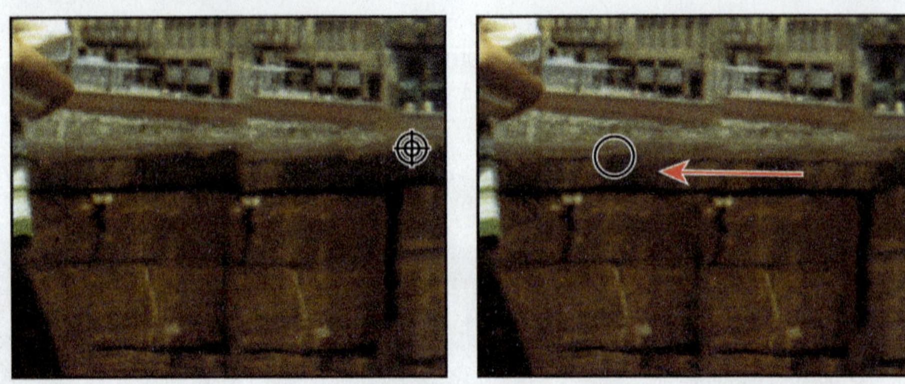

Each time you click the Clone Stamp tool, it begins again with a new source point, in the same relationship to the tool as the first stroke you made. That is, if you begin painting further right, it samples from stone that is further right than the original source point. That's because Aligned is selected in the Options bar. Deselect Aligned if you want to start from the same source point each time.

4. Select a source point where the bottom of the bridge wall is even, and then drag the Clone Stamp tool across the bottom of the wall where you patched it.
5. Select a smaller brush size, and deselect Aligned. Then select a source point over the rightmost windows in the lowest row on the building you patched. Click across to create accurate windows there.

6. Repeat step 5 to make any adjustments you want to apply to the lowest area of the building and the wall that runs in front of it.
7. If you like, you can use a smaller brush size to touch up the stones in the patched portion of the wall.
8. Save the changes to the file, and leave it open.

Sharpening the Image

The last task you might want to do when retouching a photo is to sharpen the image. There are several ways to sharpen an image in Photoshop, but the Smart Sharpen filter gives you the most control. Because sharpening can emphasize artifacts, you'll remove those first.

Try It!

1. Zoom in to about **400%** to see the boy's shirt clearly. The colored dots you see are artifacts of the scanning process.
2. Choose Filter > Noise > Dust & Scratches.
3. In the Dust & Scratches dialog box, leave the default settings with a Radius of **1** pixel and Threshold at 0, and click OK.

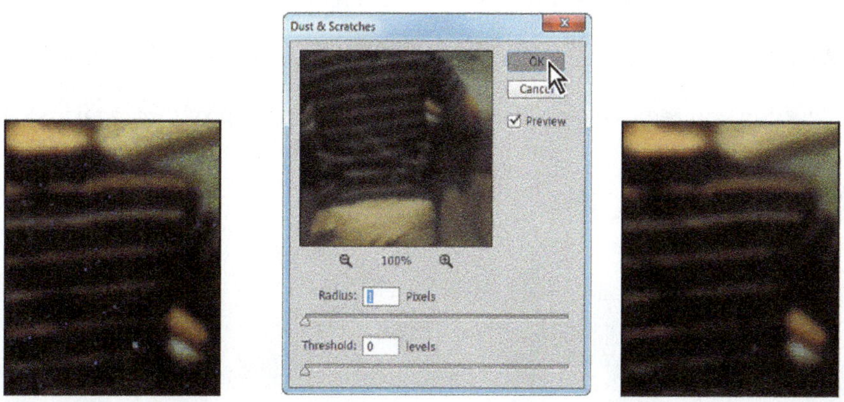

   The Threshold value determines how dissimilar the pixels should be before they are eliminated. The Radius value determines the size of the area searched for dissimilar pixels. The default values are great for tiny dots of color like the ones in this image.

4. Now that the artifacts are gone, you can sharpen the image.
5. Choose Filter > Sharpen > Smart Sharpen.
6. In the Smart Sharpen dialog box, make sure that Preview is selected, so you can see the effect of settings you adjust in the image window.

   You can drag inside the preview window in the dialog box to see different parts of the image, or use the plus and minus buttons below the thumbnail to zoom in and out.

7. Make sure Lens Blur is chosen in the Remove menu.

   You can choose to remove Lens Blur, Gaussian Blur, or Motion Blur in the Smart Sharpen dialog box. Lens Blur provides finer sharpening of detail and reduced sharpening halos. Gaussian Blur increases contrast along the edges in an image. Motion Blur reduces the effects of blur that resulted from the camera or the subject moving when the photo was taken.

8. Drag the Amount slider to about **60%** to sharpen the image.

9. Drag the Radius slider to about **1.5**.

   The Radius value determines the number of pixels surrounding the edge pixels that affect the sharpening. The higher the resolution, the higher the Radius setting should usually be.

10. When you're satisfied with the results, click OK to apply the Smart Sharpen filter.

11. Save the changes to **L8_start_xx.psd**, and close the file.

Comprehension Check

1. What does resolution mean?
2. What does the Crop tool do?
3. How can you adjust the tone and color of an image in Photoshop?
4. What tools can you use to remove blemishes in an image?
5. How can you remove digital artifacts such as colored pixels from an image?

Lesson 9 Overview

In this lesson, you will learn about:

- Evaluating a Photograph
- Measuring Light
- Recognizing Camera Settings
- Exploring Bracketing
- Transfer Photos to a Computer
- Understand Safety Considerations
- Using the Rule of Thirds
- Explaining Fair Use and Appropriation

Commercial photography includes any career in which you take photographs for commercial use, which means to make money. Some examples include sports photographers, food photographers, or portrait photographers, all of whom might sell their photos for a variety of uses such as magazines, Web sites, posters, brochures, or merchandise.

In this lesson, you will learn the basics of how to capture a photographic image. The process of creating a photograph is nearly the opposite of the process of creating vector illustrations. For instance, when you begin to create a vector illustration, you start with a blank page (or a white Adobe Illustrator artboard). Vector illustration is an additive process—you add dots, lines, or shapes to the composition. Photography necessitates a process of selective reduction. Instead of adding to the empty canvas, photographers frame their surroundings to capture just the right moment in time. Compositional design elements are still active within the frame, but technological components relating to the camera referred to as the hardware—play a large role in the resulting image.

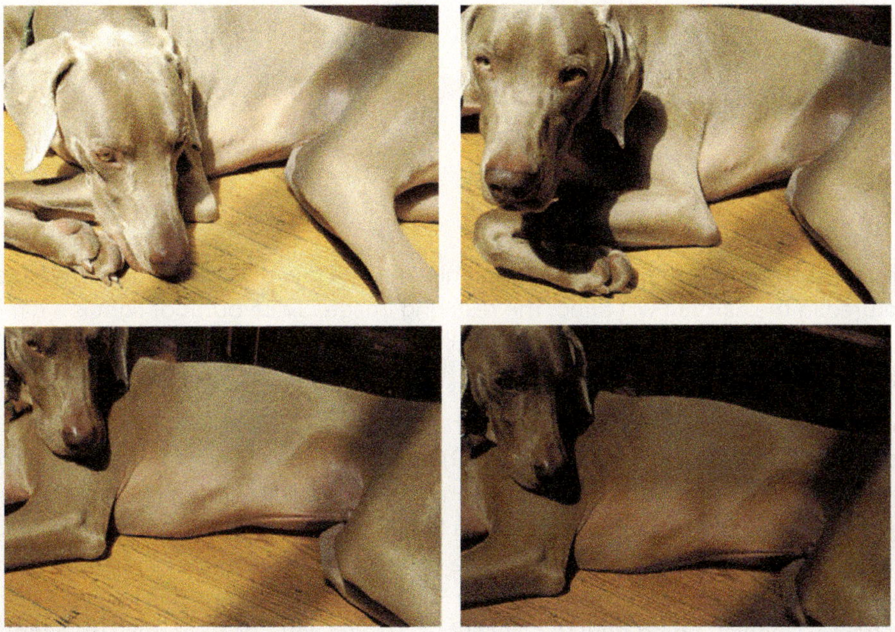

Composition

The way elements in an image are organized and arranged in relation to one another.

Layout

The way graphics are organized relative to other objects, text, and white space on a page, canvas, frame, or screen.

Digital Single Lens Reflex Camera (DSLR)

A digital still image camera that uses a single lens reflex (SLR) mechanism.

Evaluating a Photograph

Creating a successful image requires an understanding of how to use photographic **composition** and **layout**.

A successful photograph demonstrates the principles of design to achieve the artist's desired effect. Recall that the principles include:

- Balance
- Proportion
- Emphasis
- Repetition
- Contrast
- Unity
- Harmony
- Variety

When evaluating an image, consider the following:

- The composition
- The artist's intent
- How it impacts you emotionally
- The layout
- The level of technical success

Measuring Light

Light is essential for creating a photographic image. How the light is measured and captured in the camera will affect the resulting image. Since outdoor light is a direct product of the sun and moon, the amount of natural light in a photograph also relates to the time of day.

The amount of light required to make a photograph is measured with a meter. In the predigital era, some single-lens reflex (SLR) cameras had built-in light meters, while large-format cameras did not. External light meters are still used today in photography studios. Digital SLR cameras include a built-in light meter. The light meter registers the amount of light that's either in the center of the frame, averaged throughout the frame, or—for some cameras with the "spot" option—at a specific location within the frame. Understanding how to adjust your camera settings to comply with the light meter specifications requires you to understand the role of the f-stop and shutter speed camera controls. The light meter reading will show you how much light will be required to make a legible exposure for a balanced combination of f-stop and shutter speed settings. Generally, the purpose of your exposure will be to present photographic details at the extreme areas of contrast in the image. That means you'll want to capture details in the highlights and details in the shadows.

If you're shooting in automatic mode or can't control these settings, you'll simply point and shoot, and then hope for the best. Be careful when composing images in high-contrast lighting situations. Avoid shooting at or near noon, when the sun and shadows are strongest. And avoid low-light situations.

If you're working in manual mode, once you know how much light you need, balance the f-stop and shutter speed settings. Your choices about these two settings will depend on the depth of field (in the case of aperture) and movement (shutter speed) you want to include.

Some cameras let you create photographs in "aperture priority" or "shutter speed priority" modes. This means you can choose which of those two features you want to control. The camera will set the opposing lighting variable according to the choice you make.

Camera Mechanics

Basic operations take place when you create a photograph with your digital camera. There may be many adjustments to the camera that you can make, if your camera gives you control over them. These will have a direct result on the aesthetics of the resulting photograph. Most cameras also have an automatic setting, which lets you simply point and shoot. Even if you're just pressing the button, each of the following steps will take place.

Try It!

1. Before shooting, consider adjusting the white balance, ISO, and file size settings. Or, just let the camera do that work for you. (Your camera might not allow you to control some of these settings.)
2. Frame a scene by placing your eye to the viewfinder or by peering at the LCD screen on the back of the camera. Many DSLRs don't allow use of the LCD during shooting. If you have both options, consider the pros and cons of each.
3. After the image is framed, decide whether to shoot in automatic or manual mode. Do you want the camera to control the amount of light on the sensor, or do you want to control it by balancing the relationship between the f-stop (the diameter of the aperture) and the shutter speed (the quickness of the shutter release)? You'll learn more about f-stop and shutter speed settings in the next step.
4. Press the shutter release button. Hold the camera tightly and try to eliminate body movement.
5. The shutter will open, and the aperture will enlarge or decrease according to the f-stop settings.
6. Light will be recorded on the digital sensor.
7. The shutter will close based on the duration of time indicated by the shutter speed settings.
8. You can preview your image immediately as it is saved on a memory card.

Note:

Some of the information in the **Camera Mechanics** exercise won't apply to your situation if you're using a point-and-shoot camera or a mobile device. However, if you have access to a consumer-level or prosumer-level (not quite professional but a step above the consumer level) digital camera or a *digital single lens reflex (DSLR) camera* you will be able to step through the *Camera Mechanics* exercise. These types of cameras offers the photographer some degree of or even full control over light registration.

f-stop

Also known as f-number, focal ratio, or f-ratio, it governs the diameter of the aperture.

Shutter

Limits the time over which light is admitted.

Shutter Speed

The duration of the shutter release.

Aperture

A hole or an opening through which light travels.

LCD versus Viewfinder: Where Should You Look While Framing a Photograph?

This choice is dictated by personal preference and limitations presented by the type of camera you're using. When using a DSLR, you might use the viewfinder. However, on an iPhone, you must use the LCD.

LCD	Viewfinder
Accurately represents the framed image space	Can be slightly inaccurate in consumer cameras due to what is called "parallax", as the viewfinder location is slightly above and to the left of the lens
Can lead to instability: since you'll hold the camera away from your face to see through the viewfinder, the camera is less stable than it would be if you were holding it closer to your balanced body.	Often leads to greater stability: you'll hold the camera to your face while making the photograph. Remember to square your hips and be still while you shoot.
Drains battery power	No extra battery power is required for composing through the viewfinder.

Recognizing Camera Settings

The following items are elements you might be able to control when capturing a photograph. Where you find these settings depends on your camera. Read your camera's manual, or at least view the page containing the illustration of the camera and its settings! Did you lose it (or throw it away with the box)? Most manuals can be downloaded from the manufacturer's Web site.

Try It!

1. **File Size, Compression**, and/or **File Format**. These typically appear in the camera menu or function area.

   Even if your camera isn't terribly fancy, you may have a choice of creating small, medium, or large images, or you might even have a specific set of resolutions, via pixel dimensions or megabytes, to choose from in the File or Camera menu.

   You also might be able to choose to shoot in JPG, TIFF, or even RAW mode. Shooting in RAW mode yields the most information and adaptability, but processing a RAW image is outside the scope of this book. If you can choose between shooting in JPG or TIFF modes, you should know that the JPG will be more compressed (and usually a smaller file size) than the TIFF.

2. **ISO**. ISO typically appears on the Camera or Function menu.

   The ISO rating is analogous to what was once referred to as the film speed. Silver nitrate is the light-sensitive chemical found in film. The amount of silver in the film stock directly correlates to its ISO rating.

   A low ISO rating (25 or 50 in special films, 100 or 200 in the kind of film you can purchase at the drug store) indicates that there's little silver nitrate in the film. This in turn means that you'll need a lot of light in order to register the image on the film. If you're shooting outside on a bright day, set the ISO to a low setting. What's the advantage of using a super low ISO setting? In the film world, you'll see less film grain in the resulting print. In the digital world, the same rule applies—though we'll just call the film grain "digital noise." If you're shooting in a studio and you want to create a high-quality print devoid of noise, use the lowest ISO your camera offers and set up plenty of lights.

   A high ISO rating (800, 1600, 3200 in special films, 400 in common film stocks) indicates that there's a large quantity of silver nitrate in the film. This in turn means that you'll need little light in order to register the image on the film. If you're shooting indoors, in the late evening, or at night, you'll probably need to set the ISO to a high setting. The advantages of using a high ISO setting are that you have greater flexibility in low-light situations. However, you'll see the grain of the film or some digital noise in your files.

   White Balance. Along with ISO, this typically appears on the camera or function menu.

Setting the white balance on your camera, if you're able, will ensure that the whites appear a true white, and that the rest of the colors in the spectrum of the photographs are not the victims of a nasty "color cast".

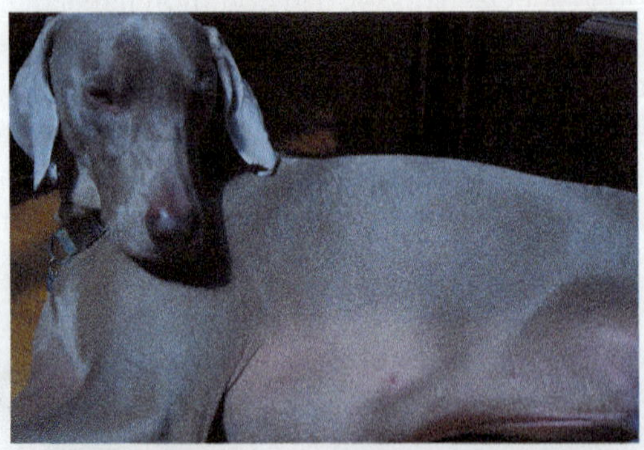

The following are typical (self-evident) settings or icons you might find on a menu or function area. Match the white balance lighting to your situation: Auto (A-WB), Daylight (sunshine icon), Cloudy (cloud icon), Tungsten (lightbulb icon), and Night (moon or flash icon).

Aperture. If you can control the aperture, you'll typically do so with a dial or button near the top of the camera body.

The aperture is the size of the opening that light travels through the lens to the digital sensor. The wider the aperture opens, the more light you'll send to the digital sensor , and vice versa. The aperture's diameter size is controlled by the f-stop. Here's the tricky part: the smaller the f-stop number, the wider the aperture is open.

Understanding F-Stop Values

The trick is to remember that the f-stop is a ratio, which means that the f-stop number you select on your camera refers to the denominator of a fraction where the numerator is 1. There is an inverse relationship between the size of the number and the size of the aperture opening. A small denominator corresponds to a big ratio (or a wide aperture).

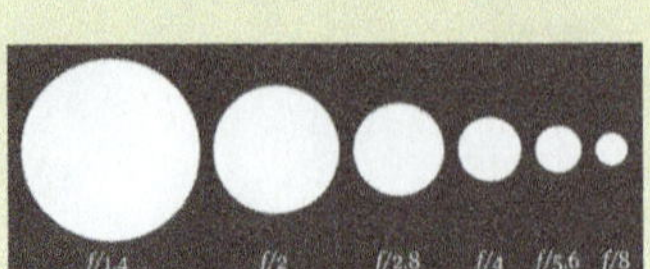

3. **Depth of Field**. This term refers to amount of an image before and beyond the focus point that will be in focus. When the aperture is wide open (for example, f/2) the resulting image has a small area of focus; a large f-number (for example, f/22) generates a large area of focus in the image. Photographers refer to this optical phenomena as "depth of field." Shallow depth of field is created with lower f-stop numbers, while greater depth of field is seen in photographs made with larger f-stop numbers.

4. **Shutter Speed**. If you can control the shutter speed, you'll typically do so with a dial or a button near the top of the camera body.

   The shutter speed indicates how quickly (or slowly) the shutter will open and close. In automatic mode with a reasonable amount of light, the shutter will probably release at about 1/60th of a second.

   Anything above 1/60th of a second (which might just be indicated by the number "60" on your digital camera) is considered somewhat fast. A fast shutter speed will appear to "freeze" time, showing a racecar, for instance, without the streaks of its movement.

Shutter Speed and Shaky Photographs

Your photographs will not display movements due to your physical inability to remain completely still at a shutter speed of 1/60th of a second or less (1/125th of a second, 1/250th of a second, and so on). With practice, you can probably even seem to hold the camera still at 1/30th of a second. Some people claim to be able to get a still image while hand-holding the camera at 1/15th of a second. If you plan to shoot at a slower shutter speed, use a tripod or steady the camera without human interference.

5. **Exposure Value** (EV or E/V). If you can't control the f-stop or shutter speed, you may be able to alter the exposure value, typically accessed by a button on the back of the camera near the LCD. This button will normally allow you to take a photograph with slightly lighter and darker exposure values. On some cameras, you can press a Plus (+) or Minus (-) button; on others, you just spin a dial to move across a sliding scale. Altering the exposure value is an essential skill to learn so you can bracket your exposures while you're still learning to create photographs.

Aperture Priority or Shutter Speed Priority?

Many prosumer-level cameras offer the ability to shoot in aperture or shutter speed priority. This is likely to be a setting listed on a dial (A or S). If your goal is to create an image with shallow depth of field, for instance, you might shoot in aperture priority mode and set the f-stop to a low number. The camera would then adjust the shutter speed for you, based on the light meter reading that it detects. Alternatively, perhaps you want to create a "freeze frame" of your friend as she dives from a high platform. You might shoot in shutter speed priority mode and set the shutter speed to a low fraction (maybe 1/125th of a second or 1/250th of a second). In this case, the camera would control the f-stop according to the light meter.

Exploring Bracketing

Bracketing is one of the first lessons new photographers learn. Since you're drawing with light when you create a photograph, the exposure of light that you set in your camera has one of the biggest visual impacts on the photograph. Bracketing is a method of increasing and decreasing the exposure value on the same scene in order to understand the visual results of an array of exposure values in a particular lighting situation. If you're new to photography, bracketing in as many lighting situations as you can will help you understand how light will register in the visual image made by your camera.

Try It!

1. On any camera where you can control the exposure value, use the bracketing technique by shooting the same scene at least three times. First, take a photograph using the most accurate exposure value according to your light meter (built in to DSLRs or likely whatever the automatic mode will indicate on consumer cameras). Then create another photograph of the same scene with one stop of additional light (a single shutter speed setting or f-stop setting). Follow this by creating one more photograph of the same scene by decreasing the amount of light to the sensor by one stop (a single shutter speed setting or f-stop setting in the opposite direction), starting from the "center" or original metered reading.

Note:

If you're only bracketing with three images, watch out for digital cameras that include half-stops. It's best to bracket at least five to eight times if you're new to the concept. You'll learn how your camera operates by experimenting.

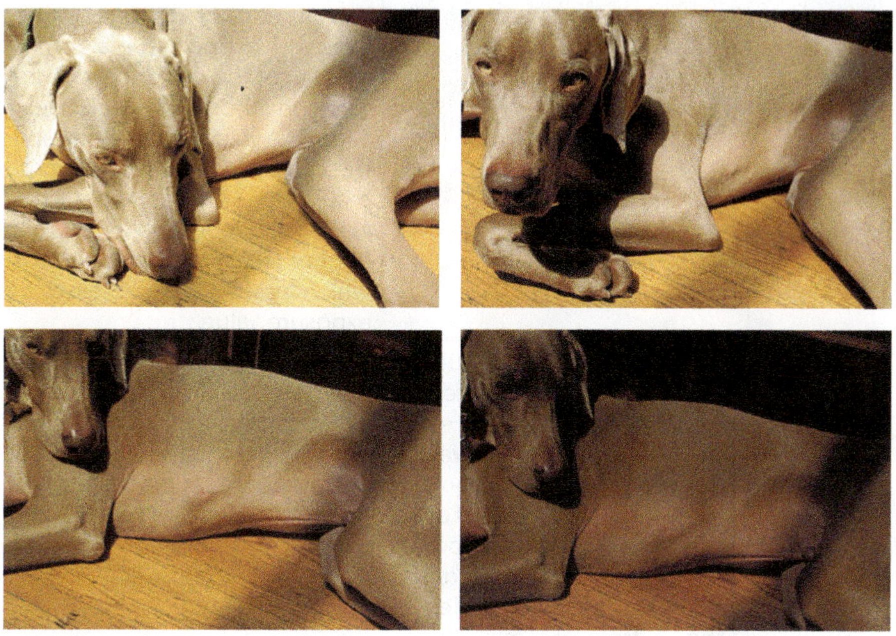

Common Bracketing Settings

	DSLR **If you can control the f-stop and shutter speed settings, use the following list.**	**Consumer Camera** **If you simply have the Exposure Value (EV or E/V) button on your camera, use the following list.**
Photo 1	Use the most accurate exposure value according to your light meter. You may need to manually adjust your shutter speed or f-stop value, or both, to achieve a balanced meter reading.	Use the most accurate exposure value according to your light meter. You'll probably see in the Exposure Value (EV or E/V) area of your camera settings that there's a dotted or dashed line, or perhaps a series of vertical straight lines with an indicator (a dot, usually) of the current exposure value. In automatic mode, the exposure value will likely fall in the center of the line. Pressing the EV button (or spinning a dial) will let you register that dot to the right or left of the center mark, which increases or decreases the exposure value.
Photo 2	Lighten the exposure value by one f-stop or by one notch on the shutter speed scale. For instance, if Photo 1 was taken at 1/60th of a second, take Photo 2 at 1/30th of a second to lighten the exposure value by one notch down on the shutter speed scale. (The shutter will remain open longer, allowing more light to register on the digital sensor.) Or, if Photo 1 was taken at f/5.6, take Photo 2 at f/4 to increase the amount of light through a wider aperture.	Lighten the exposure value by one notch to the right of the center on the exposure value line. You'll have to figure out how to add and subtract a notch on the EV scale.
Photo 3	Now decrease the exposure value. Create a photograph that's darker by one f-stop or one notch on the shutter speed scale. For instance, if Photo 1 was taken at 1/60th of a second, take Photo 3 at 1/125th of a second to darken the exposure value by one notch up on the shutter speed scale. Or, if Photo 1 was taken at f/5.6, take Photo 3 at f/8 to decrease the amount of light through a narrower aperture.	Darken the exposure value by one notch to the left of center on the exposure value line.

Transferring Images to a Computer

You can transfer photos from a digital camera to a computer in one of two ways:

- Digital cameras normally come with a USB cable that connects the camera to the computer's USB port. Once the camera is connected to your computer, a window should automatically open that displays the camera's contents. Select the photos you want to copy to the computer, specify the location to which you want to save the files, and click OK to begin the transfer.
- You can remove the SD (secure digital) memory card inside your camera, insert it in a digital card reader (similar to a flash drive), and then insert the reader into your computer's USB port. Copy the photos using the same process as with a USB cable.

Understanding Safety Considerations

When working with a digital camera, keep these safety guidelines in mind:

- If the camera feels hot or begins to smoke, discontinue use and turn it off immediately. If you have a warranty, check directions on where to send the camera for repairs. If you don't have a warranty, you may need to take it to a camera repair shop.
- If you're on rough or unstable terrain, use a tripod to avoid moving around and risking a slip or fall.
- Be careful when handling the camera's batteries, especially if you notice any leakage.
- Avoid taking the camera apart and handling any of the electronic components, as they may cause an electrical shock.
- Do not use a camera underwater unless it is made specifically for that use.
- Do not use a camera in dangerous or threatening environments, such as fire scenes and severe weather situations, such as tornadoes and floods.
- Be careful when taking photos of the sun as staring at it through the viewfinder can be as dangerous as staring at it with the naked eye.
- If you're taking photos of other people, do not use flash photography too close to the eyes as it may cause temporary blindness. Don't stage photos in unsafe locations, such as on a ledge or in areas with heavy traffic.

Using the Rule of Thirds

In addition to your camera setting choices, you'll be making decisions while creating a composition. As you can imagine, there are a lot of technical and aesthetic choices to make while creating powerful photographic imagery. In this section, you'll learn to see the compositional space using crop guides that make visible the "rule of thirds." This is a common way to understand the photographic frame, which is most often a two-dimensional environment with a 3:2 ratio. (4:3 and 16:9 are also common ratios among a variety of digital media.) The premise of the rule of thirds is to evenly divide the frame by two horizontal and two vertical lines before composing the subject matter along the intersections of those guides.

Ratios

A ratio is a relationship between pairs of numbers. For instance, if you're cooking rice at a 1:2 ratio with water, you'll add one part of rice to the pot for every two parts of water. Instead of instructing someone to cook one cup of rice with two cups of water, it's more scalable to advise the ratio.

Get Closer and Watch the Edges

Two additional pieces of advice are not specified by the rule of thirds:

- Get closer. In other words, physically move your body and your camera closer to your subject.
- Watch the edges of the frame. The viewer shouldn't be left in no-man's-land at the edges of the frame. Be conscious about using the full frame to tell your visual story.

One desired result of the rule of thirds is the elimination of the number one newbie mistake: centering the subject in the middle of the frame. You'll also start to see and weigh the visual balance of your subject matter by thirds, bringing more tension and energy to the overall composition. The more you're aware of the compositional space, the more likely you'll be to create a composition that leads the eye to your desired focal point.

Some cameras have a rule of thirds grid that you can superimpose in the viewfinder to see the guides while you're creating the photograph. In this exercise, you'll see how to use this compositional structure in Photoshop to assist you during post-production editing.

Try It!

1. Open the file **L9_start.psd** from the data files for this lesson.
2. A lousy composition has been selected for you to work with in this lesson. Where are the first and second focal points? What's happening at the edges of the frame? Notice that the middle dog and the large branch are two main areas of focus. Where are they positioned in the frame? The top of the frame is full of distracting information: the cone, the volleyball net, and the houses in the background are all unnecessary to the activity in the primary focal area. In the next step, you'll reframe this image.
3. Choose the Crop tool from the Tools panel and set the tool options to Unconstrained Select View: Rule of Thirds in the Options panel.

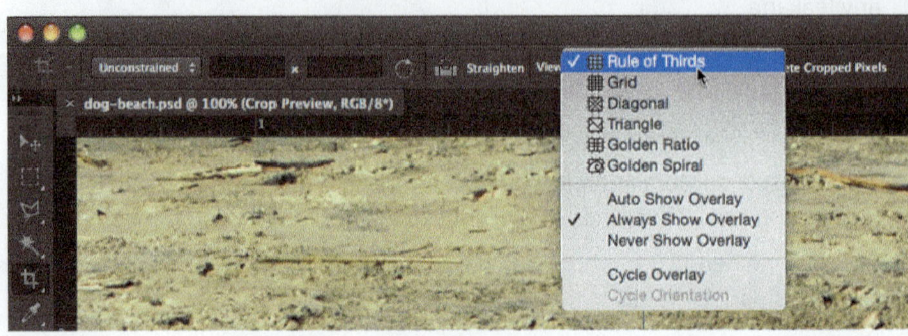

Workspace > Essential

Open Photoshop and set the workspace to Essentials by selecting it from the pull-down menu in the Application Frame or by choosing the Window > Workspace > Essentials. (Note: You may need to choose Window > Workspace > Reset Essentials.)

4. Pull the Crop anchor at the middle of the top frame down so the top of the frame touches the tip of the red dog's tail.
5. Notice where the rule of thirds guides are located on the image. The branch is located precisely in the central square. You'd rather see main elements on one of the vertical or horizontal lines than inside what would be a cell if you think of the grid as a table. Move the crop guide on the left edge of the frame toward the middle of the image until the branch is more or less aligned on the left vertical rule of thirds guide.

6. Eliminate some of the bottom area of the image, just as you did with the top—the information at the bottom is simply distracting the viewer from the activity. Move the bottom crop guide toward the top of the image, keeping the idea of a two-thirds to one-third compositional ratio in mind. Move the bottom crop guide is adjusted so that the Weimaraner's front left paw is planted on the top horizontal guide.

7. You can continue to adjust the crop guides until you're satisfied with the crop. Notice that while you're cropping the image, the Layers panel indicates that you're in a Crop Preview. Click the Commit Current Crop Operation button in the Options panel when you're finished.

8. Save the file as **L9_start_xx.psd** in the location where your teacher instructs you to store the files for this lesson, and close the file.

Careers in Photography

Photographers work in a variety of industries in different types of settings. For example, they might work in a studio or they might work on location, which could be anywhere!

Photographers must know how to use technical equipment including cameras and photo editing software programs, and must understand the use of settings such as lighting, field depth, subject motion, film type, and film speed. They must also use technical terminology.

Although a photographer with talent may be successful with just a high school diploma, many employers require a two- or four-year college degree. There are numerous industry certifications available, as well as internships, apprenticeships, and on-the-job training, which can all help build skills for career success.

Hourly wages range from $10.50 to $22.63. According to projections from the Bureau of Labor Statistics, the employment of photographers is expected to grow 4% through 2020. Growth is limited due to the increasing availability of high-quality, easy-to-use equipment, which has led to a surge in the number of amateur photographers.

Explaining Fair Use and Appropriation

Not all visual works are protected by copyright laws. In your collages and photo manipulations, you're free to use images that are in the public domain. These include official media created by the U.S. government, much of the content in the Library of Congress (LOC), and works that have an expired copyright (the death of the author plus 70 years for U.S. authors). Online collections including the LOC Web site and its Flickr stream, NASA's image gallery, as well as Wikimedia Commons are excellent resources for finding and downloading these types of images or media, although it is always your responsibility to determine the copyright.

In addition to the public domain and expired copyrights, some artists actively contribute to a growing collection of media licensed with alternative mechanisms to the traditional U.S. copyright. Creative commons licenses allow artists to set specific guidelines in regard to how their work can be shared, transformed, or redistributed, both commercially and noncommercially. Similarly, some software developers create open-source software, which means they make the source code for their programs available to the public so users can change the way it works.

Fair Use

The fair use doctrine is important for media makers because it's the part of the U.S. copyright law that permits the use of previously published materials, provided that a particular set of conditions are met. When you use previously published work, it's considered to be a *derivative* of the original. Here are the four criteria that a judge or jury would use to determine if your use is legitimately fair:

The purpose of the derivative work. For instance, a collage made by an instructor that will not be sold or distributed beyond the classroom is probably fair, while one inserted into a commercial publication is likely to be ruled in violation.

The nature of the content of the original. Factual content can legitimately be reused, whereas creative content is considered to be intellectual property.

How much of the original work is used in the derivative. For visual works, there is no set guideline for how much you are allowed to use. But, if the transformative quality (not quantity) of the new work is hard to recognize, your work may be so similar to the original that it seems to use "too much" of it.

The effect of the new work on the actual or potential market value of the original. If the new work defames the original or lessens the value of the original work, the use would not be considered fair.

Commercial artists and designers must be very careful in regard to using prior published works. As a general rule, you should always seek permission from the author, even if the work is licensed in a way that suggests redistribution is permissible.

Appropriation

Appropriation is a conceptually rich practice of borrowing, reclaiming, and transforming an original work of culture that informs and inspires artists who express their ideas in a variety of media formats. Though appropriation can be found in visual culture throughout recorded history, many artists learn of the concept through early 20th century art: Pablo Picasso and Georges Braque's mixed-media Cubist collages and Marcel Duchamp's readymades (see the sidebar on Duchamp's *Fountain*), or mid-century works such as Andy Warhol's *Campbell's Soup Cans*. The intentional act of appropriation as a means of creating transformative visual culture has become even more prevalent in the age of digital media.

Artists and designers often borrow images, media, formats, or ideas from prior recognizable works in visual culture. The word "appropriation," however, means more than just the simple action of borrowing. To appropriate is to borrow and to transform. In this way, appropriation (when successful or obvious) will help your work meet the third criterion in the fair use test.

Reminder: If you're creating appropriated work for commercial purposes, be sure that you have permission to modify the original work.

Comprehension Check

1. Explain photographic composition and layout and why they are important.
2. Identify five camera settings and what they do.
3. What is bracketing?
4. What is the Rule of Thirds and how does it impact composition?
5. Compare and contrast the principles of fair use, open source, and creative commons.
6. List and explain basic safety considerations when using digital photography equipment.

Review Project

For this project, you will need a digital camera and a USB cable or SD card reader. Review the information on camera settings discussed in this lesson and check them on your camera. Review the rule of thirds and other photo composition techniques you learned about. Then, take several photos of a subject that interests you. Transfer the photos to your computer using either the USB cable or a card reader.

In Photoshop, open one of the photos and apply enhancements that you think will improve the look of the image. Save the file as **L9_review_xx.psd** in the location where your teacher instructs you to save files for this lesson. Exchange your photo with a partner. Provide comments and suggestions on how your partner's photo could be improved. Return the photo and make adjustments to your photo, as desired. Close the file and then close Photoshop.

Lesson 10 Overview

In this lesson, you will learn about:

- Making Digital Repairs
- Creating a Hoax
- Making Tonal Repairs with Dodge and Burn
- Making a Layer Mask

In this lesson, you'll explore various tools for healing and cloning parts of an image, and add a simple layer mask to blend image features.

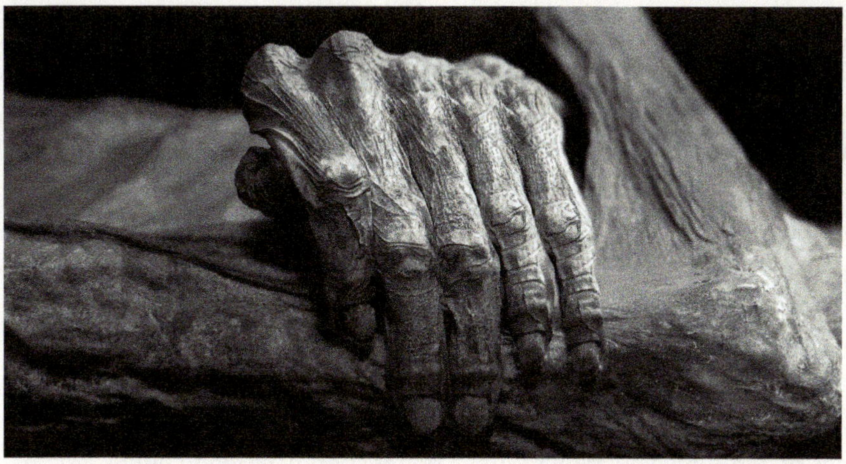

Making Digital Repairs

The repair tools are grouped together in the Photoshop Tools panel with the Spot Healing Brush tool. As you learned in Lesson 8, two useful tools for making repairs are the Spot Healing Brush tool and the Clone Stamp tool.

The Spot Healing Brush tool functions as a fix-it paintbrush. You simply click on any part of the image, and the brush attempts to *repair* (or correct uneven tones in) the area based on a sample of nearby pixels. Of course, it's never a good idea to modify your original image. So when using these tools, it is a good idea to copy the background layer to preserve the original file.

The Clone Stamp tool also takes the form of a brush, but using it is a two-step operation. When cloning, Photoshop needs to understand what you're cloning and where the clone should be applied. So you'll need to sample an original source and then brush the sample into a new location. The sampling part of the Clone Stamp operation can sometimes be tricky to learn, but once you understand how the tool works you'll be able to repair just about anything.

The Healing Brush tool is essentially a combination of the Spot Healing Brush tool and the Clone Stamp tool: it lets you sample a source and tries to even tones and blemishes based on nearby pixel information.

With these tools, basic photo repairs can be made quickly and easily. However, manipulating photographic imagery has ethical implications for photojournalists and others in the digital communications field.

Instances of photo manipulation to "get a better shot" have led to firings (for instance, Bryan Patrick from the *Sacramento Bee*) and loss of credibility (the infamous *National Geographic* cover of the Egyptian pyramids in 1982 where a horizontal image was smooshed into a vertical cover space).

Creating a Hoax

While it is important to handle digital manipulations with caution and care, artists often use these tools to create commentary on popular media and historic subject matter. For instance, Josh Azzarella's still and video works use manipulation to revise historic events by way of deletion. In his still image, *Untitled #15 (Tank Man)*, Azzarella re-creates the scene from Tiananmen Square, originally photographed by Associated Press photographer Jeff Widener. In Widener's image, the man is face-to-face with several Type 59 tanks during the Tiananmen Square protests of 1989. However, in Azzarella's image, the tanks are removed, and the man is left isolated in the middle of the street, seemingly out of the way of danger. Similarly, *Untitled #7* (16mm) is an 11-second loop showing President John F. Kennedy driving near the grassy knoll but never experiencing the fatal bullet wound. The footage of JFK riding in the car is haunting for contemporary viewers who know where the drive leads, even though it never quite gets there. While these examples of revision and manipulation aren't meant to hoax or deceive the viewer (after all, we know what the artist is up to), the strategies for image manipulation are the same as those used to create a photographic hoax.

Try It!

Remove Dust and Blemishes

1. Choose File > Open, to open the **L10_start.psd** file from the data files for this lesson. This portrait of President John F. Kennedy Is from the U.S. Navy and considered in the public domain.

2. In the Layers panel, drag the background layer to the Create a new layer icon at the bottom of the panel.

3. Unlock the background layer by clicking on the lock icon. Double-click the "background" name and rename it **original**. Rename the background copy **spot healing.**

   Choose the Spot Healing Brush tool from the Tools panel. If necessary, click the spot healing layer in the Layers panel to make it active.

> **Note:**
>
> Keep a copy of the original file in the Layers panel when working on repairs. Naming your files as you work will keep the panel organized and help you work efficiently as the size of the list increases.

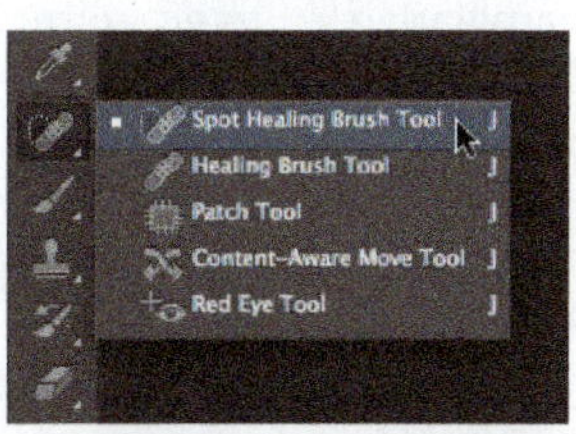

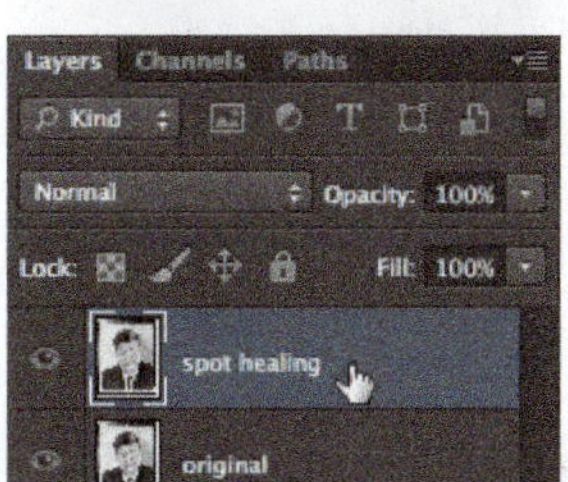

Always check a tool's options before using it. For the Spot Healing Brush tool, you can change the brush size and hardness (or softness) level, the mode (leave that on normal), and the type. Click the pull-down menu next to the set brush size and make sure that the Hardness level is set to 0, as you'll want to use a soft brush for this procedure. Further to the right on the Options panel, click the Content Aware radio button so the Spot Healing Brush tool will use image data in areas near where you click to try to match image details.

4. Place the Spot Healing Brush tool on or near the blemish on JFK's right cheek. (Don't click yet.) You might zoom in as much as 300% before making the first repair. The brush size is easily changed while you're working by pressing the hot keys, which are an open bracket ([) to reduce the brush size and a close bracket (]) to enlarge the brush size. Use the key commands to make the brush size just larger than the blemish. Then click one time. The Spot Healing Brush tool should replace the blemish with even skin tones in one simple click. Again, double-check that you're working on the spot healing layer!
5. While you have an enlarged view of the image, you'll notice dust on his dark jacket and also on the negative in the area surrounding his head. You may also find other minor blemishes on his skin tones. Repair all of this slowly. Use just one click at a time for each spot. Don't click and drag. Change the brush size according to the size of the blemish so that the brush is just barely larger than it.
6. Always review your modifications at a zoom level of 100% (or actual size). Click the eye icon next to the spot healing layer in the Layers panel to hide and show the layer. You should see your repairs disappear (showing the original image with all its imperfections). Click the eye icon again to redisplay the layer showing the adjustments you have made.
7. Save the file as **L10_start_xx.psd** in the location where your teacher instructs you to store the files for this lesson, and leave it open.

Cursor Icons

If you don't see a circle representing the size of the brush in Photoshop, check your Photoshop preferences. The brush cursor should be set in the Photoshop menu > Preferences > Cursors. Choose Normal Brush Tip and make sure you didn't leave the Caps Lock key depressed.

Zoom Tool

You can easily access the Zoom tool while working with most other tools by pressing the spacebar plus the Command keys. Click in the area you want to enlarge. To zoom out, press spacebar plus Command and Option keys (Mac) and spacebar plus Control and Alt keys (Windows).

Hand Tool

Use the Hand tool to move the image around the screen while you're zoomed in. You're not moving any part of the image file; you're simply changing your view.

History Is Full of Revisions

Repairs will inevitably leave you clicking on the Photoshop file hundreds of times. It's easy to become click-crazy in the process. Familiarize yourself with the History panel, as you'll come to rely on this handy Photoshop archive. There are three things you need to know about using the History panel:

Access the History panel by selecting Window > History or clicking the History icon along the strip of panels on the right side of the Application window.

By default, Photoshop may save only 50 of your previous clicks or steps. You'll want to increase this when doing this type of work. Choose Edit > Preferences > Performance. On the right side of the dialog box, enter 99 in the History States text field. The more clicks or previous states you save, the more RAM you'll use. If your computer is slow or you're lacking RAM, you may want to skip this step.

To go back a step or two, or five, click once on the name of each of the previous steps in the History panel until your file appears in the state that you want to begin working on anew. There's nothing else you need to click. Simply begin working again, and the History panel will create new steps, overwriting the grayed-out step or steps that you're leaving out of your process.

Making Tonal Repairs with Dodge and Burn

Now you'll focus on repairing the eye area. Since you've already done a once-over with the Spot Healing Brush tool for dust, scratches, and major blemish repairs, you'll do this additional, localized work on a separate layer. In this exercise, you'll place a copy of JFK's eyes on a new layer that you'll modify with the Dodge and Burn tools. If you've never printed a negative in the darkroom, the analogy between this tool and common darkroom practices might be vague. When dodging an area of the sensitized paper during an exposure to light in a black-and-white wet lab, for instance, a common exposure time for the adjustment might be about 10 percent of the total exposure. So, you might start with the Exposure Value set at 10% in the Dodge tool options. Of course, this value varies from negative to negative (or print to print), so it's common to make a best guess when using this tool.

Try It!

1. Choose the Lasso tool from the Tools panel. This tool lets you make a free-form selection around any part of the image. It's not a good tool to use when you need to perform a precise selection, but it's perfect for quickly isolating a general area of the image.

2. Draw a loose circle all the way around the left eye area, including a bit above the eyebrows. Be sure to begin and end the selection at the same point so that Photoshop knows the complete area of the selection. You'll see flickering dashed lines surrounding the selected area, often referred to as "marching ants." Now you'll add a selected area around the right eye to the current selection. Press and hold the Shift key while drawing a circular shape around the right eye area with the Lasso tool—you might notice an additional, tiny plus sign near the bottom of the tool icon. You should have two sets of marching ants on the image, one surrounding each eye.

Note:

Why not use the Spot Healing Brush tool here? You could work with the Spot Healing Brush tool to correct the eye bags, but the truth is that there should be a little shadow beneath the eyes in this photograph. In this situation, correcting the tones by burning and dodging will maintain the integrity of the image.

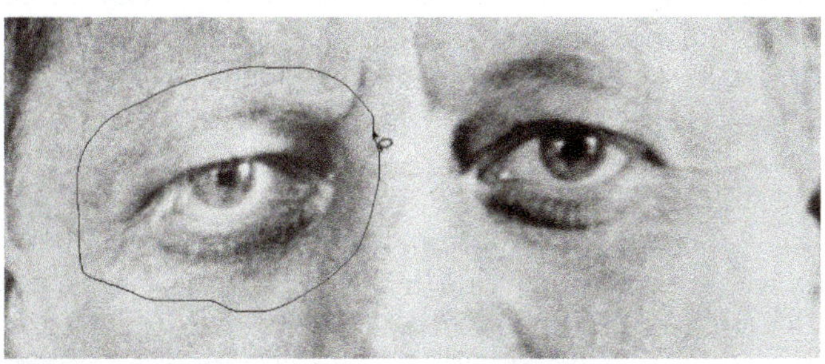

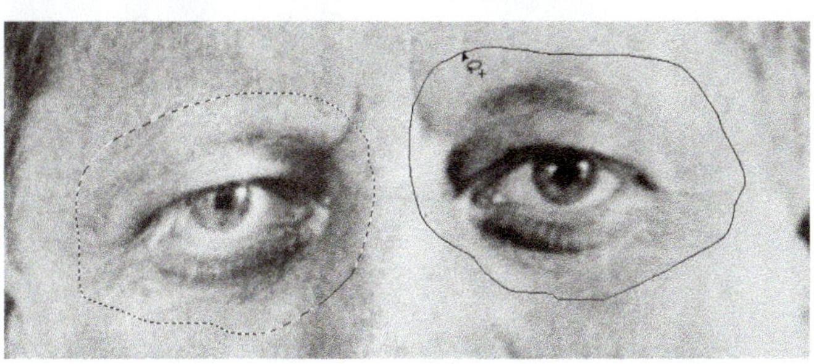

Adding and Deleting within Selections

You can add to any selection using one of the Photoshop selection tools by pressing the Shift key. If you want to add extra area to an existing selection, you'll have to begin the "new" part of the selected area from within the existing selection. If you want to subtract part of an existing selection, press and hold the Option key while starting the "deleted" area of the selection from outside the existing selection. This is much more easily demonstrated than understood by reading text.

3. Make sure the spot healing layer is active. Drag the layer to the New Layer icon at the bottom of the panel. Rename the new layer **eyes**. Copying the selection from the repaired layer saves you from having to "re-repair" any parts of the image that you have already "healed."

4. JFK's wrinkles aren't too extreme, so leave those alone in this image. However, his eye bags are a bit dense. In opposition to this, his eyebrows (especially his left brow) are so light they barely register. Use the Dodge tool to lighten the shadow areas beneath the eyes and the Burn tool to darken the brows. Click the Dodge tool, located a couple of tools above the Type tool in the Tools panel.

5. Make sure the eyes layer is active (eye icon should be displayed). Set the brush Hardness value to 0 if necessary. Select Shadows from the Range pull-down menu, as the eye bags are shadows you'll want to lighten. Now you need to estimate a reasonable dodging exposure value. The general rule is that you can always brush the Dodge tool over an area more than once, so it's better to err on the side of a lower value. Remember to zoom in and set the brush size so it's just about the same size or larger than the shadow area you're targeting (use the [and] hot keys). Brush the bags to conceal them. Select View > Fit On Screen to evaluate your results. The modification should not be extreme. Modifying the photograph in this way will make the president appear slightly less tired. Your modification should be believable!

6. The eyes layer should still be active. Click and hold down on the Dodge tool and switch to the Burn tool. Choose Highlights from the Range pull-down menu in the Options bar. Play with the exposure value (try using 10%) and make a quick brushstroke over JFK's left eyebrow to darken it. Change the exposure value if necessary, and repeat.

7. Review your modifications at actual size. Click the eye icon next to the eyes layer to toggle between hiding and showing the layer.

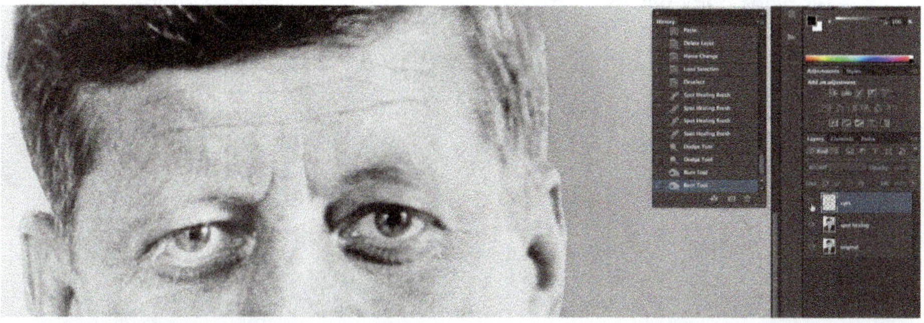

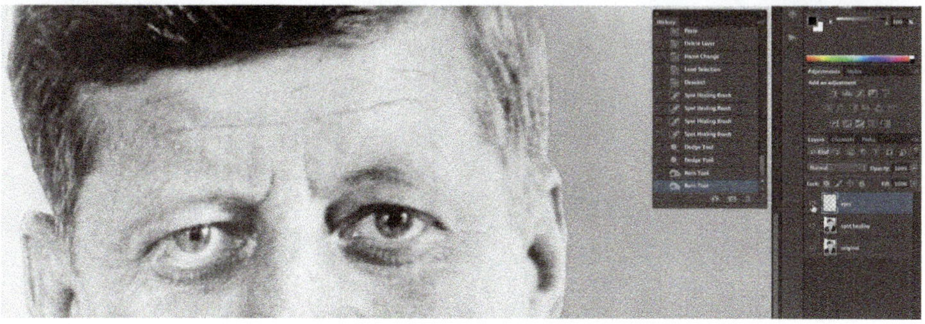

8. Save your file and leave it open.

Adding a Layer Mask

You'll use the Spot Healing Brush tool again, but this time a minor adjustment to the layer will help the change seem believable.

Try It!

1. Draw a loose selection around the forehead with the Lasso tool, making sure to avoid the eye area you just modified. However, you'll want to include the area between the eyes in your selection. Activate the spot healing layer. (Remember: this part of the image doesn't exist on the eyes layer that you were just working on, and to copy it, you need to activate the layer where the pixels are saved.)

2. Drag the spot healing layer to the New Layer icon at the bottom of the panel, and rename the layer **forehead**.

3. The new layer will paste directly above the active layer in the Layers panel. Drag the forehead layer above the *eyes* layer in the panel to rearrange the stacking order of the layers. Any modifications you make on this layer should be visible in the event that there's overlap with the eyes when selecting the forehead. Toggle the forehead layer on and off (use the eye icon) to make sure that the eyes retain their adjustments.

4. Repair the forehead layer moderately with the Spot Healing Brush tool. Don't make it perfect—JFK's facial age should be close to the reality of his wrinkles. When you're finished, reduce the layer Opacity to 70%. This will bring some of the wrinkles back without emphasizing them in that area of image.

5. Review your modifications at actual size, save the changes to the file, and close the file.

Comprehension Check

1. Identify Photoshop's repair tools.
2. What does the Clone Stamp do and how do you use it?
3. What are the ethical implications of repairing images digitally?

End-of-Chapter Activities

Chapter Review

1. What is a context menu?
2. What are two methods you can use to undo actions in Photoshop?
3. List the eight general steps used when retouching photos in Photoshop?
4. What is the difference between resolution and image size?
5. What do Curves and Levels adjustments do?
6. What is depth of field?
7. What is bracketing?

Multiple Choice

1. What is the file extension for a Photoshop document?
   a. .tif
   b. .jpg
   c. .ai
   d. .psd
2. Which panel changes based on the tool that is selected?
   a. Options bar
   b. Menu bar
   c. Panel menu
   d. Workspace
3. What is the name of the default Phtotoshop workspace?
   a. Typography
   b. Photography
   c. Painting
   d. Essentials
4. The Crop tool can be used to do all except which of the following?
   a. Straighten
   b. Trim
   c. Scale
   d. Skew
5. Which tool should be used when removing dust and scratches?
   a. Clone Stamp tool
   b. Content-aware Patch
   c. Spot Healing Brush
   d. Eyedropper

Chapter 3 – Portfolio Builder

It's a Hoax! Adding an Extra Mummy Finger

In this exercise, you'll add an extra mummy finger using the Clone Stamp tool. This tool functions similarly to the Spot Healing Brush tool, but you're responsible for the location of the source and the repair area. You'll work with a hard-edged and soft-edged brush in this exercise and clean your work with a layer mask.

DIRECTIONS

1. Open **PB3.psd** in Photoshop from the data files for this lesson.
2. Save the file as **PB3_xx.psd** in the location where your teacher instructs you to store the file for this lesson.
3. Set the workspace to Essentials.
4. In the Layers panel, Click the Create a new layer button. Unless you clicked the button more than once, the layer's default name is Layer 1. Double-click the Layer 1 name and rename it **finger**.
5. Choose the Clone Stamp tool from the Tools panel In the Options panel, set the brush option to 250 pixels and changed the Hardness value to 85%. Since you'll be copying pixels with this tool, you'll want to use a brush that isn't too soft. The soft edges often blur the pixel information, which you want to keep sharp, at least during the copying portion of this process. Keep the Mode set to Normal and the Opacity and Flow at 100%. If necessary, check the Aligned Sample box. Remember, you'll sample first with this tool and then clone. If you check the Align box, you're telling Photoshop to keep the sample area aligned with the cloning area. You'll see that it makes sense to keep the source and clone aligned. Finally, choose All Layers from the pull-down menu.
6. Zoom in. Make sure the finger layer is active on top of the last knuckle. Press the Option key (Mac) or Alt key (Windows) and click just once in this location. Don't drag the mouse. You just told Photoshop that this is the area that you want to sample as you clone the new finger.
7. Move the mouse to the right of the last knuckle and down a little bit to align it with a plausible location for a new knuckle. The Clone Stamp tool provides a preview of what the cloned image will look like in your composition. Click and drag downward, tracing the finger, until you reach the end of the fingernail.

   Since fingers don't stay the same size from the knuckle to the nail, there are extra parts of the cloned finger that obstruct the view of the original composition through which the viewer can tell that the image has been manipulated. In this exercise, you'll use a layer mask to hide extra parts surrounding the cloned finger.
8. In the Layers panel, activate the finger layer and then press the Add Layer Mask button at the bottom of the panel. You'll see a new icon in the Layers panel—a white square next to the layer icon of the finger.
9. The layer mask is used to hide or show parts of a layer. Since the finger layer contains only the extra, cloned finger, the mask will affect only this image data. You could work with the Eraser tool to delete image data, but instead, try working in a nondestructive way to simply hide (rather than delete) pixels. Layer masks operate in white (show the layer content), black (hide the layer content), and shades of gray (make the layer content partially hidden). Choose the Brush tool and select black as the foreground color.
10. View the Brush tool options. Set the Hardness value to 0, as you'll want to use a soft-edged brush. Leave the Mode set to Normal and the Opacity and Flow at 100%.

11. Before you add black paint to the layer mask (which will indicate which parts of the finger layer should be hidden), make sure that the mask is active in the Layers panel. You can click once on the Layer icon or on the mask. Notice that whichever is activated has white edges around its icon. When you're sure that the mask is active, paint black using your soft brush around the edges of the finger where you want to hide the extra image details.
12. Notice that the layer mask now contains an abstract black painting on its white background. Option-click (Mac) or Alt-click (Windows) on the layer mask icon in the Layers panel to show just the mask in your composition—you may notice that the name of the file indicates that you're viewing the Layer Mask in the title area. The black areas of the composition are hidden. The white areas are revealed. Look for gaps between the black and white areas.
13. You may want to review those parts of the composition and add more black or white paint to fill in the gaps. This is an easy way to clean the mask because you can really see how the image details are being treated. Option-click (Mac) or Alt-click (Windows) on the Mask icon in the Layers panel again to resume the normal working mode and continue to modify the layer mask, before you complete your think necessary. Remember to view the image at actual size as you work.
14. When you are satisfied with the look of the hand, save the image, close it, and then close Photoshop.

Chapter 3 – Critical Thinking

Demonstrate Knowledge of Photographic Composition and Layout

With your digital camera, take a series of at least three photographs of the same scene making use of different lighting situations in which you expose the image for the highlight areas. Bracket these exposures (see the Try It exercise on pp. 245-246) so that you can then open the images and create a Levels adjustment layer to recover the shadows and expand the tonal range.

1. Transfer the photos from your camera to your computer using either a USB cable connection or an SD card reader.
2. Open each photo in Photoshop naming the documents as follows and saving in the location where your teacher instructs you to store the files for this lesson:
   - **CT3_1_xx.psd**
   - **CT3_2_xx.psd**
   - **CT3_3_xx.psd**
3. Make any necessary adjustments with the Crop tool to improve the composition of each image.
4. Apply a Levels adjustment layer to each image to improve shadows and improve the tonal range.
5. Save the files and then close them.

Chapter 4

Printing & Imaging with Photoshop

Lesson 11 | Working with Type

Lesson 12 | Producing and Printing Consistent Color

Lesson 13 | Exploring 3D Features in Photoshop

End-of-Chapter Activities

Lesson 11 Overview

In this lesson, you will learn about:

- Adding Guides to Position Type
- Adding Point Type
- Making a Clipping Mask and Applying a Shadow
- Creating Type on a Path
- Warping Point Type
- Designing Paragraphs of Type
- Adding a Rounded Rectangle
- Adding Vertical Text
- Developing New Skills

Typographic design, or typography, is the art of arranging type so text can be easily read and understood. It involves positioning the type, selecting a typeface, or font, setting the type size and other attributes, and adjusting the spacing between lines. Type in Photoshop consists of mathematically defined shapes that describe the letters, numbers, and symbols of a typeface. Many typefaces are available in more than one format; the most common formats being Type 1 or PostScript fonts, TrueType, and OpenType.

When you add type to an image in Photoshop, the characters are composed of pixels and have the same resolution as the image file—zooming in on characters shows jagged edges. However, Photoshop preserves the vector-based type outlines and uses them when you scale or resize type, save a PDF or EPS file, or print the image to a PostScript printer. As a result, you can produce type with crisp, resolution-independent edges, apply effects and styles to type, and transform its shape and size.

Using Guides to Position Type

Photoshop lets you add horizontal and vertical guides to help you position type precisely. You can also create a **clipping mask** from shapes, letters, or even other layers. In this exercise, you will add guides and use type to create a clipping mask to allow an image in another layer to show through the letters. In effect, you are clipping the artwork to conform to the shape of the object (or mask).

The **L11_start.psd** file includes a background layer, which will be the foundation for your typography. You'll start by zooming in on the work area and using ruler guides to help position the type.

> **Clipping Mask**
>
> An object or a group of objects whose shape masks other artwork so that only the areas that lie within the clipping mask are visible.

Try It!

1. Start Photoshop.
2. Choose File > Open to open the **L11_start.psd** file from the data files for this lesson. Save the file as **L11_start_xx.psd** in the location where your teacher instructs you to store the files for this lesson.
3. Choose Typography from the Workspace Switcher in the Options bar.

4. Choose View > Fit On Screen to see the whole cover clearly.
5. Choose View > Rulers to display rulers along the left and top borders of the image window.

6. Drag a vertical guide from the left ruler to the center of the cover (4.25").

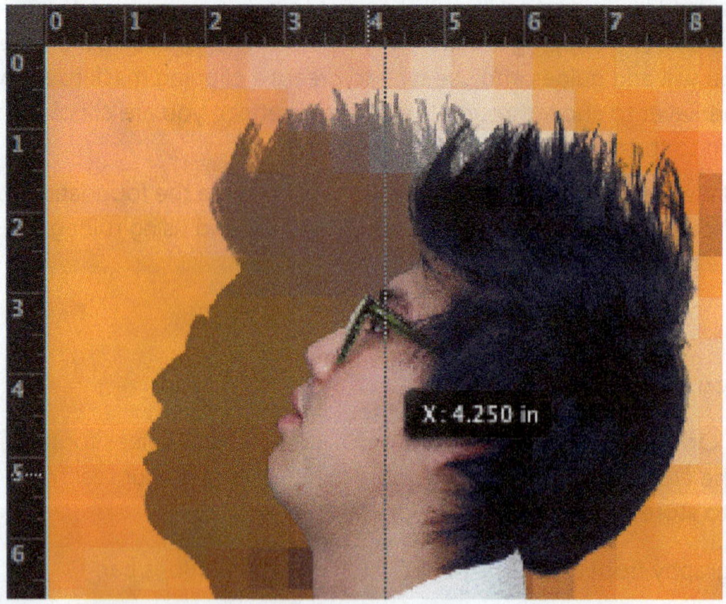

7. Save the **L11_start_xx.psd** file and leave it open.

Adding Point Type

Now you're ready to add type to the composition. You can create horizontal or vertical type anywhere in an image. You can enter **point type** (a single letter, word, or line) or **paragraph type**. You will do both in this lesson. First, you'll create point type.

Point type
A single letter, word, or line.

Paragraph type
Multiple lines of text within a bounding box.

Try It!

1. In the Layers panel, select the Background layer.
2. Select the Horizontal Type tool and, in the Options bar, do the following:
   - Choose a serif typeface, such as Minion Pro Regular, from the Font Family pop-up menu.
   - Type 144 pt for the Size, and press Enter or Return.
   - Click the Center Text button.

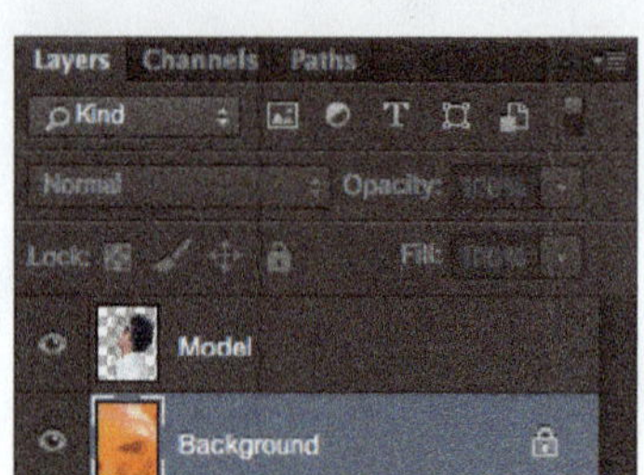

3. In the Character panel, change the Tracking value to 100.

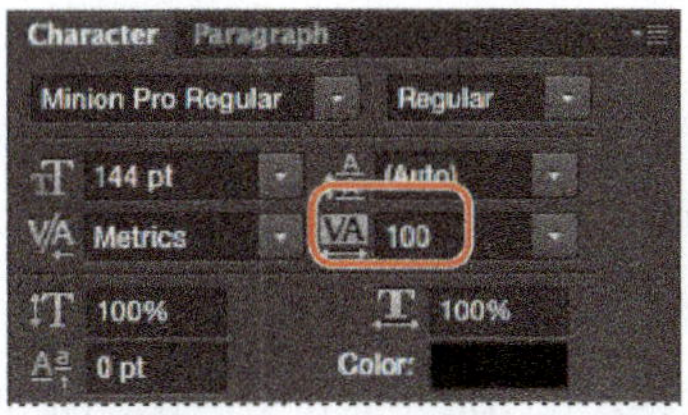

The Tracking value specifies the overall space between letters, which affects the density in a line of text.

4. Click on the center guide between the 2" and 3" ruler settings to set an insertion point, and type **DIGITAL** in all capital letters. Then click the Commit Any Current Edits button in the Options bar.

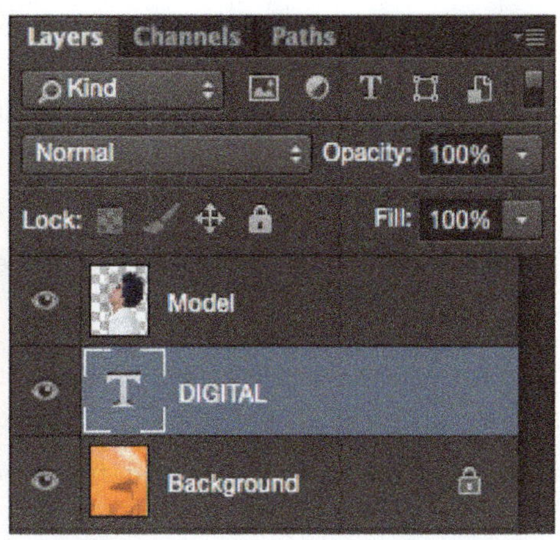

The word "DIGITAL" is added to the cover, and it appears in the Layers panel as a new type layer named DIGITAL. You can edit and manage the type layer as you would any other layer. You can add or change the text, change the orientation of the type, apply anti-aliasing, apply layer styles and transformations, and create masks. You can move, restack, and copy a type layer, or edit its layer options, just as you would for any other layer.

The text is big enough, but not modern enough, for this magazine's style. You'll apply a different font.

5. Select the Horizontal Type tool, and select the "DIGITAL" text.

6. Open the Font Family pop-up menu in the Options bar. Move the cursor over the fonts, either with the mouse or using arrow keys.

   When the cursor is over a font name, Photoshop applies that font to the selected text so you can preview the font in context.

7. Select Myriad Pro Semibold, and then click the Commit Any Current Edits button in the Options bar.

8. Select the Move tool, and drag the "DIGITAL" text to move it to the top of the cover, if it's not there already.

9. Choose File > Save to save **L11_start_xx.psd** and leave it open.

Making a Clipping Mask and Applying a Shadow

You added the letters in black, the default text color. However, you want the letters to appear to be filled with an image of a circuit board, so you'll use the letters to make a clipping mask that will allow another image layer to show through.

Try It!

1. Choose File > Open, and open the **circuit_board.tif** file, which is in the data files for this lesson.

2. Choose Window > Arrange > 2-Up Vertical. The **circuit_board.tif** and **L11_start_xx.psd** files appear onscreen together. Click the **circuit_board.tif** file to ensure that it's the active window.

3. With the Move tool selected, hold down the Shift key as you drag the Background layer from the Layers panel onto the center of the **L11_start_xx.psd** file.

   Pressing Shift as you drag centers the **circuit_board.tif** image in the composition.

   A new layer—Layer 1— appears in the Layers panel for the **L11_start_xx.psd** file. This new layer contains the image of the circuit board, which will show through the type. But before you make the clipping mask, you'll resize the circuit board image, as it's currently too large for the composition.

4. Close the **circuit_board.tif** file without saving any changes.

5. In the **L11_start_xx.psd** file, select Layer 1, and then choose Edit > Transform > Scale.

6. Grab a corner handle on the bounding box for the circuit board. Press Alt+Shift (Windows) or Option+Shift (Mac) as you resize it to approximately the same width as the area of text.

   Pressing Shift retains the image's proportions; Alt or Option keeps it centered.

7. Reposition the circuit board so that the image covers the text, and press Enter or Return to confirm the transformation.

8. Double-click the Layer 1 name, and change it to **Circuit Board**. Then press Enter or Return, or click away from the name in the Layers panel, to apply the change.

9. Select the Circuit Board layer, if it isn't already selected, and choose Create Clipping Mask from the Layers panel menu.

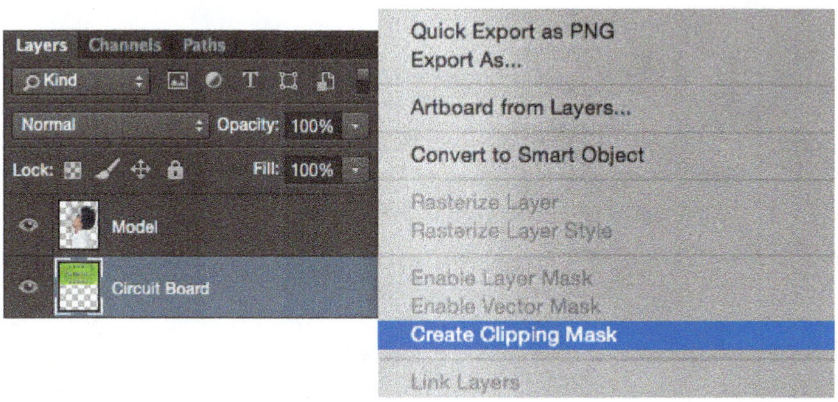

The circuit board now shows through the DIGITAL letters. A small arrow in the Circuit Board layer and the underlined type layer name indicate the clipping mask is applied. Next, you'll add an inner shadow to give the letters depth.

10. Select the DIGITAL layer to make it active. Then, click the Add A Layer Style button at the bottom of the Layers panel, and choose Inner Shadow from the pop-up menu.

11. In the Layer Style dialog box, change the Blend Mode to Multiply, Opacity to 48%, Distance to 18, Choke to 0, and Size to 16. Then click OK.

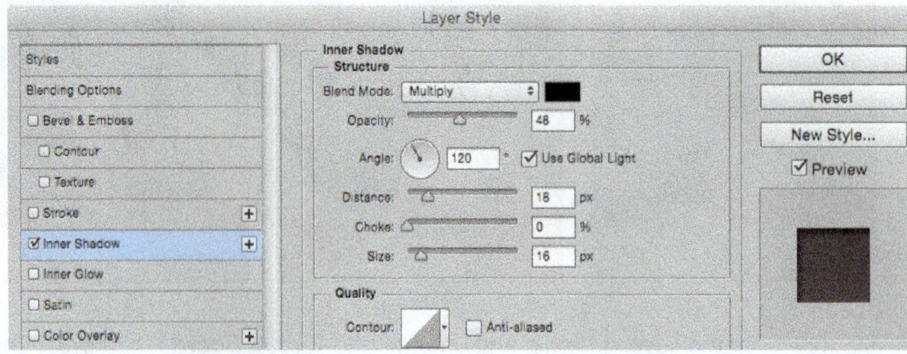

12. Save the **L11_start_xx.psd** file and leave it open.

Creating Type on a Path

In Photoshop, you can create type that follows along a path that you create with a pen or shape tool. The direction the type flows depends on the order in which anchor points were added to the path. When you use the Horizontal Type tool to add text to a path, the letters are perpendicular to the baseline of the path. If you change the location or shape of the path, the type moves with it.

You'll create type on a path to make it look as if questions are coming from the model's mouth. We've already created the path for you.

Try It!

1. In the Layers panel, select the Background layer.
2. Select the Paths tab in the Layers panel group.
3. In the Paths panel, select the path named Speech Path.

   The path appears to be coming out of the model's mouth.

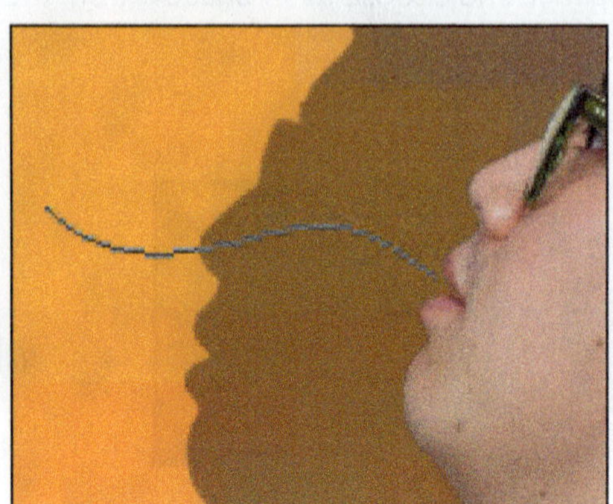

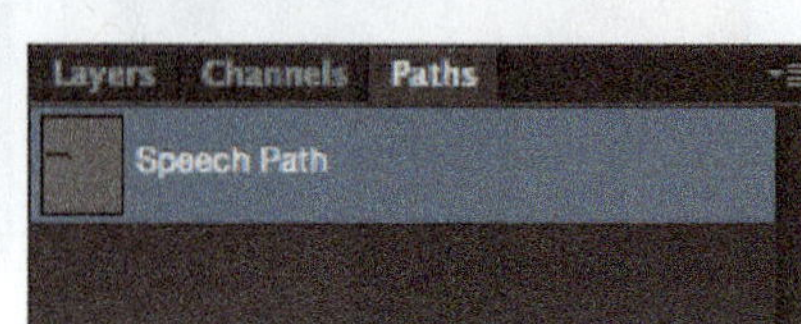

4. Select the Horizontal Type tool.

5. In the Options bar, click the Right Align Text button.

6. In the Character panel, select the following settings:
   - Font Family: Myriad Pro Regular
   - Font Style: Regular
   - Font Size: 16 pt
   - Tracking: -10
   - Color: White
   - All Caps

7. Move the Type tool over the path. When a small slanted line appears across the I-bar, click the end of the path closest to the model's mouth, and type **what's new with games?**

8. Select the word "**games**" and change its font style to Bold. Click the Commit Any Current Edits button in the Options bar.

9. Click the Layers tab to bring it forward. In the Layers panel, select the **What's new with games?** layer, and then choose Duplicate Layer from the Layers panel menu. Name the new layer **What's new with music?**, and click OK.

   Photoshop creates a duplicate text layer, hiding the text you typed earlier.

10. With the Type tool, select "**games**" and replace it with **music** (don't worry that the text is overlapping). Click the Commit Any Current Edits button in the options bar.

11. Choose Edit > Free Transform Path. Rotate the left side of the path approximately 30 degrees, and then shift the path up above the first path, and a little to the right, as in the image below. Click the Commit Transform button in the Options bar.

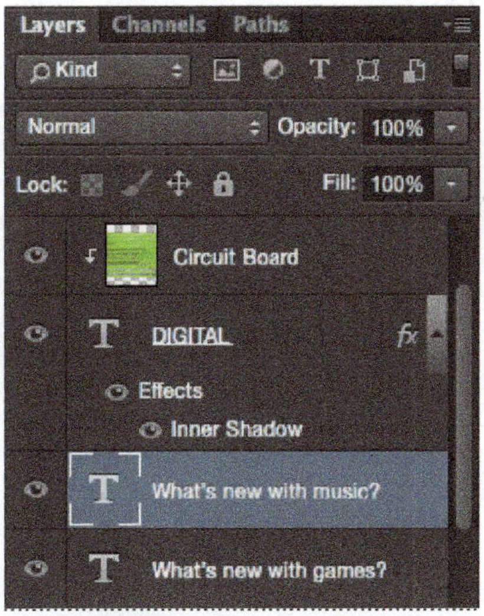

12. Repeat steps 9–11, replacing the word "**games**" with **phones**. Rotate the left side of the path approximately -30 degrees, and move it below the original path.

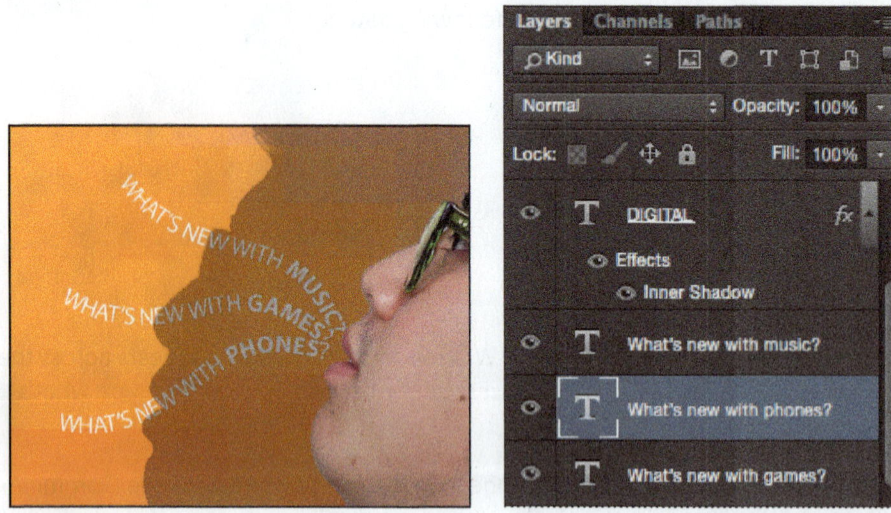

13. Save the **L11_start_xx.psd** file and leave it open.

Warping Point Type

> **Warping**
> Distorting type to conform to a shape, such as an arc or wave.

The text on a curvy path is more interesting than straight lines would be, but you'll warp the text to make it more playful. **Warping** lets you distort type to conform to a variety of shapes, such as an arc or a wave. The warp style you select is an attribute of the type layer—you can change a layer's warp style at any time to change the overall shape of the warp. Warping options give you precise control over the orientation and perspective of the warp effect.

Try It!

1. Scroll or use the Hand tool to move the visible area of the image window so that the sentences to the left of the model are in the center of the screen.

2. Right-click (Windows) or Control-click (Mac OS) the **What's new with games?** layer in the Layers panel, and choose Warp Text from the context menu.

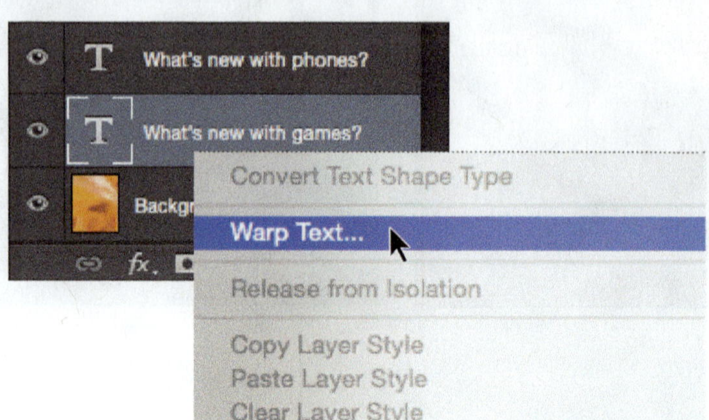

3. In the Warp Text dialog box, choose Wave from the Style menu, and select the Horizontal option. Specify the following values: Bend +33%; Horizontal Distortion -23%; and Vertical Distortion +5%. Then click OK.

   The Bend slider specifies how much warp is applied. Horizontal Distortion and Vertical Distortion determine the perspective of the warp.

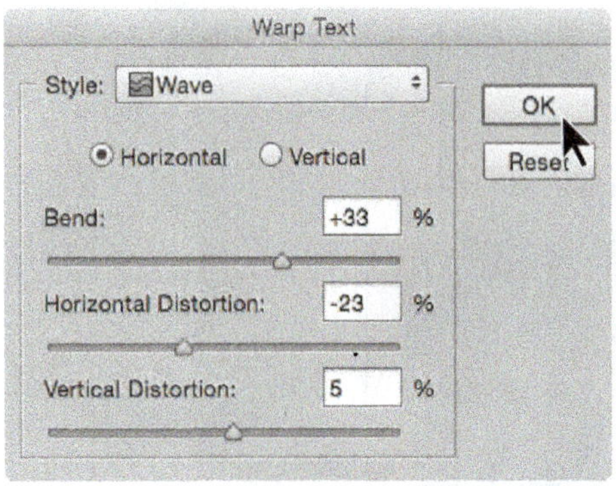

   The words "What's new with games?" appear to float like a wave on the cover.

4. Repeat steps 2 and 3 to warp the other two text layers you typed on a path.

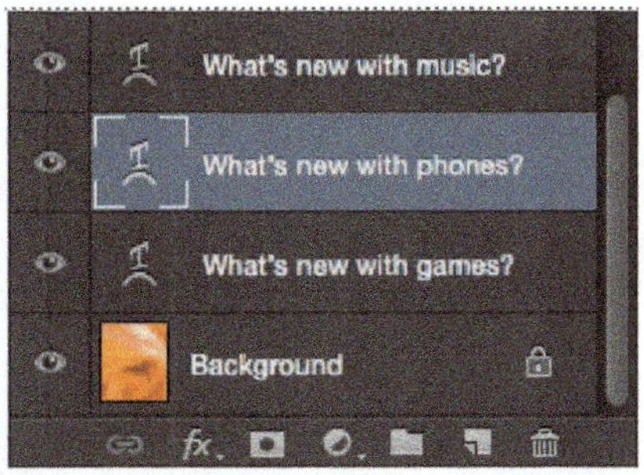

5. Save the **L11_start_xx.psd** file and leave it open.

Designing Paragraphs of Type

All of the text you've written on this cover so far has been a few discrete words or lines—point type. However, many designs call for full paragraphs of text. You can design complete paragraphs of type in Photoshop; you can even apply paragraph styles. You don't have to switch to a dedicated page layout program for sophisticated paragraph type controls.

Adding Guides

You will add paragraphs to the cover in Photoshop. First, you'll add some guides to the work area to help you position the paragraph.

Try It!

1. Drag a guide from the left vertical ruler, placing it approximately 1/4" from the right side of the cover.

   Drag a guide down from the top horizontal ruler, placing it approximately 2" from the top of the cover.

2. Save the **L11_start_xx.psd** file and leave it open.

Adding Paragraph Type from a Sticky Note

You're ready to add the text. In a real design environment, the text might be provided to you in a word processing document or the body of an email message, which you could copy and paste into Photoshop. Or you might have to type it in. Another easy way to add a bit of text is for it to be attached to the image file in a sticky note, as we've done for you here.

Try It!

1. Select the Move tool, and then double-click the yellow sticky note in the lower right corner of the image window to open the Notes panel. Expand the Notes panel, if necessary, to see all the text.

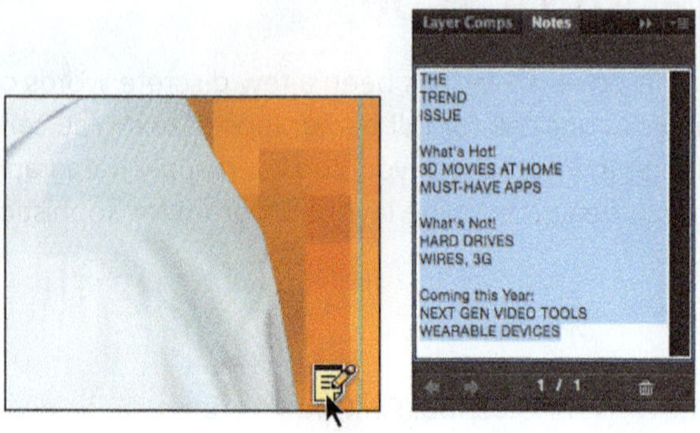

2. In the Notes panel, select all the text. Press Ctrl+C (Windows) or Command+C (Mac) to copy the text to the clipboard. Close the Notes panel.
3. Select the Model layer. Then, select the Horizontal Type tool.
4. Press Shift as you click where the guidelines intersect, about 1/4" from the right edge and 2" from the top of the cover. Continue to hold the Shift key as you start to drag a text box down and to the left. Then release the Shift key and continue dragging until the box is about 4 inches wide by 8 inches high, the top and right edges aligned with the guides you just added.
5. Press Ctrl+V (Windows) or Command+V (Mac) to paste the text. The new text layer is at the top of the Layers panel, so the text appears in front of the model.

   The pasted text is 16 pts, and it's right-aligned, because those were the latest text settings you'd used.
6. Select the first three lines ("The Trend Issue"), and then apply the following settings in the Character panel:
   - Font Family: Myriad Pro (or another sans serif font)
   - Font Style: Regular
   - Font Size: 70 pt
   - Leading: 55 pt
   - Tracking: 50
   - Color: White
7. Select just the word "Trend," and change the Font Style to Bold.

You've formatted the title. Now you'll format the rest of the text.

8. Select the rest of the text you pasted. In the Character panel, select the following:
   - Font Family: Myriad Pro
   - Font Style: Regular
   - Font Size: 22 pt
   - Leading: 28 pt
   - Tracking: 0
   - Deselect All Caps

   The text looks good, but it's all the same. You'll make the headlines stand out more.
9. Select the "What's Hot!" text, and then change the following in the Character panel:
   - Font Style: Bold
   - Font Size: 28 pt
10. Repeat step 9 for the "What's Not" and "Coming this year" subheads.
11. Select "Coming this year" and all the text that follows it. Then, in the Character panel, change the text color to Black.
12. Finally, click the Commit Any Current Edits button in the Options bar.
13. Save the **L11_start_xx.psd** file and leave it open.

Adding a Rounded Rectangle

You're almost done with the text for the magazine cover. All that remains is to add the volume number in the upper right corner. First, you'll create a rectangle with rounded corners to serve as a background for the volume number.

Try It!

1. Select the Rounded Rectangle tool, hidden beneath the Rectangle tool, in the Tools panel.
2. Draw a rectangle in the space above the letter "L" in the upper right corner of the cover, placing its right edge along the guide.
3. In the Properties panel, type 67 px for the width, and then make sure the stroke width is 3 pt.
4. Click the fill color swatch in the Properties panel, and select the Pastel Yellow Orange swatch in the third row.

   By default, all the corners in the rectangle have the same radius, but you can adjust the radius for each corner separately. You can even return to edit the corners later if you want to. You'll change the rectangle so that only the lower left corner is rounded and the others are right angles.

5. Unlink the corner radius values in the Properties panel. Then change the bottom left corner to 16 px, and set all the others to 0 px.

6. With the Move tool, drag the rectangle to the top of the image so it hangs down like a ribbon and its right edge is next to the ruler guide.

7. Select Show Transform Controls in the Options bar. Drag the bottom of the rectangle down so that it's close to the letter "L." You want the rectangle to be long enough to contain the text. Then click the Commit Transform button.

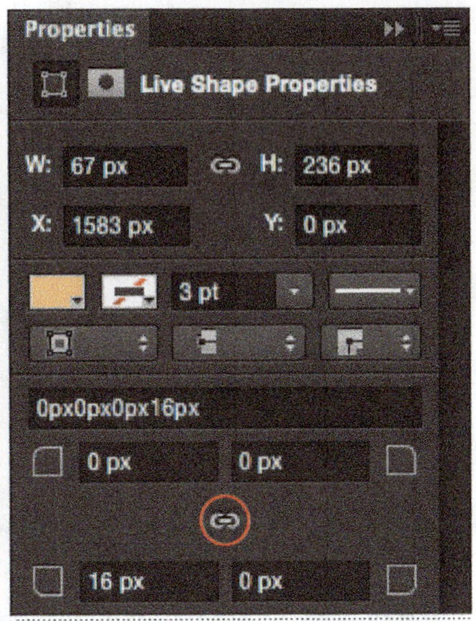

8. Save the **L11_start_xx.psd** file and leave it open.

Adding Vertical Text

You're ready to add the volume number on top of the ribbon.

Try It!

1. Choose Select > Deselect Layers. Then select the Vertical Type tool, which is hidden under the Horizontal Type tool.

2. Press the Shift key, and click inside the rectangle you just created.

   Pressing the Shift key as you click ensures that you create a new text box instead of selecting the title.

3. Type VOL 9.

   The letters are too large to view. You'll need to change their size to see them.

4. Choose Select > All, and then, in the Character panel, select the following:
    - Font Family: a sans-serif typeface, such as Myriad Pro
    - Font Style: a light or narrow style, such as Light Condensed
    - Font size: 15 pt
    - Tracking: 10
    - Color: Black

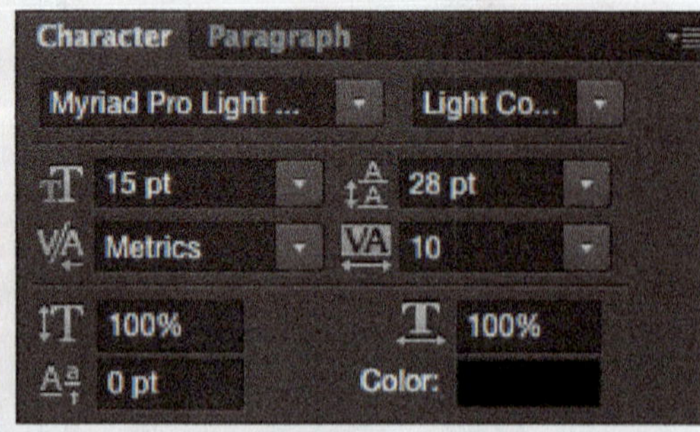

5. Click the Commit Any Current Edits button in the Options bar. Your vertical text now appears as the layer named VOL 9. Use the Move tool to center it in the ribbon, if necessary.

    Now, you'll clean up a bit.

6. Click the note to select it. Then right-click (Windows) or Control-click (Mac), and choose Delete Note from the context menu; click Yes to confirm that you want to delete the note.

7. Hide the guides and then press Ctrl+; (Windows) or Command+; (Mac). Zoom out to get a nice look at your work.
8. Choose File > Save to save your work.

   You've added and stylized all of the type on the Digital magazine cover. Now that the magazine cover is ready to go, you'll flatten it and prepare it for printing.
9. Choose File > Save As. In the Save As dialog box, rename the file **L11_start_xx_flattened**, and click Save. Click OK if you see the Photoshop Format Options dialog box.

   Keeping a layered version lets you return to the **L11_start_xx.psd** file in the future to edit it.
10. Choose Layer > Flatten Image.
11. Choose File > Save to save the file **L11_start_xx_flattend.psd**, then close the image window.

Careers in Computer Software Engineering

If you enjoy playing video games in your free time, you might consider pursuing a career as a computer software engineer. These workers research and design computer programs, creating applications to meet specific user needs. They might design software to help run a factory, to keep track of hospital patient files, or to create 3-D designs. They could create software for guiding missiles or saving an arcade princess. While they often have strong programming skills, software engineers are more concerned with creating and designing new applications rather than writing the actual code that makes those applications run. As such, their jobs require a balance of artistic vision, imagination, and technical skills.

Because computers are used in nearly every facet of life, the need for software engineers is great, and average earnings are relatively high. In fact, the profession is expected to grow much faster than average compared to other occupations over the next ten years. While there are a few examples of computer whiz kids who make their fortunes right out of high school, most computer software engineers have a bachelor's degree or higher.

Developing New Skills

There are many ways to develop new skills. Once you have a job, co-workers and supervisors often provide on-the-job training simply by showing you how to improve the way you do your regular tasks, or teaching you new skills.

Your company might also offer other opportunities for education and training, including:

- Specialized courses, such as a seminar on how to use Web-based storage for data management employees. You may receive certification after completing some of these courses.
- Professional development, which is training in your chosen career. Teachers are usually required to participate in professional development to learn about new trends in education and advancements in their area of expertise, or to prepare for certification exams.
- Tuition reimbursement programs, which means that if you take a class, your company will pay the tuition costs. You can take classes at a local college on nights or weekends to earn a degree or certification, or simply to learn new skills that might help you advance.

Developing new skills and receiving additional education, licensure, and certificates prepares you for new responsibilities and helps you achieve career, academic, and life goals. It makes you a more valuable worker and helps you grow as a person.

Comprehension Check

1. What is a clipping mask?
2. What effect does warping have on type?
3. List three ways you can develop new skills once you are working in a career.

Review Project

Research a career in the Web and Digital Communications pathway that interests you. Gather information on the job responsibilities, average annual salary, education requirements, and any certifications or other training required. Then, search for an image that you feel represents the job. Be sure to note the source of the image. Using the information you have gathered and the image, create a help wanted ad for the job. Pay special attention to your treatment of type to make sure the ad is easy to read and understand. Share your ad with the class.

Lesson 12 Overview

In this lesson, you will learn about:

- Preparing an Image for the Printer
- Finalizing an Image for Printing
- Checking and Correcting Image Problems
- Exploring Color Management
- Identifying Out-of-Gamut Colors
- Adjusting Color and Tone
- Converting an Image to CMYK
- Specifying Color Management Settings
- Proofing an Image
- Saving an Image as a CMYK EPS File
- Printing a CMYK Image from Photoshop
- Recognizing Printing Issues
- Reviewing Color Modes
- Exploring Printing Technology

After you've edited an image to get the effect you want, you probably want to share or publish it in some way. Ideally, you've been editing with the final output in mind, and you've managed file resolution, colors, file size, and other aspects of the image accordingly. But as you prepare to output the file, you have another opportunity to make sure your image will look its best.

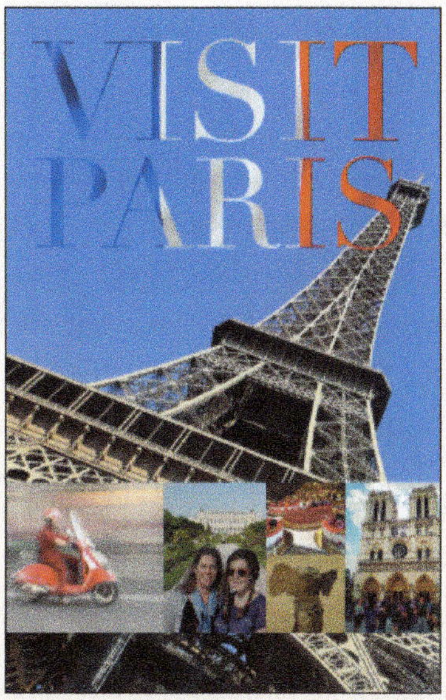

Preparing an Image for the Printer

If you plan to print the image—whether you'll print it to your own inkjet printer or send it to a service provider for professional printing—you should perform the following tasks for the best results. (Many of these tasks are described in greater detail later in this lesson.)

- Determine the final destination. Identify if it will be printed to a PostScript printer, an inkjet printer, an offset press, or some other device. If you're working with a service provider, ask what format they prefer; often, they request a PDF file.
- Verify that the image resolution is appropriate. For professional printing, the resolution should be 300 dpi when the image size matches the intended output size. For an inkjet printer, you may get the best results with a 300-dpi image, but you might also get good results with a lower resolution; if you own the printer, you can experiment with settings to find what works best. Generally, 300 dpi is a safe resolution for most printed output.
- Do a "zoom test:" Take a close look at the image. Zoom in to check and correct sharpness, color, noise, and other issues that can affect the final printed image quality.
- Allow for bleeds if you're sending an image for professional printing: If any color runs to the edge of the image, extend the canvas by 1/4 inch on all sides to ensure that the color is properly printed even if the trim line is not exact. Your service provider can help you determine whether you have bleeds and how to prepare your file to ensure it prints correctly.
- Unless you're printing to an inkjet printer, convert the file to CMYK. Note: Some high-quality printers are inkjets; ask your service provider what color space your image should be saved in.
- Flatten the file to reduce its size for faster transfer and printing speeds. Make sure you keep an unflattened copy of the original so you can make changes or reuse the content later, if necessary. Photoshop prompts you to merge layers when you convert to CMYK.
- Soft-proof the image to ensure the colors will print as you expect them to.

Finalizing an Image for Printing

You'll prepare an 11"x17" travel poster for professional printing. The Photoshop file is quite large, because it contains several layers and has a resolution of 300 dpi, which is necessary for quality printing.

Restore Default Preferences

First, start Photoshop, and restore its default preferences.

Try It!

1. Start Photoshop, and then immediately hold down Ctrl+Alt+Shift (Windows) or Command+Option+Shift (Mac) to restore the default preferences.

2. When prompted, click Yes to delete the Adobe Photoshop Settings file.
3. Choose File > Open, to open the **L12_start.psd** file from the data files for this lesson.

   Because the file is large, it may open slowly, depending on your system.
4. Choose File > Save As, and save the file as **L12_start_xx.psd** in the location where your teacher instructs you to store the files for this lesson, and leave it open.

   Click OK in the Photoshop Format options dialog box.

Checking and Correcting Image Problems

When you've finished editing an image, it is important to take a few minutes to make sure everything is appropriate for your output device and that you haven't overlooked any potentially problematic details. Start with the image resolution.

Try It!

1. Choose Image > Image Size.
2. Verify that the width and height are the final output size -11" in width and 17" in height-and that the resolution is 300 dpi.
3. Click OK to close the dialog box.

   Next, you'll look closely at the image and correct any problems. When you prepare your own images for printing, zoom in and scroll to view the entire image closely.
4. Select the Zoom tool in the Tools panel, and zoom in on the photos in the lower third of the poster.

   The photo of tourists is flat and a little muddy-looking.
5. Select the Tourists layer in the Layers panel, click the Adjustments tab to display the Adjustments panel, and then click the Curves button to add a Curves adjustment layer.

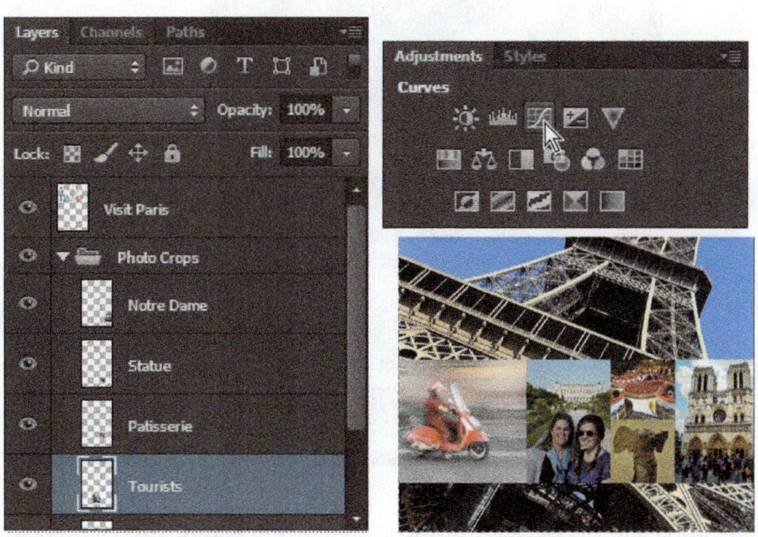

6. Click the Clip To Layer button at the bottom of the Properties panel to create a clipping mask.

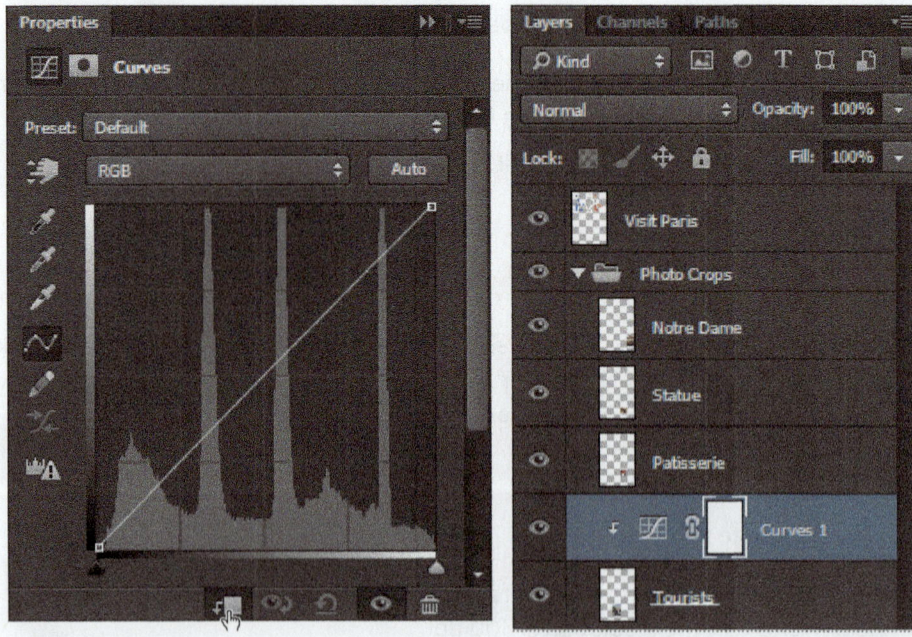

The clipping mask ensures that the adjustment layer affects only the layer directly below it in the Layers panel.

7. In the Properties panel, select the White Point eyedropper tool, and then click the light area of the building behind the tourists to brighten and correct the color in the image.

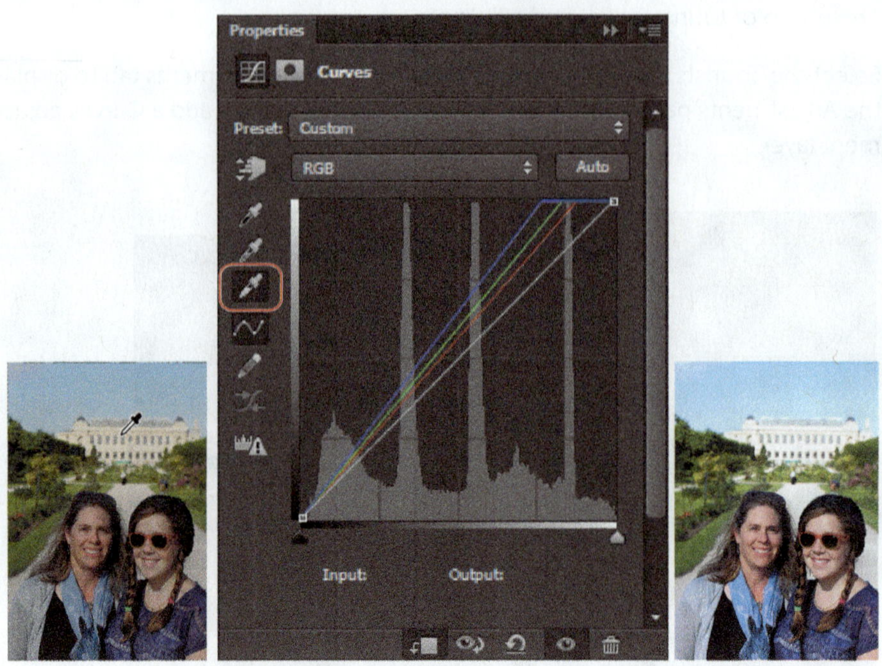

The image of tourists looks better. But the image of the statue appears flat and lacks contrast. You'll fix that with a Levels adjustment layer.

8. Select the Statue layer in the Layers panel, and then click the Levels icon in the Adjustments panel to add a Levels adjustment layer.

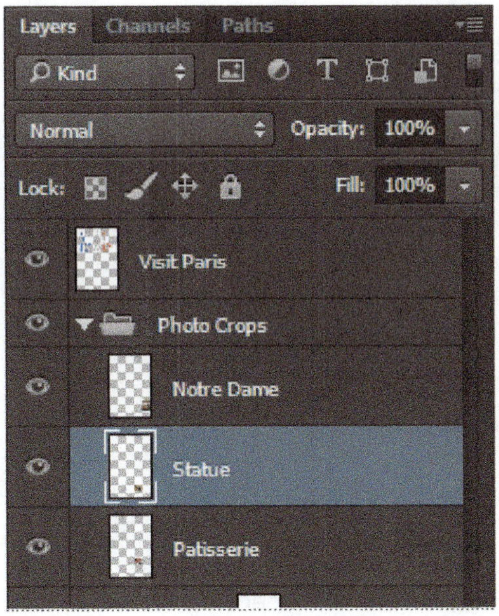

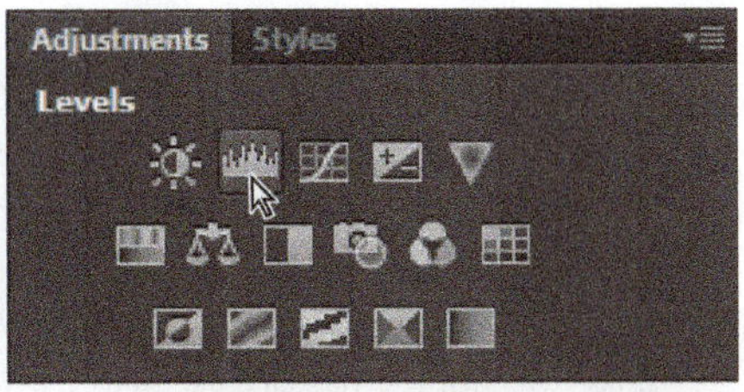

9. Click the Clip To Layer button at the bottom of the Properties panel to create a clipping mask, so that the adjustment layer affects only the Statue layer.

10. In the Properties panel, click the Calculate A More Accurate Histogram button to refresh the histogram display.

    Cached histogram data displays more quickly, but is often less accurate. It's a good idea to refresh the histogram before you make edits based on information in it.

11. Move the sliders to punch up the image. Enter the values 31, 1.6, and 235 as shown in the figure below.

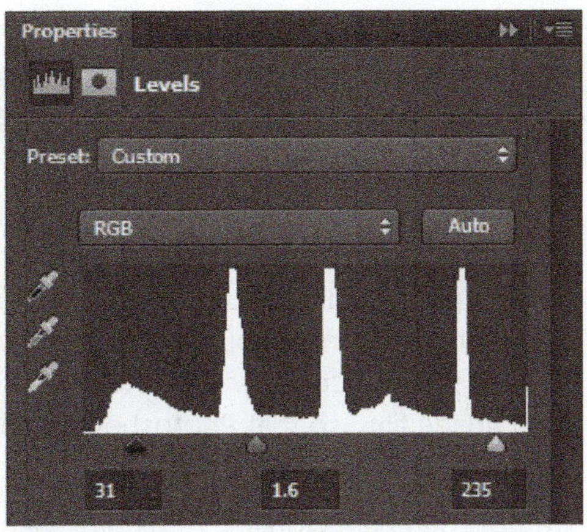

12. Save the **L12_start_xx.psd** file and leave it open.

Hexadecimal Values for Color

In Adobe® Photoshop® and other graphics programs, RGB mode assigns a value to each pixel. The values range from 0 to 255, for a total of 256 colors. Black (no color) is assigned the value of 0, and white (full color) is given a value of 255. Since RGB mode is based on three colors, one value needs to be assigned to the red, another to the green, and another to the blue to make another color. For example, one shade of bright red is made using a value of 246 for red, 20 for green, and 50 for blue. The three values are programmed into the computer using the hexadecimal value system for color so the desired color displays onscreen or in print.

About Color Management

Gamut
Range of colors

Because the RGB and CMYK color models use different methods to display colors, each reproduces a different **gamut**, or range, of colors. For example, RGB uses light to produce color, so its gamut includes neon colors, such as those you'd see in a neon sign. In contrast, printing inks excel at reproducing certain colors that can lie outside the RGB gamut, such as some pastels and pure black.

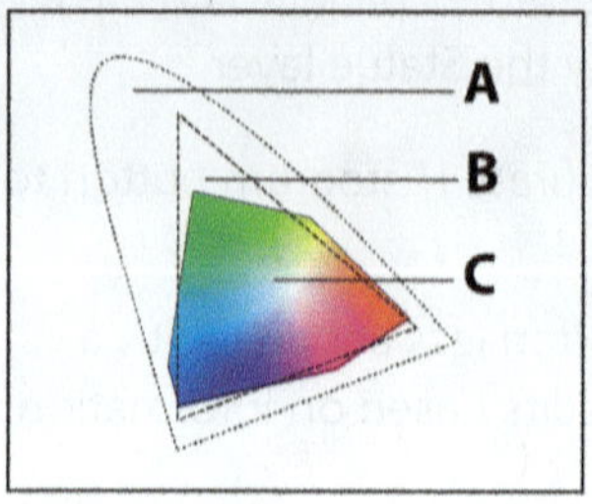

A. Visible colors
B. RGB
C. CMYK

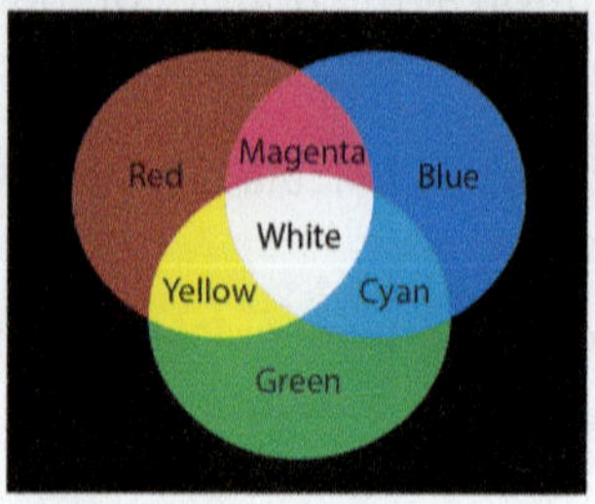

RGB (monitor)

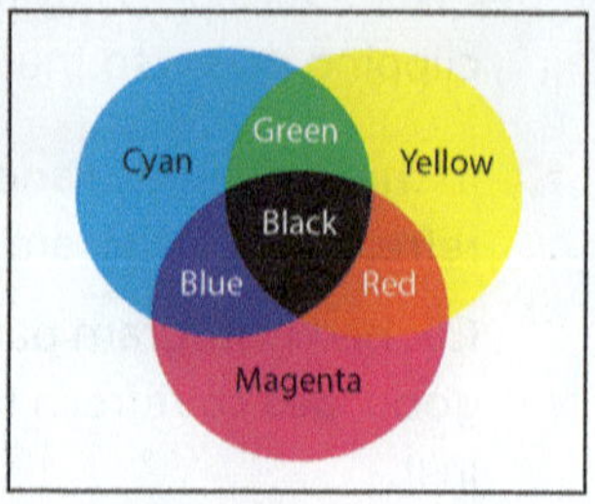

CMYK (printer)

Color Space
A conceptual tool for understanding the color capabilities of a particular device or digital file.

But not all RGB and CMYK gamuts are alike. Each monitor and printer model differs, and so each displays a slightly different gamut. For example, one brand of monitor may produce slightly brighter blues than another. The **color space** for a device is defined by the gamut it can reproduce.

The color management system in Photoshop uses International Color Consortium (ICC)-compliant color profiles to convert colors from one color space into another. A color profile is a description of a device's color space, such as the CMYK color space of a particular printer. You specify which profiles to use to accurately proof and print your images. Once you've selected the profiles, Photoshop can embed them into your image files, so that Photoshop and other applications can accurately manage color for the image.

Before you begin working with color management, you should calibrate your monitor. If your monitor doesn't display colors accurately, color adjustments you make based on the image you see on your monitor may not be accurate. For information about calibrating your monitor, see Photoshop Help.

Identifying Out-of-Gamut Colors

Colors on a monitor are displayed using combinations of red, green, and blue light (called RGB), while printed colors are typically created using a combination of four ink colors—cyan, magenta, yellow, and black (called CMYK). These four inks are called process colors because they are the standard inks used in the four-color printing process.

Most scanned photographs contain RGB colors within the CMYK gamut, so changing them to CMYK mode converts all the colors with relatively little substitution. Images that are created or altered digitally, however, often contain RGB colors that are outside the CMYK gamut—for example, neon-colored logos and lights.

Before you convert an image from RGB to CMYK, you can preview the CMYK color values while still in RGB mode.

Try It!

1. Choose View > Gamut Warning to see out-of-gamut colors. Photoshop builds a color-conversion table, and displays a neutral gray in the image window where the colors are out of gamut.

   Because the gray can be hard to spot in the image, you'll convert it to a more visible color.

2. Choose Edit > Preferences > Transparency & Gamut (Windows) or

   Photoshop CC > Preferences > Transparency & Gamut (Mac OS).

3. Click the color sample in the Gamut Warning area at the bottom of the dialog box. Select a vivid color, such as purple or bright green, and click OK.

4. Click OK to close the Preferences dialog box.

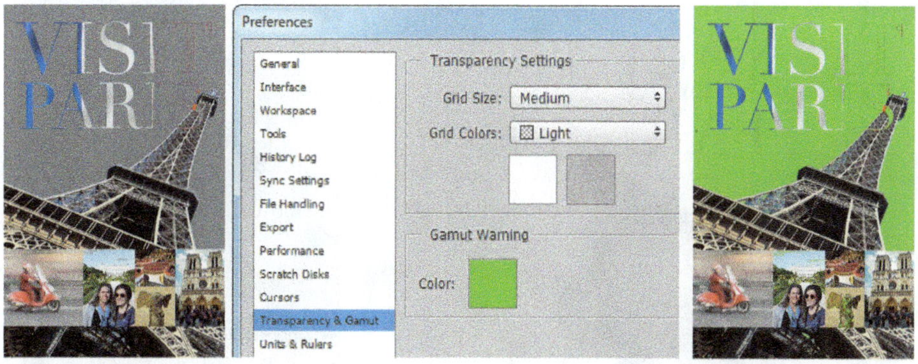

   The bright new color you chose appears instead of the neutral gray as the gamut warning color.

5. Choose View > Gamut Warning to turn off the preview of out-of-gamut colors.

6. Save the **L12_start_xx.psd** file and leave it open.

Adjusting Color and Tone

The next step in preparing an image for output is to make any necessary color and tonal adjustments. In this exercise, you'll add some tonal and color adjustments to correct an off-color scan of the original poster.

So that you can compare the image before and after making corrections, you'll start by making a copy.

Try It!

1. Choose Image > Duplicate, and click OK to duplicate the image.
2. Choose Window > Arrange > 2 Up Vertical so you can compare the images as you work.

   You'll adjust the hue and saturation of the image to move all colors into gamut.
3. Select L12_start_xx.psd (the original image) to make it active, and then select the Visit Paris layer in the Layers panel.
4. Choose Select > Color Range.
5. In the Color Range dialog box, choose Out Of Gamut from the Select menu, and then click OK.

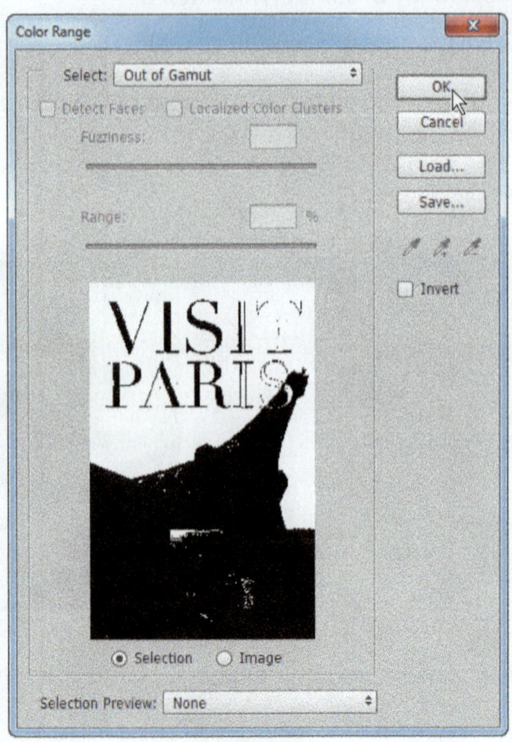

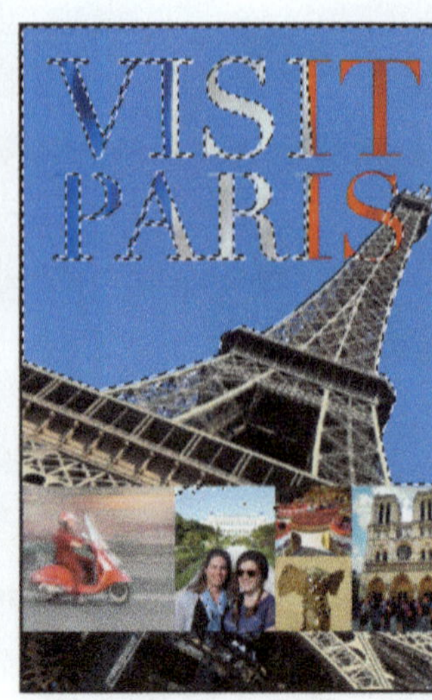

The areas that were marked as out of gamut earlier are now selected, so you can make changes that affect only those areas.

6. Choose View > Extras to hide the selection while you work with it.

   The selection border can be distracting. When you hide extras, you no longer see the selection, but it's still in effect.

7. Click the Hue/Saturation button in the Adjustments panel to create a Hue/Saturation adjustment layer. (Choose Window > Adjustments if the panel isn't open.) The Hue/Saturation adjustment layer includes a layer mask, created from your selection.

8. In the Properties panel, do the following:

   - Leave the Hue setting at the default value.
   - Drag the Saturation slider until the intensity of the colors looks more realistic (we used -14).
   - Drag the Lightness to the left to darken (we used -2).

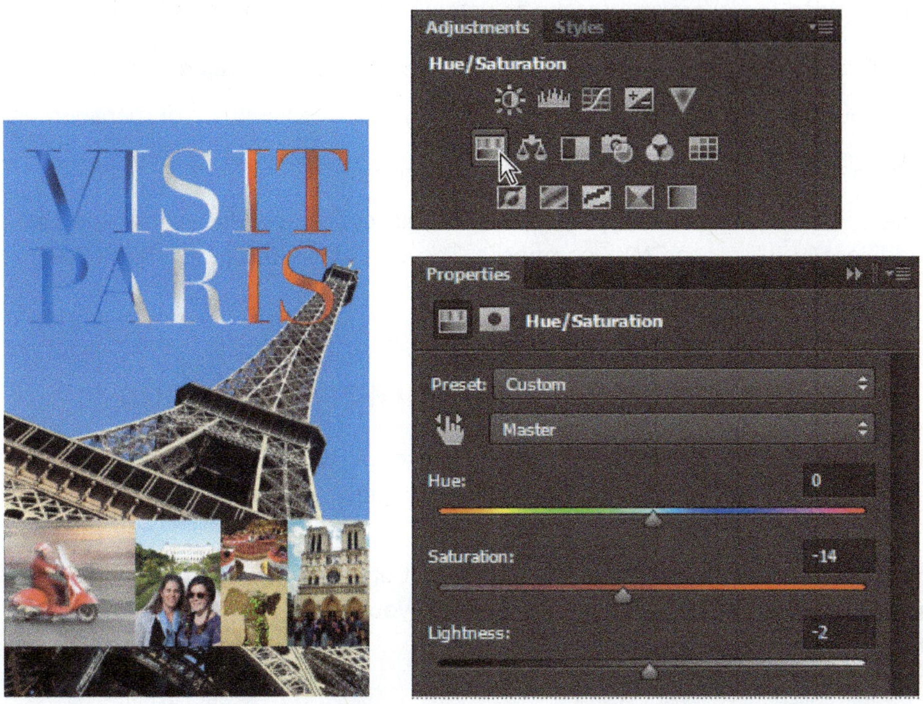

9. Choose View > Gamut Warning. You have removed most of the out-of-gamut colors from the image. Choose View > Gamut Warning again to deselect it.

10. Close the duplicate image file without saving it.

11. Save the **L12_start_xx.psd** file and leave it open.

Converting an Image to CMYK

It's generally a good idea to work in RGB mode as long as possible. Converting between modes causes color values to be rounded—and therefore less accurate if you convert multiple times. Once you've made any last-minute corrections, you're ready to convert the image to CMYK. If you think you may want to output the image to an inkjet printer or distribute it digitally later, save a copy in RGB mode before converting to CMYK mode.

Try It!

1. Click the Channels tab to bring the Channels panel to the front.

   The image is currently in RGB mode, so there are three channels listed: red, green, and blue. The RGB channel is not actually a channel, but a composite of all three.

2. Choose Image > Mode > CMYK Color.
3. Click Merge in the message that warns you that you might lose some adjustment layers.

   Adjustment layers are lost when you convert the color mode from RGB to CMYK. Merging the layers ensures the adjustments you made are preserved.

4. Click OK in the message about the color profile used in the conversion.

   You'll learn more about color profiles when you work with color management.

5. Save the **L12_start_xx.psd** file and leave it open.

The Channels panel now displays four channels: cyan, magenta, yellow, and black. Additionally, it lists the CMYK composite. The layers were merged during conversion, so there is only one layer in the Layers panel.

Specifying Color Management Settings

In order to accurately preview your colors onscreen, you need to set up color management in Photoshop. Most of the color management controls you need are in the Color Settings dialog box.

By default, Photoshop is set up for RGB as part of a digital workflow. If you are preparing artwork for print production, however, you'll want to change the settings to be more appropriate for printing.

You'll create customized color settings.

Try It!

1. Choose Edit > Color Settings to open the Color Settings dialog box.

   The bottom of the dialog box interactively describes each option.

2. Move the pointer over each part of the dialog box, including the names of areas (such as Working Spaces), the menu names, and the menu options. As you move the pointer, Photoshop displays information about each item.

   Now, you'll choose a set of options designed for a print workflow, rather than an online workflow.

3. Choose North America Prepress 2 from the Settings menu. The working spaces and color-management policy options change for a prepress workflow. Then click OK.

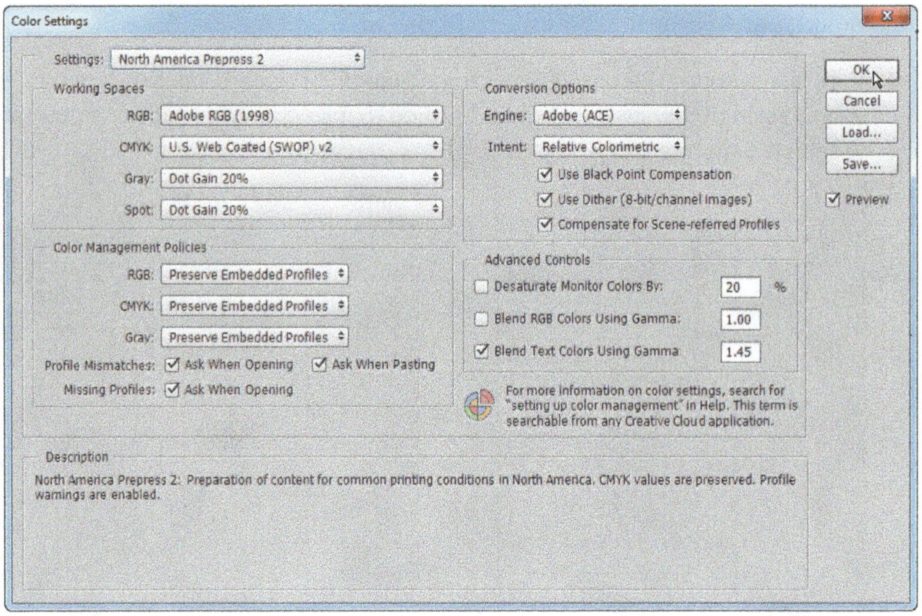

4. Save the **L12_start_xx.psd** file and leave it open.

Proofing an Image

You'll select a proof profile so that you can view a close onscreen representation of what an image will look like when printed. An accurate proof profile lets you proof on the screen (**soft proof**) for printed output.

A **proof profile** (also called a **proof setup**) defines how the file is going to be printed, and adjusts the onscreen appearance accordingly. Photoshop provides a variety of settings that can help you proof images for different uses, including print and display on the Web. For this lesson, you'll create a custom proof setup. You can then save the settings for use on other images that will be output the same way.

Soft Proof

Proofing for printed output on screen.

Proof Profile or Proof Setup

Settings that define how something will be printed

Try It!

1. Choose View > Proof Setup > Custom. The Customize Proof Condition dialog box opens. Make sure Preview is selected.

2. From the Device To Simulate menu, choose a profile that represents the final output device, such as that for the printer you'll use to print the image. If you don't have a specific printer, the profile Working CMYK–U.S. Web Coated (SWOP) v2, the current default, is generally a good choice.

3. If you've chosen a different profile, make sure Preserve CYMK Numbers is *not* selected.

   The Preserve CMYK Numbers option simulates how colors will appear if they're not converted to the output device color space.

4. Make sure Relative Colorimetric is selected for the Rendering Intent.

   A rendering intent determines how the color is converted from one color space to another. Relative Colorimetric, which preserves color relationships without sacrificing color accuracy, is the standard rendering intent for printing in North America and Europe.

5. If it's available for the profile you chose, select Simulate Black Ink. Then deselect it, and select Simulate Paper Color; notice that selecting this option automatically selects Simulate Black Ink.

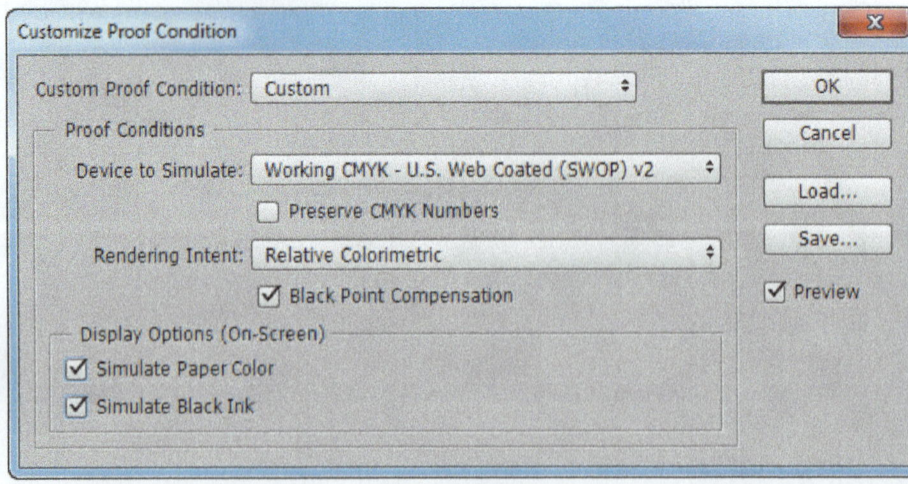

   Notice that the image appears to lose contrast. Paper Color simulates the dingy white of real paper, according to the proof profile. Black Ink simulates the dark gray that actually prints to most printers, instead of solid black. Not all profiles support these options.

6. Toggle the Preview option to see the difference between the image as it is displayed on screen and as it will print, based on the profile you selected. Then click OK.

7. Save the **L12_start_xx.psd** file and leave it open.

Saving the Image as a CMYK EPS File

Many professional printers request that Photoshop images be submitted in EPS format. You'll save this image as an EPS file in CMYK mode.

Try It!

1. Choose File > Save As.
2. In the Save As dialog box, do the following, and then click Save:
   - Choose Photoshop EPS from the Save as type menu.
   - Under Color, select Use Proof Setup. Don't worry about the warning icon; you'll save a copy.
   - Accept the filename **L12_start_xx.eps**.

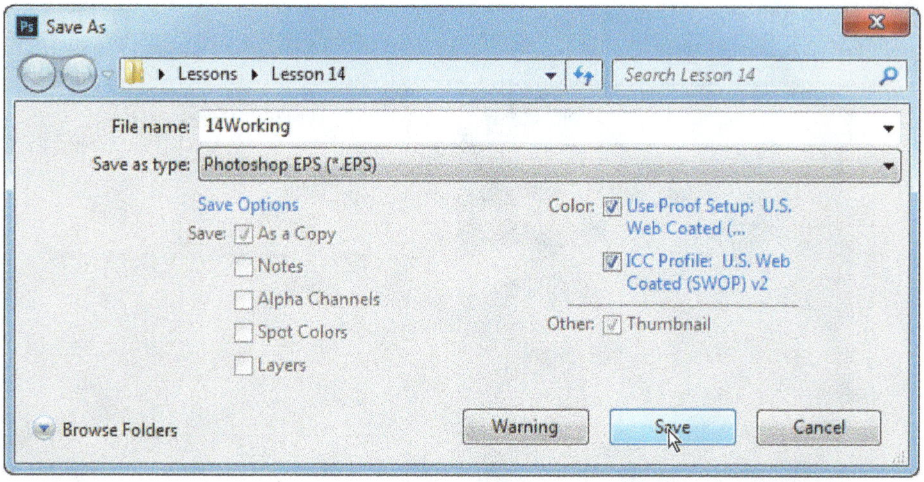

3. Click OK in the EPS Options dialog box that appears.
4. Save and then close the **L12_start_xx.psd** file.
5. Choose File > Open, to open the **L12_start_xx.eps** from the location where your teacher instructs you to store the files for this lesson, and leave it open.

Printing a CMYK Image from Photoshop

If you're printing an image directly from Photoshop, use the following guidelines for best results:

- Print a **color composite**, often called a **color comp**, to proof your image. A color composite is a single print that combines the red, green, and blue channels of an RGB image (or the cyan, magenta, yellow, and black channels of a CMYK image). This indicates what the final printed image will look like.
- Set the parameters for the halftone screen.
- Print separations to make sure the image separates correctly.
- Print to film or **plate**.

Color composite or color comp

A single print that combines the red, green, and blue channels in an RGB image or the cyan, magenta, yellow, and black channels of a CMYK image indicating what the final image will look like.

Plate

A separate sheet printed for each ink.

When you print color separations, Photoshop prints a separate sheet, or plate, for each ink. For a CMYK image, it prints four plates, one for each process color. In this exercise, you'll print color separations.

Try It!

1. With the **L12_start_xx.eps** image open from the previous exercise, choose File > Print.

   By default, Photoshop prints any document as a composite image. To print this file as separations, you need to explicitly instruct Photoshop in the Print dialog box.

2. In the Photoshop Print Settings dialog box, do the following:
   - In the Color Management area, choose Separations from the Color Handling menu.
   - Click Print.

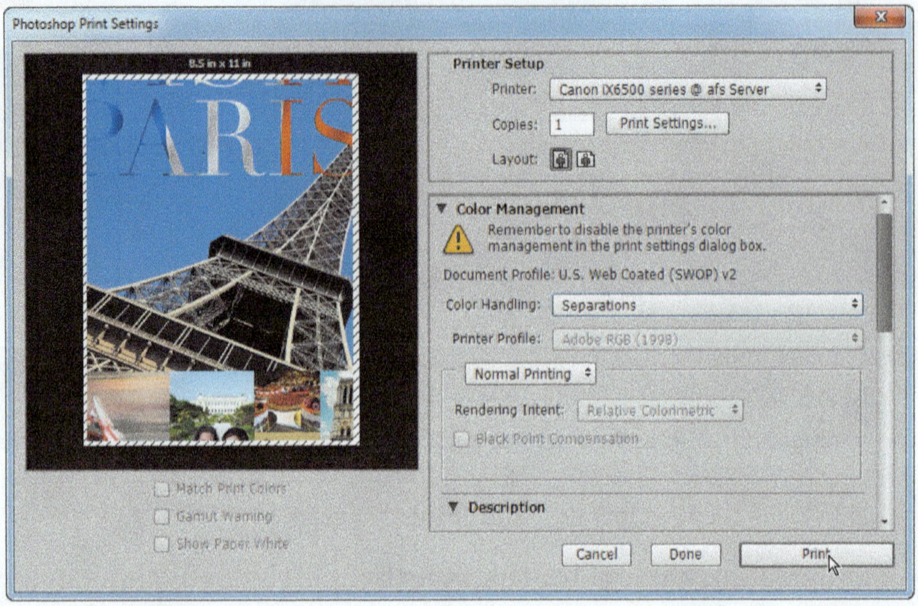

3. Close the file without saving and close Photoshop.

This lesson has provided an introduction to printing and producing consistent color from Photoshop. If you're printing on a desktop printer, you can experiment with different settings to find the best color and print settings for your system. If you're preparing images for professional printing, consult with your print service provider to determine the best settings to use. For more information about color management, printing options, and color separations, see Photoshop Help.

Printing to a Desktop Inkjet Printer

Many consumer-level inkjet printers do a good job printing photographs and other image files. The precise settings available vary from printer to printer, but when you're printing images from Photoshop to a desktop inkjet printer, you'll get the best results if you do the following:

- Make sure the appropriate printer driver is installed, and that you've selected it.
- Use the appropriate paper for your intended use. Special photographic and coated papers are a good choice when you're printing photos for framing.
- Select the correct paper source in the printer settings. The printer lays ink differently on different types of paper. If you're using photographic paper, make sure you've selected it in the printer settings.
- Select the image quality in the printer settings. For framed prints, you probably want to print the highest quality. If you're printing a proof to get a sense of the color, you may want to select a lower quality for speedier printing and to use less ink.

Recognizing Printing Issues

File Compression and Graphics

Graphics files can be very large. When they are stored on the computer, the images are often compressed, or saved in a format requiring less space. This saves disk space and decreases the time it takes to send images via the Internet.

When a file is compressed, the program performing the compression replaces certain pieces of information with shorter codes. This makes the file smaller.

In **lossless compression**, information is removed in such a way that all of it can later be fully restored without introducing errors. This process results in a perfect copy of the file that is about one third of the original size. Lossless compression is a good choice for reducing files with graphics, text, or computer code.

In **lossy compression**, some information is permanently removed from the file in such a way that it cannot be restored to its original state. Lossy compression can reduce a file to one fiftieth or less of its former size. It is best for reducing the size of video and audio files.

Lossless Compression

Information is removed in such a way that all of it can later be fully restored without introducing errors.

Lossy Compression

Information is permanently removed from the file in such a way that it cannot be restored to its original state.

Color Depth

Color Depth

The number of colors that can be displayed on a monitor at one time

The more colors or shades of gray an image contains, the sharper and more detailed it will look. The number of colors that can be displayed on a monitor at one time is the **color depth**. Most modern computer monitors can display millions of colors. Because the computer must store more bits of information for each color pixel, more memory is needed to store colors than to store black and white alone.

Resolution Issues

When creating or modifying graphics, it is important to work with the proper resolution. A graphic's resolution should be determined by how that graphic will be displayed—the output.

If a graphic is to be viewed on-screen only, the resolution need not be higher than 72 dpi or 96 dpi. A 300-dpi graphic looks the same on-screen as a 72-dpi version of the same file. Increasing the dpi does not improve on-screen appearance. Because a 72- or 96-dpi file is smaller, it will display more quickly.

Reviewing Color Modes

Color modes determine which and how many colors are available for creating computer graphics.

Bitmap Mode

When it comes to color modes, bitmap refers to a 1-bit, or black-and-white, image.

Grayscale Mode

When working in grayscale mode, the computer can display 256 different shades of gray to represent the colors, shades, and textures in an image.

RGB Mode

Look closely at a television picture, and you may notice that it is made up of tiny clusters of dots. Each cluster has one red, one green, and one blue dot. When these three colors are combined in various ways, they produce different colors.

RGB mode allows each of these three colors to have 8 bits of information, resulting in 256 different shades each of the colors red (R), green (G), and blue (B). Color computer monitors use RGB color to display graphics, so RGB mode is used to design on-screen graphics such as those for the Internet.

CMYK Mode

In CMYK mode, a combination of four colors in different densities produces other colors. Variations of cyan (greenish-blue), magenta (purplish-red), yellow, and black (known as K) are combined to produce new colors.

CMYK mode is used to design graphics that will be printed on a printing press. Each of the four color values in a CMYK graphic is assigned to one of the four inks. These inks are then used on the printing press to print a full-color piece.

But what if you wanted to display a CMYK graphic on a monitor? To view a CMYK graphic on the screen, the computer has to convert it to RGB. This is why printed graphics may look different from an on-screen preview of the image.

Psychological Effects of Color

Some people give a lot of weight to the psychological effects and associations of color, while others prefer to use color based solely on the visual impact. The psychological implications of color can be very complex and subtle. They also vary from culture to culture, so you should try to learn something about your audience when making color choices. However, there are some basic associations with colors to take into account when designing. You can manipulate these associations by slightly altering hue, saturation, and value.

The warm colors—red, orange, and yellow—have associations ranging from anger, agitation, and excitement to warmth, security, and new growth. Red is often associated with passion and with aggression. Yellow has strong associations with sunlight, warmth, and growth and, at the same time, can be considered cowardly or sickly. The cool colors of blue, green, and purple are generally thought to be calming and peaceful and are associated with stability, but they can also evoke sadness and despair. Blue often connotes authority and stability, but can serve equally well to invoke the sky and dreamlike, soothing states. Green has taken on a whole new range of associations with the interest in environmental issues. Black connotes stability, power, authority, and death and is often considered sinister or evil. White is usually associated with purity and light. However, many of these associations as different in other cultures. For instance, in some cultures purple, rather than black, is used in mourning. In India, white has negative associations as well as positive; in Japan, white is connected with death. In all cases, you need to consider your audience and do some research before making assumptions about color associations.

You will want to be particularly aware of certain color combinations commonly used in our society and make conscious decisions about how to use them. For example, green and red will always mean Christmas in the United States (and in many countries). Orange and black are associated with

Halloween. These associations don't necessarily restrict you from using those color combinations; just be aware of the potential underlying messages. Use of colors also changes just like fashion. Pay attention to the "fashionable" colors of the season, not with pressure to use them, but to be aware of what they are when making choices. For example, if you're designing a building's signage system, then you might not want to use a color that will be trendy.

Also keep in mind that approximately 8 percent of men and .5 percent of women are colorblind. If your message is dependent entirely on the use of color, you may be losing part of your audience. Try to make sure that, even if color is a major design component, it is still possible for a viewer to understand the information if they see only shades of gray.

Comprehension Check

1. What steps should you follow to reproduce color accurately?
2. What is a gamut?
3. What is a color profile?
4. Why do graphics files often need compression?
5. Why is RGB mode used to design computer graphics?

Review Project

Start Photoshop and open the birthday card file you worked with in Lesson 7 of Chapter 3 named **L7_start_xx.psd**. Save the file as **L12_review_xx.psd** in the location where your teacher instructs you to store the files for this lesson. Review the steps presented at the beginning of this lesson for how to prepare an image for the printer. Do the following to prepare the birthday card for printing:

- Leave the final output size as is but change the resolution to 300 dpi.
- Make adjustments to the color and tone as you feel is necessary.
- Identify out-of-gamut colors and make adjustments accordingly.
- Convert the image to CMYK and change color management settings, if necessary.
- Proof the image.
- Save it as a CYMK EPS file (using the same name) and, with your instructor's permission, print it. Close the file and then close Photoshop.

Lesson 13 Overview

In this lesson, you will learn about:

- Exploring the 3D Environment
- Positioning 3D Elements
- Printing a 3D File
- Exporting a 3D Object
- Using Communication Skills

This lesson explores 3D features, which are available only if your video card has at least 512MB of dedicated VRAM and supports OpenGL 2.0, and if OpenGL 2.0 is enabled on your computer. To learn about your video card, choose Edit > Preferences > Performance (Windows) or Photoshop CC > Preferences > Performance (Mac). Information about your video card is in the Graphics Processor Settings area of the dialog box.

In this lesson, you'll create a three-dimensional luggage tag.

Exploring the 3D Environment

Applying three-dimensional effects can create a whole new perspective on your images. Photoshop includes several basic tools that make it easy to rotate, resize, and position 3D objects. The 3D tools in the Options bar manipulate the object itself. The Camera widget in the lower left corner of the application window allows you to view a 3D scene from different angles.

You can use the 3D tools whenever a 3D layer is selected in the Layers panel. A 3D layer behaves like any other layer—you can apply layer styles, mask it, and so on. However, a 3D layer can be quite complex.

Unlike a regular layer, a 3D layer contains one or more **meshes**. A mesh defines the 3D object. For example, in the following exercise, the mesh is the cone shape. Each mesh, in turn, includes one or more **materials**—the appearance of a part or all of the mesh. Each material includes one or more **maps**, which are the components of the appearance. There are nine typical maps, and there can be only one of each kind; however, you can also use custom maps. Each map contains one **texture**—the image that defines what the maps and materials look like. The texture may be a simple bitmap graphic or a set of layers. The same texture might be used by many different maps and materials.

In addition to meshes, a 3D layer also includes one or more **lights**, which affect the appearance of 3D objects and remain in a fixed position as you spin or move the object. A 3D layer also includes **cameras**, which are saved views with the objects in a particular position. The **shader** creates the final appearance based on the materials, object properties, and renderer.

That may all sound complicated, but the most important thing to remember is that the 3D tools in the Options bar move an object in 3D space and the Camera widget moves the cameras that view the object.

You'll start by creating a simple 3D object from a plain colored layer.

Mesh

Defines the 3D object.

Materials

The appearance of a part or all of the mesh.

Maps

The components of the appearance of a 3D object.

Texture

The image that defines what the maps and materials look like.

Lights

Affects the appearance of 3D objects and remain in fixed positions as you spin or move the object.

Cameras

Saved views with the objects in a particular position.

Shader

Creates the final appearance based on the materials, object properties, and renderer.

Try It!

1. In Photoshop, choose File > New and select Default Photoshop Size . Click OK to accept the default values.

2. Choose Select > All to select the entire background layer.

3. Choose Edit > Fill. In the Fill dialog box, choose Color from the Contents menu, and then select a vivid blue color in the Color Picker. Click OK to close the Color Picker, and click OK again to close the Fill dialog box.

4. Choose Select > Deselect.

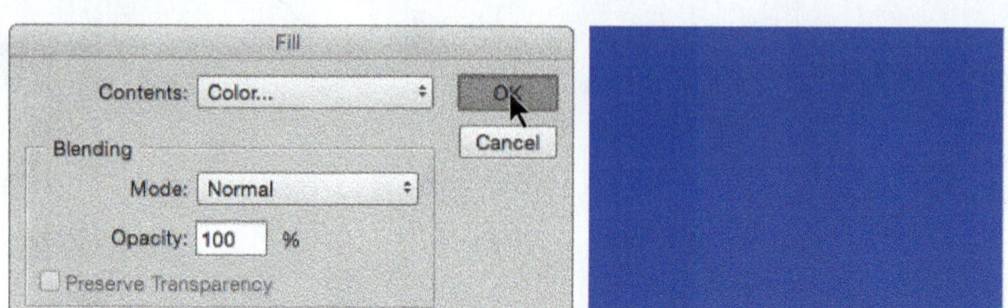

5. Choose 3D > New Mesh From Layer > Mesh Preset > Cone. If you see a message asking whether you want to switch to the 3D workspace, click Yes.

   Click OK in the Embedded Profile Mismatch dialog box accepting the defaults.

   Your blue layer becomes a blue cone. Photoshop displays a grid, a Secondary View window, a Camera widget, and other 3D resources. Now that you have a 3D object, you can use the 3D tools.

6. In the Tools panel, select the Move tool.

   All the 3D capabilities are embedded into the Move tool, which recognizes when a 3D layer is selected and enables the 3D tools.

7. Select the Pan the 3D Camera tool in the 3D Mode area of the Options bar.

8. Click the edge of the cone, or just outside it, and drag to move it from side to side or up and down. Return the cone to the center. (If you click the cone itself, Photoshop recognizes the 3D Axis widget, and switches to the tool that corresponds with the active area of the widget, which you'll learn about shortly.)

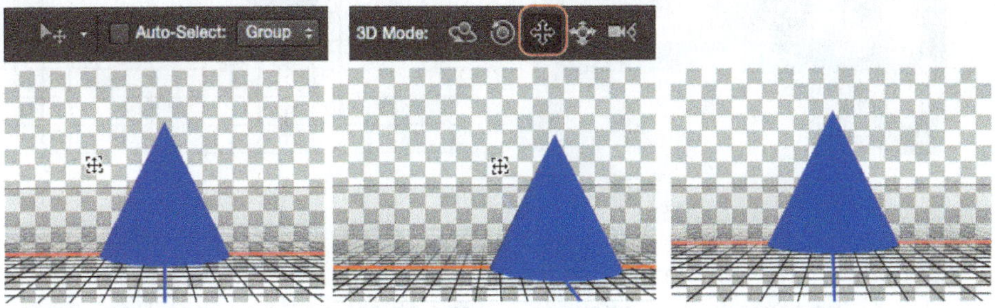

9. Select the Orbit the 3D Camera tool in the Options bar, and then click and drag the cone to rotate the view. Experiment with the other tools to see how they affect the view of the object.

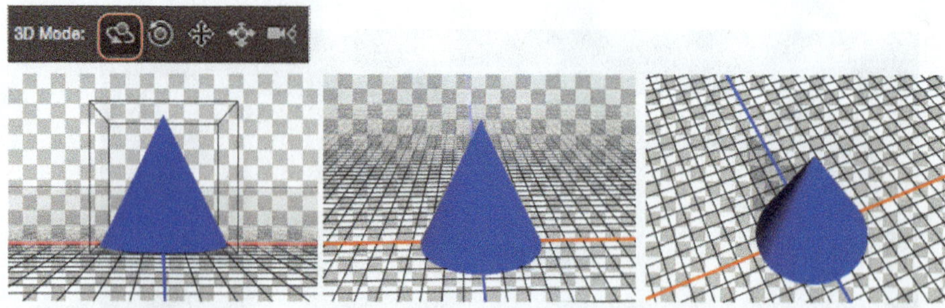

10. With the Move tool, click the cone to select it.

    When you select a 3D object, Photoshop displays the colorful 3D Axis widget, with green, red, and blue representing different axes. Red represents the x axis, green represents the y axis, and blue represents the z axis. (Hint: Think of RGB color to remember the order.)

    If you hover the mouse over the center box until it turns yellow, you can click the box and drag to scale the object uniformly. Click an arrow to move the object along that axis; click the curved handle just before the arrow to rotate on that axis; click the smaller handle to scale along that axis.

11. Rotate, scale, and move the cone using the widget.

12. Right-click (Windows) or Control-click (Mac OS) the Camera widget in the lower left corner of the application window (it has two axes visible), and choose Top.

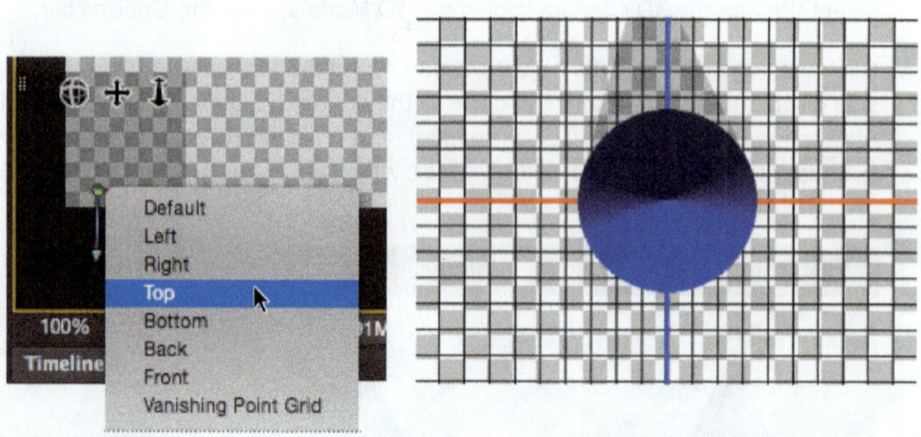

    Options on the Camera menu determine the angle from which you see the object. The camera angle changes, but the object itself does not. Don't be fooled by its relationship to the background; the background is not 3D, so it remains in place when Photoshop moves the camera for the 3D object.

13. Choose other camera views to see how they affect the perspective.

14. When you're done experimenting, close the file. You can save your creation if you want to, or close without saving.

Positioning 3D Elements

Now that you've gotten a feel for the 3D tools, you'll use them to position the text on a luggage tag.

Try It!

1. Choose File > Open, to open the **L13_start_xx.psd** file from the data files for this lesson.

   Click OK on the Embedded Profile Mismatch dialog box accepting the default settings.

2. Save the file as **L13_start_xx.psd** in the location where your teacher instructs you to store the files for this lesson, and leave it open. Click OK in the Photoshop Format Options dialog box.

   This file contains two 3D elements: the text and the tag itself. Currently, the text is in an awkward position, overlapping the tag. You'll start by centering it.

3. Make sure the Move tool is selected in the Tools panel.

4. Click the front of the "Visit Paris" text to activate the 3D Axis widget.

5. Hover the pointer over the tip of the green arrow until the Move On Y Axis tool tip appears.

6. Click the tip of the green arrow, and drag the type down until it's centered vertically on the red tag.

7. Click the tip of the red arrow, and drag the type to the right so that it's horizontally centered on the red tag.

   Your tag is ready to print.

Printing a 3D File

When you think of printing, you usually think of producing a flat page of two-dimensional text and images. They may be high-quality, amazing images, but you can't see them from different angles, and what you hold in your hand remains a piece of paper or other relatively simple media.

3D printers open up a whole new world of printing opportunities. Instead of printing an image of a thing, you can print the thing itself. The possibilities are endless, including medical uses, prototyping, and creative enterprises such as making jewelry and one-of-a-kind souvenirs.

3D printers were once the province of well-funded labs, but have recently become much more accessible. In many cities, you can use one at a "maker" or do-it-yourself (DIY) space, a shared workshop area where, for a fee, you can use many advanced resources. If you don't have a 3D printer yourself or easy access to one, you can also send your 3D creations to online vendors who will print them using the material you specify and mail them to you.

You can create 3D objects in Photoshop—or import 3D objects that have been created elsewhere—and print them directly from Photoshop.

Specifying 3D Print Settings

You don't use the standard Print dialog box to print 3D objects from Photoshop. And before you print, you need to make sure the settings are appropriate.

Try It!

1. Choose 3D > 3D Print Settings.

   The Properties panel displays the 3D print settings, and the image window shows a preview of your 3D object. The preview shows you how it will look when printed, based on the printer you select.

2. Choose Shapeways from the Print To menu in the Properties panel.

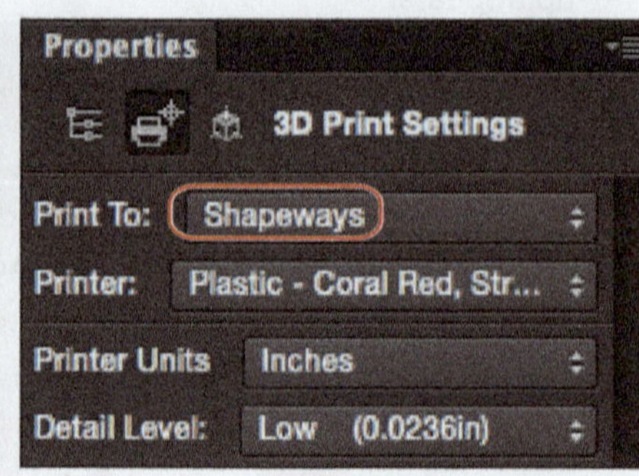

   Shapeways is an online vendor that prints 3D objects and mails them to you for a fee. There are other online vendors, but Shapeways is easiest to use because you can choose its printers directly within Photoshop. If you use another vendor, ask them for instructions for printing from Photoshop.

   If you own a 3D printer, choose Local from the Print To menu, and then choose your printer from the Printer menu. If your printer isn't listed on the menu, choose Get Latest Printers from the Print To menu, and then download the profiles for all supported printers.

3. Choose Plastic - Alumide from the Printer menu. Plastic alumide is a plastic that simulates metal.

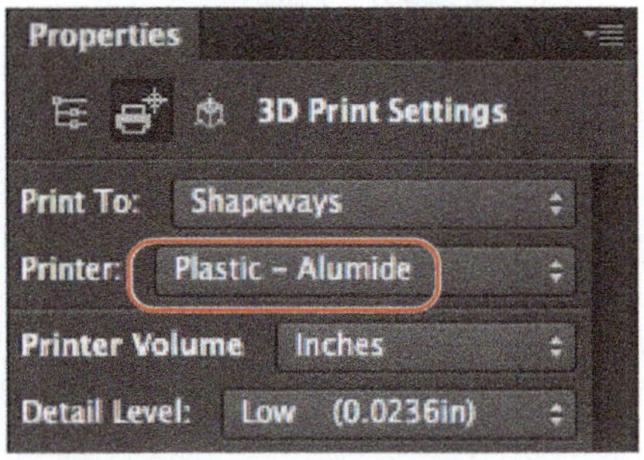

When you choose Shapeways from the Print To menu, the Printer menu lists dozens of material options. The material you select affects the appearance and cost of the object you print.

The preview of the 3D object changes in the image window to reflect the choices you've made. When you choose Plastic - Alumide, the preview shows a silver-gray tag with extruded text.

4. Make sure Inches is selected in the Printer Units menu to specify how printer volume should be measured.

   3D printers have different capacities, and it's important to consider whether your object will fit within the printer's volume. The Printer Units values are dimmed, because you can't change them; they describe the volume for the printer you've chosen. The Scene Volume values reflect the size of your 3D scene (in this case, a single object). If the Show checkbox is selected, the preview shows a cube outline to represent the printer volume that the scene lies within.

   If the scene volume is larger than the printer volume, click Scale To Print Volume in the Properties panel to reduce its size so that your printer can print it. In this case, the scene volume is comfortably smaller than the printer volume.

5. Choose Medium from the Detail Level menu. This option determines how detailed the preview image is.

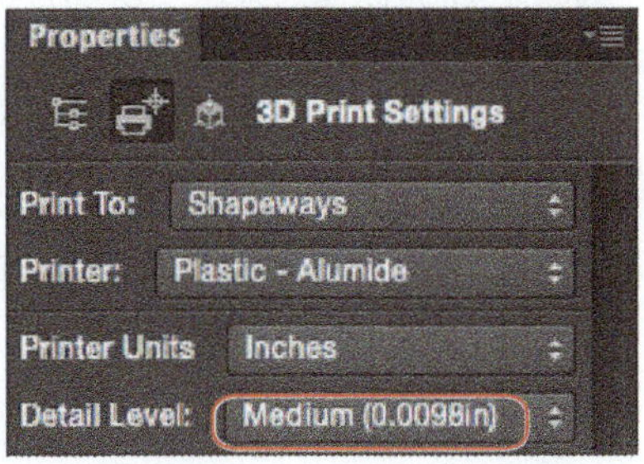

The Surface Detail options preserve bump maps and other texture and opacity settings when you print. You can leave those options selected, though there are no bump maps or opacity settings in this object.

You're ready to print.

6. Save the **L13_start_xx.psd** file and leave it open.

Exporting a 3D Object

Printing a 3D object is a little more complicated than printing a two-dimensional image. It's not that much more challenging for the person doing the printing, but Photoshop has to do a lot of behind-the-scenes calculations.

Raft

A base for a 3D object to print on.

Scaffolding

Supports portions of the 3D object so they don't collapse while the rest of the object is printed.

3D printers build objects from the bottom. If you're printing a cube, for example, or another object with a significant base, the printer can create it without further support. However, many 3D objects are irregularly shaped, and the bottom of the object may actually be a set of disconnected surfaces. For example, think of a model of an animal. The bottom of the animal is composed of the four separate feet. In order to print such an object, the printer requires a support structure. That structure typically includes a **raft**, which provides a base to print from, and **scaffolding**, which supports portions of the object so they don't collapse while the rest of the object is being printed.

When you choose 3D Print, Photoshop prepares the object for printing, and calculates any necessary raft and scaffolding as well.

Try It!

1. Choose 3D > 3D Print, or click the Start Print icon at the bottom of the Properties panel.

   Photoshop displays a progress bar as it prepares the print job.

2. Click OK in the dialog box that informs you that the estimated price may differ from the final purchase price.

3. In the Photoshop 3D Print Settings dialog box, review the estimated price and print size.

   Click options in the Preview area of the dialog box to see the size, shadows, raft, scaffolding, and other aspects of the job. This object requires no raft or scaffolding, so those options are dimmed.

   Use the 3D tools at the top of the dialog box to see your object from different angles.

   Printing prices vary dramatically depending on the material you choose. You can click Cancel, choose a different printer, and then let Photoshop calculate the price again. You've made no commitments at this point in the process.

4. Click Export.
5. Click Save in the Save dialog box.

   Photoshop saves the 3D print file information in the L13_start_xx.psd file.
6. When you're prompted to upload your file to the Shapeways site for printing, click Yes to continue to the site, or click No to stop the process.
7. If you continue to the Shapeways site, sign in if you have an account, or create one if you don't. (Creating an account is free.)
8. On the Shapeways Web site, click Upload. When prompted, select the file you just saved and click Choose. It will be in the location where your teacher has you save your files, called L13_start_xx.stl.zip. Then click Upload.

   Shapeways uploads and unzips the file. It displays the object and lists possible materials and their prices.

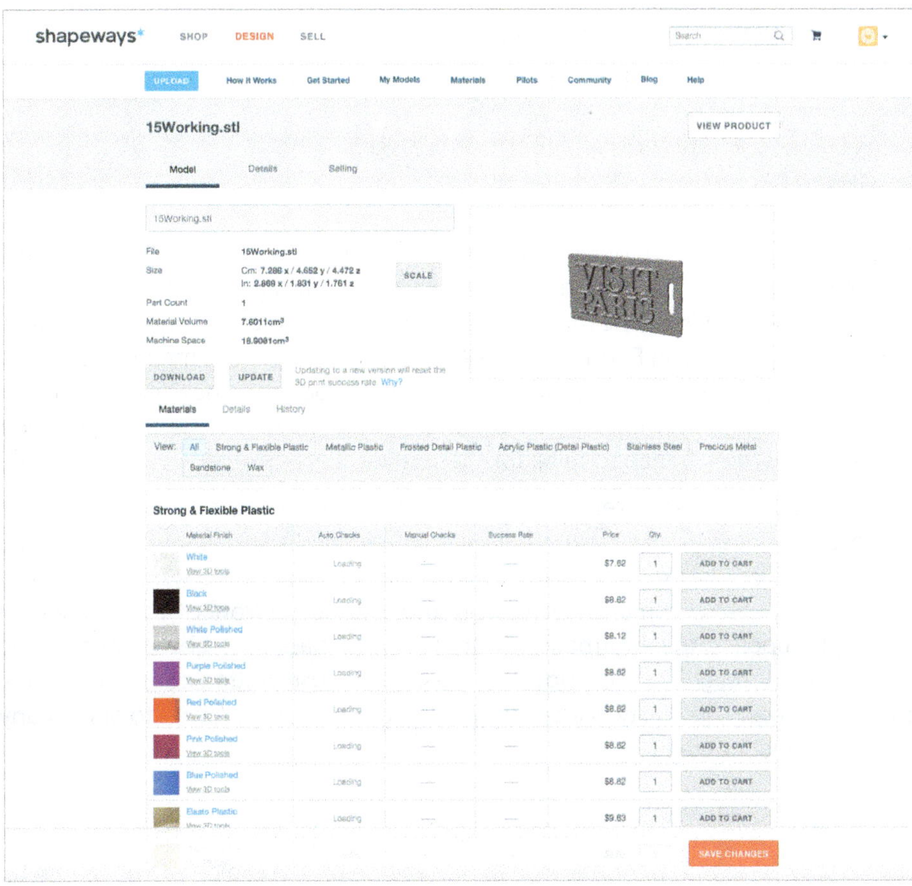

9. Click Add To Cart next to the material you want to print, and then follow the on-screen instructions to place your order. The printed object will be shipped to you.

10. Save the **L13_start_xx.psd** file and close Photoshop.

Using Communication Skills

Using Written Communication

Historians believe that the printing press, invented by Johannes Gutenberg in 1440, was the single most important invention of all time. Most agree that its invention marks the transition from the Middle Ages to the Renaissance, a period of artistic and intellectual revival in Europe. Why is that? The printing press made it easier and cheaper to create printed communications such as books and newspapers, and this in turn allowed for information to spread more easily. When people can read books for themselves, they began to think for themselves.

Before the printing press, creating written communications was a time-consuming and costly business. Books were usually written by hand and paper was scarce and expensive. Written communications were therefore rare. These days, you are surrounded by written communications, from the textbook in front of you to the notes in your notebook to the information written on your class whiteboard or your teacher's Web site or blog. Everyone now has the ability to use written communications to transfer ideas. This ability will be integral—necessary or essential—to almost any career you might enter.

Reading

Why do you think it is important to learn how to read? If you did not know how to read, you would have to learn all of your ideas from people speaking to you. Reading allows you to learn on your own. You can learn ideas that were developed and written down in the past, even centuries ago.

Reading will be essential for your career. Whether you want to be an animator, Web developer, or social networking specialist, you will need to read every day you are on the job.

There are different ways to read, depending on what you are reading. You can read passively or critically.

- Passive reading is the kind of reading you do for entertainment, such as when you read a magazine or a comic book. In this kind of reading, you are just taking in information or following the plot.
- When you read critically, you take time to really think about what is written and why. Critical reading happens when you are actively engaging the subject as you read.

The difference between passive and critical reading is like the difference between listening to your friend talk and having a debate with her. When you read critically, you are having a debate with the text. Here are the steps to critical reading:

- Determine the best reading strategy for the text. This means that you need to figure out whether to skim the text, read closely for detail, or read for meaning or critical analysis.
- As you read, stop and think about what is being said and try to put it in your own words or rephrase it from your own point of view.
- Take notes while you're reading to make sure you are understanding and remembering the main points.

Writing

Like peanut butter and jelly, reading and writing go together. In fact, you cannot do critical reading without also writing. But not all writing is the kind you do in English or Creative Writing class. Jotting down notes and texting a message to a friend also count as writing.

Writing is something you get better at with practice. You can think of words as being like tools. Writers who are just learning to write use simple words to communicate their ideas, just as beginning builders start with basic tools to put together small projects. The more words you learn and the more you learn how to put them together, the bigger the projects you can build.

Just like learning any skill, learning to write is an ongoing process. You should always expect to get better, and accept constructive criticism—suggestions from others on how to improve your writing—and consider how it can make you a better writer.

Like reading, writing well will be essential in almost any career you choose. While you are employed, you may have regular writing tasks such as preparing letters to clients, creating written reports for customers, or writing memos to your co-workers. You might also have to write a letter of resignation, if you have decided to change from one job or career to another. This is a letter that expresses your reasons for leaving and your appreciation for your former employer.

Before you send or submit any written material you should check it and evaluate it to make sure it is accurate, valid, and truthful. You should check for proper grammar, spelling, and punctuation. You should also make sure the terminology–words–you select are right, and that you are using them correctly.

Using Verbal Communication

You were born with the ability to learn how to speak and understand others. This ability to use and understand language is something that all human beings have, and it is something that makes us unique among all other animals on the planet.

Of course, just because you know how to talk does not mean you know how to speak well. Even if you were the smartest person in the world, it would be very hard for you to get the career you want if others did not understand you.

Mastering the art of verbal communication is a very important part of getting the career you want, because you will have to use this skill to convince an employer to hire you. You will also have to use verbal communication every day on the job, no matter what it is.

Effective Communication

You can communicate effectively by using a six-step process:

1. *Be clear*. The receiver is more likely to get your message if you deliver it in a way he or she can understand. Speak slowly. Consider who you are talking to. You probably use different language when you talk to a teacher than when you talk to a friend. You might even use a completely different type of communication. For example, you probably talk to your teacher face to face, but you might text your friend.

2. *Be personal*. Use the other person's name so there's no doubt who you are talking to. Use an "I" statement—a statement that starts with the word "I"—to frame the statement in terms of you and your goals. An "I" statement indicates that you are taking responsibility for your thoughts and feelings. It helps the receiver understand your point of view and respond to you.

3. *Be positive*. Phrase your message in positive terms. Say what you want, not what you don't want. For example, say, "I want to leave at 3:30," instead of saying, "I don't want to leave at 4:00."

4. *Get to the point*. Follow the "I" statement with an explanation of the message you are sending. Explain how or why you feel a certain way, or how or why you think a certain thing. For example, say, "I want to leave at 3:30. I think that will give us enough time to get there without having to rush."

5. *Listen to the response*. Pay attention and use active listening techniques to make sure you hear the response.

6. *Think before you respond*. Make sure you understand the message. Repeat it, if necessary, and ask questions for clarification. Use critical thinking to make sure you are not letting emotions and preconceived ideas get in the way.

Different Types of Verbal Communication

The ways you speak to your friends, your parents, your teachers, or your siblings differ greatly. For instance, you might get in trouble with your teachers if you spoke with them as if they were your friends. On the other hand, speaking to your friends as if they were your teachers wouldn't be any fun.

Just as you use different types of verbal communication when speaking to your friends and your parents, you use different types of verbal communication when speaking to people with whom you relate on the job, such as your boss, your co-workers, your customers, and your subordinates—the people you supervise.

- Your boss has a higher rank in the company than you do and has control over your job. When communicating with a boss, you usually use a formal style of verbal communication. You show deference—courteous regard or respect—by using her title and refraining from jokes or casual remarks you might use with a friend. You must also recognize that your boss has the final say on most matters, and so you must know when to agree with her decisions, even if you disagree with them personally.
- Your co-workers, or colleagues, have the same rank in the company that you do. This does not mean that you should joke around with them as you do with your friends. It also does not mean you should use the same style of verbal communication you would use with your boss. You can speak to them more casually.
- Your customers are the source of your business. When communicating with customers, remember the old saying, "the customer is always right." This means that in order to be successful, you must respect your customers and speak with them positively.
- If you supervise others in the company, you communicate with them using the respect that is due to any worker. You can also use an assertive or positive style of verbal communication, so that they know exactly what is expected of them.

Not only is what you say important, but so is how you say it. In addition to the different ways you can verbally communicate with others in the work-place, you can use different tones to make your meaning clear. These include:

- Assertive speech, which includes action verbs such as "should," "does," and "will."
- Aggressive speech, which you should avoid in the workplace, since it can lead to arguments or hurt feelings. An example of aggressive speech would be, "You better help me now!"
- Passive speech, which is usually best to use when you also want to show respect or deference. Examples of passive speech include words such as "can," "might," and "could." What do you think it takes to be an effective communicator?

Understanding Nonverbal Communication

Body language is a different type of nonverbal communication that everyone uses every day, sometimes without knowing it. Did you ever notice that if you didn't do your homework somehow your teacher knows it and calls on you anyway? Your body language may be giving you away. Body language can be either positive or negative. It can show you are confident and prepared, or that you are unsure or afraid.

Here are some other ways you can communicate using positive body language.

- *Watch your posture.* Stand up and sit straight without bending backward, and keep your shoulders square with the person to whom you are speaking. If sitting, you may lean slightly forward to show that you are interested in what the other person has to say.

- *Open arms communicate an open mind.* Standing or sitting with your arms at your sides or in front of you indicates that you are open and receptive to your conversation partner's ideas.
- *Active hand gestures indicate active debate.* This means that you move your hands to show and demonstrate ideas. Why is this important? Because it shows that you are actively engaged in the conversation, not just passively hearing and responding.
- *Maintain adequate eye contact.* This does not mean you must lock eyes with the person you are speaking with at all times. It does mean that you must at least meet his eyes when he looks at you.

Finally, one other way to communicate without speaking or writing is to use visual aids—pictures, graphs, charts, or anything without words that conveys your ideas. Visual aids can often deliver a clearer or more easily understood message than written or verbal communication.

Comprehension Check

1. How does a 3D layer differ from other layers in Photoshop?
2. How can you change the camera view?
3. Which color represents each axis on the 3D Axis widget?
4. How do you print a 3D object?
5. Why is good communication key to your success in finding a career?

Review Project

Select a career in the Web and Digital Communications pathway that interests you. (Refer to the help wanted ad you created in the Lesson 11 Review Project, if desired.) In your word processor, write a short report on the tasks and responsibilities that would require you to employ effective verbal, nonverbal, and written communication skills, and possess strong reading skills. Share your report with a partner.

End-of-Chapter Activities

Directions: **Match each vocabulary term in the left column with the correct definition in the right column.**

1. Clipping Mask
2. point type
3. text warping
4. paragraph type
5. lossy compression
6. color depth
7. gamut
8. color space
9. proof profile
10. lossless compression

A. distorting type to conform to a shape, such as an arc or wave

B. compression format in which some information is permanently removed

C. a single letter, word, or line

D. compression format in which all information is kept

E. range of colors

F. settings that define how something will be printed

G. an object or group whose shape masks other artwork

H. multiple lines of text within a bounding box

I. a conceptual tool for understanding the color capabilities of a particular device or file

J. colors shown on a monitor at one time

Review Project

As a class, discuss how graphics can be used both to make a publication look better and to help convey a message. Select a topic that interests you and have it approved by your teacher. Then, use graphics software to create an image that could be used on a Web page about your topic. Make sure the image would both enhance the appearance of the page and convey a message about the topic. Deliver an informal oral presentation of your graphic to a partner or to the class. As a class, display and discuss the images.

Chapter 4 – Portfolio Builder

Designing a billboard

In this exercise, you will use Photoshop to design a billboard for a city zoo. You will include clip art, text, and colors to create an attention-getting design.

DIRECTIONS

1. Before beginning, find an image of a baby elephant and of tiger cubs on the Internet and download them to the location where you are storing files for this lesson.
2. Open the elephant photo in Photoshop, and crop as close to the elephant as possible, and resize the picture to approximately 3.0" high by 4.0" wide.
3. Open the cubs photo and crop as close to the cubs as possible, and resize the picture to approximately 2.5" high by 4.0" wide.
4. Save both images with names of your choice and make sure to select .TIFF as the file format for both. Close the files.
5. In Photoshop, create a new document with the following settings:
   - Name: **PB_4_xx**
   - Preset: U.S. Paper
   - Size: Letter
   - Width: 11 inches
   - Height: 8.5 inches
   - Color Mode: RGB
6. Display the rulers and the gridlines.
7. Use the Place Embedded command to insert the photo of the baby elephant.
8. Align the picture in the middle of the page vertically, with its left border about 1" from the left edge of the page.
9. Use the Place Embedded command to insert the photo of tiger cubs.
10. Align the picture in the middle of the page vertically, with its right border about 1" from the right edge of the page.
11. Insert a text box approximately 1.5" high by 9" wide above the pictures.
12. Set the font in the text box to Arial, bold, 48 points, and type **Come See Our New Arrivals!**
13. Center the text in the text box.
14. Center the text box horizontally.
15. Draw a rectangle with rounded corners below the other objects, centered horizontally. Size it to approximately 1.0" high by 5.0" wide.
16. Add text to the rectangle, and, using 26-point Arial Black, type **Townsville City Zoo**, centered in the text box.
17. Draw another text box below the rounded rectangle, with no border or fill, and centered horizontally. Size it to approximately 0.5" high by 5.0" wide.
18. Set the font to 20-point Arial and type **123 Elm Street—Open 7 days a week!**, centered in the text box.
19. Apply a solid light green background to the slide or canvas.
20. Select the rounded rectangle and the text box within it, change the font color to black, and apply a green fill and a black outline.
21. Adjust the zoom and check the alignment and position of objects.
22. From the View > Proof Setup > choose Custom.

    The Customize Proof Condition dialog opens. In the following steps, you will choose proofing settings for your specific output device.
23. Check Preview, then from the Device to Simulate menu, choose the correct color profile for your printer and paper—the profile that you either downloaded from the manufacturer's Web site or installed with your printer driver file
24. Uncheck Preserve RGB Numbers, if available, to allow Photoshop to simulate how the colors will look when converted to the output profile.

25. Choose a Rendering Intent to control how colors will change as the image is shifted to the output profile.

    It is recommended that you choose either Perceptual or Relative Colorimetric.

    To compare these options, choose them one by one and look at your document onscreen—or even better, output a test print for each one and compare the results.

26. Check Black Point Compensation to allow adjustments to be made for differences in the black point among different color spaces.

    With this option chosen, the full dynamic range of the image color space is mapped to the full dynamic range of the color space of your output device.

    With this option off, black areas in the image may display or print as grays. For an inkjet proof, we recommend checking this option.

27. *Optional*: For Display Options (On-Screen), check Simulate Paper Color to preview the white of the printing paper, as defined in the chosen printer profile, or if you're going to print the file on uncoated paper, check Simulate Black Ink to preview the full range of black values that the printer profile can produce.

28. To save your custom proof setup, click Save, enter a name, keep the .psf extension, keep the default location (the Proofing folder), then click Save.

29. Your newly saved proof setup appears on the Customize Proof Condition menu. Click OK. The setup is now also available on the View > Proof Setup sub-menu for use at any time, and View > Proof Colors is checked automatically so you can study the soft proof onscreen. (While Proof Colors is checked, the color profile that is currently chosen on the Proof Setup submenu is also listed in the document tab.)

    Remember, the Proof Setup options control only how Photoshop simulates colors onscreen. Colors in the file won't actually be converted to the chosen profile until you physically output the document to an inkjet printer or convert it to a different color mode (such as from RGB to CMYK).

30. With your teacher's permission, print the file.

31. Close the file, saving all changes, and exit the program.

Chapter 4 – Critical Thinking

Demonstrate Redesign Skills

Using your skills in Photoshop, redesign an event poster that you see in your neighborhood. Search telephone or lighting poles, coffee shops, store bulletin boards, and other public areas for amateur event posters.

1. Create a letter size Photoshop document and name it **CT_4_xx.psd**.
2. Redesign the poster using your design and typography skills.
3. Save the file as **CT_4_xx.psd** in the location where your teacher instructs you to store the files for this lesson.

Chapter 5

Working with Animation

Lesson 14 | Getting Acquainted with Adobe Flash

Starting Flash and Creating a New Document
Getting to Know the Workspace
Working with the Library Panel
Working with the Timeline
Inserting Frames
Organizing Layers in a Timeline
Using the Properties Inspector
Using the Tools Panel
Undoing Steps in Flash
Previewing Your Movie
Modifying the Content and Stage
Saving a Movie

Lesson 15 | Working with Graphics in Flash

Creating Shapes in Flash
Selecting Strokes and Fills
Editing Shapes
Changing Strokes and Fills
Using Gradient and Bitmap Fills
Grouping Objects
Using Variable-Width Strokes
Creating Transparencies
Creating and Editing Text
Matching the Color of an Existing Object
Adding Hyperlinks
Aligning and Distributing Objects
Converting and Exporting Art

Lesson 16 | Working with Symbols

Importing Illustrator Files
Identifying Symbols
Creating Symbols
Importing Photoshop Files
Editing and Managing Symbols
Changing the Size and Position of Instances
Changing the Color Effect of Instances
Using Display Options
Using Blending Effects
Exporting as Bitmap
Applying Filters for Special Effects
Positioning in 3D Space

Lesson 17 | Animating Symbols

Examining Animation in Flash
Animating Position
Using the Controller to Preview the Animation
Changing the Pacing and Timing
Animating Transparency
Animating Filters
Animating Transformations
Changing the Path of a Motion
Swapping Tween Targets
Creating Nested Animations
Setting Easing
Creating Frame-by-Frame Animation
Animating 3D Motion
Testing a Movie

End-of-Chapter Activities

Lesson 14 Overview

In this lesson, you will learn about:

- Starting Flash and Creating a New Document
- Getting to Know the Workspace
- Working with the Library Panel
- Working with the Timeline
- Inserting Frames
- Organizing Layers in a Timeline
- Using the Properties Inspector
- Using the Tools Panel
- Undoing Steps in Flash
- Previewing Your Movie
- Modifying the Content and Stage
- Saving a Movie

Computer animation is the process of creating animated images using computer graphics. While mostly used in media and entertainment industries, computer animation is also used in many other types of businesses for many different purposes. For example, it is used for instruction and demonstrations in medicine, and to create models of products, buildings, and designs in fields such as architecture and mechanics.

Adobe® Flash® is a multimedia authoring and computer animation program. You use it to design vector graphics and animation that you can publish on a Web site, in a Web application, or use in a video game. Developing skills with Adobe Flash can lead to a career as a multimedia artist or animator. In this lesson, you explore the Flash program interface and practice using basic Flash tools to create graphics and animations.

Starting Flash and Creating a New Document

Adobe Flash is a nonlinear editing system that allows you to place, replace, move, and manipulate animation clips to produce a new series of motions and effects. It gives you great flexibility in creating and modifying your animations. Linear editing was developed for working with video tape and film. It requires selecting, arranging, and modifying clips in a predetermined, ordered sequence. Each desired clip has to be isolated and recorded (or *dubbed*) onto a master tape. Linear editing is economical and has application to projects in which you simply want to add a clip to the end of another. But today, the standard is nonlinear editing. This chapter focuses on Flash's nonlinear editing capabilities

The first time you start Flash you'll see a Welcome screen with links to standard file templates, tutorials, and other resources. In this lesson, you'll create a simple animation to showcase a few vacation snapshots. You'll add a background, photos, and a title, and in the process you'll learn about positioning elements on the **Stage** and placing them along the **Timeline** so they appear one at a time, in sequence. You'll begin learning how to use the Stage to organize your visual elements spatially, and how to use the Timeline to organize your elements temporally.

> **Stage**
> The rectangular area where content such as graphics displays.
>
> **Timeline**
> The element used to organize and control the movement of objects over time.

Try It!

1. Start Adobe Flash Professional. In Windows, choose Start > All Programs > Adobe Flash Professional CC. In Mac, click Adobe Flash CC in the Adobe Flash CC folder in the Applications folder.

2. Choose File > New.

   The New Document dialog box opens.

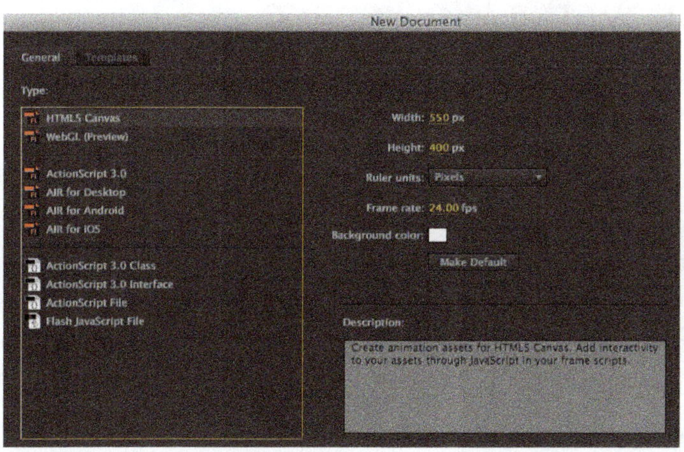

3. Under the General tab, choose the first option, HTML5 Canvas.

   HTML5 is a **markup language** used for structuring and presenting content on the World Wide Web. The other options in the New Document dialog box target different playback technologies. For example, WebGL is a document type for animation that takes advantage of hardware-accelerated support for graphics within HTML. ActionScript 3.0 is a document type that targets the Flash Player. AIR for Android and AIR for iOS are documents configured for playback with AIR on an Android or Apple mobile device. AIR for Desktop is a document configured for playback with AIR on a Mac or Windows desktop.

> **Markup language**
> A set of codes used to format online content.

4. On the right side of the dialog box, you can choose the dimensions of the Stage by entering new pixel values for the Width and Height. Enter **800** for Width and **600** for Height. Keep the Ruler units as Pixels.

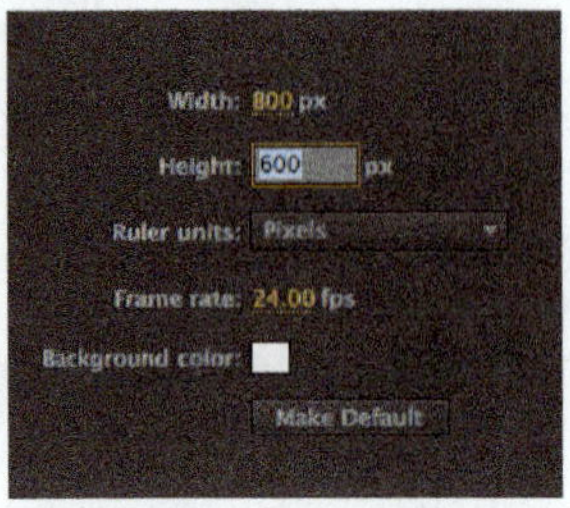

Leave the Frame rate and Background color for the Stage at their default settings. You can always edit these document properties, as explained later in this lesson.

5. Click OK.

Flash creates a new HTML5 Canvas document with all the specified settings.

6. Choose File > Save. Name the file **L14_start_xx**, and from the File Format/Save as type pull-down menu, choose Flash document (*.fla). Save it in the location where your teacher instructs you to store the files for this lesson, and leave it open.

Saving your file right away is a good working habit that ensures your work won't be lost if the application or your computer crashes. The extention .fla identifies the file as the Flash source file.

Note:

Be aware that once you select the file type/format for your animation, you cannot easily convert it to another format. For example, you can't convert an ActionScript 3.0 document into a WebGL document. However, you can use standard copy and paste commands to move your content from one document to another. The exception is converting an ActionScript 3.0 document into an HTML5 Canvas or a WebGL document, which Flash Pro supports.

Getting to Know the Workspace

The Adobe Flash Professional work area includes the command menus at the top of the screen and a variety of tools and panels for editing and adding elements to your movie. You can create all the objects for your animation in Flash, or you can import elements you've created in Adobe Illustrator, Adobe Photoshop, Adobe® After Effects®, or other compatible applications.

By default, Flash displays the menu bar, Timeline, Stage, Tools panel, Properties inspector, Edit bar, and a few other panels. As you work in Flash, you can open, close, dock, undock, and move panels around the screen to fit your work style or your screen resolution.

Choosing a New Workspace

Flash also provides a few preset panel arrangements that may better suit the needs of particular users. The various workspace arrangements are listed in the Workplace switcher pull-down menu at the top right of the Flash workspace or in the top menu under Window > Workspaces.

Try It!

1. Click the Essentials button at the upper-right corner of the Flash workspace and choose a new workspace.

   The various panels are rearranged and resized according to their importance in the chosen workspace. For example, the Animator and Designer workspaces put the Timeline at the top for easy and frequent access.

   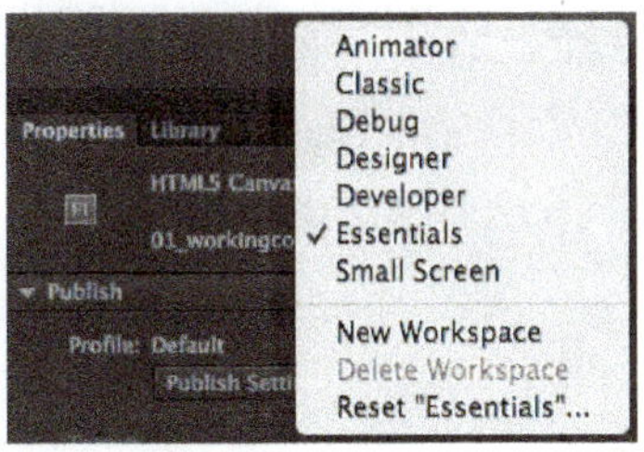

2. If you've moved some of the panels around and you want to return to one of the prearranged workspaces, choose Window > Workspaces > Reset and the name of the preset workspace.

3. To return to the default workspace, choose Window > Workspaces > Essentials. In this book, we'll be using the Essentials workspace.

4. Save the changes to **L14_start_xx.fla**, and leave it open.

About the Stage

The big white rectangle in the middle of your screen is called the Stage. As with a theater stage, the Stage in Flash is the area that viewers see when a movie is playing. It contains the text, images, and video that appear on the screen. Move elements on and off the Stage to place them in and out of view. You can use the rulers (View > Rulers) or grids (View > Grid > Show Grid) to help you position items on the Stage. Additionally, you can use the Align panel and other tools you'll learn about in the lessons in this chapter.

By default, you'll see the gray area off the Stage where you can place elements that won't be visible to your audience. The gray area is called the **Pasteboard**. To see just the Stage, choose View > Pasteboard to deselect the option. For now, leave the option selected.

Pasteboard

The gray area around the Stage in Flash where you can store elements you do not want to display on the Stage.

To scale the Stage so that it fits completely in the application window, choose View > Magnification > Fit in Window. You can also choose different magnification view options from the pop-up menu just above the Stage.

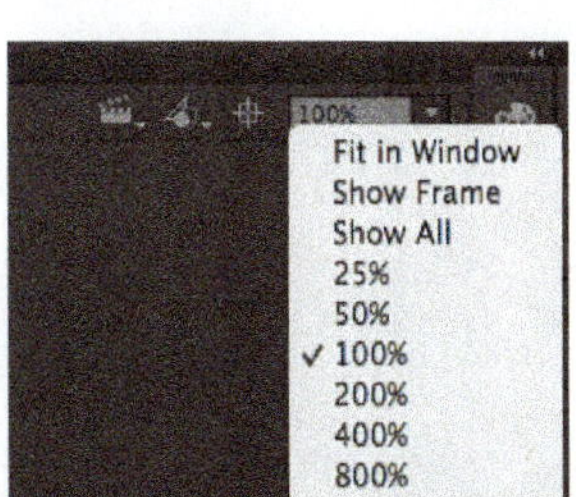

Changing the Stage Properties

Now you'll change the color of the Stage. The Stage color, along with other document properties such as the Stage dimensions and frame rate, are available in the Properties inspector, which is the vertical panel just to the right of the Stage.

Try It!

1. At the bottom of the Properties inspector, note that the dimensions of the current Stage are set at 800 x 600 pixels, which you chose when you created the new document.

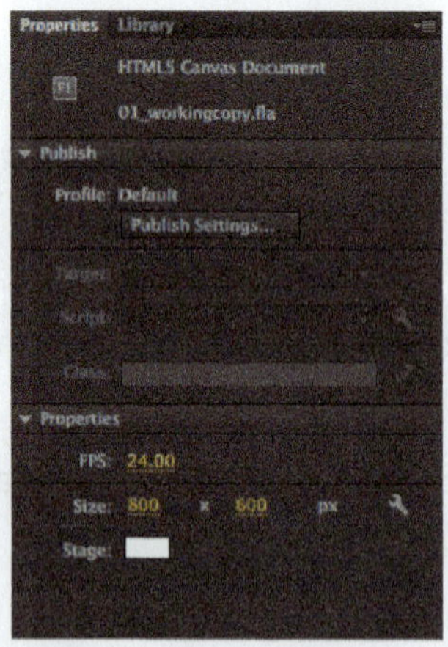

2. Click the Background color button next to the Stage and choose dark gray (#333333).

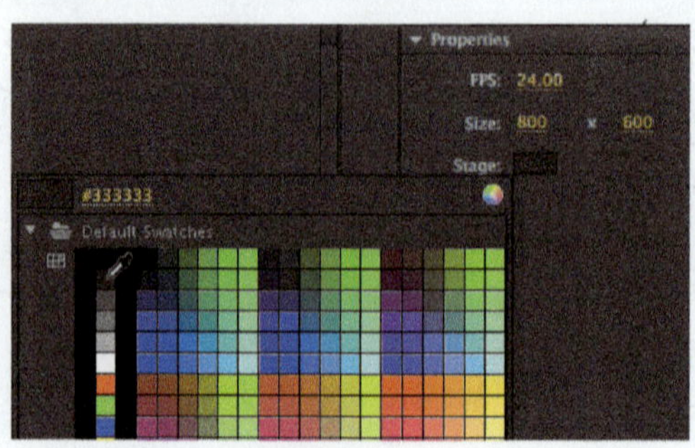

Your Stage is now a different color. You can change the Stage properties at any time.

3. Save the changes to **L14_start_xx.fla**, and leave it open.

Working with the Library Panel

The Library panel is accessible from a tab just to the right of the Properties inspector. The Library panel is where you store and organize symbols created in Flash, as well as imported files, including bitmaps, graphics, sound files, and video clips. **Symbols** are graphics used frequently for animation and for interactivity.

Symbols

Graphics used frequently for animation and interactivity.

About the Library Panel

The Library panel lets you organize library items in folders, see how often an item is used in a document, and sort items by type. When you import items into Flash, you can import them directly onto the Stage or into the library. However, any item you import onto the Stage is also added to the library, as are any symbols you create. You can then easily access the items to add them to the Stage again, edit them, or examine their properties.

To display the Library panel, click the Library panel tab, choose Window > Library, or press Command+L (Mac) or Ctrl+L (Windows).

Importing an Item to the Library Panel

Often, you'll create graphics directly with Flash's drawing tools and save them as symbols, which are stored in the library. Other times you'll import media such as JPEG images or MP3 sound files, which are also stored in the library. In this lesson, you'll import several images into the library to be used in the animation.

Try It!

1. Choose File > Import > Import to Library. In the Import to Library dialog box, select the **background.png** file from the data files for this lesson, and click Open.

   Flash imports the selected PNG image and places it in the Library panel.

2. Continue importing **photo1.jpg, photo2.jpg**, and **photo3.jpg** from the data files for this lesson. Don't import the last image, **photo4.jpg**. You'll use that image later in this lesson.

   You can also hold down the Shift key to select multiple files and import all of the images at once.

3. The Library panel displays all the imported images with their filenames and a thumbnail preview. These images are now available to be used in your Flash document.

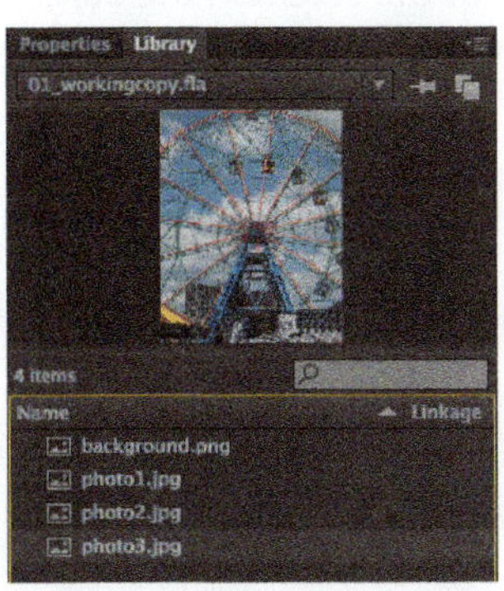

4. Save the changes to **L14_start_xx.fla**, and leave it open.

Adding an Item from the Library Panel to the Stage

To use an imported image, simply drag it from the Library panel onto the Stage.

Try It!

1. Choose Window > Library to open the Library panel if it isn't already open.
2. Select the **background.png** item in the Library panel, drag it onto the Stage, and place it approximately in the center of the Stage.
3. Save the changes to **L14_start_xx.fla**, and leave it open.

Working with the Timeline

Frame

An individual image within a sequence of images.

Playhead

The red vertical line on the Timeline that indicates the current frame.

Frame rate

The number of frames that play per second.

The Timeline is located below the Stage. Like films, Flash documents measure time in **frames**. As the movie plays, the **playhead**, shown as a red vertical line, advances through the frames in the Timeline. You can change the content on the Stage for different frames. To display a frame's content on the Stage, move the playhead to that frame in the Timeline.

At the bottom of the Timeline, Flash indicates the selected frame number, the current **frame rate**, and the time that has elapsed so far in the movie.

Using Layers

Like Photoshop, the Flash Timeline contains layers, which you can use to organize the artwork in your document. At the moment, your project has only one layer, which is called Layer 1. Think of layers as multiple film strips stacked on top of one another. Each layer can contain a different image that appears on the Stage, and you can draw and edit objects on one layer without affecting objects on another layer. The layers are stacked in the order in which they overlap each other, so that objects on the bottom layer in the Timeline are on the bottom of the stack on the Stage. You can hide, lock, or show the contents of layers as outlines by clicking the dots in the layer under the layer option icons.

Renaming a Layer

It's a good idea to separate your content on different layers and name each layer to indicate its contents so that you can easily find the layer you need later.

1. Select the existing layer, called Layer 1, in the Timeline.
2. Double-click the name of the layer to rename it and type **background**.

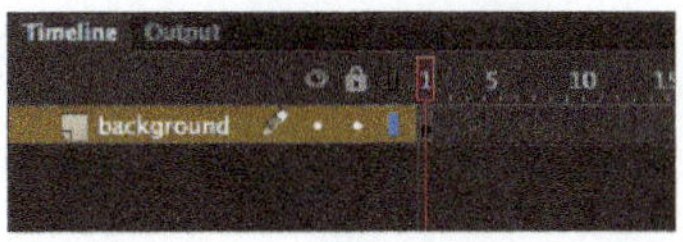

3. Click outside the name box to apply the new name.
4. Click the lock icon to lock the layer. Locking a layer prevents you from accidentally making changes to it.

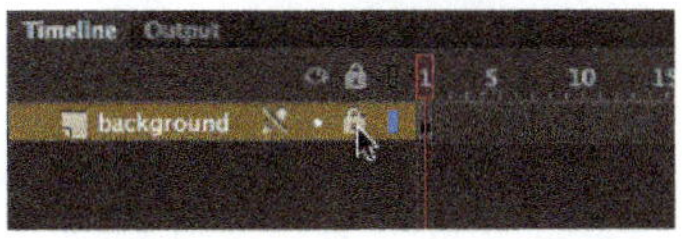

   The pencil icon with a diagonal slash that appears after the layer name indicates that you can't make edits to the layer because it is locked.

5. Save the changes to **L14_start_xx.fla**, and leave it open.

Adding a Layer

A new Flash document contains only one layer, but you can add as many layers as you need. Objects in the top layers will overlap objects in the bottom layers.

Try It!

1. Select the background layer in the Timeline.
2. Choose Insert > Timeline > Layer. You can also click the New Layer button below the Timeline. A new layer appears above the background layer.
3. Double-click the new layer to rename it and type **photo1**. Click outside the name box to apply the new name.

   Your Timeline now has two layers. The background layer contains the background photo, and the newly created photo1 layer above it is empty.

4. Select the photo1 layer, if necessary.
5. Choose Window > Library to open the Library panel if it isn't already open.

6. Drag the photo1.jpg from the library onto the Stage.

The photo1 JPEG appears on the Stage and overlaps the background image.

7. Choose Insert > Timeline > Layer, or click the New Layer button below the Timeline to add a third layer.
8. Rename the third layer **photo2**.
9. Save the changes to **L14_start_xx.fla**, and leave it open.

Note:

If you don't want a layer, you can easily delete it by selecting it and then clicking the Delete button below the Timeline.

If you want to rearrange your layers, click and drag any layer to move it to a new position in the layer stack.

Inserting Frames

So far, you have a background photo and another overlapping photo on the Stage, but your entire animation consists of only a single frame. To create more time on the Timeline and make this animation run for a longer duration, you must insert additional frames.

Try It!

1. Select frame 48 in the background layer.

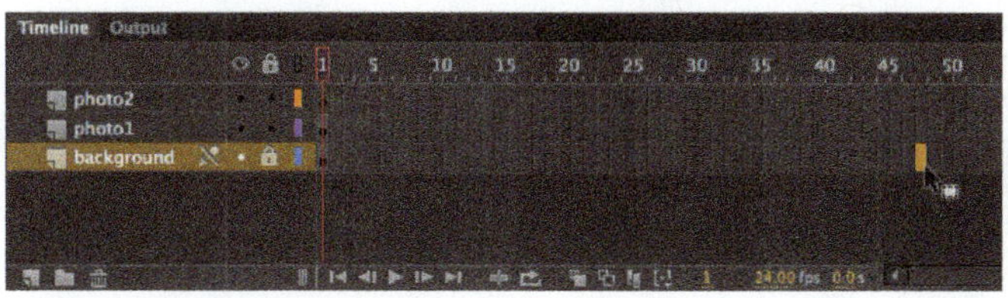

2. Choose Insert > Timeline > Frame (F5). You can also right-click/Ctrl-click and choose Insert Frame from the context menu that pops up.

   Flash adds frames in the background layer up to the selected frame 48.

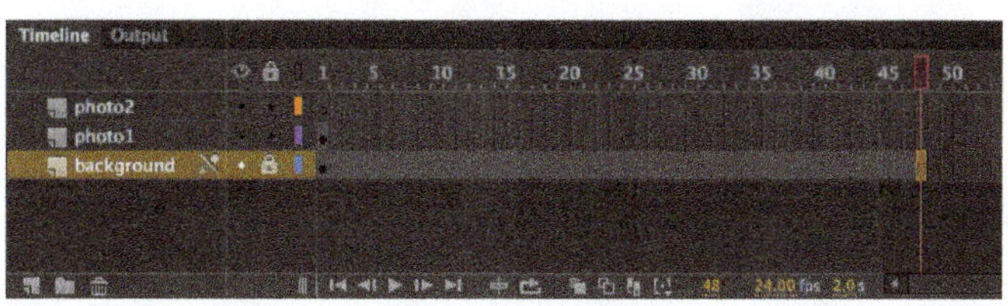

3. Select frame 48 in the photo1 layer.
4. Choose Insert > Timeline > Frame (F5). You can also right-click/Ctrl-click and choose Insert Frame from the context menu.

   Flash adds frames in the photo1 layer up to the selected frame, frame 48.

5. Select frame 48 in the photo2 layer and insert frames on this layer.

   You now have three layers, all with 48 frames on the Timeline. Since the frame rate of your Flash document is 24 frames per second, your current animation lasts 2 seconds.

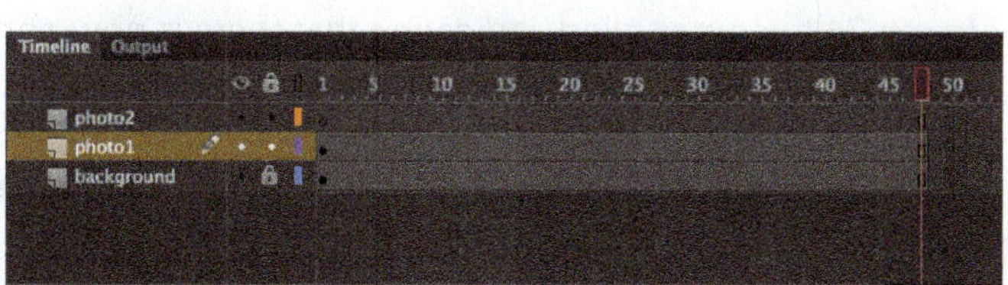

6. Save the changes to **L14_start_xx.fla**, and leave it open.

Creating a Keyframe

Keyframe

A frame that indicates a change or transition.

Note:

You can hold down the Shift key to select multiple frames on the Flash Timeline. If you have several layers and want to insert frames into all of them, click on the frame in the first layer to select it, then hold down the Shift key and click on the frame in the last layer. All the frames between the layers will be selected. You can also simply click and drag where you want to add frames. Then choose Insert > Timeline > Frame.

A **keyframe** is a frame that indicates a change in content on the Stage. Keyframes are marked on the Timeline as a circle. An empty circle means there is nothing in that particular layer at that particular time. A filled-in black circle means there is something in that particular layer at that particular time. The background layer, for example, contains a filled keyframe (black circle) in the first frame. The photo1 layer also contains a filled keyframe in its first frame. Both layers contain photos. The photo2 layer, however, contains an empty keyframe in the first frame, indicating that it is currently empty.

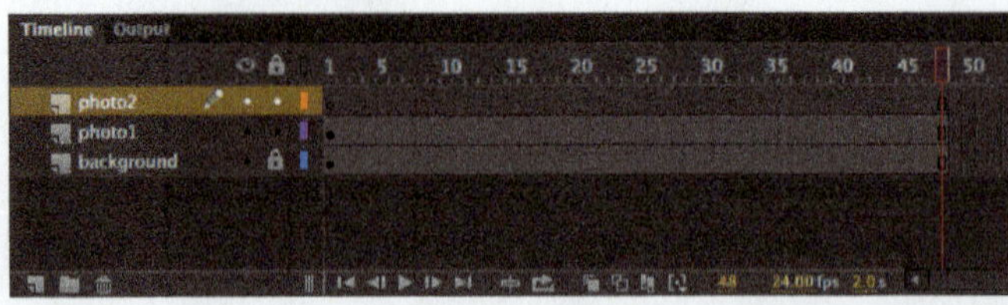

You'll insert a keyframe in the photo2 layer at the point in time when you want the next photo to appear.

Try It!

1. Select frame 24 on the photo2 layer. As you select a frame, Flash displays the frame number beneath the Timeline.
2. Choose Insert > Timeline > Keyframe (F6).

   A new keyframe, indicated by an empty circle, appears in the photo2 layer in frame 24.

3. Select the new keyframe at frame 24 in the photo2 layer.
4. Drag photo2.jpg from your library onto the Stage.

   The empty circle at frame 24 becomes filled, indicating that there is now content in the photo2 layer. At frame 24, your photo appears on the Stage. You can click and drag the red playhead from the top of the Timeline to **scrub**, or show, what's happening on the Stage at any point along the Timeline. You'll see that the background photo and photo1 remain on the Stage throughout the Timeline, but photo2 appears only at frame 24.

Scrub

Clicking and dragging the playhead back and forth to preview the animation

5. Save the changes to **L14_start_xx.fla**, and leave it open.

   Understanding frames and keyframes is essential for mastering Flash. Be sure you understand how the photo2 layer contains 48 frames with 2 keyframes—an empty keyframe at frame 1 and a filled keyframe at frame 24.

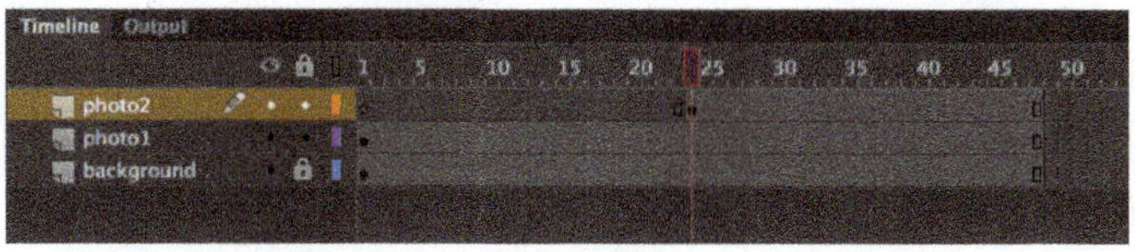

Moving a Keyframe

If you want photo2.jpg to appear later or earlier in time, you need to move the keyframe in which it appears closer or further to the right on the Timeline. You can easily move any keyframe along the Timeline by simply selecting it and then dragging it to a new position.

Try It!

1. Select the keyframe in frame 24 on the photo2 layer.
2. Move the mouse pointer slightly, and you'll see a box icon appear near the pointer, indicating that you can reposition the keyframe.
3. Click and drag the keyframe to frame 12 in the photo2 layer.

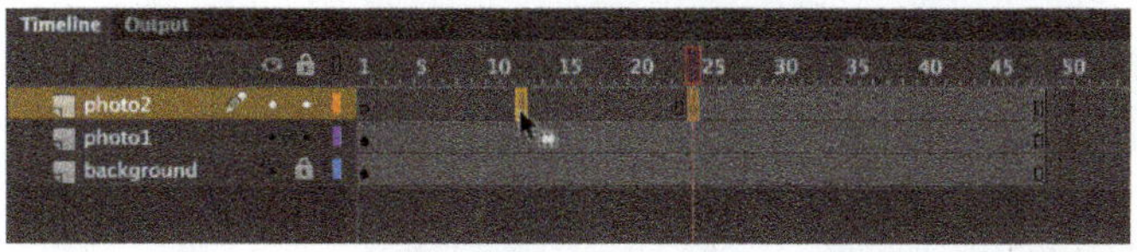

   The photo2.jpg image now appears on the Stage much earlier in the animation.

4. Save the changes to **L14_start_xx.fla**, and leave it open.

> **Note:**
>
> If you want to remove a keyframe, do not press the Delete key! Doing so will delete the contents of that keyframe on the Stage. Instead, select the keyframe and choose Modify > Timeline > Clear Keyframe (Shift+F6). Your keyframe will be removed from the Timeline

Organizing Layers in a Timeline

At this point, your working Flash file has only three layers: a background layer, a photo1 layer, and a photo2 layer. You'll be adding additional layers for this project, and as in most other projects, you'll end up having to manage multiple layers. Layer folders help you group related layers to keep your Timeline organized and manageable, just like you make folders for related documents on your desktop. Although it may take some time to create the folders, it will save you time later because you'll know exactly where to look for a specific layer.

Creating Layer Folders

For this project, you'll continue to add layers for additional photos, and you'll place those layers in a layer folder.

Try It!

1. Select the photo2 layer and click the New Layer button at the bottom of the Timeline.
2. Name the layer **photo3**.
3. Insert a keyframe at frame 24.
4. Drag photo3.jpg from the library onto the Stage.

You now have four layers. The top three contain photos of scenes from Coney Island that appear at different keyframes.

5. Select the photo3 layer and click the New Folder icon at the bottom of the Timeline.

   A new layer folder appears above the photo3 layer.

6. Name the folder **photos**.
7. Save the changes to **L14_start_xx.fla**, and leave it open.

Adding Layers to Layer Folders

Now you'll add the photo layers to the photos folder. As you arrange layers, remember that Flash displays the content in the layers in the order in which they appear in the Timeline, with the top layer's content at the front and the bottom layer's content at the back.

Try It!

1. Drag the photo1 layer into the photos folder.

   Notice how the bold line indicates the destination of your layer. When you place a layer inside a folder, Flash indents the layer name.

   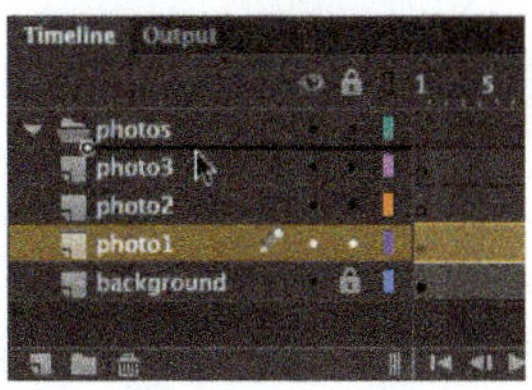

2. Drag the photo2 layer into the photos folder.
3. Drag the photo3 layer into the photos folder.

   All three photo layers should be in the photos folder.

   You can collapse the folder by clicking the arrow just to the left of the folder name. Expand the folder by clicking the arrow again. Be aware that if you delete a layer folder, you delete all the layers inside that folder as well.

4. Save the changes to **L14_start_xx.fla**, and leave it open.

Cut, Copy, Paste, and Duplicate Layers

When managing multiple layers and layer folders, you can rely on cut, copy, paste, and duplicate layer commands to make your workflow easier and more efficient. All the properties of the selected layer are copied and pasted, including its frames, its keyframes, any animation, and even the layer name and type. You can also copy and paste layer folders and their contents.

To cut or copy any layer or layer folder, simply select the layer and right-click/Ctrl-click the layer. In the contextual menu that appears, choose Cut Layers or Copy Layers.

Right-click/Ctrl-click on the Timeline again, and choose Paste Layers. The layer or layers that you cut or copied are pasted into the Timeline. Use Duplicate Layers to copy and paste in one operation.

You can also cut, copy, paste, or duplicate layers from the top Flash menu. Choose Edit > Timeline > and choose Cut Layers, Copy Layers, Paste Layers, or Duplicate Layers.

Using the Properties Inspector

The Properties inspector gives you quick access to the attributes you're most likely to need. What appears in the Properties inspector depends on what you've selected. For example, if nothing is selected, the Properties inspector includes options for the general Flash document, including changing the Stage color or dimensions; if you've selected an object on the Stage, the Properties inspector shows its x and y coordinates and its width and height, among other information. You'll use the Properties inspector to move your photos on the Stage.

Positioning an Object on the Stage

You'll begin by moving the photos with the Properties inspector. You'll also use the Transform panel to rotate the photos.

Try It!

1. At frame 1 of the Timeline, select the photo1.jpg image that you dragged onto the Stage in the photo1 layer. A blue outline indicates that the object is selected.
2. In the Properties inspector, type 50 for the X value and 50 for the Y value. Press Enter (Windows)/Return (Mac) to apply the values. You can also click and drag your mouse pointer over the X and Y values to change their values. The photo moves to the left side of the Stage.

The X and Y values are measured on the Stage from the upper-left corner. X begins at 0 and increases to the right, and Y begins at 0 and increases downward. The registration point (the point from which Flash makes measurements) for imported photos is at the upper-left corner.

3. Choose Window > Transform to open the Transform panel.
4. In the Transform panel, select Rotate, and type -12 in the Rotate box, or click and drag over the value to change the rotation. Press Enter (Windows)/Return (Mac) to apply the value.

   The selected photo on the Stage rotates 12 degrees counterclockwise.

5. Select frame 12 of the photo2 layer. Now click on photo2.jpg on the Stage.

6. Use the Properties inspector and Transform panel to position and rotate the second photo in an interesting way. Use X=200, Y=40, and a Rotate of 6 to give it some contrast with the first photo.
7. Select frame 24 in the photo3 layer. Now click on photo3.jpg on the Stage.
8. Use the Properties inspector and Transform panel to position and rotate the third photo in an interesting way. Use X=360, Y=65, and a Rotate of −2 so all your photos have visual variety.
9. Save the changes to **L14_start_xx.fla**, and leave it open.

Using the Tools Panel

The Tools panel—the long, narrow panel on the far right side of the work area—contains selection tools, drawing and type tools, painting and editing tools, navigation tools, and tool options. You'll use the Tools panel frequently to switch to tools designed for the task at hand. Most often, you'll use the Selection tool, which is the black arrow tool at the top of the Tools panel, for selecting and clicking on items on the Stage or the Timeline. When you select a tool, check the options area at the bottom of the panel for more options and other settings appropriate for your task.

Note:
When images are scaled or rotated in Flash, they may appear jagged. You can smooth them out by double-clicking the bitmap icon in the Library panel. In the Bitmap Properties dialog box that appears, select the Allow Smoothing option.

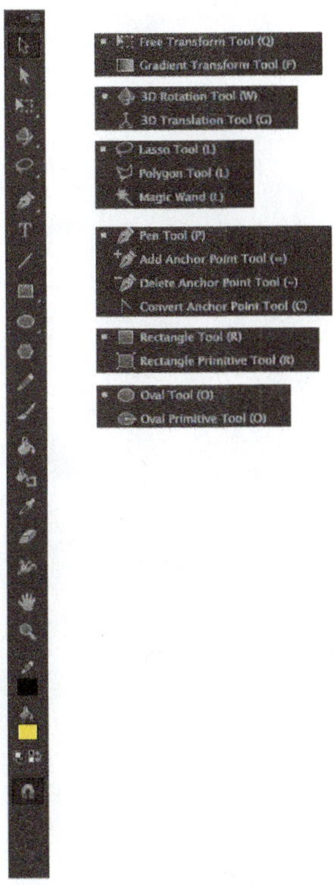

Selecting and Using a Tool

When you select a tool, the options available at the bottom of the Tools panel and the Properties inspector change. For example, when you select the Rectangle tool, the Object Drawing mode and Snap To Objects options appear. When you select the Zoom tool, the Enlarge and Reduce options appear.

The Tools panel contains too many tools to display all at once. Some tools are arranged in hidden groups in the Tools panel; only the tool you last selected from a group is displayed. A small triangle in the lower-right corner of the tool's button indicates that there are other tools in the group. Click and hold the icon for the visible tool to see the other tools available, and then select one from the pop-up menu.

You'll use the PolyStar tool to add a little decoration to your short animation.

Try It!

1. Select the top layer folder in the Timeline, and then click the New Layer button.
2. Name the new layer **stars**.
3. Lock the other layers below it so you don't accidentally move anything into them.
4. In the stars layer, move the playhead to frame 36 and the select frame 36.
5. Choose Insert > Timeline > Keyframe (F6) to insert a new keyframe at frame 36 in the stars layer.
6. In the Tools panel, select the PolyStar tool, which is indicated by the hexagon shape.

7. In the Properties inspector, click the square next to the pencil icon, which indicates the color of the outline. The square should be white with a diagonal red line through it, indicating that no outline color is applied. If not, click the square and then click the white icon with the red line..

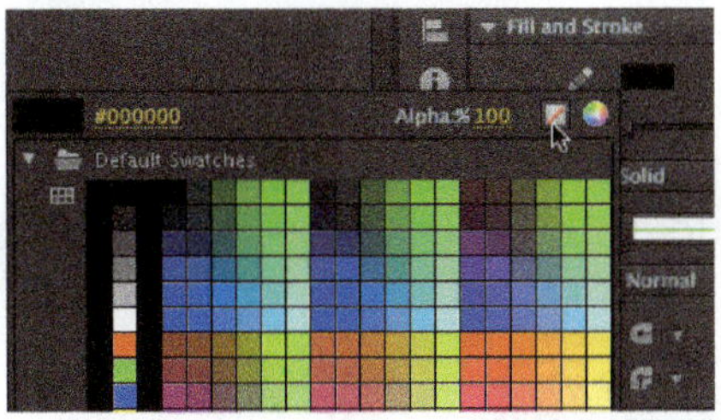

8. Click the colored square next to the paintbucket icon, which indicates the color of the fill, and choose a bright, cheery color such as yellow. You can click on the color wheel at the upper right to access the Adobe Color Picker, or you can change the Alpha percentage at the upper right, which determines the level of transparency.

9. In the Properties inspector, click the Options buttons under Tool Settings.

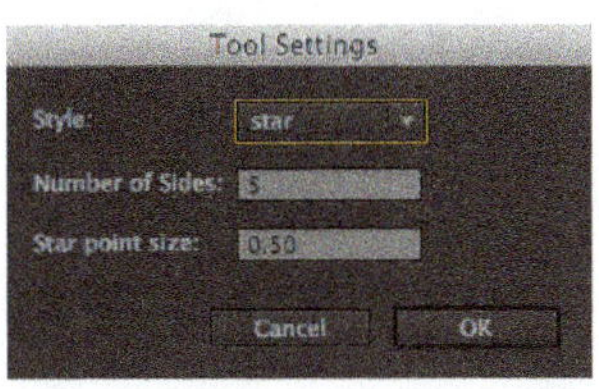

The Tool Settings dialog box appears.

10. For Style, choose star. If necessary, change theNumber of Sides to 5 and the Star point size to 0.50. Click OK.

    The options determine the shape of your star.

11. Make sure the empty keyframe in frame 36 of the stars layer is selected. Click on the Stage where you want to begin adding a star, and drag to change the width of your star. Move your cursor around the first click to rotate the star. Make multiple stars of different sizes and with different angles of rotation.

12. Exit the PolyStar tool by selecting the Selection tool.

13. Use the Properties inspector or the Transform panel to reposition or rotate your stars on the Stage, if desired. Or, choose the Selection tool and simply click to select a star and drag it to a new position on the Stage. The X and Y values in the Properties inspector update as you drag the star around the Stage.

14. Save the changes to **L14_start_xx.fla**, and leave it open.

Undoing Steps in Flash

In a perfect world, everything would go according to plan. But sometimes you need to move back a step or two and start over. You can undo steps in Flash using the Undo command or the History panel.

To undo a single step in Flash, choose Edit > Undo or press Command/Ctrl+Z. To redo a step you've undone, choose Edit > Redo.

The easiest way to undo multiple steps in Flash is to use the History panel, which displays a list of the last 100 steps you've performed. Closing a document clears its history. To access the History panel, choose Window > History.

For example, if you aren't satisfied with the newly added stars, you can undo your work and return your Flash document to a previous state.

Try It!

1. Choose Edit > Undo to undo the last action you made. You can choose the Undo command multiple times to move backward as many steps as are listed in the History panel. You can change the maximum number of Undo commands by selecting Flash/Edit > Preferences.
2. Choose Window > History to open the History panel.
3. Drag the History panel slider up to undo the step(s) below it. Steps that you remove are dimmed in the History panel. To add a step back, move the slider back down.

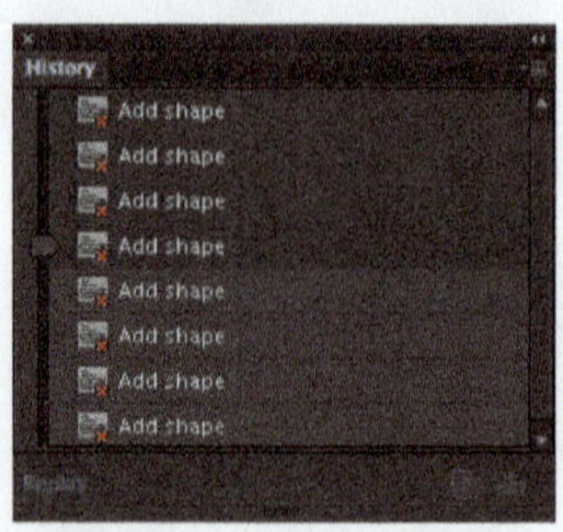

4. Save the changes to **L14_start_xx.fla**, and leave it open.

Previewing Your Movie

As you work on a project, it's a good idea to preview it frequently to ensure that you're achieving the desired effect. To quickly see how an animation or movie will appear to a viewer, choose Control > Test Movie > In Browser. You can also press Command+Return (Mac) or Ctrl+Enter (Windows) to preview your movie.

Try It!

1. Choose Control > Test.

   Flash creates the required published files in the same location as your FLA file and opens and plays the animation in your default browser.

   Flash automatically loops your movie in this preview mode.

2. If you don't want the animation to loop when you test your movie, in Flash, choose File > Publish Settings, and deselect the Loop timeline option.
3. Close the browser window and return to Flash.
4. Save the changes to **L14_start_xx.fla**, and leave it open.

Modifying the Content and Stage

When you first started this lesson, you created a new file with the Stage set at 800 pixels by 600 pixels. However, your client may later tell you that they want the animation in several different sizes to accommodate different layouts. For example, they'd like to create a smaller version with a different aspect ratio for a banner ad. Or, they may want to create a version that will run on AIR for Android devices, which has specific dimensions.

Fortunately, you can modify the Stage even after all your content is put in place. When you change the Stage dimensions, Flash provides the option of scaling the content so that it increases or decreases in proportion to the Stage size.

Stage Resizing and Content Scaling

You'll create another version of this animated project with different Stage dimensions.

Try It!

1. At the bottom of the Properties inspector, note that the dimensions of the current Stage are set at 800 x 600 pixels. Click the Edit button next to the Stage size (the wrench icon).

   The Document Settings dialog box appears.

2. In the Width and Height boxes, enter new pixel dimensions. Enter 400 for the Width and 300 for the Height.

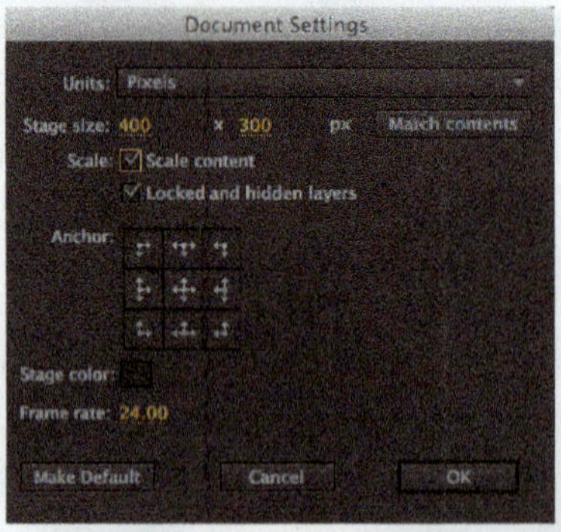

   Notice that as you enter new values for the Width and the Height, the option to Scale content with Stage becomes enabled.

3. Check the option to Scale content with Stage.

   Do not select an Anchor option. By default, no anchor is selected. The Anchor option lets you choose the origin from which your content is resized, if the proportions of the new Stage are different.

4. Click OK.

   Flash modifies the dimensions of the Stage and automatically resizes all the content. If your new dimensions are not proportional to the original size, Flash will resize everything to maximize the content to fit. This means that if your new Stage size is wider than the original, there'll be extra Stage space to the right. If your new Stage size is taller than the original, there'll be extra Stage space on the bottom.

5. Choose File > Save As. Choose the .fla file type and name the file **L14_start_resized_xx**, and leave it open.

   You now have two Flash files, identical in content but with different Stage dimensions. Close this file and reopen **L14_start_xx.fla** to continue this lesson.

Saving a Movie

A mantra in multimedia production is "save early, save often." Applications, operating systems, and hardware crash more often than anyone wants, and at unexpected and inconvenient times. You should always save your movie at regular intervals to ensure that, if a crash does happen, you won't have lost too much of your time.

Flash can help alleviate much of the worry over lost work. The Auto-Recovery feature creates a backup file in case of a crash.

Using Auto-Recovery for a Backup

The Auto-Recovery feature is a preference set for the Flash application and applies to all documents.

Try It!

1. Choose Edit> Preferences.

   The Preferences dialog box displays.

2. If necessary, choose the General category from the left column.
3. Select the Auto-Recovery option, if it's not already selected, and enter a time (in minutes) for the interval that Flash creates a backup file.
4. Click OK.
5. Save the changes to **L14_start_xx.fla**, and leave it open.

Saving an XFL document

You've already saved your Flash movie as an FLA file, but you can also save it in an uncompressed format known as XFL. The XFL format is actually a folder of files rather than a single document. The XFL file format exposes the contents of your Flash movie so that other developers or animators can easily edit your file or manage its assets without having to open the movie in the Flash application. For example, all the imported photos in your Library panel appear in a Library folder within the XFL format. You can edit the library photos or swap them with new photos. Flash will make the substitutions in the movie automatically.

Try It!

1. Choose File > Save As.
2. Name the file **L14_start_copy_xx** and choose Flash Uncompressed Document (*.xfl). Click Save.

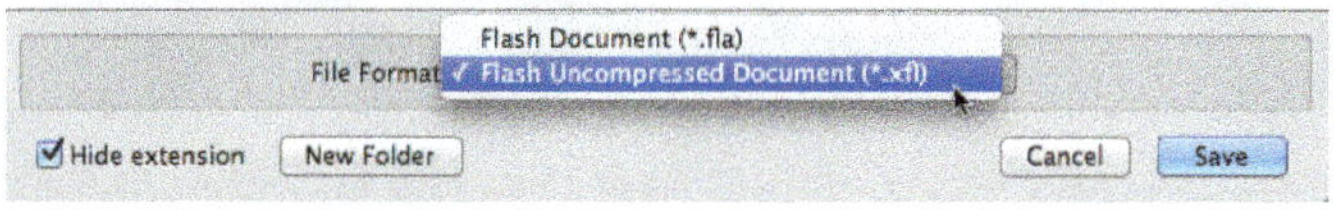

   Flash creates a folder named L14_start_copy_xx, which contains all the files for your Flash movie.

3. Close the Flash document by choosing File > Close.

Modifying an XFL document

In this exercise, you'll modify the Library folder of the XFL document to make changes to your Flash movie.

Try It!

1. In your file management program, open the LIBRARY folder inside the **L14_start_copy_xx** folder.

   The folder contains all the photos you imported into your Flash movie.

2. Select the **photo3.jpg** file and delete it.
3. Drag the photo4.jpg file from the data files for this lesson and move it to the LIBRARY folder inside the L14_start_copy_xx folder. Rename photo4.jpg as **photo3.jpg**.
4. Swapping out photo3.jpg with a new image in the LIBRARY folder automatically makes the change in the .xfl file.
5. From the L14_start_copy_xx folder, double-click the XFL document to open it in Flash.

   The last image in keyframe 24 of your Timeline has been swapped with the new photo.

6. Save and close the document, and then exit Flash.

Preparing a Multimedia or Animation Project

Creating an effective multimedia or animation requires thought, organization, and precision. You could just sit down and start drawing, but you are more likely to succeed if you follow these preparation steps first.

1. Client Meeting

The first step is to meet with the client to discuss the project. You must find out exactly what the client expects, wants, and is willing to pay for. Be prepared to use the information you collect to draft a proposal or concept which you will submit to the client for approval. This process ensures that both you and the client understand each other and agree on the scope of the project. At this point, you should know the technical specifications for the final product, including the budget, length, and delivery format..

2. Develop the Story

After the initial concept has been approved or decided upon, writers develop the story in the form of a script or screenplay. Story is critical. The highest production values cannot save a project with an inadequate story. Without a solid story, there are only elements thrown randomly at the screen, leaving the viewer confused, bored, and in most cases, unsatisfied.

A key component of developing the story is identifying the audience. Who are you trying to reach? Who do you want to watch the finished product? Knowing who your audience is will help you select the appropriate images and language for that audience. For example, if your audience is medical professionals, you would not select images and terminology that are playful and silly.

Another key component of the story is the character design. Character design is more than just the way the character looks. It includes the character's personality traits, movements, and voice. Memorable characters are unique, but have a way of connecting with the audience.

3. Create a Storyboard

With the script approved, the director will work with story artists to continue to flesh out the story in the form of **storyboards**, or a sequence of drawings that help pre-visualize the story.

Storyboard

A sequence of drawings that help previsualize the story.

Storyboards are more than just sketches of what is described in the script. They play a role in how shots are framed and can help set the pace of the entire animation. They may include notes for suggestions on direction or sound. Artists often refer back to the storyboards during a production to ensure that they don't stray too far from the original goal. Some of the best elements of any story are conceived during this stage of production. Skipping the storyboarding stage can prevent you from further refining the story and can delay production.

4. Plan for Audio

Will your project include narration? Dialog? Music? Most effective animations do. If you do not plan ahead, you may find yourself backtracking and adjusting to make the audio and visual content align.

Scratch tracks

Also known as scratch voices, temporary voices created for the animatic phase.

Scratch Voice Recording

If the animation will include dialog, the next step is to record temporary voices called **scratch tracks** or scratch voices. These are just stand-in voices performed by any willing member of the production crew.

Scratch voices provide the director and editor with placeholders for the final dialogue. They can also be useful in testing how shots play out with audio before committing to final dialogue and the pacing of scenes.

Although scratch voices are almost always replaced later in production, sometimes they don't need to be. If the director enjoys one of these early performances enough, the scratch voice could end up being used in the final.

Animatic

An animated storyboard with voice overs, used to flesh out the story.

Voice Recording

At the voice recording stage of production, the story and **animatics** have been locked, and the producer and director should already have actors cast for all the voices.

Once recorded, the voices are later assembled into the edit so that the timing can be locked, and the audio files are delivered to the animators. These recordings directly influence the timing in the scenes and help drive the performance the animators will create in the final frames of the animation. It can be extremely helpful to record video of the voice recording sessions to help aid the animators when they are trying to capture the characters' expressions at key moments.

Music and Sound

In most cases audio engineers work simultaneously with the rest of the crew by starting to develop the music and sound effects as early as the animatic has been locked. These masters of sound open up a whole new level of awesome into an animation.

Comprehension Check

1. What is the difference between a linear and nonlinear editing system?
2. In Flash, what is the Stage?
3. What's the difference between a frame and a keyframe?
4. What's a hidden tool, and how can you access it?
5. Name two methods to undo steps in Flash, and describe them.
6. What is a storyboard? Find three examples of storyboards from your favorite animated films.
7. What is an animatic and why is it important?

Review Project

In this project, you will use what you have learned in this lesson to create a short animation on a vacation you have taken, or one you would like to take. You will need to scan your own photos or download stock photos or clip art from online resources. Use storyboards to plan your animation. Then, create your animation and save it as **L14_review_xx.fla** in the location where your teacher instructs to save files for this lesson. Add shapes or other objects for interest. Preview your movie in your browser. Make any modifications, if necessary, and then share it with your class.

Lesson 15 Overview

In this lesson, you will learn about:

- Creating Shapes in Flash
- Selecting Strokes and Fills
- Editing Shapes
- Changing Strokes and Fills
- Using Gradient and Bitmap Fills
- Grouping Objects
- Using Variable-Width Strokes
- Creating Transparencies
- Creating and Editing Text
- Matching the Color of an Existing Object
- Adding Hyperlinks
- Aligning and Distributing Objects
- Converting and Exporting Art

You can use rectangles, ovals, and lines to create interesting, complex graphics and illustrations in Flash. Edit their shapes and combine them with gradients, transparencies, text, and filters for even greater expressive possibilities.

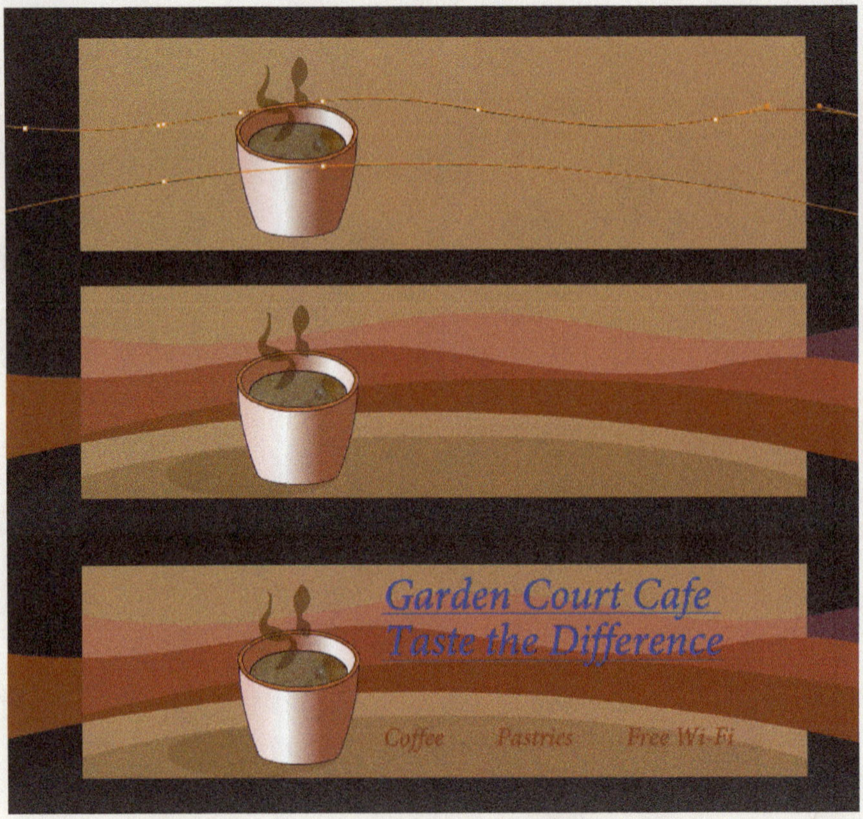

Creating Shapes in Flash

Flash includes several drawing tools, which work in different drawing modes. Many of your creations will begin with simple shapes such as rectangles and ovals, so it's important that you're comfortable drawing them, modifying their appearance, and applying fills and strokes.

Working with Strokes and Fills

Every graphic in Flash starts with a shape. A shape consists of two components: the **fill**, or the insides of the shape; and the **stroke**, or the outline of the shape.

Fill

The insides of the shape.

Stroke

The outlines of the shape.

The fill and the stroke function independently of each other, so you can modify or delete either without affecting the other. For example, you can create a rectangle with a blue fill and a red stroke, and then later change the fill to purple and delete the red stroke entirely. You'll be left with a purple rectangle without an outline. You can also move the fill or stroke independently, so if you want to move the entire shape, make sure that you select both its fill and stroke.

Start by creating your Flash document for this lesson.

Try It!

1. In Flash, choose File > New. In the New Document dialog box, choose ActionScript 3.0.
2. On the right-hand side of the dialog box, make the Stage size **700** pixels by **200** pixels, and change the color of the Stage by clicking the icon next to Background color and then clicking the #CC9966 color swatch. Click OK.
3. Choose File > Save. Name the file **L15_start_xx,** save it in the location where your teacher instructs you to store the files for this lesson, and leave it open.

Using the Rectangle Tool

A coffee cup is essentially a cylinder, which is a rectangle with an oval at the top and an oval at the bottom. You'll start by drawing the rectangular body. It's useful to break down complicated objects into their component parts to make drawing them easier.

Try It!

1. In the Tools panel, select the Rectangle tool. Make sure the Object Drawing mode icon is *not* selected.
2. Choose a stroke color and a fill color from the bottom of the Tools panel. Choose #663300 (dark brown) for the stroke and #CC6600 (light brown) for the fill.
3. On the Stage, draw a rectangle that is a little taller than it is wide.

   You'll specify the exact size and position of the rectangle in step 6.
4. Select the Selection tool.

5. Drag the Selection tool around the entire rectangle to select it. When a shape is selected, Flash displays it with white dots. You can also double-click a shape, and Flash will select both the stroke and fill of the shape.

6. In the Properties inspector, type **130** for the width and **150** for the height. Press Enter (Windows) or Return (Mac) to apply the values.

7. Save the changes to **L15_start_xx.fla**, and leave it open.

> **Note:**
>
> Each color has a hexadecimal value in Flash, HTML, and many other applications. The six digits after the # sign represent the red, green, and blue contributions to the color.

Using the Oval Tool

Now you'll create the opening at the top and the rounded bottom.

Try It!

1. In the Tools panel, choose the Oval tool.

2. Make sure the Snap to Objects option at the bottom of the Tools panel is enabled. This option forces shapes that you draw on the Stage to snap to each other to ensure that lines and corners connect to one another.

3. Click inside the rectangle and drag across it to make an oval inside the rectangle. The Snap to Objects option makes the sides of the oval connect to the sides of the rectangle.

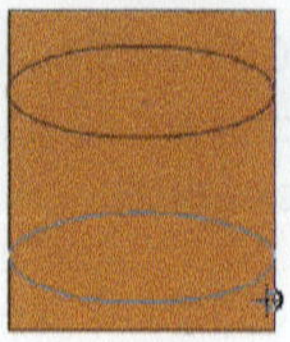

4. Draw another oval near the bottom of the rectangle.

5. Save the changes to **L15_start_xx.fla**, and leave it open.

Selecting Strokes and Fills

> **Note:**
>
> Flash applies the default fill and stroke to the rectangle and oval, which are determined by the last fill and stroke you applied.

To modify an object, you must first be able to select different parts of it. In Flash, you can make selections using the Selection, Subselection, or Lasso tool. Typically, you use the Selection tool to select an entire object or a section of an object. The Subselection tool lets you select a specific point or line in an object. With the Lasso tool, you can make a freeform selection.

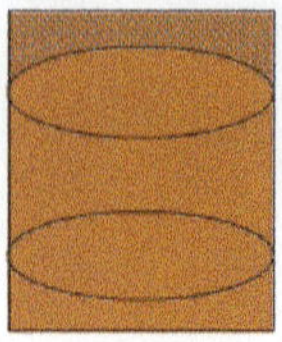

Now, you'll make the rectangle and ovals look more like a coffee cup.

You'll use the Selection tool to delete unwanted strokes and fills.

1. In the Tools panel, select the Selection tool.
2. Click the fill above the top oval to select it.

   Flash highlights the shape above the top oval.

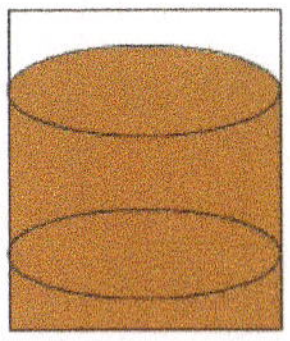

3. Press the Delete key.

   Flash deletes the shape.
4. Select each of the three line segments above the top oval and press the Delete key.

   Flash deletes the individual strokes, leaving the top oval connected to the rectangle.
5. Now select the fill and strokes below the bottom oval, as well as the inside arc at the bottom of the cup, and press the Delete key.

   The remaining shape appears as a cylinder.

6. Save the changes to **L15_start_xx.fla**, and leave it open.

Note:

Hold down the Shift key when making selections to select multiple fills or strokes together.

Editing Shapes

When drawing in Flash, you'll often start with the Rectangle and Oval tools. But to create more complex graphics, you'll use other tools to modify those base shapes. The Free Transform tool, the Copy and Paste commands, and the Selection tool can help transform the plain cylinder into a coffee cup.

Using the Free Transform Tool

The coffee cup will look more realistic if you taper the bottom rim. You'll use the Free Transform tool to change its overall shape. With the Free Transform tool, you can change an object's scale, rotation, or skew (the way it is slanted), or distort an object by dragging control points around a bounding box.

Try It!

1. In the Tools panel, select the Free Transform tool.
2. Drag the Free Transform tool around the cylinder on the Stage to select it.

   Transformation handles appear on the cylinder.

3. Press Command/Ctrl+Shift as you drag one of the lower corners inward. Holding these keys while dragging lets you move both corners the same distance simultaneously.

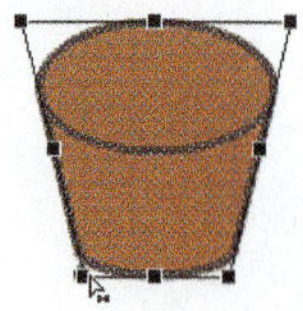

4. Click outside the shape to deselect it.

   The bottom of the cylinder is narrow, and the top is wide. It now looks more like a coffee cup.

5. Save the changes to **L15_start_xx.fla**, and leave it open.

Using Copy and Paste

Use Copy and Paste commands to easily duplicate shapes on the Stage. You'll set the surface level of the coffee by copying and pasting the top rim of the coffee cup.

Try It!

> **Note:**
>
> If you press the Option or Alt key while moving one of the control points, Flash scales the selected object relative to its transformation point, represented by the circle icon. You can move the transformation point anywhere, even outside the object. Press Shift to constrain the object proportions. Press Command/Ctrl to deform the object from a single control point.

1. Select the Selection tool. Hold down the Shift key and select the top arc and bottom arc of the coffee cup opening.

2. Choose Edit > Copy (Command/Ctrl+C). The top strokes of the oval are copied.

3. Choose Edit > Paste in Place (Shift+Command/Ctrl+V).

   A duplicate oval appears on the Stage, exactly where you copied it.

4. In the Tools panel, select the Free Transform tool.

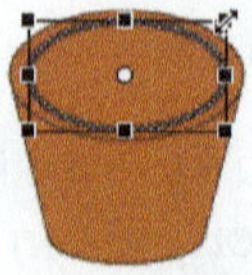

   Transformation handles appear on the oval.

5. Press the Shift key as you drag the corners inward. Make the oval about 10 percent smaller. Pressing the Shift key lets you change the shape uniformly so the oval maintains its aspect ratio.

   The top edge of the coffee cup is in place.

6. Choose Edit > Paste in Place (Shift+Command/Ctrl+V) one more time.
7. Choose the Free Transform tool. Hold down the Shift key and drag the corners inward to shrink another oval.
8. Drag the oval over the rim of the coffee cup so it overlaps the front lip. You can also press the Down Arrow key to nudge the selected oval down the Stage.
9. Click outside the selection to deselect the oval.
10. Select the lower portions of the smaller oval and delete it.

    Your coffee cup now is filled with coffee!
11. Save the changes to **L15_start_xx.fla**, and leave it open.

Changing Shape Contours

With the Selection tool, you can push and pull lines and corners to change the overall contours of any shape. It's a fast and intuitive way of working with shapes.

Try It!

1. In the Tools panel, select the Selection tool.
2. Move your mouse pointer close to one of the sides of the coffee cup.

   A curved line appears near your pointer, indicating that you can change the curvature of the stroke.
3. Click and drag the stroke outward.

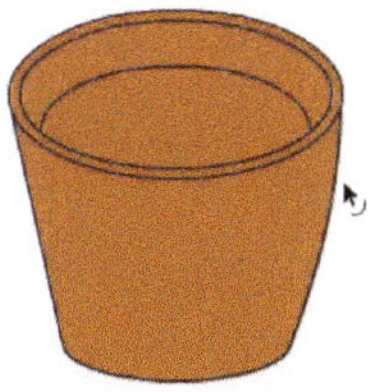

   The sides of the coffee cup bend, giving the coffee cup a slight bulge.
4. Click and drag the other side of the coffee cup outward slightly.

   The coffee cup now has a more rounded body.
5. Save the changes to **L15_start_xx.fla**, and leave it open.

Changing Strokes and Fills

If you want to change the properties of any stroke or fill, you can use the Ink Bottle tool or the Paint Bucket tool. The Ink Bottle tool changes stroke colors; the Paint Bucket tool changes fill colors.

Try It!

1. In the Tools panel, select the Paint Bucket tool.
2. In the Properties inspector, choose a darker brown color (#663333) for the Fill color.
3. Click the top surface of the coffee that is inside the cup.

   The fill of the top oval changes to the darker brown color.

4. In the Tools panel, select the Ink Bottle tool.
5. In the Properties inspector, choose a darker brown color (#330000) for the Stroke color.
6. Click the top stroke above the surface of the coffee.

   The stroke around the surface of the coffee changes to a darker brown color.

7. Save the changes to **L15_start_xx.fla**, and leave it open.

> **Note:**
>
> If your Paint Bucket tool changes the fill in surrounding areas, there may be a small gap that allows the fill to spill over. Close the gap, or at the bottom of the Tools panel, choose different gap sizes to close for your Paint Bucket tool.

> **Note:**
>
> You can also select a stroke or a fill and change its color in the Properties inspector without using the Paint Bucket or Ink Bottle tool.

Flash Drawing Modes

Flash provides three drawing modes that determine how objects interact with one another on the Stage and how you can edit them. By default, Flash uses Merge Drawing mode, but you can enable Object Drawing mode or use the Rectangle Primitive or Oval Primitive tool to use Primitive Drawing mode.

Merge Drawing Mode

In this mode, Flash merges drawn shapes, such as rectangles and ovals, where they overlap, so that multiple shapes appear to be a single shape. If you move or delete a shape that has been merged with another, the overlapping portion is permanently removed.

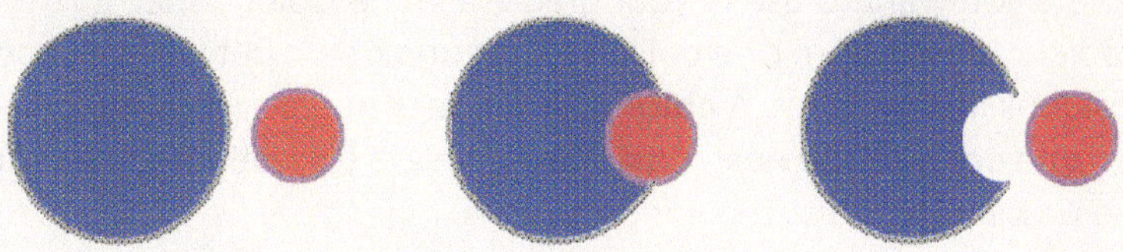

Object Drawing Mode

In this mode, Flash does not merge drawn objects; they remain distinct and separate, even when they overlap. To enable Object Drawing mode, select the tool you want to use, and then click the Object Drawing icon in the options area of the Tools panel.

To convert an object to merged shapes (Merge Drawing mode), select it and press Command/Ctrl+B. To convert a shape to an object (Object Drawing mode), select it and choose Modify > Combine Objects > Union.

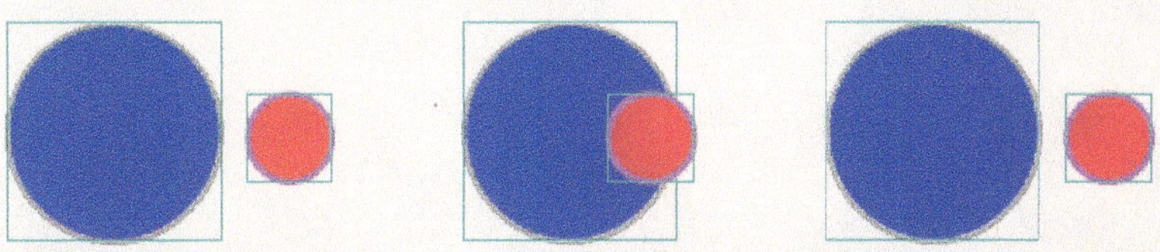

Primitive Drawing Mode

When you use the Rectangle Primitive tool or the Oval Primitive tool, Flash draws the shapes as separate objects. Unlike regular objects, however, you can modify the corner radius and start and end angle of rectangle primitives, and adjust the inner radius of oval primitives using the Properties inspector.

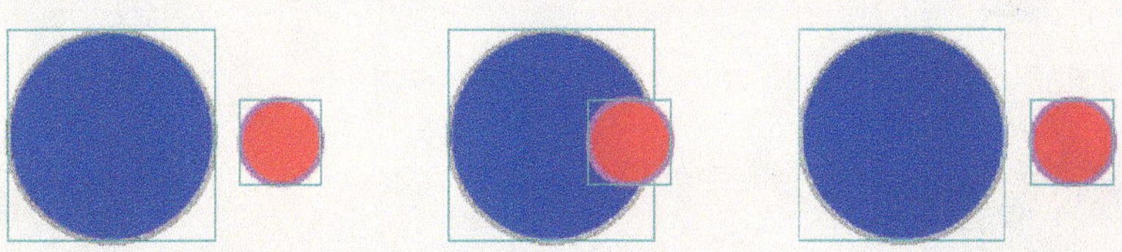

Using Gradient and Bitmap Fills

So far, you have used solid colors for fills, but you can also use a gradient or a bitmap image (such as a JPEG file) as a fill.

Gradient

One color gradually changing to another.

Linear gradient

Color changes horizontally, vertically, or diagonally.

Radial gradient

Color changes moving outward from a central focal point.

Color pointer

Determines where the gradient changes from one color to the next.

In a **gradient**, one color gradually changes into another. Flash can create **linear** gradients, which change color horizontally, vertically, or diagonally; or **radial** gradients, which change color moving outward from a central focal point.

For this lesson, you'll use a linear gradient fill to add three-dimensionality to the coffee cup. To give the appearance of a top layer of foaming cream, you'll import a bitmap image to use as the fill. You can import a bitmap file in the Color panel.

Creating Gradient Transitions

You'll define the colors you want to use in your gradient in the Color panel. By default, a linear gradient moves from one color to a second color, but you can use up to 15 color transitions in a gradient. A **color pointer** determines where the gradient changes from one color to the next. Add color pointers beneath the gradient definition bar in the Color panel to add color transitions.

You'll create a gradient that moves from tan to white to dark tan on the surface of the coffee cup to give it a rounded appearance.

Try It!

1. Choose the Selection tool. Select the fill that represents the front surface of the coffee cup.

2. Open the Color panel (Window > Color). In the Color panel, choose the Color type menut and select Linear gradient.

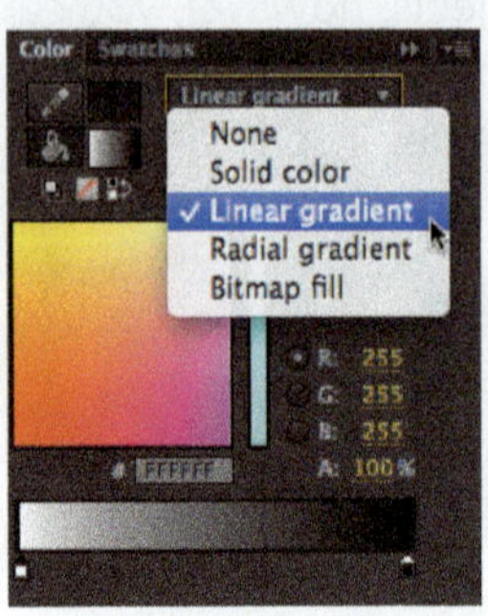

The front surface of the coffee cup is filled with a color gradient from left to right.

3. Select the color pointer on the left of the color gradient in the Color panel (the triangle above it turns black when selected), and then type **FFCCCC** in the Hex value field to specify a light tan color. Press Enter/Return to apply the color. You can also choose a color from the color picker or double-click the color pointer to choose a color from the color swatches.

4. Select the far-right color pointer, and then enter **B86241** for a dark tan color. Press Enter/Return to apply the color.

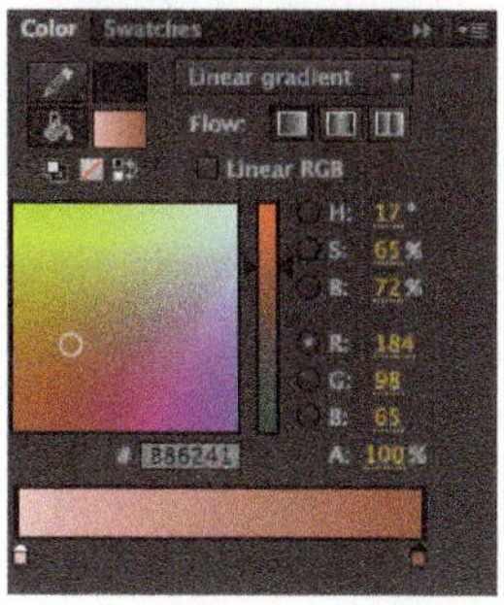

The gradient fill for the coffee cup gradually changes from light tan to dark tan across its surface.

5. Click beneath the gradient definition bar to create a new color pointer.

6. Drag the new color pointer to the middle of the gradient.

7. Select the new color pointer, and then type **FFFFFF** in the Hex value field to specify white for the new color. Press Enter/Return to apply the color.

The gradient fill for the coffee cup gradually changes from light tan to white to dark tan.

8. Deselect the fill on the Stage by clicking elsewhere on the Stage. Choose the Paint Bucket tool and make sure the Lock Fill option at the bottom of the Tools panel is deselected.

   The Lock Fill option locks the current gradient to the first shape to which it was applied so that subsequent shapes extend the gradient. You'll want a new gradient for the back surface of the coffee cup, so the Lock Fill option should be deselected.

9. With the Paint Bucket tool, select the back surface of the coffee cup.

   Flash applies the gradient to the back surface.

10. Save the changes to **L15_start_xx.fla**, and leave it open.

Using the Gradient Transform Tool

In addition to choosing colors and positioning the color pointers for a gradient, you can adjust the size, direction, or center of a gradient fill. To squeeze the gradient in the front surface and reverse the gradient in the back surface, you'll use the Gradient Transform tool.

Try It!

> **Note:**
>
> To delete a color pointer from the gradient definition bar, simply drag it off the bar.

1. Select the Gradient Transform tool. (The Gradient Transform tool is grouped with the Free Transform tool.)

2. Click the front surface of the coffee cup. Transformation handles appear.

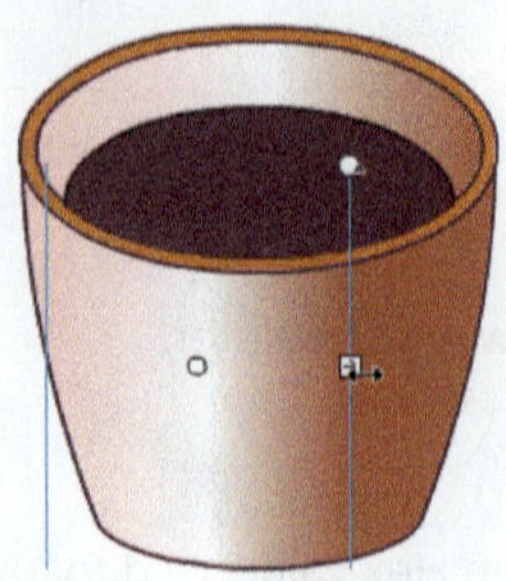

3. Drag the square handle on the side of the bounding box inward to squeeze the gradient tighter. Drag the center circle to move the gradient to the left so the white highlight is positioned slightly left of center.
4. Now click the back surface of the coffee cup. Transformation handles appear.
5. Drag the round handle on the corner of the bounding box to rotate the gradient 180 degrees so the gradient fades from dark tan on the left to white to light tan on the right.
   The coffee cup now looks more realistic because the shadows and highlights make it appear that the front surface is convex and the back surface is concave.
6. Save the changes to **L15_start_xx.fla**, and leave it open.

Adding a Bitmap Fill

You'll make this cup of coffee a little fancier by adding a frothy layer of cream. You'll use a JPEG image of foam as a bitmap fill.

Try It!

1. Select the top surface of the coffee with the Selection tool.
2. Choose Window > Color to open the Color panel.

3. Select Bitmap fill from the Color type menu.

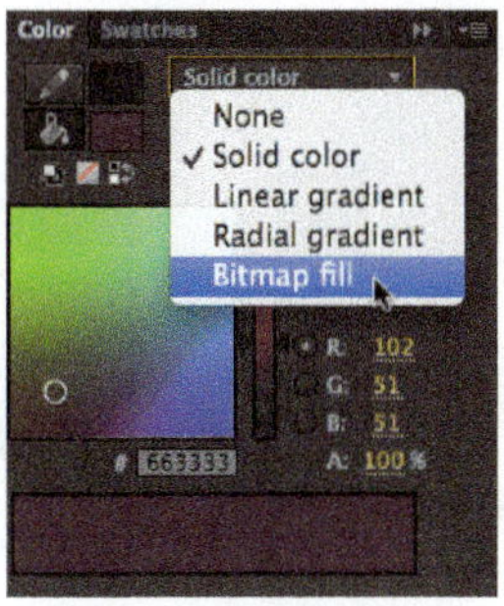

4. In the Import to Library dialog box, navigate to the **coffeecream.jpg** file from where the data files are save for this lesson.

5. Select the **coffeecream.jpg** file and click Open.

   The top surface of the coffee fills with the foam image.

6. The cup of coffee is complete! Rename the layer containing your completed drawing **coffee cup**. All that's left to do is to add some hot steam.

7. Save the changes to **L15_start_xx.fla**, and leave it open.

Note:

Move the center circle to change the center of the gradient; drag the arrow circle to rotate the gradient; or drag the arrow in the square to stretch the gradient.

Grouping Objects

Now that you're finished creating your cup of coffee, you can make it into a single group. A group holds together a collection of shapes and other graphics to preserve their integrity. When the elements that compose the coffee cup are grouped, you can move them as a unit without worrying that the cup might merge with underlying shapes. Use groups to organize your drawing.

Try It!

1. Choose the Selection tool.

2. Drag around the cup of coffee to select all its parts.

3. Choose Modify > Group.

   The cup of coffee is now a single group. When you select it, a blue outline indicates its bounding box.

4. If you want to change any part of the cup of coffee, double-click the group to edit it.

   Notice that all the other elements on the Stage dim, and the Edit bar above the Stage displays Scene 1 Group. This indicates that you are now in a particular group and can edit its contents.

5. Click the Scene 1 icon in the Edit bar at the top of the Stage, or double-click an empty part of the Stage, and return to the main scene.

6. Save the changes to **L15_start_xx.fla**, and leave it open.

Using Variable-Width Strokes

You can apply many different styles of lines to your strokes. In addition to a solid line, you can choose dotted, dashed, or ragged, or even customize your own. In addition, you can create lines with variable widths and edit the variations with the new Width tool.

In this lesson, you'll use the Pencil tool to create variable-width lines to represent the steam wafting off the coffee.

Adding Variable-Width Lines

Now you'll add some whimsical lines above your coffee illustration to give it some personality.

Try It!

1. On the Timeline, insert a new layer and name it **coffee aroma**. You'll draw your lines in this layer.

2. In the Tools panel, select the Pencil tool. Choose the Smooth option at the bottom of the panel.

3. In the Properties inspector, choose a dark brown color at 50% Alpha value.

4. For Stroke, enter **15** for stroke size. For Style, choose Solid, and for Width, choose the thick and thin profile, Width Profile 2.

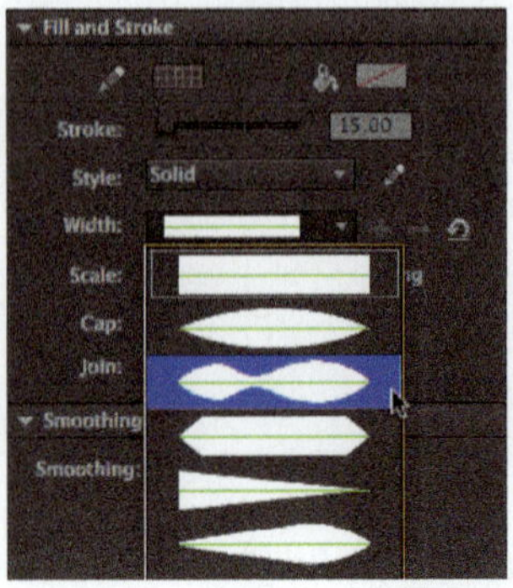

5. Draw a few wavy lines above the coffee.

Flash renders a line with a thick-and-thin width. Although it appears as a complicated shape, the entire object is a single selectable stroke.

6. Save the changes to **L15_start_xx.fla**, and leave it open.

Editing the Width of Lines

You can finesse where the bulges appear in your lines, and how much of a bulge there is. Use the Width tool to make those edits.

Try It!

1. In the Tools panel, choose the Width tool.
2. Move your mouse pointer over one of your variable-width strokes.
3. Anchor points appear along the line to show you where the thick and thin portions of the line are located.

Note:

Edit variable-width lines as you would any other stroke. Use the Selection or Subselection tool to bend the curves or move the anchor points.

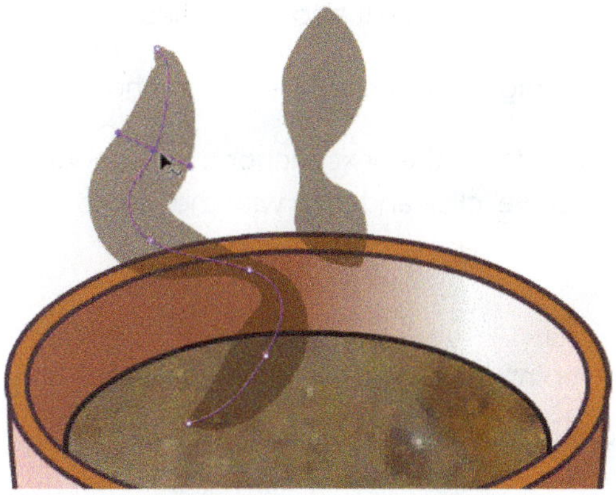

4. Click and drag the handles at any anchor point to change the width of the line. Exaggerate some of the restrictions and bulges.
5. Click and drag the anchor point along the stroke to move its location.
6. Click and drag anywhere along the stroke to add a new anchor point and define the width at that location. Flash displays a small plus sign next to your pointer to indicate that you can add an anchor point.
7. Save the changes to **L15_start_xx.fla**, and leave it open.

Creating Curves with the Pen Tool

You've used the Width tool to pull and push on the edges of shapes to intuitively make curves. For more precise control, you can use the Pen tool.

Now you'll create a soothing, wavelike background graphic.

Try It!

1. Choose Insert > Timeline > Layer, and name the new layer **dark brown wave**.
2. Drag the layer to the bottom of the layer stack.

> **Note:**
>
> To delete an anchor point of a variable-width line, click to select the anchor point, and press the Delete key.

> **Note:**
>
> Hold down the Option/Alt key when you want to modify only one side of a variable-width line.

3. Lock all the other layers.
4. In the Tools panel, select the Pen tool.
5. Set the Stroke color to a dark brown.

   The other attributes from the previous exercise will also be applied.
6. Begin your shape by clicking on the Stage to establish the first anchor point.
7. Click on another part of the Stage to indicate the next anchor point in your shape. When you want to create a smooth curve, click and drag with the Pen tool.

   A handle appears from the anchor point, indicating the curvature of the line.
8. Continue clicking and dragging to build the outline of the wave. Make the wave wider than the Stage.
9. Close your shape by clicking the first anchor point.
10. Select the Paint Bucket tool.
11. Set the Fill color to a dark brown.

12. Click inside the outline you just created to fill it with color and delete the stroke.

13. Save the changes to **L15_start_xx.fla**, and leave it open.

> **Note:**
>
> Don't worry about making all the curves perfect. It takes practice to get used to the Pen tool. You'll also have a chance to refine your curves in the next part of the lesson.

Editing Curves with the Selection and Subselection Tools

Your first try at creating smooth waves probably won't be very good. Use the Selection tool or the Subselection tool to refine your curves.

Try It!

1. Choose the Selection tool.
2. Hover over a line segment and look at the curve that appears near your pointer. This indicates that you can edit the curve. If a corner appears near your pointer, this indicates that you can edit the vertex.

3. Drag the curve to edit its shape.
4. In the Tools panel, select the Subselection tool.
5. Click on the outline of the shape.
6. Drag the anchor points to new locations or move the handles to refine the overall shape.

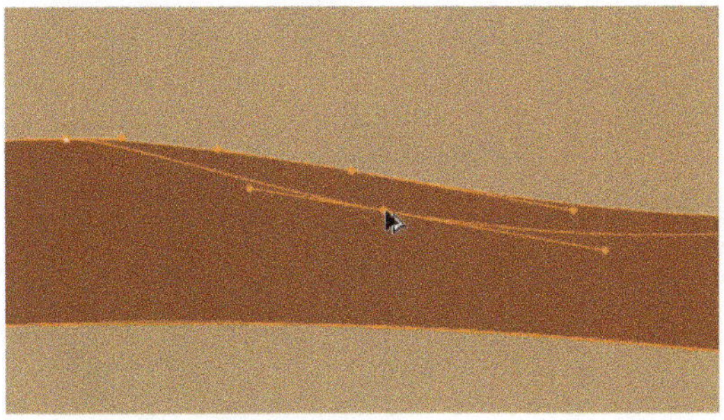

7. Save the changes to **L15_start_xx.fla**, and leave it open.

Deleting or Adding Anchor Points

Use the hidden tools under the Pen tool to delete or add anchor points as needed.

Try It!

1. Press and hold on the Pen tool to access the hidden tools under it.

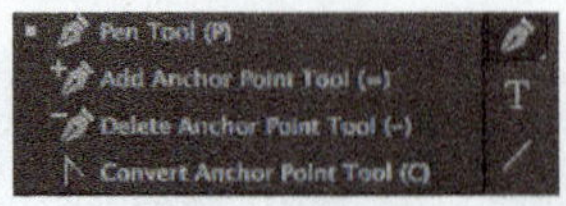

2. Select the Delete Anchor Point tool.
3. Click an anchor point on the outline of the shape to delete it.
4. Select the Add Anchor Point tool.
5. Click on the curve to add an anchor point.
6. Save the changes to **L15_start_xx.fla**, and leave it open.

Creating Transparencies

Next, you'll create a second wave to overlap the first wave. You'll make the second wave slightly transparent to create more overall depth. You can apply transparency to either the stroke or the fill. Transparency is measured as a percentage and is referred to as alpha. An alpha of 100% indicates that a color is totally opaque, whereas an alpha of 0% indicates that a color is totally transparent.

Try It!

1. Select the shape in the dark brown wave layer.
2. Choose Edit > Copy.
3. Choose Insert > Timeline > Layer, and name the new layer **light brown wave**.

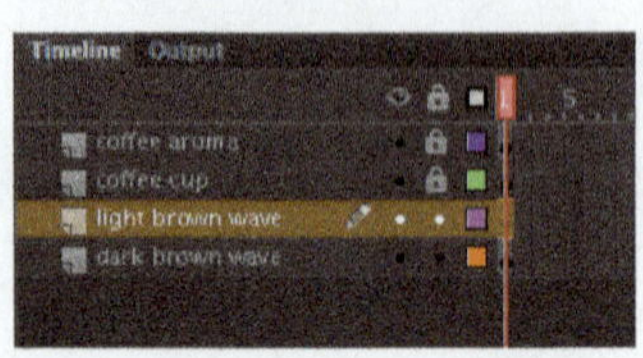

4. Choose Edit > Paste in Place (Command/Ctrl+Shift+V).

   The Paste in Place command puts the copied item in the exact same position from where it was copied.

5. Choose the Selection tool and move the pasted shape slightly to the left or to the right so the crests of the waves are somewhat offset.

6. Select the fill of the shape in the light brown wave layer.

7. Choose Window > Color to open the Color panel. Set the fill color to a slightly different brown hue (**#CC6666**), and then change the Alpha value to **50%**.

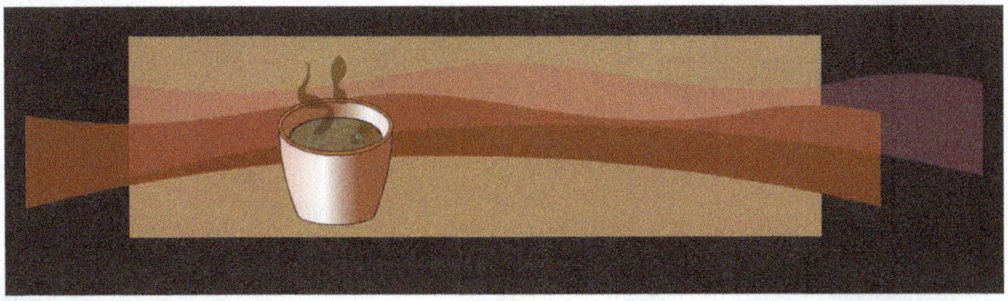

   The color swatch in the Color panel previews your newly selected color. Transparencies are indicated by the gray grid that you can see through the transparent color swatch.

8. Save the changes to **L15_start_xx.fla**, and leave it open.

Adding Shadows

Transparent fills are effective for creating shadows, which can provide a sense of depth for your illustration. You'll add a cast shadow for your coffee mug and another decorative shadow at the bottom of the Stage.

Try It!

1. Choose Insert > Timeline > Layer, and name the new layer **shadow**.

2. Choose Insert > Timeline > Layer again, and name the second new layer **big shadow**.

3. Drag the shadow layer and the big shadow layer to the bottom of the layer stack.

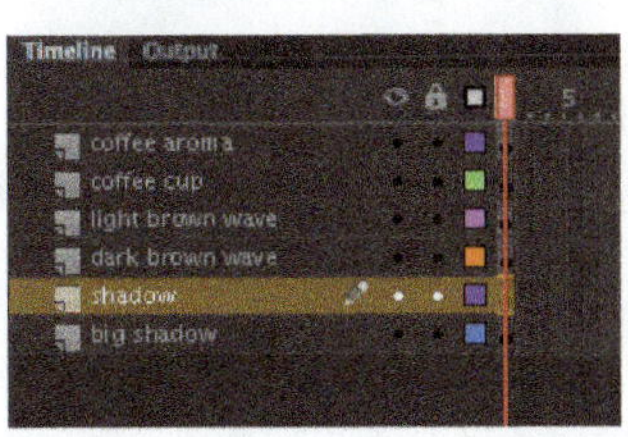

4. Choose the Oval tool.

5. For the Stroke, choose none, and for the Fill, choose a dark brown color (#663300) with a 15% Alpha value.

Note:

You can also change the transparency of a shape from the Properties inspector by clicking the Fill Color icon and changing the Alpha value in the pop-up color menu.

6. In the shadow layer, draw an oval that sits just under the coffee mug.

7. In the big shadow layer, draw a larger oval where its top edge covers the bottom of the Stage.

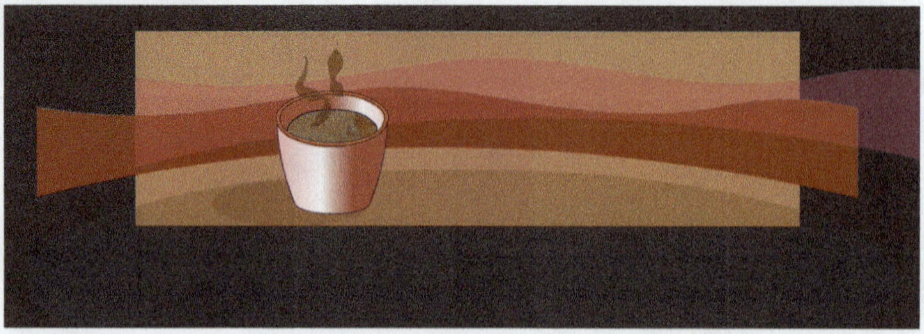

The overlapping transparent ovals add a rich, layered appearance to the illustration.

8. Save the changes to **L15_start_xx.fla**, and leave it open.

Creating and Editing Text

Now let's add text to complete this illustration. An ActionScript 3.0 Flash document has three text options: Static Text and two more advanced options, Dynamic Text and Input Text. Use Static Text for display. Use Dynamic or Input Text when you want to control the text with ActionScript.

When you create Static text on the Stage and publish your project, Flash automatically includes all the necessary fonts to display the text correctly. That means you don't have to worry about your audience having the required fonts to see the text as you intended it.

Using the Text Tool

You'll create your text with the Text tool.

Try It!

1. Select the top layer.
2. Choose Insert > Timeline > Layer, and name the new layer **text**.
3. Choose the Text tool.

4. In the Properties inspector, select Static Text.

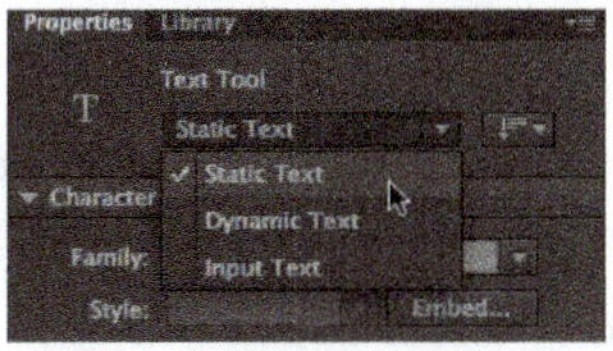

5. Under the Character options, choose a font, style, size, and color that look appealing to you.

   Under the Paragraph options, you have additional choices for formatting the text, such as justification or spacing. Choose values there or accept the defaults.

6. Click on the Stage and begin typing. Enter **Garden Court Cafe Taste the Difference**. Alternatively, you can click and drag out a text box to define the maximum width of your text.

7. Exit the Text tool by choosing the Selection tool.

8. Add three more pieces of text in a smaller font size on the Stage in the same layer: **Coffee, Pastries,** and **Free Wi-Fi**.

9. Save the changes to **L15_start_xx.fla**, and leave it open.

Matching the Color of an Existing Object

If you want to match a color exactly, you can use the Eyedropper tool to sample a fill or a stroke. After you click on an object with the Eyedropper tool, Flash automatically provides you with the Paint Bucket tool or the Ink Bottle tool with the selected color and associated properties that you can apply to another object.

You'll use the Eyedropper tool to sample the color of one of the decorative background waves and apply it to the three pieces of smaller text.

Try It!

1. In the Tools panel, choose the Selection tool.
2. Hold down the Shift key and select all three of the smaller pieces of text: Coffee, Pastries, and Free Wi-Fi.
3. Choose the Eyedropper tool.
4. Click on the fill of the shape in the dark brown wave layer.

The three selected pieces of text change color to match the fill of the dark brown wave layer. Using the same colors helps to unify the composition.

5. Save the changes to **L15_start_xx.fla**, and leave it open.

Note:

You can also use the Eyedropper tool to sample the color and properties of a fill or stroke and apply it to another shape.

Adding Hyperlinks

Adding hyperlinks to text makes your content interactive. Next, you'll add a hyperlink to the tagline in this coffee illustration to take readers to the coffee Web site.

1. Double-click the Garden Court Cafe box and select the text, **Garden Court Cafe Taste the Difference**.

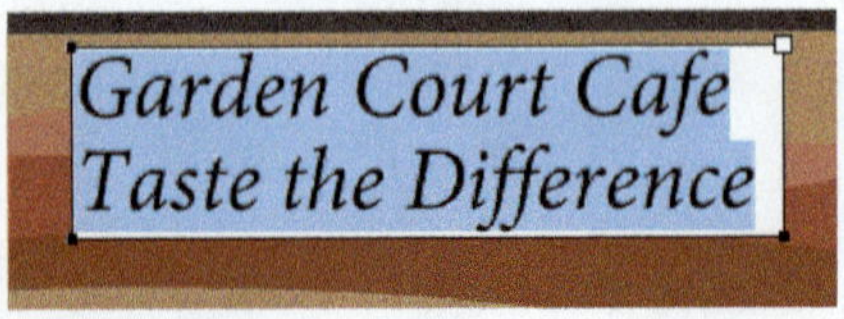

2. In the Properties inspector, expand the Options section, and enter **http://** in the Link field. This will launch your browser when clicked, but it will not take you to an actual Web site.

3. In the Target field, choose _blank.

The Target options determine where the URL loads; in this case, a blank browser window.

4. Exit the Text tool.

   Flash underlines the text to show you that it is hyperlinked. The underline won't show in the final published file.

5. Choose Control > Test Movie > in Flash Professional.

   Flash exports a SWF (small Web format) file and displays it in a new window.

6. Click the hyperlinked tagline text.

   Your default browser launches with the specified URL.

7. Save the changes to **L15_start_xx.fla**, and leave it open.

Aligning and Distributing Objects

Finally, you'll tidy up the text so the layout is organized. Although you can use rulers (View > Rulers) and grids (View > Grid > Show Grid) to help position objects, you'll use the Align panel, which is more effective when you're dealing with multiple objects. You'll also rely on the smart guides that appear when you move objects around the Stage.

Aligning Objects

The Align panel, as you might guess, aligns any number of selected objects horizontally or vertically. It can also distribute objects evenly.

Try It!

1. Choose the Selection tool.
2. Select the first small piece of text, **Coffee**.
3. Move the text to the left until smart guides appear. Align the left edge of the selected text with the left edge of the larger text above it.
4. Select the third small piece of text, **Free Wi-Fi**.
5. Move the text to the right until smart guides appear. Align the right edge of the selected text with the right edge of the larger text above it.

6. Select all three small pieces of text.

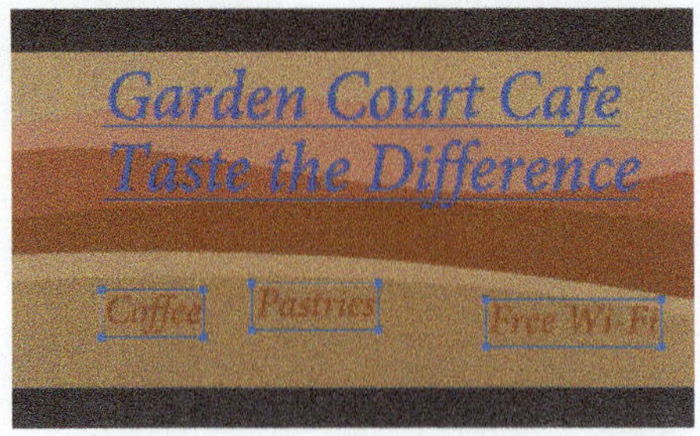

7. Open the Align panel (Window > Align).

8. Deselect the Align to Stage option, if it is already selected. Click the Align Bottom Edge button.

   Flash aligns the bottom edges of the text.

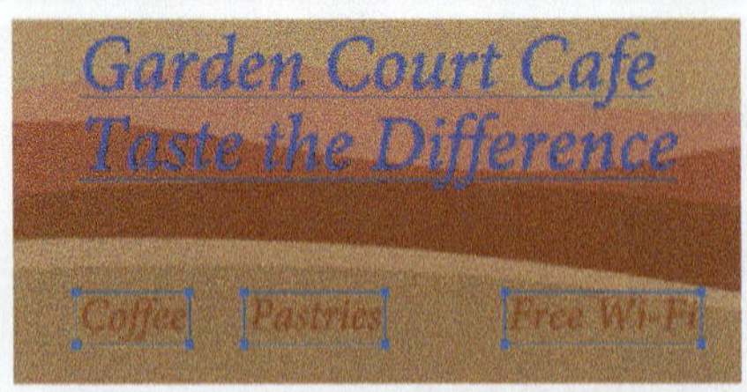

9. Click the Space Evenly Horizontally button.

   Flash moves the selected text so that the spaces between them become uniform.

10. Save the changes to **L15_start_xx.fla**, and leave it open.

Note:

You might have to lock the lower layers so you don't accidentally select the shapes in the lower layers.

Converting and Exporting Art

You've completed your composition, made up of a simple illustration and layered design and text elements. You may still need to take additional steps, however, in order to optimize it for display in the final, published playback environment.

Converting Vector Art to Bitmap Art

Vector art, especially art with complex curves, shapes and line styles, can be processor-intensive and can take its toll on mobile devices, where performance suffers. An option called Convert to Bitmap provides a way to turn selected artwork on the Stage into a single bitmap, which can be less taxing on the processor.

Once you've converted the object to a bitmap, you can move it without worrying about it merging with underlying shapes. However, the graphics are no longer editable with Flash's editing tools.

1. Choose the Selection tool.

2. Select the wavy coffee aroma lines in the coffee aroma layer, and the coffee group in the coffee cup layer.

3. Choose Modify > Convert to Bitmap.

   Flash converts the cup of coffee and wavy lines to a single bitmap and stores the bitmap in the Library panel.

4. Choose Edit > Undo (Command/Ctrl+Z) several times to undo the conversion to bitmap and revert your coffee mug and aroma strokes to vector graphics.

5. Save the changes to **L15_start_xx.fla**, and leave it open.

Exporting Art to SVG

Scalable Vector Graphics (SVG) is a common format for displaying vector graphics in a browser. You can export your final composition from Flash as SVG, embedding or linking any bitmap images.

1. Choose File > Export > Export Image.

2. For File Format, choose SVG Image (*.svg) and click Save.

3. In the ExportSVG dialog box that appears, choose Embed for the Image Location option.

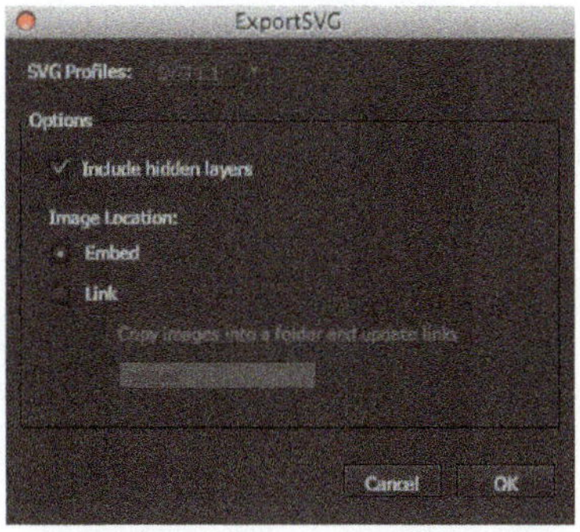

The Image Location options determine whether your bitmap images are encoded into the SVG file or kept as separate files and linked to your SVG. Embedding images creates larger SVG files, while linking allows you to swap and edit the images easily.

4. Click OK.

   Flash exports the SVG file with the coffeecream.jpg image encoded in the text file.

5. Open the SVG file in a browser.

6. Save the changes to **L15_start_xx.fla**, and close Flash.

Your browser renders the image, and all the vector information is preserved. Use your browser's zoom function (View > Zoom In) to examine the composition closer. The curves remain sharp even up close, and all the text is still selectable.

Careers in Animation

Individuals who study multimedia art and animation work as illustrators, 3D animators, animation directors, animation producers, digital artists, creative directors, and media producers. These professionals have strong computer skills as well as training and expertise in areas such as video, film, audio, and graphics. Their work is incorporated into video games, movies, music videos, television or Internet commercials, Web sites, and other products.

Essential skills include teamwork, effective communication, problem-solving, time-management, and critical thinking. They benefit from a strong background in fine arts and design as well as computers and electronics.

Most multimedia artists and animators have a four-year bachelor's degree. There are numerous industry certifications available, including many issued by Adobe, Inc. for demonstrating proficiency using the Adobe Creative Cloud products. Obtaining certifications will increase your appeal to employers and improve your chances for career success.

On average, people in this field earn about $34.00 per hour. The Bureau of Labor Statistics projects the employment of multimedia artists and animators to grow 6% through 2022. This growth is due to demand for animation and visual effects in video games, movies, Internet, and television shows.

Comprehension Check

1. What are the three drawing modes in Flash, and how do they differ?
2. What is the difference between the Paint Bucket tool and the Ink Bottle tool?
3. When would you use each of the selection tools in Flash?
4. What can you do with the Width tool?
5. What does the Align panel do?

Review Project

Start a new Flash document and save it as **L15_review_xx.fla**. Using the tools you learned about in this lesson, create a graphic that represents your favorite season of the year; for example, flowers for spring or a snowman for winter. Be creative with your use of shapes, colors, gradients, and stroke widths. Add text that identifies the season. Create a hyperlink from the text to an actual Web site that you think illustrates your favorite season. Share your graphic with the class.

Lesson 16 Overview

In this lesson, you will learn about:

- Importing Illustrator Files
- Identifying Symbols
- Creating Symbols
- Importing Photoshop Files
- Editing and Managing Symbols
- Changing the Size and Position of Instances
- Changing the Color Effect of Instances
- Using Display Options
- Using Blending Effects
- Exporting as Bitmap
- Applying Filters for Special Effects
- Positioning in 3D Space

Symbols are reusable assets that are stored in your Library panel. You can import symbols or create your own. Once you store them in the Library, you can insert them in any document. This saves you the time and effort of recreating items you use frequently, and also helps ensure consistency within a movie.

Movie clips, graphics, and buttons are three types of symbols that you will be creating and using often for special effects, animation, and interactivity. Learning how to work with symbols is an essential step to creating any animation or interactivity.

In this lesson, you'll use Illustrator graphic files, imported Photoshop files, and symbols to create an attractive static image with interesting effects.

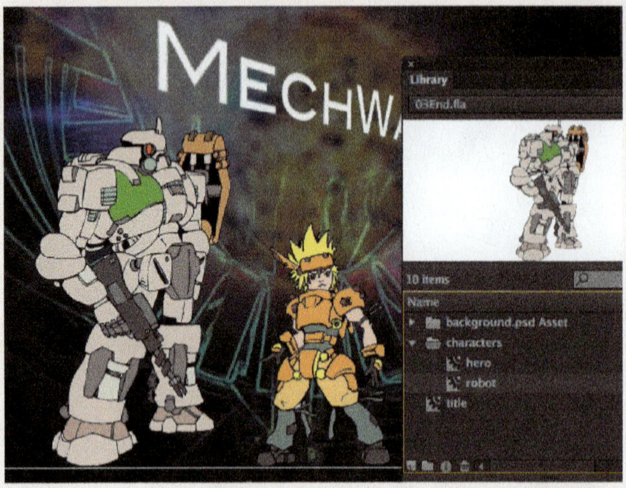

Try It!

1. Open Flash, and choose File > New. In the New Document dialog box, choose ActionScript 3.0.
2. On the right side of the dialog box, change the Stage to **600** pixels wide by **450** pixels high, and click OK.
3. Choose File > Save. Name the file **L16_start_xx,** save it in the location where your teacher instructs you to store the files for this lesson, and leave it open.

Importing Illustrator Files

As you learned in the previous lesson, you can draw objects in Flash using the Rectangle, Oval, and other tools. However, for complex drawings, you may prefer to create the artwork in another application. Flash supports a variety of graphic formats, including Adobe Illustrator files, so you can create original artwork in that application and then import it into Flash.

When you import an Illustrator file, you can choose how Flash should import the different layers of the original file as well as any text it contains. You'll import an Illustrator file that contains all the characters for the cartoon frame.

Try It!

1. Choose File > Import > Import to Stage.
2. Navigate to the data files for this lesson and select **characters.ai**.
3. Click Open.

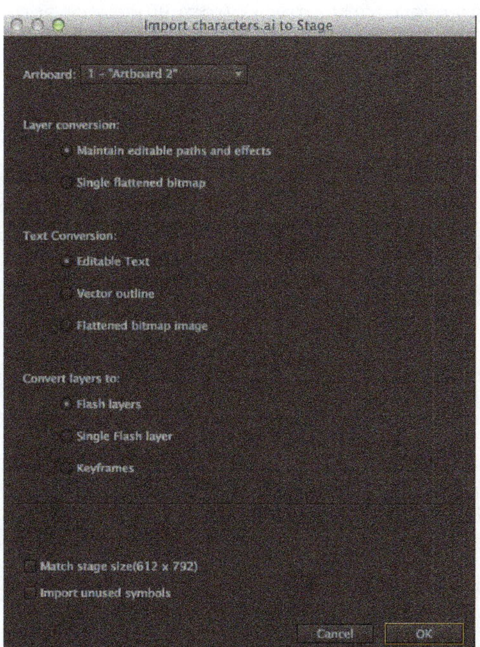

The Import to Stage dialog box appears.

4. For Layer Conversion, choose Maintain editable paths and effects.

   Maintaining editable paths and effects lets you continue to edit the vector drawing in Flash. The other option, Single flattened bitmap, imports the Illustrator artwork as a bitmap image.

5. For Text Conversion, choose Editable Text.

   The Illustrator file doesn't contain any text, so the settings here don't matter.

6. For Convert layers to, choose Flash layers.

   Flash preserves the layers from Illustrator. The Single Flash layer option flattens the Illustrator layers into one Flash layer, and the Keyframes option separates the Illustrator layers into individual Flash keyframes.

7. Click OK.

   Flash imports the Illustrator vector graphics, and all the layers from the Illustrator file also appear in the Timeline.

8. Save the changes to **L16_start_xx.fla**, and leave it open.

Using Adobe Illustrator with Flash

Flash Professional can import Illustrator files and automatically recognize layers, frames, and symbols. If you're more familiar with Illustrator, you may find it easier to design layouts in Illustrator, and then import them into Flash to add animation and interactivity.

Save your Illustrator artwork in Illustrator AI format, and then choose File > Import > Import to Stage or File > Import > Import to Library to import the artwork into Flash. Alternatively, you can even copy artwork from Illustrator and paste it into a Flash document.

Importing Layers

When an imported Illustrator file contains layers, you can import them in any of the following ways:

- Convert Illustrator layers to Flash layers
- Convert Illustrator layers to Flash keyframes
- Convert all Illustrator graphics to a bitmap
- Convert all Illustrator layers to a single Flash layer

Importing Symbols

Working with symbols in Illustrator is similar to working with them in Flash. In fact, you can use many of the same symbol keyboard shortcuts in both Illustrator and Flash: Press F8 in either application to create a symbol. When you create a symbol in Illustrator, the Symbol Options dialog box lets you name the symbol and set options specific to Flash, including the symbol type (such as movie clip) and registration point location.

If you want to edit a symbol in Illustrator without disturbing anything else, double-click the symbol to edit it in isolation mode. Illustrator dims all other objects on the artboard. When you exit isolation mode, the symbol in the Symbols panel—and all instances of the symbol—is updated accordingly.

Use the Symbols panel or the Control panel in Illustrator to assign names to symbol instances, break links between symbols and instances, swap a symbol instance with another symbol, or create a copy of the symbol.

Copying and Pasting Artwork

When you copy and paste (or drag and drop) artwork between Illustrator and Flash, the Paste dialog box appears. The Paste dialog box provides import settings for the Illustrator file you're copying. You can paste the file as a single bitmap object, or you can paste it using the current preferences for AI files. Just as when you import the file to the Stage or the Library panel, when you paste Illustrator artwork, you can convert Illustrator layers to Flash layers.

Identifying Symbols

A **symbol** is a reusable asset that you can use for special effects, animation, or interactivity. Symbols can reduce the file size and download time for many animations because they can be reused. You can use a symbol countless times in a project, but Flash includes its data only once.

Symbols are stored in the Library panel. When you drag a symbol to the Stage, Flash creates an instance of the symbol, leaving the original in the Library. An **instance** is a copy of a symbol located on the Stage. You can think of a symbol as an original photographic negative, and the instances on the Stage as prints of the negative. With just a single negative, you can create multiple prints.

It's also helpful to think of symbols as containers. Symbols are simply containers for your content. A symbol can contain a JPEG image, an imported Illustrator drawing, or a drawing that you created in Flash. At any time, you can go inside your symbol and edit it, which means changing or replacing its contents.

Each of the three kinds of symbols in Flash is used for a specific purpose. You can tell whether a symbol is a graphic, button, or movie clip by looking at the icon next to it in the Library panel.

Symbol

A reusable asset that you can use for special effects, animation, or interactivity.

Instance

A copy of a symbol located on the Stage.

Movie Clip Symbols

Movie clip symbols are among the most powerful and flexible kinds of symbols. When you create animation, you will typically use movie clip symbols. You can apply filters, color settings, and blending modes to a movie clip instance to enhance its appearance with special effects.

A movie clip symbol also contains its own independent Timeline. You can have an animation inside a movie clip symbol just as easily as you can have an animation on the main Timeline. This makes very complex animations possible; for example, a butterfly flying across the Stage can move from left to right as well as have its wings flapping independently of its movement.

Most important, you can control movie clips with ActionScript to make them respond to the user. For instance, a movie clip can have drag-and-drop behavior.

Button Symbols

Button symbols are used for interactivity. They contain four unique keyframes that describe how they appear when the mouse is interacting with them. However, buttons need ActionScript functionality to make them do something.

You can also apply filters, blending modes, and color settings to buttons.

Graphic Symbols

Graphic symbols are the most basic kind of symbol. Although you can use them for animation, you'll rely more heavily on movie clip symbols.

Graphic symbols are the least flexible symbols, because they don't support ActionScript and you can't apply filters or blending modes to a graphic symbol. However, in some cases when you want an animation inside a graphic symbol to be synchronized to the main Timeline, you'll find graphic symbols useful.

Creating Symbols

There are two main ways to create a symbol. The first is to have nothing on the Stage selected, and then choose Insert > New Symbol. Flash enters symbol-editing mode, where you can begin drawing or importing graphics for your symbol.

The second way is to select existing graphics on the Stage, and then choose Modify > Convert to Symbol (F8). Whatever is selected will automatically be placed inside your new symbol.

Both methods are valid; which one you use depends on your particular workflow preferences. Most designers prefer to use Convert to Symbol (F8) because they can create all their graphics on the Stage and see them together before making the individual components into symbols.

For this lesson, you'll select the different parts of the imported Illustrator graphic, and then convert the various pieces to symbols.

Try It!

1. On the Stage, select just the cartoon character in the hero layer.
2. Choose Modify > Convert to Symbol (F8).
3. Name the symbol **hero** and select Movie Clip for the Type.
4. Leave all other settings as they are. The Registration icon indicates the center point (x=0, y=0) and transformation point of your symbol.

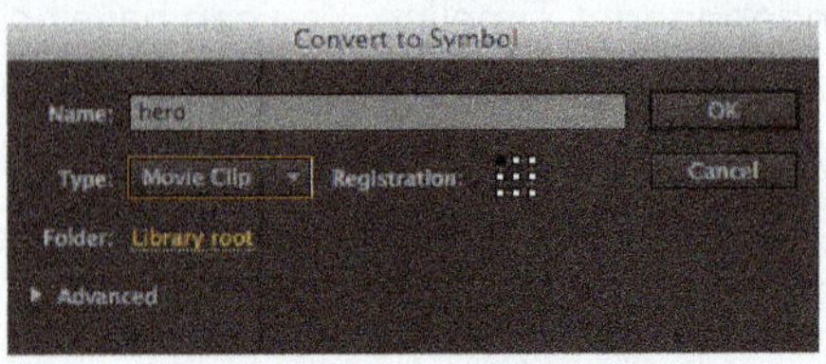

5. Click OK. The hero symbol appears in the Library.
6. Select the other cartoon character in the robot layer and convert it to a movie clip symbol as well. Name it **robot**.

   You now have two movie clip symbols in your Library and an instance of each on the Stage as well.
7. Save the changes to **L16_start_xx.fla**, and leave it open.

Importing Photoshop Files

You'll import a Photoshop file for the background. The Photoshop file contains two layers with a blending effect. A blending effect can create special color mixes between different layers. You'll see that Flash can import a Photoshop file with all the layers intact and retain most of the blending information as well.

Try It!

1. Select the top layer in your Timeline.
2. Choose File > Import > Import to Stage.
3. Navigate to the data files for this lesson and select **background.psd**. You might need to select Photoshop as the file type in order to see it in the data files folder.
4. Click Open.

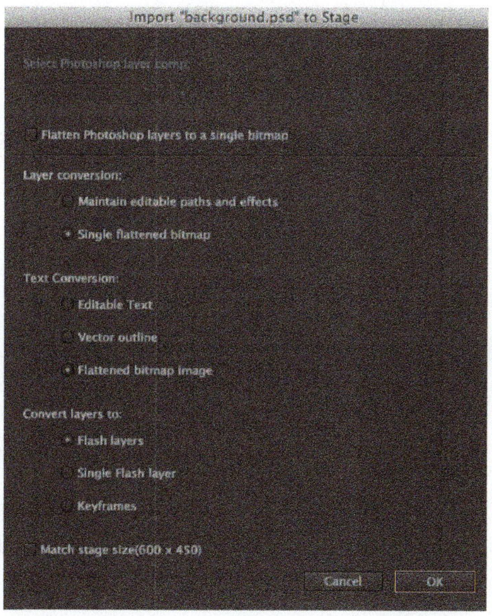

   The Import to Stage dialog box appears.
5. For Layer conversion, choose Maintain editable paths and effects.

   Flash preserves the Lighten blend effect from Photoshop.
6. For Text conversion, choose Editable Text.

   The Photoshop file doesn't contain any text, so the settings here don't matter.

7. For Convert layers to, choose Flash layers.

   Flash preserves the layers from Photoshop. The Single Flash layer option flattens the Photoshop layers into one Flash layer, and the Keyframes option separates the Photoshop layers into individual Flash keyframes.

   You also have the option of changing the Flash Stage size to match the Photoshop canvas. However, the current Stage is already set to the correct dimensions (600 pixels x 450 pixels).

8. Click OK. The two Photoshop layers are imported into Flash and placed on separate layers on the Timeline.

   Flash automatically converts the Photoshop images into movie clip symbols and saves them in your Library. The movie clip symbols are contained in the Library folder named **background.psd** Asset.

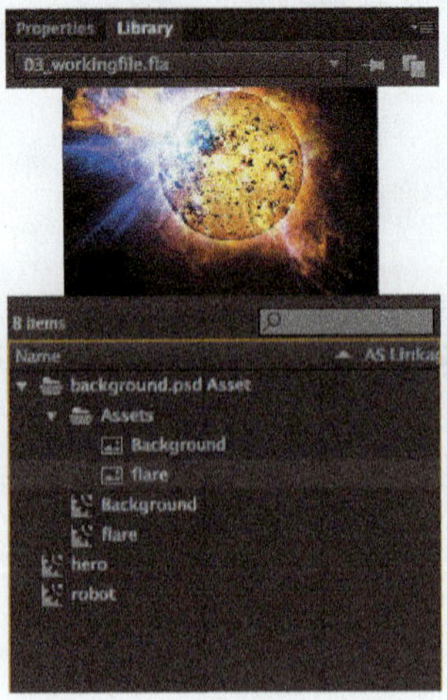

All the blending and transparency information is preserved. If you select the image in the flare layer, you'll see that the Blending option under the Display section in the Properties inspector is set to Lighten.

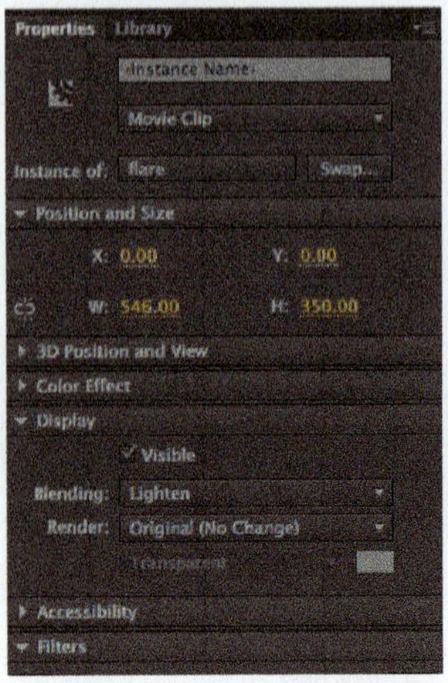

9. Drag the robot and hero layers to the top of the Timeline so they overlap the background layers.
10. Save the changes to **L16_start_xx.fla**, and leave it open.

Editing a Photoshop File from Flash

If you want to edit your Photoshop files, you don't have to go through the entire import process again. You can edit any image on the Stage or in the Library panel in Adobe Photoshop or any other image-editing application. Right-click/Ctrl-click an image on the Stage or an image in the Library and choose Edit with Adobe Photoshop to edit in Photoshop, or select another Edit with option to choose your preferred application. Flash launches the application, and once you have saved your changes, your image is immediately updated in Flash. Make sure that you right-click/ Ctrl-click an image on the Stage or Library, and not the movie clip.

Editing and Managing Symbols

You now have multiple movie clip symbols in your Library and several instances on the Stage. You can better manage the symbols in your Library by organizing them in folders. You can also edit any symbol at any time. If you decide you want to change the color of one of the robot's arms, for example, you can easily go into symbol-editing mode and make that change.

Adding Folders and Organizing the Library

Try It!

1. In the Library panel, right-click/Ctrl-click in an empty space and select New Folder. Alternatively, you can click the New Folder button at the bottom of the Library panel, or click in the panel's upper right menu and click New Folder.

   Flash creates a new folder in your Library.
2. Name the folder **characters**.

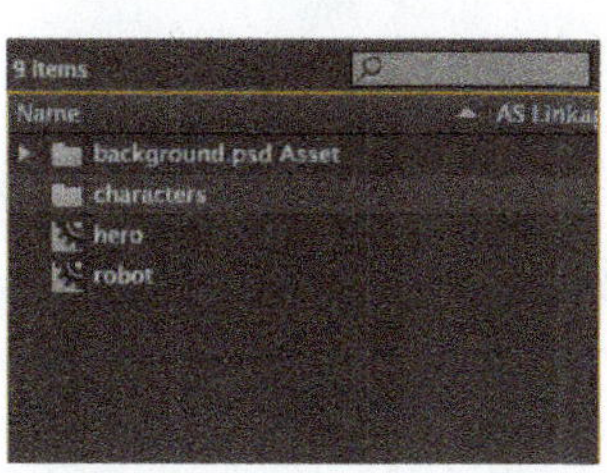

3. Drag the hero and robot movie clip symbols into the characters folder.

   You can collapse or expand folders to hide or view their contents and keep your Library organized.
4. Save the changes to **L16_start_xx.fla**, and leave it open.

Editing a Symbol from the Library

Try It!

1. Open the characters folder and double-click the robot movie clip symbol icon in the Library. Make sure you double-click the icon and not the symbol name.

   Flash takes you to symbol-editing mode. In this mode, you can see the contents of your symbol. Notice that the Edit bar at the top of the Stage tells you that you are no longer in Scene 1 but are inside the symbol named robot.

2. Double-click the drawing to edit it. Choose an individual shape in the drawing and double-click it as many times as necessary to drill down until it is selected..

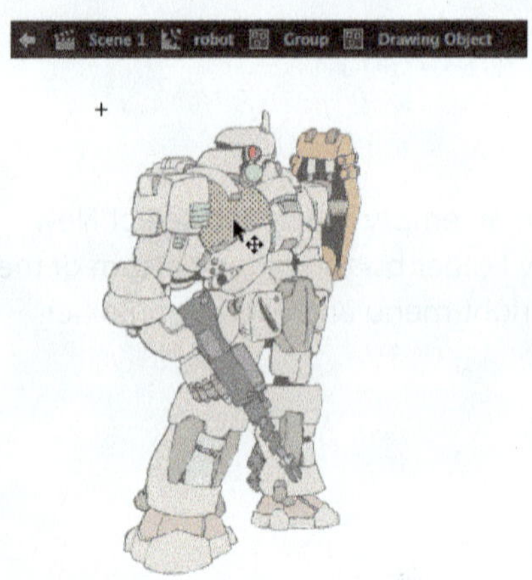

3. Choose the Paint Bucket tool. Select a new fill color and apply it to the shape on the robot drawing.

4. Click on Scene 1 on the Edit bar above the Stage to return to the main Timeline.

   The movie clip symbol in the Library reflects the changes you made. The instance on the Stage also reflects the changes you made to the symbol. All instances of the symbol will change if you edit the symbol.

5. Save the changes to **L16_start_xx.fla**, and leave it open.

Editing a Symbol in Place

You may want to edit a symbol in context with the other objects on the Stage. You can do so by double-clicking an instance on the Stage. You'll enter symbol-editing mode, but you'll also be able to see the symbol's surroundings. This editing mode is called editing in place.

Try It!

1. Using the Selection tool, double-click the robot movie clip instance on the Stage.

   Flash dims all other objects on the Stage and takes you to symbol-editing mode. Notice on the Edit bar that you are no longer in Scene 1 but are inside the robot symbol.

2. Double-click the drawing to edit it. Double-click another individual shape as many times as necessary to drill down until the shape is selected.

3. Choose the Paint Bucket tool. Select a new fill color and apply it to the shape on the robot drawing.

4. Click on Scene 1 on the Edit bar above the Stage to return to the main Timeline. You can also double-click with the Selection tool any part of the Stage outside the graphic to return to the next-higher group level.

   The movie clip symbol in the Library panel reflects the changes you made. The instance on the Stage also reflects the changes you made to the symbol.

5. Save the changes to **L16_start_xx.fla**, and leave it open.

Breaking Apart a Symbol Instance

If you no longer want an object on the Stage to be a symbol instance, you can use the Break Apart command to return it to its original form.

Try It!

1. Select the robot instance on the Stage.

2. Choose Modify > Break Apart.

   Flash breaks apart the robot movie clip instance. What's left on the Stage is a group, which you can break apart further to edit.

3. Choose Modify > Break Apart again.

   Flash breaks apart the group into its individual components, which are smaller drawing objects.

4. Choose Modify > Break Apart one more time.

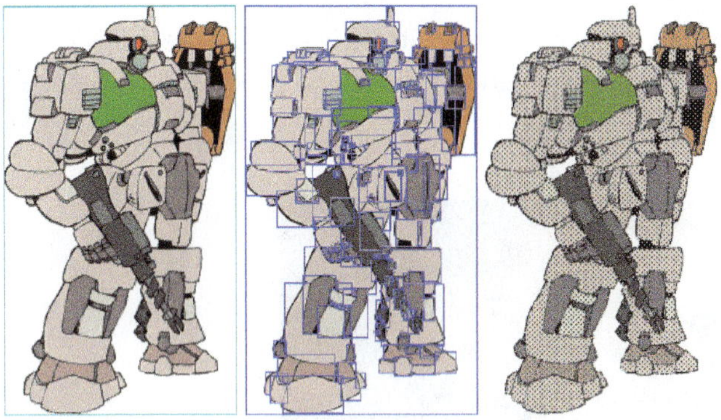

Flash breaks apart the drawing objects into shapes.

5. Choose Edit > Undo three times to return your robot to a symbol instance.

6. Save the changes to **L16_start_xx.fla**, and leave it open.

Changing the Size and Position of Instances

You can have multiple instances of the same symbol on the Stage. Now you'll add a few more robots to create a small robot army. You'll learn how to change the size and position (and even rotation) of each instance individually.

1. Select the robot layer in the Timeline.

2. Drag another robot symbol from the Library onto the Stage.

   A new instance appears.

3. Choose the Free Transform tool.

   Control handles appear around the selected instance.

4. Drag a control handle on the side of the selection to flip the robot so it is facing in the other direction.

5. Hold down the Shift key and drag a handle on the corner of the selection to reduce the size of the robot.

6. Drag a third robot from the Library onto the Stage. With the Free Transform tool, flip the robot, resize it, and make it overlap the second robot. Move the characters into an attractive arrangement.

The robot army is growing! Notice how edits to an instance do not change the Library symbol, and do not change other instances. On the other hand, edits to the Library symbol change all of its instances.

7. Save the changes to **L16_start_xx.fla**, and leave it open.

Using Rulers and Guides

You may want to be more precise in your placement of symbol instances. In a previous lesson, you learned how to use the X and Y coordinates in the Properties inspector to position individual objects. You have also learned to use the Align panel to align several objects to each other.

Another way to position objects on the Stage is to use rulers and guides. Rulers appear on the top and left edge of the Pasteboard to provide measurement along the horizontal and vertical axes. Guides are vertical or horizontal lines that appear on the Stage but do not appear in the final published movie.

Try It!

1. Choose View > Rulers (Option+Shift+Command+R [Mac]/Alt+Shift+R [Windows]).

   Horizontal and vertical rulers measuring in pixels appear along the top and left edges of the Pasteboard. As you move objects on the Stage, tick marks indicate the bounding box positions on the rulers.

2. Click the top horizontal ruler and drag a guide onto the Stage.

   A colored line appears on the Stage that you can use as a guide for alignment.

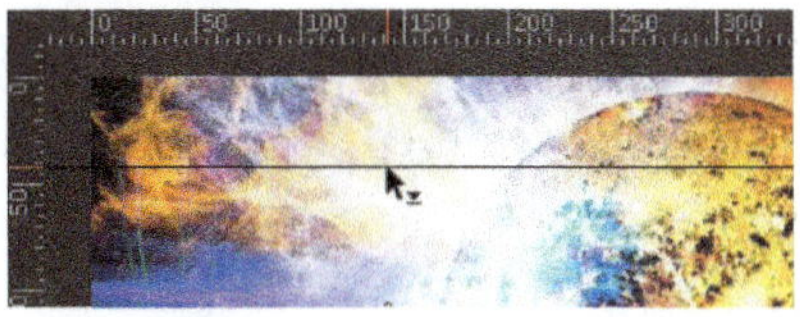

3. Double-click the guide with the Selection tool.

   The Move Guide dialog box appears.

4. Enter **435** as the new pixel value of the guide. Click OK.

   The guide is repositioned 435 pixels from the top edge of the Stage.

5. Choose View > Snapping. If necessary, click > Snap to Guides to select it.

   Objects will now snap to any guides on the Stage.

   Drag the robot instance and the hero instance so their bottom edges align with the guide.

6. Save the changes to **L16_start_xx.fla**, and leave it open.

Changing the Color Effect of Instances

The Color Effect option in the Properties inspector allows you to change several properties of any instance. These properties include brightness, tint, and alpha.

Brightness controls how dark or light the instance appears, **tint** controls the overall coloring, and **alpha** controls the level of opacity. Decreasing the alpha value decreases the opacity and increases the amount of transparency.

Brightness

How dark or light the instance appears.

Tint

The overall coloring of an instance.

Alpha

The level of opacity of an instance.

Changing the Brightness

Try It!

1. Using the Selection tool, click the smallest robot on the Stage.
2. In the Properties inspector, click the Color Effect panel and from the Style box, select Brightness.

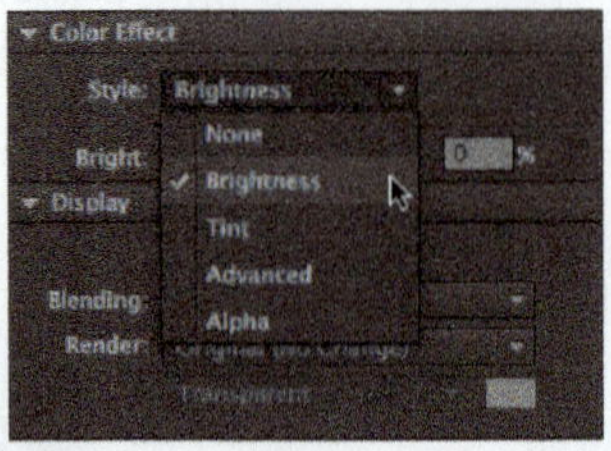

3. Drag the Bright slider to –40%.

   The robot instance on the Stage becomes darker and appears to recede into the distance.

4. Save the changes to **L16_start_xx.fla**, and leave it open.

Changing the Transparency

Try It!

1. Select the glowing orb in the flare layer.
2. In the Properties inspector, choose Alpha from the Color Effect Style menu.

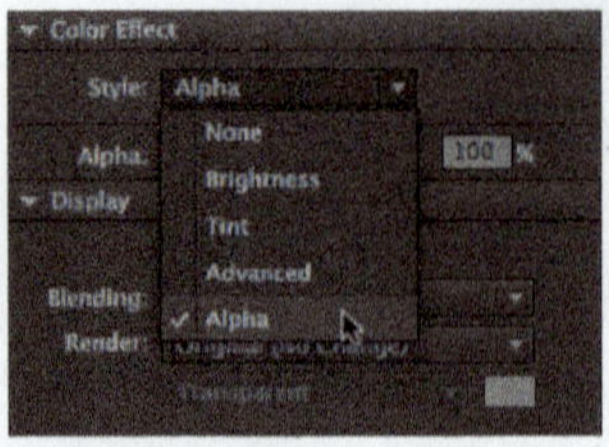

3. Drag the Alpha slider to a value of 50%.

   The orb in the flare layer on the Stage becomes more transparent.

4. Save the changes to **L16_start_xx.fla**, and leave it open.

Using Display Options

The Display section in the Properties inspector for movie clips offers options for controlling the instance's visibility, blending, and rendering.

Using the Visible Option for Movie Clips

The Visible property makes objects either visible or invisible to the audience. You can directly control the Visible property of movie clip instances on the Stage by selecting or deselecting the option in the Properties inspector.

Try It!

1. Select the Selection tool.
2. Select one of the robot movie clip instances on the Stage.
3. In the Properties inspector, under the Display section, notice that the Visible option is selected by default, meaning that the instance is visible.

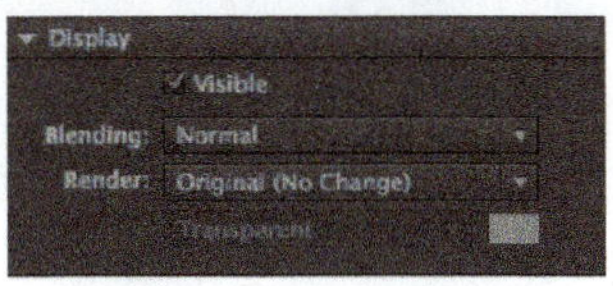

4. Deselect the Visible check box.

   The selected instance becomes invisible.

   The instance is present on the Stage, and you can still move it to a new position, but the audience won't be able to see it. Use the Visible option to turn instances on or off during the course of your movie, rather than deleting them entirely. You can also use the Visible option to position invisible instances on the Stage in order to make them visible later with ActionScript, the coding language of Flash.

5. Select the Visible option to make the robot visible on the Stage again.
6. Save the changes to **L16_start_xx.fla**, and leave it open.

Using Blending Effects

Blending refers to how the colors of an instance interact with the colors below it. You saw how the instance in the flare layer had the Lighten option applied to it (carried over from Photoshop), which integrated it more with the instance in the Background layer.

There are many kinds of Blending options. Some have surprising results, depending on the colors in the instance and the colors in the layers below it. Experiment with all the options to understand how they work. The following figure shows some of the Blending options and their effects on the robot instance over a blue-black gradient.

Exporting as Bitmap

The robots and the hero character in this lesson are movie clip symbols containing complex vector graphics imported from Illustrator. Vector art can be processor-intensive, and can take its toll on performance and playback. A rendering option called Export as Bitmap can help. The Export as Bitmap option renders the vector art as a bitmap, reducing the performance load (but increasing memory use). The movie clip remains as editable vector graphics in the Flash file, however, so you can still modify the artwork.

Try It!

1. Select the Selection tool.
2. Select the hero movie clip instance on the Stage.
3. In the Properties inspector in the Display section, click the Render drop-down arrow and choose Export as Bitmap.

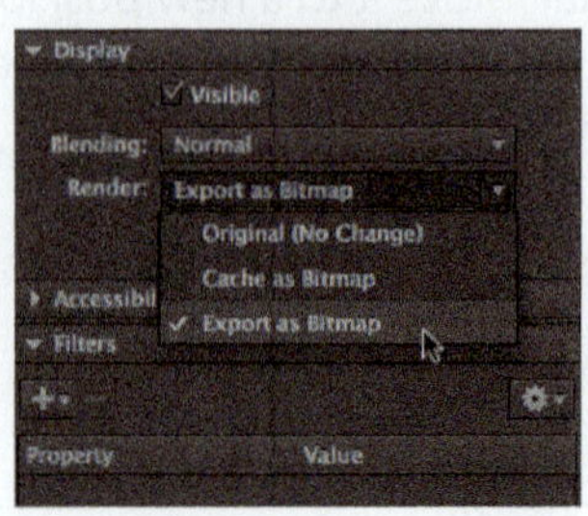

The hero movie clip instance appears as it will be rendered when published. You may see a slight "softening" of the illustration because of the rasterization of the art.

4. In the pull-down menu under the Render options, leave the selection as Transparent.

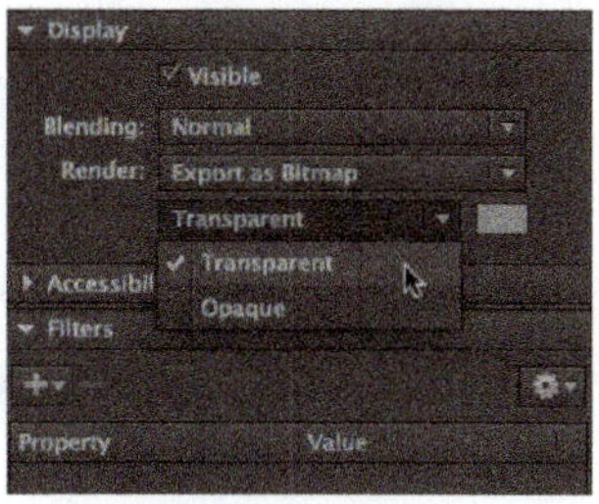

The Transparent option renders the background in your movie clip symbol as transparent. Alternately, you can choose Opaque and pick a color for the background of your movie clip symbol.

5. Save the changes to **L16_start_xx.fla**, and leave it open.

Applying Filters for Special Effects

Filters are special effects that you can apply to movie clip instances. Several filters are available in the Filters section of the Properties inspector. Each filter has different options that can refine the effect.

Filters

Special effects that you can apply to movie clip instances.

Try It!

1. Select the glowing orb in the flare layer.
2. In the Properties inspector, expand the Filters section.
3. Click the Add filter button at the top of the Filters section and select Blur.

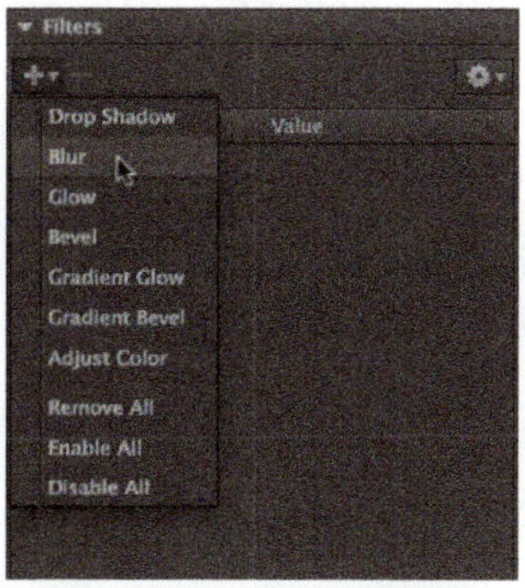

The Blur filter appears in the Filters window with options for Blur X and Blur Y.

4. If they aren't linked already, click the link icons next to the Blur X and Blur Y options to link the blur effect in both directions.

5. Set the Blur X and Blur Y value to **10** pixels.

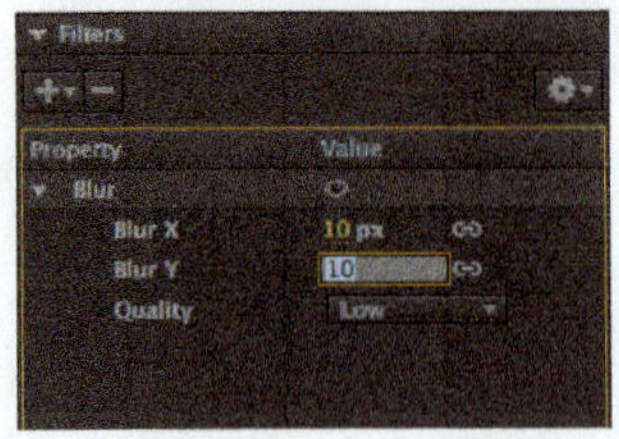

The instance on the Stage becomes blurry, helping to give an atmospheric perspective to this scene.

6. Save the changes to **L16_start_xx.fla**, and leave it open.

Positioning in 3D Space

You also have the ability to position and animate objects in real three-dimensional space. However, objects need to be movie clip symbols to be moved in 3D. Two tools allow you to position objects in 3D: the 3D Rotation tool and the 3D Translation tool. The Transform panel also provides information for position and rotation.

Understanding the 3D coordinate space is essential for successful 3D placement of objects. Flash divides space using three axes: the x, y, and z axes. The x axis runs horizontally across the Stage with x=0 at the left edge. The y axis runs vertically with y=0 at the top edge. The z axis runs into and out of the plane of the Stage (toward and away from the viewer) with z=0 at the plane of the Stage.

Changing the 3D Rotation of an Object

You'll add some text to your image, but to add a little more interest, you'll tilt it to put it in perspective. Think about the beginning text introduction to the *Star Wars* movies, and see if you can achieve a similar effect.

1. Insert a new layer at the top of the layers stack and rename it **text**.

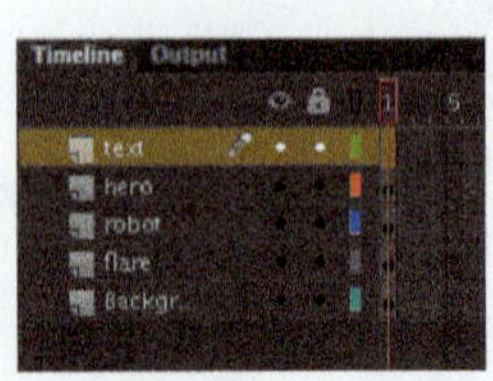

2. Choose the Text tool from the Tools panel.

3. In the Properties inspector, choose Static Text, and select a large-size font with an interesting color that will add some pizzazz. Your font might look different from what's shown in this lesson, depending on the fonts available on your computer.

4. Click on the Stage in your text layer and begin typing your title **MechWars**.

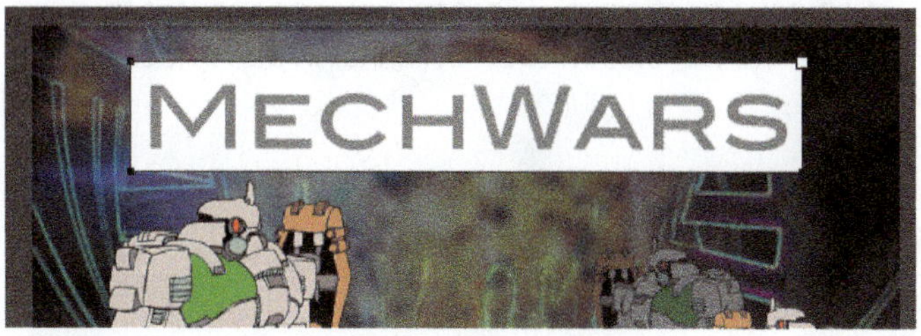

5. To exit the Text tool, select the Selection tool.
6. With the text still selected, choose Modify > Convert to Symbol (F8).
7. In the Convert to Symbol dialog box, enter **title** for the Name and choose Movie Clip for Type. Click OK.

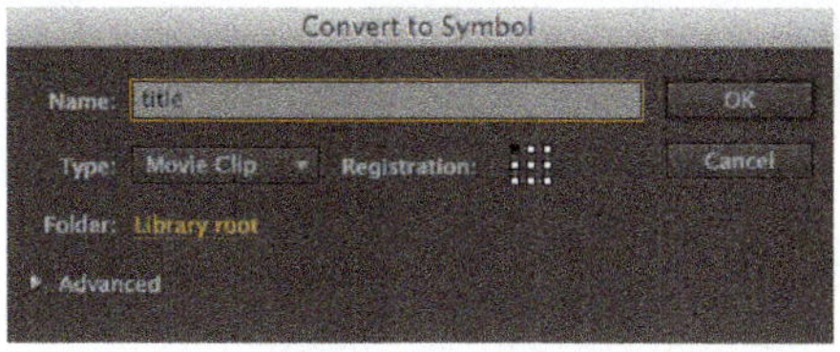

   Your text is put into a movie clip symbol, and an instance remains on the Stage.

8. Choose the 3D Rotation tool.

   A circular, multicolored target appears on the instance. This is a guide for the 3D rotation. It's useful to think of the guides as lines on a globe. The red longitudinal line rotates your instance around the x axis. The green line along the equator rotates your instance around the y axis. The circular blue guide rotates your instance around the z axis.

9. Click one of the guides—red for x, green for y, or blue for z—and drag your mouse in either direction to rotate your instance in 3D space.

   You can also click and drag the outer orange circular guide to freely rotate the instance in all three directions.

10. Save the changes to **L16_start_xx.fla**, and leave it open.

Changing the 3D Position of an Object

In addition to changing an object's rotation in 3D space, you can move it to a specific point in 3D space. Use the 3D Translation tool, which is hidden under the 3D Rotation tool.

Try It!

1. Choose the 3D Translation tool.
2. Click on your text.

   A guide for the 3D translation appears on the instance. The red guide represents the x axis, the green is the y axis, and the blue is the z axis.

3. Click one of the guide axes and drag your mouse in either direction to move your instance in 3D space. Notice that your text stays in perspective as you move it around the Stage.
4. Save the changes to **L16_start_xx.fla**, and leave it open.

Resetting the Transformation

If you've made a mistake in your 3D transformations and you want to reset the rotation of your instance, you can use the Transform panel.

Try It!

1. Choose the Selection tool and select the instance that you want to reset.
2. Choose Window > Transform to open the Transform panel.

   The Transform panel shows all the values for the x, y, and z angles and positions.

3. Click the Remove Transform button in the lower-right corner of the Transform panel.

   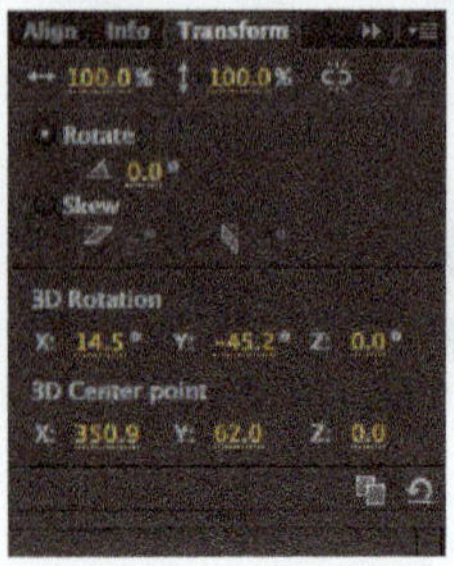

   The selected instance returns to its original rotation.

4. Save the changes to **L16_start_xx.fla**, and leave it open.

Understanding the Vanishing Point and the Perspective Angle

Objects in 3D space represented on a 2D surface (such as the computer screen) are rendered with perspective to make them appear as they do in real life. Correct perspective depends on many factors, including the **vanishing point** and the **perspective angle**, both of which can be changed in Flash.

The vanishing point determines where on the horizon parallel lines of a perspective drawing converge. Think of railroad tracks and how the parallel tracks converge to a single point as they recede into the distance. The vanishing point is usually at eye level in the center of your field of view, so the default settings are exactly in the middle of the Stage. You can, however, change the vanishing point setting so it appears above or below eye level, or to the right or left.

The perspective angle determines how quickly parallel lines converge to the vanishing point. The greater the angle, the quicker the convergence, and therefore, the more severe and distorted the illustration appears.

Perspective

The art of representing three-dimensional objects on a two-dimensional surface.

Vanishing point

The point in a perspective image where parallel lines that move off into the distance seem to converge on the horizon.

Perspective angle

The angle at which parallel lines used to indicate perspective converge.

Try It!

1. Select the title object on the Stage.
2. In the Properties inspector, expand the 3D Position and View section.

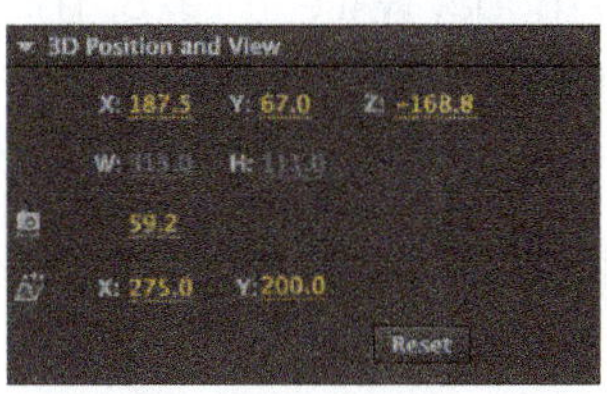

3. Click and drag on the X and Y values of the Vanishing Point to change the vanishing point, which is indicated on the Stage by intersecting gray lines.
4. To reset the Vanishing Point to the default values (to the center of the Stage), click the Reset button.
5. Click and drag on the Perspective Angle value to change the amount of distortion. The greater the angle, the more the distortion.

Now, you will test the movie in your browser to see how it appears if it were placed on a Web page.

6. Click Control > Test Movie > In Browser. Your browser should open automatically and display the scene.

7. Close your browser, save the changes to **L16_start_xx.fla**, and close Flash.

A Brief History of Animation

It is possible that the earliest animations were drawn on the walls of caves as sequences of pictures showing action, such as a hunt. Paintings in Egyptian tombs that are 4,000 years old show the sequence of athletic competitions. These were all attempts to show motion in art.

People started developing technology to display animation around the middle of the 19th century. Devices such as the Phenakistoscope (1831) and Zoetrope (1834) used different methods to create the illusion of movement. John Barnes Linnett patented the first flip book, called a kineograph, in 1868. The first known animated projection on a screen was created in France in 1877 by a science teacher named Charles-Émile Reynaud. He called it the Praxinoscope.

In 1908, the first hand-drawn animated film was created by Emile Cohl. Shortly there-after animated short films, typically called "cartoons" became its own industry. These short animations were shown in movie theaters before and between feature films.

In 1923, Walt Disney opened his studio. He released Steamboat Willie in 1928. The animated film was the first to feature Mickey Mouse, and to incorporate sound. Warner Brothers Cartoons was founded in 1933. The first fully computer-animated film was Pixar Animation Studio's Toy Story.

Comprehension Check

1. What is a symbol, and how does it differ from an instance?

2. Name two ways you can create a symbol.

3. When you import an Illustrator file, what happens if you choose to convert layers to Flash layers? To keyframes?

4. How can you change the transparency of an instance in Flash?

5. What are the two ways to edit symbols?

Review Project

Conduct research to learn about the history and evolution of animation. Look for information on how animation has influenced society. Evaluate the information you find for accuracy and validity. Create a poster illustrating your findings. Present it to a partner or to the class.

Lesson 17 Overview

In this lesson, you will learn about:

- Examining Animation in Flash
- Animating Position
- Using the Controller to Preview the Animation
- Changing the Pacing and Timing
- Animating Transparency
- Animating Filters
- Animating Transformations
- Changing the Path of a Motion
- Swapping Tween Targets
- Creating Nested Animations
- Setting Easing
- Creating Frame-by-Frame Animation
- Animating 3D Motion
- Testing a Movie

Animation is the illusion of motion. You accomplish this by sequencing images that change over time. You can use Flash to change almost any aspect of an object over time—position, color, transparency, size, rotation, and more.

Examining Animation in Flash

Animation

The movement, or change, of objects through time.

Easing

The way an object accelerates or decelerates.

Motion tweens

Create animation for changes in position on the Stage and for changes in size, color, or other attributes.

Animation is the movement, or change, of objects through time. Animation can be as simple as moving a box across the Stage from one frame to the next. It can also be much more complex. As you'll see in this lesson, you can animate many different aspects of a single object. You can change an object's position on the Stage, change its color or transparency, change its size or rotation, or animate the special filters that you saw in the previous lesson. You also have control over an object's path of motion, and even its **easing**, which is the way an object accelerates or decelerates.

Motion tweening is the basic technique of creating animation with symbol instances. **Motion tweens** create animation for changes in position on the Stage and for changes in size, color, or other attributes. Motion tweens require you to use a symbol instance. If the object you've selected is not a symbol instance, Flash will automatically ask to convert the selection to a symbol.

Flash also automatically separates motion tweens on their own layers, which are called Tween layers. There can be only one motion tween per layer without any other element in the layer. Tween layers allow you to change various attributes of your instance at different key points over time. For example, a spaceship could be on the left side of the Stage at the beginning keyframe and at the far-right side of the Stage at an ending keyframe, and the resulting tween would make the spaceship fly across the Stage.

Tweening

The smooth transition between keyframes.

The term "tween" comes from the world of classic animation. Senior animators would be responsible for drawing the beginning and ending poses for their characters. The beginning and ending poses were the keyframes of the animation. Junior animators would then come in and draw the "in-between" frames, or do the "in-betweening." Hence, "**tweening**" refers to the smooth transitions between keyframes.

Preparing the Project File for Animation

The Flash file that you work with in this lesson contains a few animated elements already or partially completed. Each of the six layers in the file contains an animation. The figure below identifies the layers by name and the folders in which they are organized.

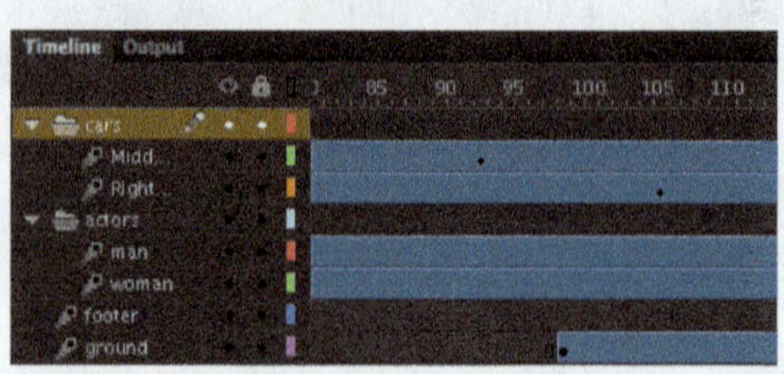

You'll be adding more layers to create an animated cityscape, refining the animation of one of the actors, as well as adding a third car and a 3D title. All the necessary graphic elements have been imported into the Library panel. The Stage is set at a generous 1280 pixels by 787 pixels, and the Stage color is black. You might need to choose a different view option to see the entire Stage.

Try It!

1. Open Flash, and then open the **L17_start.fla** file in the data files for this lesson. This file is an ActionScript 3.0 document that is partially completed and already contains many of the graphic elements imported into the Library for you to use.

2. From the view options above the Stage, choose Fit in Window, or View > Magnification > Fit in Window, so that you can see the entire Stage on your computer screen.

3. Choose File > Save As. Name the file **L17_start_xx**, save it in the location where your teacher instructs you to store the files for this lesson, and leave it open.

Animating Position

You'll start this project by animating the cityscape. It will begin slightly lower than the top edge of the Stage, and then rise slowly until its top is aligned with the top of the Stage.

Try It!

1. Lock all the existing layers so you don't accidentally modify them. Create a new layer above the footer layer and rename it **city**.

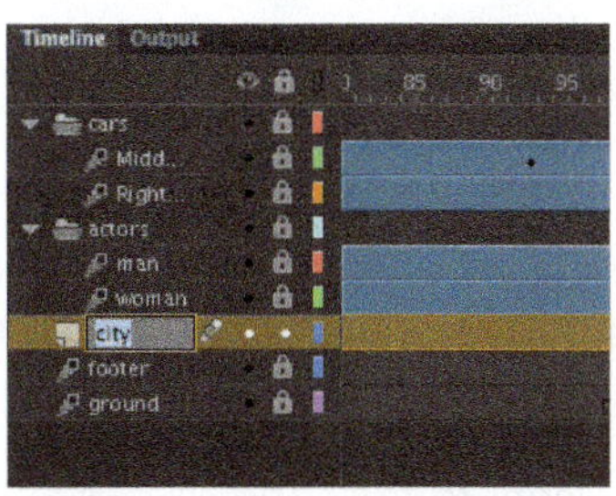

2. Drag the bitmap image called cityBG.jpg from the bitmaps folder in the Library panel to the Stage.

3. In the Properties inspector, set the value of X to 0 and the value of Y to 90.

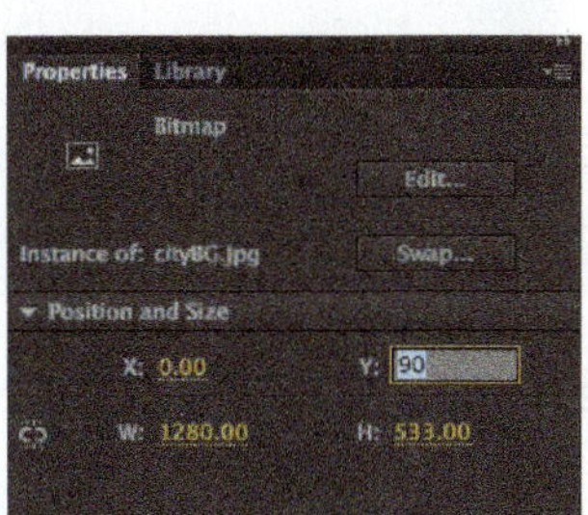

This positions the cityscape image just slightly below the top edge of the Stage.

4. Right-click/Ctrl-click on the cityscape image and choose Create Motion Tween. From the menu bar, you can also select Insert > Motion Tween.

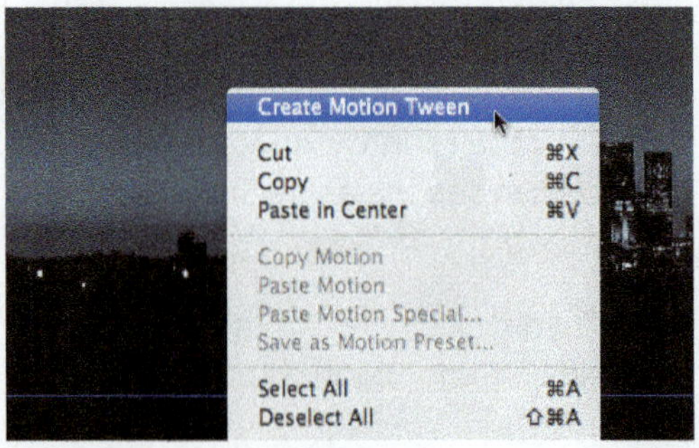

A dialog box appears warning you that your selected object is not a symbol. Motion tweens require symbols. Flash asks if you want to convert the selection to a symbol so it can proceed with the motion tween. Click OK.

Flash automatically converts your selection to a symbol, and stores it in your Library panel. Flash also converts the current layer to a Tween layer so you can begin to animate the instance. Tween layers are distinguished by a special icon in front of the layer name, and the frames are tinted blue. Tween layers are reserved for motion tweens, and hence, no drawing is allowed on a Tween layer.

5. Move the red playhead to the end of the tween span at frame 190.

6. Select the instance of the cityscape on the Stage, and while holding down the Shift key, move the instance up the Stage.

7. Holding down the Shift key constrains the movement to right angles.

8. For more precision, set the value of Y to 0 in the Properties inspector.

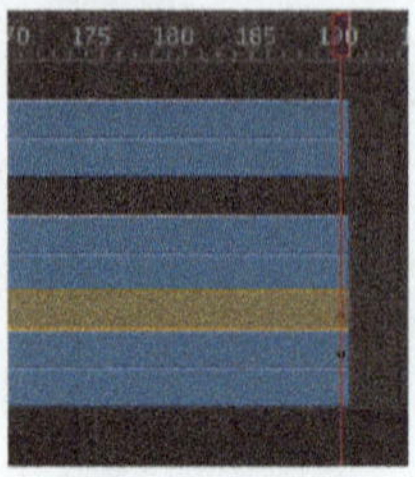

A small black diamond appears in frame 190 at the end of the tween span. This indicates a keyframe at the end of the tween.

Flash smoothly interpolates the change in position from frame 1 to frame 190 and represents that motion with a motion path.

9. Drag the red playhead back and forth at the top of the Timeline to see the smooth motion. You can also choose Control > Play (Enter) to make Flash play the animation.

   Animating changes in position is simple, because Flash automatically creates keyframes at the points where you move your instance to new positions. If you want to have an object move to many different points, simply move the red playhead to the desired frame, and then move the object to its new position. Flash takes care of the rest.

10. Save the changes to **L17_start_xx.fla**, and leave it open.

Using the Controller to Preview the Animation

The Controller panel allows you to play, rewind, or go step-by-step backward or forward through your Timeline to review your animation in a controlled manner.

Use the playback controls that are integrated at the bottom of the Timeline, or choose the playback commands from the Control menu.

Try It!

1. Click any of the playback buttons on the Controller below the Timeline to go to the first frame, go to the last frame, play, stop, or move forward or backward one frame.

2. Choose the loop option at the bottom of the Timeline and click the play button.

   The playhead loops, allowing you to see the animation over and over for careful analysis.

3. Move the front or rear brackets on the Timeline to define the range of frames that you want to see looped.

   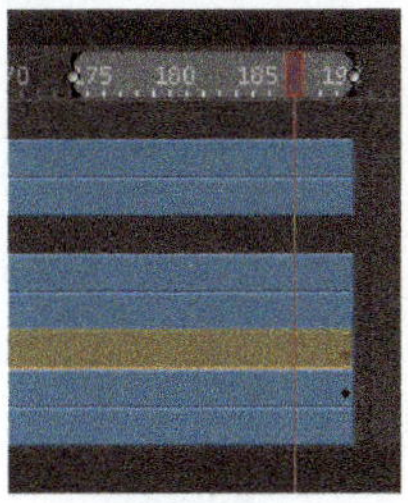

   The playhead loops within the bracketed frames. Click the loop option again to turn it off.

4. Save the changes to **L17_start_xx.fla**, and leave it open.

Changing the Pacing and Timing

You can change the duration of the entire tween span or change the timing of the animation by clicking and dragging keyframes on the Timeline.

Changing the Animation Duration

If you want the animation to proceed at a slower pace (and thus take up a longer period of time), you need to lengthen the entire tween span between the beginning and end keyframes. If you want to shorten the animation, you need to decrease the tween span. Lengthen or shorten a motion tween by dragging the ends on the Timeline.

Try It!

1. Move your mouse pointer close to the end of the tween span in the city layer.

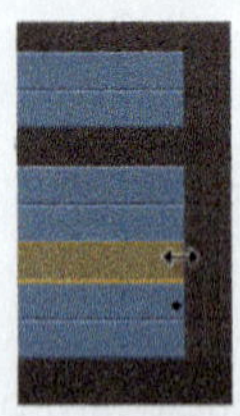

   Your cursor changes to a double-headed arrow, indicating that you can lengthen or shorten the tween span.

2. Click and drag the end of the tween span back toward frame 60.

   Your motion tween shortens to 60 frames, reducing the time it takes the city-scape to move.

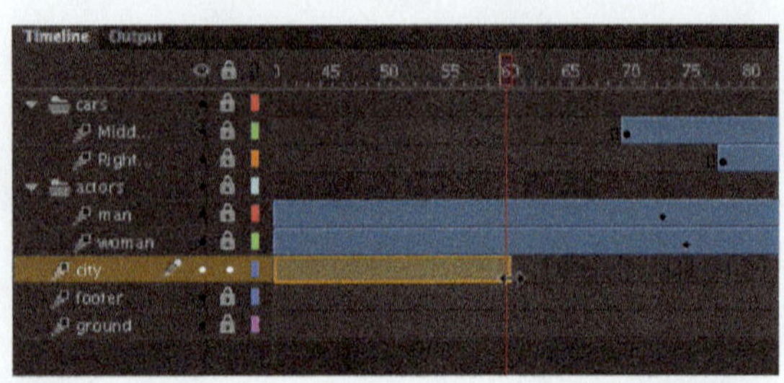

3. Move your mouse pointer close to the beginning of the tween span (at frame 1).

4. Click and drag the beginning of the frame span forward to frame 10.

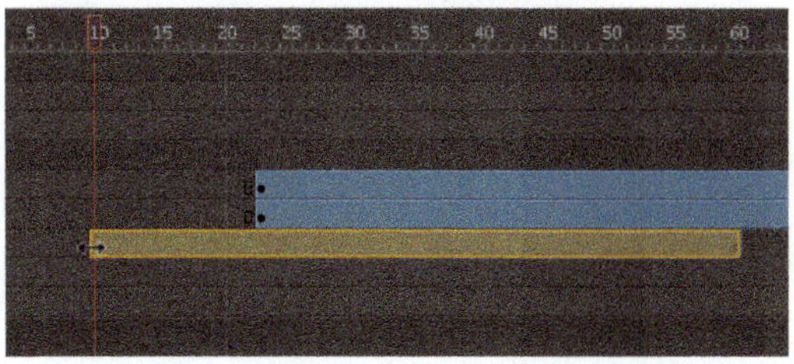

Your motion tween begins at an earlier time, so it now plays only from frame 10 to frame 60.

5. Save the changes to **L17_start_xx.fla**, and leave it open.

Adding Frames

You'll want the last keyframe of your motion tween to hold for the remainder of the animation. Add frames by Shift-dragging the end of a tween span.

Try It!

1. Move your mouse pointer close to the end of the tween span.
2. Hold down the Shift key, and click and drag the end of the tween span forward to frame 190.

   The last keyframe in the motion tween remains at frame 60, but Flash adds frames to frame 190.

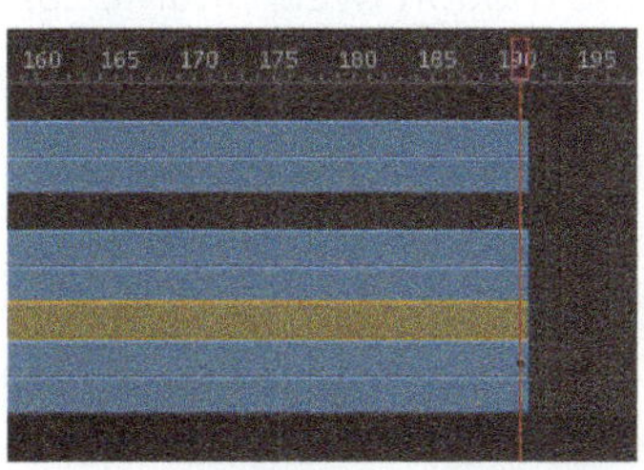

3. Save the changes to **L17_start_xx.fla**, and leave it open.

Moving Keyframes

If you want to change the pacing of an animation, you can select individual keyframes, then click and drag the keyframes to new positions.

Try It!

1. Click the keyframe at frame 60.

   The keyframe at frame 60 is selected. A tiny box appears next to your mouse cursor, indicating that you can move the keyframe.

2. Click and drag the keyframe to frame 40.

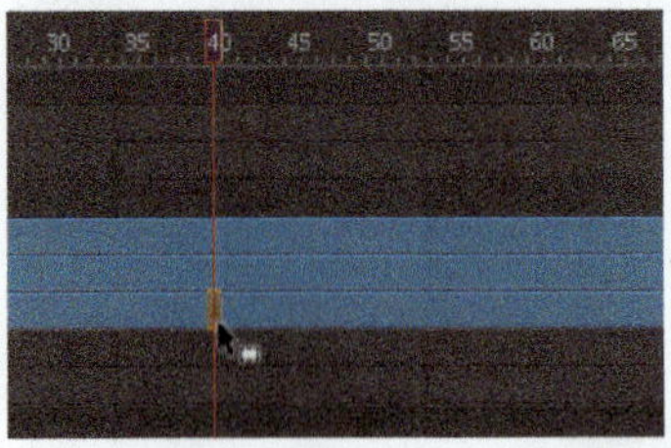

The last keyframe in the motion tween moves to frame 40, so the motion of the cityscape proceeds quicker.

3. Save the changes to **L17_start_xx.fla**, and leave it open.

Animating Transparency

In the previous lesson, you learned how to change the color effect of any symbol instance to change the transparency, tint, or brightness. You can change the color effect of an instance in one keyframe and change the value of the color effect in another keyframe, and Flash will automatically display a smooth change, just as it does with changes in position.

You'll change the cityscape in the beginning keyframe to be totally transparent but keep the cityscape in the ending keyframe opaque. Flash will create a smooth fade-in effect.

Try It!

1. Move the red playhead to the first keyframe of the motion tween (frame 10).

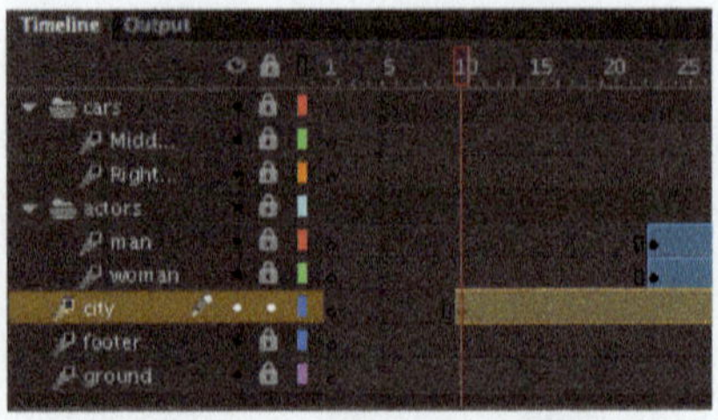

2. Select the cityscape instance on the Stage.
3. In the Properties inspector, choose the Alpha option under Color Effect.

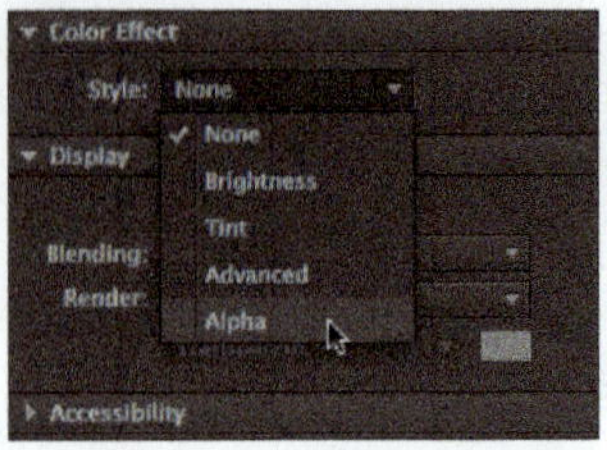

4. Set the Alpha value to 0%.

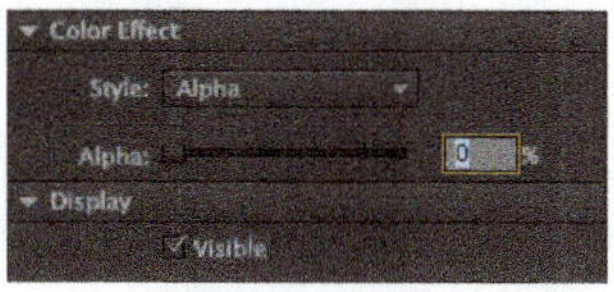

The cityscape instance on the Stage becomes totally transparent.

5. Move the red playhead to the last keyframe of the motion tween (frame 40).

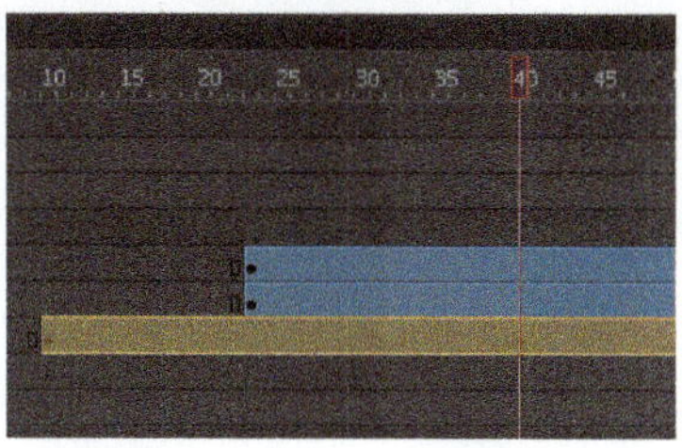

6. Select the cityscape instance on the Stage.
7. In the Properties inspector, under Color Effect, set the Alpha value to **100%**.

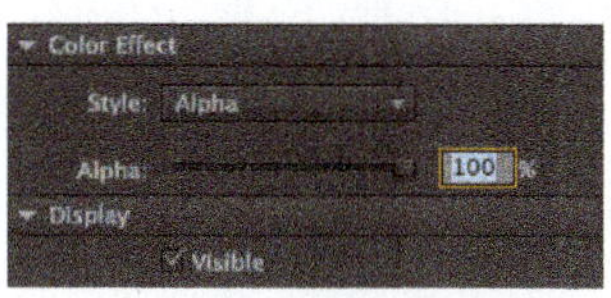

The cityscape instance on the Stage becomes totally opaque.

8. Preview the effect by choosing Control > Play (Enter).

   Flash interpolates the changes in both position and transparency between the two keyframes.

9. Save the changes to **L17_start_xx.fla**, and leave it open.

Animating Filters

Filters, which give instances special effects such as blurs and drop shadows, can also be animated. You'll refine the motion tween of the actors next by applying a blur filter to one of them to make it appear as if the camera changes focus. Animating filters is no different from animating changes in position or changes in color effect. You simply set the values for a filter at one keyframe and set different values for the filter at another keyframe, and Flash creates a smooth transition.

Try It!

1. Make the actors layer folder on the Timeline visible.
2. Lock all the layers on the Timeline except the woman layer.
3. Move the red playhead to the beginning keyframe of the motion tween in the woman layer—at frame 23.
4. Select the instance of the woman on the Stage. You won't be able to see her because she has an alpha value of 0% (totally transparent). Click on the upper-right side of the Stage to select the transparent instance.

5. In the Properties inspector, expand the Filters section.
6. Click the Add filter button at the top of the Filters section and select Blur.

Flash applies the Blur filter to the instance.

7. In the Filters section of the Properties inspector, make sure that the link icons are intact to constrain the blur values to both the x and y directions equally. Set the X and Y Blur values to **20** pixels.

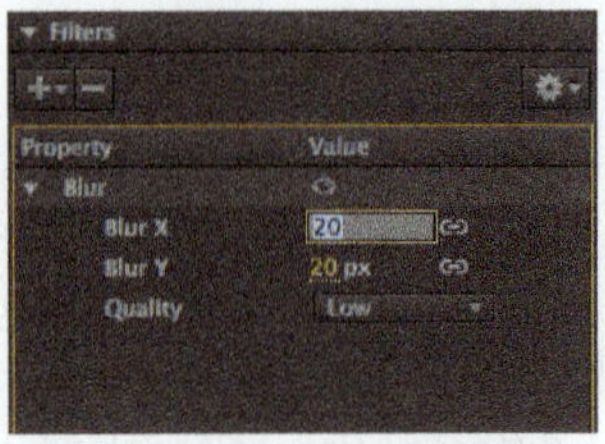

8. Move the red playhead across the entire Timeline to preview the animation.

   The 20-pixel Blur filter is applied to the woman instance throughout the motion tween.

9. Right-click/Ctrl-click on the woman layer at frame 140, and choose Insert Keyframe > Filter.

Flash establishes a keyframe for filters at frame 140.

10. Move the red playhead to frame 160, right-click/Ctrl-click on the woman layer, and choose Insert Keyframe > Filter.

    Flash establishes another keyframe for filters at frame 160.

11. Select the instance of the woman on the Stage at frame 160.

12. In the Properties inspector, change the value of the Blur filter to X=0 and Y=0.

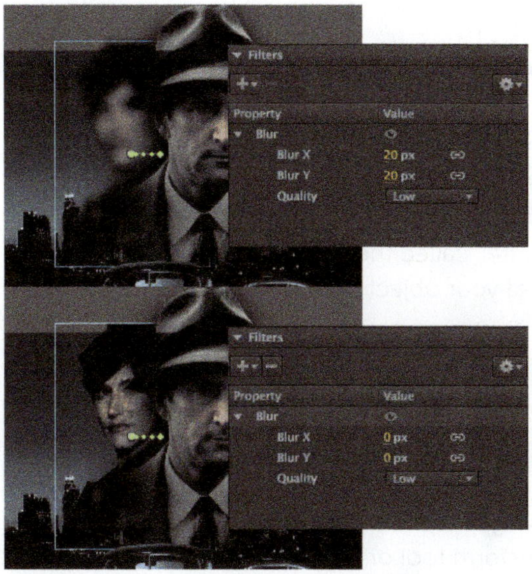

The Blur filter changes from the keyframe at frame 140 to the keyframe at 160. Flash creates a smooth transition from a blurry instance to an in-focus instance.

13. Save the changes to **L17_start_xx.fla**, and leave it open.

Understanding Property Keyframes

Changes in properties are independent of one another and do not need to be tied to the same keyframes. That is, you can have a keyframe for position, a different keyframe for the color effect, and yet another keyframe for a filter. Managing many different kinds of keyframes can become overwhelming, especially if you want different properties to change at different times during the motion tween. Fortunately, Flash provides a few helpful tools for keyframe management.

When viewing the tween span, you can choose to view the keyframes of only certain properties. For example, you can choose to view only the Position keyframes to see when your object moves. Or, you can choose to view only the Filter keyframes to see when a filter changes. Right-click/Ctrl-click on a motion tween in the Timeline, choose View Keyframes, and then select the desired property among the list. You can also choose All or None to see all the properties or none of the properties.

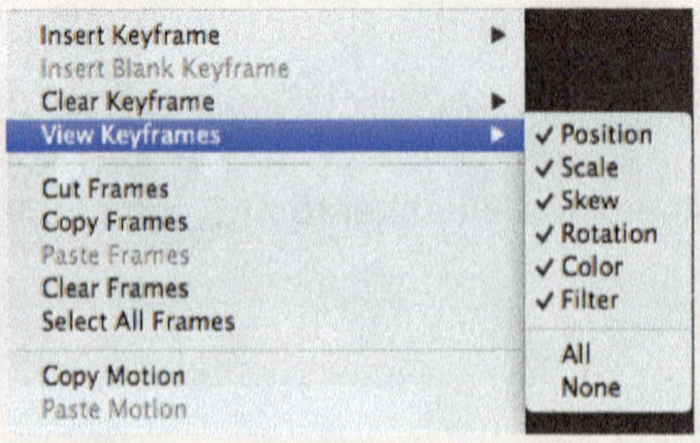

When inserting a keyframe, you can also insert a keyframe specific to the property you want to change. Right-click/Ctrl-click on a motion tween in the Timeline, choose Insert Keyframes, and then select the desired property.

You can also view an advanced panel, called the Motion Editor, to see and edit how the different properties of your object change over the course of the motion tween.

Animating Transformations

Now you'll learn how to animate changes in scale or rotation. These kinds of changes are made with the Free Transform tool or with the Transform panel. You'll add a third car to the project. The car will start small, and then become larger as it appears to move forward toward the viewer.

Try It!

1. Lock all the layers on the Timeline.

2. Insert a new layer inside the cars folder and rename it **Left_car**.

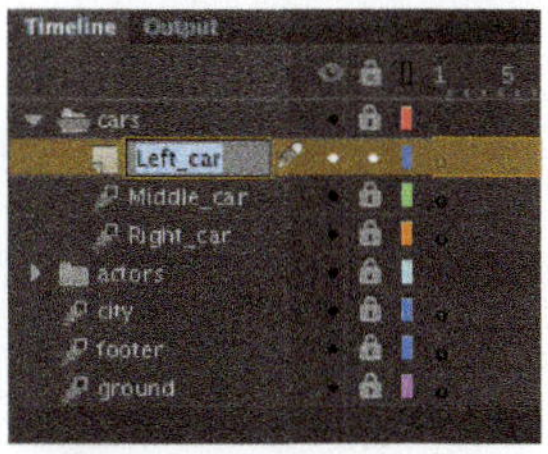

3. Select frame 75 and insert a new keyframe (F6).

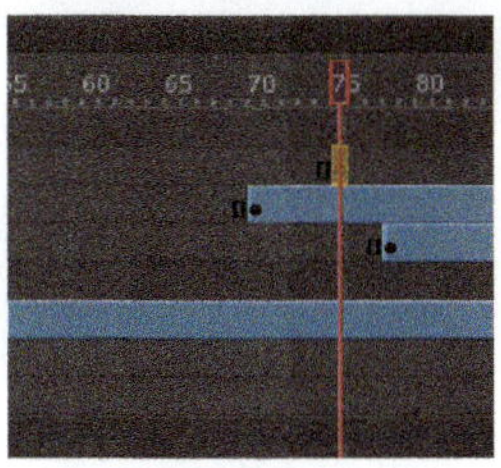

4. Drag the movie clip symbol called carLeft from the Library panel to the Stage at frame 75.
5. Select the Free Transform tool.

   The transformation handles appear around the instance on the Stage.
6. While holding down the Shift key, click and drag a corner handle inward to make the car smaller.
7. In the Properties inspector, make sure that the width of the car is about 400 pixels.
8. Alternatively, you can use the Transform panel (Window > Transform) and change the scale of the car to about 29.4%.
9. Move the car to its starting position at about X=710 and Y=488.
10. In the Properties inspector, select Alpha for the Color Effect.
11. Set the value of the Alpha to 0%.

    The car becomes totally transparent.

12. Right-click/Ctrl-click the car on the Stage and select Create Motion Tween.

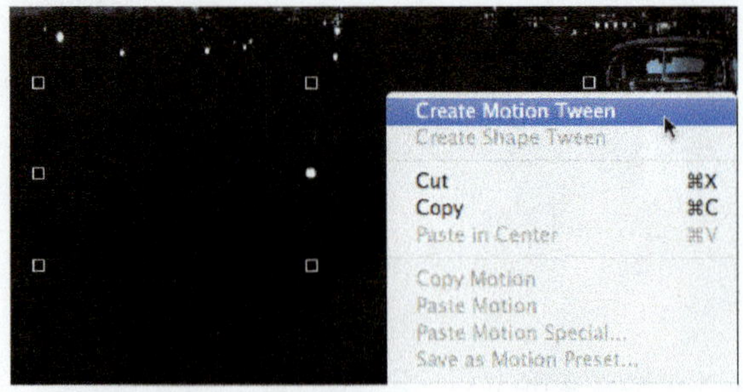

The current layer becomes a Tween layer.

13. Move the red playhead on the Timeline to frame 100.

14. Select the transparent instance of the car on the Stage, and in the Properties inspector, change the Alpha value to 100%.

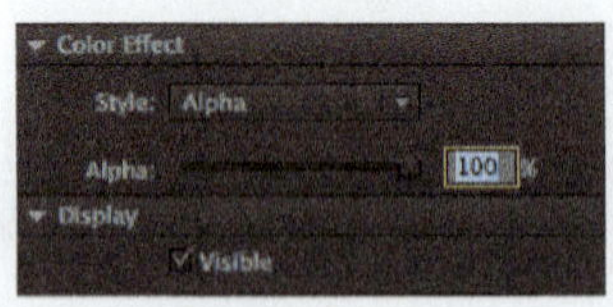

A new keyframe is automatically inserted at frame 100 to indicate the change in transparency.

15. Select the Free Transform tool.

16. While holding down the Shift key, click and drag a corner handle outward to make the car larger. For more precision, use the Properties inspector and set the dimensions of the car to width=1380 pixels and height=445.05 pixels.

17. Position the car at X=607 and Y=545.

18. Move the Left_car layer in between the Middle_car and Right_car layers so that the car in the center overlaps the cars on the side.

    Flash tweens the change in position and the change in scale from frame 75 to frame 100. Flash also tweens the change in transparency from frame 75 to frame 100.

19. Save the changes to **L17_start_xx.fla**, and leave it open.

Motion Presets

If your project involves creating identical motion tweens repeatedly, Flash provides a panel called Motion Presets that can help. The Motion Presets panel (Window > Motion Presets) can store any motion tween so you can apply it to different instances on the Stage.

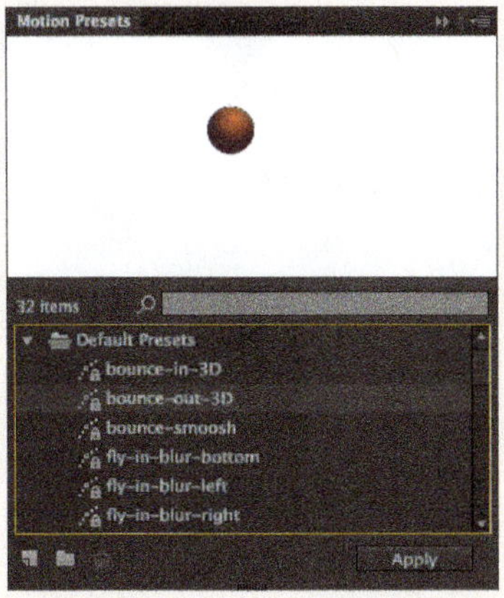

For example, if you want to build a slide show where each image fades out in the same manner, you can save that transition to the Motion Presets panel.

1. Select the first motion tween on the Timeline or the instance on the Stage.
2. In the Motion Presets panel, click the Save selection as preset button at the bottom of the panel. Alternatively, right-click/Ctrl-click on the motion tween and choose Save as Motion Preset.
3. Name your motion preset, and it will be saved in the Motion Presets panel.
4. Select a new instance on the Stage and choose the motion preset.
5. Click Apply, and Flash will apply your saved motion preset to the new instance.

Flash provides a number of motion presets that you can use to quickly build sophisticated animations without much effort.

Changing the Path of a Motion

The motion tween of the left car that you just animated shows a colored line with dots indicating the path of the motion. You can edit the path of the motion easily to make the car travel in a curve, or you can move, scale, or rotate the path just like any other object on the Stage.

To better demonstrate how you can edit the path of the motion, the students will use a sample file that contains a single Tween layer with a rocket ship moving from the top left of the Stage toward the bottom right.

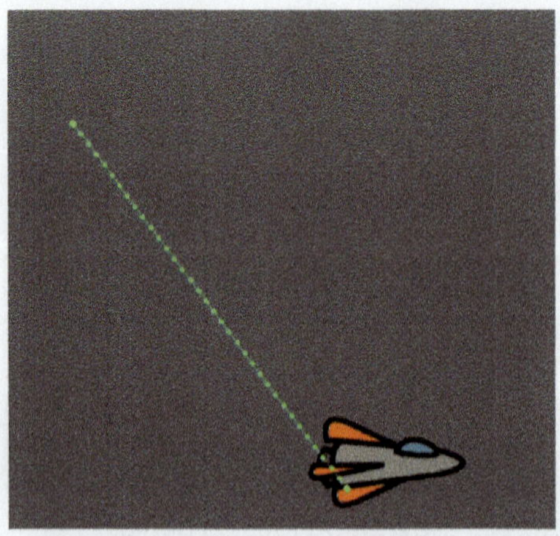

Moving the Path of the Motion

You will move the path of the motion so the relative movement of the rocket ship remains the same, but its starting and ending positions change.

Try It!

1. 1. Click File > Open, navigate to the data files for this lesson, and open **L17_start2.fla**. Save the file as **L17_start2_xx.fla**.
2. Choose the Selection tool.
3. Click on the path of the motion to select it.

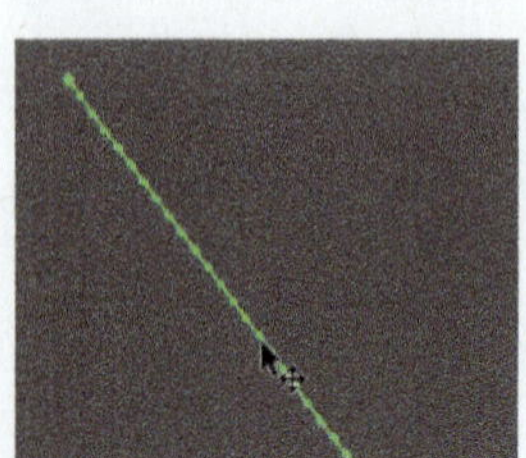

The path of the motion becomes highlighted.

4. Click and drag the motion path to move it to a different place on the Stage.

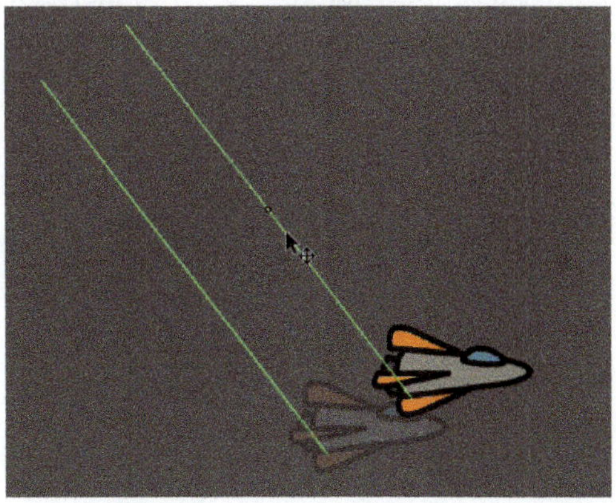

The relative motion and timing of the animation remain the same, but the starting and ending positions are relocated.

5. Save **L17_start2_xx.fla**, and leave it open.

Changing the Scale or Rotation of a Path

You can also manipulate the path of the object's motion using the Free Transform tool.

Try It!

1. Select the path of the motion.
2. Choose the Free Transform tool.

   Transformation handles appear around the path of the motion.
3. Scale or rotate the path of the motion as desired. You can make the path smaller or larger, or rotate the path so the rocket ship starts from the bottom left of the Stage and ends at the top right.

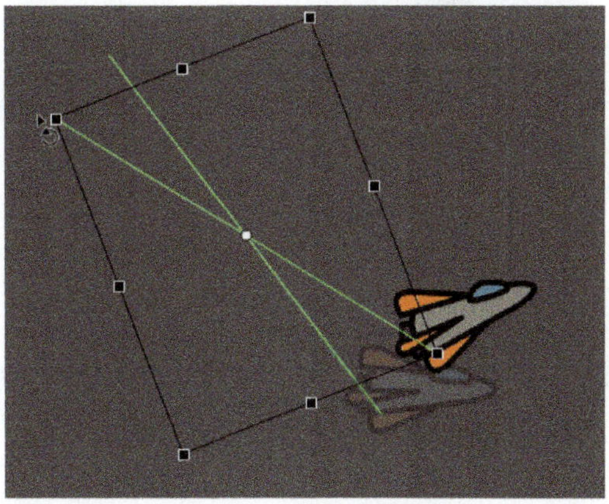

4. Save the changes to **L17_start2_xx.fla**, and leave it open.

Editing the Path of a Motion

Making your objects travel on a curved path is a simple matter. You can either edit the path with Bezier precision using anchor point handles, or you can edit the path in a more intuitive manner with the Selection tool.

Try It!

1. Choose the Convert Anchor Point tool, which is hidden under the Pen tool.

2. Click the starting point or the ending point of the motion path on the Stage and drag the control handle out from the anchor point.

   The handle on the anchor point controls the curvature of the path.

3. Choose the Subselection tool.

4. Click and drag the handle to edit the curve of the path. Make the rocket ship travel in a wide curve.

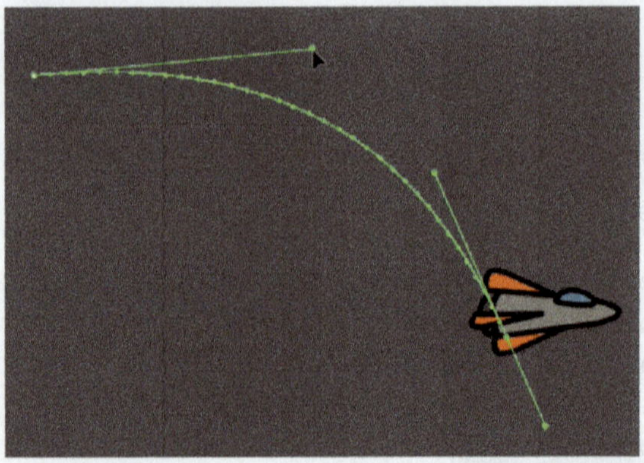

5. Save the changes to **L17_start2_xx.fla**, and leave it open.

Orienting Objects to a Path

Sometimes the orientation of the object traveling along the path is important. In the motion picture splash page project, the orientation of the car is constant as it rumbles forward. However, in the rocket ship example, the rocket ship should follow the path with its nose pointed in the direction in which it is heading. The Orient to path option in the Properties inspector gives you this option.

Try It!

1. Select the motion tween on the Timeline.
2. In the Properties inspector, under Rotation, select the Orient to path option.

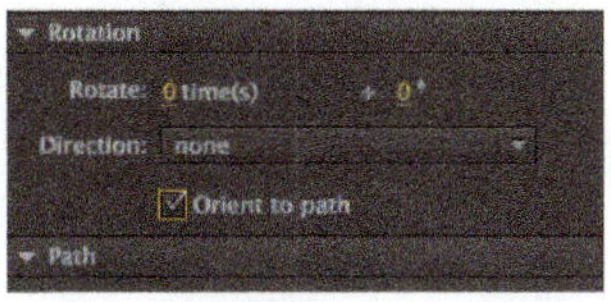

   Flash inserts keyframes for rotation along the motion tween to orient the nose of the rocket ship to the path of the motion.

3. Save the changes to **L17_start2_xx.fla**, and leave it open.

Swapping Tween Targets

The motion tween model in Flash Professional is object-based. This means that an object and its motion are independent of each other, and you can easily swap out the target of a motion tween. If, for example, you'd rather see an alien moving around the Stage instead of a rocket ship, you can replace the target of the motion tween with an alien symbol from your Library panel and still preserve the animation.

Try It!

1. Drag the movie clip symbol of the alien from the Library panel onto the rocket ship.

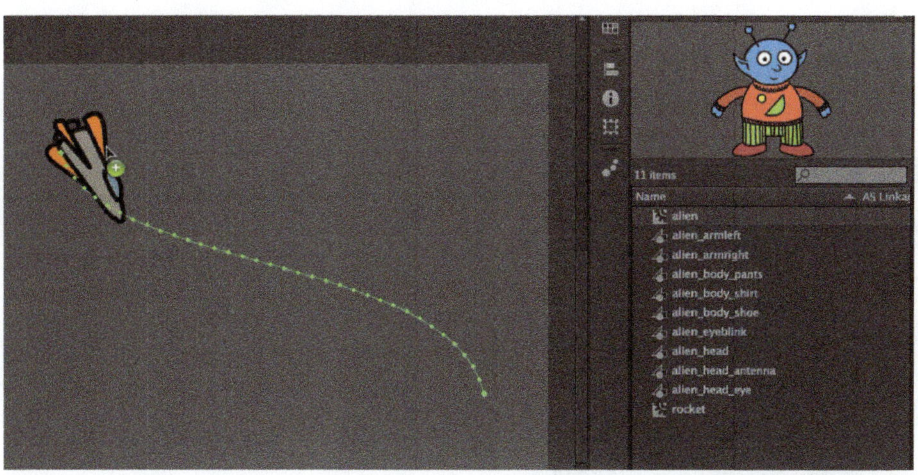

> **Note:**
>
> You can also swap instances in the Properties inspector. Select the object that you want to swap on the Stage. In the Properties inspector, click the Swap button. In the dialog box that appears, choose a new symbol and click OK. Flash will swap the target of the motion tween.

2. Flash asks if you want to replace the existing tween target object with a new object. Click OK.

Flash replaces the rocket ship with the alien. The motion remains the same, but the target of the motion tween has changed.

3. Save the changes to **L17_start2_xx.fla**, and leave it open.

Creating Nested Animations

> **Nested animations**
>
> An animation contained inside a movie clip symbol.

Often, an object that is animated on the Stage will have its own animation. For example, a butterfly moving across the Stage will have an animation of its wings flapping as it moves. Or the alien that you swapped with the rocket ship could be waving his arms. These kinds of animations are called **nested animations**, because they are contained inside the movie clip symbols. Movie clip symbols have their own Timeline that is independent of the main Timeline.

In this example, you'll make the alien wave his arms inside the movie clip symbol, so he'll be waving as he moves across the Stage.

Creating Animations Inside Movie Clip Symbols

Try It!

1. In the Library panel, double-click the alien movie clip symbol icon.

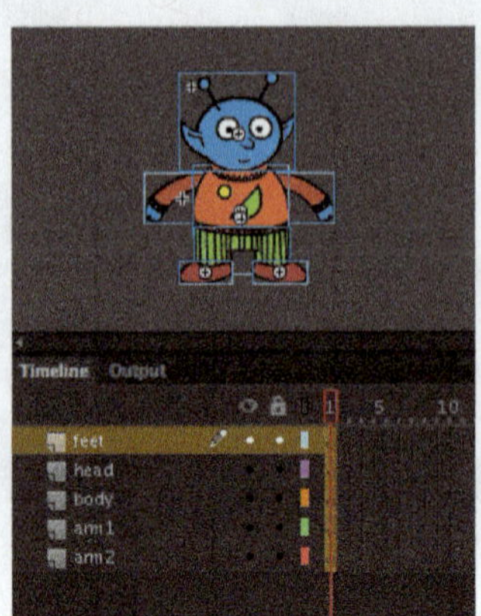

You are now in symbol-editing mode for the alien movie clip symbol. The alien appears in the middle of the Stage. In the Timeline, the parts of the alien are separated in layers.

2. Choose the Selection tool.
3. Right-click/Ctrl-click the alien's left arm and choose Create Motion Tween.

   Flash converts the current layer to a Tween layer and inserts 1 second's worth of frames so you can begin to animate the instance.

4. Choose the Free Transform tool.
5. Drag the corner rotation control point near the hand to rotate the arm upward to the alien's shoulder height.

   Flash inserts a keyframe at the end of the motion tween. The left arm rotates smoothly from the resting position to the outstretched position.

6. Move the red playhead back to frame 1.
7. Now create a motion tween for the alien's other arm. Right-click/Ctrl-click his right arm and choose Create Motion Tween.

   Flash converts the current layer to a Tween layer and inserts 1 second's worth of frames so you can begin to animate the instance.

8. Choose the Free Transform tool.
9. Drag the corner rotation control point near the hand to rotate the arm upward to the alien's shoulder height.

   Flash inserts a keyframe at the end of the motion tween. The arm rotates smoothly from the resting position to the outstretched position.

10. Select the last frame in all the other layers and insert frames (F5) so that the head, body, and feet all remain on the Stage for the same amount of time as the moving arms.

11. Click the Scene 1 button in the Edit bar at the top of the Stage to exit symbol-editing mode.

    Your animation of the alien raising his arms is complete. Wherever you use the movie clip symbol, the alien's nested animation will continue to play.

12. Preview the animation by choosing Control > Test.

    Flash opens a window showing the exported animation. The alien moves along the motion path while the nested animation of his arms moving plays and loops.

13. Save the changes to **L17_start2_xx.fla**, and then close it.

Setting Easing

As you learned earlier in this lesson, easing refers to the way in which a motion tween proceeds. You can think of easing as acceleration or deceleration. An object that moves from one side of the Stage to the other side can start off slowly, then build up speed, and then stop suddenly. Or, the object can start off quickly, and then gradually slow to a halt. Your keyframes indicate the beginning and end points of the motion, but the easing determines how your object gets from one keyframe to the next.

A simple way to apply easing to a motion tween is from the Properties inspector. Easing values range from –100 to 100. A negative value creates a more gradual change from the starting position (known as an ease-in). A positive value creates a gradual slowdown (known as an ease-out).

Splitting a Motion Tween

Easing affects the entire span of a motion tween. If you want the easing to affect only frames between keyframes of a longer motion tween, you should split the motion tween. For example, return to the L17_start_xx.fla file of the cinematic animation. The motion tween of the car in the Left_car layer begins at frame 75 and ends at frame 190, at the very end of the Timeline. However, the actual movement of the car starts at frame 75 and ends at frame 100. You'll split the motion tween so you can apply an ease to the tween just from frames 75 to 100.

Try It!

1. If necessary, open the **L17_start_xx.fla** file. In the Left_car layer, select frame 101, which is the frame just after the second keyframe where the car ends its movement.

2. Right-click/Ctrl-click on frame 101 and choose Split Motion.

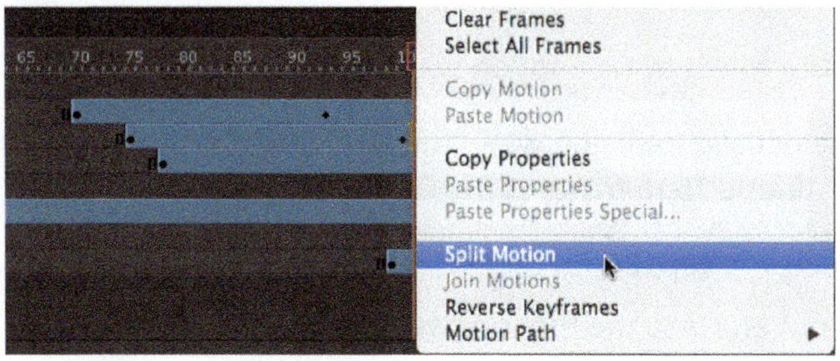

Flash cuts the motion tween into two separate tween spans. The end of the first tween is identical to the beginning of the second tween.

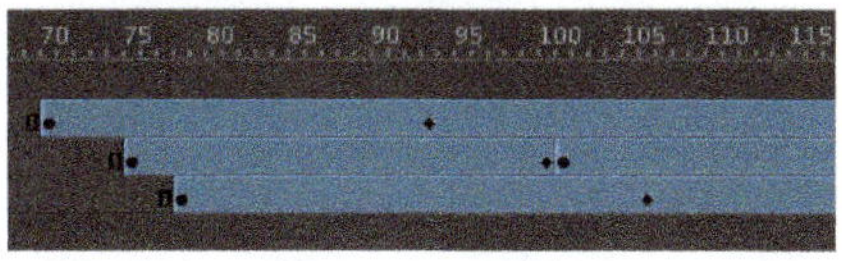

3. In the Middle_car layer, select frame 94, right-click/Ctrl-click, and choose Split Motion.

   Flash cuts the motion tween into two separate tween spans.

4. In the Right_car layer, select frame 107, right-click/Ctrl-click, and choose Split Motion.

   Flash cuts the motion tween into two separate tween spans. The motion tweens of all three cars are split.

5. Save the changes to **L17_start_xx.fla**, and leave it open.

Setting Eases of a Motion Tween

You'll apply an ease-in to the motion tweens of the approaching cars to give them a sense of weight and decelerate as real cars would.

Try It!

1. In the Middle_car layer, select any frame between the first and second keyframes of the first motion tween (frame 70 to frame 93).

2. In the Properties inspector, enter **100** for the Ease value.

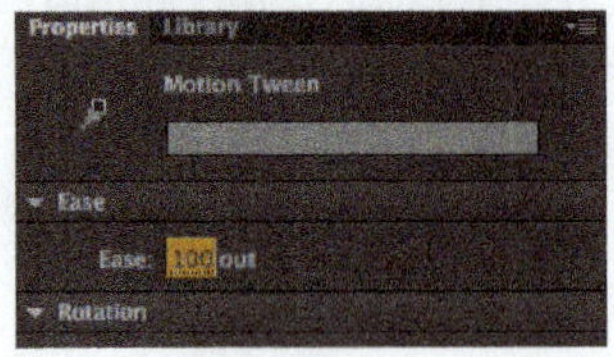

Flash applies an ease-out effect to the motion tween.

3. In the Left_car layer, select any frame between the first and second keyframes of the first motion tween (frame 75 to frame 100).
4. In the Properties inspector, enter **100** for the Ease value.

   Flash applies an ease-out effect to the motion tween.
5. In the Right_car layer, select any frame between the first and second keyframes of the first motion tween (frame 78 to frame 106).
6. In the Properties inspector, enter **100** for the Ease value.

   Flash applies an ease-out effect to the motion tween.
7. Enable the Loop Playback option at the bottom of the Timeline, and move the front and rear markers to bracket frames 60 to 115.
8. Click Play (Return/Enter).

   Flash plays the Timeline in a loop between frames 60 and 115 so you can examine the ease-out motion of the three cars.
9. Save the changes to **L17_start_xx.fla**, and leave it open.

Creating Frame-by-Frame Animation

Cel Animation

A traditional form of animation similar to a flipbook except the images are drawn on transparent sheets and then recorded to film.

Flipbook

A primitive form of animation where images are drawn on pages in a book and the image appears to move when the pages are flipped.

Frame-by-frame animation refers to the illusion of movement created by seeing the incremental changes between every keyframe. It's the closest to traditional hand-drawn **cel animation**, and it's just as tedious. In Flash, you can change a drawing in every keyframe, and create a frame-by-frame animation.

A **flipbook** is similar to a frame-by-frame animation except that it is done on paper. A flipbook is a primitive form of animation where a series of images are drawn from one page to the next and the image varies gradually. When the pages are flipped the image appears to move.

Frame-by-frame animations increase your file size rapidly because Flash has to store the contents for each keyframe. Use frame-by-frame animation sparingly.

In the next section, you'll insert a frame-by-frame animation inside the carLeft movie clip symbol to make it move up and down in a jittery fashion. When the movie clip loops, the car will rumble slightly to simulate the idle of the motor.

Inserting a New Keyframe

The frame-by-frame animations inside the carMiddle and carRight movie clip symbols have already been done. You'll finish the animation for the carLeft symbol.

Try It!

1. In the Library panel, double-click the carRight movie clip symbol to examine its completed frame-by-frame animation.
2. Inside the carRight movie clip, three keyframes establish three different positions for the car and its headlights. The keyframes are spaced unevenly to provide the unpredictable up and down motion.
3. In the Library panel, double-click the carLeft movie clip symbol.

   You enter symbol-editing mode for the carLeft symbol.

4. Select frame 2 in both the lights layer and the smallRumble layer.
5. Right-click/Ctrl-click and choose Insert Keyframe (F6).
6. Flash inserts a keyframe in frame 2 of the lights layer and the smallRumble layer. The contents of the previous keyframes are copied into the new keyframes.
7. Save the changes to **L17_start_xx.fla**, and leave it open.

Changing the Graphics

In the new keyframe, change the appearance of the contents to create the animation.

1. In frame 2, select all three graphics on Stage (Edit > Select All, or Command/Ctrl+A) and move them down the Stage 1 pixel. You can use the Properties inspector or press the Down Arrow key to nudge the graphics by 1 pixel.

   The car and its headlights move down slightly.

2. Next, repeat the process of inserting keyframes and changing the graphics. For a random motion like an idling car, at least three keyframes are ideal.
3. Select frame 4 in both the lights layer and the smallRumble layer.
4. Right-click/Ctrl-click and choose Insert Keyframe (F6).

   Flash inserts a keyframe in frame 4 of the lights layer and the smallRumble layer. The contents of the previous keyframes are copied into the new keyframes.
5. Select all three graphics on Stage (Edit > Select All, or Command/Ctrl+A) and move them up the Stage 2 pixels. You can use the Properties inspector or press the Up Arrow key twice to nudge the graphics by 2 pixels.

   The car and its headlights move up slightly.
6. Test the idling motion by enabling the Loop Playback option at the bottom of the Timeline and click Play (Return/Enter).
7. Save the changes to **L17_start_xx.fla**, and leave it open.

Animating 3D Motion

Finally, you'll add a title and animate it in 3D space. Animating in 3D presents the added complication of a third (z) axis. When you choose the 3D Rotation or 3D Translation tool, you need to be aware of the Global Transform option at the bottom of the Tools panel. The Global Transform option toggles between a global option (button depressed) and a local option (button raised). Moving an object with the global option on makes the transformations relative to the global coordinate system, whereas moving an object with the local option on makes the transformations relative to itself.

Try It!

1. Click on Scene 1 in the Edit bar to return to the main Timeline. Insert a new layer at the top of the layer stack and rename it **title**.
2. Lock all the other layers.
3. Insert a new keyframe at frame 120.
4. Drag the movie clip symbol named movietitle from the Library panel onto the Stage.

   The movietitle instance appears in your new layer in the keyframe at frame 120.
5. Position the title at x=180 and y=90.
6. Right-click/Ctrl-click on the movie title and choose Create Motion Tween.

   Flash converts the current layer to a Tween layer so you can begin to animate the instance.
7. Move the red playhead to frame 140.

8. Select the 3D Rotation tool.
9. Deselect the Global Transform option at the bottom of the Tools panel.
10. Click and drag the title to rotate it around the y-axis (green) so that its angle is at about –50 degrees. You can check the rotation values in the Transform panel (Window > Transform).

11. Move the red playhead to the first keyframe at frame 120.
12. Click and drag the title to rotate it around the y-axis in the opposite direction so that the instance looks like just a sliver.

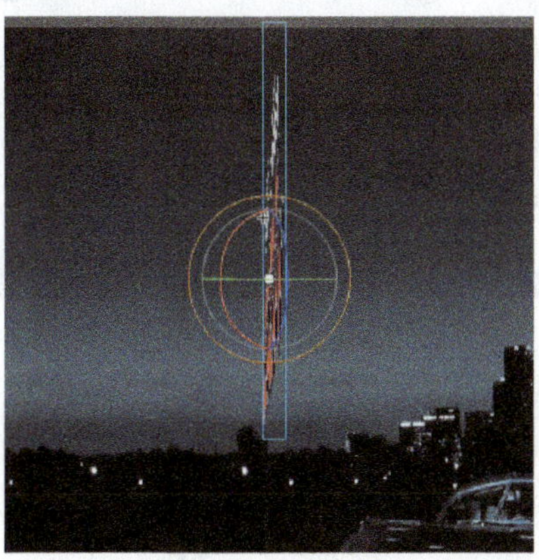

Flash motion-tweens the change in the 3D rotation, so the title appears to swing in three dimensions.

13. Save the changes to **L17_start_xx.fla**, and leave it open.

Testing a Movie

You can quickly preview your animation by "scrubbing" the red playhead back and forth on the Timeline or by choosing Control > Play. You can also use the integrated Controller at the bottom of the Timeline.

However, to preview your animation as your audience will see it and to preview any nested animations within movie clip symbols, you should test your movie.

1. Choose Control > Test.

   Flash exports the published files—in this case, a SWF file—and saves it in the same location as your FLA file. The SWF file is the compressed, final Flash media that you would embed in an HTML page to play in a browser with the Flash Player. Flash displays the SWF file in a new window with the exact Stage dimensions and plays your animation.

2. To exit Test Movie mode, click the Close window button.

   You can also preview your animation by choosing Control > Test Movie > in Browser, and Flash will export a SWF file and open it automatically in your default browser.

3. Save the changes to **L17_start_xx.fla**, and close Flash.

Generating PNG Sequences and Sprite Sheets

While you can create sophisticated animations to play as a SWF file with the Flash Player, you can also use Flash's powerful tools to create your animation and export it as a series of images for use in other environments. For example, animations with HTML5 or on mobile devices often rely on sequential PNG files or a single file that packs all the images organized in rows and columns, known as a sprite sheet. The sprite sheet is accompanied by a data file that describes the position of each image, or sprite, in the file.

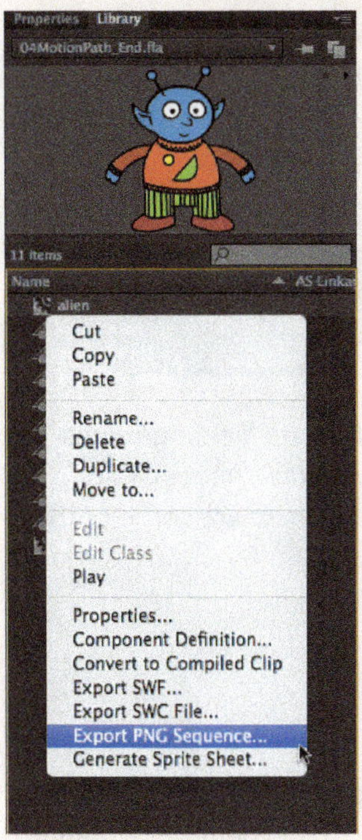

Generating either PNG sequences or a sprite sheet of your animation is easy. First, your animation must be within a movie clip symbol. In the Library panel, right-click/Ctrl-click the symbol and choose Export PNG Sequence.

Next, you select the destination on your hard drive for your images and the dimensions of your images.

For a sprite sheet, right-click/Ctrl-click the symbol and choose Generate Sprite Sheet. The Generate Sprite Sheet dialog box that appears provides different options, such as sizing, background color, and the particular data format.

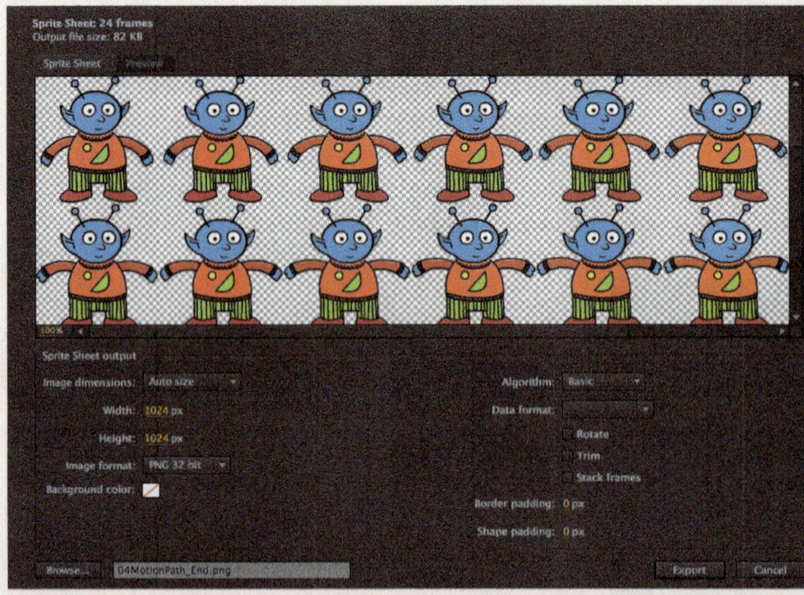

Click Export to output the sprite sheet and data file. The data file determines what kind of development environment you'll use your sprite sheet in. For example, JSON, Starling, cocos2D, and Adobe's Edge Animate are some of the data formats available.

Academic Planning

Can you name one thing you can do to increase the amount of money you will earn in your lifetime? How about graduating from high school? Even better, graduating from college!

High school graduation might seem very far away. The thought of studying for so many years, of taking—and passing—so many classes, might feel like a heavy burden. But the benefits of success are worth the effort. Graduates are more likely to be hired than non-graduates. They earn more money, are healthier, and live better lifestyles. Completing your education is one of the best things you can do for yourself and your career. Academic planning can help you reach that goal.

- Fold a piece of paper in half. On one side, make a list of jobs you think you could get without a high school diploma. On the other side, list jobs you think you could not get without a high school diploma. As a class, discuss which jobs offer better benefits and rewards.

Recognizing the Value of School

Finishing school is an investment in your future. Studies show that people who stay in school have higher self-esteem, better physical health, and a more positive attitude. They are more likely to have a job, and they earn more money.

School is an opportunity. When you stay in school, you can learn new things, meet new people, and try new activities. You can practice skills you will need when you graduate, such as getting along with others, speaking up for yourself, and being on time for appointments.

Why School Matters

School also provides an opportunity to prepare for a career. Core subjects such as reading, writing, and math are vital for the career-search process. Science, social studies, music, art, technology, family and consumer sciences, and sports all help you gain knowledge and build skills you will need to succeed at work, such as teamwork, leadership, and problem solving. School clubs and organizations also help you build skills for future success.

Why Dropping Out Is Not Cool

You might think dropping out of school to get a job is a good idea. Maybe you need money. Maybe you are tired of going to class. Maybe you think you are ready to live like a grownup. However, when you are not in school, you will be expected to pay your own rent, pay for your own transportation, and pay for your own food. If a company does hire you, it will likely pay you about 35 percent less than if you had graduated.

A dropout—someone who leaves school without receiving a diploma—is more likely to be poor, receive assistance from the government, and be a single parent. Dropouts are more likely to commit crimes and go to jail, to suffer from depression, and to have substance abuse problems.

How Education Affects Employment

Education teaches you skills and information you need to get and keep a job. Think about this: Most companies will not hire an employee who has not graduated from high school. Some will not hire an employee who has not graduated from college. If a company does hire dropouts, it usually pays them less than it pays graduates.

Employers assume that graduates have certain characteristics that dropouts don't have. If a graduate and a dropout apply for the same job, the employer thinks that the graduate:

- Knows how to read and write
- Understands basic math
- Can communicate with others
- Knows how to solve problems
- Has a good work ethic
- Has a positive attitude
- Is self-disciplined
- Is motivated to succeed

Note:

According to the U.S. Census Bureau, the average dropout can expect to earn an annual income of $20,241. A high school graduate, on the other hand, can expect to make about $30,500 a year, and those with a bachelor's degree can expect to make more than $50,000 a year.

Meeting Career Goals

Developing strong academic skills can help you in any career you choose. What skills can you acquire and strengthen in school in order to achieve your career goals?

- Prioritize assignments and manage your time to complete them.
- Listen carefully and follow instructions.
- Enroll in courses related to the career you want to pursue.

What habits in school might interfere with achieving your career goals?

- Cram for a test the night before it's scheduled.
- Socialize and talk a lot during class.
- Enroll in easy classes so you can get a good grade and improve your GPA.

What other academic skills can help you meet your career goals?

Comprehension Check

1. What are two requirements of a motion tween?
2. What kinds of properties can a motion tween change in an ActionScript 3.0 document?
3. What are property keyframes, and why are they important?
4. How can you edit the path of an object's motion?
5. What does easing do to a motion tween?
6. List at least three benefits of staying in school.

End-of-Chapter Activities

Chapter Review

1. How is a frame-by-frame animation similar to a flip book?
2. Explain why storyboarding is important when planning your animation.
3. What is the difference between the Stage and the Pasteboard?
4. Distinguish between an object that is opaque and one that is transparent.
5. How can you change the duration of an animation?

Chapter 5 – Portfolio Builder

Part 1 – Turn a Dragonfly into a Butterfly

DIRECTIONS

In the first part of this activity, you will shape-tween a dragonfly vector outline into a butterfly.

1. Start Flash and open the **PB5-1.fla** from the data files for this lesson.
2. Save the file as **PB5-1_xx.fla** in the location where your teacher instructs you to store the file for this lesson.
3. Click on the keyframe holding the butterfly, and drag that keyframe to frame 30 of the dragonfly layer.

   You should now have the dragonfly vector artwork showing up from frame 1 to frame 29.

   When the playback head hits frame 30, the butterfly appears.
4. Right-click anywhere in the span between the dragonfly and butterfly, and choose Create Shape Tween from the menu.

   The vectors should tween when you move the playback head.
5. To control the path of the tween, click on the dragonfly keyframe, and then choose Modify > Shape > Add Shape Hint.
6. Drag the lettered dot to the tip of the dragonfly wing.
7. On the butterfly keyframe, move the same dot to the corresponding wing tip of the butterfly vector.
8. Repeat as needed, anchoring different areas of the vector until it tweens symmetrically. You may need to restart the hinting by choosing Modify > Shape > Remove All Hints.
9. Publish your file for submission. To publish a .swf file, choose File > Publish Settings. Be sure a Flash player is selected in the Target menu. Also make sure that the Flash (.swf) option is selected in the Publish area at the left of the Publish Settings dialog box. Click the Publish button at the bottom of the dialog box.

   The output .swf file will be written to the location specified in the Output File field.
10. Save the changes to your file, close the project, and leave Flash open.

Part 2 – Animate a SImple Timer

DIRECTIONS

In the second part of this activity, you will create a simple timer animation with a rotating hand.

1. Open **PB5-2.fla** from the data files for this lesson.
2. Save the file as **PB5-2_xx.fla** in the location where your teacher instructs you to store the file for this lesson.
3. Use the element provided in the library to create a graphic symbol that includes the clock face and the clock hand.
4. Using a tween on the graphic symbol's Timeline, animate the spinning hand of the clock 360 degrees.
5. Duplicate the graphic symbol as a movie clip.
6. Place the two symbols on the main Timeline next to each other.
7. Extend the main Timeline or remove frames to make the main Timeline half the length of a complete rotation.
8. Test the movie, and observe the difference between the two symbols.
9. Save the changes to your project file and close Flash.

Chapter 5 – Critical Thinking

Recall the L17_start2 file with the rocket and alien that you worked with in Lesson 17. Working in teams, use that file as the basis for creating an animation for a new movie "starring" the alien and its rocket. Use the four-step process for preparing an animation project that was discussed in Lesson 14. You can import graphics and images from other sources to add characters and other visual enhancements. Add text as desired and apply animation to various objects. Save the file as CT5_xx.fla. Test the movie in your browser, and share with the class.

Chapter 6

Exploring Audio/Video Production

Lesson 18 | Touring Premiere Pro CC
Exploring Nonlinear Editing in Premiere Pro
Defining the Standard Digital Video Workflow
Touring the Premiere Pro Workspace
Customizing the Workspace
Exploring Preferences
Solving Problems

Lesson 19 | Recording and Capturing Audio/Video Assets
Exploring Video Script Production
Shooting Video
Taking Quality Video
Capturing Video for Editing in Premiere Pro
Protecting Copyright

Lesson 20 | Setting Up a Project
Creating a Premiere Pro Project File
Setting Up a Sequence
Identifying Audio Track Types

Lesson 21 | Importing Media
Exploring Importing Assets
Using a Tapeless Workflow
Finding Assets with the Media Browser
Importing Images
Recording a Scratch Narration Track
Exploring Laws Regarding the Use of Technology

Lesson 22 | Organizing Media
Setting the Default Editing Workspace
Exploring the Project Panel
Working with Bins
Identifying Personal and Professional Qualities

Lesson 23 | Essentials of Video Editing
Using the Source Monitor
Navigating the Timeline
Creating a Sequence
Moving Clips
Extracting and Deleting Segments

Lesson 24 | Adding Transitions
Exploring the Use of Transitions
Adding Video Transitions

Lesson 25 | Creating Titles
Working with Text
Creating Titles from Scratch

Lesson 26 | Exporting Frames, Clips, and Sequences
Sharing Your Project
Examining Export Options
Working with Adobe Media Encoder
Configuring the Export
Queuing the Export
Identifying Teamwork and Leadership

Lesson 27 | Working with Adobe Audition
Capturing Audio Files
Configuring Audition for Audio Capture and Editing
Exploring the Audition Workspace
Navigating in the Audition Workspace
Editing Audio Clips

End-of-Chapter Activities

Lesson 18 Overview

In this lesson, you will learn about:

- Exploring Nonlinear Editing in Premiere Pro
- Defining the Standard Digital Video Workflow
- Touring the Premiere Pro Workspace
- Customizing the Workspace
- Exploring Preferences
- Solving Problems

There's enormous demand for high-quality video content, and you're working in an ever-changing landscape of old and new technologies. Despite all this rapid change, however, the goal of video editing is the same as it was in the early days of cinema: You want to take your footage and shape it, guided by your original vision, so that you can communicate ideas and understanding with your audience.

Adobe® Premiere Pro® is video editing software that supports the latest technology and cameras with powerful tools that are easy to use and that integrate perfectly with almost every type of media, as well as a wide range of third-party plug-ins and other post-production tools.

In this lesson you will learn about the main components in the Premiere Pro interface and how to create custom workspaces. You will also explore editing and workflow procedures and concepts.

Exploring Nonlinear Editing in Premiere Pro

There are two basic type of video editing processes: linear and nonlinear. **Linear editing** was developed for working with video tape. It required selecting, arranging, and modifying images and sound in a predetermined, ordered sequence. Each desired video clip had to be isolated and recorded (or dubbed) onto a master tape. Linear editing is economical and has application to projects in which you simply want to add a video clip to the end of another. But today, the standard is nonlinear editing.

Premiere Pro is a **nonlinear editing system** (NLE). Like a word processor, Premiere Pro lets you place, replace, and move footage anywhere you want in your final edited video. You can also adjust any parts of the video clips you use at any time. You don't need to perform edits in a particular order, and you can make changes to any part of your video project at any time.

Nonlinear editing system (NLE)

Editing system that allows you to place, replace, and move footage anywhere you want in your final edited video.

Linear editing

The process of editing video sequentially, in a predetermined, ordered sequence.

With Premiere Pro, you combine multiple clips to create a sequence that you can change simply by clicking and dragging with your mouse. You can edit any part of your sequence, in any order, and then change the contents, move clips so that they play earlier or later in the video, blend layers of video together, add special effects, and more.

You can even combine multiple sequences and jump to any moment in a video clip without needing to fast-forward or rewind. It's as easy to organize the clips you're working with as it is to organize files on your computer.

Premiere Pro supports both tape and tapeless media formats, including XDCAM EX, XDCAMHD 422, DPX, DVCProHD, AVCHD (including AVCCAM and NXCAM), AVC-Intra, and DSLR video. It also has native support for the latest in raw video formats, including media from RED, ARRI, and Blackmagic cameras.

Defining the Standard Digital Video Workflow

As you gain editing experience, you'll develop your own preference for the order in which to work on the different aspects of your project. Each stage requires a particular kind of attention and different tools. Also, some projects call for more time spent on one stage than another.

Whether you skip through some stages with a quick mental check or spend hours (even days!) dedicated to perfecting an aspect of your project, you'll work through the following steps:

1. Acquire the video. This can mean recording original footage or gathering assets for a project.
2. Capture (transfer or ingest) the video to your hard drive. With tape-based formats, Premiere Pro (with the appropriate hardware) can convert the video into digital files. With tapeless media, Premiere Pro can read the media directly, with no need for conversion. If you're working with tapeless media, be sure to back up your files to a second location because physical drives sometimes fail unexpectedly.
3. Organize your clips. There can be a lot of video content to choose from in your project. Spend the time to organize clips together into special folders (called bins) in your project. You can add color labels and other metadata (additional information about the clips) to help keep things organized.

4. Combine the parts of the video and audio clips you want as a sequence and add them to the Timeline.

5. Place special transition effects between clips, add video effects, and create combined visual effects by placing clips on multiple layers (tracks).

6. Create titles or graphics, and add them to your sequence in the same way you would add video clips.

7. Mix your audio tracks to get the combined level just right, and use transitions and effects on your audio clips to improve the sound.

8. Export your finished project to videotape, to a file for a computer or for Internet playback, to a mobile device, or to a DVD or Blu-ray Disc.

Premiere Pro supports each of these steps with industry-leading tools.

Touring the Premiere Pro Workspace

It's helpful to begin by getting familiar with the editing interface so you can recognize the tools as you work with them in the following lessons. To make it easier to configure the user interface, Premiere Pro offers workspaces. Workspaces quickly configure the various panels and tools onscreen in ways that are helpful for particular activities, such as editing, special effects work, or audio mixing.

Try It!

1. Launch Premiere Pro.

To Launch Premiere Pro in Macintosh:

Do one of the following:

- On the startup drive, open the Applications > Adobe Premiere Pro folder, then double-click the Adobe Premiere Pro application icon.
- Click the Premiere Pro application icon in the Dock.
- To launch Premiere Pro by opening a file, double-click a Premiere Pro file icon or drag a Premiere Pro file icon over the application icon in the Dock.
- Press F4 on the keyboard, then click the Premiere Pro application icon.

To Launch Premiere Pro in Windows:

Do one of the following:

- In Windows 8, display the Start screen, then click the tile for Adobe Premiere Pro.
- In Windows 10, click the Start button, choose All Programs, then click Adobe Premiere Pro.

1. On the welcome screen of Premiere Pro, you can start a new project or open a saved one.

2. Click Open Project.

3. In the Open Project window, open **L18_start.prproj** from the data files for this lesson.

4. Save the file as **L18_start_xx.prproj** in the location where your teacher instructs you to store the files for this lesson, and leave the file open.

All Premiere Pro project files have a .prproj extension

> **Note:**
>
> You may be prompted with a dialog asking where a particular file is. This will happen when the original files are saved on a hard drive (or hard drive letter) different from the one you're using. You'll need to identify the storage location. In this case, navigate to the assets files for this lesson and select the file that the dialog is prompting you to open. Premiere Pro will remember this location for the rest of the files.

The Workspace Layout

Before you begin, make sure you're using the default Editing workspace.

Try It!

1. Choose Window > Workspaces > Editing.
2. Choose Window > Workspaces > Reset to Saved Layout.
3. Click Yes in the Reset Workspace dialog, if necessary.
4. Save the file and leave it open.

Although it might look confusing at first, the Premiere Pro interface is designed to make video editing easy. The principal elements are shown here.

A. Project panel
B. Media Browser panel (hidden)
C. Info panel (hidden)
D. Effects panel (hidden)
E. Audio Clip Mixer panel (hidden)
F. Timeline panel
G. Clips panel
H. Source Monitor panel
I. Program Monitor panel
J. Effect Controls panel (hidden)
K. Tools panel

Each workspace item appears in its own panel, and multiple panels can be combined into a single frame. Some items with common industry terms stand alone, such as Timeline, Audio Clip Mixer, and Program Monitor. The main user interface elements are as follows:

- **Timeline panel:** This is where you'll do most of your actual editing. You view and work on **sequences** in the Timeline panel. One strength of sequences is that you can nest them (place sequences inside other sequences). In this way, you can break up a production into manageable chunks or create unique special effects.

> **Sequence**
>
> An edited video segment or entire project that you are working on.

- **Tracks:** You can layer—or *composite*—video clips, images, graphics, and titles on an unlimited number of tracks. Tracks in Premiere Pro are similar to layers in Photoshop and Flash. Video clips on upper video tracks cover whatever is directly below them on the Timeline. Therefore, you need to give clips on higher tracks some kind of transparency or reduce their size if you want clips on lower tracks to show through.
- **Monitor panels:** You use the Source Monitor (on the left) to view and select parts of clips (your original footage). To view a clip in the Source Monitor, double-click it in the Project panel. The Program Monitor (on the right) is for viewing your current sequence.
- **Project panel:** This is where you place links to your project's media files: video clips, audio files, graphics, still images, and sequences. You can use bins—similar to folders—to organize your assets.
- **Media Browser:** This panel allows you to browse your hard drive to find footage. It's especially useful for file-based camera media.
- **Effects panel:** This panel contains all the clip effects you will use in your sequences, including video filters, audio effects, and transitions. It's docked, in this workspace, with the Project panel. Effects are grouped by type to make them easier to find.

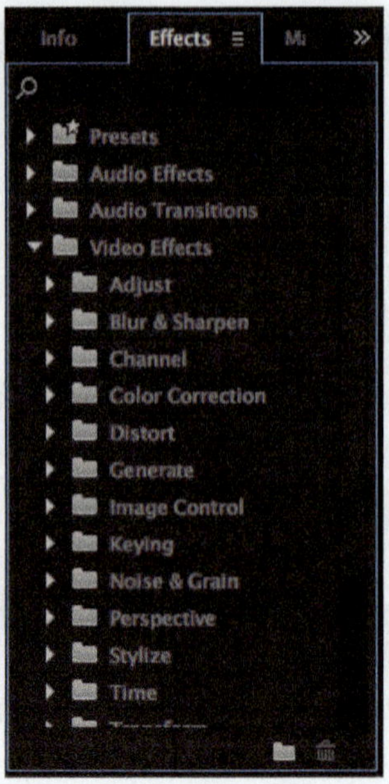

- **Audio Clip Mixer:** This panel (docked, by default, with the Source, Metadata, and Effect Controls panels) is based on audio production studio hardware, with volume sliders and panning knobs. There is one set of controls for each audio track on the Timeline. The adjustments you make are applied to audio clips. There's also a dedicated Audio Track Mixer, for applying audio adjustments to tracks.

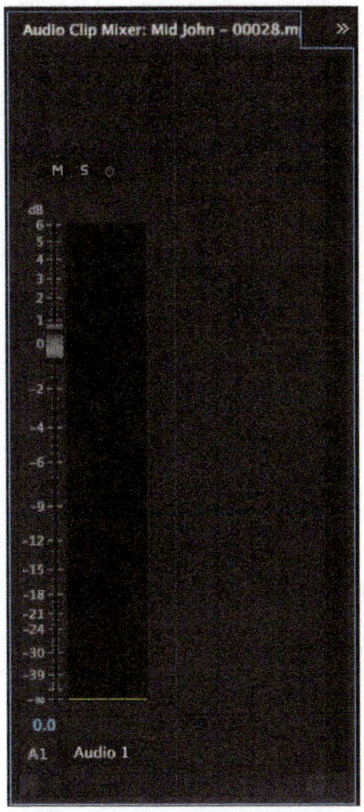

- **Effect Controls panel:** This panel (docked, by default, with the Source, Audio Clip Mixer, and Metadata panels) displays the controls for any effects applied to a clip you select in a sequence. Motion, Opacity, and Time Remapping controls are always available for visual clips. Most effect parameters are adjustable over time.

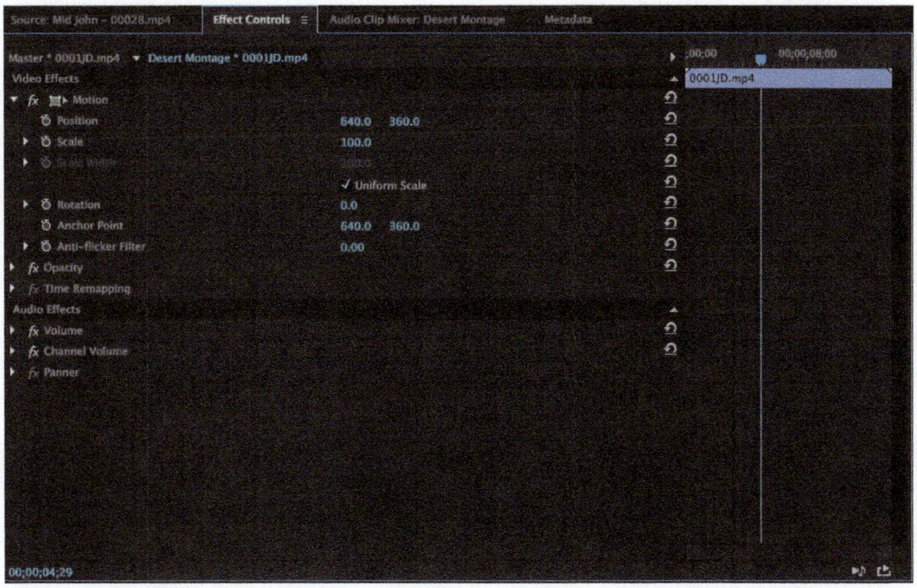

- **Tools panel:** Each icon in this panel represents a tool that performs a specific function, typically a type of edit in a sequence. The Selection tool is context-sensitive, which means it changes appearance to indicate the function that matches the positioning. If you find your pointer doesn't work as you expect, it might be because you have the wrong tool.

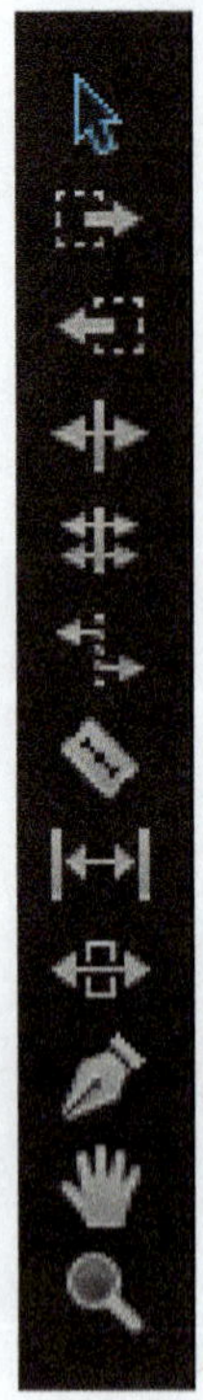

- **Info panel:** The Info panel (docked, by default, with the Project panel and Media Browser) presents useful information about any asset you select in the Project panel or any clip or transition selected in a sequence.
- **History panel:** This panel (docked, by default, with the Effects and Info panels) tracks the steps you take and lets you back up easily. It's a kind of visual Undo list. When you select a previous step, all steps that came after it are also undone.

Customizing the Workspace

Note:

As you move a panel, Premiere Pro displays a drop zone. If the panel is a rectangle, it will go into the selected frame as an additional tab. If it's a trapezoid, it will go into its own frame.

In addition to customizing the default workspaces (based on tasks), you can adjust the position and location of panels to create a workspace that works best for you. You can then store a workspace or even create multiple workspaces for different tasks.

- As you change the size of a frame, other frames change size to compensate.
- All panels within frames are accessible via tabs.
- All panels are dockable—you can drag a panel from one frame to another.
- You can drag a panel out of a frame to become a separate floating panel.

In this exercise, you'll try all these functions and save a customized workspace.

Try It!

1. Click the Source Monitor panel (selecting its tab if necessary), and then position your pointer on the vertical divider between the Source Monitor and the Program Monitor. Then, drag left and right to change the sizes of those frames. You can choose to have different sizes for your video displays.
2. Now place the pointer on the horizontal divider between the Source Monitor and the Timeline. Drag up and down to change the sizes of these frames.
3. Click the gripper area in the upper-left corner of the tab for the Effects panel (to the left of the name), and drag it to the middle of the Source Monitor to dock the Effects panel in that frame.

   When many panels are combined in a single frame, you may not be able to see all the tabs. A navigation slider appears above the tabs to navigate between them. Slide it left or right to reveal hidden tabs. You can also display a panel by choosing it in the Window menu.
4. Drag the Effects drag handle to a point near the right of the Project panel to place it in its own frame.

   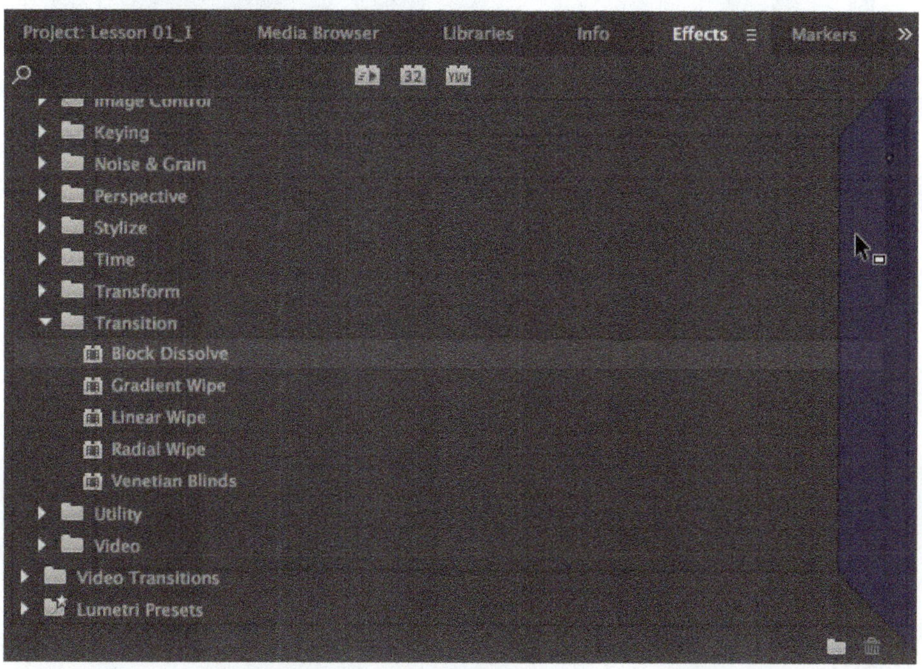

   The drop zone is a trapezoid that covers the right portion of the Project panel. Release the mouse button, and your workspace should look something like the example.

   You can also pull panels out into their own floating panel.
5. Click the Source Monitor's drag handle, and hold down the Control (Windows) or Command (Mac) key while dragging it out of its frame. Its drop zone image is much more distinct, indicating that you are about to create a floating panel.

6. Drop the Source Monitor anywhere, creating a floating panel. Resize it by dragging from a corner or a side like any other panel.

7. As you gain experience, you might want to create and save the layout of your panels as a customized workspace. To do so, choose Window > Workspace > New Workspace. Type a name, and click OK.

8. If you want to return a workspace to its default layout, choose Window > Workspaces > Reset To Saved Layout. To return to a recognizable starting point, choose the preset Editing workspace and reset it now.

9. Save the changes to **L18_start_xx.prproj** and leave it open.

Exploring Preferences

The more you edit video, the more you'll want to customize Premiere Pro to match your specific needs. There are several types of preferences, all grouped into one panel for easy access. Preferences will be covered in depth as they relate to the individual lessons in this book. Let's look at a simple one.

Try It!

1. Choose Edit > Preferences > Appearance (Windows) or Premiere Pro > Preferences > Appearance (Mac).

2. Drag the Brightness slider to the left or right to suit your needs. When you're done, click OK, or click Cancel to return to the default setting.

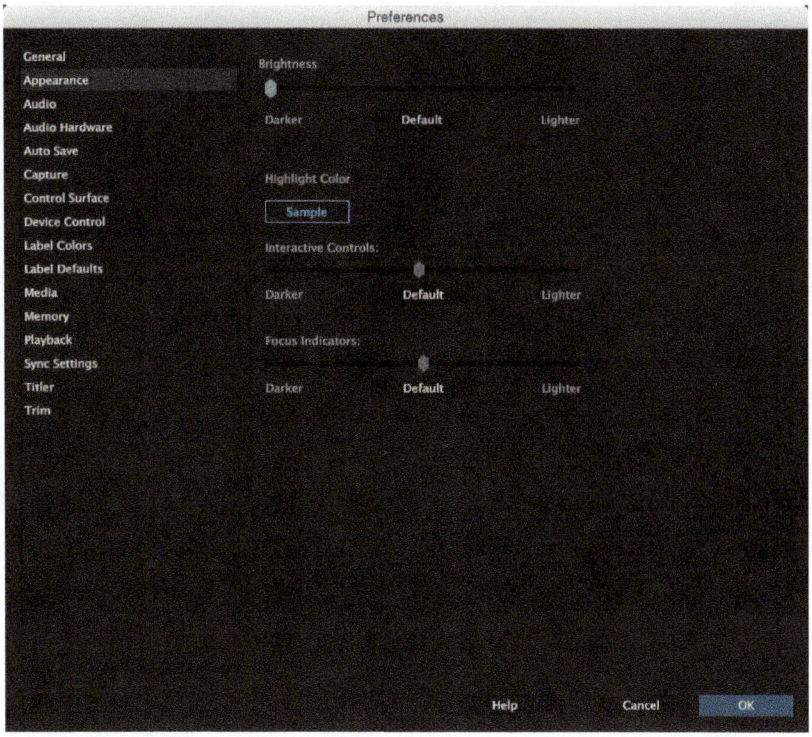

The default brightness is a neutral gray to help you see colors correctly.

3. Switch to the Auto Save preferences.

   Imagine if you had worked for hours and then there was a power cut. If you hadn't saved recently, you'd have lost a lot of work.

   Premiere Pro automatically saves a backup copy of your project file while you work, in case of system failure. Premiere Pro is integrated with Adobe Creative Cloud, so an additional backup project file can be saved to your Creative Cloud shared files folder if you check the box in this dialog box.

4. Click Cancel.

5. Save the changes to **L18_start_xx.prproj**, and close the Premiere Pro project file.

Moving, Backing Up, and Syncing User Settings

User preferences include a number of important options. The defaults work well in most cases, but as you become more familiar with the editing process, it's likely you'll want to make a few adjustments.

Premiere Pro includes the option to share your user preferences between multiple machines: When installing Premiere Pro, you will have entered your Adobe ID to confirm your software license. You can use the same ID to store your user preferences in Creative Cloud, allowing you to sync and update them from any installation of Premiere Pro.

You can sync your preferences on the Welcome screen by choosing Sync Settings Now, or you can sync your preferences while working with Premiere Pro by choosing File > Sync Settings > Sync Settings Now (Windows) or Premiere Pro > Sync Settings > Sync Settings Now (Mac).

This new option to sync preferences between multiple machines makes it easier than ever to move your creative work from one location to another.

Video Editing Platforms

The tools to edit video have gone through a remarkable change since the days of tape-to-tape linear editing. Linear editing used at least two videotape recorders to copy each shot from the camera source to the program tape one by one. It required the editor to place each shot in the order it was meant to be seen.

If a shot needed to be added to an early part of a program, the rest of the program from that point on needed to be edited again. The editor had to have a clear game plan on how the program and each shot should be laid out. Creating a simple effect like a dissolve required the second shot to be copied on another video tape to be played back on a third videotape player to be played back simultaneously to perform the effect.

Editing on a computer in a nonlinear editing (NLE) system allows the editor to move shots around in any order they need without losing any previous work.

In the 1990s, the film and television industry began to adopt editing on NLEs. The two most popular editing systems at the time were Avid and Lightworks. Avid Technology, Inc., still holds the title of the standard for professional editing systems in film and TV production.

Lightworks is also still around, and although not as popular or widely used as Avid Media Composer, it is one of the most affordable editing programs.

In 1999, Apple, Inc. released Final Cut Pro, an NLE designed to work without any additional software. Digital video (DV) cameras could be connected to a Mac computer using a FireWire cable to capture picture and sound without any loss of quality.

Final Cut Pro was sold at a fraction of the price of the established competitors, which caused a disruption and a bit of a divide in the industry. Video production companies and documentarians used Final Cut Pro because of its affordability and ease of use, where TV and film editors continued to use Avid's editing applications because of their established base, support, and reliability.

The same year Final Cut Pro was released, Sonic Foundry released Vegas Pro, a Windows-only NLE, which was acquired by Sony in 2003.

The team that originally created Final Cut Pro was hired by Adobe Systems, Inc., to create another entry in the competition, Adobe Premiere (now Adobe Premiere Pro), which was released in 2003.

The adoption and use of each video-editing solution ebbs and flows as each system comes out with new versions with new features. It is difficult to say which solution is the right one to use, since factors such as budget and choice of operating system apply differently for each user and each production.

To add yet another set of options for editing your project, mobile apps for phones and tablets are becoming more powerful and capable of handling high-quality video to create professional-level projects. Apple iMovie for iOS becomes more feature-rich with each update. Film editor Dan Lebental, A.C.E. (Iron Man, 2008), developed TouchEdit, a video-editing app used on professional productions and fitting into established workflows. Adobe recently announced its own editor for the iOS platform, Premiere Clip.

The market for the tools to deliver your message using video is being flooded by new and creatively designed solutions. It can be overwhelming.

Ultimately, if you choose to pursue a professional career in postproduction, you should learn as many platforms as you can. The evolutionary history of postproduction tools proves that nothing settles and unexpected change lurks around every corner.

Solving Problems

A **problem**, or challenge, is a difficulty that you must resolve before you can make progress. In any career, you will be faced with problems. Sometimes you will have to confront problems on your own, but often you will be working as part of a team to solve problems. Learning to recognize problems and the steps for solving them will help you advance in school, in your relationships with other people, and in your career.

> **Problem**
>
> An obstacle between you (or your team) and a goal.

There is a five-step process you can use to identify and solve problems. Developing problem-solving skills will help you move forward to achieve your goals:

1. Identify the problem. You must be honest, acknowledge the problem, and determine how it is blocking your ability to progress.
2. Consider all possible solutions. There may be an obvious solution, or there may be many possible solutions. Write down as many as you can think of.
3. Identify the consequences of each solution. Write down how each possible solution might affect you, other people, and other situations. Will it cause more problems? Will it be expensive?
4. Select the best solution. The best solution offers the best possible opportunity for you to move forward and make progress.
5. Evaluate the solution, process, and outcome. After you implement your solution, take the time to look back to see what worked and what did not work.

A key component of problem-solving is the ability to use critical thinking skills to recognize the problem and determine the best solution. **Critical thinking** is when you are honest, rational, and open-minded about a situation while choosing the best course of action. It is when you consider all possible options as well as other points of view. You look at information objectively, which means fairly and without influence.

> **Critical thinking**
>
> The ability to be honest, rational, and open-minded about a situation while choosing the best course of action.

Comprehension Check

1. Why is Premiere Pro considered a nonlinear editor?
2. Describe the basic video-editing workflow.
3. What is the Media Browser used for?
4. Can you save a customized workspace?
5. What is the purpose of the Source Monitor? What is the purpose of the Program Monitor?
6. How can you drag a panel to its own floating panel?
7. List the five steps in the problem-solving process.
8. Explain critical thinking.

Lesson 19 Overview

In this lesson, you will learn about:

- Exploring Video Script Production
- Shooting Video
- Taking Quality Video
- Capturing Video for Editing in Premiere Pro
- Protecting Copyright

With Adobe Premiere Pro you can make professional-looking videos. To do that, you need to start with high-quality raw material. This lesson gives you tips for developing a script, recording great video and audio, and then getting that video and audio into Adobe Premiere Pro.

```
EXT. EAST SIDE HELIPAD - DAY

Jimmy waits, alone. He takes a vial of pills out of his
pocket, opens it and swallows two, dry.

Gillespie and Morrow appear. The three men cross to where
their prisoner, GRIFFIN, waits for them in the custody of two
Riker's Island guards.

                    GILLESPIE
          Sure we can't stick around a couple
          extra days? We could bring them up
          to date on what we've been doing,
          like cultural ambassadors.

Morrow signs the guards' voucher for their prisoner.

                    GUARD ONE
          Thank you, Sir.

The guards take off. Gillespie tries to get a rise out of
Griffin, who stares intently at Jimmy.

                    GILLESPIE
          Comfortable?

                    MORROW
              (re: the pilot)
          He'll shuttle you to JFK. You're
          traveling to China first class.

                    GILLESPIE
              (impressed)
          First class...

                    MORROW
          Hong Kong PD will meet you at
          Beijing and ferry you to the
          island. Once you drop him off,
          you're done. Good luck. See you in
          a few days.

                    JIMMY
              (uncertain)
          Thanks.

                                        CUT TO:
```

Exploring Video Script Production

Screenplay

A script that indicates specifically what the audience will see and hear, specifically what the audience is seeing on screen and hearing on the audio track.

A **screenplay** (or teleplay) is a script, or written version of a show. It indicates what the audience is seeing (what is on screen) and hearing (on the audio track). In other words, it is a list of images that must be recorded and sounds that will accompany them. Because of this, a screenplay reads like the combination of a novel and a technical document like the blueprint of a house.

The Components of a Screenplay

Screenplays are technical documents that should include the following elements:

- Scene heading, which is also called a slugline
- Scene description
- Transition
- Communication

Sluglines

Slugline

A heading in a screenplay that identifies when and where a scene takes place.

Every scene must start with a **slugline**, which is a capitalized heading that provides three key pieces of information: the setting, which is either interior (INT.) or exterior (EXT.), the location, and the time of day. You skip a line before and after each slugline to designate a new scene starting.

Here's an example:

INT. CROWDED SCHOOL HALLWAY – DAY

Scene descriptions

Scene descriptions describe the scene exactly the way the camera shows it to us. Unlike novels, which can take us inside the mind of their characters, it's important in scripts to describe the picture on the screen *visually* and avoid phrases like "Luis and Marco have been best friends for years," using instead, for example, "Luis and Marco give each other a secret handshake," which is something we can see or hear on film.

When you write a screen description, use the present tense, and include only the most important details. Be brief and clear, telling us just what we need to know to get across the necessary information in the scene. Insert a blank line between paragraphs and keep paragraphs to no more than six lines. One rule of thumb is to break each paragraph where you want the camera to cut.

Each time a new character is introduced, type the character name in all uppercase letters. You may also capitalize certain words for emphasis, such as sound effects.

Transitions

Transitions

Instructions in a script that tell the reader how you want to go from scene to scene.

Transitions, or screen breaks, tell the reader *how* you want to go from scene to scene. There should be one at the end of every scene. As with sluglines, you skip a line before and after each transition.

Except for FADE IN: at the front of a script, you place transitions flush right along the right margin of the page so they stand out. They look like this on the page:

```
FADE IN:
CUT TO:
DISSOLVE TO:
FADE TO BLACK.
```

Here are some descriptions of the major transitions and what they are used for:

- CUT TO: means one shot begins exactly where the previous one ends with no overlap of the visuals.
- FADE IN: means a fade from a black screen into the first shot of the movie.
- FADE OUT: (or FADE TO BLACK) is usually the last shot of a film, where the image gradually disappears into the blackness. Fade-ins and outs take us into the story as if we were transporting across dimensions to another world where this narrative is beginning, which involves someone who seems like us. They may also feel as if we are falling asleep into the dream of the show. Occasionally, a show might fade to black and then leave the screen black for a moment before fading up into the EXT. scene. This (along with other elements) may suggest a passage of time, though it would be up to the writer/director to then clarify how much time has passed.
- DISSOLVE TO: is when a shot disappears (fades out) as another shot appears (fades in) and the two shots overlap and occupy the screen together for a moment. This is typically used to connect two images in some way, such as when a singer on the left side of the screen singing a duet dissolves into their partner singing along with them on the other side of the screen and the two characters, apart in "space," are united graphically onscreen and seem to be looking at each other.

  A dissolve can be used for many purposes. Its main attribute is that it is not a cut; it has a different feeling, particularly based on the length of the dissolve, and may require the audience to wonder why the show is going from shot to shot or scene to scene in a different way.
- WIPE TO: is when a line moves across the screen, usually either horizontally, vertically, or diagonally, and it lays one shot down on top of another as it goes.

Communication

The three main types of communication in a screenplay are as follows:

Dialogue: One character speaks to another, several characters speak to each other, or a character addresses a group. Unless your characters can read minds, this will involve synchronization between their words and the image of their mouths.

Narration or voiceover: Either a character from the piece or the omniscient (all-knowing) narrator who is not part of the story speaks directly to the audience without being seen. This is written as follows: JENNY (VO) or JENNY (OC) or JENNY (NARRATION), where OC means off-camera.

Interior monologue: The characters "speak" to themselves. Usually, we hear their thoughts over an image of their face. When you write dialog, you include the speaker's name, written in all uppercase letters, followed by the vocal direction (if the speaker is off screen) in parentheses. The vocal direction might be (VO) for voice over (OS) for off screen. Below the speaker's name, in parentheses, include the personal direction telling the speaker any emotion or physical action that should be attached to the dialog.

Below the personal direction you type the actual dialog.

The following illustration shows a script for a one page scene.

```
EXT. EAST SIDE HELIPAD - DAY

Jimmy waits, alone. He takes a vial of pills out of his
pocket, opens it and swallows two, dry.

Gillespie and Morrow appear. The three men cross to where
their prisoner, GRIFFIN, waits for them in the custody of two
Riker's Island guards.

                    GILLESPIE
          Sure we can't stick around a couple
          extra days? We could bring them up
          to date on what we've been doing,
          like cultural ambassadors.

Morrow signs the guards' voucher for their prisoner.

                    GUARD ONE
          Thank you, Sir.

The guards take off. Gillespie tries to get a rise out of
Griffin, who stares intently at Jimmy.

                    GILLESPIE
          Comfortable?

                    MORROW
              (re: the pilot)
          He'll shuttle you to JFK. You're
          traveling to China first class.

                    GILLESPIE
              (impressed)
          First class...

                    MORROW
          Hong Kong PD will meet you at
          Beijing and ferry you to the
          island. Once you drop him off,
          you're done. Good luck. See you in
          a few days.

                    JIMMY
              (uncertain)
          Thanks.

                                                   CUT TO:
```

Script Breakdowns

When a script is in preproduction, the unit production manager or line producer marks up the script using various colored highlighters to determine exactly what is going to be needed to record every scene. Then, as the scenes are scheduled for shooting, he or she determines when the individual cast, crew, and objects will be required to be on the set to shoot.

As the first assistant director creates a production board and a shooting schedule based on the number of script pages in a particular scene and a certain location, they determine what they need and by when. The line producer and unit production manager attend to the many technical details necessary to be ready to shoot.

Charts of all the required elements for a particular shooting day, called a *script breakdown*, detail everything that is necessary and accountable for each day of shooting.

Often, when it comes to costumes, props, and so forth, line producers will try to get multiples or doubles of whatever they need because things happen, and they need to *be prepared*.

The script breakdown is a complete list of all the categories involved in the production of a particular scene:

- Locations
- Actors
- Background actors (extras)
- Props
- Costumes
- Vehicles
- Stunt performers
- Makeup and hair

In the finished script breakdown, each of these necessary elements has been color-coded and organized by category for each individual scene.

There are software applications such as Movie Magic Scheduling and Jungle Software that allow you to create script breakdowns fairly easily. Not all crews go to the trouble to create script breakdowns. Most prefer simple lists of cast, crew, props, and so on. But there's no denying that your production, however big or small, will run more smoothly if the producer releases, in advance, a complete list of what is required to shoot and when it is needed.

Formatting a Script

Although screenplays are now usually prepared using word-processing software, such as Microsoft Word, they are still formatted the way they were when typewriters were in use. Whether you are writing a script for a 30-second online video or for a full-length feature film, there are formatting specifications you should use:

- Font: 12-point Courier New. This translates to approximately one page for one minute of screen time.
- Page margins: Left: 1.5 inches; Right, Top, and Bottom: 1 inch
- Element positions:
    - The Scene Heading should be 1.5 inches (15 spaces) from the left edge of the page.
    - The Action should be 1.5 inches (15 spaces) from the left edge of the page.
    - The Character's name should be 3.7 inches (37 spaces) from the left edge of the page.

- The Dialogue should be 2.5 inches (25 spaces) from the left edge of the paper and end 2.5 inches (25 spaces) from the right edge of the paper.
- Parentheticals should be 3.1 (31 spaces) from the left edge of the paper and end 2.9 inches (29 spaces) from the right edge of the paper.
- Transitions should be 1 inch (10 spaces) from the right of the page.
- Page numbers should be 1 inch from the edge of the right page.

- Line spacing:
  - Double-space between the SCENE HEADING and ACTION.
  - Double-space between ACTION PARAGRAPHS.
  - Double-space between ACTION and CHARACTER NAME.
  - Single-space between CHARACTER NAME and DIALOUGE.
  - Double-space between DIALOGUE and the next CHARACTER NAME
  - Single-space between CHARACTER NAME and PARENTHETICALS
  - Single-space between PARENTHETICAL and DIALOGUE

If you are submitting your script to a client or producer, include a title page. Type the script title in all uppercase letters and center it vertically and horizontally. Leave a double line space, type the word "by", leave another double line space, and type your name. In the lower right hand corner, right-align your name, mailing address, phone number, and email address.

Examining Tools for Working with Audio and Video

Audio (sound) and video (movies and animations) are essential components of multimedia. You will need these tools to work with multimedia.

- Video camera: Video cameras (also called video recorders) range widely in price and features. You can shoot quality video with a camera that has full manual image control and audio control and XLR audio inputs. Some of the more expensive cameras offer bigger imaging chips and interchangeable lenses.
- Tripod: A tripod is useful for not only recording video but also serves as a handy platform to put your camera on instead of laying it on the ground when you're not recording.
- Microphone(s): On-camera mics (the ones built into the video camera) can be useful for reference but they capture all the sound in the environment and, if you're shooting from a distance, they might not pick up the audio you're hoping to record. There are several types of microphones available. These include handheld mics like those used in public address systems; shotgun mics which are placed on a boom pole to get the mic close to the sound source, while keeping it out of the camera frame; and lavalier microphones, or body mics that are clipped to clothing. If they are not built in, microphones are connected to a camera or audio recorder with cables. The most common cable used in

professional audio recording is a cable that has XLR connectors with three pins at each end. XLR connectors allow for a balanced audio connection and therefore longer-distance runs with less noise in the signal. Lavalier mics can be part of a wireless kit that consists of a transmitter, which stays with the "talent," and a receiver, which is connected to the audio or video recording device.

- Headphones: Over-ear headphones are more suitable than earbuds. Keep in mind that with a good pair of headphones, what you hear will sound good even at low volumes.
- Lights: Even if you're shooting outdoors or in a well-lit indoor location, lighting is important to the quality and ambience of your video. Incandescent and halogen lights are the most commonly used.
- Audio recorder (for recording audio only): Portable digital recorders come in the following formats: solid state, which use flash memory; hard disk drive, which record to an internal or external hard disk; CD, or compact disc, which record to CD-Rs; and direct-to-computer, which requires a computer with a microphone and analog-to-digital converter that sends the signal into the computer via FireWire or a USB connection.
- Sound card: A sound card is a special expansion board that allows the computer to input, edit, and output sounds. Audio—whether voices, music, or sound effects—is entered into the computer through the input jacks on the sound card. Once audio is captured on the computer's hard drive, you can edit and work with it. You can then play it through the computer's speakers or headphones, or save it to a disc. You can also send it to another audio device using the sound card's output jack. Full-featured cards even include optical inputs and outputs for digital sound and special software for mixing sound.
- Video capture board: Video signals, such as those from television programs or movies, have to be converted into a format that computers understand. This is done with a video capture board, a special card that plugs into a computer. You can transfer video to the capture board from video cameras, digital cameras, and other sources.

After video and audio are saved to the computer's hard drive, you can combine them in new ways. You do this work with a video editor program, such as Premiere Pro.

Safety Considerations

When working with audio- and video-recording equipment, keep these safety guidelines in mind:

- If the device feels hot or begins to smoke, discontinue use and turn it off immediately.
- If you're on rough or unstable terrain, use a tripod to avoid moving around and risking a slip or fall.
- Be careful when handling batteries, especially if you notice any leakage.
- Avoid taking the equipment apart and handling any of the electronic components, as they may cause an electrical shock.
- Do not use the equipment underwater unless it is made specifically for that use.
- Do not use the equipment in dangerous or threatening environments, such as fire scenes and severe weather conditions, such as tornadoes and floods.

In addition, you must always be aware of ethical issues when recording audio and video. Some guidelines to consider include the following:

- Respect the privacy of others. Almost always, you should obtain permission and consent from the subjects involved in your recording. When the subject is a public figure, you may not need their permission to record.
- Do not record audio or video that harasses, bullies, or defames another individual.
- Do not portray others in a false or misleading way.
- Be sure to distinguish clearly between what is fact and what is your opinion.
- Adhere to copyright laws. Obtain permission and/or provide attribution for any work you use that was created by another individual.
- Comply with community guidelines posted by video-sharing Web sites.

Taking Quality Video

With your video recorder of choice in hand, it's time to venture out and shoot videos. The better the video segments you capture, the better the completed project will be. Following are some tips for shooting quality video.

Get an Establishing Shot

An establishing shot sets a scene in one image. Although super wide shots work well (aerials in particular), consider other points of view: a shot from the cockpit of a race car, a close-up of a scalpel with light glinting off its surface, or a shot of paddles dipping frantically in roaring white water. Each grabs the viewer's attention and helps tell your story.

Shoot Plenty of Video

Videotape is cheap and expendable, and digital video is limited only by the amount of storage space you have.. Shoot a lot more raw footage than you'll put in your final production. Five times as much is not unusual. Giving yourself that latitude might help you grab shots you would have missed otherwise.

Adhere to the Rule of Thirds for Good Composition

It's called the rule of thirds, but it's more like the rule of four intersecting lines. When composing your shot, think of your viewfinder as being crisscrossed by two horizontal and two vertical lines. The center of interest should fall along those lines or near one of the four intersections, not the center of the image.

Consider all those family photos where the subject's eyes are smack dab in the center of the photo. Those are not examples of good composition.

Another way to follow the rule of thirds is to look around the viewfinder as you shoot, not just stare at its center. Check the edges to see whether you're filling the frame with interesting images. Avoid large areas of blank space.

Keep Your Shots Steady

You want to give viewers the sense they're looking through a window or, better yet, are there with your subjects on location. A shaky camera shatters that illusion. When possible, use a tripod. The best "sticks" have fluid heads that enable you to make smooth pans or tilts.

If it's impractical to use a tripod, try to find some way to stabilize the shot: Lean against a wall, put your elbows on a table, or place the video recorder on a solid object.

Follow the Action

This might seem obvious, but keep your viewfinder on the ball (or sprinter, speeding police car, surfer, conveyor belt, and so on). Your viewers' eyes will want to follow the action, so give them what they want.

One nifty trick is to use directed movement as a pan motivator. That is, follow a leaf's progress as it floats down a stream, and then continue your camera motion past the leaf—panning—and widen out to show something unexpected: a waterfall, a huge industrial complex, or a fisherman.

Use Trucking Shots

Trucking or dolly shots move with the action. For example, hold the camera at arm's length right behind a toddler as she motors around the house, put the camera in a grocery cart as it winds through the aisles, or shoot out the window of a speeding train.

Find Unusual Angles

Getting your camera off your shoulder, away from eye level, leads to more interesting and enjoyable shots. Ground-level shots are great for frolicking lambs or cavorting puppies. Shoot up from a low angle and down from a high angle. Shoot through objects or people while keeping the focus on your subject.

Lean Forward or Backward

The zoom lens can be a crutch. A better way to move in close or away from a subject is simply to lean in or out. For example, start by leaning way in with a tight shot of someone's hands as he works on a wood carving; then, while still recording, lean way back (perhaps widening your zoom lens as well) to reveal that he is working in a sweatshop full of folks hunched over their handiwork.

Get Wide and Tight Shots

Our eyes work like medium-angle lenses. So, we tend to shoot video that way. Instead, grab wide shots and tight shots of your subjects. If practical, get close to your subject to get the tight shot rather than use the zoom lens. Not only does it look better, but the proximity leads to clearer audio.

Note:

Matched action keeps the story flowing smoothly while helping to illustrate a point.

Shoot Matched Action

Consider a shot from behind a pitcher as he throws a fastball. He releases it, and then it smacks into the catcher's glove. Instead of a single shot, grab two shots: a medium shot from behind the pitcher showing the pitch and the ball's flight toward the catcher, and a tight shot of the catcher's glove. It's the same concept for an artist: Get a wide shot of her applying a paint stroke to a canvas, and then move in for a close shot of the same action. You'll edit them together to match the action.

Get Sequences

Shooting repetitive action in a sequence is another way to tell a story, build interest, or create suspense. A bowler wipes his hands on a rosin bag, dries them over a blower, wipes the ball with a towel, picks up the ball, fixes his gaze on the pins, steps forward, swings the ball back, releases it, slides to the foul line, watches the ball's trajectory, and then reacts to the shot.

Instead of simply capturing all this in one long shot, piecing these actions together in a sequence of edits is much more compelling. You can easily combine wide and tight shots, trucking moves, and matched action to turn repetitive material into attention-grabbing sequences.

Avoid Fast Pans and Snap Zooms

Fast pans and zooms fall into MTV and amateur video territory. Few circumstances call for such stomach-churning camera work. In general, it's best to minimize all pans and zooms. As with a shaky camera, they remind viewers they're watching TV.

If you do zoom or pan, do it for a purpose: to reveal something, to follow someone's gaze from his or her eyes to the subject of interest, or to continue the flow of action (as in the floating leaf example earlier). A slow zoom in, with only a minimal change to the focal length, can add drama to a sound bite. Again, do it sparingly.

Shoot Cutaways

Avoid jump cuts by shooting cutaways. A jump cut is an edit that creates a dis- connect in the viewer's mind. A cutaway—literally, a shot that cuts away from the current shot—fixes jump cuts.

Cutaways are common in interviews where you might want to edit together two 10-second sound bites from the same person. Doing so would mean the interviewee would look like he suddenly moved. To avoid that jump cut—that sudden disconcerting shift—you make a cutaway of the interview. That could be a wide shot, a handshot, or a reverse-angle shot of the interviewer over the interviewee's shoulder. You then edit in the cutaway over the juncture of the two sound bites to cover the jump cut.

The same holds true for a soccer game. It can be disconcerting to simply cut from one wide shot of players on the field to another. If you shoot some crowd reactions or the scoreboard, you can use those cutaways to cover up what would have been jump cuts.

Use Lights

Lights add brilliance, dazzle, and depth to otherwise bland and flat scenes. Consider using an onboard camera fill light and, if you have the time, money, patience, or personnel, a full lighting kit with a few colored gels.

In a pinch, do whatever you can to increase available light. Open curtains, turn on all the lights, or bring a couple of desk lamps into the room. Keep in mind one caveat: Low-light situations can be dramatic, and flipping on a few desk lamps can destroy that mood in a moment.

Grab Good Sound Bites

Your narrator presents the facts. The people in your story present the emotions, feelings, and opinions. Don't rely on interview sound bites to tell the who, what, where, when, and how. Let those bites explain the why.

In a corporate backgrounder, have the narrator say what a product does, and let the employees or customers say how enthusiastic they are about that product.

Your narrator should be the one to say, "It was opening night, and this was her first solo." Let the singer, who is recalling this dramatic moment, say, "My throat was tight, and my stomach was tied in knots."

In general, even though your interviews might take forever, use only short sound bites in your final production. Use those bites as punctuation marks, not paragraphs.

Get Plenty of Natural Sound

Think beyond images. Sound is tremendously important. Listen for sounds you can use in your project. Even if the video quality is mediocre, grab that audio.

Your camera's onboard microphone is not much more than a fallback. Consider using additional microphones: shotgun mics to narrow the focus of your sound and avoid extraneous noise, lavalieres tucked out of sight for interviews, and wireless mics when your camera can't be close enough to get just what you need.

Plan Your Shoot

When you consider a video project, plan what you need to shoot to tell the story. Videotaping a soccer championship match, a corporate backgrounder, or a medical procedure each requires planning to ensure success. Know what you want your final video project to say, and think of what you need to videotape to tell that story.

Even the best laid plans and most carefully scripted projects might need some adjusting once you start recording in the field. No matter how you envision the finished project, be willing to make changes as the situation warrants.

Capturing Video for Editing in Premiere Pro

In order to edit video that is not already stored in a file format, you must capture or digitize it. (In some programs, capture is synonymous with ingest.)

Capturing is used with live video or video on tape. Premiere Pro saves captured footage to a storage device as files, and imports the files into projects as clips.

Digitizing is used to convert analog video into a digital form so it can be saved as a file.

All that Adobe Premiere Pro does during digital video (DV) capture is to place the video data in a movie file "wrapper" without changing the original DV data.

The capture process in the analog world takes several steps: transfer, conversion, compression, and wrapping. Your camera transfers the video and audio as analog data to a video capture card. That card's built-in hardware converts the waveform signal to a digital form, compresses it using a codec (compression/decompression) process, and then wraps it in the AVI file format on Windows systems or in the QuickTime format for users working on a Mac.

Three DV-Capturing Scenarios

Premiere Pro offers tools to take some of the manual labor out of the capturing process. Three basic approaches exist:

- Capture your entire videotape as one long clip.
- Log each clip's In and Out points for automated batch capturing.
- Use the scene detection feature in Premiere Pro to automatically create separate clips whenever you press the Pause/Record button on your video camera.

To do this exercise, you will need a DV camcorder. You can work with HDV or with a professional-level camcorder with a Serial Digital Interface (SDI) connector and a specialized video capture card.

Premiere Pro handles HDV and SDI capture with the same kind of software device controls used with a standard DV camcorder. SDI requires an extra setup procedure.

If you have an analog camcorder, you need a video capture card that supports S-Video or composite video connectors. The only option with most analog camcorders is to manually start and stop recording. Most analog capture cards do not work with remote device control or have timecode readout, so you can't log tapes, do batch capture, or use the scene detection feature.

The Shot: Composing for Meaning

The placement of the camera and the type of lens used do a lot to help tell your story. When motion pictures got into the storytelling business at the start of the 20th century, directors just placed actors in front of the camera and had them act. The result was a filmed play, and the camera was mostly used as a recording device.

These days, media creators use the camera in countless ways to add energy to a scene or to comment on the action. Here are some things to think about when deciding where to put your camera.

Shot

Camera angle.

A **shot** here is defined as a camera angle—move the camera or change the lens and you're changing the shot—and it can be defined in many different ways as you will see. Here are some preliminary definitions and categorizations.

Shots Defined by Size

Some shots are defined by width, or the lateral range of subjects or action captured in the frame. Each shot plays a role in the sequence of shots that comprise a scene, is a part of the way one or more subjects are framed, or determines where the director wants the audience's attention focused at a given time

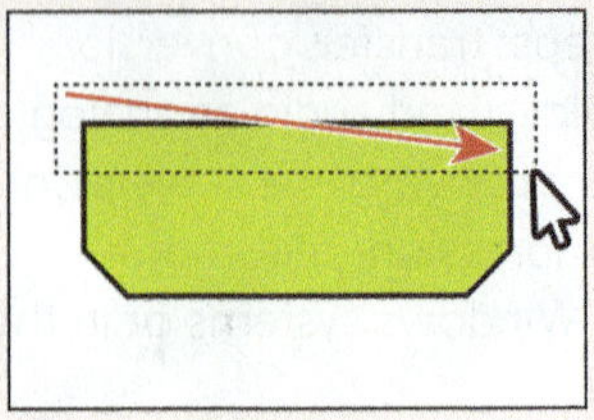

Wide Shot (WS)

A wide shot is a short-lens shot used to establish space, as in a master shot, or a whole location, as in the opening of a film. One of the key things video producers want to do, especially in the beginning of their project, is to establish where it is taking place and then again, once the location changes, to reestablish that.

Full Shot

A full shot gives a full-body view of the subject. The top of the frame is slightly above the subject. The bottom of the frame is just underneath the subject's feet. The shot allows the viewer to see the relationship between the subject and the location of the scene.

3/4 Shot

A 3/4 shot (pronounced "three-quarter") is slightly closer than a full shot. The bottom of the frame cuts off at around the knees. The shot is loose enough to see enough of the subject's full body movement, without bringing attention to the placement of the subject in the surrounding space.

Medium Shot (MED)

A medium shot is a head and upper-body shot, where the bottom of the frame cuts off at around the waist of the subject. It may be considered the workhorse of media creation since many directors use it most commonly to handle dialogue-heavy scenes. More than 50 percent of most films are medium shots.

Medium Close-up (MCU)

A medium close-up is like a medium shot, showing the head and the upper body, yet the bottom of the frame cuts off halfway between the waist and the shoulders.

Close-up (CU)

In a close-up, the face of the character fills the frame, with the bottom of the frame cutting off right below the subject's shoulders. This brings the audience very close to the character in a way that can seem uncomfortable or claustrophobic, which is why it is mostly saved for scenes of emotional importance or to convey suspense.

Extreme Close Up (ECU)

A macro lens is used to magnify something in extreme close-up and make it fill the screen, for example, an ant on someone's skin or a blade of grass. Showing the audience something closer than they would ever typically see it can have a disquieting effect on the audience.

Long Shot (LS)

The main action is far away from the camera in a long shot. This makes the audience look into the shot to figure out what is happening, and it can also be used to contrast a character with their environment.

Two-Shot

The two-shot can be an MS, CU, or WS where two characters speak to each other and both their faces are featured in the shot.

Note:

Before beginning the next section you will need to record some footage on a tape-based video camera (camcorder).

Over-the-Shoulder (OTS)

This is a type of two-shot used frequently for conversations. Over-the-shoulder shots are generally done in pairs, each one focusing on a character on one side of the frame and the listener's shoulder on the other side as if the camera was sitting on it like a parrot on a pirate.

Capturing an Entire Tape

To capture an entire tape, follow these steps.

Try It!

> **Note:**
>
> Windows might note that you've powered up your camera by displaying a Digital Video Device connection message. Mac OS may start a default associated application, such as iMovie.

1. Connect the camcorder to your computer.
2. Turn on your camcorder and set it to playback mode: VTR or VCR. Do not set it to camera mode.

Use AC, Not a Battery

When capturing video, power your camcorder from its AC adapter, not its battery. Here's why: When using a battery, camcorders can go into sleep mode, and the battery will often run out before you're done.

Project Settings for SDI or HDV

This lesson assumes you are recording from a DV camcorder: standard 4:3 format or widescreen anamorphic 16:9 screen ratio. If you are working with SDI or HDV, you need to start Premiere Pro, click New Project, and select the preset project settings that match your camcorder.

Try It!

1. Start Premiere Pro and click New Project. Save the file as **L19_start_xx.prproj** to the location where your teacher instructs you to store your files for this lesson, and leave it open.
2. Connect your camcorder to your computer using the FireWire or USB connector cables that came with the camera.
3. Choose File > Capture to open the Capture panel.
4. Insert a tape into your camcorder. You will be prompted to give the tape a name.
5. Type a name for your tape in the text box. Be sure not to give two tapes the same name; Premiere Pro remembers clip in/out data based on tape names.

> **Note:**
>
> To help you identify buttons, in the Capture panel move the pointer over them to see tool tips.
>
> If you are capturing HDV video, the video is not displayed in the Capture panel as it is being recorded.

6. Use the VCR-style device controls in the Capture panel to play, fast-forward, rewind, pause, and stop your tape. If you have never used a computer to control a camcorder, this will seem pretty cool.
7. Try some of the other VCR-style buttons:
   - Shuttle (the slider toward the bottom) enables you to move slowly or zip quickly—depending on how far you move the slider off center—forward or backward through your tape.
   - Single-frame Jog control (below the shuttle slider)
   - Step Forward and Step Back, one frame at a time
   - Slow Reverse and Slow Play
8. Rewind the tape to its beginning or to wherever you want to start recording.
9. In the Setup area of the Logging tab, note that Audio and Video is the default setting. If you want to capture only audio or only video, change that setting.
10. Click the Tape button in the Capture area of the Logging tab or the Record button in the Capture panel to start recording.

    You'll see (and hear) the video in the Capture panel and on your camcorder. Since there is a slight delay during capture, you'll hear what sounds like an echo. Feel free to turn down the speaker on either your camcorder or your computer.
11. Click the red Record button or the black Stop button when you want to stop recording.

    The Save Captured Clip dialog box appears.
12. Give your clip a name (add descriptive information if you want) and click OK.

    Adobe Premiere Pro stores all the clips you capture in the folder where you save your project.

    You can change the default location by choosing Project > Project Settings > Scratch Disks (Windows) or Premiere Pro > Project > Project Settings > Scratch Disks (Mac).
13. Save the **L19_start_xx.prproj** file and leave it open.

Using Batch Capture and Scene Detection

When you perform a batch capture, you log the In and Out points of a number of clips and then have Premiere Pro automatically transfer them to your computer.

Use the logging process to critically view your raw footage. You want to look for "keeper" video, the best interview sound bites, and any natural sound that will enhance your production.

The purpose of using a batch capture is threefold: to better manage your media assets, to speed up the video capture process, and to save hard disk space (one hour of DV consumes roughly 13 GB). If you batch capture all your clips, you may use the combination of the Premiere Pro project file (which is relatively small) and the MiniDV tapes as a backup of your project. To re-edit the project, simply open the project file and recapture the clips.

Using a Clip-Naming Convention

Think through how you're going to name your clips. You might end up with dozens of clips, and if you don't give them descriptive names, it'll slow down editing.

You might use a naming convention for sound bites such as "Bite-1," "Bite-2," and so forth. Adding a brief descriptive comment, such as "Bite-1 Laugh," will help.

Here are the steps to follow.

Try It!

1. In the Capture panel, click the Logging tab.
2. Change the Handles setting (at the bottom of the Logging tab) to 30 frames.

   This adds 1 second to the start and finish of each captured clip, which will give you enough head and tail frames to add transitions without covering up important elements of the clip.

   When changing the Handles value, you can click the current number and type a new figure, or you can simply position your pointer over the Handles number and drag left or right to lower or raise the value. This method of changing a numeric value works throughout Premiere Pro.

> **Note:**
>
> Handles are extra frames at the beginning and end of a clip. For example, adding 30 frames as handles would add 1 second of video to the start and end of your clips. This can be useful for transitions.

3. In the Clip Data area of the Logging tab, give your tape a unique name.
4. Log your tape by rewinding and then playing it.
5. When you see the start of a segment you want to transfer to your computer, stop the tape, rewind to that spot, and click the Set In button in the Timecode area of the Logging tab.
6. When you get to the end of that segment (you can use Fast Forward or simply Play to get there), click Set Out. The in/out times and the clip length will appear.
7. Click Log Clip to open the Log Clip dialog box.
8. Change the clip name, if needed, and add appropriate notes if you want; then click OK.

   That adds this clip's name with its in/out times and tape name information to the Project panel (with the word "Offline" next to it). You'll go there later to do the actual capture.
9. Log clips for the rest of your tape using the same method.

   Each time you click Log Clip, Premiere Pro automatically adds a number to the end of your previous clip's name. You can accept or override this automated naming feature.
10. When you've finished logging your clips, close the Capture panel.

    All your logged clips will be in the Project panel, with the offline icon next to each.
11. In the Project panel, select all the clips you want to capture.

12. Choose File > Batch Capture.

    A very simple Batch Capture dialog box opens, allowing you to override the camcorder settings or add more handle frames.

13. Leave the Batch Capture options unselected and click OK.

    The Capture panel opens, as does another little dialog box telling you to insert the proper tape (in this case, it's probably still in the camcorder).

14. Insert the tape and click OK.

    Premiere Pro now takes control of your camcorder, cues up the tape to the first clip, and transfers that clip and all other clips to your hard drive.

15. When the process is complete, take a look at your Project panel to see the results. The offline icon is now a movie icon, and your footage is ready to be edited.

16. Save the **L19_start_xx.prproj** file and leave it open.

Using Scene Detection

Instead of manually logging In and Out points, you might want to use the scene detection feature. Scene detection analyzes your tape's time/date stamp, looking for breaks such as those caused when you press the camcorder's Pause button while recording.

When scene detection is on and you perform a capture, Premiere Pro automatically captures a separate file at each scene break it detects. Scene detection works whether you are capturing an entire tape or just a section between specific In and Out points.

To turn on scene detection, do either of the following:

- Click the Scene Detect button (below the Record button in the Capture panel).
- Select the Scene Detect option in the Capture area of the Logging tab.

Then you can either set In and Out points and click Record or cue your tape to wherever you want to start capturing and click Record. In the latter case, click Stop when done.

Your clips will show up in the Project panel. You don't need to batch capture them—Adobe Premiere Pro captures each clip on the fly. Adobe Premiere Pro then names the first captured clip by putting a "01" after the name you put in the Clip Name box and increments the number in each new clip name by one.

Note:

Automatic scene detection isn't available for HDV or HD assets.

Tackling Manual Analog Movie Capture

If you need to transfer analog video—consumer-level VHS, SVHS, Hi-8, or professional-grade video such as Beta SP—you need a video capture card with analog inputs. Most analog capture cards have consumer-quality composite connectors as well as S-Video and sometimes top-of-the-line component connections.

Check your card's documentation for setup and compatibility issues.

With analog video, you have only one capture option—to do it manually.

Try It!

1. Open the Capture panel (File > Capture).

2. Use the controls on the camcorder to move the videotape to a point several seconds before the frame you want to begin capturing.

3. Press the Play button on the camcorder and then click the red Record button in the Capture panel.
4. When your clip has been captured, click the Stop button in the Capture panel and on the camcorder. Your clip will show up in the Project panel.
5. Save the **L19_start_xx.prproj** file and then close it.

Capturing HDV and HD Video

> **Note:**
>
> HDV video is not displayed in the Capture panel while the video is being captured.

You can capture HDV video in the same way as DV video: by connecting the HDV camcorder or deck to your computer via IEEE 1394. When you start a new HDV project, select the appropriate HDV project preset and capture as described for DV video.

HD video requires an SDI card in your computer to connect the coaxial interface from the HD camcorder to your computer. The vendor that supplies the SDI card will typically install additional HD presets into Adobe Premiere Pro as part of its installation.

If you have ventured into tapeless camcorders such as the Panasonic P2 or Sony XDCAMs, the capture process is eliminated altogether.

Project Planning and Management

By now, you've probably realized that creating a digital media project, such as a video, requires a lot of planning, organization, and management. A good manager uses a four-step process to make thoughts and ideas become reality:

1. First, you figure out what needs to be done. You identify the purpose of the project and who it is for, or its audience. This may involve a series of meetings with a client or other stakeholders in which you assess problems that might arise and set goals. Based on the information you gather, you develop a proposal or concept that outlines the scope of the project and identifies the budget, length, and delivery format.
2. Then you develop an action plan with a timeline for completing key parts of the project. You identify and acquire resources, assign responsibilities, and set milestones. You develop the story in the form of a script or screenplay and further define the audience needs. You might flesh out the story in the form of storyboards. You might also need to identify audio needs and requirements.
3. Next, you put the plan into action and execute tasks according to its timeline. You create script breakdowns, if necessary, to detail each task. You monitor the plan to make sure it is going the way you expect. You might even need to make revisions and changes along the way.
4. Finally, you look back to assess and evaluate. Did the plan work the way you expected? Did you achieve your goal? What lessons did you learn?

Comprehension Check

1. What are the basic tools you will need for shooting and capturing a video?
2. Summarize safety procedures you should follow while using digital audio and video equipment.
3. Why are cutaway shots so useful?
4. What does scene detection do when selected?
5. During the capture process, how do you add extra frames to ensure you have enough footage for transitions?

Review Project 1

With a partner, write a script for a video in which a reporter interviews an "expert" on proper ethics in recording and capturing video. Read your script to the class.

Review Project 2

In teams of three to four, plan a video project on a school- or career-related topic. For example, you might create a video on a school club or organization to which you belong, or the steps for researching and planning a career. Use the four-step process discussed in this lesson to plan and manage the project. Create a word processing file in which you document how you will complete each step in the process. Trade documents with another team. Review the other team's plan and provide feedback on how you think it could be improved.

Lesson 20 Overview

In this lesson, you will learn about:

- Creating a Premiere Pro Project File
- Seting Up a Sequence
- Identifing Audio Track Types

Before you begin editing, you need to create a new project and choose some settings for your first sequence. If you're not familiar with video and audio technology, all the options might be a little overwhelming. Luckily, Adobe Premiere Pro gives you easy shortcuts. Plus, the principles of video and sound reproduction are the same no matter what you're creating.

It's just a question of knowing what you want to do. To help you plan and manage your projects, this lesson contains information about formats and video technology. You may decide to revisit this lesson later, as your familiarity with Premiere Pro grows.

In this lesson, you'll learn how to create a new project and choose sequence settings that tell Premiere Pro how to play your video and audio clips.

Creating a Premiere Pro Project File

A Premiere Pro project file stores links to all the video and sound files—aka clips—used in your Premiere Pro project. A project file also has at least one sequence—that is, a series of clips that play, one after another, with special effects, titles, and sound, to form your completed creative work. You'll choose which parts of your clips to use and in which order they'll play. The beauty of editing with Premiere Pro is that you can change your mind about almost anything.

Starting a new Premiere Pro project is simple. You create a new project file, choose a sequence preset, and get on with editing.

The sequence settings control the way Premiere Pro plays your video and audio clips. To speed things up, you can use a built-in preset to choose sequence settings and then make adjustments if you need to.

You need to know the kind of video and audio your camera records, because your sequence settings will usually be based on your original source footage. To make it easier for you to choose the right settings, Premiere Pro sequence presets are named after different camera recording formats. If you know which video format your camera records, you'll know what to choose.

Note:

Premiere Pro project files have the file extension .prproj.

Note:

Many of the terms used in Premiere Pro come from film editing, including the term clip. In traditional film editing, film editors cut a piece of celluloid with a clipper and then put the piece aside for use in the edit.

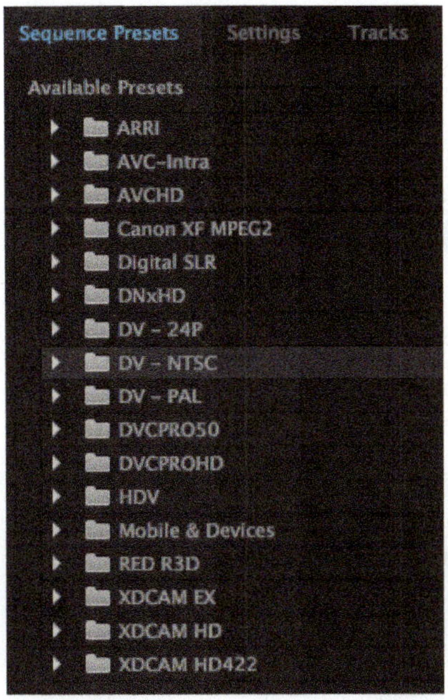

In this lesson, you'll learn how to create a new project and choose sequence settings that tell Premiere Pro how to play your clips. You'll also learn about different kinds of audio tracks, what preview files are, and how to open projects created in Apple Final Cut Pro and Avid Media Composer.

Note:

Presets preselect several settings, saving you time. You can use an existing sequence preset or create a new one for use next time.

Setting Up a Project

Let's begin by creating a new project.

Try It!

1. Launch Premiere Pro. The Welcome screen appears.

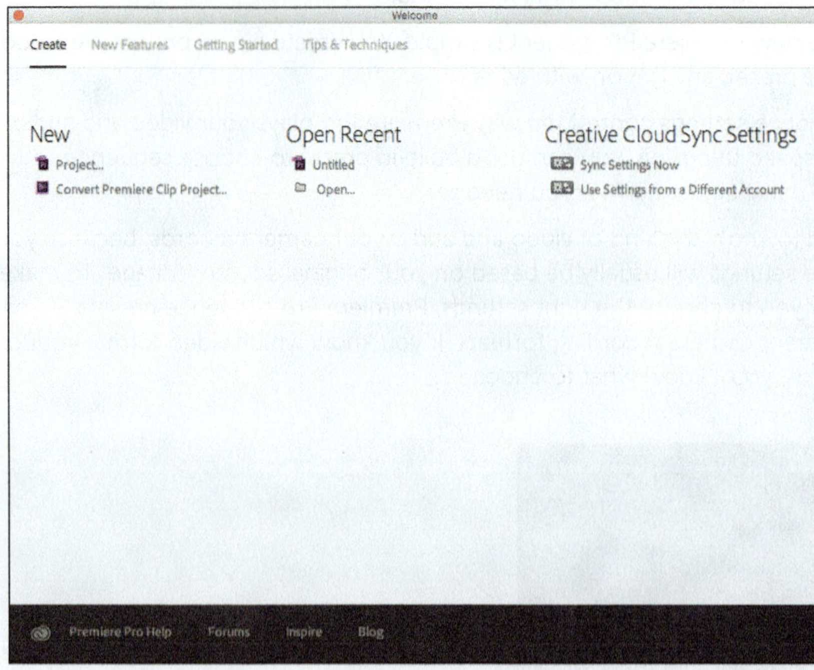

There are several buttons in this window:

- New Project: Opens the New Project dialog.
- Open Recent: Lets you browse to an existing project file and open it to continue working on it.
- Creative Cloud Sync Settings Now: Allows you to synchronize your user preferences with those you store in Creative Cloud. This makes it easy to move from one editing system to another.

2. Click New Project to open the New Project dialog.

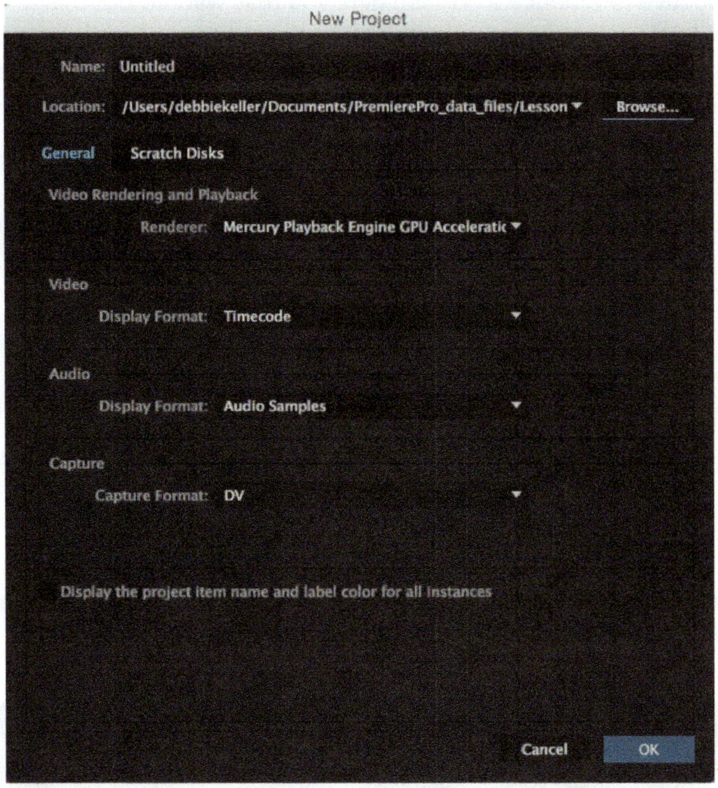

This dialog box has two tabs: General and Scratch Disks. All of the settings in this dialog box can be changed later. In most cases, you'll want to leave them as they are. Let's take a look at what they mean.

Note:

You'll notice that tabbed panels and dialog boxes appear a lot in Premiere Pro. They are a useful way of packing extra options into a smaller space.

Video Display Format

There are four options for Video Display Format. The correct choice for a given project largely depends on whether you are working with video or film as your source material.

When a camera records video, it captures a series of still images of the action. If there are enough images captured each second, it looks like moving video when played back. Each picture is called a frame, and the number of frames each second is usually called frames per second (fps).

The fps will vary depending on your camera/video format and settings. It could be any number, including 23.976, 24, 25, 29.97, 50, or 59.94 fps. Some cameras allow you to choose between more than one frame rate, with different options for accompanying frame sizes.

The choices are as follows:

- **Timecode:** This is the default option. Timecode is a universal standard for counting hours, minutes, seconds, and individual frames of video. The same system is used by cameras, professional video recorders, and nonlinear editing systems all around the world.

- **Feet + Frames 16mm or Feet + Frames 35mm:** If your source files are captured from film and you intend to give your editing decisions to a lab so they can cut the original negative to produce a finished film, you may want to use this standard method of measuring time. Rather than measuring time, this is the number of feet plus the number of frames since the last foot. It's a bit like feet and inches but with frames rather than inches. Because 16mm film and 35mm film have different frame sizes (and so different numbers of frames per foot), there's an option for each.
- **Frames:** This option simply counts the number of frames of video, starting at 0. This is sometimes used for animation projects and is another way that labs like to receive information about edits for film-based projects. For this exercise, leave Video Display Format set to Timecode.

Project Files Settings

In addition to choosing where new media files are created, Premiere Pro also allows you to choose the location for storing Auto Save files. These are additional copies of your project file that are created automatically while you work.

If you need to go back to an earlier version of your project, you can open one of these additional copies. If you store your Auto Save files in a different location than your project file, they serve as a useful backup in case of system failure.

For this project, we recommend you leave all your scratch disks set to the default option: Same as Project.

Try It!

1. Click in the Name box and name your new project **L20_start__xx**.
2. Click the Browse button; then choose the location where your teacher instructs you to store the files for this lesson, and leave it open.
3. If your project is set up correctly, the General and Scratch Disks tabs in your New Project window should look identical to the screens shown here. If the settings match, click OK to create the project file. If not, go back and make the necessary changes and then click OK.

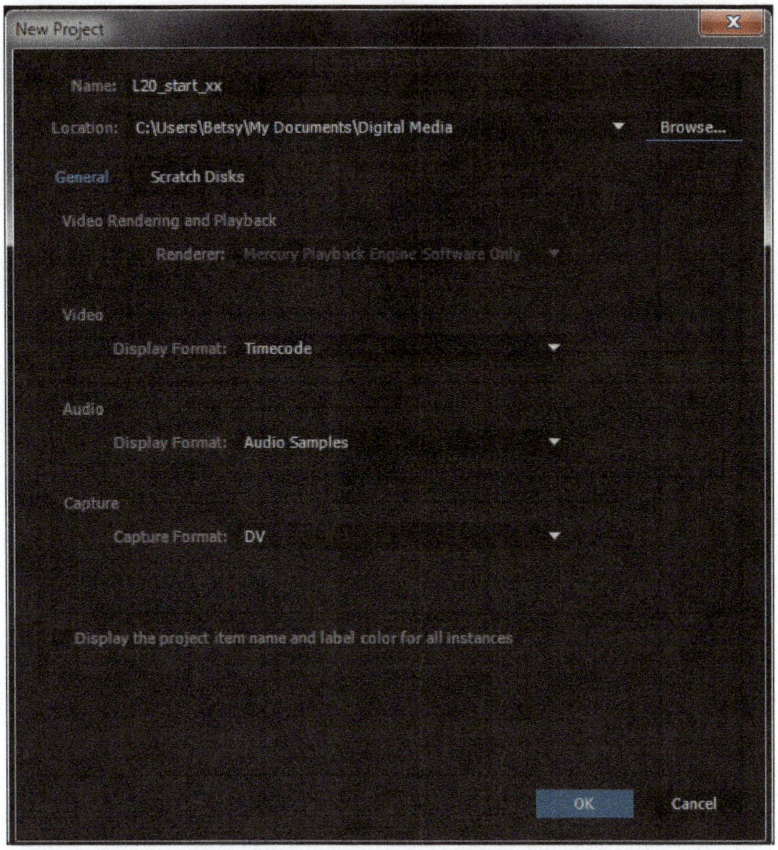
New Project
Name: L20_start_xx
Location: C:\Users\Betsy\My Documents\Digital Media
Browse...
General
Scratch Disks
Video Rendering and Playback
Renderer: Mercury Playback Engine Software Only
Video
Display Format: Timecode
Audio
Display Format: Audio Samples
Capture
Capture Format: DV
Display the project item name and label color for all instances
OK
Cancel

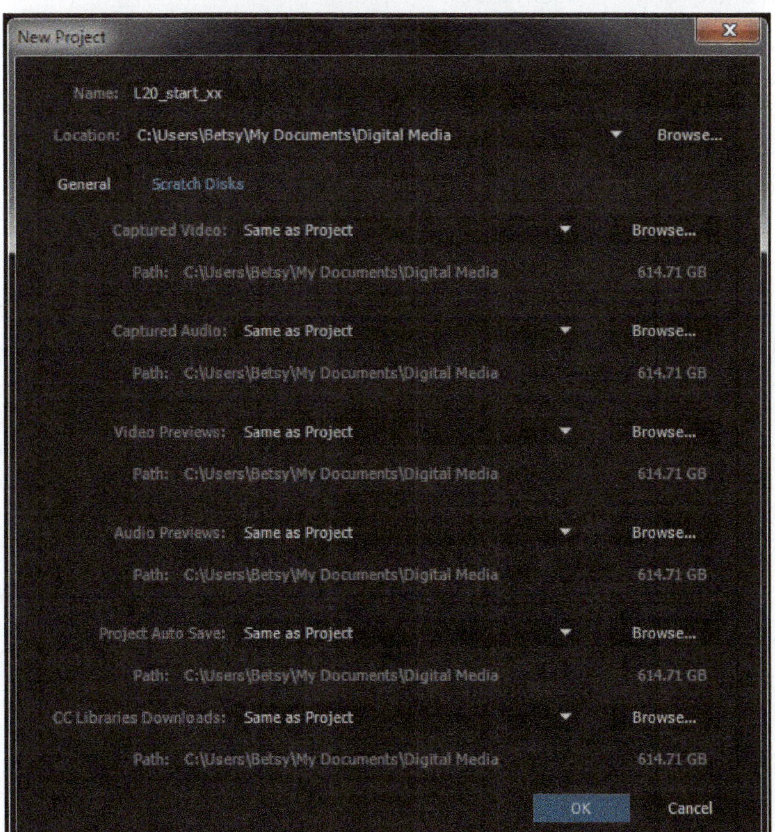
New Project
Name: L20_start_xx
Location: C:\Users\Betsy\My Documents\Digital Media
Browse...
General
Scratch Disks
Captured Video: Same as Project
Browse...
Path: C:\Users\Betsy\My Documents\Digital Media
614.71 GB
Captured Audio: Same as Project
Browse...
Path: C:\Users\Betsy\My Documents\Digital Media
614.71 GB
Video Previews: Same as Project
Browse...
Path: C:\Users\Betsy\My Documents\Digital Media
614.71 GB
Audio Previews: Same as Project
Browse...
Path: C:\Users\Betsy\My Documents\Digital Media
614.71 GB
Project Auto Save: Same as Project
Browse...
Path: C:\Users\Betsy\My Documents\Digital Media
614.71 GB
CC Libraries Downloads: Same as Project
Browse...
Path: C:\Users\Betsy\My Documents\Digital Media
614.71 GB
OK
Cancel

Careers in the Audio/Video Technology Pathway

The audio/video technology pathway in the Arts, Audio/Video Technology, and Communications career cluster prepares you for careers in fields that manufacture, sell, rent, design, install, integrate, operate, and repair the equipment of audio-visual communications. It includes the presentation of sound, video and data in such venues as offices, convention centers, classrooms, theme parks, and stadiums, as well as workers who edit film and video.

Some typical job titles include motion picture projectionists, film and video editors, sound engineering technicians, and audio and video equipment technicians.

Education requirements vary depending on the position. For example, projectionists may only need a high school diploma or GED while film and video editors require a four-year bachelor's degree in a related field. According to the Bureau of Labor Statistics, the annual median salary for broadcast and sound engineers is about $41,000. For film and video editors, it is about $57,000.

It is possible to earn certifications for some careers in this pathway. For example, Adobe offers certifications for showing profiency with its video editing software. Avid Technology, Inc. offers certification for showing proficiency with its non-linear digital editing system. Some industry associations also offer certifications, including the Society of Broadcast Engineers, the National Institute for Certification in Engineering Technologies, and the International Association of Lighting Management Companies.

The job outlook in this pathway is very strong. According to the Bureau of Labor Statistics, employment of audio/video technology workers is expected to grow by up to 35% through 2020.

Setting Up a Sequence

In your Premiere Pro projects you will create sequences, into which you'll place video clips, audio clips, and graphics. If necessary, Premiere Pro adapts video and audio clips that you put into a sequence so they match the settings for that sequence. Each sequence in your project can have different settings, and you'll want to choose settings that match your original media as precisely as possible. Doing so reduces the work your system must do to play back your clips, improves real-time performance, and maximizes quality.

Note:

If the first clip you add to a sequence does not match the playback settings of your sequence, Premiere Pro asks if you would like to change the sequence settings automatically to fit.

If you're editing a mixed-media format project, you may have to make careful choices about which format to match with your sequence settings. You can mix formats easily but playback performance is best when the sequence settings match.

Creating a Sequence that Automatically Matches Your Source

If you're not sure what sequence settings you should choose, don't worry. Premiere Pro has a special shortcut to create a sequence based on your original media.

At the bottom of the Project panel, there is a New Item menu. You can use this menu to create new items, such as sequences and titles.

To automatically create a sequence that matches your media, drag and drop any clip (or multiple clips) in the Project panel onto this New Item menu button. Premiere Pro creates a new sequence with the same name as the clip and a matching frame size and frame rate. Now you're ready to start editing, and you can be confident your sequence settings will work with your media.

If the Timeline panel is empty, you also can drag a clip (or multiple clips) into it to create a sequence automatically.

Choosing the Correct Preset

Premiere Pro can play back and work with a very wide range of video and audio formats and will often play back mismatched formats smoothly.

However, when Premiere Pro has to adjust video for playback because of mismatched sequence settings, your editing system must work harder to play the video, and this will impact real-time performance. It's worth taking the time before you start editing to make sure you have sequence settings that closely match your original media files.

The essential factors are always the same: The number of frames per second, the frame size (the number of pixels in the picture), and the audio format. If you turn your sequence into a file, then the frame rate, frame size, and audio format will match the settings you choose here. When you output to a file, you can choose to convert your sequence to any format you like.

If you know exactly which settings you need, Premiere Pro gives you access to all the options to configure a sequence. If you're not so sure, you can choose from a list of presets.

Click the New Item menu button on the Project panel, and choose Sequence.

The New Sequence dialog box has three tabs: Sequence Presets, Settings, and Tracks. We'll start with Sequence Presets.

The Sequence Presets tab makes setting up a new sequence much easier. When you choose a preset, Premiere Pro chooses settings for your sequence that closely match a particular video and audio format. After choosing a preset, you can tweak these settings on the Settings tab.

You'll find a wide range of preset configuration options for the most commonly used and supported media types. These settings are organized based on camera formats (with specific settings inside a folder named after the recording format).

Click the disclosure triangle to see specific settings in a group. These settings are typically designed around frame rates and frame sizes. Let's look at an example.

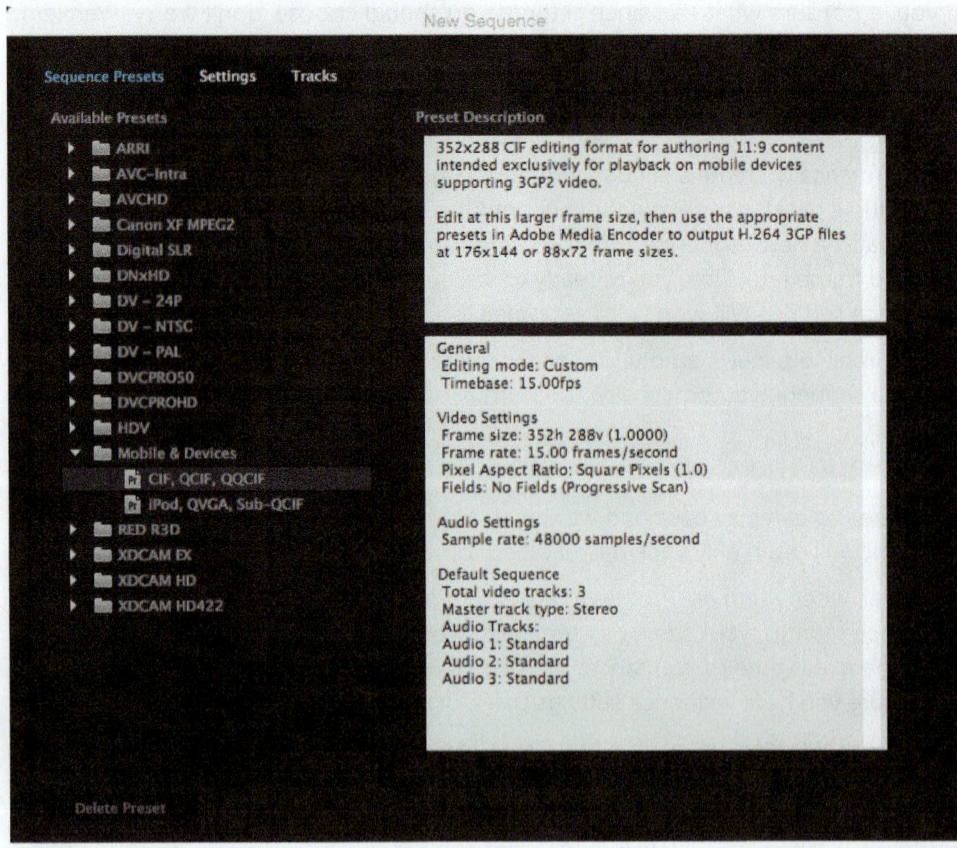

The Sequence Presets tab makes setting up a new sequence much easier. When you choose a preset, Premiere Pro chooses settings for your sequence that closely match a particular video and audio format. After choosing a preset, you can tweak these settings on the Settings tab.

You'll find a wide range of preset configuration options for the most commonly used and supported media types. These settings are organized based on camera formats (with specific settings inside a folder named after the recording format).

Click the disclosure triangle to see specific settings in a group. These settings are typically designed around frame rates and frame sizes. Let's look at an example.

Try It!

1. Click the New Item button in the Project panel and select Sequence.
2. Click the disclosure triangle next to the group AVCHD.

   You can now see three subfolders, based on frame sizes and interlacing methods. Remember that video cameras can often shoot video using resolutions of HD, as well as different frame rates and recording methods. The media used for the next exercise will be AVCHD at 720p and a frame rate of 25fps.

3. Click the disclosure triangle next to the 720p subgroup.

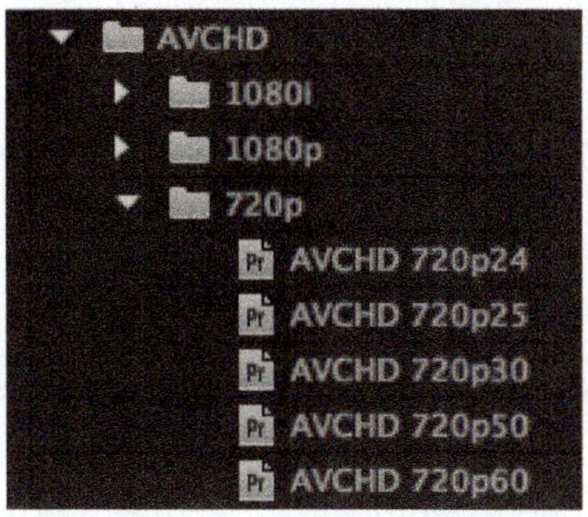

4. To best match the footage we'll be using, choose the AVCHD 720p25 preset by clicking its name. Click OK.

5. Save the **L20_start_xx.prprog** file and close the project file.

Capture Format Settings

It's most common to record video as data files you can work with immediately. However, if you're working with archival material, you might need to capture from videotape.

The Capture Format settings menu tells Premiere Pro what tape format you are using when capturing video to your hard drive through your computer's FireWire port.

DV and HDV Capture

Premiere Pro can capture from DV and HDV cameras using the FireWire connection on your computer, if it has one. FireWire is also known as IEEE 1394 and i.LINK.

FireWire is a convenient connection for tape-based media because it uses one cable to transmit video and sound, device control (so your computer can tell the video deck to play, fast-forward, pause, and so on), and timecode information.

Third-party Hardware Capture

Not all video decks use a FireWire connection, so you may need additional third-party hardware installed to be able to connect your video deck for capture.

If you have additional hardware, you should follow the directions provided by the manufacturer to install it. Most likely you'll install software supplied with your hardware, and this will discover that Premiere Pro is installed on your computer, automatically adding extra options to this menu and other menus.

Follow the directions provided with your third-party equipment to configure new Premiere Pro projects.

For more information about video capture hardware and video formats supported by Premiere Pro, visit www.adobe.com/products/premiere/extend.html.

Ignore this setting for now because we will not be capturing.

Identifying Audio Track Types

Track

A layer in a video editing program where video or audio clips are placed.

When you add a video or audio clip to a sequence, you'll put it on a **track**. Tracks are horizontal areas in the sequence that hold clips in a particular position in time. If you have more than one video track, any video clips placed on an upper track will appear in front of clips on a lower track. For example, if you have text or a graphic on your second video track and a video clip on your first video track, you'll see the text or graphic in front of the video.

The Tracks tab of the New Sequence dialog allows you to preselect the track types for the new sequence.

All audio tracks are played at the same time, creating a complete audio mix. To create the mix, position your audio clips on different tracks, lined up in time. Narration, sound bites, sound effects, and music can be organized by putting them on different tracks. You can easily rename tracks, making it easier to find your way around your sequence. Premiere Pro lets you specify how many video and audio tracks will be added when the sequence is created. You can add and remove audio or video tracks later, but you can't change your Audio Master setting.

You can choose from several audio track types. Each track type is designed for specific types of audio. When you choose a particular track type, Premiere Pro gives you the right controls to make adjustments to the sound, based on the number of audio channels. For example, Stereo clips need different controls than 5.1 Surround clips. When you add a clip to a sequence that has both video and audio, Premiere Pro makes sure the audio part goes to the right kind of track. You can't accidentally put an audio clip on the wrong kind of track; Premiere Pro will automatically create the right kind of track if one doesn't exist.

Audio Tracks

Audio tracks are the horizontal areas where you'll put your audio clips. The types of audio tracks available in Premiere Pro are as follows:

- **Standard:** These tracks are for both mono and stereo audio clips.
- **5.1:** These tracks are for audio clips with 5.1 audio (the kind used for surround sound mixes).
- **Adaptive:** Adaptive tracks are for both mono and stereo audio, and give you precise control over the output routing for each audio channel. For example, you could decide the track audio channel 3 should be output to your mix in channel 5. This workflow is commonly used for multilingual broadcast TV.
- **Mono:** This track type will accept only mono audio clips.

Protecting Copyright

Copyright

A series of rights that the creator of any piece of media automatically has in regard to that media.

Recall that when you use someone else's work without permission, you are violating copyright law. As a media creator, you are also protected by copyright laws. If you see the little © symbol to the right of an image it has as much power as the S on Superman's chest. **Copyright** is one of the single most important concepts for the novice media creator to grasp. It actually refers to a series of rights that the creator of any piece of media automatically has in regard to that media, including the following:

- The right to produce or reproduce the copyrighted work
- The right to prepare derivative works based upon the work
- The right to distribute copies of the work to the public
- The right to perform a copyrighted work publicly
- The right to display the copyrighted work publicly

This means that if you write, compose, or design something, you are the one who has the right to exploit that work commercially and to make money from its reproduction. Naturally, if someone disputed your copyright claim and it came down to a lawsuit, the hearing board would try to determine which parts of your work are both original and yours.

The U.S. Copyright Act of 1976 (and a few pieces of legislation since) clarifies the protections that are guaranteed to the owner of a copyrighted work. Technically, you own the copyright to anything you create from the moment you write it, as long as you're not infringing on the copyright of someone else.

However, to protect your copyright or to simply clarify that you are the one who created the work, it may be worthwhile for you to register your work with the U.S. Copyright Office. You simply send them a copy of your completed work along with their fee, which depends on what type of work it is, and they will protect it.

It would naturally help, of course, if you were ever to bring a lawsuit for infringement against another party for violating your copyrighted work, to have a copy of your work on file with the U.S. Copyright Office.

Additionally, the Writers' Guild of America (WGA), an organization that protects the rights of writers, will register your script as a sort of protective backup to the copyright office. As a professional writer, when you try to sell your script, a lot of potential buyers may see it over a short period of time, so you may want it to be as protected as it can be.

Certain types of work like TV shows, films, screenplays, songs, paintings, and computer software are protected by copyright. Certain designs would be considered trademarks rather than original artwork but would then be protected by trademark law. A *trademark* is another type of intellectual property—a symbol, sign, or expression that is associated with a commercial product or a corporate entity.

Other original work like fashion designs can be copyright-protected; however, the original aspects of certain types of work sometimes need to be challenged in a court for some larger determination to be made about what is truly original.

Comprehension Check

1. What is the purpose of the Settings tab in the New Sequence dialog?
2. How should you choose a sequence preset?
3. What is timecode?

4. What options are available inside Premiere Pro to capture video from tape with no additional third-party hardware?

5. Name four different types of audio clips.

Review Project

Working with a partner, select a career in the Web and Digital Communications pathway. Conduct research to learn details about the selected career, including educational requirements, job outlook, and the types of companies that hire such workers. When your research is complete, write a script for a video that demonstrates a job interview for the selected career. Read your script to the class and listen to their scripts. Evaluate the scripts for content and effectiveness.

Lesson 21 Overview

In this lesson, you will learn about:

- Importing Assets
- Using a Tapeless Workflow
- Finding Assets with the Media Browser
- Importing Images
- Recording a Scratch Narration Track
- Exploring Laws Regarding the Use of Technology

To edit your video assets, you need to import media files into your project. This might include video footage, animation files, narration, music, atmospheric sound, graphics, or photos. Everything you include in a sequence must be imported before it can be used.

Because Adobe Premiere Pro can work with so many types of assets, it offers multiple methods for browsing and importing media.

In this lesson, you'll learn to import media assets into Premiere Pro CC. For most files, you'll use the Adobe Media Browser, a robust asset browser that works with all the media types you may need to import into Premiere Pro. You'll also learn about special cases such as importing graphics.

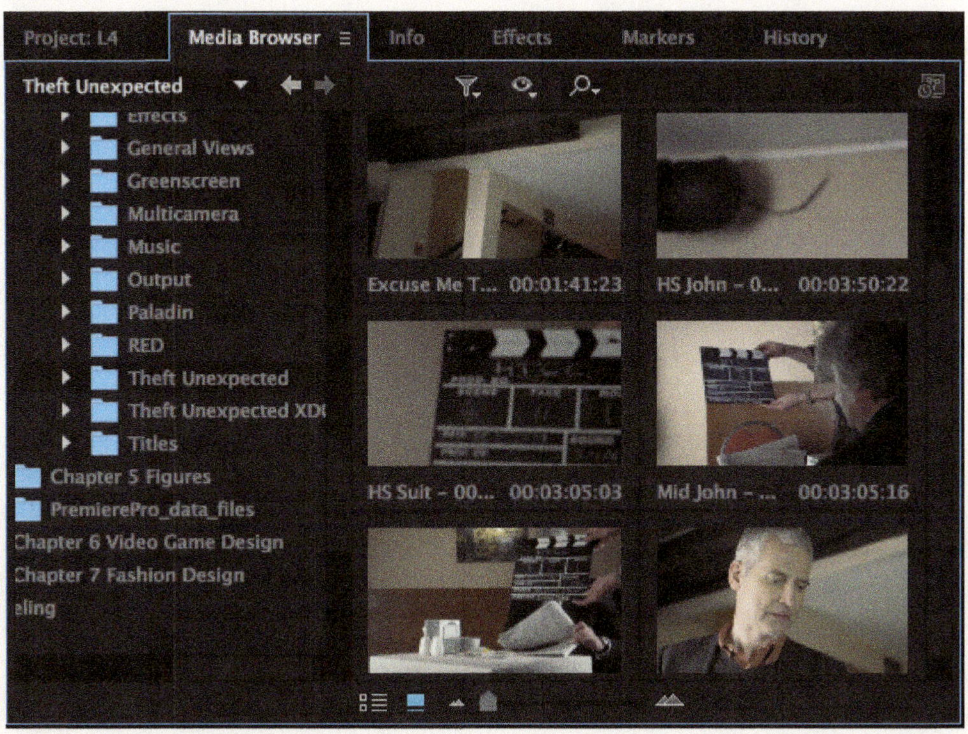

Importing Assets

When you import items into a Premiere Pro project, you are creating a link from the original media file to a pointer that lives inside your project. This means you are not actually modifying the original files; you're just manipulating them in a nondestructive manner. For example, if you choose to edit only part of a clip into your sequence, you're not deleting the unused media.

You'll import media into Premiere Pro in two principal ways:

- Standard importing by choosing File > Import
- Using the Media Browser panel

Let's explore the benefits of each.

When to Use the Import Command

Note:

Another way to open the Import dialog box is to simply double-click an empty area of the Project panel.

Using the Import command is straightforward (and may match what you're used to from other applications). To import any file, just choose File > Import.

You can also use the keyboard shortcut Control+I (Windows) or Command+I (Mac) to open the standard Import dialog box.

This method works best for self-contained assets such as graphics and audio, especially if you know exactly where those assets are stored and you want to quickly navigate to them. This importing method is not ideal for file-based camera footage, which often uses complex folder structures with separate files for audio, video, and important additional data. For camera-originated media, you'll instead use the Media Browser.

When to Use the Media Browser

The Media Browser is a robust tool for reviewing your media assets and then importing them into Premiere Pro. The Media Browser shows the fragmented files you might get from a digital video camera as whole clips; you'll see each recording as a single clip, with the video and audio combined, regardless of the recording format.

This means you can avoid dealing with complex camera folder structures and instead work with easy-to-browse icons and metadata. Being able to see this metadata (which contains important information, such as clip duration, recording date, and file type) makes it easier to select the correct clip from a long list.

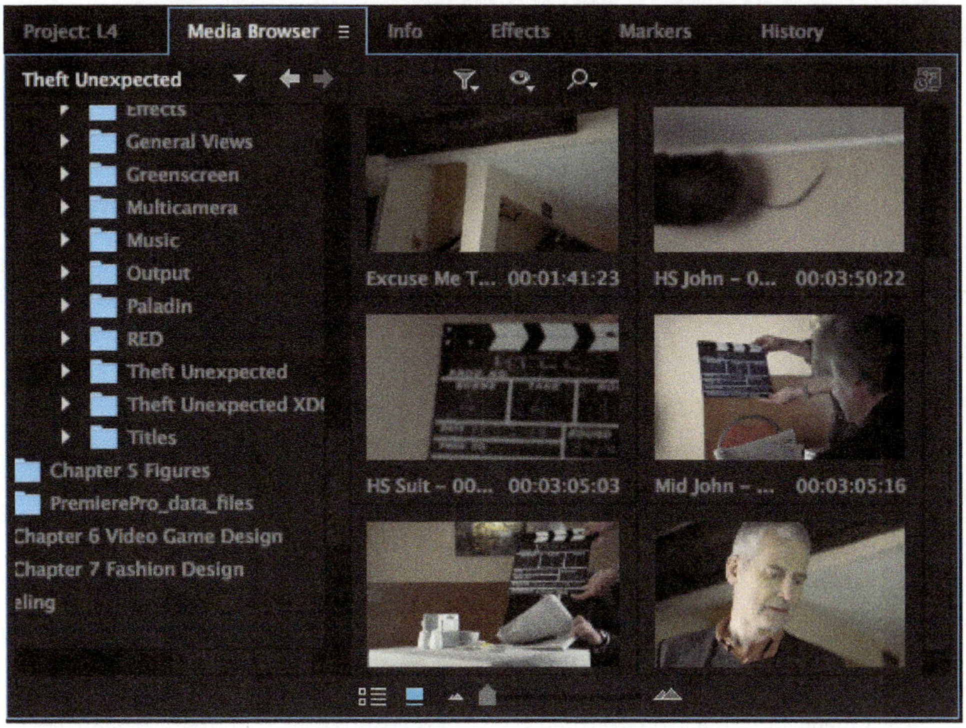

By default, you'll find the Media Browser in the lower-left corner of your Premiere Pro workspace (if your workspace is set to Editing). It's docked in the same frame as the Project panel. You can also quickly access the Media Browser by pressing Shift+8.

You can position the Media Browser elsewhere onscreen by dragging it, or you can undock it and make it a floating panel by clicking the panel menu in the upper-right corner and choosing Undock Panel.

You'll find that working in the Media Browser is not significantly different from browsing using your computer's file management program. There are a series of navigation folders on the left side and buttons to navigate forward and backward at the top. You can use the Up Arrow and Down Arrow keys to select items within a list and the Left Arrow and Right Arrow keys to move further along a file directory path (such as stepping into a folder to examine its contents).

The major benefits of the Media Browser include the following:

- Narrowing the display to a specific file type, such as JPEG, Photoshop, XML, or AAF.
- Autosensing camera data—AVCHD, Canon XF, P2, RED, ARRIRAW, Sony HDV, or XDCAM (EX and HD)—to correctly display the clips.
- Viewing and customizing the kinds of metadata to display.
- Correctly displaying media that has spanned clips across multiple camera media cards. This is common in professional cameras, and Premiere Pro will import the files as a single clip even if a longer video file filled one card and continued on a second one.

Note:

If you need to use assets from another Premiere Pro project, you can import that project into your current one. Just use the Media Browser to locate it; once you double-click a project, Premiere Pro will reveal all of its assets and its bin structure. You can then navigate through it to select individual clips and sequences or drag the whole project into your current project.

Using a Tapeless Workflow

> **Tapeless workflow**
>
> Also known as a file-based workflow, the process of importing video from a tapeless camera, editing it, and exporting it.

A **tapeless workflow** (also known as a file-based workflow) is simply the process of importing video from a tapeless camera, editing it, and exporting it. Premiere Pro CC makes this especially easy because it does not require the media from these tapeless formats to be converted before editing. Premiere Pro can edit tapeless formats (such as P2, XDCAM, AVCHD, and even formats from DSLRs that shoot video) natively with no conversion.

For best results when working with your own camera media, follow these guidelines:

- Create a new folder for each project.
- Copy the camera media to your editing hard drive with the existing folder structure intact. Be sure to transfer the complete data folder directly from the root directory of the card. For best results, you can use the transfer application that is often included by the camera manufacturer for moving your video clips. Visually inspect it to ensure that all media files have been copied and that the card and new copied folder sizes match.
- Clearly label the copied folder of the media with the camera information, including card number and date of shoot.
- Create a second copy of the cards on a physically separate, second drive.
- Ideally, create a long-term archive using another backup method, such as Blu-ray disc, LTO tape, and so on.

Finding Assets with the Media Browser

Using the Media Browser is an easy way to locate and import assets in Premiere Pro.

Try It!

1. Open Premiere Pro, and open **L21_start.prproj** from the data files for this lesson.
2. Choose File > Save As.
3. Rename the file **L21_start_xx.prproj,** save it in the location where your teacher instructs you to store the files for this lesson, and leave it open.

4. Choose Window > Workspace > Editing. Then choose Window > Workspace > Reset Current Workspace, and click Yes.

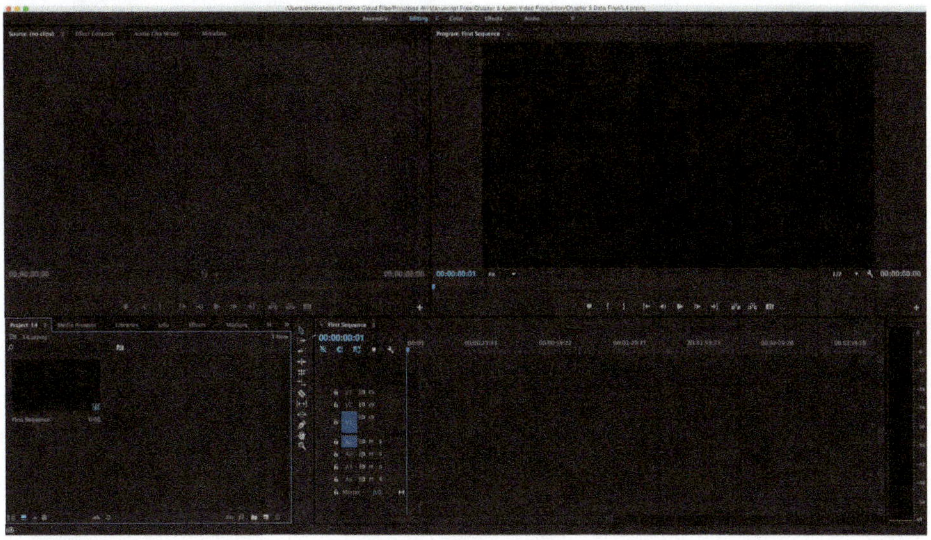

5. Click the Media Browser (it should be docked with the Project panel by default). Make it larger by dragging its right edge to the right.

6. To make the Media Browser easier to see, place your mouse pointer over the panel and then press the ` (grave) key (it is often in the upper-left corner of a keyboard).

   The Media Browser panel should now fill the screen. You may need to adjust the width of columns to make it easier to see items.

7. Using the Media Browser, navigate to the folder for the data files for this chapter. You will see individual lesson files as well as a series of folders.. You can open each folder by double-clicking. Double-click the Theft Unexpected folder.

8. Drag the resize slider in the lower-left corner of the Media Browser to enlarge the thumbnails of the clips. You can use any size you like.

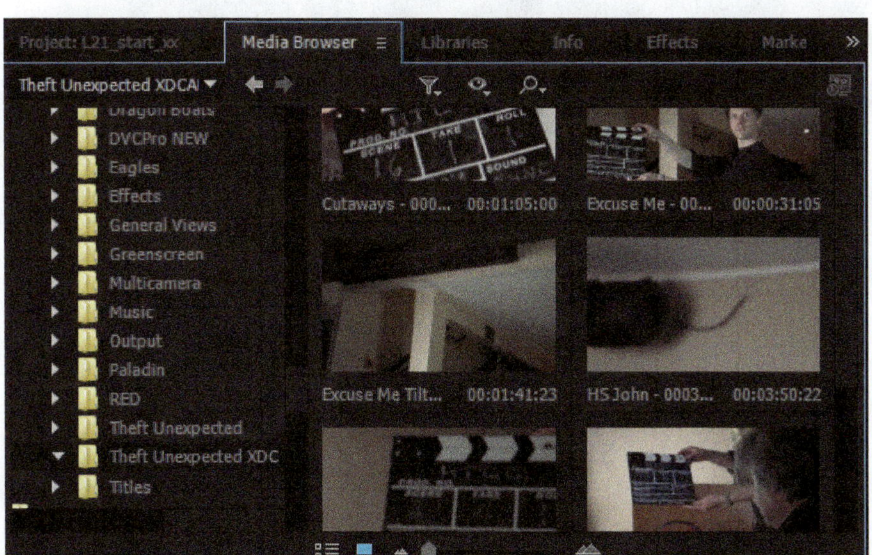

9. Click the Theft Unexpected folder, and then click any clip in the folder to select it.

   You can now preview the clip using keyboard shortcuts.

10. Press the L key to play a clip.

11. To stop playback, press the K key.

12. To play backwards, press the J key.

13. Experiment with playing back other clips. If the volume of your computer is turned up, you should be able to hear the audio playback clearly.

    You can press the J or L keys multiple times to increase the playback rate for fast previews. Use the K key or the spacebar to pause.

14. Now you'll import all of these clips into your project. Press Control+A (Windows) or Command+A (Mac) to select all of the clips.

15. Right-click one of the selected clips and choose Import.

Alternatively, you can drag all of the selected clips onto the Project panel's tab and then down into the empty area to import the clips.

16. Press the ` (grave) key to restore the Media Browser to its original size. Then switch to the Project panel.
17. Click File > Import. Navigate to the data files for this chapter, select the Stills folder, and then click Import Folder.
18. Save the file and leave it open.

Importing Images

A multimedia project includes graphics as well as sound and video (and may also include animation). Graphics have become an integral part of the modern video edit. People expect graphics to both convey information and add to the visual style of a final edit. Fortunately, Premiere Pro can import just about any image and graphic file type. Support is especially excellent when you use the native file formats created by Adobe's leading graphic tools, Adobe Photoshop and Adobe Illustrator.

Note:

Filter the assets you're looking for by using the Files of Type menu in the Media Browser.

The Media Browser filters out non-media files, making it easier to browse for video or audio assets.

Importing Flattened Adobe Photoshop Files

Anyone who works with print graphics or does photo retouching has probably used Adobe Photoshop. It's the workhorse of the graphic design industry. Adobe Photoshop is a powerful tool with great depth and versatility, and it's becoming an increasingly important part of the video production world. Let's explore how to properly import two files from Adobe Photoshop.

To start, you'll import a basic Adobe Photoshop graphic.

Try It!

1. Click the Project panel to select it.
2. Choose File > Import, or press Control+I (Windows) or Command+I (Mac).
3. Navigate to the data files for this lesson.
4. Select the file **Theft_Unexpected.psd**, (it may be stored in a folder named Graphics), and click Open.

   The graphic is a simple logo file and imports into the Premiere Pro project.
5. Save the file and leave it open.

Importing Layered Adobe Photoshop Files

Adobe Photoshop can also create graphics using multiple layers. Layers are similar to tracks in your Timeline and allow for separation between elements. You can import Photoshop layers into Premiere Pro individually to allow for isolation or animation.

Try It!

1. Double-click an empty area of the Project panel to open the Import dialog box.
2. Navigate to the data files for this lesson.
3. Select the file **Theft_Unexpected_Layered.psd**, (again, it may be stored in a folder named Graphics) and click Import.
4. A new dialog box opens, giving you a choice of how to interpret the layered file. There are four ways to import the file, controlled by a pop-up menu in the Import Layered File dialog box:

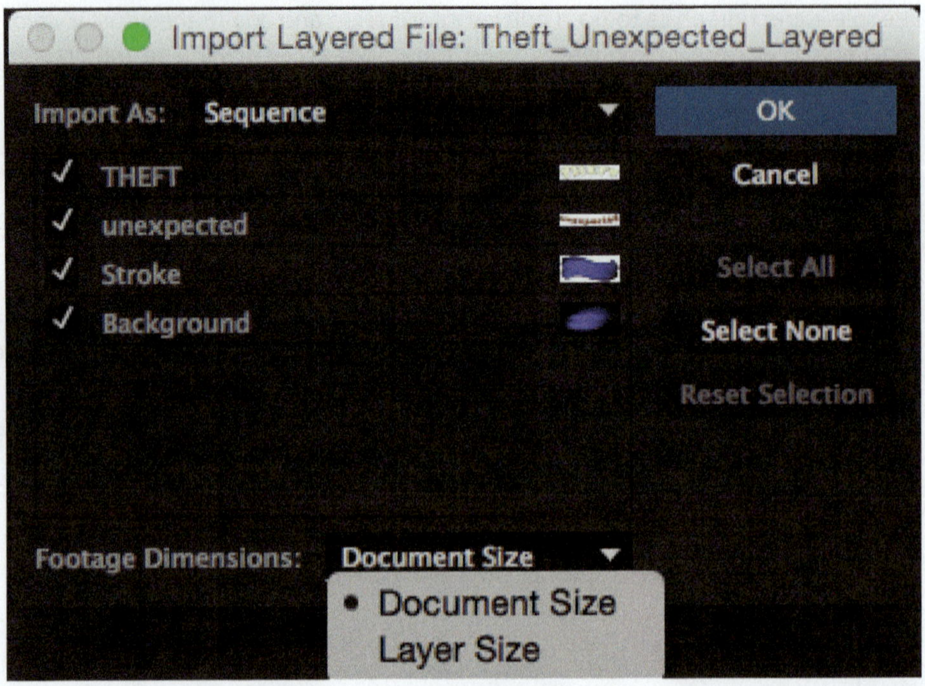

- **Merge All Layers:** Merges all layers, importing the file into Premiere Pro as a single, flattened clip.
- **Merged Layers:** Merges only the layers you select into a single, flattened clip.
- **Individual Layers:** Imports only the layers you select, with each layer becoming a separate clip in a bin.
- **Sequence:** Imports only the layers you select, each as a single clip. Premiere Pro also then creates a new sequence (with its frame size based on the imported document) containing each layer on a separate track (that matches the original stacking order).

  Choosing Sequence or Individual Layers allows you to select one of the following options from the Footage Dimensions menu:

- **Document Size:** Brings the selected layer in at the size of the original Photoshop document.

- **Layer Size:** Matches the frame size of the clips to the frame size of their content in the original Photoshop file. Layers that do not fill the entire canvas will be cropped tightly, as transparent areas are removed. They'll also be centered in the frame, losing their original relative positioning.

5. For this exercise, choose Sequence and use the Document Size option. Click OK.
6. Looking in the Project panel, locate the new bin Theft_Unexpected_Layered. Double-click it to open it and reveal its contents.
7. Double-click the sequence Theft_Unexpected_Layered to load it.

   You may want to switch to list view to see the clips more easily.
8. Examine the sequence in the Timeline panel. Try turning the visibility icons off and on for each track to see how the layers are isolated.

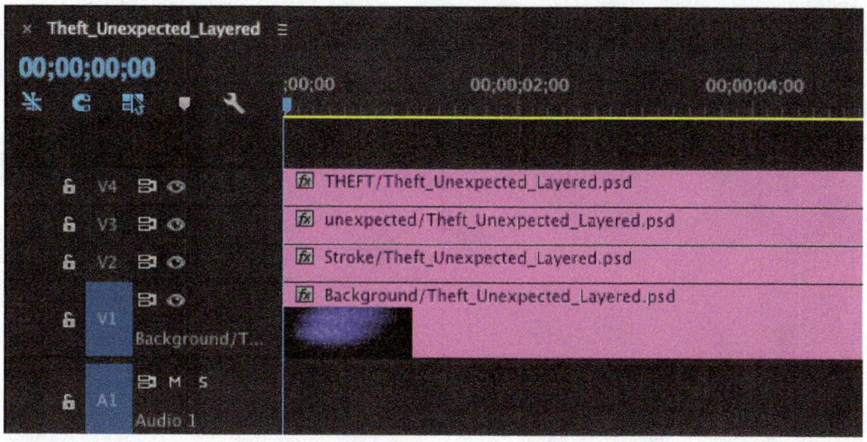

9. Save the file and leave it open.

Recording a Scratch Narration Track

Many times, you may be working with a video project that has a narration track. While most choose to eventually get these recorded by professionals (or at least recorded in a location quieter than their desks), you can record temporary audio, called a scratch track, right into Premiere Pro.

This can be helpful if you need something to edit your video to, especially as it will give you a sense of timing for your edits.

Here's how to go about recording a scratch audio track.

Try It!

1. You will need something to read for your recording. Keep it short--only a few sentences will be necessary to demonstrate how to capture the audio. If you're not using a built-in microphone, make sure your external microphone is properly connected to your computer. You may need to see the documentation for your computer or sound card.

2. Choose Edit > Preferences > Audio Hardware (Windows) or Premiere Pro > Preferences > Audio Hardware (Mac) to properly configure your microphone so Premiere Pro can use it. Use one of the choices from the Default Device pop-up menu, such as System Default Input/Output or Built-in Microphone/Built-in Output, and click OK.

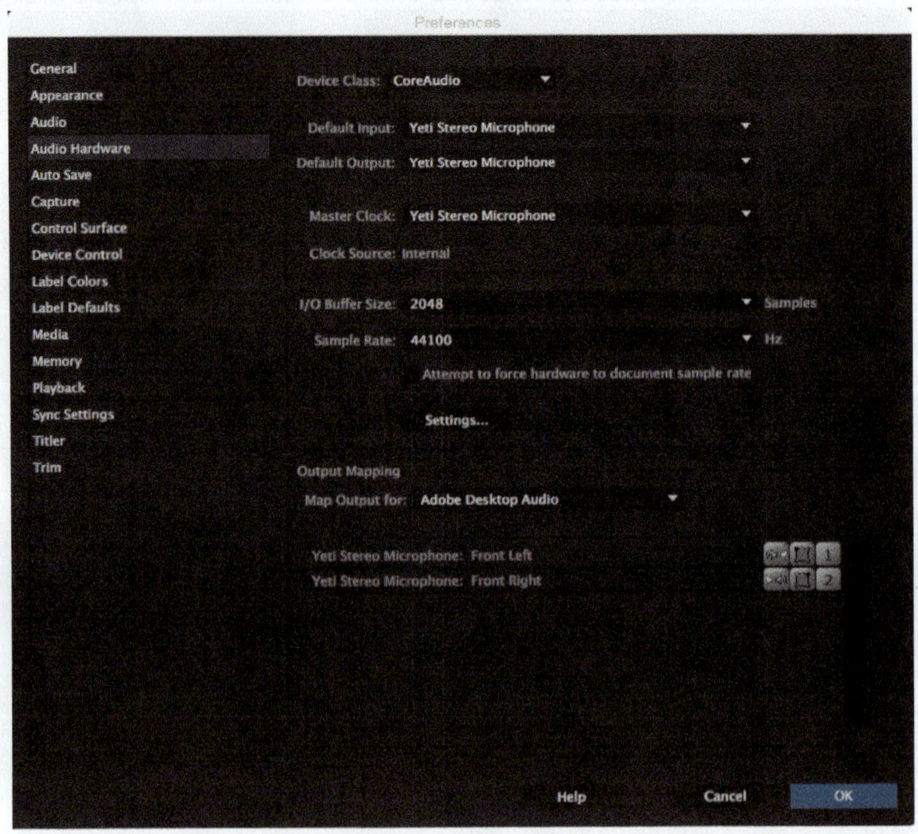

3. Turn down the speakers on your computer to prevent feedback or echo.

4. Open a sequence, and select an empty track in the Timeline.

5. Choose Window > Audio Track Mixer (which is likely to be docked in the same frame as your Source Monitor).

6. In the Audio Track Mixer, click the Enable Track For Recording icon (R) for the track you have chosen.

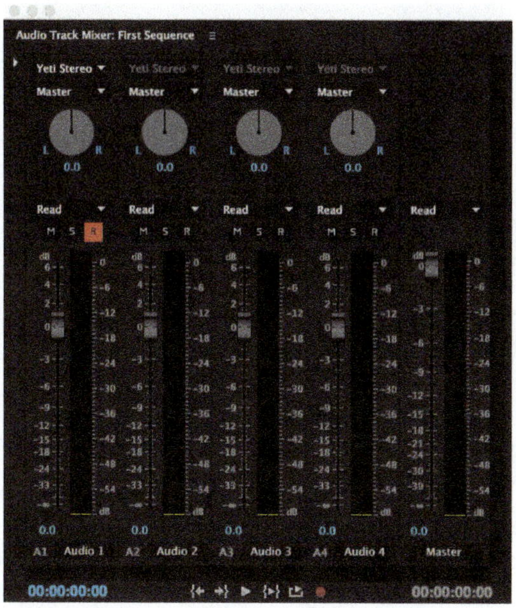

7. Choose the recording input channel from the Track Input Channel menu, at the top of the Audio Track Mixer.

8. Click the Record button at the bottom of the Audio Track Mixer to enter Record mode.

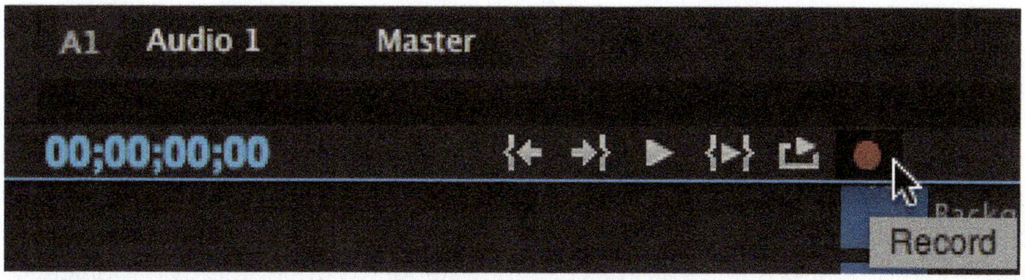

9. Click the Play button to start recording. Read the passage you selected.

10. If the levels are too loud or too quiet, you can adjust the track volume fader up (louder) or down (quieter) as you record. If you see the red indicators at the top of the VU meters light up, you likely have distortion. A good target to aim for is loud audio registering near 0 dB and quiet audio registering around –18 dB.

11. Click the Stop icon to stop recording.

12. Locate both instances of the recorded audio. The newly recorded audio appears both on the audio track in the Timeline and as a clip in the Project panel. You can select the clip in the Project panel and rename it or delete it from your project.

13. Save the file and close Premiere Pro.

Note:

Premiere Pro CC allows you to customize the Timeline by adding and removing buttons on the track headers (the far left of the Timeline panel). You can add a Voice-over Record button that begins recording audio immediately.

Exploring Laws Regarding the Use of Technology

As you create and use digital information, it is important that you comply with relevant laws. You have already explored ethical use of technology and copyright laws. Other regulations for compliance issues relevant to this cluster include:

- The First Amendment to the U.S. Constitution
- Federal Communications Commission regulations
- The Freedom of Information Act
- Liability Laws

The First Amendment

The First Amendment to the Constitution guarantees rights to certain freedoms, including freedom of speech and freedom of the press. That means that the government cannot persecute individuals or organizations who express their opinions.

Of course, when the Constitution was written, this amendment applied to speech, writing, and print, as there was no digital information. Now, the U.S. Supreme Court has expanded its interpretation to include broadcasting, the Internet, and other digital forms of expression.

There are some instances, however, where freedom of speech is not protected. They include defamation, which is when you make false statements that damage another person's reputation; true threats, which is when you threaten to commit a crime; face-to-face personal insults deliberately used to provoke a fight; obscenity; child pornography; and misleading commercial advertising.

Federal Communications Commission Regulations

The Federal Communications Commission (FCC) is a U.S. government agency that regulates the radio, television, and telephone industries, including communications by radio, television, wire, satellite, and cable. This includes Internet and smartphone communications. Among other things, the FCC issues operating licenses for radio and television stations and enforces decency standards under the Communications Decency Act (CDA) of 1996.

Two key features of FCC regulations include:

- The FCC cannot censor broadcast stations
- The FCC can punish, usually by fine, a broadcast station if someone transmits obscene or indecent language

In early 2015, the FCC adopted the Open Internet rule, which prohibits Internet access providers from blocking, impairing, or impeding access to lawful content online. It reinforces the concept of Net Neutrality, which means that you can develop products and services for the Internet without having to ask someone else for permission.

The Freedom of Information Act

The Freedom of Information Act (FOIA) is a U.S. law that gives you the right to request access to records from any federal agency. According to the law, federal agencies must disclose information unless it falls into one of nine categories that protect specific interests, such as personal privacy, national security, and law enforcement.

The Office of Information Policy at the Department of Justice is responsible for monitoring compliance with the FOIA .

Liability Law

Liability means being legally responsible for something. Liability laws are the laws that determine who is responsible or at fault when something goes wrong. Much of liability law has to do with personal injury, such as when someone rear-ends your car or falls in your driveway. Other liability laws concern products. Product liability laws are the legal rules concerning who is responsible for defective or dangerous products. Most liability laws are set at the state level, and vary depending on the state you are in.

There is an area of liability law that covers publishers and distributors of information, including broadcasters, printers, and Internet providers. It involves determining if these publishers or distributors are protected by the First Amendment or if they are liable under the FCCs decency standards. For example, a Web site publisher may be liable for posting defamatory information. However, an Internet service provider might not be liable for hosting a forum where users post defamatory comments.

Other Relevant Regulations

Most of the industries in the Information Technology career cluster are regulated by the above laws and agencies. In other words, they are protected by the First Amendment and liable under the CDA. In response to consumer concerns, many have adopted self-regulating policies. Self-regulation is when an industry sets regulations for itself rather than waiting for the government to do so. For example, both the motion picture and video gaming industries have ratings systems to identify violent or adult content. In addition, the video gaming industry has a code of marketing that regulates how they advertise and market games to children.

Comprehension Check

1. What is one advantage of using the Media Browser rather than the File > Import method to import tapeless media?
2. When you're importing a layered Photoshop file, what are the four different ways to import the file?
3. What keys can you use to play back video and sound clips?
4. What is protected by the First Amendment?
5. What is regulated by the FCC?
6. What is the Freedom of Information Act?
7. What is self-regulation and how does the video gaming industry use it?

Review Project

Conduct research to learn more about the laws that apply to industries in the Information Technology career cluster. Evaluate your sources for accuracy and validity. Select one law and create a presentation that explains it. Remember to properly cite your sources. Share your presentation with a partner or with the class.

Lesson 22 Overview

In this lesson, you will learn about:

- Setting the Default Editing Workspace
- Exploring the Project Panel
- Working with Bins
- Identifing Personal and Professional Qualities

Once you have imported video and sound assets to your project, you'll want to begin looking through your footage and adding clips to a sequence. Before you do, it's well worth spending a little time organizing the assets you have. Doing so can save you hours of time hunting for things later.

When you have lots of clips in your project, imported from several different media types, it can be a challenge to stay on top of everything and always find that magic shot when you need it.

In this lesson, you'll learn how to organize your clips using the Project panel, which is the heart of your project. You'll create special folders, called *bins*, to divide your clips into categories. You'll also learn about adding important metadata and labels to your clips.

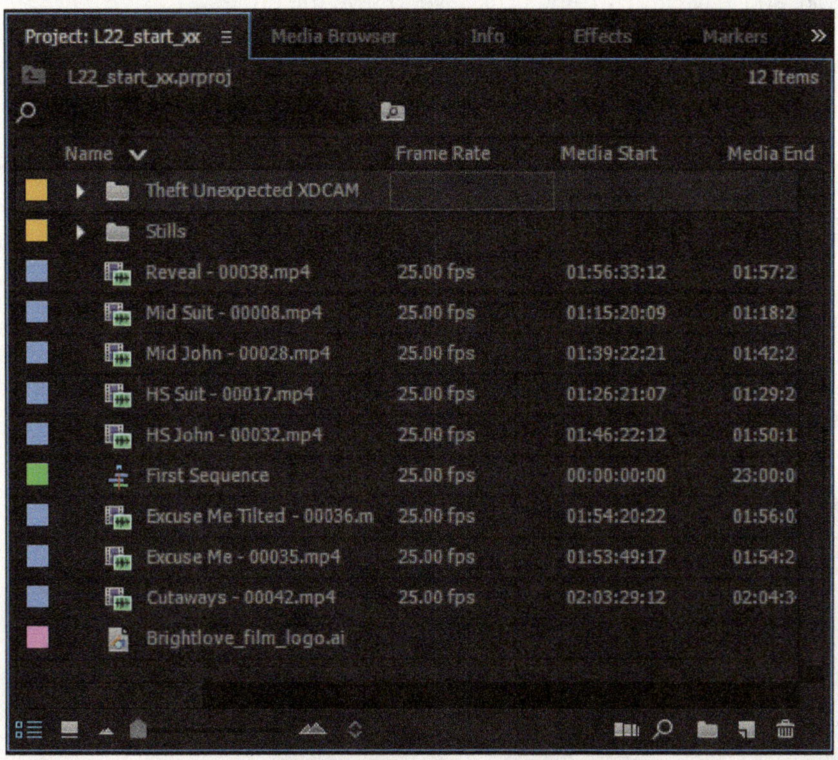

Set the Default Editing Workspace

Before you begin, make sure you're using the default Editing workspace.

Try It!

1. For this lesson, you'll use the project file you used in Lesson 21, **L21_start_xx.prproj.** If the project is not already open, open it from the location where your teacher has you save your files.
2. Choose Window > Workspaces > Editing.
3. Choose Window > Workspaces > Reset to Saved Layout.
4. Choose File > Save As.
5. Rename the file **L22_start_xx.prproj**.
6. Choose the location where your teacher instructs you to store the files for this lesson, and leave it open, and click Save to save the project.

Exploring the Project Panel

Bin

A folder used for storing and organizing media clips in Premiere Pro.

Anything you import into your Premiere Pro project will appear in the Project panel. As well as giving you excellent tools for browsing your clips and working with their metadata, the Project panel has special folders, called bins that you can use to organize everything.

Everything that appears in a sequence must be in the Project panel. If you delete a clip in the Project panel that is already used in a sequence, the clip will automatically be removed from the sequence. Premiere Pro will warn you if deleting a clip will affect an existing sequence.

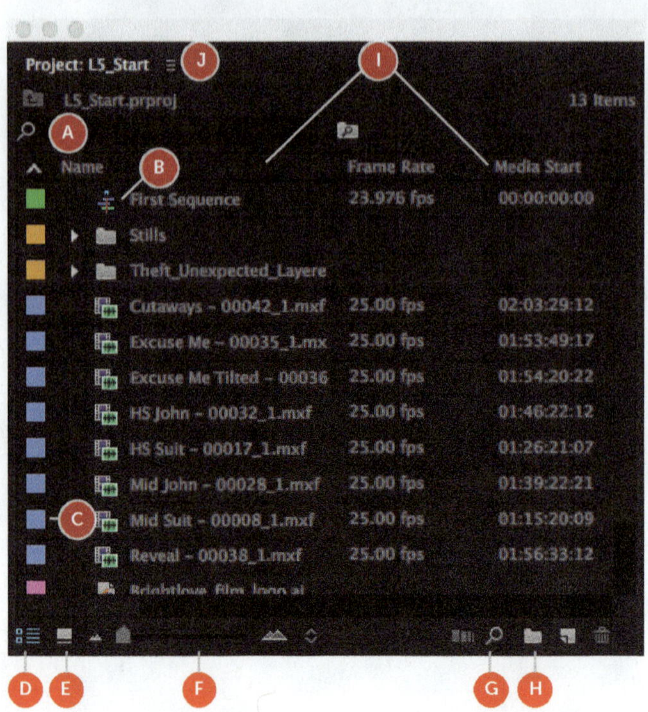

G. Filter Bin Content menu
H. Sequence
I. Clip
J. List View
K. Icon View
L. Zoom
M. Find
N. New bin
O. Headings
P. Panel menu

As well as acting as the repository for all of your clips, the Project panel gives you important options for interpreting media. All of your footage will have a frame rate (frames per second, or fps) and a pixel aspect ratio (pixel shape), for example. You may want to change these settings for creative reasons.

You could, for example, interpret video recorded at 60fps as 30fps to achieve a 50% slow-motion effect. You might also receive a video file that has the wrong pixel aspect ratio setting.

Premiere Pro uses metadata associated with footage to know how to play it back. If you want to change the clip metadata, you can do so in the Project panel.

Working with Bins

Bins allow you to organize clips by dividing them into groups.

Just like folders on your hard drive, you can have multiple bins inside other bins, creating a folder structure as comprehensive as your project requires.

There's an important difference between bins and folders on your hard drive: Bins exist only inside your Premiere Pro project file to organize your media within your project. You won't find individual folders representing project bins on your hard drive.

Creating Bins

Try It!

1. Click the New Bin button at the bottom of the Project panel.

   Premiere Pro creates a new bin and automatically highlights the name, ready for you to rename it. It's a good habit to name bins as soon as you create them.

2. We have already imported some clips from a film, so let's give them a bin. Name the new bin **Theft Unexpected**.

   You can also create a bin using the File menu.

3. Make sure the Project panel is active, choose File > New > Bin, and name the new bin **PSD Files**.

   You can also make a new bin by using a shortcut menu.

4. Right-click a blank area in the Project panel and choose New Bin. Name the new bin **Illustrator Files**.

   Finally, you can use shortcut keystrokes.

5. Make sure the Project panel is active but no existing bins are selected. Press the keyboard shortcut Control+B (Windows) or Command+B (Mac) to make another bin. Name the bin **Sequences**.

6. Save the changes to **L22_start_xx.prproj**, and leave it open.

Using Bins

If your Project panel is set to List view, bins are displayed in name order among the clips.

Try It!

1. Import the clip **Brightlove_film_logo.ai** from the data files (see the Graphics folder) into the Illustrator Files bin.
2. Import **Theft_Unexpected.psd** from the data files into the PSD Files bin.
3. In the Project panel, drag the sequence named **First Sequence** into the Sequences bin.
4. Drag all of the remaining clips into the Theft Unexpected bin.
5. Save the changes to **L22_start_xx.prproj**, and leave it open.

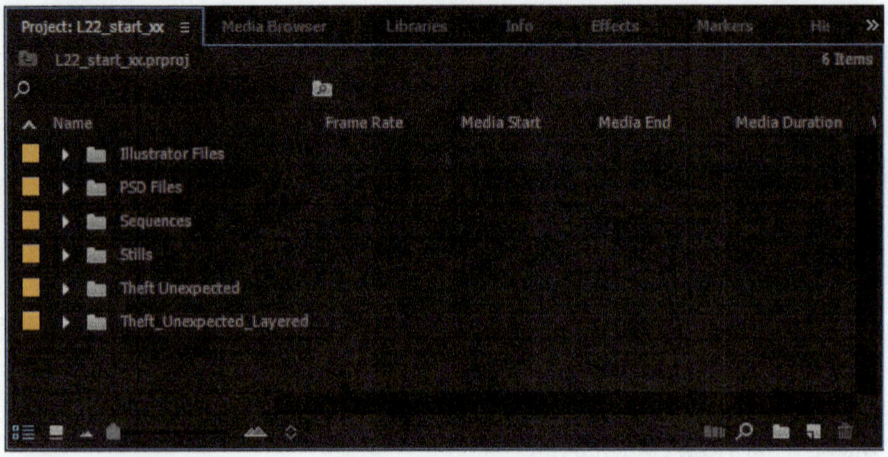

You should now have a nicely organized Project panel, with each kind of clip in its own bin.

Copying a Clip to a Bin

Notice that you can also copy and paste clips to make extra copies if this suits your organizational system. You have a Photoshop document that might be useful for the Theft Unexpected content. Let's make an extra copy.

Try It!

1. Click the disclosure triangle for the PSD Files bin to display the contents.
2. Right-click the Theft_Unexpected.psd clip, and choose Copy.
3. Click the disclosure triangle for the Theft Unexpected bin to display the contents.
4. Right-click the Theft Unexpected bin, and choose Paste.

   Premiere Pro places a copy of the clip in the Theft Unexpected bin.
5. Save the changes to **L22_start_xx.prproj**, and close Premiere Pro.

Identifying Personal and Professional Qualities

Personal qualities are the traits that make you unique. You demonstrate your personal qualities by the way you act and the things you say. These qualities influence the way other people see you and the way you see yourself.

Most people have both positive and not-so-positive personal qualities. It is the positive personal qualities that will help you build relationships with others and succeed in your career. That's because the qualities that make you successful in other areas of your life, make you successful at work, too. Employers look to hire people who exhibit both positive personal qualities and professional qualities.

Some positive qualities you can develop and demonstrate include the following:

- Flexibility, which is a willingness to compromise or adapt.
- Open-mindedness, which is a willingness to try new things or to hear and consider new ideas.
- Initiative, which is a willingness to take charge or to act in order to accomplish a goal.
- Active listening skills, which means that you listen attentively to speakers to make sure you hear and understand the message they are sending.
- A willingness to learn new knowledge and skills, which shows others that you are helpful, curious, and interested in expanding your abilities.
- Pride in quality work, which shows others that you recognize the importance of performing to a high level and are willing to put in the effort to do so.
- Strong oral and written communications skills, which means you have the ability to speak and write effectively in order to get your message across to others.
- Interpersonal skills, which means the ability to communicate and relate to other people in a positive way.
- Leadership, which is the ability to take charge and encourage others to work together to achieve goals.
- Teamwork, which is the ability to cooperate and work with others to achieve goals.
- Appreciation for diversity, which is the ability to understand and respect people from different cultures and backgrounds as well as those who have different values and opinions.
- Ability to manage conflict, which means you can help yourself and others recognize disagreements and cope with them in a respectful and honest way.
- Customer service skills, which means the ability to assist and advise customers and clients in a positive, helpful way.
- Work ethic, which is behavior that shows you respect your employer, your co-workers, your clients, and your responsibilities.
- Adaptability, which is the ability to change in order to function more effectively in a particular situation or environment.

You are not stuck with the same personal qualities for your whole life. You can work to build positive qualities and eliminate the negative ones.

Comprehension Check

1. What is a bin?
2. How do you create a new bin?
3. Why might you copy a clip from one bin to another?
4. What are personal qualities?
5. List and describe three positive personal qualities that will help you succeed in your career.

Review Project

Make a chart that lists at least five positive personal qualities and explains how you can demonstrate these qualities in school or in a career. With a partner, select one and create a short video that illustrates the selected quality. Be sure to adhere to safety guidelines and procedures in recording video that were discussed in Lesson 19.

Lesson 23 Overview

In this lesson, you will learn about:

- Using the Source Monitor
- Navigating the Timeline
- Creating a Sequence
- Moving Clips
- Extracting and Deleting Segments

This lesson will teach you the core editing skills you will use again and again when creating sequences with Premiere Pro.

Editing is much more than choosing shots. You'll choose your cuts precisely, placing clips in sequences at exactly the right point in time and on the track you want (to create layered effects), adding new clips to existing sequences, and removing old ones.

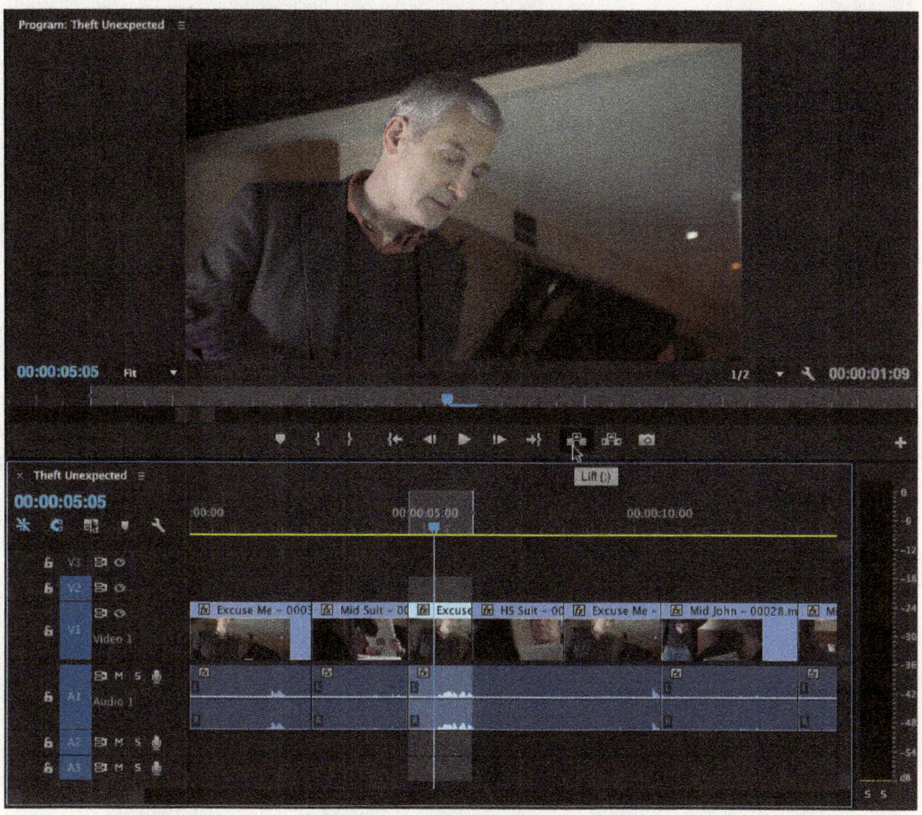

Using the Source Monitor

The Source Monitor is the main place you'll go to when you want to check your assets before including them in a sequence.

When you view video clips in the Source Monitor, you watch them in their original format. They will play back with their frame rate, frame size, field order, audio sample rate, and audio bit depth exactly as they were recorded.

When you add a clip to a sequence, Premiere Pro conforms it to the sequence settings. This means the frame rate and audio type might be adjusted so that all the clips in the sequence play back the same way.

As well as being a viewer for multiple file types, the Source Monitor provides important additional functions. You can use two special kinds of markers, called In points and Out points, to select part of a clip for inclusion in a sequence. You can also add comments in the form of markers that you can refer to later or use to remind yourself about important facts relating to a clip. You might include a note about part of a shot you don't have permission to use, for example.

Before you begin, make sure you're using the default Editing workspace.

Try It!

1. For this lesson, you'll use the project file you used in **Lesson 22, L22_start_xx.prproj.** Start Premiere Pro if necessary and open it from the location your teacher has you save your files.

2. Choose Window > Workspaces > Editing.

3. Choose Window > Workspaces > Reset to Saved Layout.

4. Choose File > Save As.
5. Rename the file **L23_start_xx.prproj**. Save the project in the location where your teacher instructs you to store the files for this lesson, and leave it open.

Timecode Information

At the bottom left of the Source Monitor, a timecode display shows the current position of the playhead in hours, minutes, seconds, and frames (00:00:00:00).

For example, 00:15:10:01 would be 0 hours, 15 minutes, 10 seconds, and 1 frame.

Note that this is based on the original timecode for the clip, which probably does not begin at 00:00:00:00.

At the bottom right of the Source Monitor, a timecode display shows the duration of your clip. By default, this shows the whole clip duration, but later you'll be adding special marks to make a partial selection.

Loading a Clip

To load a clip, do the following.

Try It!

1. In the Project panel, hold down the Control (Windows) or Command (Mac) key and double-click the Theft Unexpected bin icon. To navigate back to the Project panel contents, click the Navigate Up icon beside the project name.
2. Double-click a video clip, or drag and drop a clip into the Source Monitor.

   Premiere Pro displays the clip in the Source Monitor, ready for you to watch it and add markers.
3. Position your mouse pointer so that it is over the Source Monitor, and press the ` (grave) key. The panel fills the Premiere Pro application frame, giving you a larger view of the video clip. Press the ` (grave) key again to restore the Source Monitor to its original size.
4. Save the changes to **L23_start_xx.prproj**, and leave it open.

Loading Multiple clips

Next you'll create a selection of clips to work with in the Source Monitor.

Try It!

1. Click the Recent Items menu at the top left of the Source Monitor, and choose Close All.

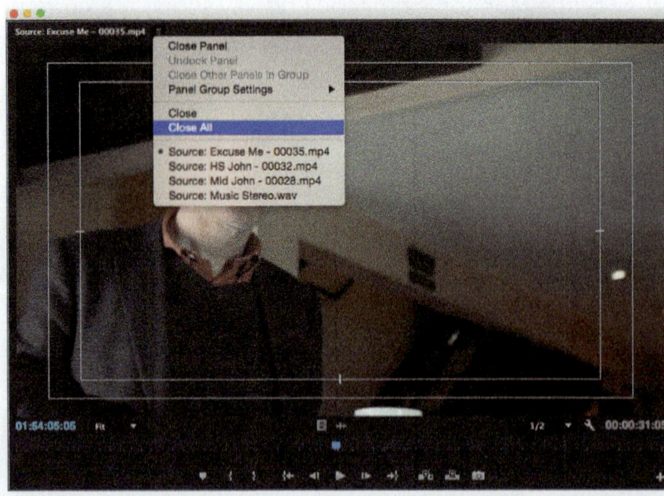

2. Click the List View button on the Theft Unexpected bin, and make sure the clips are displayed in alphabetical order by clicking the Name heading.
3. Select the first clip, Cutaways, and then hold down the Shift key and click the clip Mid John - 00028.

   This makes a selection of multiple clips in the bin.
4. Drag the clips from the bin to the Source Monitor.

   Now the clips selected will be displayed in the Source Monitor Recent Items menu. You can use the menu to choose which clip to view.
5. Save the changes to **L23_start_xx.prproj**, and leave it open.

Safe Margins

Old-style CRT monitors crop the edges of the picture to achieve a clean edge. If you're producing video for a CRT monitor, click the Settings (wrench icon) button at the bottom of the Source Monitor and choose Safe Margins. Premiere Pro displays white outlines over the image.

The outer box is the action-safe zone. Aim to keep important action inside this box so that when the picture is displayed, edge cropping does not hide what is going on.

The inner box is the title-safe zone. Keep titles and graphics inside this box so that even on a badly calibrated display, your audience will be able to read the words.

Click the Settings button at the bottom of the Source Monitor and choose Safe Margins to turn them off.

Essential Playback Controls

Let's look at the playback controls.

Try It!

1. Double-click the shot Excuse Me in the Theft Unexpected bin to open it in the Source Monitor.

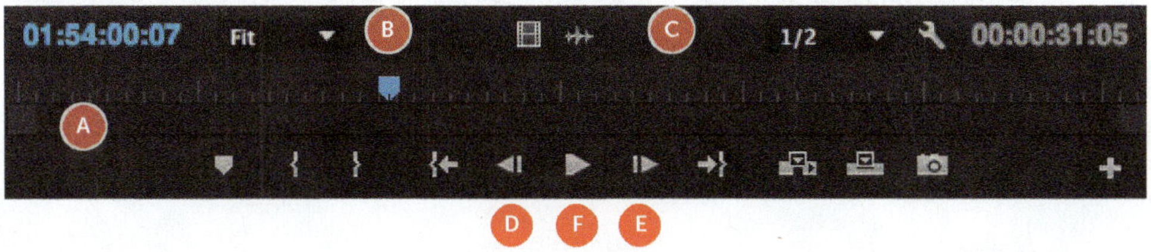

A. Navigator
B. Playhead
C. Time ruler
D. Step Back 1 Frame
E. Step Forward 1 Frame
F. Play-Stop toggle

7. At the bottom of the Source Monitor, there's a blue playhead marker. Drag it along the bottom of the panel to view different parts of the clip. You can also click wherever you want the playhead to go, and it will jump to that spot.

8. Below the Time Ruler and the playhead, there's a scroll bar that doubles as a Zoom control. Drag one end of the scroll bar to zoom in on the clip navigator.

9. Click the Play-Stop button to play the clip. Click it again to stop playback. You can also use the spacebar to play and stop playback.

10. Click the Step Back 1 Frame and Step Forward 1 Frame buttons to move through the clip one frame at a time. You can also use the Left Arrow and Right Arrow keys on your keyboard.

11. Try using the J, K, and L keys to play your clip.

12. Save the changes to **L23_start_xx.prproj**, and leave it open.

Source Monitor Controls

As well as playback controls, there are some important additional buttons in the Source Monitor.

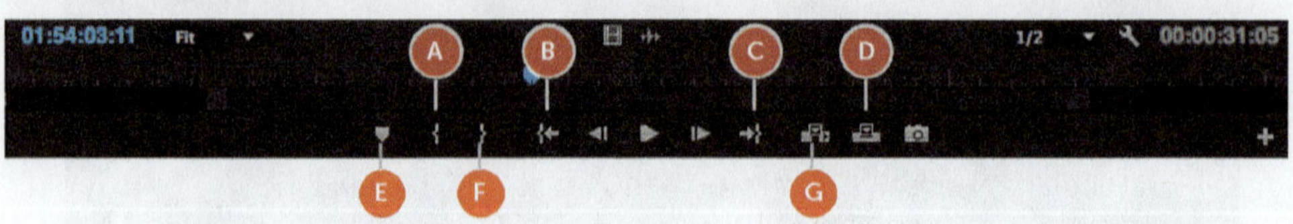

A. Mark In
B. Go to In
C. Go to Out
D. Overwrite
E. Add Marker
F. Mark Out
G. Insert

- **Add Marker:** Adds a marker to the clip at the location of the playhead. Markers can provide a simple visual reference or store comments.
- **Mark In:** Sets the beginning of the part of the clip you intend to use in a sequence. You can have only one In point. A new In point will automatically replace the existing one.
- **Mark Out:** Sets the end of the part of the clip you intend to use in a sequence. You can have only one Out point. A new Out point will automatically replace the existing one.
- **Go to In:** Moves the playhead to the clip In point.
- **Go to Out:** Moves the playhead to the clip Out point.
- **Insert:** Adds the clip to the sequence currently displayed in the Timeline panel using the insert edit method.
- **Overwrite:** Adds the clip to the sequence currently displayed in the Timeline panel using the overwrite edit method.

Adjusting Audio Channels

Premiere Pro has advanced audio management features. You can create complex sound mixes and selectively target output audio channels with original clip audio. You can produce mono, stereo, 5.1, and even 32-channel sequences with precise control over the routing of audio channels.

If you're just starting out, you'll probably want to produce sequences mastered in stereo using stereo clips. In this case, the default settings are most likely exactly what you need.

When recording audio with a professional camera, it's common to have one microphone record onto one audio channel and a different microphone record onto another audio channel. These are the same audio channels that would be used for regular stereo audio, but they now contain completely separate sound.

Your camera adds metadata to the audio to tell Premiere Pro whether the sound is meant to be mono (separate audio channels) or stereo (channel 1 audio and channel 2 audio combined to produce the complete stereo sound).

You can tell Premiere Pro how to interpret audio channels when new media files are imported by going to Edit > Preferences > Audio (Windows) or Premiere Pro > Preferences > Audio (Mac).

If the setting was wrong when you imported your clips, it's easy to tell Premiere Pro how to correctly interpret the audio channels.

Try It!

1. Right-click the Reveal clip in the Theft Unexpected bin, and choose Modify > Audio Channels.

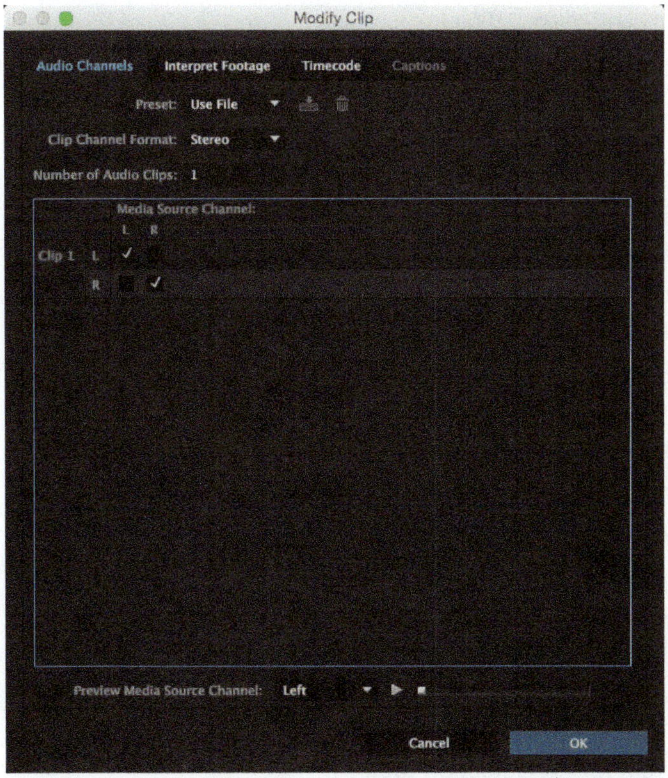

2. This clip is set to use the file's metadata to identify the channel format for the audio. Click the Preset menu, and change it to Mono.

   Premiere Pro switches the Channel Format menu to Mono. You'll see that the Left and Right source channels are now linked to tracks Audio 1 and Audio 2. This means that when you add the clip to a sequence, each audio channel will go on a separate track, allowing you to work on them independently.

3. Click OK.

4. Save the changes to **L23_start_xx.prproj**, and leave it open.

Navigating the Timeline

The Timeline panel in Premiere Pro is the canvas on which you develop your video content. The Timeline is where you will add clips to your sequences, make editorial changes to them, add visual and audio special effects, mix soundtracks, and add titles and graphics.

Here are a few facts about the Timeline panel:

- You view and edit sequences in the Timeline panel.
- You can open multiple sequences at the same time, and each will be displayed in its own Timeline panel.
- The terms sequence and Timeline are often used interchangeably, as in "in the sequence" or "on the Timeline."
- You can have up to 99 video tracks. Upper video tracks play "in front" of lower ones, so you would normally place graphics clips on tracks above background video clips.
- You can have up to 99 audio tracks that all play at the same time to create an audio mix. Audio tracks can be mono (1 channel), stereo (2 channels), 5.1 (6 channels), or adaptive—with up to 32 channels.
- You can change the height of Timeline tracks to gain access to additional controls and thumbnails on your video clips.
- Each track has a set of controls, shown on a track header, that change the way it functions.
- Time always moves from left to right on the Timeline.
- The Program Monitor shows you the contents of the currently displayed sequence at the position of the playhead.
- For most operations on the Timeline, you will use the standard Selection tool. However, there are several other tools that serve different purposes, and each tool has a keyboard shortcut. If in doubt, press the V key. This is the keyboard shortcut for the Selection tool.

- You can zoom in and out of the Timeline using the + and – keys at the top of your keyboard to get a better view of your clips. If you press the \ key, Premiere Pro toggles the zoom level between your current setting and showing your whole sequence. You can also double-click the navigator at the bottom of the Timeline panel to view the whole timeline.

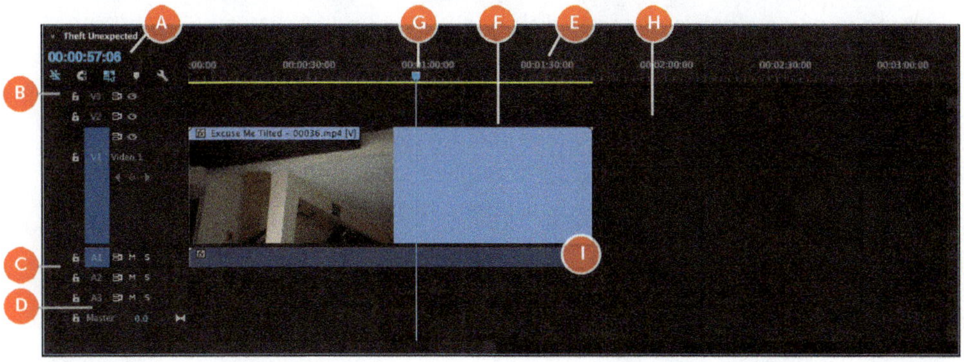

E. Timecode
F. Track selection
G. Track lock
H. Source tracks
I. Time ruler
J. Clip video
K. Playhead
L. Clip audio
M. Track

Creating a Sequence

A sequence is a series of clips that play, one after another—sometimes with multiple blended layers, and often with special effects, titles, and audio—making a complete film.

You can have as many sequences as you like in a project. Sequences are stored in the Project panel, just like clips. They have their own icon.

Let's make a new sequence for our Theft Unexpected drama.

Try It!

1. In the Theft Unexpected bin, drag the clip Excuse Me (not Excuse Me Tilted) onto the New Item button at the bottom of the panel.
2. This is a shortcut to make a sequence that perfectly matches your media. Premiere Pro creates a new sequence, and automatically names it after the clip you selected.

   The sequence is highlighted in the bin, and it is a good idea to rename it right away.
3. Right-click the sequence in the bin, and choose Rename. Name the sequence **Theft Unexpected**.

   The sequence is automatically open, and it contains the clip you used to create it. This works for our purposes, but if you had used a random clip to perform this shortcut, you might choose to select it in the sequence and delete it now (by pressing the Delete key).
4. Close the sequence by clicking the **x** on its name tab in the Timeline panel. Save the changes to **L23_start_xx.prproj**, and close the project.

Using Thumbnails to Create a Storyboard

The term **storyboard** usually describes a series of drawings that show the intended camera angles and action for a film. Storyboards are often quite similar to comic strips, though they usually include technical information, such as intended camera moves, lines of dialogue, and sound effects.

You can use clip thumbnails in a bin as storyboard images. Arrange the thumbnails by dragging and dropping them in the order in which you would like the clips to appear in your sequence, from left to right and from top to bottom. Then drag and drop them into your sequence, or use a special automated edit feature to add them to your sequence with transition effects.

Splitting a Clip

It's also common to add a clip to a sequence and then realize you need it in two parts. Perhaps you want to take just a section of a clip and use it as a cutaway, or maybe you want to separate the beginning and the end to make space for new clips.

You can split clips in several ways:

- Use the Razor tool, with the keyboard shortcut C. If you hold the Shift key while clicking with the Razor tool, you'll add an edit to clips on every track.
- Make sure the Timeline panel is selected, go to the Sequence menu, and choose Add Edit. Premiere Pro adds an edit, at the location of your playhead, to clips on any tracks that are turned on. If you have selected clips, Premiere Pro adds the edit only to the selected clips.
- If you go to the Sequence menu and choose Add Edit to All Tracks, Premiere Pro adds an edit to clips on all tracks, regardless of whether they are turned on.
- Use the Add Edit keyboard shortcuts. Press Control+K (Windows) or Command+K (Mac) to add an edit to selected tracks or clips, or press Shift+Control+K (Windows) or Shift+Command+K (Mac) to add an edit to all tracks regardless of selection.

Clips that were originally continuous will play back seamlessly unless you move them or make separate adjustments to different parts.

The Kuleshov Effect

Media influences human emotions in many ways. Sometimes it is the story itself that evokes feelings such as happiness, sadness, or even anger. Sometimes it is the way the media is created. Simply adding music or color can change the way people react to video, animation, or images. Soviet film pioneer Lev Kuleshov developed the theory of editing that is the core foundation of the motion picture, which we know as the **Kuleshov effect**.

Kuleshov Effect
Creating a new meaning from two images that do not have an intentional connection.

The Kuleshov effect is the phenomenon that two images, having no intentional connection or relation to one another, will create new meaning and interpretation simply by being seen sequentially, or juxtaposed. Many filmmakers, including Alfred Hitchcock—who referred to the Kuleshov effect as pure editing—believed that the juxtaposition of shots, more than the composition of any individual shot, was the truest magic of cinema.

The most popular example of Kuleshov's demonstration of this theory starts with a close-up shot of a man, an actor who stares off-screen with a blank or ambiguous expression. By cutting this shot together with a shot of a bowl of soup, then back to the man, the effect is the audience perceives that the man is hungry. The same shot of the man intercut with the shot of a child in a coffin gives the illusion that the man is sad.

The Kuleshov effect: hunger

The Kuleshov effect: sadness

Is the man actually feeling any of the suggested emotions? Does it really matter? What matters is that the audience naturally looks for a connection in the images, which means that you as a storyteller have a powerful tool for bypassing your audience's rationality and reaching them via their subconscious mind. Just remember to use it responsibly.

Moving Clips

Insert edits and overwrite edits add new clips to sequences in dramatically different ways. Insert edits push existing clips out of the way, whereas overwrite edits simply replace them.

When moving clips using the Insert mode, you may want to ensure you have the sync locks on for your tracks to avoid any possible loss of sync.

Let's try a few techniques.

Dragging Clips

At the top left of the Timeline panel, you'll see the Snap button. When snapping is enabled, clip segments snap automatically to each other's edges. This simple but useful feature will help you position clip segments accurately.

Try It!

1. Start Premiere Pro, and open **L23_start2.prproj** from the data files for this lesson.
2. Save the file as **L23_start2_xx.prproj** in the location where your teacher instructs you to store the files for this lesson.
3. Click the last clip on the Timeline, HS Suit, and drag it a little to the right.

   Because there are no clips after this one, you simply introduce a gap before the clip. No other clips are affected.

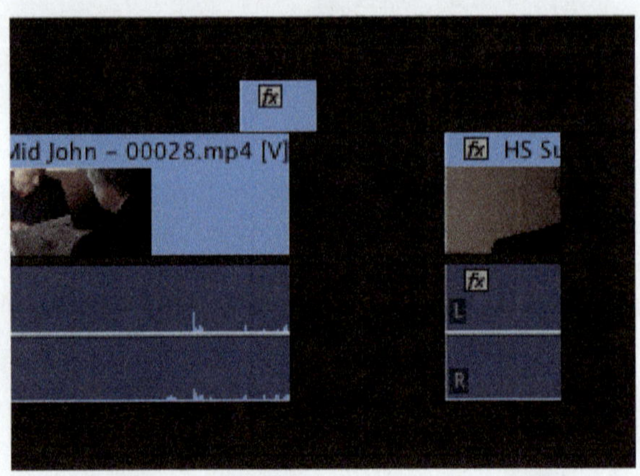

4. Drag the clip back to its original position. If you move the mouse slowly and if Snap mode is on, you'll notice that the clip segment slightly jumps into position. When this happens, you can be confident it is perfectly positioned. Notice that the clip also snaps to the end of the cutaway shot on Video 2.
5. Drag the clip to the left so it's positioned earlier in the Timeline. Slowly drag the clip until it snaps to the end of the clip before. When you release the mouse button, the clip simply replaces the end of that clip.

   When you drag and drop clips, the default mode is Overwrite.
6. Undo to restore the clip to its original position.
7. Save the changes to **L23_start2_xx.prproj**, and leave it open.

Nudging Clips

Many editors prefer to use the keyboard as much as possible, minimizing the use of the mouse. Working with the keyboard is often faster.

It's common to move clip segments inside a sequence by using the arrow keys in combination with a modifier key, nudging the selected items left and right in time, or up and down between tracks.

You won't be able to nudge linked video and audio clips on V1 and A1 up and down until you separate them, or unlink them, because the separator between the video and audio tracks blocks the movement.

Premiere Pro includes many keyboard shortcut options, some of which are available, but not yet assigned keys. You can set these up, prioritizing the use of available keys to suit your workflow.

Rearranging Clips in a Sequence

If you hold the Control (Windows) or Command (Mac) key while you drag clips on the Timeline, Premiere Pro uses Insert mode instead of Overwrite mode.

The HS Suit shot around 00:00:20:00 might work well if it appeared before the previous shot—and it might help us hide the poor continuity between the two shots of John.

Try It!

1. Verify the Theft Unexpected sequence is active in the Timeline panel.
2. Drag and drop the HS Suit clip to the left of the clip before it. The left edge of the HS Suit clip should line up with the left edge of the Mid Suit clip.
   Once you have begun dragging, hold the Control key (Windows) or Command key (Mac). Release the key after you've dropped the clip.

3. Play the result. This creates the edit you want, but it introduces a gap where the clip HS Suit used to be.

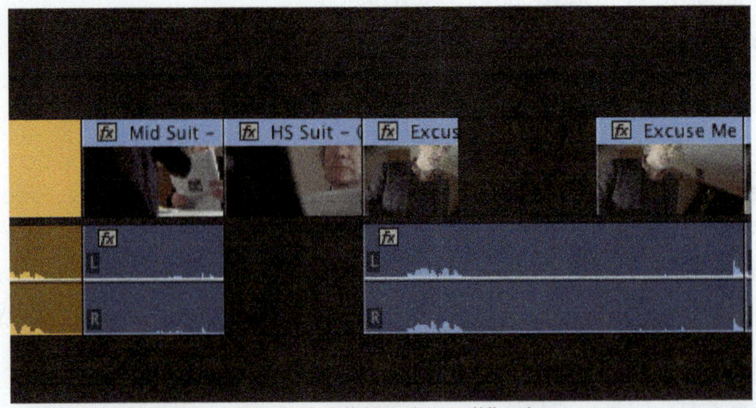

Let's try that again with an additional modifier key.

4. Use the Undo command to restore the clips to their original positions.
5. Holding Control+Alt (Windows) or Command+Option (Mac), drag and drop the HS Suit clip to the beginning of the previous clip again.

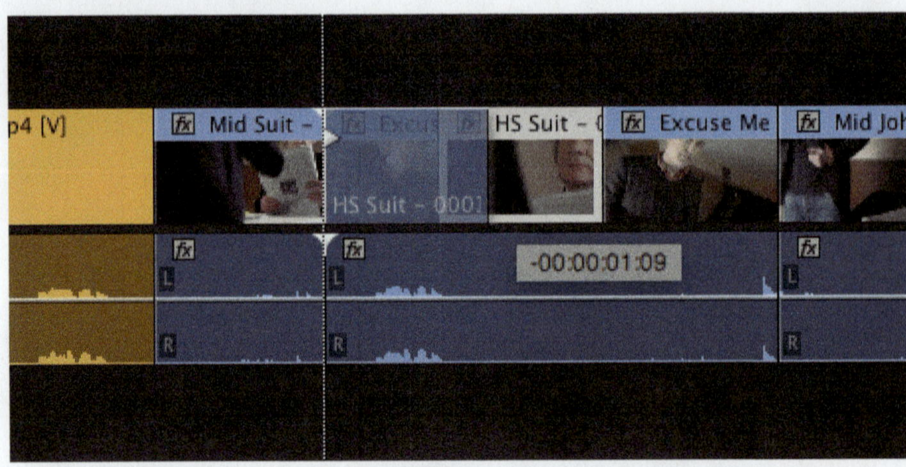

This time, no gap is left in the sequence.

6. Play through the edit to see the result.
7. Save the changes to **L23_start2_xx.prproj**, and leave it open.

Using the Clipboard

You can copy and paste clip segments on the Timeline just as you might copy and paste text in a word processor.

Try It!

1. In a sequence, select any clip segment (or segments) you want to copy, and then press Control+C (Windows) or Command+C (Mac) to add them to the clipboard.

2. Position your playhead where you would like to paste the clips you copied, and press Control+V (Windows) or Command+V (Mac).

3. Save the changes to **L23_start2_xx.prproj**, and leave it open.

Premiere Pro adds copies of the clips to your sequence based on the tracks you enable. The lowest enabled track receives the clip (or clips).

Extracting and Deleting Segments

Now that you know how to add clips to a sequence and how to move them around, all that remains is to learn how to remove them. Once again, you'll be operating in Insert or Overwrite mode.

There are two ways of selecting parts of a sequence you want to remove. You can use In and Out points combined with track selections, or you can select clip segments. If you use In and Out points, selecting clips overrides selecting tracks, so you can ignore track selection if you make careful clip selections.

You will still be working with a selected amount of time, but selecting clips can be quicker than selecting tracks.

Lift

A lift edit will remove the selected part of a sequence, leaving blank space. It's similar to an overwrite edit but in reverse.

You'll need to set In and Out points on the Timeline to select the part that will be removed. You can do this by positioning the playhead and pressing I or O. You can also use a handy shortcut.

Try It!

1. Open the sequence Theft Unexpected 03 in the Sequences bin. This sequence has some unwanted extra clips. They have different label colors to make them easier to identify.

2. Position the playhead so that it's somewhere over the first additional clip, Excuse Me Tilted.

3. Make sure the Video 1 track header is turned on, and press X.

   Premiere Pro automatically adds an In point and an Out point that match the beginning and end of the clip. You'll see a highlight that shows the selected part of the sequence.

   The correct tracks are already selected, so there's no need to do anything else to prepare for the lift edit. In fact, because you have selected a clip, the track selection has no effect anyway. The edit you're about to perform will apply to the selected clip.

4. Click the Lift button at the bottom of the Program Monitor, or press the ; key.

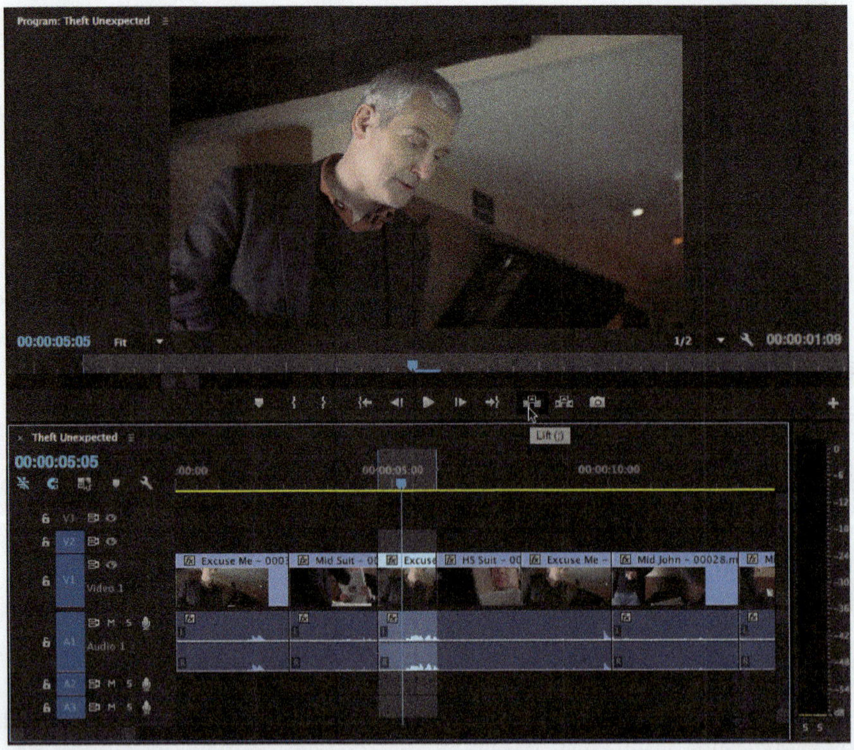

Premiere Pro removes the part of the sequence you selected, leaving a gap behind. This might be fine on another occasion, but in this instance you don't want the gap. You could right-click inside the gap and choose Ripple Delete, but for this exercise you'll use an extract edit.

5. Save the changes to **L23_start2_xx.prproj**, and leave it open.

Extract

An extract edit removes the selected part of your sequence and does not leave a gap. It's similar to an insert edit, but in reverse.

Try It!

1. Undo the last edit.

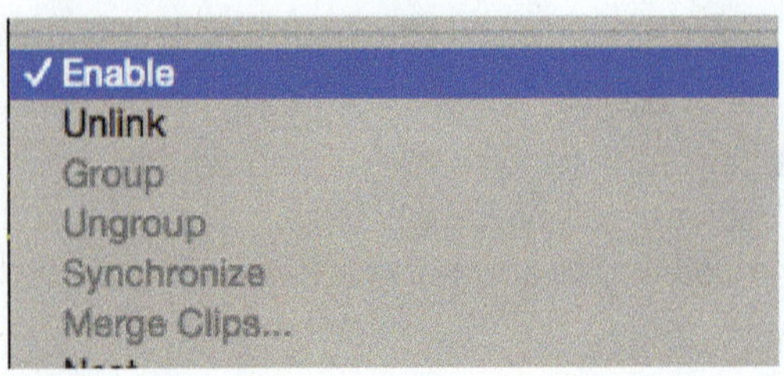

2. Click the Extract button at the bottom of the Program Monitor, or press the ' (apostrophe) key.

   This time, Premiere Pro removes the selected part of the sequence and doesn't leave a gap.

3. Save the changes to **L23_start2_xx.prproj**, and leave it open.

   There are also two ways of removing clips by selecting segments: Delete and Ripple Delete.

4. Click the second unwanted clip, Cutaways, and try these two options:
   - Pressing the Delete key removes the selected clip (or clips), leaving a gap behind. This is the same as a lift edit.
   - Pressing Shift+Delete removes the selected clip (or clips) without leaving a gap behind. This is the same as an extract edit. If you're using a Mac keyboard without a dedicated Delete key, use the Function key to convert the Backspace key into a Delete key.

The result seems similar to what is achieved using In and Out points because you used the In and Out points to select a whole clip. You can use In and Out points to choose any parts of clips, while selecting clip segments and pressing Delete will remove whole clips.

5. Save the changes to **L23_start2_xx.prproj**, and then close Premiere Pro.

Comprehension Check

1. When dragging clips into the Source Monitor, what modifier key (Control/Command, Shift, or Alt) should you use to make an insert edit rather than an overwrite edit?
2. In which panel do you view and edit sequences?
3. What is the difference between an extract edit and a lift edit?
4. What is the difference between the Delete and Ripple Delete functions? What do In and Out points do?
5. What is the difference between an overwrite edit and an insert edit?

Review Project

Select a media clip or image that you think has emotional impact. Write a paragraph explaining why, and present it to a partner or to the class.

Lesson 24 Overview

In this lesson, you will learn about:

- Exploring the Use of Transitions
- Adding Video Transitions

Transitions can help create a seamless flow between two video or audio clips. Video transitions are often used to signify a change in time or location. Audio transitions provide a useful way to avoid abrupt edits that jar the listener.

In this lesson, you'll learn to use transitions.

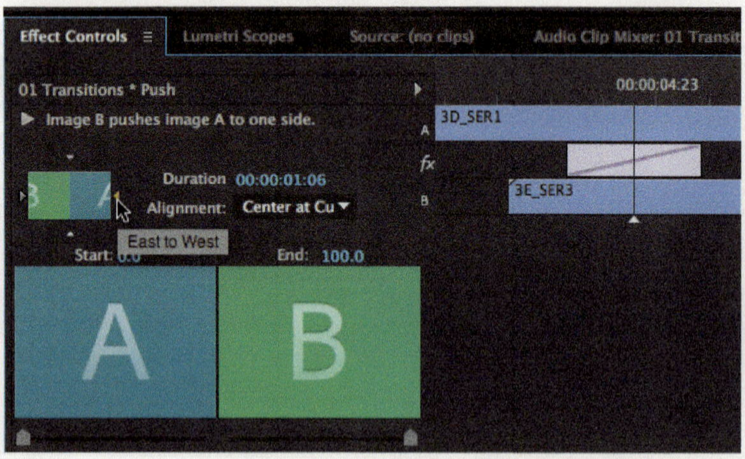

Exploring the Use of Transitions

Adobe Premiere Pro offers several special effects and preset animations to help you bridge neighboring clips in the Timeline. These transitions—such as dissolves, page wipes, dips to color, and so on—provide a way to ease viewers from one scene to the next. Occasionally, a transition can also be used to grab viewers' attention to signify a major jump in the story.

Transition

In video and audio editing, a bridge from the end of one clip to the beginning of the next clip.

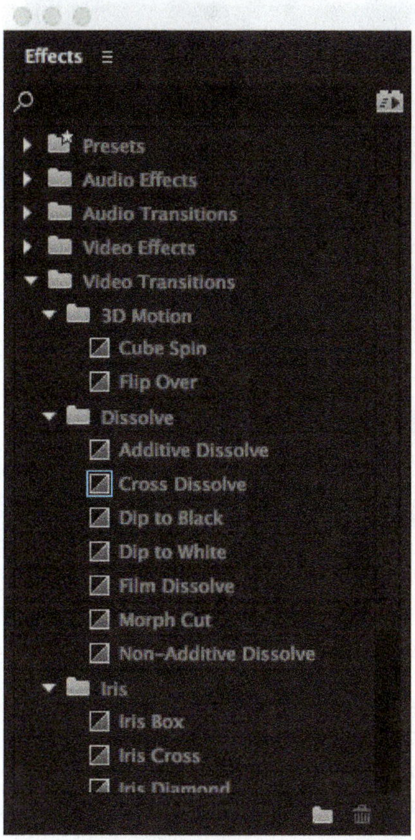

Adding transitions to your project is an art. Applying them starts simply enough; it's a mere drag-and-drop process. The skill comes in their placement, length, and parameters, such as direction, motion, and start/end locations.

Most transition work takes place in the Effect Controls panel. In addition to the various options unique to each transition, the Effect Controls panel displays an A/B timeline. This feature makes it easy to move transitions relative to the edit point, change the transition duration, and apply transitions to clips that don't have sufficient head or tail frames (additional content to provide an overlap). You can also apply a transition to a group of clips.

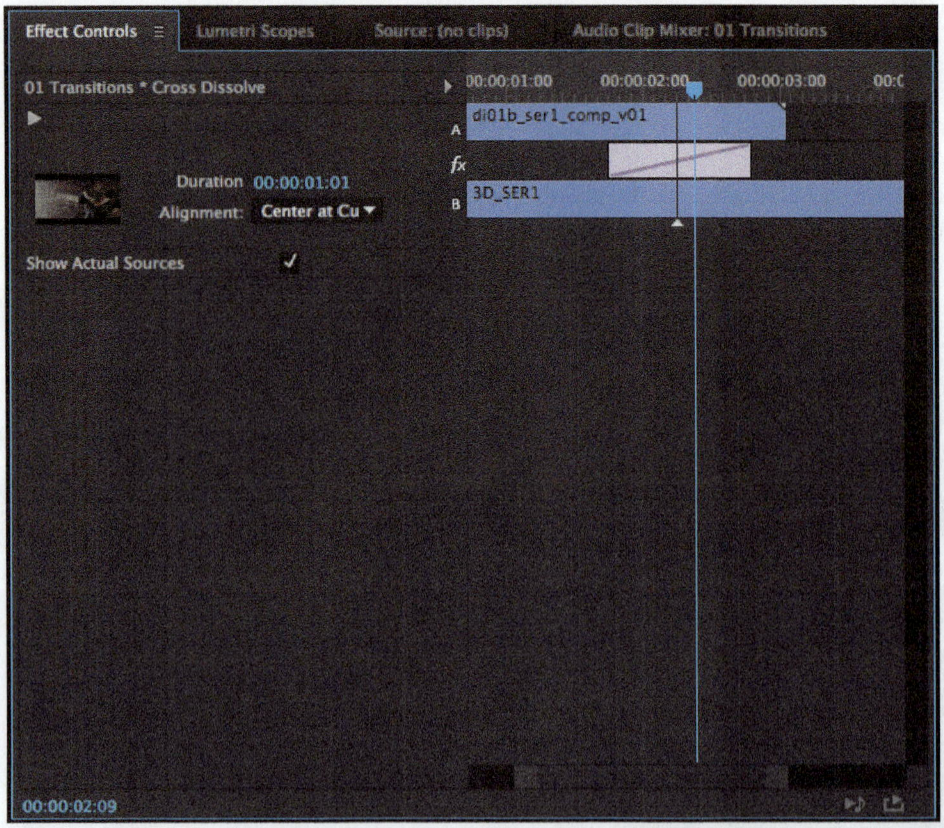

When to Use Transitions

Transitions are most effective when you have no options other than making a distracting edit that makes your sequence appear jarring when viewed. For example, you may switch from indoors to outdoors in a video, or you may jump forward in time by several hours. An animated transition or a dissolve helps the viewer understand that time has passed or that the location has changed.

Transitions are a standard storytelling tool in video editing. For many years, viewers have become used to seeing transitions applied in standard ways, such as the changing of one section to another in a video or the slow fade to black at the end of a scene. The key with transitions is to use restraint.

Best Practices with Transitions

Many editors have a tendency to overuse transitions. Some come to rely on them as a crutch and think that they add visual interest. But that can be a mistake.

Think of transitions as seasoning or spice. When added in small amounts and at the right time, they can make a meal tastier and more enjoyable. When overdone, they can quickly ruin that meal. Keep this in mind when you're applying transitions to your projects.

Jump cut
A jarring or abrupt edit..

Watch some TV news stories. Most use cuts-only edits. You'll rarely see any transitions. Why? The principal reason for the lack of transitions is that they can be distracting. If a TV news editor uses one, it's for a purpose. Their most frequent use in newsroom editing bays is to take what would have been a jarring or abrupt edit—often called a **jump cut**—and make it more palatable.

That's not to say transitions don't have their place in carefully planned stories. They do smooth the change between scenes, and they can send a clear message to the audience.

Adding Video Transitions

Premiere Pro contains several video transitions (plus three audio transitions). You'll find two types of video transitions inside Premiere Pro. The most commonly used transitions are those in the Video Transitions group. These are organized into seven categories based on style. You'll also find additional transitions in the Video Effects group in the Effects panel. These are meant to be applied to an entire clip and can be used to reveal the footage (typically between its start and end frame). This second category works well for superimposing text or graphics.

Applying a Single-Sided Transition

The easiest transition to understand is one that applies to just one end of a single clip. This could be a fade from black on the first clip in a sequence or a dissolve into an animated graphic that leaves the screen on its own.

Try It!

1. Start Adobe Premiere Pro CC, and open the project **L24_start.prproj** from the data files for this lesson.
2. Save the file as **L24_start_xx.psd** in the location where your teacher instructs you to store the files for this lesson, and leave it open.
3. Choose Window > Workspaces > Effects.

   This changes the workspace to the preset that was created to make it easier to work with transitions and effects.
4. If necessary, click the Effects panel to make it active.
5. Make sure the sequence, 01 Transitions is open. This sequence has four video clips. The clips have long enough handles for transitions to be applied.
6. In the Effects panel, open the Video Transitions > Dissolve bin. Find the Film Dissolve effect.

   You can use the Search field, at the top of the panel, to locate the effect by name, or you can manually open the folders of effects.
7. Drag and drop the effect onto the start of the first video clip. You can set the effect only to Start at Cut for the first clip.

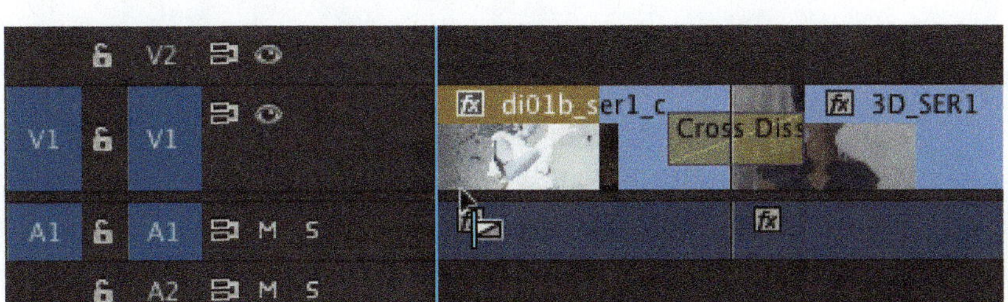

8. Drag the Film Dissolve effect onto the end of the last video clip.

   The Dissolve icon shows that the effect will start before the end of the clip and complete by the time it reaches the clip's end.

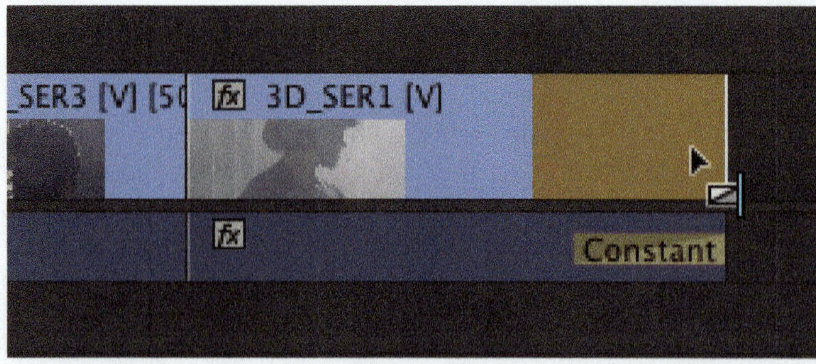

   Because you are applying the Film Dissolve transition onto the ends of clips, where there is no connected clip, the picture dissolves into the background of the Timeline (which happens to be black).

   Transitions of this kind don't extend the clip (using the handle) because the transition doesn't reach past the end of the clip.

9. Play the sequence to see the result.

   You should see a fade from black at the start of the sequence and a fade to black at the end.

10. Save the changes to **L24_start_xx.prproj**, and leave it open.

Applying a Transition between Two Clips

Let's apply transitions between several clips. For the purposes of exploration, we'll break the rules and try a few different options.

Try It!

1. Continue working with the previous sequence, 01 Transitions.

   To make the transition you are about to apply easier to see, you need to zoom in closer to the Timeline.

2. Move the playhead to the edit point between clip 1 and clip 2 on the Timeline, and then press the equal sign (=) three times to zoom in fairly close.

3. Drag the Dip to White transition from the Dissolve category onto the edit point between clip 1 and clip 2.

4. Next, drag the Push transition from the Slide category onto the edit point between clip 2 and clip 3.
5. Click the Push transition effect on the Timeline and go to the Effect Controls panel. Change the direction of the clip from West to East to East to West.

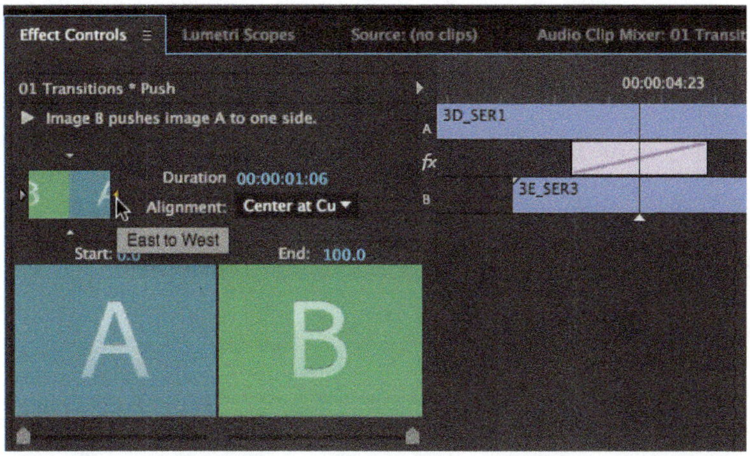

6. Drag the Flip Over transition from the 3D Motion category onto the edit point between clip 3 and clip 4.
7. Review the sequence by playing it from beginning to end.

   Having watched this sequence, you can probably see why it's a good idea to use transitions with restraint.

   Let's try replacing an existing effect.
8. Drag the Split transition from the Slide category onto the existing effect between clip 2 and clip 3. The new transition replaces the old one.
9. Select the Split transition on the Timeline. In the Effect Controls panel, set Border Width to 7 and Anti-aliasing Quality to Medium to create a thin black border at the edge of the wipe.

   The anti-aliasing effect reduces potential flicker when the line animates.

10. Watch the sequence to see the new transition.

    Transitions have a default duration, which is measured in frames, not seconds. This means the frame rate of your sequence will change the time it will take to play a transition. The default transition duration can be changed to match your sequence settings in the General tab of the Preferences panel.

11. Choose Edit > Preferences > General (Windows) or Premiere Pro > Preferences > General (Mac).

12. This is a 24-frames-per-second sequence, so enter a value of 24 frames for Video Transition Default Duration and click OK. Because this matches the frame rate of the sequence, the default duration is now 1 second.

13. Save the changes to **L24_start_xx.prproj**, and close Premiere Pro.

The existing transitions stay the same, but any future ones you add will have the new duration. Be sure to update this value to match your specific needs if you're using 25, 30, or 60 fps sequence settings, keeping in mind that few transitions employed by professional editors are actually a full second in duration.

Comprehension Check

1. What is a jump cut?
2. How do you track down a transition by name?
3. How do you replace a transition with another one?
4. How do you change the duration of a transition?

Lesson 25 Overview

In this lesson, you will learn about:

- Working with Text
- Creating Titles from Scratch

While you will rely upon audio and video sources as the primary ingredients for building a sequence, you will often need to incorporate text into your project. The Adobe Premiere Pro CC Titler is a powerful tool set for text and shape creation.

You can use the Titler in Premiere Pro to create text and shapes. These objects can be placed above video or used as stand-alone clips to convey information to an audience.

Lower-third

Name and title displayed on the lower portion of the viewable region.

Bumpers

Text used to identify sections of longer video.

Working with Text

Text is very effective when you need to convey information quickly to your audience. For example, you can identify a speaker in your video by superimposing their name and title during the interview (often called a **lower-third**). You may also use text to identify sections of a longer video (often called **bumpers**) or to acknowledge the cast and crew (with credits).

Text, properly used, is clearer than a narrator and allows for information to be presented in the middle of dialogue. Text can be used to reinforce key information.

Premiere Pro has a versatile Titler tool. It offers you a range of text editing and shape creation tools that you can use to design effective titles. You can use the fonts loaded on your computer.

You can also control opacity and color and insert graphic elements or logos created using other Adobe applications, such as Adobe Photoshop or Adobe Illustrator.

Exploring the Titler Window

Let's start with some preformatted text and modify it. This is a good way to get an overview of the powerful features of the Premiere Pro Titler. Later in this lesson, you'll build titles from scratch.

Try It!

1. Open the **L25_start.prproj** from the data files for this lesson.

   The sequence 01 Seattle should already be open. If not, open it now.

2. Save the file as **L25_start_xx.prproj** in the location where your teacher instructs you to store the files for this lesson.

3. Go to Window > Workspaces > Effects.

4. Choose Window > Workspaces > Reset to Saved Layout.

5. Double-click the clip Title Start, in the Project panel.

   This is a Premiere Pro title, so it opens in the Titler, with the title displayed over the current frame in the Program Monitor. The text object should be selected by default; if not, click once to choose it.

   Here's a quick rundown of the Titler's panels:

   - **Title Tools panel:** These tools select objects, set text position, define text boundaries, set text paths, and select geometric shapes.
   - **Title Designer panel:** This is where you build and view text and graphics.
   - **Title Properties panel:** Here you'll find text and graphic options, including font characteristics and effects.
   - **Title Actions panel:** You'll use these to align, center, or distribute text and groups of objects.
   - **Title Styles panel:** Here you'll find preset text styles.

A. Title Tools panel
B. Title Actions panel
C. Title Styles panel
D. Title Designer panel
E. Title Properties panel

6. Click a few thumbnails in the Styles panel to acquaint yourself with the default styles available.

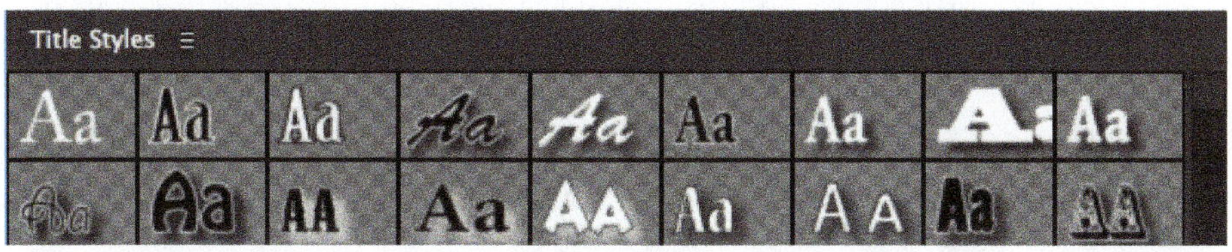

Each time you click a style, Premiere Pro changes the selected text object to that style. Some of the styles are so large that some of the text disappears off-screen; we'll adjust these settings shortly.

7. Choose the style Adobe Garamond White 90, the seventh from the left.

This style works with the background.

8. Click the Font Browser menu at the top of the Titler. This is a duplicate of the Font Browser menu in the Properties panel.

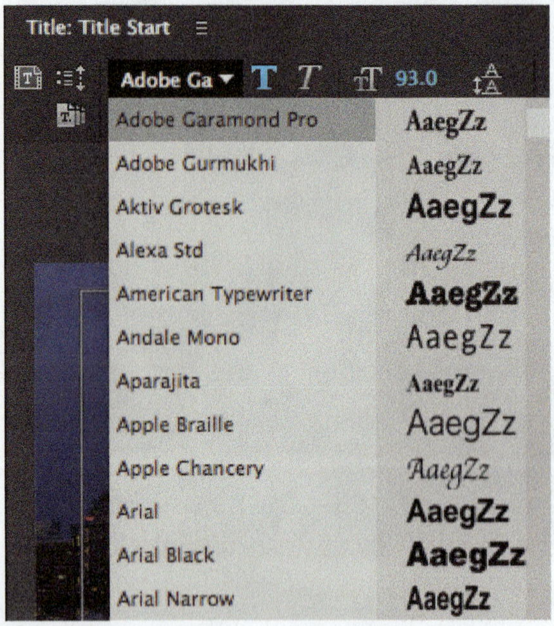

9. Scroll through the fonts. Each time you choose a new font, the text updates. If you click into the menu without using the dropdown option, you can use the Up Arrow and Down Arrow keys on your keyboard to choose different fonts.

10. Click the Font Family menu in the Title Properties panel, on the right side of the Titler. This is another way to change fonts. Experiment with changing the font through this panel. You can also experiment with the Font Style menu.

11. When you've finished experimenting, choose Adobe Caslon Pro (or a similar-looking font) from the Font Family menu. Choose Bold from the Font Style menu to make the text easier to read.

12. Change the font size to 140 by typing 140 into the Font Size field or by dragging the Size number until it reaches 140. When you do this, it's likely the text will be hidden. This is because it no longer fits inside the text box.

13. Resize the text box by dragging the top handle of the bounding box with the Selection tool.

14. In the Title Designer panel, click the Center button to center the text.

15. In the Title Properties panel, change Tracking to 3.0. Tracking changes the spacing between the characters.

    Let's make the drop shadow more pronounced and easier to read.

16. In the Title Properties panel, below the Shadow option. Change Shadow Distance to 10, Shadow Size to 15, and Shadow Spread to 45. You can enter numbers into each field or drag the numbers to scrub their values.

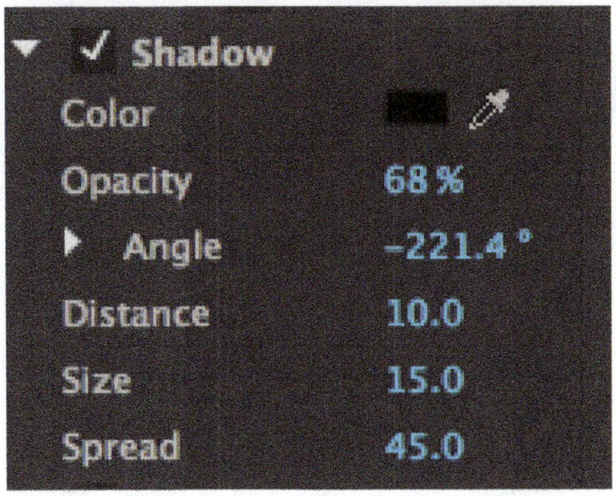

17. In the Title Actions panel in the Center section, click the Horizontal Center and Vertical Center buttons to align the text object to the absolute center of the screen.

    Your screen should look like this.

18. Drag the Titler floating window to the right—far enough to be able to see the Project panel.

19. In the Project panel, double-click Title Finished to load it in the Titler.

20. Your text should look similar to the Title Finished text.

21. Close the Titler by clicking the x in the upper-right corner (Windows) or the Close button in the upper-left corner (Mac).

22. Drag the Title Start clip from the Project panel to the Video 2 track on the Timeline, stretch it so it matches the length of the video clip, and drag the playhead through it to see how it looks over that video clip.

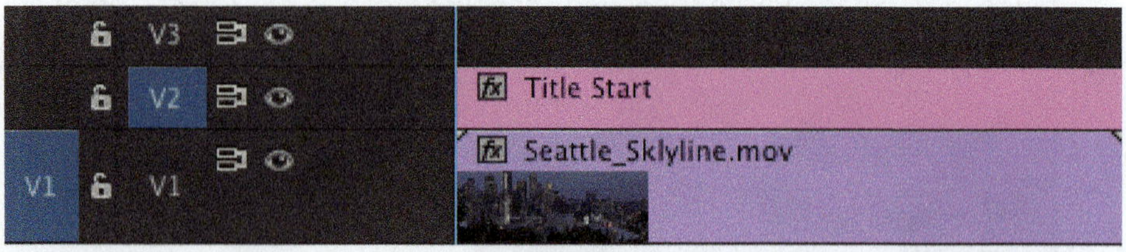

23. Save the changes to **L25_start_xx.prproj**, and leave it open.

Action-safe margin

The outside margin that shows 90 percent of the viewable area, video that takes place outside this region may not be seen.

Title-safe zone

The outside margin that shows 80 percent of the viewable area; text outside this area may not be seen.

Safe Title Margin

When you're designing in the Titler, you'll see a series of two nested boxes. The first box shows you 90 percent of the viewable area, which is considered the **action-safe margin**. Things that fall outside this box may get cut off when the video signal is viewed on a CRT television monitor. Be sure to place all critical elements that are meant to be seen (like a logo) in this region.

The second box, which is 80 percent of the viewable area, is called the **title-safe zone.** Just as this book you're reading has margins to keep the text from getting too close to the edge, it's a good idea to keep text inside the innermost, or title-safe, zone. This will make it easier for your audience to read the information.

Creating Titles from Scratch

When you create a title, you'll need to make some choices about how the text is displayed. The Titler panel offers three approaches to creating text, each offering both horizontal and vertical text-direction options:

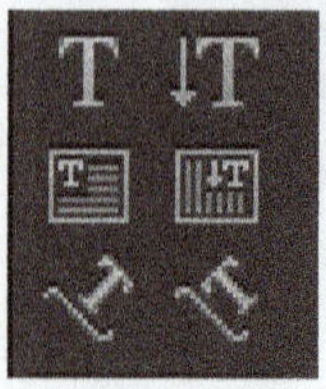

- Point text: This approach builds a text bounding box as you type. The text runs on one line until you press Enter (Windows) or Return (Mac) or until you choose Title > Word Wrap. Changing the shape and size of the box changes the shape and size of the text.

- Paragraph (area) text: You set the size and shape of the text box before entering text. Changing the box size later displays more or less text but does not change the shape or size of the text.
- Text on a path: You build a path for the text to follow by clicking points in the text screen to create curves and then adjusting the shape and direction of those curves using the handles.

In the Title Tools panel, you can select a tool from the left or right column. This determines whether the text will appear horizontally or vertically.

Adding Point Text

Now that you have a basic understanding of how to modify and design a title, let's build one from scratch, working with a new sequence.

You'll create a new title to help promote a tourist destination.

Try It!

1. If the Title panel is open, close it and then open the sequence 02 Cliff.
2. Open the New Title dialog by choosing File > New > Title or by pressing Control+T (Windows) or Command+T (Mac).
3. Type **The Dead Sea** in the Name box, and click OK.

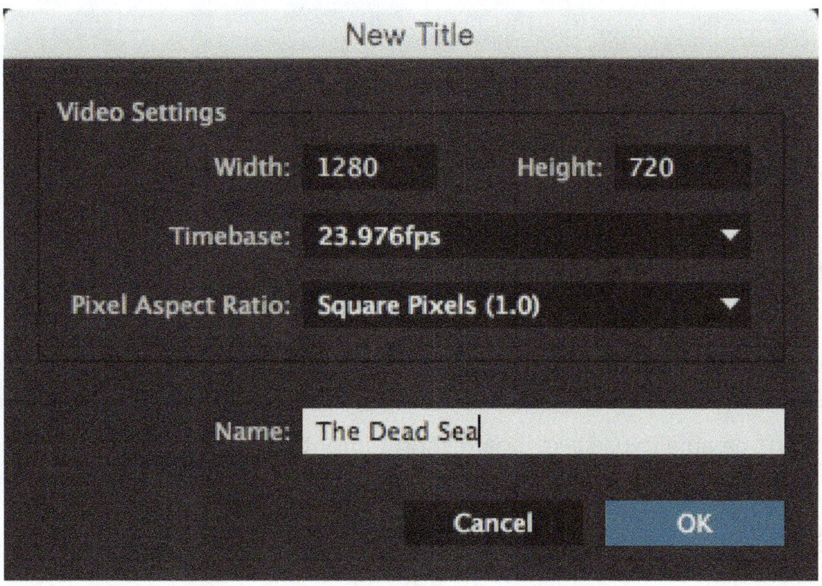

Try changing the background video frame by dragging the timecode next to the Show Background Video button. You can also move the Timeline playhead to change the background image in the Titler, but it may be hidden by the Titler frame.

4. Click the Show Background Video button to hide the video clip.

   The background now shows a grayscale checkerboard, which represents transparency. If you reduce the opacity of text or graphics, you'll see some of the background show through.

5. Click the Myriad Pro White 25 style, highlighted here.

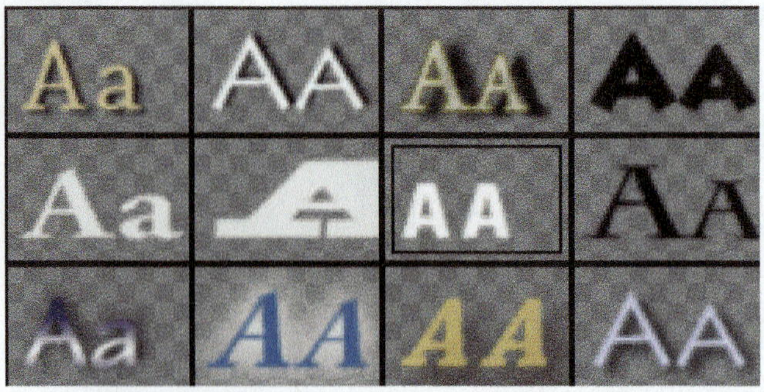

6. Click the Type tool (shortcut T), and click anywhere in the Title Designer.

   The Type tool creates point text.

7. Type **THE DEAD SEA** to match the text in the figure.

8. Click the Selection tool, in the upper-left corner of the Title Tools panel. Handles appear on the text bounding box.

   You won't be able to use a keyboard shortcut for the Selection tool, because you're typing into a text bounding box.

9. Drag the corners and edges of the text bounding box. Notice that the settings for Font Size, Width, and Height change as you do. Hold the Shift key to constrain the text so it scales uniformly.

10. Hover the pointer just outside a corner of the text box until a curved pointer appears. This allows you to rotate the text box. Drag to rotate the bounding box off its horizontal orientation.

11. With the Selection tool still active, click anywhere in the bounding box and drag the text and its bounding box somewhere else in the Title Designer.

    Adjust the size, rotation, and position of the text using the techniques you've learned so far.

12. Click the Show Background Video button to redisplay the background video. Close the Titler window if necessary.

13. Drag The Dead Sea clip from the Project panel to the Video 2 track on the Timeline, stretch it so it matches the length of the video clip, and drag the playhead through it to see how it looks over that video clip.

14. Save the changes to **L25_start_xx.prproj**, and close Premiere Pro.

Comprehension Check

1. What are the differences between point text and paragraph (or area) text?

2. Why display the title-safe zone?

3. What are some of the things you can do in the Title Properties panel?

4. What are the three types of titles you can create with the Titler?

Lesson 26 Overview

In this lesson, you will learn about:

- Sharing Your Project
- Examining Export Options
- Working with Adobe Media Encoder
- Configuring the Export
- Queuing the Export
- Identifing Teamwork and Leadership

One of the best things about editing video is the feeling you have when you can finally share it with your audience. Adobe Premiere Pro offers a wide range of export options to record your projects to tape or convert them to additional digital files.

Exporting your project is the final step in the video production process. Adobe Media Encoder offers multiple high-level output formats. Within those formats you have dozens of options and can also export in batches.

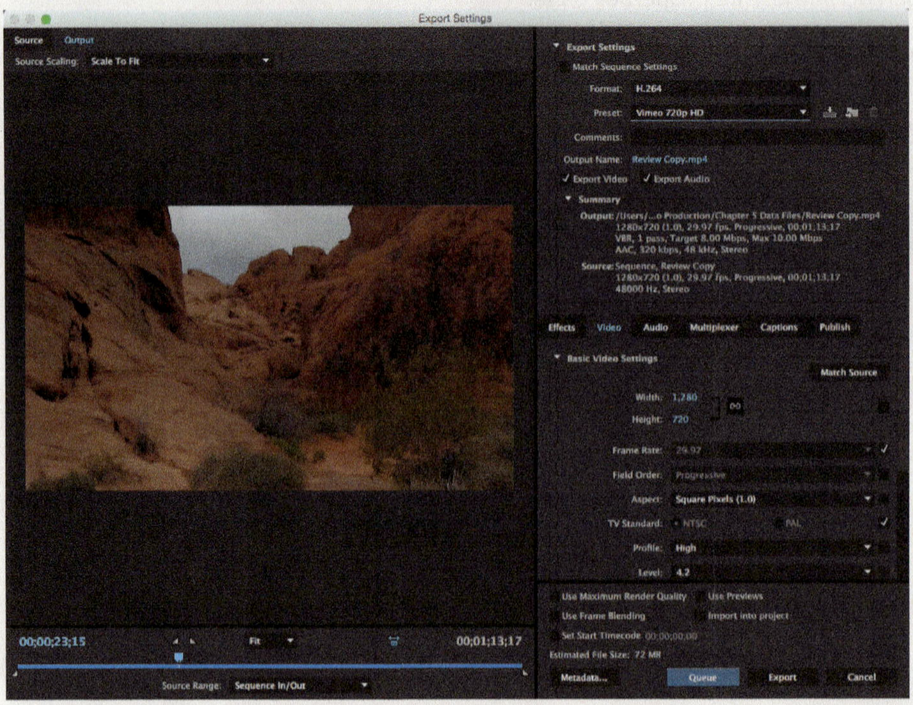

Sharing Your Project

How you share or deliver your project to your client or audience depends on the how you intend to distribute it. Some video-editing applications have direct upload options to online video-hosting services such as YouTube or Vimeo.

Just like with the process of transcoding media for editing, conversion to a more compressed codec for Internet delivery such as H.264, called **encoding**, is needed to keep file size down for quick transfer. Because of the nature of the encoding process, compressing media into a smaller file size while maintaining an acceptable quality can be time-consuming, especially if you have a long program.

Once compressed, you will have a single file, containing all the edited clips, titles, graphics, effects, and audio in one neat compact stream, ready to be delivered through the Internet, stored on the cloud, or copied onto a flash drive or external hard drive.

Nowadays, the primary form of media distribution is digital files. To create these files, you can use Adobe Media Encoder. Adobe Media Encoder is a stand-alone application that handles file exports in batches, so you can export in several formats simultaneously and process in the background while you work in other applications, including Premiere Pro and Adobe After Effects.

Examining Export Options

Whether you've completed a project or you just want to share an in-progress review, you have a number of export options:

- You can select a whole sequence as a single file to post to the Internet or burn to a disk.
- You can export a single frame or a series of frames to post to the Internet or attach to an email.
- You can choose audio-only, video-only, or full audio/video output.
- Exported clips or stills can be reimported back into the project automatically for easy reuse.
- You can play out directly to videotape.

Beyond choosing an export format, you can set several other parameters as well:

- You can choose to create files in a similar format, and at the same visual quality and data rate as your original media, or you can compress them to a smaller size for distribution on disk or the Internet.
- You can transcode your media from one format to another to make it easier to exchange with other people involved in the post-production process.
- You can customize the frame size, frame rate, data rate, or audio and video compression techniques if a particular preset doesn't fit your needs.

You can use exported files for further editing, in presentations, as streaming media, or as sequences of images to create animations.

Working with Adobe Media Encoder

Adobe Media Encoder is a stand-alone application that can be run independently or launched from inside Premiere Pro. One advantage of using Adobe Media Encoder is that you can send an encoding job directly from Premiere Pro and then continue working on your edit as the encoding is processed. If your client asks to see your work before you finish editing, Adobe Media Encoder can produce the file without interrupting your flow.

Choosing a File Format for Export

It can be a challenge to know how to deliver your finished work. Ultimately, choosing delivery formats is a process of planning backwards; find out how the file will be presented and it's usually straightforward to identify the best file type for the purpose.

Very often, clients will have a delivery specification you must follow, making it easy to select the right options for encoding.

Premiere Pro and Adobe Media Encoder can export to many formats. Following is a list of formats and when you should use them.

- **AAC Audio:** The Advanced Audio Coding format is the audio-only format that is most often used with H.264 encoding.
- **AIFF:** The Audio Interchange File Format is an audio-only file format popular on the Mac.
- **AS-11:** This format is based on MXF (see below), with precise configuration for broadcast television delivery. If you're producing content for TV, you might be asked to deliver in this format.
- **DNxHD MXF OP1a:** This format is included primarily for providing compatibility with Avid editing systems. It is, however, a high-quality, cross-platform file format for professional editing.
- **DPX:** DPX (Digital Picture Exchange) is a high-end image sequence format for digital intermediate and special effects work.
- **H.264:** This is the most flexible and widely used format today, with many presets for devices such as the iPod and Apple TV and TiVo Series3 SD and HD, and for services such as YouTube and Vimeo. H.264 files can be played on smartphones or used as high-quality, high-bit-rate intermediate files for work in other video editors.
- **JPEG:** This setting creates a sequential series of still images.
- **MP3:** This compressed audio format is popular because it produces a relatively small file that still sounds good to the ear.
- **MPEG2:** This older file format is primarily used for DVDs and Blu-ray Discs. Presets in this group allow you to produce files that can be distributed for playback on your own or other computers. Many broadcasters use MPEG2 as a format for digital delivery.
- **MPEG2-DVD:** This creates a DVD-compliant MPEG2 video and audio file for standard-definition discs.
- **MPEG4:** This produces lower-quality H.263 3GP files for playback on older cellphones.

- **QuickTime:** This container format can store media using one of several codecs. QuickTime files use the .mov extension, regardless of the codec. It is the preferred format for use on Macintosh computers.
- **Waveform Audio:** This uncompressed audio file format is popular on Windows computers using the .wav formats.

The following formats are available only in Windows:

- **AVI:** Like QuickTime files, this "container format" can store files using one of several codecs. While not officially supported by Microsoft for a number of years, AVI files are still in widespread use.
- **Windows BMP:** This is an uncompressed, rarely used still-image format.
- **Animated GIF and GIF:** These compressed still-image and animated formats are used primarily on the Internet. They're available only on the Windows version of Premiere Pro.
- **Uncompressed Microsoft AVI:** This is a very high-bit-rate intermediate format that is not widely used and is available only on the Windows version of Premiere Pro.
- **Windows Media:** This produces WMV files for playback using the Windows Media Player, and is ideal for Microsoft Silverlight applications (Windows only).

Configuring the Export

To export from Premiere Pro with Adobe Media Encoder, you'll need to queue the project. The first step is to use the Export Settings dialog to make choices about the file you're going to export.

Try It!

1. Start Premiere Pro, and open **L26_start.prproj** from the data files for this lesson.
2. Save the file as **L26_start_xx.prproj** in the location where your teacher instructs you to store this lesson.
3. Make sure the Review Copy sequence is open, and go to File > Export > Media.

   It's best to work through the Export Settings dialog box from the top down. Choose your format and presets first, then pick the output, and finally decide whether you'd like to export audio, video, or both.
4. Choose H.264 from the Format menu. This is a popular choice for files you'll upload to online video Web sites.

> **Note:**
>
> The settings tabs displayed in the Export Settings dialog change depending on the format you choose. Most of the critical options are contained on the Format, Video, and Audio tabs.

5. In the Preset menu, choose Vimeo HD 720p.

   These settings match the frame size and frame rate of the sequence. The codec and data rate match the requirements for the Vimeo.com Web site.

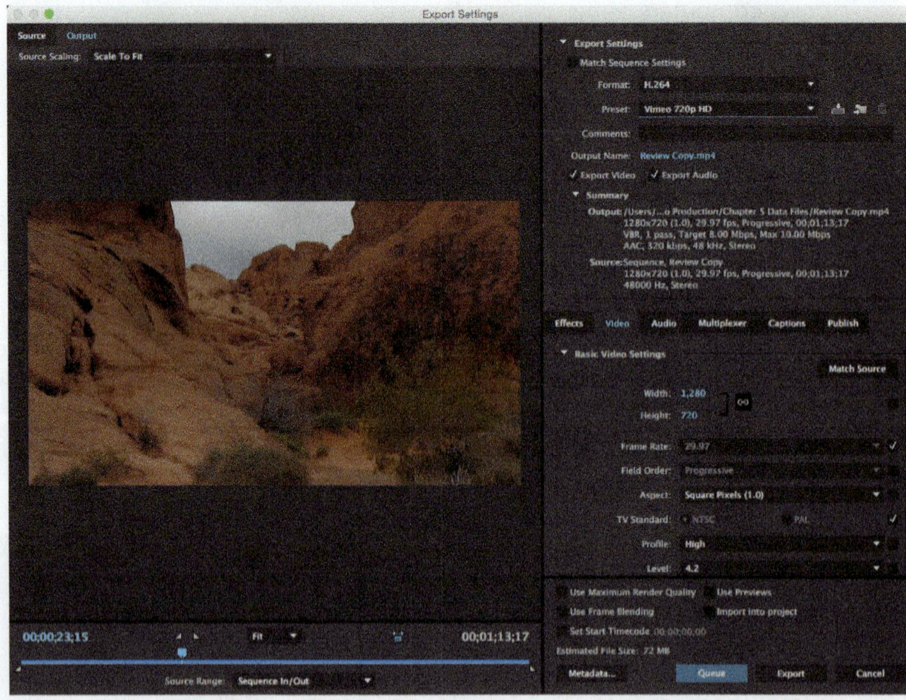

6. Click the output name (the blue text), and rename the file **Review Copy 03.mp4**. Save it to the same destination where you are saving the files for this lesson.
7. Examine the Summary information text to check your choices.
8. Click Export.

   Here's an overview of the various tabs displayed under Summary:

   - **Effects:** You can add a number of useful effects and overlays as you output your media.
   - **Video:** The Video tab allows you to adjust the frame size, frame rate, field order, and profile. The default settings are based on the preset you chose, but you can change them to anything you like.
   - **Audio:** The Audio tab allows you to adjust the bit rate of the audio and, for some formats, the codec. The default settings are based on the preset you chose, but you can change them to anything you like.
   - **Multiplexer:** These controls let you determine whether the encoding method is optimized for compatibility with a specific device (like an iPod or PlayStation Portable). This can also control if the video and audio are combined or delivered as separate files.
   - **FTP:** This tab lets you to enter the details of an FTP server to which to automatically upload the new video file when it has finished encoding. If you create your own preset, this FTP information is included. FTP (File Transfer Protocol) is a standard way to transmit files to a server.

- **Use Maximum Render Quality:** Consider enabling this setting when scaling from larger image sizes to smaller image sizes. This option requires more RAM, which can dramatically slow down the output. This option is usually not needed except when scaling the image and seeking the highest possible quality.
- **Use Previews:** When you render special effects, preview files are produced that look like your original footage combined with the effects. If you enable this option, the preview files will be used as the source for the new export. This can save a significant amount of time that would otherwise be spent rendering the effects again. The result might be lower quality, depending on the sequence preview files format.
- **Queue:** Click the Queue button to send the file to Adobe Media Encoder, which will open automatically, allowing you to continue working in Premiere Pro while the export takes place.
- **Export:** Select this option to export directly from the Export Settings dialog box rather than sending the file to the Adobe Media Encoder queue. This is a simpler workflow and usually a faster export, but you won't be able to edit in Premiere Pro until the export is complete.

9. Click the Queue button to send the file to Adobe Media Encoder, which starts up automatically.
10. Save the changes to **L26 _start_xx.prproj**, and close Premiere Pro.

Career Spotlight: Video Director

A video director is responsible for directing the work of the cast and crew during the production of a video. Directors interpret scripts, select the cast, and manage rehearsals. If necessary, they approve the sets, costumes, choreography, and music.

A few directors succeed in the motion picture industry, but many work for businesses creating training and marketing videos. Many are self-employed, which means they must work hard to promote themselves to get new jobs.

Video directors must prove they have skill and talent. They must also manage a diverse team of people, including actors, producers, and writers, and keep track of the budget. Most attend college to study theater arts, while taking advantage of opportunities to direct videos while in school. They may start their careers as an assistant director.

Use the Internet, a library, or career center to research the responsibilities, education and training requirements, and salary range of a video director. Write a video script for a biography of a successful video director. If possible, turn the script into an actual video, or perform it with a team of classmates.

Identifying Teamwork and Leadership

A team is a group of two or more people who work together to achieve a common goal. When you are part of a team, you have access to all the knowledge, experience, and abilities of your teammates. Together you can have more ideas, achieve more goals, and solve more problems.

Many professionals in the Web and Digital Communications pathway work in teams. For example, audio and video technicians must work with the entire production team to produce a product. Members of an effective team:

- Listen to each other
- Respect each other's opinions
- Recognize each other's skills and abilities
- Share the work load
- Share responsibility

Developing Leadership Characteristics

Even when all members of a team have an equal role in decision making and problem solving, it is important to have a leader. A leader is a type of manager who knows how to use available resources to help others achieve their goals.

Leaders exhibit positive qualities that other people respect, such as self-confidence, honesty, effective listening and speaking skills, decisiveness, respect for others, and open-mindedness. They are organized and supportive of the other team members

Although you might have heard that someone is a "born leader," that's not usually the case. Becoming a leader takes time and patience. Leaders have to prove that they can make decisions, set goals, and solve problems. You can develop leadership characteristics by recognizing and modeling positive leadership qualities. One way to do this is by participating in student leadership and professional development opportunities. For example, you can join clubs and activities such as your school newspaper, yearbook, drama club, or audio-visual club, and volunteer for leadership roles. You might also join a career technical student organization (CTSO) such as SkillsUSA. CTSOs offers members a range of individual and group programs, activities, and competitions designed to build professional skills as well as leadership qualities.

Qualities of an Effective Team Member

While a strong leader is important to the success of a team, team members must also be committed to the group's success. An effective team member helps teammates if they need help, does not blame teammates for problems or mistakes, and offers ideas and suggestions instead of criticism. Effective team member use critical-thinking skills and interpersonal skills to identify and solve problems and achieve their goals.

You are a good team member if you are:

- Open minded
- Willing to compromise
- Cooperative
- Friendly
- Trustworthy

Teamwork Through Technology

Technology plays an important role in the way team members communicate and interact with each other. Collaboration technologies allow teams to share ideas, conduct meetings, and solve problems without any of their members having to leave their desk! E-mail and text messaging are commonly used in the workplace. Other technologies that are growing in popularity include the following:

- Videoconferencing: An online meeting in which participants can see and hear each other on computer or television screens. Videoconferences require equipment such as cameras, a fast network connection, and video screens or computer monitors. A Web-based videoconference allows participants to connect to a Web server, identify themselves, and then join the meeting. Some videoconference programs allow screen-sharing, which means the presenter can share his computer screen or even control the screens of other computers in the conference.
- Blogs and Wikis: A blog—or Weblog—is a type of Web page diary. People create blogs to share their thoughts and opinions. A blog is stored on a Web server, like a Web page, and the owner usually updates it on a regular basis. Anyone with access to the Internet can read the blog. Often, blogs provide a way for readers to comment on the blog content. A wiki is a collaborative Web page. Anyone can edit or create content on the page.
- Internet Relay Chat (IRC): An Internet service that enables users to join chat groups, called channels, and enter into live, or real-time, conversations.

Comprehension Check

1. What Internet-ready export options are available in Adobe Media Encoder?
2. What encoding format should you use when exporting to most mobile devices?
3. Must you wait for Adobe Media Encoder to finish processing its queue before working on a new Premiere Pro project?
4. List at least five qualities of an effective leader.
5. List at least five qualities of an effective team member.
6. What technologies can you use to collaborate with others and gather information?

Review Project

In teams of four or five, work together to plan, develop, and create a video that identifies and promotes a club or organization at your school. Target the video to an audience of middle school students who will be attending your school in the future. Assign each team member the responsibility to lead and manage one aspect of the project. Collaborate as a team to plan the schedule, develop the script, shoot the video, and acquire necessary media resources. Then, organize the oral, written, and graphic information you have collected for use in the project. Compile and edit the content to create your final project. Then, modify the script language and the project design so that you can use the video for a different audience, such as parents.

As you work through the project development process, use critical thinking to solve problems and interpersonal skills to resolve conflict. At key points of the process, ask another team to review and evaluate your work. Use their advice to improve your work. Present your video to the class.

Lesson 27 Overview

In this lesson, you will learn about:

- Capturing Audio Files
- Configuring Audition for Audio Capture and Editing
- Exploring the Audition Workspace
- Navigating in the Audition Workspace
- Editing Audio Clips

Adobe Audition CC is a digital audio editing program that you can use to record, edit, mix, and restore audio files. Audition provides all the tools you need to mix multiple tracks of narration, dialogue, music, and sound effects to create professional-grade audio compositions. In addition to its editing functionality, Audition integrates smoothly with Premiere Pro, so you can edit audio within your video projects.

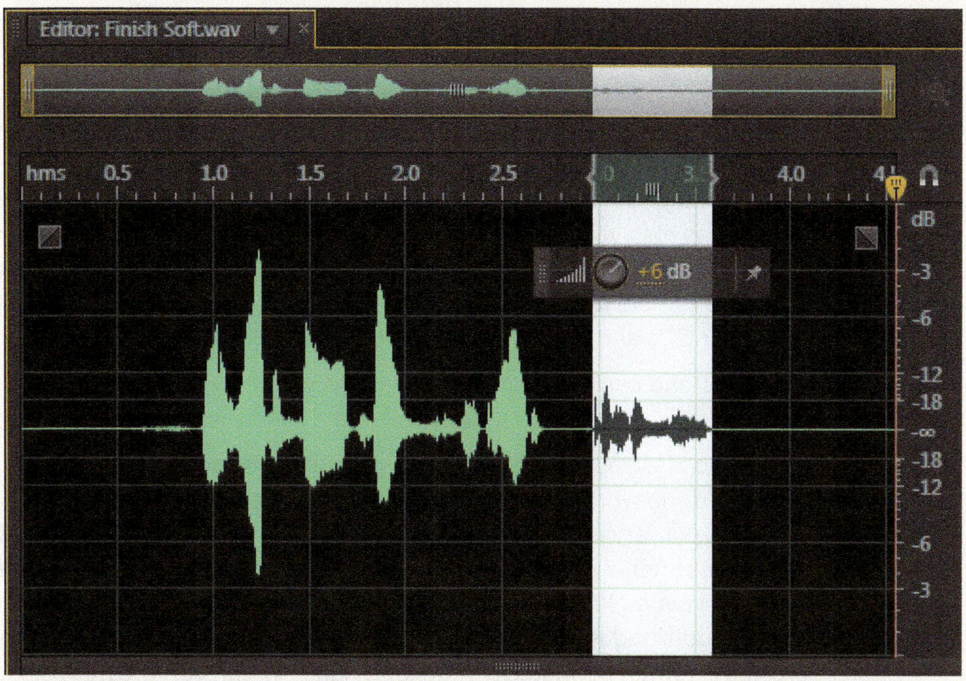

Capturing and Working with Audio

Sound card

Device use to convert audio signals into digital data that your computer and Audition can recognize

Audio interface

External piece of hardware used to convert audio.

Drivers

Handle communications between your computer and audio hardware.

Capturing audio to a computer requires converting audio signals into digital data that your computer and your audio-editing program can recognize. Similarly, playback requires converting that digital data back to analog audio so you can hear it. The device that performs these conversions is usually called a **sound card** when it's built into the computer or an **audio interface** if it's an external piece of hardware. Both include analog to digital (A/D) and digital to analog (D/A) converters. In addition, software **drivers** handle communications between your computer and audio hardware.

You can capture audio sound bites in much the same manner as you capture video.

- Connect the audio source, such as a portable audio recorder or microphone, to the computer's audio input jack using the cables that were bundled with the source. This is typically a USB cable or FireWire.
- If you're not using internal speakers, plug headphones (or earbuds) into the computer's line-level output.
- Open your digital audio-editing program, such as Adobe Audition. Configure the program settings according to the equipment you are using. Set the latency and sample rate values. Latency determines the delay that audio experiences as it passes through the computer. Low values result in less delay through the system, whereas high values increase stability. Sample rate refers to the number of samples or "snapshots" taken of the signal and is measured in hertz/second. The higher the sample rate, the better the sound will be. A value of 44,100 is the sample rate for CDs and most consumer digital audio.
- Arrange frames and panels in your workspace as you do with video capture and editing.
- Open the audio files you want to edit, and use the tools for editing as desired. When you are done working with a file, you can save it in various formats for use on various delivery platforms. Common formats are MP3, which is suitable for the Web or portable media players; Wave PCM (shortened to WAV), which is the audio format on Windows; WMA (Windows Media Audio), which stores compressed audio and is more common for today's devices; AIFF, which is the standard audio format on Mac OS; Monkey's Audio, which compresses files to roughly half their original size; and MP2, which is popular in radio broadcasting.

Configuring Audition

The following exercises assume you are working in Adobe Audition CC, Adobe's digital audio editing program. Before you start, you should configure your system's audio inputs and outputs according to the hardware you are using. You will also need to set preferences and configure settings in Audition as well. These include the device class (usually MME), the default input and output devices, the latency value (200ms for most computers), the sample rate (44100 is standard), and channel mapping.

Testing Inputs and Outputs

Connect your audio source to your computer. If you are not using speakers, plug the earbuds/headphones into the computer's line-level output. Test these connections to ensure that the inputs and outputs are set up properly.

Try It!

1. Start Audition.
2. Choose File > New > Audio File to create a new file in the Waveform Editor. A dialog box appears.

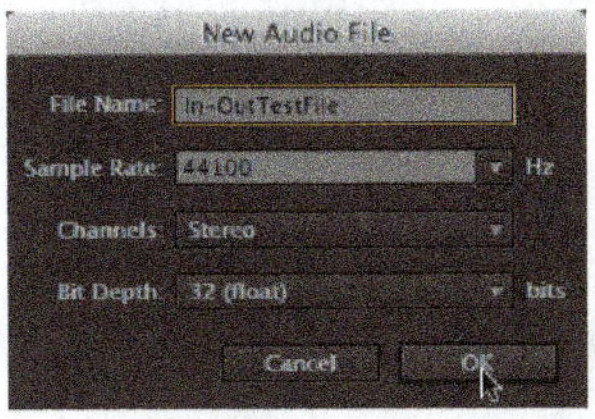

3. Name the file **In-OutTestFile**. The sample rate should default to the value you selected in Preferences.
4. Choose the number of channels. Their inputs will default to what you specified in Preferences. If you choose Mono, only the first channel of the input channel pair will be recorded.

   The bit depth represents the project's internal bit depth, not the bit resolution of your interface's converters. This resolution will be used to calculate changes in volume, effects, and the like, so choose the highest resolution, which is 32 (float).
5. Click OK to close the dialog box.
6. In the Transport panel in the lower left of the Audition window, click the red Record button, and then start playback from your audio source. If all connections are defined and all levels are set properly, you'll see a waveform being drawn in the Waveform Editor window. Record several seconds of audio.
7. Click the Move Playhead to Previous button in the Transport panel, or drag the playhead (also called the *current time indicator [CTI]*) back to the beginning of the file. Click Play, and you should hear what you recorded in your chosen output device (internal speakers, earbuds, or headphones). Click the Stop button to end playback.
8. Now test recording and playback in the Multitrack Editor. Choose File > New > Multitrack session. A dialog box appears.

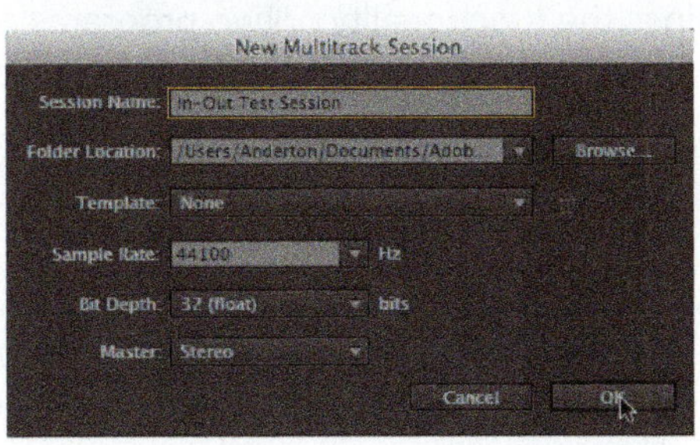

9. Name the file **In-Out Test Session**. For template, choose None. The sample rate should default to the value you selected in Preferences.
10. As with the Waveform Editor, choose the highest resolution of 32 (float), and then choose the number of output channels (Stereo) for the Master Track.

11. Click OK to close the dialog box.

12. Arm a track by clicking the R (Record) button. Start playing your audio source; the channel's meter should indicate a signal. Note that the input will connect automatically to the default input; however, if you click the input field's right arrow, you can choose just one input for mono tracks or you can open the hardware section under Preferences if you have a multi-input audio interface and want to choose an input other than the default.

13. Click the Transport Record button. If all connections are defined and all levels are set properly, you'll see a waveform being drawn in the Multitrack Editor window. Record several seconds of audio.

14. Click the Transport Move Playhead to Previous button, or drag the playhead back to the beginning of the file. Click Play, and you should hear what you recorded in your chosen output device (internal speakers, earbuds, headphones, or monitoring system). Click the Transport Stop button to end playback.

15. Click File > Close All. If you are asked if you want to save the files, click No. Leave Audition open for the next exercise.

The Audition Workspace

Audition's workspace has the same look and functionality as Premiere Pro and other Adobe graphics applications. It consists of frames and panels that you can arrange and customize to suit your needs. You can also choose various ways to navigate through Audition's Waveform Editor and Multitrack Editor.

Audition's Dual Personality

A unique aspect of Audition is that it combines the functionality of two programs within a single piece of software:

- A Waveform Editor that can perform highly detailed and sophisticated editing
- A Multitrack Editor for creating multitrack music productions

The two sections are interrelated in that audio can move freely between the two environments. Audio in the Multitrack Editor can be transferred to the Waveform Editor for detailed editing and then transferred back. Files brought into the Waveform Editor can be tweaked prior to making them the basis of a multitrack project.

Both editors have highly customizable workspaces that you can optimize for any of Audition's uses—not just editing or multitrack productions, but also audio for video, sound library development, audio restoration, sound effects creation, and even forensics. This lesson concentrates on the Waveform Editor, but operations in the Multitrack Editor are similar, and in many cases identical.

Try It!

1. With Audition open, click File > Open. Navigate to the data files for this lesson, and open the file **L27_start.aif**.

2. Choose Window > Workspace > Classic.

3. To make sure the workspace uses the stored version, choose Window > Workspace > Reset "Classic."

4. A dialog box asks if you want to reset Classic to its original layout. Click Yes.

5. Click on the waveform, which is within the waveform's Editor panel.

6. If you want to see more of the waveform's Editor panel, click the panel's left border, and drag to the left to widen the panel.

7. Increase the panel's height by clicking the panel's lower line and dragging down. Return the panel's lower line to its original location.

   As you have seen, every panel has a tab at the top. Click the menu drop-down button to the right of the tab name, and choose Close Panel to hide the panel. (You can always reopen a panel from the Window menu if you need it later.)

8. The Selection/View panel toward the lower right probably isn't needed right now, so click its Close box to free up some more space. Note how the Zoom panel expands to take up the space.

   Every panel is housed in a frame. You can save space by grouping several panels into the same frame to create a collection of panels that has tabs across the top.

9. Click a panel tab to select the panel. You can drag a selected panel to a different location in the window. Click the Time panel's tab and drag it to the right of the Zoom panel's tab. A strip containing this tab turns blue to indicate it is a "drop zone" where a panel can be dropped.

10. Release the mouse button; the Time and Zoom panels are now within a tabbed frame.

11. Click the Transport panel's gripper (the section where you can click and drag a panel to move it), and drag it into the blue drop zone strip that already has the Zoom and Time tabs. Now the Zoom, Transport, and Time panels are all within a tabbed frame.

12. Click the Zoom tab, then the Time tab, and then the Transport tab. Note that the original double rows of Transport buttons are now arranged as a single row, which allows more space for increasing the Editor panel's height.

13. With the Transport tab showing, click in the Editor panel. Click its lower border and drag down until the Transport panel is just high enough to show all the Transport buttons. Click the Time tab and then the Zoom tab, and note that they've also been resized to fit.

14. To create even more space, move the Levels panel to the left of the Audition Workspace. Click the Levels panel gripper, and drag it to the Audition Workspace's left edge, to the left of the waveform's Editor. Now you can drag the bottom of the Editor panel down even further.

15. Choose File > Close. If you are asked if you want to save changes, click No. Leave Audition open for the next exercise.

Navigating in the Audition Workspace

There are three main elements to navigation in the Audition Workspace:

- Navigating to desired files and projects so you can open them, typically using Audition's Media Browser
- Navigation related to playing back and recording audio within the Waveform Editor and Multitrack Editor
- Navigating visually within the Waveform Editor and Multitrack Editor (zooming in and out to specific parts of the file)

Navigating to Files and Projects

For Mac and Windows, Audition adopts standard navigation menu protocols (such as Open and Open Recent) for navigating within the computer to find specific files and projects.

Try It!

1. If necessary, open Audition, navigate to the data files for this lesson, and open the file **L27_start.aif**. Or as a shortcut, choose File > Open Recent > **L27_start.aif**.

2. Choose File > Open Append > To Current.

3. Navigate to the data files for this lesson, choose **String_Harp.wav**, and click Open.

4. The file you selected is appended to the end of the current waveform in the Waveform Editor.

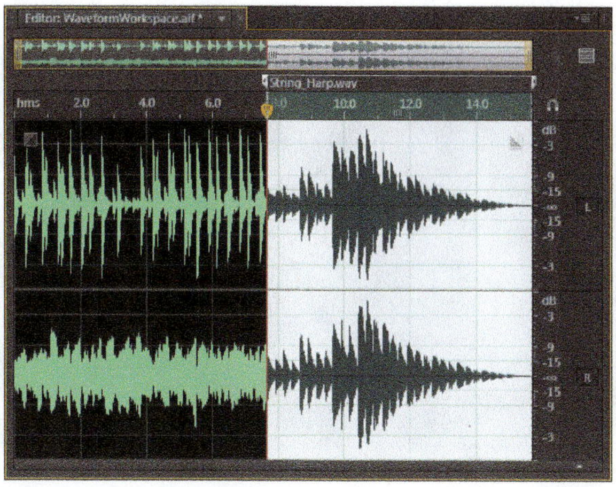

5. Choose File > Open Append > To New.

6. Navigate to the data files for this lesson, choose **String_Harp.wav**, and then click Open.

7. The file you selected opens in a new Waveform Editor view. It does not replace the previously loaded file, and you can select either one using the Editor panel's drop-down menu.

8. Choose File > Close All, and then select No To All in the dialog box. Leave Audition open for the next exercise.

Navigating with the Media Browser

The Media Browser is an enhanced version of the browsing options offered on the Windows and Macintosh operating systems. You should be familiar with it from working in Premiere Pro.

Once you locate a file, you can drag it into the Waveform Editor or Multitrack Editor window.

Try It!

1. Choose Window > Workspace > Default.

2. Choose Window > Workspace > Reset "Default." Click OK in the confirmation dialog box.

3. Click the Media Browser panel's tab or gripper, and drag the panel outside of the workspace to float it. This isn't necessary but makes it easy to extend the size to see all the available options in the Media Browser. Drag the window to the right to extend it.

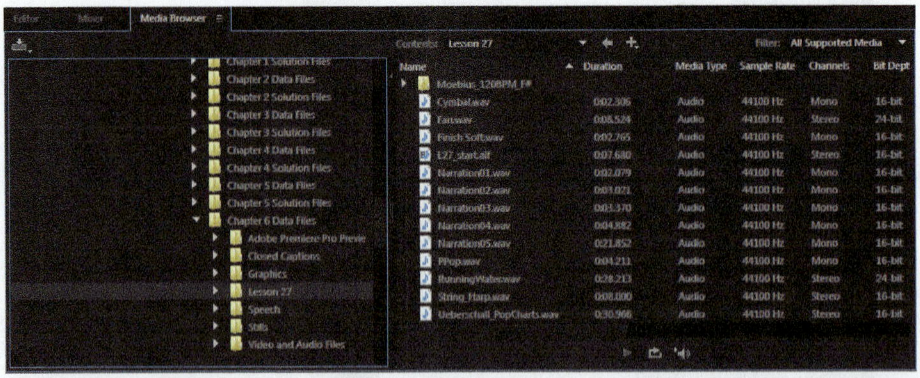

4. The left Media Browser column shows the drives mounted to your computer. Clicking any of these drives displays its contents in the right column. You can also click a drive's disclosure triangle to reveal its contents.

5. In the left column, navigate to the data files for this lesson. Click its disclosure triangle to expand it, and then click the **Moebius_120BPM_F#** folder.

   The folder's audio files are shown in the right column. Note how additional subcolumns show file attributes, such as duration, sample rate, channels, and more.

6. You can change subcolumn widths. Click the divider line between two subcolumns, and drag left or right to change the width.

7. You can rearrange the order of subcolumns. Click a column name, like Media Type. Drag it left or right to position it. This feature is helpful because you can drag the columns containing the information you need the most to the left side, so the data is visible even if the window isn't fully extended to the right.

8. Another Media Browser advantage is that you can listen to the files as you browse, thanks to the Preview Transport. If it's not visible, choose Show Preview Transport from the drop-down menu in the Media Browser tab. Click the Auto-Play button with the speaker icon; you'll then be able to hear a file play when you click it. Click the Stop button to stop the recording.

9. Choose Window > Workspace > Reset "Default." Leave Audition open for the next exercise.

Navigating within Files and Sessions

Once you're in the Waveform Editor or Multitrack Editor, you'll want to be able to navigate within the Editor to locate or edit specific sections. Audition has several tools you can use to do this.

Try It!

1. Using the File > Open command or the Media Browser, navigate to the data files for this lesson, and open the file **L27_start.aif**.

2. Drag the left border of the Editor window so you can see all the Transport and Zoom buttons at the bottom.

3. Click about a third of the way into the waveform and drag to about two-thirds of the way through the waveform to create a selection. Notice the playhead at the top at the beginning of the selection.

4. Click anywhere in the waveform to deselect the selection. Leave the file open for the next exercise.

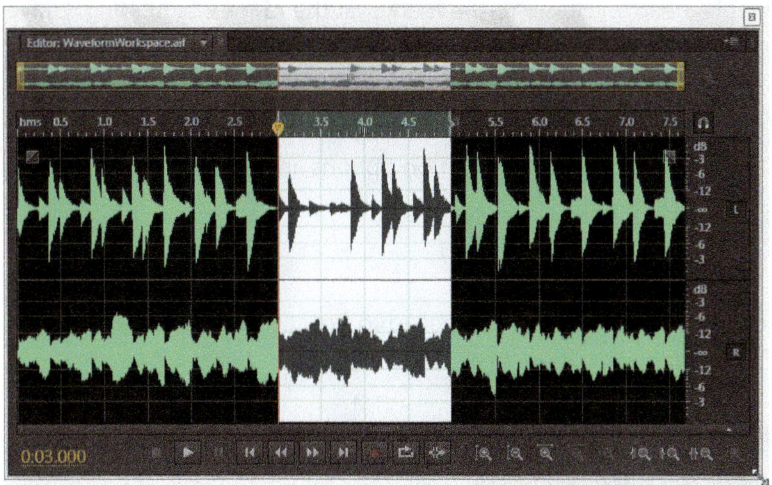

Navigation with Markers

You can place markers (also called cues) within the Waveform Editor and Multitrack Editor to indicate specific places you want to navigate to immediately. For example, in a Multitrack project, you might place markers before a verse and chorus so you can jump back and forth between them. In the Waveform Editor, you might place markers to indicate places where edits are required.

1. Choose Window > Markers to open the Markers panel.

2. Click in the waveform toward the beginning, around 1.0 second.

3. Press M to add a marker at the playhead location and add the marker to the list of markers in the marker window.

4. Now click in the waveform at around 3.0 seconds. As an alternate way to add a marker, click the Add Cue Marker button in the Markers panel.

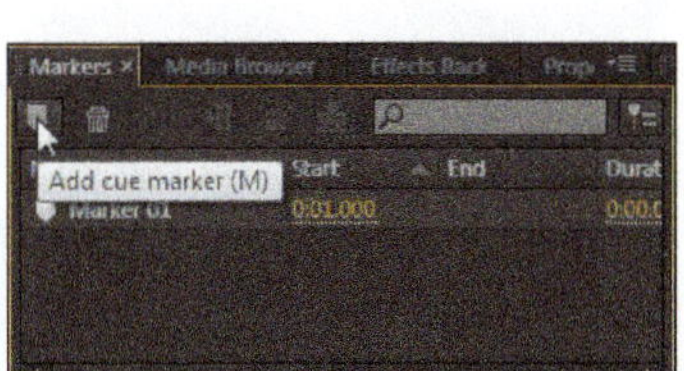

5. You can also mark a selection. Click around 5.0 and continue to drag right to 6.0 to create a selection. Press M to mark the selection. Note that the Markers panel shows a different symbol to indicate that this Range marker is marking a selection.

6. You can also convert the Range marker to an individual marker at the selection start. Right-click (Control-click) on either the start or end of the Range marker, and then choose Convert to Point. You will then see a single marker around 5.0.

7. There are several ways to navigate among markers. Double-click any marker in the Markers panel list, and the playhead will jump to that marker. With Range markers, the playhead will jump to the marker at the range's beginning. Leave the file open for the next exercise.

Navigation with the Transport

The Transport controls offer several navigation options, including navigation using markers.

Try It!

1. In the Editor panel, click the Move Playhead to Previous button. The playhead moves to Marker 2.

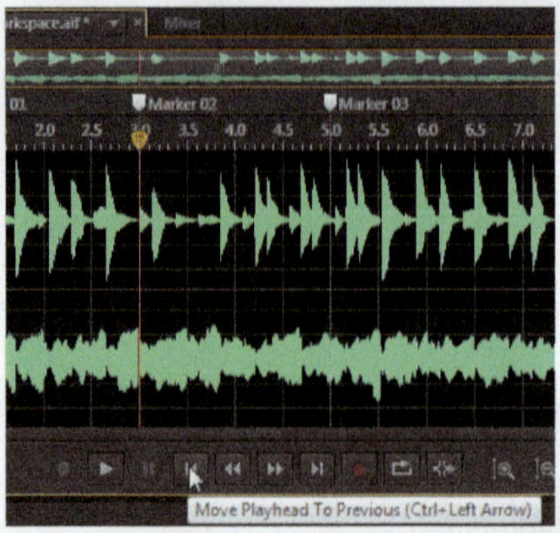

2. Click the Move Playhead to Previous button again. The playhead moves to Marker 1. Click the Move Playhead to Previous button once more, and the playhead moves to the beginning of the file.

3. Click the Move Playhead to Next button (the button to the left of the Record button with the red dot) four times. The playhead steps to each marker until it reaches the end of the file.

4. To move the playhead backward in the file without dragging the playhead or using markers, click and hold the Rewind button in the Transport until the playhead is in the desired location. You'll hear audio during the scrolling process. Rewind back to the beginning.

5. Click the Play button (the second Transport button from the left with the right arrow). Playback begins.

6. As soon as the playhead passes the first marker, click the Move Playhead To Next button. The playhead jumps to the second marker. Click the Move Playhead To Next button again, and the playhead jumps to the third marker.

7. Right-click (Control-click) the Transport Play button and choose Return Playhead to Start Position on Stop. With this option selected, clicking Stop will return the playhead to where it started. With this option deselected, the playhead will stop at the position it had when you clicked the Stop button.

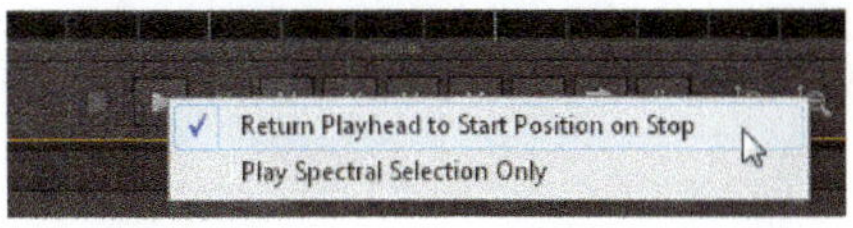

8. Click File > Close to close the L27_start.aif file. Click No when you are asked if you want to save changes. Leave Audition open for the next exercise.

Editing Audio Files

Audition makes it easy to cut, paste, copy, trim, fade, and apply other edits to audio files. You can also zoom in to make extremely precise edits while seeing a zoomed-out version in the overview window at the top.

You can open multiple files in Adobe Audition, which are stacked behind each other in the main Waveform view. Individual files are selected via the Editor panel drop-down menu for file selection.

Try It!

1. With Audition open, in the Files panel, click the Open file button. Navigate to the data files for this lesson, select the file **Narration01**, and then click Open.

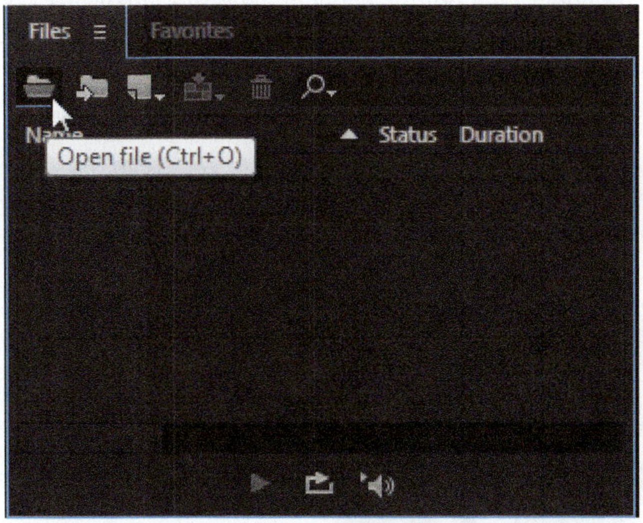

2. To open multiple files simultaneously, choose File > Open, and navigate to the data files for this lesson. Select **Narration02**, and then Shift-click on **Narration05**. Four files are selected. (To select noncontiguous files, press Ctrl-click [Command-click] on each file you want to load.)

3. Click Open. Audition loads the selected files and displays the list of files in the Files panel.

4. In the Files panel, double-click one of the Narration files to display it in the Waveform Editor. Click the Play button to listen to the recording.

5. Click the Editor panel's file selector drop-down menu (in its tab, to the right of the panel name) to see a list of the files you loaded. Click on any of these files to select it and open it in the Waveform view.

6. Open the file **Finish Soft.wav** from the data files for this lesson. Leave Audition open for the next exercise.

Selecting a Region for Editing and Changing its Level

To begin editing your audio, you need to start by choosing a file and specifying which parts of that file you want to edit.

Try It!

1. If **Finish Soft.wav** isn't the currently loaded waveform, click on the Editor panel drop-down menu to see a list of recent files loaded into Audition. Select **Finish Soft.wav**, and it will load into the Editor panel.

2. Click the Play button to hear the file play from start to finish.

   Note how the words "to finish" are softer than the other words. Sometimes when you're recording narration, a drop in volume can occur at the end of phrases. You can fix this in Audition.

3. Click at the beginning of the words "**to finish**," and then drag to the end (or click at the end and drag to the beginning). You've now selected those words for editing, as indicated by a white background. You can fine-tune the selection by clicking on the region's right or left border, either in the Waveform view or time-line, and dragging. Note that upon selecting a region, a heads-up display (HUD) with a small volume control appears automatically.

4. Click on the HUD's volume control and drag upward to increase the volume level to +6dB. To preview this change, click Play. Then click anywhere in the wave-form to deselect the selection, move the playhead to the beginning, and click Play to hear the change in context.

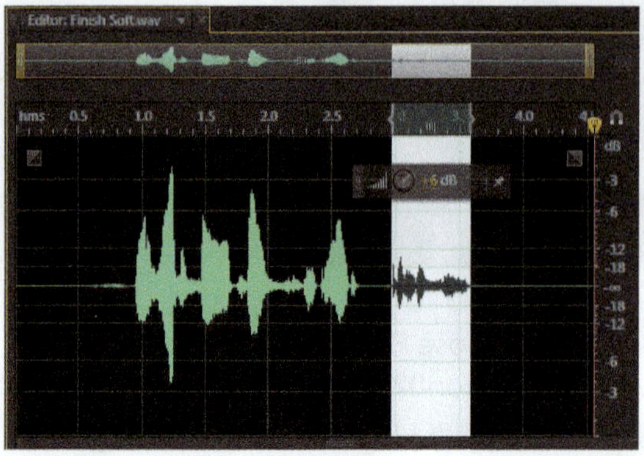

5. If the level is good, you're done. If not, choose Edit > Undo Amplify, or press Ctrl+Z (Command+Z). Then you can vary the level and audition the results again, as you did in the previous step.

6. When you're satisfied with the level, click anywhere in the waveform to deselect the region. Audition will retain any volume changes, because they occur as soon as you change the level, and they will be retained unless you undo the edit.

7. Make sure the **Finish Soft.wav** clip is selected in the Files panel. Click File > Save As. In the Save As dialog box, rename the file **Finish Soft_xx.wav**, and navigate to the location where your teacher instructs you to save files for this lesson. Click OK. Leave Audition open for the next exercise.

Cutting, Deleting, and Pasting Audio Regions

Cutting, deleting, and pasting audio regions is particularly useful with narration audio files because you can remove unwanted sounds from your narration, like coughs or "umms," tighten up spaces, increase spaces between words and phrases, and even rearrange the dialogue if needed. In this next exercise, you'll edit the narration file Narration05.wav so it flows logically and doesn't have unwanted sounds. Here's what the narration says:

"First, once the files are loaded, select the file you, uh, want to edit from the drop-down menu. Well actually, you need to go to the File menu first, select open; then choose the file you want to edit. Remember; you can (clears throat) open up, uh, multiple files at once."

You'll get rid of the uhs and throat clearing, and rearrange the narration to say:

"Go to the File menu first; select open; then choose the file you want to edit. Remember: you can open up multiple files at once. Once the files are loaded, select the file you want to edit from the drop-down menu."

Try It!

1. In the Files panel, double-click the file **Narration05.wav** to open it in the Waveform Editor.

2. Click File > Save As. Click File > Save As. In the Save As dialog box, rename the file **Narration05_xx.wav** in the location where your teacher instructs you to save files for this lesson. Click OK.

3. Play the file until you reach the first "**uh**." Stop the Transport, and click and drag across the "**uh**" to select it.

   To hear what the file will sound like after you delete the "uh," click in the timeline several seconds prior to the region, and then click Skip Selection (the rightmost transport button). Click the Transport Play button; the file will play up to the region start, and then seamlessly skip to the region end and resume playback.

4. Choose Edit > Delete to delete the "**uh**."

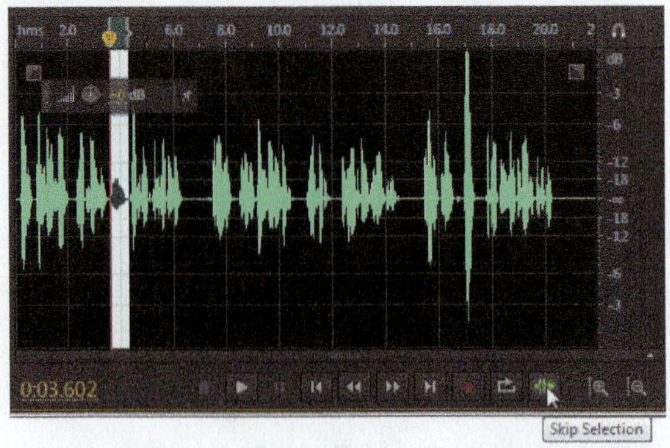

When you invoke this command (Delete), you may not see any visual difference when zoomed out, because the adjustments are often very minor. However, Audition is indeed moving the region boundaries as defined by the command; you can verify this by zooming in to the waveform so you can see the results with more accuracy.

5. Play the recording from the beginning and listen for the unwanted throat clearing. Click somewhat before the throat clearing section and slightly after it. Click the Skip Selection button and then replay the section. When you are satisfied with the edit, press the Del key on your keyboard as a shortcut.

6. Now delete the second "uh" that's in the audio. This occurs after the throat clearing noise you just removed. You may need to zoom in to be more precise in your editing.

   Notice that deleting this "uh" results in too tight a transition between the words before and after the "uh" (you also have to be careful not to cut off too much of the beginning of the word "multiple").

7. Undo your last cut (press Ctrl+Z [Command+Z]). Instead of deleting the "uh," you'll insert silence instead to produce a better result. To do this, select the "uh" and choose Edit > Insert > Silence. A dialog box appears denoting the length of the silence, which will equal the region length you defined. You could edit this, but simply click OK.

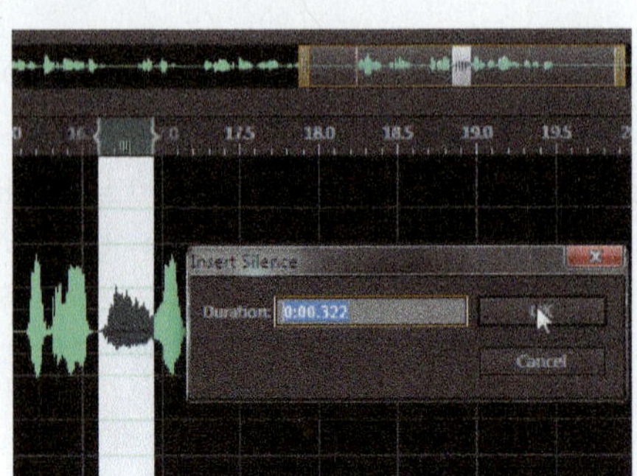

8. If the silent gap is too long or too short, redefine it. You may have to test and redefine several times to get it right. When you are satisfied with the edit, choose Edit > Delete. The gap is now shorter.

9. Save the **Narration05_xx.wav** file and leave Audition open for the next exercise.

Now that you've fixed some of the verbal glitches, let's change the sentence structure into a more coherent narration.

Cutting and Pasting with Multiple Clipboards

You're probably familiar with the computer's clipboard. In a word processing program, you typically copy a sentence to the clipboard and then paste it from the clipboard to somewhere else in the text. Audition's clipboard feature works similarly but it has five clipboards so you can temporarily store up to five different pieces of audio for pasting later. You'll put that feature to good use when making additional edits to the Narration05 file.

Try It!

1. Select the part of the file that says, "**Once the files are loaded, select the file you want to edit from the drop-down menu.**"

2. Choose Edit > Set Current Clipboard and select Clipboard 1 (it will likely already be selected). You can also select this clipboard by pressing Ctrl+1 (Command+1).

3. To remove the phrase and store it in Clipboard 1, choose Edit > Cut, or press Ctrl+X (Command+X) to place the phrase in Clipboard 1. The word (Empty) will no longer appear next to the Clipboard 1 name.

4. Select the part of the file that says, "**Go to the file menu first; select open; then choose the file you want to edit.**" You might find it helpful to mark beginning and end points with markers.

5. Press Ctrl+2 (Command+2) to make Clipboard 2 the current clipboard (you could also choose Edit > Set Current Clipboard and select Clipboard 2).

6. Choose Edit > Cut to place the phrase in Clipboard 2.

7. Select the part of the file that says, "**Remember; you can open up multiple files at once.**"

8. Press Ctrl+3 (Command+3) to make Clipboard 3 the current clipboard.

9. Choose Edit > Cut to place the phrase in Clipboard 3.

10. Save the **Narration05_xx** file and leave it open for the next exercise.

Now you have a separate clip for each phrase, which will make it easy to place the phrases in a different order. The goal is to end up with "Go to the file menu first; select open; then choose the file you want to edit. Remember; you can open up multiple files at once. Once the files are loaded, select the file you want to edit from the drop-down menu."

Try It!

1. Select all the leftover bits of audio in the Narration05 file (or simply press Ctrl+A [Command+A]), and press the Delete key. This clears all the audio and places the playhead at the file's beginning.

2. Clipboard 2 contains the introduction you want. Press Ctrl+2 (Command+2) to select that clipboard, and then choose Edit > Paste or press Ctrl+V (Command+V).

3. Disable Skip Selection, return the playhead to the beginning of the file, and then click Play to confirm you have the desired audio.

4. Click within the Waveform view to deselect the pasted audio. Otherwise, subsequent pasting will replace the selected region.

5. Click where you want to insert the next phrase.

   For this Try It, you'll place it at the end of the existing audio.

6. Clipboard 3 has the desired middle section for this project. Press Ctrl+3 (Command+3), and then press Ctrl+V (Command+V).

7. Repeat steps 4 and 5.

8. Clipboard 1 has the desired ending for this project. Press Ctrl+1 (Command+1), and then press Ctrl+V (Command+V).

   Play the file to hear the rearranged audio. For further practice, you can do the following:

   - Tighten up spaces between words by selecting a region and pressing Ctrl+X (Command+X) or Delete, or choosing Edit > Cut.
   - Add more space between words by placing the playhead where you want to insert silence (don't drag; just click on the desired point in the timeline) and choosing Edit > Insert > Silence. When a dialog box appears, enter the desired duration of silence in the format minutes:seconds.hundredths of a second.

9. Click File > Close All. Close Audition.

Comprehension Check

1. What is the function of a sound card?
2. What is the difference between capturing audio and audio playback?
3. Provide at least two examples of an audio source.
4. Summarize the process for capturing audio and/or sound bites.
5. In which formats can you save an audio file for exporting? When would you use each?

Review Project

Create a "how-to" audio clip, similar to the one you worked on in this lesson. Think of something you know how to do that you could teach others how to do;

for example, how to use a template to create a resume, or how to open a savings account, or even how to make salsa. Prepare a script with instructions. Using a microphone or other device, record your instructions. If necessary, capture the audio clip to your computer. Open and edit the clip in Audition. When you are finished, save and export it in a format of your choice and share it with the class.

End-of-Chapter Activities

Review Questions

1. Describe the differences between a linear and a nonlinear editing system.
2. Identify and explain the stages in a standard digital video workflow.
3. Explain the impact of audio and video selection on human emotions. Provide at least three examples from movies you have seen.
4. Describe eight different tips for shooting quality video.
5. List and describe the components of a script/screen play.
6. Describe the steps for capturing or ingesting media into Premiere Pro.
7. What is the difference between point text, paragraph text, and text on a path.
8. What are at least two ways you can develop leadership qualities?

Multiple Choice

1. The payment you make to register your work with the U.S. Copyright Office is known as what?
   a. Copyright clearance
   b. Intellectual property
   c. Copyright fee
   d. Release form
2. What is the term for existing work that belongs to somebody else?
   a. Derivative works
   b. Copyrighted material
   c. Patented material
   d. Authorized content
3. What is the term for content that no longer has a copyright attached to it?
   a. Royalty free
   b. Out of copyright
   c. Patent free
   d. Fair use
4. When should you seek copyright clearance?
   a. Always
   b. Only if it is a short extract
   c. Only if it is a long extract
   d. Always, unless it comes under the fair use doctrine
5. Which of the following industry terms are used for transferring media from your camera ready for editing? (select all answers that apply)
   a. Ingest
   b. Transforming
   c. Capturing
   d. Editing

6. What type of shot moves with the action?
   a. Lower-third
   b. Rule of thirds
   c. Trucking
   d. Leaning in and out
7. What is the term for a technique that sets the scene in one image?
   a. Tight shot
   b. Establishing
   c. Rule of thirds
   d. Close-up
8. What type of shot is typically used to show detail in a face?
   a. Tight shot
   b. Wide shot
   c. Rule of thirds
   d. Close-up
9. Typically, what part of the screen is used to provide informational text during an interview or news item?
   a. Upper-third
   b. Lower-third
   c. Middle-third
   d. Center
10. What tool can you use in Audition to mark spots in the waveform that you want to navigate to immediately?
    a. Markers
    b. Playheads
    c. Levels
    d. Tracks

Chapter 6 – Portfolio Builder

Complete the following steps to begin editing a Premiere Pro project. The project file has been started for you and all the assets organized in bins.

DIRECTIONS

1. Launch Adobe Premiere Pro and open **PB6.prproj** from the data files for this lesson.
2. Save your project as **PB6_xx.prproj** and save in the location where your teacher instructs you to store the files for this lesson.
3. Choose Window > Workspaces > Editing.
4. Choose Window > Workspaces > Reset to Saved Layout
5. In the Interview bin, marquee-select the clips **Interview_03.mp4** through **Interview_08.mp4**.
6. Click and drag the selected clips into the sequence, directly to the right of the existing clip.
7. Make sure the edge of the new clips snaps to the edge of the existing clip.
8. Drag the playhead to the beginning of the sequence, or press the Home key.
9. Press the spacebar to begin playback, and then stop playback after the first clip.
10. Park the playhead at 00:00:05:00.
11. Zoom in on your Timeline by pressing the equal (=) key on your main keyboard (not the numeric keypad) three times.
12. Drag the playhead to the right and then back to the left again, so you can hear where he says the word *and*.
13. Click on the Collapse-Expand Track triangle to twirl down Audio 1.
14. Hover your pointer over the divider line between Audio 1 and Audio 2 until it changes shape, and then drag downward to stretch Audio 1 vertically in the Timeline.
15. Drag the playhead back and forth over the word *and* so you can identify it in the audio waveform.
16. Park the playhead at 05:17.
17. In the Program Monitor, click the Mark In button.
18. Park the playhead at 06:04.
19. In the Program Monitor, click the Mark Out button.
20. Now let's remove the video and audio from this region of time. Click the Extract button.
21. Drag the playhead to the beginning of the sequence, or press the Home key.
22. Make sure that the Program Monitor is set to show the entire frame.
23. Press the spacebar to play back the first 15 seconds of the edit, and then stop playback.
24. Press the backslash (\) key to zoom the sequence to fit the Timeline panel.
25. In the Project panel, double-click the **Live** bin to open it.
26. Select **Live_01.mp4**. Hold down the Shift key and select **Live_25-60.mp4**. This will select all clips in between.
27. Click the Toggle Track Output button for Video 2 to make it invisible.
28. Click the Toggle Track Output button for Video 2 again to make it visible.
29. Close the Live bin by selecting it and pressing Command+W (Ctrl+W).
30. Press the backslash (\) key to zoom your sequence to fit the Timeline panel.
31. Click the last clip on the Timeline in Video 2, **Live_25-60.mp4**, to select it.
32. Click and drag the clip to the beginning of Video 2.
33. Choose Edit > Undo to undo your Overwrite edit.
34. Click the last clip on the Timeline in Video 2, **Live_25-60.mp4**, to select it.
35. While holding down the Command (Ctrl) key, click and drag the clip to the beginning of Video 2. Notice how the pointer changes while you do this.
36. Choose Edit > Undo to undo your Insert edit.
37. Toggle on the Lock button on both Video 1 and Audio 1.

38. Click the last clip on the Timeline in Video 2, **Live_25-60.mp4**, to select it.
39. While holding down the Command (Ctrl) key, click and drag the clip to the beginning of Video 2.
40. Click the next-to-last clip on Video 2, **Live_23-60.mp4**.
41. While holding down the Command (Ctrl) key, click and drag the clip so it lines up with the beginning of the **Live_01.mp4** clip on Video 2.
42. Release the mouse button.
43. Select the **Live_02.mp4** clip on your Timeline, and while holding down the Command (Ctrl) key, drag it to the beginning of the **Live_01.mp4** clip and drop it there.
44. Move the playhead to the beginning of the sequence, and start playback to review your changes.
45. Stop playback.
46. Press the backslash key (\) to show your entire sequence.
47. Select the clip at the end, Live_24-60.mp4.
48. Press the Delete key. The clip is deleted from your sequence.
49. Find what is now the second-to-last clip in Video 2, Live_21.mp4, and select it.
50. Press the Delete key.
51. Zoom in to your Timeline by pressing the equal (=) key.
52. Click on the gap between Live_20.mp4 and Live_22.mp4.
53. Right-click on this selection and choose Ripple Delete. Live_22.mp4 automatically moves to the left and fills in the gap.
54. Select the Live_01.mp4 clip on your Timeline.
55. Right-click on the clip and choose Ripple Delete.
56. In the Project panel, twirl open the Audio bin.
57. Double-click the file **Can't_Listen_Edited_Even.aif** to load it into the Source Monitor.
58. Press the spacebar to preview the audio file.
59. In the Timeline, click the disclosure triangle on the Audio 1 track to collapse the track and hide its waveform.
60. In the Source Monitor, click and drag the Drag Audio Only button to the Audio 2 track on your Timeline.
61. Make sure the beginning of the audio file lines up with the beginning of the sequence, and then release your mouse button.
62. Adjust the playhead to the beginning of your sequence. Press the spacebar to preview the sequence with the new audio added. Stop playback when you're finished previewing.
63. Choose Window > Audio Mixer > **Afrolicious Promo Edit 01**. The Audio Mixer panel appears.
64. With the sequence playing back, click and drag down the volume fader for Audio 2 in the Audio Mixer until the volume is low enough so you can hear Joey's voice clearly. This will be in the area of –12dB.
65. Press the spacebar to stop playback.
66. Press Command+S (Ctrl+S) to save your project and then close Premiere Pro.

Chapter 6 – Critical Thinking

Write a Script and Create a Visual Poem

The Visual Poem project is designed to allow you to stretch your imagination and exercise your style and creativity to demonstrate your skills in visual storytelling. The concept is simple: Make a video that visualizes the ideas, images, and language of a poem written by a notable poet or author.

Directions

1. Choose a poem from a notable poet or author or write your own. You can also ask your teacher for suggestions!
2. Analyze the poem. Write a few sentences describing what the poem means to you and what you think the poet intended it to mean. This might require some research.
3. Script it out. For each line of the poem, describe what actions and/or images would be ideal to express the ideas, meaning, theme, and subtext beyond what just the words mean. Use the script format you learned about in this chapter.
4. Storyboard it! Using the description for each shot written in your script, draw out what those images should actually look like on the screen.
5. Plan your shoot. Create every single document that a professional production would require. That means a schedule, a budget, and a script breakdown for every scene.
6. Shoot beautiful images. Having scheduled enough time, experiment with the controls of the camera. Be curious and try things that you think you might not even use in the finished video. If it doesn't work, don't use it!
7. Create a Premiere Pro project and name it **CT6_xx.prproj**.
8. Start your edit by laying down the voiceover. Edit the appropriate image over each line of the poem. If you have more than one shot per line, try cutting them in. If it works well with the pace and rhythm of the poem and how you performed it, then be happy you shot more than you thought you needed.
9. Read the poem out loud into a microphone. Record a voiceover narration by delivering a performance of the poem that uses appropriate tone, emphasis, volume, and pacing.
10. Add sound effects and music that you created and recorded or are royalty-free.
11. Export the video in a format of your choice that allows you to share it with your class, and others, if desired.
12. Save the file and then close Premiere Pro.

Chapter 7

Designing Web Pages with Adobe Dreamweaver CC

Lesson 28 | Creating and Formatting Web Pages

Exploring the Dreamweaver Workspace
Creating a Web Site
Understanding Web Design Guidelines
Adding Keywords to a Web Site
Understanding HTML and XHTML
Adding Text to a Web Site
Importing Text to a Web Site
Editing Text
Formatting Text with the CSS Designer

Lesson 29 | Adding Links and Digital Media to Web Pages

Creating Links
Previewing a Web Site
Applying Colors and Rules
Inserting Graphics on a Web Page
Inserting Animation on a Web Page
Working with Audio and Video
Publishing a Site

End-of-Chapter Activities

Lesson 28 Overview

In this lesson, you will learn about:

- Exploring the Dreamweaver Workspace
- Creating a Web Site
- Understanding Web Design Guidelines
- Adding Keywords to a Web Site
- Understanding HTML and XHTML
- Adding Text to a Web Page
- Importing Text to a Web Page
- Formatting Text and Working with CSS Styles

Adobe Dreamweaver CC is a widely used Web site design program. Combining sophisticated design tools with an easy-to-use interface, Dreamweaver makes it simple for anyone to create and manage many types of Web sites.

Dreamweaver offers design environments that are friendly to both new and experienced designers. A new user does not have to be HTML literate to create a Web site in Dreamweaver. Dreamweaver's Design view, Code view, and Live view give you different ways to view your work and the Files panel allows you to easily organize and manage your site's pages and assets.

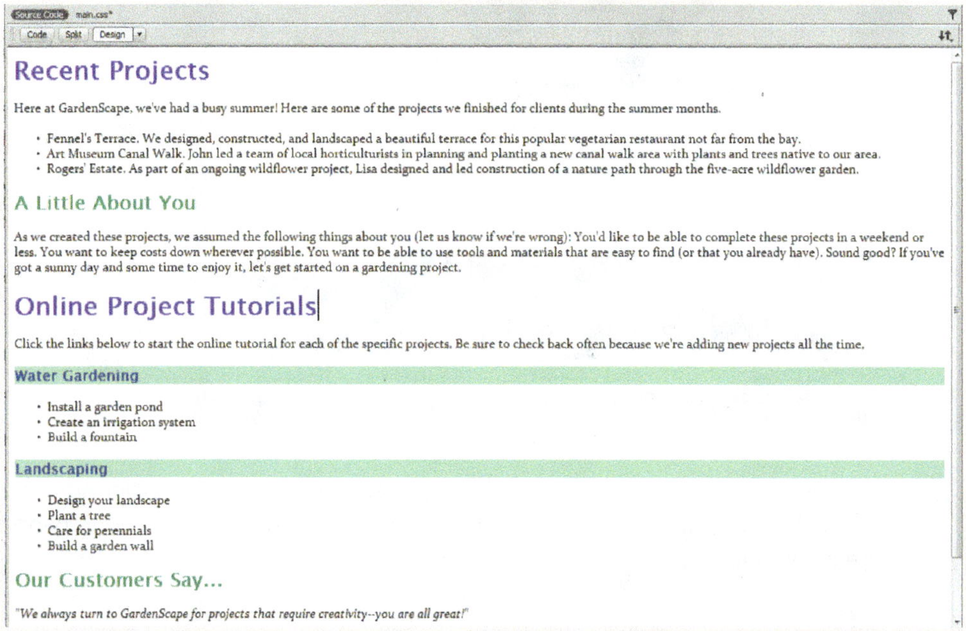

Exploring the Dreamweaver Workspace

When you start Dreamweaver CC, a Welcome screen opens, providing options for you to obtain stock images and to open brief tutorials on commonly used features. Close the Welcome screen to display the Dreamweaver Document window. You will see the menu bar at the top, and grouped panels along the right side of the screen. Notice the Files panel. This is the control center for your Web site, where you can see the files and other assets it contains. It functions in much the same way as your computer's file management program. You can create folders and subfolders within your site's root folder, open and save pages, and drag objects from the panel to a Web page.

A. Files panel
B. Workspace switcher

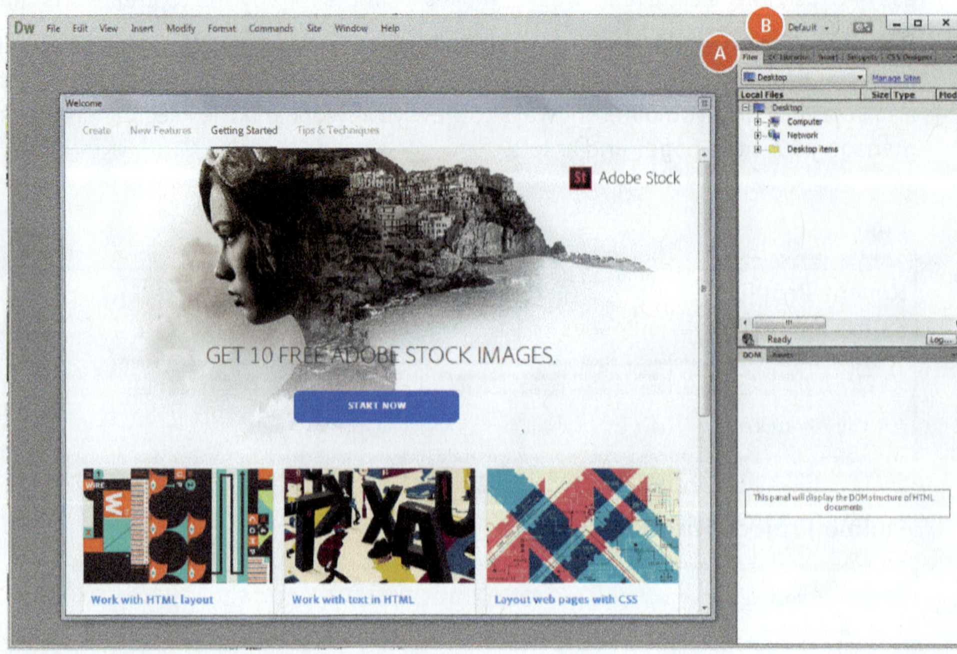

You should be familiar with the concept of panels from working in other Adobe applications in this course. In the Document window, you can open a Web page or create a new site.

Try It!

3. Start Adobe Dreamweaver CC. In Windows, choose Start > All Programs > Adobe Dreamweaver CC. On the Mac, click Adobe Dreamweaver CC in the Adobe Dreamweaver CC folder in the Applications folder.

4. Open a Web page. Click File > Open. In the Open dialog box, navigate to the data files for this lesson, open the **lillysgarden** folder, and double-click the **index.html** file. This is a Web page for a Web site under construction.

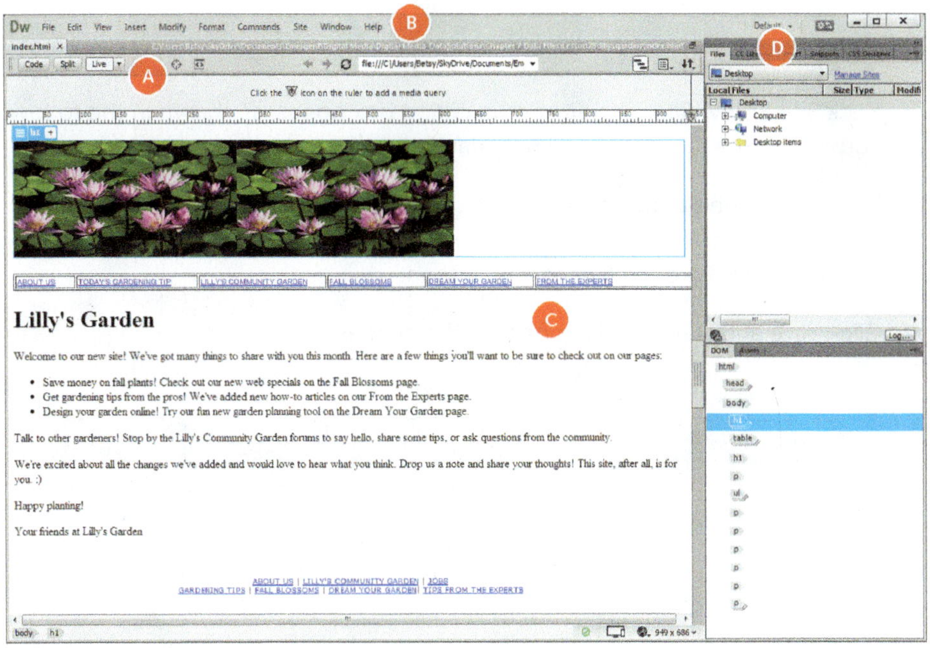

E. View buttons
F. Menu bar
G. Document window
H. Panel group

9. Click Window > Properties to open the Properties panel.
10. Click in the **Lilly's Garden** heading and view the properties shown for this heading in the Property inspector. Also notice the HTML tags for the heading in the status bar.
11. Collapse the Properties panel and all panels at the right side of the screen.
12. Open and close the panels at the right side of the screen. You can open panels by selecting them from the Window menu.
13. Rearrange the workspace by dragging the Properties panel into the Document window and docking the Files panel at the bottom of the Properties panel.
14. Click the Workspace switcher button and select the Beginner workspace option. Click the Workspace switcher again and return to the Default workspace.
15. Click File > Close. Close the document without saving it and leave Dreamweaver open for the next exercise.

Creating a Web Site

Dreamweaver simplifies the creation process by making it easy for you to begin designing your site. Initially you will be asked to provide a name and folder for the site, and later on, when you're ready to post the files to your server and publish online, you will be prompted to provide additional information that relates to the server technology.

Before you begin, you will find it helpful to plan your Web site. Identify the number of pages you need and do a simple sketch to show how the pages are linked and what content they will provide. This sketch will serve as a map as you begin creating your site and will save you time in deciding what content you need and where to place it.

Try It!

1. Click Site > New Site. The Site Setup dialog box opens, as shown in the following figure. The Site tab is selected by default.
2. Enter the name **gardenscape**. This is the root folder for your site. Click the Browse for folder button and navigate to the location where your teacher instructs you to store the files for this lesson.
3. Click Save and leave the file open for the next exercise.

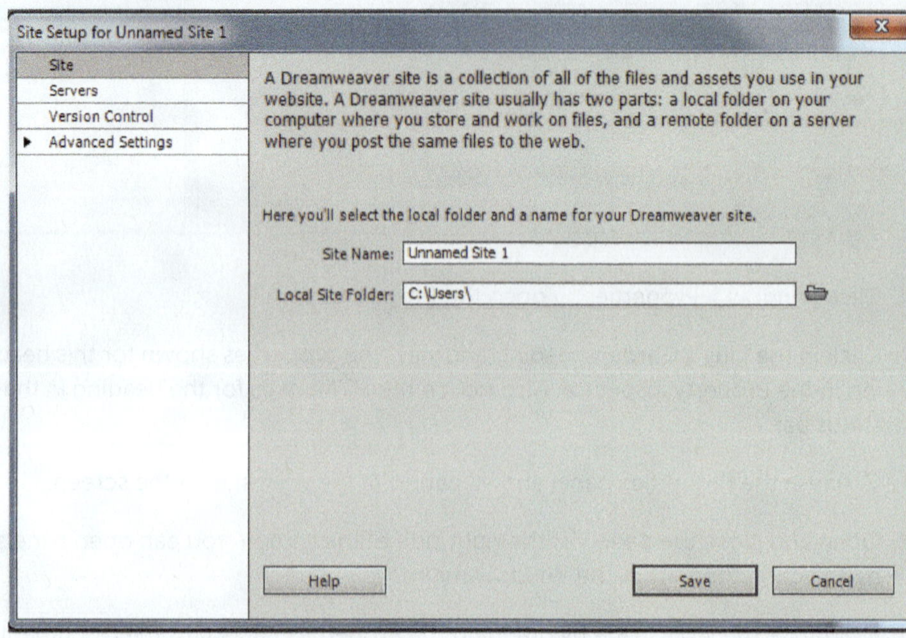

Create Web Pages

Your Web site content appears on documents stored within the Web site. These documents become the Web pages that visitors open when the Web site is published on a Web server.

Try It!

1. Click File > New to open the New Document dialog box.

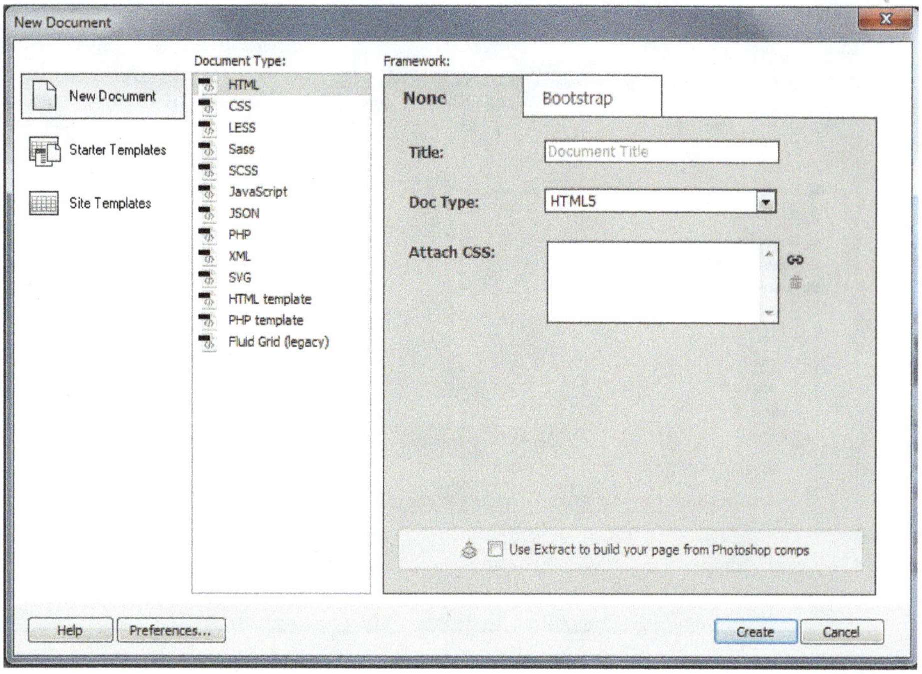

2. Select New Document. For the Document Type, the most common selection is the HTML option. Choosing this selection creates a blank page that uses XHTML to display page elements. Some types of Web content, such as content that changes dynamically based on certain controls on the page, require different selections. Click HTML, if necessary.
3. As part of the page creation process, you should also give each page a title. A page's title appears in the title bar of the browser when the page is opened. Enter **Home**.
4. Click Create.

5. Before you begin adding content to a new page, you need to save it. Click File > Save (or Save As). The Save As dialog box opens.

   The process of saving a document in Dreamweaver is very similar to saving files in any Windows program: Give the new file a name and specify the location where it will be stored. The Site Root button in the Save As dialog box makes it easy to jump right to the folder that contains your site files. This is especially handy when you are opening an existing file from a location outside your site and saving it to your root folder.

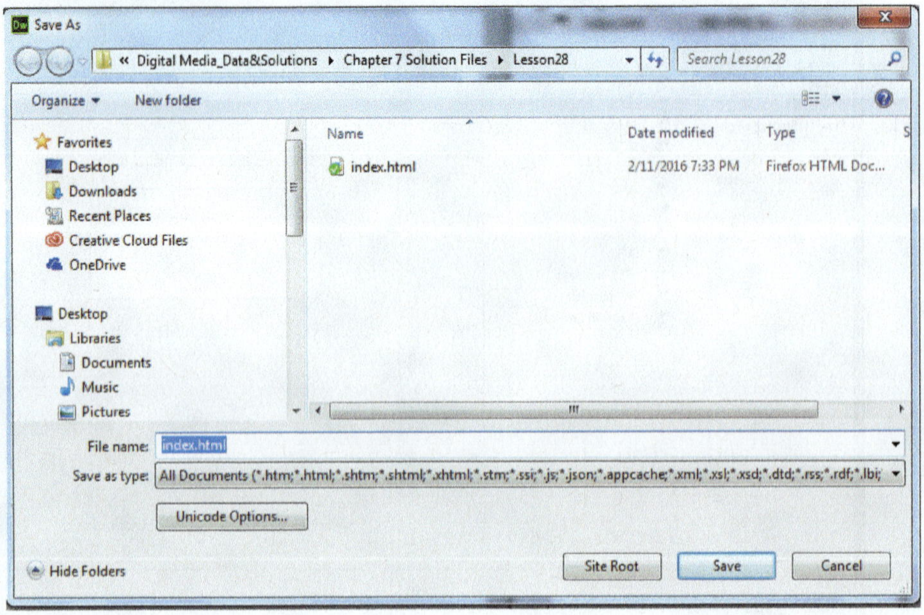

6. Enter **index.html** as the File name. Click the Site Root button and then click Save. After you save a page, the title bar shows the file folder and file name.

   Many servers expect the home page of a Web site to be named index.htm or index.html. The home page is the first page that opens in a Web site. This page usually gives general information about the site and includes links to other pages in the site.

7. Create another page. Click File > New, select HTML as the Document Type, and enter **GardenScape Services** as the title. Click Create.

8. Click File > Save As. Enter **services.html** as the File name. Click the Site Root button and then click Save.

9. Click File > New, select HTML as the Document Type, and enter **Contact Us** as the title. Click Create.

10. Click File > Save As. Enter **contactus.html** as the File name. Click the Site Root button and then click Save.

As you add pages or open existing pages, each page is opened in a tab in the Document window and in the Files panel. Click a page tab to select the page so that you can work with it.

View Site Files

The Files panel gives you easy access to your Web site and its files and folders. The Files panel group also includes the Assets panel, which allows you to track colors, images, and objects used in a site.

Try It!

1. If the Files panel is not displayed, click Window > Files.
2. Click the Expand/Collapse button in the right corner of the Files panel.
3. If there is a plus sign beside the gardenscape site folder, click it to display its pages. If there is a minus sign, click it to hide the pages.
4. With the pages displayed, double-click the services page. Notice that its tab becomes active in the Document window. Leave the site open for the next exercise.

Understanding Web Design Guidelines

Dreamweaver is an application that encourages creativity, and it gives you considerable support and assistance as you work to bring your ideas to life. Before jumping in and starting your site design, however, you may want to consider some design guidelines that can help you turn out professional quality pages.

- **Know your audience.** Who will be visiting your site? Thinking through what they expect to see— and then surpassing their expectations —will ensure a successful browsing experience for users.
- **Name your pages well.** Search engines pick up the titles you use—the title of your site as well as page titles. Make your titles clear and easy to understand.
- **Be consistent.** Consistency in color, graphics, and placement helps your visitor understand your site.
- **Make your site easy to navigate.** When visitors come to your Web site, they should be able to tell from your home page how to get around your site and find the features they need.
- **Pay attention to connection speed.** If it takes too long to download your Web site, your visitors will not return. Time is valuable, both theirs and yours.
- **Keep it simple.** Clean lines and clear, easy-to-read content are features you always should keep in mind when building your site.
- **Be unique.** When you copy another designer's site ideas, you are not only plagiarizing but also limiting your own ideas and site potential.
- **Take it easy.** Resist the temptation to overdo your site by loading it up with large image files or media objects. The more you add, the more you may affect your site download times. And visitors love fast-loading sites.

- **Respect your visitors.** Make sure your site looks professional from the very first moment it is online. Don't fall into the habit of posting a "construction guy" graphic or similar icon to notify your visitors that your site is under construction. If your visitors are visiting your site for information, when they don't find what they are looking for, they likely will look elsewhere

Adding Keywords to a Web Site

Keywords

Words or phrases that describe the site content and which are scanned by search engines to create the links that bring visitors to the site.

To make sure others can find and visit your site, you can supply **keywords** on your pages that search engines use to index a site in their databases. You add keywords to the Head section of a site. Think carefully about the keywords you enter to make sure they summarize the important content on your Web site, and be selective. Some search engines accept only a specific number of keywords and ignore keywords altogether if too many are supplied.

Try It

1. In the gardenscape site, click the index.html tab in the Document window.
2. Click Insert > HTML > Keywords.
3. Add the following keywords, separating them with a comma: **landscaping services, garden design**.
4. Click OK.

Understanding HTML and XHTML

HTML (Hypertext Markup Language)

The code used to create Web pages

HTML Tags

Formal name for HTML markup element. HTML tags appear inside angle brackets (< >).

XHTML (Extensible Hypertext Markup Language)

The current version of HTML that combines HTML structure with XML power and flexibility.

XML (Extensible Markup Language)

A type of markup language, similar to HTML, that enables designers to create their own data tagging system and structure.

If you choose, you can create a Web site in Dreamweaver without ever having to work directly in HTML at all. But any person interested in learning Web design really needs a basic understanding of HTML. HTML skills help you understand what's going on behind the scenes on your pages and give you the ability to better control the styles and attributes of page elements. What's more, with HTML you add keywords to your pages, which enables people searching on the Web to find your site. HTML5 is the most recent version of HTML.

About HTML and XHTML

HTML (Hypertext Markup Language) is a scripting language—or code—you use to create pages that can be viewed with a Web browser. Nearly every item on a Web page—including text, formatting, pictures, and other page elements—is controlled by HTML coding. Unlike some programming languages, HTML is text-based and easy to read and follow. Even developers with little programming experience can read and generally understand what's happening in HTML code.

Dreamweaver supports **XHTML (Extensible Hypertext Markup Language)**. XHTML is a reformulation of HTML4 that uses **XML (Extensible Markup Language)**. XML is a language that uses tags to structure information, similar to HTML. Unlike HTML, however, XML allows you to create your own tags to fit your information more specifically. XHTML was developed to answer a need for a stricter version of HTML that could be used to deliver content across a wide variety of devices: not merely computer browsers, but also mobile phones, laptops, PDAs, and so on. XHTML combines the standard HTML structure with the power and flexibility of XML.

The value of using a program such as Dreamweaver is that you do not have to work with HTML, XHTML, or XML in order to create Web content. Dreamweaver automatically applies the correct coding (also known as *markup*) as you select features from its menus and panels. As you become more proficient with Dreamweaver, however, you may find that you want to "tweak" the code for a specific page element. Knowing the basics of HTML coding can help you to trouble shoot page display problems and easily modify page elements. The following information gives you a brief tutorial in HTML basics.

HTML Document Structure

HTML documents have a standard structure that consists of two sections: a Head section and a Body section. The Head section contains information that browsers need to display the Web page, such as the page title and the character set used to create the page. None of the information in the Head section appears in the browser except the page title, which displays in the browser's title bar.

The Body section contains the actual Web page content, such as the page's headings, paragraphs, and pictures.

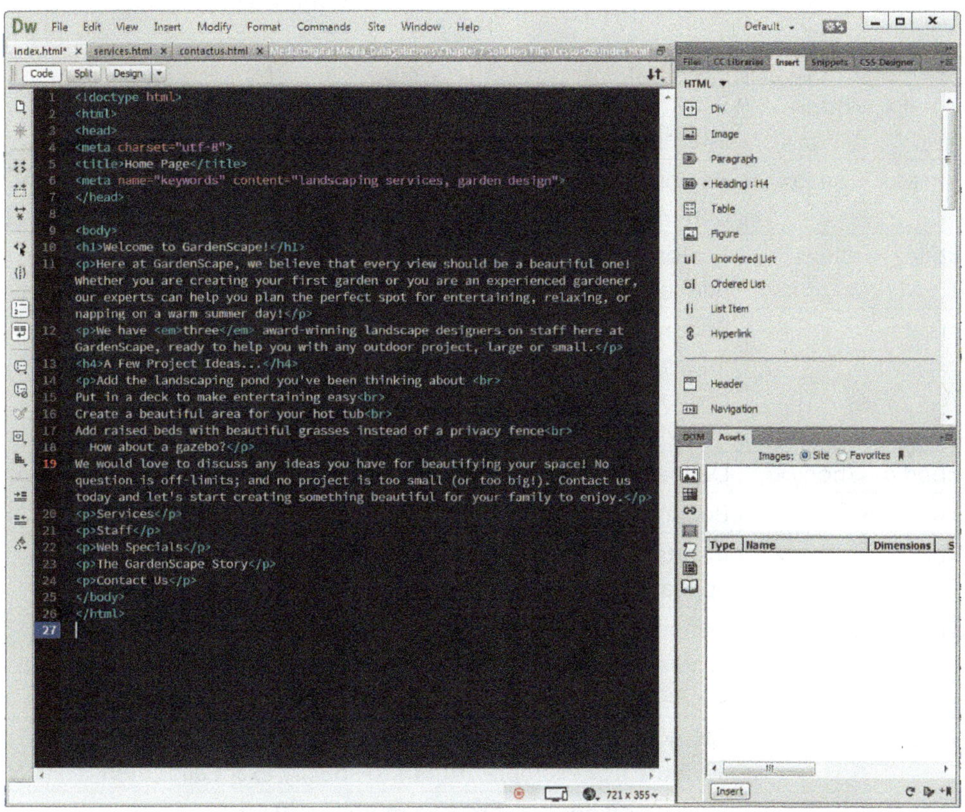

HTML coding instructions are delivered to the browser by means of **HTML tags**. As you can see in the figure, HTML tags have a specific structure, or syntax:

- The first part of an HTML tag is the left wicket (<).

> **Note:**
> HTML tags may be written with all capital letters or all lowercase letters. Dreamweaver's tags are all lowercase, so that convention will be used in this book.

- Next is the tag element, or name, such as title or h2.
- Last is the right wicket (>).

Most HTML codes require both an opening tag and a closing tag. The opening tag instructs the browser to begin displaying a format or feature (for example, <title>). The closing tag usually has the same syntax as an opening tag, but also contains a closing switch (/) before the tag element (for example, </title>). Text that appears between an opening tag and a closing tag is affected by that tag.

Tags may be nested to supply additional formatting to text. For example, in the following HTML code, the word three will appear in italics in the paragraph: <p>We also have <em>three</em> award-winning landscape designers on staff!</p>.

Tag attributes modify a tag element by supplying additional instructions to the browser about how to display an element. Attributes appear within HTML tags, usually between the tag element and the right wicket. Attributes often include values that give specific instructions to the browser. Attribute values are usually enclosed in quotation marks. Typically, attributes are not repeated in closing tags.

Common HTML Tags

You can use dozens of HTML tags and attributes to create sophisticated effects on Web pages. The following table lists some of the most common tags.

Tag(s)	Result
<html> </html>	Sets the page as an HTML document so that its code can be interpreted by the browser software.
<head> </head>	Begins and ends the section that contains information on content, language, and keywords for the page.
<title> </title>	Encloses the Web page's page title. In a browser, the page's title appears in the browser's title bar.
<meta>	Records information about the current page and supplies information such as keywords that search engines use to identify your page. (Does not require a closing tag and appears in XHTML coding as <meta />.)
<body> </body>	Defines the section of the Web page that displays in a browser.
<p> </p>	Begins and ends a paragraph on the Web page.
 	Inserts a line break. (Does not require a closing tag and appears in XHTML coding as .)
<h1> </h1>	Defines the first heading level (Heading 1). Use the same syntax for other heading levels, such as <h2> </h2>, <h3> </h3>, etc.
<align> </align>	Changes the alignment of text between the tags; requires an attribute (for example, "right") to specify exact alignment.
<ol> </ol>	Begins and ends an ordered (numbered) list.
<ul> </ul>	Begins and ends an unordered (bulleted) list.
<li> </li>	Identifies each item in an ordered or unordered list.
<dl> </dl>	Begins and ends a definition list.

Tag(s)	Result
<a> </a>	Identifies a hyperlink; requires the href attribute and a value to specify the target of link.
<img> </img>	Indicates location of a picture in a Web page.

Adding Text to a Web Page

After you have set up your site and created pages, you are ready to add content. Your pages should contain a balance of text and graphics to make the pages both informative and attractive. You can display rulers on the pages so you can easily position content on the page.

A newly opened Dreamweaver document displays a blinking insertion point at the top left of the Document window. To enter text on a page, simply begin typing at the location of the insertion point. Type the text as you would in a word-processing document; there's no need to press Enter at the end of each line. Dreamweaver wraps the text automatically at the right side of the page. Press the Enter key only when you want to start a new paragraph.

Dreamweaver automatically inserts a line space after a paragraph, so you do not have to double-space between paragraphs as you might do in a word-processing document. If you do not want the default space to appear after a paragraph, you can insert a line break rather than a paragraph break.

Note:

As a general rule, Web page paragraphs do not have a first-line indent. Dreamweaver does not recognize tabs or spaces at the beginning of paragraphs.

Try It!

1. Click the tab of the index.html page in the Document window. Click in the page, click Format > Paragraph Format > Heading 1, and enter the following text: **Welcome to GardenScape!**
2. Press Enter or Return.
3. You will enter the remaining text for this page by copying and pasting from a data file. In your file management program, navigate to the data files for this lesson and open gardenscape_text.txt using a text editor (like Windows Notepad).
4. Select all the text and click Edit > Copy. Close the text editor without saving changes.

5. In the index.html page, click Edit > Paste to paste the text onto the Web page. Click File > Save to save the page.

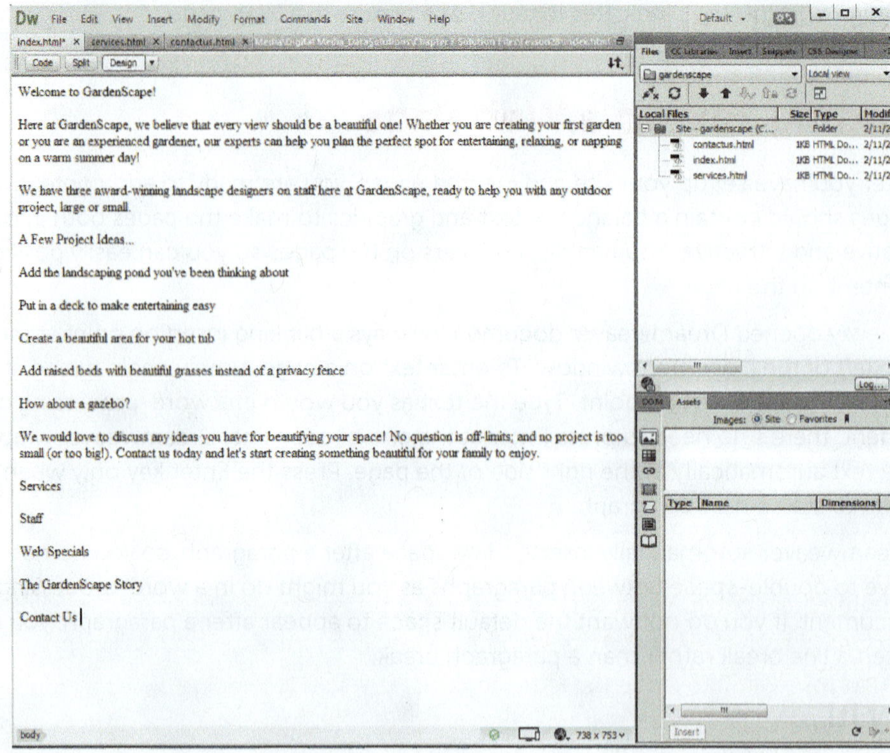

6. Click the contactus.html page tab. Type the following text:

   Contact GardenScape

   We want to hear from you! Contact us anytime by calling us at 800-555-5555. Or, e-mail one of our design experts:

   Landscaping Design: john@gardenscape.com

   Water Gardens: lisa@gardenscape.com

   Bridges and Walls: tom@gardenscape.com

   Natural Habitats: linda@gardenscape.com

7. Click File > Save, and leave the page open for the next exercise.

Use Paragraph and Heading Tags

You can format the text on a Web page with standard HTML paragraph and heading tags that control font style and size. By default, all new text is formatted with the Paragraph format. This format equates to the HTML <p> (Paragraph) tag. Heading levels are ordered from largest (Heading 1) to smallest (Heading 6).

You can apply limited formats, such as bold, italics, and bulleted or numbered lists, using the Properties panel and the Format menu options but you have much greater flexibility and control using cascading style sheets, which you will learn about later in this lesson.

Try It!

1. On the contactus.html page, select the heading. Click Format > Paragraph Format > Heading 1.
2. Display the index.html page. Click Window > Properties to open the Properties panel.
3. In the second paragraph, select the word "three." In the Properties panel, click the Italic button.
4. Click in the line, *A Few Project Ideas*, and click Format > Paragraph Format > Heading 2.
5. Select the text for the five ideas below the line, *A Few Project Ideas*.
6. Click Format > List > Unordered List to apply a bullet list style.
7. Click File > Save All, and leave the site open for the next exercise.

Use Code and Design Views

The Document window displays page content in Design view. In Design view, content looks almost identical to the way it will appear in a browser. In Live view, your page appears just like it will in a browser.

When you switch to Code view, the page content's HTML coding appears. You can write or edit HTML code while working in Code view. You can also display both views in the Document window at the same time so you can see immediately the results of your coding.

Try It!

1. Display the index.html page, if necessary.. Click the down arrow on the Design button and switch to Live view.
2. Click the Code button to display Code view.
3. Click the Split button to display both Code and Design view. Locate the HTML tags that have been applied to the text you just formatted. Also, notice the code in the Head section, where the code for keywords is entered.
4. Click the Design button to switch back to Design view. Leave the page open for the next exercise.

Importing Text to a Web Page

With Dreamweaver, it's easy to import existing text from other sources, such as Microsoft Word or Excel. The easiest way to insert Office text in a Dreamweaver page is to use the File > Import > Word Document or File > Import > Excel Document menu command. Word text inserted this way is imported into the current page, and its text is converted to HTML text indistinguishable from other HTML text on the page. Excel spreadsheet text inserted this way displays on the Dreamweaver page in tabular format that can be edited just like any other tabular material you might create using Dreamweaver's table tools.

You can also insert text using the Copy and Paste commands, as you learned earlier in this lesson. When pasting, you can choose the Paste Special command to choose from the following paste options:

- Text only pastes the copied material as basic text. Excel data pastes as a block of text without any tabular organization.
- Text with structure pastes the copied material with its basic paragraph or spreadsheet structure in place.
- Text with structure plus basic formatting pastes the copied material with structure plus any bold or italic formatting that has been applied.
- Text with structure plus full formatting pastes the copied material with structure and all applied formatting, such as font color or cell fill color.

If both the Office document and the Dreamweaver page are open on the screen at the same time, you can simply select the content you want to use and drag it from the Office document onto the Dreamweaver page. This moves the content from the Word document to the Dreamweaver page and gives you the same result as using the Text with structure plus full formatting paste option.

Opening Office HTML Files

All Microsoft Office applications include the capability to save documents in HTML format. A user can, for example, create a Word document or Excel workbook and save it as an HTML file that will display in a browser the same as any page created in Dreamweaver.

Office files that are saved in HTML format can be opened in the same way as any Dreamweaver page, using the File > Open menu command. Office HTML files are opened as complete pages, rather than being inserted on an existing page, as is the case with importing or copying.

The pages you open this way take their file names (and page titles, for Word files) from the original HTML page, but you must still save the new page as part of the site.

Word HTML pages may contain coding that is not necessary in Dreamweaver, making the files larger than necessary. To strip out unnecessary codes, use the Commands > Clean Up Word HTML menu command.

Try It!

1. Click the services.html page tab. You need to add some text to this page: Click at the beginning of the page.
2. Click File > Import > Word Document. Navigate to the data files for this lesson and double-click the **newtext.docx** Word document.

Try It!

1. GardenScape wants to add a page that will offer online tutorials for popular gardening projects. Click File > Open. Navigate to the data files for this lesson and open **projects.html**.
2. Click File > Save As, click the Site Root button to save it with the site files, and then click Save. Click Yes if a message box opens, asking if you want to update links.
3. Close the original **projects.html** data file by clicking the Close button on its tab in the Document window.
4. Display the Properties pane, if necessary, and enter a document title of **Garden Projects**.
5. Click Window > CSS Designer to display the CSS Designer panel. Click the All button, if necessary. Click Window > DOM to display the DOM panel. The DOM panel shows an HTML "tree" for the content on your page. This view helps you visually map elements in Design view or Live view with their HTML markup and the applied selectors in CSS Designer.
6. Click the Add CSS Source button and select Create a New CSS Style.

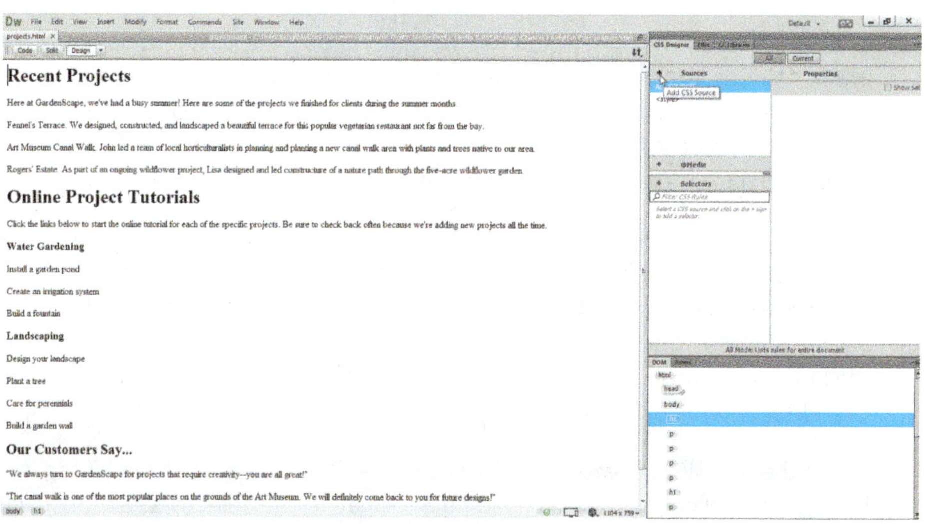

7. In the Create a New CSS File dialog box, click Browse. In the Save Style Sheet File As dialog box, click the Create New Folder button and name the folder **styles.** Open the styles folder and in the File name box, enter the style name of **main**. In the Relative to box, make sure Document is selected. Click Save. Click OK in the Create a New CSS File.
8. Select the heading *Recent Projects*. Notice the h1 tag is highlighted in the DOM panel, indicating that the text is formatted as an h1 heading.

9. In the Selectors section, click the Add Selector button and notice that *body h1* appears highlighted in the pane. Press the Up arrow key to drill down to the h1 tag. Then press Enter or Return.

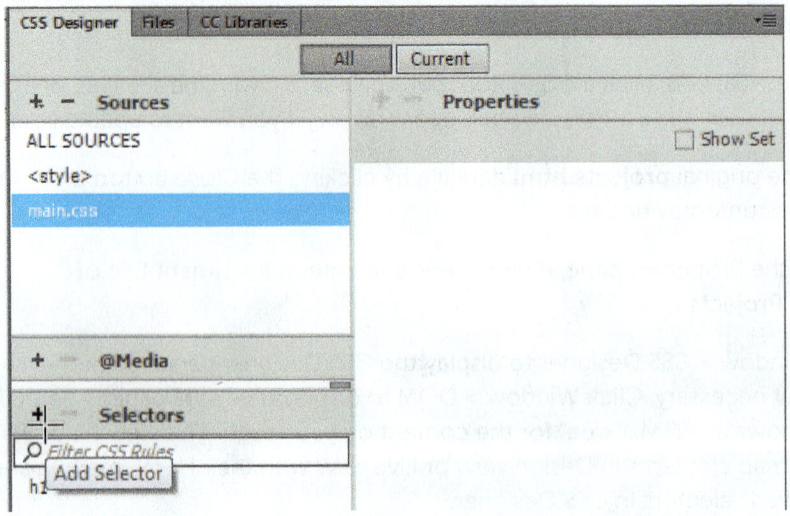

10. In the Properties section, deselect the Show Set box. The properties for the highlighted selector (h1) display.

> **Note:**
>
> The term selector in the CSS Designer refers to the terminology of CSS rules. A rule consists of the selector, which is the name of the styled element, and the declaration, which defines the style's attributes.

11. Click the Text button, and in the text formatting options, click the Set color box. In the text box, enter **#5B08B6**. Click the font family box and select the family with that contains Lucida Grande. For the font weight, click bolder. For the font size, click pt, type **24** and press Enter or Return. Notice that the formatting is applied to both h1 headings on the page.

12. Select the subheading, *Our Customers Say*. Notice in the DOM panel, that the h2 tag is highlighted indicating this is a heading 2 format. In the Selectors section, click the Add Selector button, press the Up arrow key to drill down to the h2 tag, and press Enter or Return. In the Properties section, click the Text button. Click the Set color button and enter **#009966**. Change the font-family to the Lucida Grande font family, the font-weight to bold, and the font-size to 18pt.

13. Select the text *Water Gardening*. Notice in the DOM panel, that the h3 tag is highlighted indicating this is a heading 3 format. In the Selectors section, click the Add Selector button, press the Up arrow key to drill down to the h3 tag, and press Enter or Return.

14. In the Properties section, click the Text button. Click the Set color button and enter **#003399**. Change the font-family to Lucida Grande, the font-weight to bold, and the font-size 14. The style is applied to both h3 headings on the page.

15. Click in the first sentence under the Recent Projects heading. Notice in the DOM panel that the text is formatted in the default *p* for paragraph. Click the Add Selector button. The body p tag should be highlighted. Press Enter or Return.

16. In the Properties section, click the Text button. Click the font-family box and select the font family that begins with Constantia. Click the font-size box, select pt, type **12**, and then press Enter or Return. The new font is applied to all paragraph (p) text on the page.

17. Select the list of items beneath the *Water Gardening* heading. The list is currently formatted as paragraph text but you want to change it to a bulleted list. Click Format > List > Unordered List. Repeat for the list under the *Landscaping* heading and the list of the three recently completed projects at the top of the page.

18. Select one of the unordered lists. In the CSS Designer, make sure main.css is still selected as the source. Click the Add Selector button, and press Enter or Return for the body ul li selector. In the Properties section, click the Text button. Apply the Constantia font in 12-point size to the list. All three bulleted lists are reformatted with the new style.

19. Insert a blank line before the *Online Project Tutorials* heading. Click Format > Paragraph Format > Heading 2 and type **A Little About You**. Press Enter or Return.

20. On the new line, make sure the format is set to <p> and type the following:

    As we created these projects, we assumed the following things about you (let us know if we're wrong): You'd like to be able to complete these projects in a weekend or less. You want to keep costs down wherever possible. You want to be able to use tools and materials that are easy to find (or that you already have). Sound good? If you've got a sunny day and some time to enjoy it, let's get started on a gardening project.

21. Select the three quotes from customers at the bottom of the page. Click Format > HTML Style > Italic. This applies the italic format to those three lines only, instead of to all text on the page that is in paragraph (p) format.

    You can easily modify styles by making changes in the Properties section of the CSS Designer.

22. Make sure the h3 rule is selected in the Selectors section. In the Properties section, click the Background button. Change background-color to **#9FC**.

23. Click Commands > Check Spelling and correct any spelling errors on the page.

24. Your page should look similar to the figure below. Click File > Close. Click Yes to save changes and leave the site open for the next exercise.

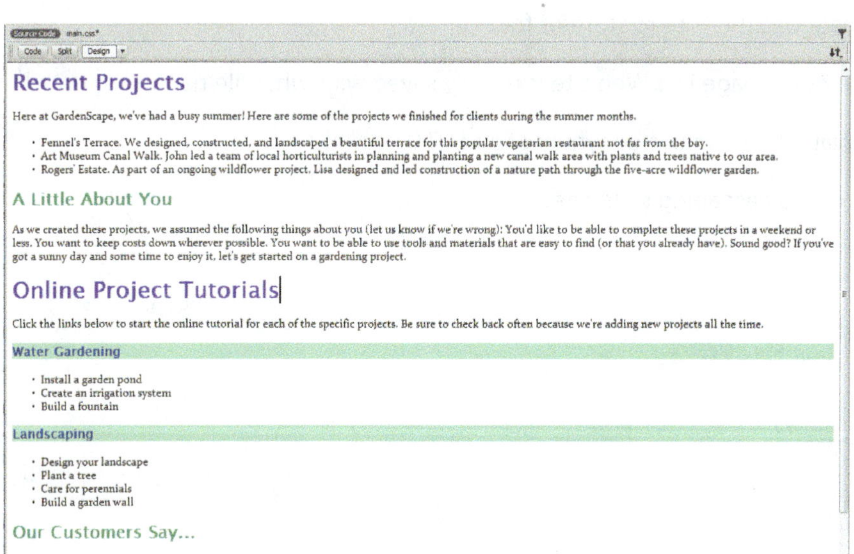

Attaching Styles to Other Pages

As was noted earlier, your CSS formats apply only to the current page; your Web site must have a valid http:// address in order for the styles to apply to all your pages. However, you can attach the styles to other pages in your site.

Try It!

1. Click the **index.html** tab to make the page active.
2. Click the Add CSS Source button in the CSS Designer and select Attach Existing CSS Style.
3. Browse to the **styles** folder in your site root folder and double-click the **main.css** file. Click OK in the dialog box. Check the page to see that styles were applied properly.
4. You want to center the heading on this page only. Select the heading. On the CSS Designer, click the Add CSS Source button and select Define in Page. With <style> selected in the Sources section, click the Add Selector button, press the Up arrow to drill down to the h1 heading, and press Enter or Return. Click the Text button in the Properties section. From the text-align options, click the Center button.
5. Attach the **main.css** file to other pages in your site. Again, review all pages to see that styles were applied properly. If necessary, make sure the main heading on all pages is formatted as an h1. On the articles.html page, format the list of topics covered in the expert articles as an unordered list. Change the title of each expert article to an h2 heading.
6. Click File > Close All. Click Yes to save changes. Then, close Dreamweaver.

Comprehension Check

1. What's the first thing you should do before you begin designing a Web site in Dreamweaver?
2. What does the "site root" refer to?
3. The home page in a Web site is usually saved with what file name?
4. Explain the structure or syntax of an HTML tag.
5. What is a cascading style sheet?

Review Project

Before you start Dreamweaver and create a new Web site, you will find it helpful to plan your Web site. In teams of three to five, select a topic in which you are all interested. This could be anything—a hobby, a sport, a community service program, an academic subject, and so forth.

Plan a Web site for the topic. Determine the content you think will appeal to visitors to your site. Identify the number of pages you need. On a poster board, do a simple sketch to show how the pages are linked and what content they will provide. Insert symbols to represent graphic images, photos, and any multimedia elements you want to include. Assign team members responsibilities in gathering the information and resources for your Web site. Add the list of assignments to the poster. You and your team will create the Web site in the Review Project at the end of the next lesson.

Lesson 29 Overview

In this lesson, you will learn about:

- Creating Links
- Previewing a Web Page
- Applying Colors, Rules, and Background Images
- Inserting Graphics on a Web Page
- Inserting Animation on a Web Page
- Working with Audio and Video
- Publishing a Site

You can integrate files that you create in other applications into your Web site. For example, you might add digital photos that you've enhanced in Photoshop, illustrations that you've created in Illustrator, and animations that you've built in Flash. You can even add audio and video clips. You can add these, and other interactive elements to your Web site to create new levels of impact and interest. These elements are an important part of the overall look and feel of the site, and are an effective tool for engaging viewers.

Your site's navigation system is equally important. Links provide connections between Web pages that allow visitors to find and navigate your site. You can create links on a Web page that link from page to page in a site, to an e-mail address, and from your site to other Web sites.

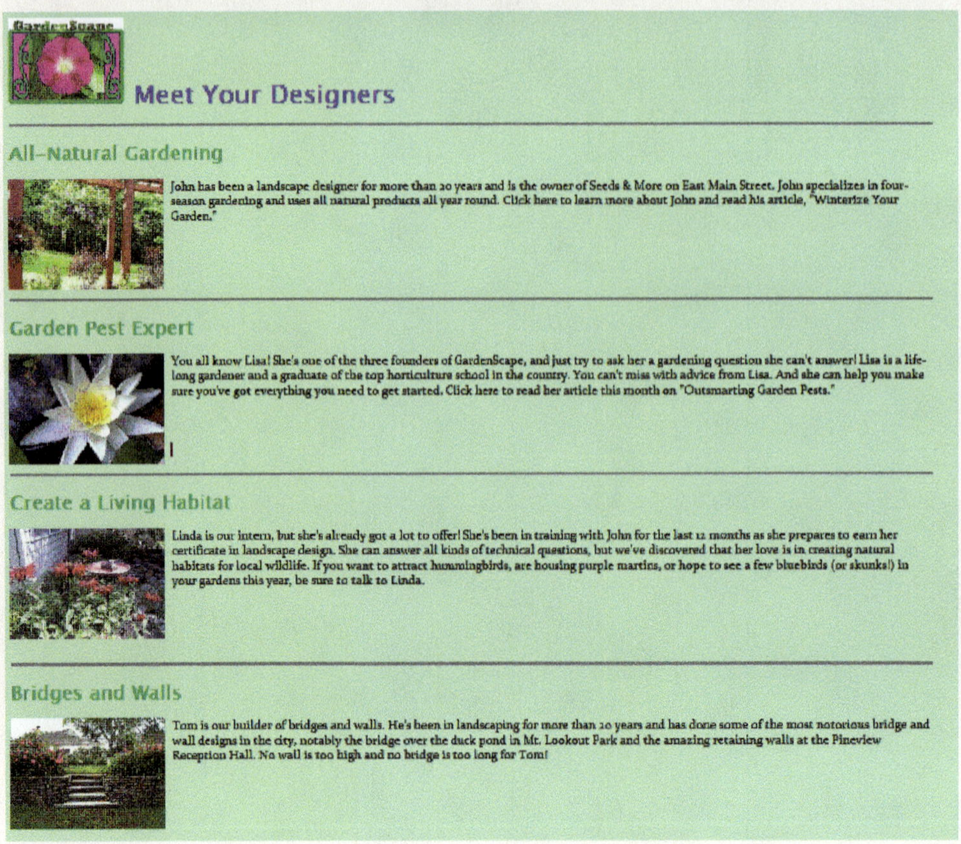

Inserting Links on a Web Page

Web sites rely heavily on **links**. Links are the means by which visitors "jump" and "browse" among Web pages and sites on the Internet. Links work by directing a browser to open a page at a specific World Wide Web address called an URL (uniform resource locator). The URL www.gardenscape.com/, for example, tells the browser to find the site and open its home page on the GardenScape server on the World Wide Web (www). Alternately, this URL could tell the browser to find the server that hosts Gardenscape, which may be one of many sites on the server (a Web server can host more than one Web site).

Links
Connections between pages in the same file or different files.

Links are typically formatted in such a way that they stand out from surrounding text so visitors can easily recognize them. They are usually in a different color and underlined.

You can create several types of links in Dreamweaver:

- Text links—links created using a word or phrase.
- Named anchor links—links from one location on a page to another location on the same page.
- E-mail links—links that open an e-mail program so a visitor can send a message to a Web site's e-mail address.
- Graphic links—links created using an image or icon on a page.

Creating a Named Anchor Link

A **named anchor**—also called a bookmark—is a specific location in a Web page (such as the top of the page). After you create a named anchor, you can create a link to help visitors navigate to that point on the page.

Named anchor
A named location in a Web page that is used for links on the same page.

Try It!

1. Start Dreamweaver. On the Files panel, click the disk drive arrow and select the **gardenscape** site that you worked on in the last lesson.
2. Double-click **articles.html** to open the page.
3. Scroll to the bottom of the page. Click after the *Pond Care and Maintenance* line and press Enter or Return.
4. Switch to Live view. The tag selector for the new paragraph should be selected. Click the Insert panel and in the HTML category, click Paragraph.

5. In the position assist interface, click Before. A new paragraph element appears in the layout, with the placeholder text *This is the content for Layout P Tag*.

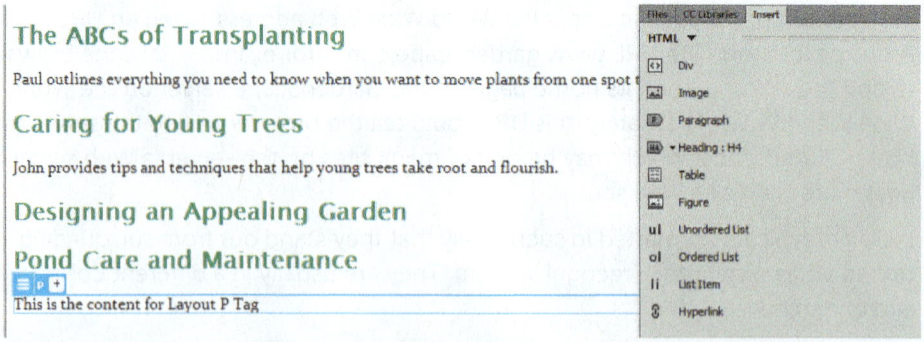

6. Double-click the Placeholder text and type **Back to Top**.
7. Select the Back to Top text. Click the Hyperlink icon and type **#top** in the Link field. Press Enter or Return. The #top code creates a link to a target within the current page.
8. Switch to Design view. Click Window > Properties.
9. Scroll to the top of the page and click before the title word Articles!

10. In the Properties panel, type **top** in the id field and press Enter/Return. Click before the title again. Notice the tag selector for the paragraph in the status bar changes to #top.

11. Click File > Save, and then close the page.

Creating Relative and Absolute Links

Links can be either *relative* or *absolute*. A **relative link** is a link to a page within your Web site. All of your Web site pages are stored together within a single folder. These pages remain in the same locations relative to each other even after a Web site is published to a Web server. An **absolute link** takes a visitor from a page within your site to a different Web site. Because the browser must open a new Web site, it needs the full URL for the page it is to open.

Relative link

A link to a page within a site; it does not include the domain name.

Absolute link

A link from a page within one site to a different Web site; it includes the complete path name in the URL.

Creating Text Links

To create a text link, select the text you want to use as the link and then use the Properties Panel Link text box to set up the link.

To create a relative link to a page in your site, type the address of the page you want to link to directly in the Link text box. You only need to type the page name, instead of the entire URL; for example, *contactus.html*. Or, click the Browse for File button to the right of the Link text box to open the Select File dialog box, which lists your Web site pages. You can also use the Point to File icon on the Property inspector to point directly to a page to which you want to link.

As soon as you complete the page name, Dreamweaver underlines and changes the color of the selected text to indicate it is a link.

If you want to create an absolute link, enter the complete URL in the Properties panel Link text box. Make sure you use the proper protocol, such as http:// or ftp://.

You can remove a link by selecting the text used as the link and clicking the Link list arrow on the Property inspector. On the list that appears, click in the blank area at the bottom of the list. You can also right-click a link and select Remove Link from the context menu.

Try It!

1. Double-click the **index.html** page in the Files panel to open it.
2. Select the text *Services*. In the Properties panel, click the Point to File button and drag it to the **services.html** page in the Files panel. Repeat this process to link the text *Projects* to the **projects.html** page and the text *Contact Us* to the **contactus.html** page.
3. Delete the text *Web Specials* and *The GardenScape Story*.
4. Enter the text **National Garden Association** just below *Contact Us*.
5. Select the text and in the Link text box, enter the URL **http://www.garden.org/**.
6. Save the index.html page and leave it open for the next exercise.

Link to E-Mail Address

One of the most helpful items to place on your site is a link to an e-mail address where your site visitors can send you questions, feedback, comments—even complaints.

When creating an e-mail link, select the text you want to use as the link and then type *mailto*: followed by the designated e-mail address in the Property inspector's Link box. Or, select the Email Link item on the Insert panel. In the Email Link dialog box, enter the e-mail address in the Email text box and click OK.

Try It!

1. On the index.html page, select the text *Contact us today* text in the paragraph below the bullet list.

2. Click the Insert panel and select Email Link.

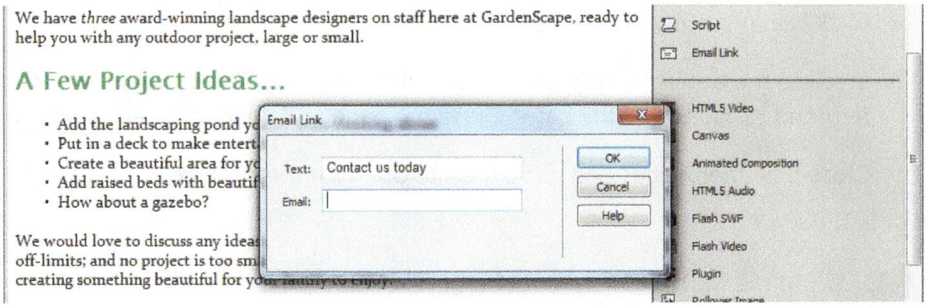

3. In the Email Link dialog box, enter the e-mail address **lisa@gardenscape.com**. Click OK.
4. On the contactus.html page, select each of the individual e-mail addresses and follow the instruction in steps 2-3 to create email links for each expert. Notice that the e-mail address will automatically be entered in the Email Link dialog box.
5. Click File > Save and leave the page open for the next exercise.

Previewing a Page

You can use the Preview in Browser feature at any time to see how your Web page will look when viewed by a site visitor. Once you have set up links, you can move from page to page in the browser to make sure the links are correct.

Try It!

1. With the index.htm page displayed, click File > Preview in Browser. Select a browser from the submenu. The page should open in the browser you selected.
2. Click the Contact Us link near the bottom of the page. Your browser should display the contactus.html page.
3. Click one of the e-mail links on the contactus.html page. A dialog box will open asking you to choose an application with which to open the link. Because this is a fictional email address, click Cancel.
4. Click the Back button and then click the National Garden Association link. Your browser should display the association's Web site. Close the site.
5. Close your Web page.

6. In Dreamweaver, close the index.html and contactus.html page and open the articles.html page.

7. Click File > Preview in Browser.

8. Scroll to the bottom of the page and click the Back to Top link. You should be returned to the top of the page. Close the page and your browser.

9. Close any open pages and leave the site open for the next exercise.

Applying Colors, Rules, and Background Images

You can add background color and images to a Web page to add interest and help communicate your message. You use the Page Properties dialog box to apply colors and images.

Try It!

1. Open the **articles.html** page and change the title at the top of the page to **Expert Articles**.

2. Click Modify > Page Properties.

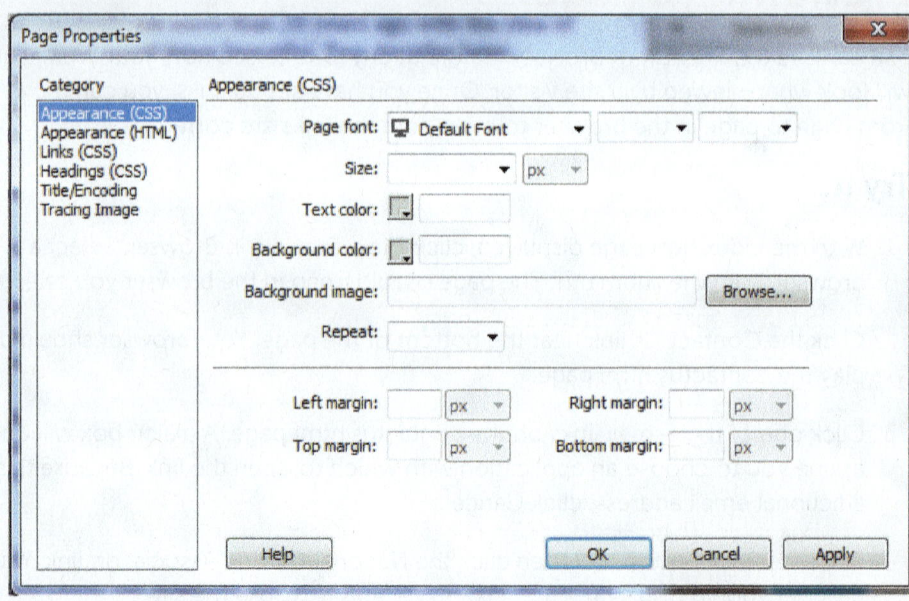

3. In the Page Properties dialog box, click the Background color box and enter **#AAFFC6**. Click OK.

4. Click File > Open. Navigate to the data files for this lesson and open the **designers.html** file.

5. Click File > Save As. Save the page in the location where your Web site files are stored. Click Yes to update links in the message box.

6. Open the Properties panel, if necessary, and enter **Meet Your Designers** as the Document Title. Change the title of the page to the same.
7. In the CSS Designer, click Add CSS Source and then click Attach Existing CSS File. Browse to the styles folder in the site root and double-click **main.css**. Click OK.
8. Change the background color of the page to the same color (#AAFFC6) you applied to the articles.html page. Apply the same background color to the **services.html** and **projects.html** pages.
9. Open **index.html** and insert the text **Our Expert Designers** between the Projects and Contact Us links at the bottom of the page. In the Properties panel, drag the Point to File icon to the **designers.html** file in the Files panel. Insert the text **Expert Articles** after the *Our Expert Designers* link. Select the text and create a link between it and the **articles.html** page.
10. Click Modify > Page Properties.
11. Click the Browse button next to the Background image box. Navigate to the data files for this lesson and double-click the **squares.jpg** image. Click OK.
12. Apply the squares.jpg background image to the **contactus.html** page.
13. Click File > Save All and leave the site open for the next exercise.

Inserting Horizontal Rules

You can add horizontal rules on your Web pages to separate sections of text. Position the cursor at the beginning or end of a paragraph and select the Horizontal Rule element on the Insert panel. If you position the cursor at the end of a paragraph, the horizontal rule is inserted below the paragraph. If you position the cursor at the beginning of a paragraph, the horizontal rule is inserted above the paragraph.

By default, a rule runs the full width of the Web page. You can change the width and height (thickness) of a rule in the Properties panel. Select the Shading checkbox in the panel to add shading to the rule that makes it look three-dimensional. Deselect this checkbox to make the rule a solid color.

Try It!

1. On the **designers.html** page, click before the heading *All-Natural Gardening*.
2. On the Insert panel, click Horizontal Rule. In the Properties panel, enter 3 in the H box and deselect the Shading checkbox.
3. Click on the rule and press Ctrl + C to copy it. Click in front of the heading *Garden Pest Expert* and press Ctrl + V to paste it. Repeat for the other two headings on the page.
4. Click File > Preview in Browser to check all your pages and links. When you are done, close your browser.

5. Save and close all open pages and leave the site open for the next exercise.

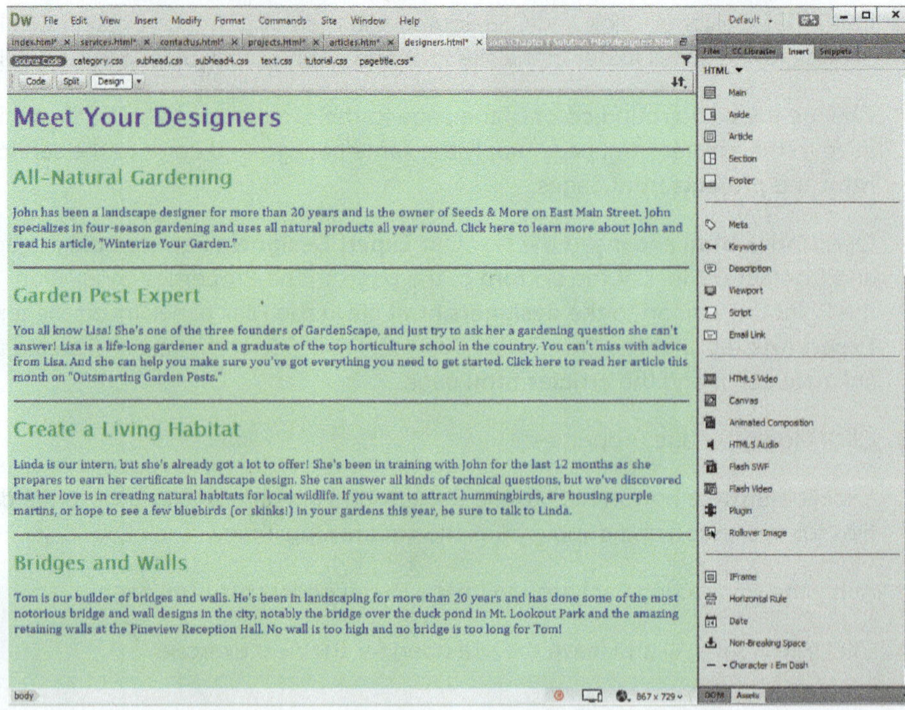

Inserting Graphics on a Web Page

The images you add to your Web sites are an important part of the overall design. Images illustrate ideas in your text, welcome the visitor to the page, or simply provide something beautiful or interesting that connects to your site content in some way.

As you add image files to your Web site, Dreamweaver prompts you to save the files to your Web site's root folder so they will be available to display in the browser.

You can store the files directly in the Web folder. However, for larger sites that may include many files, it is better site management to create a subfolder for graphic files.

You can create a subfolder in the Local Files pane of the Files panel. Right-click any file and select New Folder to insert a new folder in the site. Then type a new name for the folder, such as *images*.

Try It!

1. On the Files panel, right-click the gardenscape site name in the Local Files list and click New Folder.
2. Enter **images** as the name of the folder.
3. Drag the **squares.jpg** background image into the new images folder.
4. Open the **index.html** page. Insert a blank space before the main heading. On the Insert panel, click the Image element. The Select Image Source dialog box opens.

5. Navigate to the data files for this lesson and double-click the **gslogo.png** file. A dialog box may open telling you that the file is outside of your site's root folder. Click Yes to copy the file to the root folder.
6. In the Copy File As dialog box, the files and folders for your root folder should be displayed. Double-click the **images** folder to open it, and then click Save.
7. Click File > Save and leave the page open for the next exercise.

Adding Alternate Text

You can specify alternate text for an image. Alternate text displays in place of the image in text-only browsers. If a site visitor is using a screen reader, the alternate text is read aloud so the visitor knows the content of the image. Some browsers display alternate text as a ScreenTip when you rest the mouse pointer over the image, while other browsers, such as Firefox and Mozilla, do not.

Alternate text should be kept fairly short; Dreamweaver suggests no more than 50 characters. Search engines do pick up the alternate tags on your images, so if the keywords of your site fit the image you're displaying, feel free to include them as part of the alternate text. Don't load your alternate text with keywords, though, because that is considered bad form and could cause search engines to skip your site altogether.

Some images that you insert, such as those used to create a navigation bar, may not require alternate text. However, you should still specify a value for the Alt attribute to satisfy accessibility standards. If you don't want to enter a phrase, you can add a null value by clicking the Alternate text list arrow and selecting <empty>.

It is important to remember that images can significantly increase the size of a page and, even if a visitor is using a broadband connection, increase its download time. (This is especially true with digital photographs, which can produce very large files.) A page that loads too slowly is an inconvenience to your site visitors, so you should try to keep download times low by eliminating or reducing large image files.

The download time is based by default on a connection speed of 56.0kbps. You can set a different connection speed for this measurement in the Preferences dialog box in the Status Bar category.

Try It!

1. Click Window > Properties to display the Properties panel, if necessary
2. Click in the Alt text box and enter **GardenScape Logo** as the alternate text.

Copying an Image and Using the Library

Often, you will want to use an image repeatedly on other pages in your site. You can copy and paste the image within your site root folder.

Try It!

1. On the Files panel, open the images folder if necessary. Right-click the **gslogo.png** file, point to Edit, and then select Copy. Right-click on the images folder, point to Edit, and select Paste. Right-click the copy, point to Edit, click Rename, and enter **small_logo.png** for the new file name.
2. Open **services.html.** Click to the left of the main heading. Click and drag the **small_logo.png** file from the images folder to the left of the main heading. Supply the alternate text **link logo**.
3. In the Properties panel, change the width of the image by entering **150** in the W box. Change the height in the H box to **110**.
4. Click in the Link box, click the Point to File button and drag it to **index.html** in the Files panel. This establishes a link between the services.html page and the index.html page. In a browser, the viewer can click on the logo graphic to return to the home page.

   You can also use the Library to store and copy images. The Library feature in the Assets panel is a handy tool that saves you time and enables you to use the same elements repeatedly—while still being able to update and change them in every Web page that uses the element. This reduces creation time, especially when you are working with a team that has a variety of skills.

5. With the small logo still selected on the services page, click Modify > Library > Add Object to Library. Name the file **small_logo**.

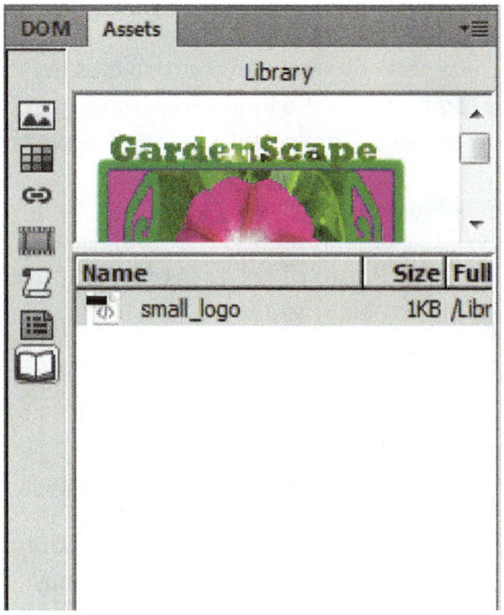

6. Open **articles.html** and drag the icon of the **small_logo** from the library to the left of the main heading.

7. Open **designers.html** and drag the **small_logo** image to the left of the main heading. Repeat for the **projects.html** and **contactus.html** pages. Now, each page contains a graphic link to the home page. Save and close all open pages and leave the site open for the next exercise.

Modifying an Image

Click an image and its properties appear in the Properties panel. Notice that a thumbnail-size version of the image appears at the left side of the panel. You can use an image to link to other pages or sites in the same way you use text. Select the image and then type the link address in the Link text box, or use the Point to File icon or Browse for File button to specify the link target. You can modify an image in the following ways:

- You can resize an image by specifying exact measurements in the W and H boxes. You must supply both a width and a height, as Dreamweaver does not automatically resize proportionally if you supply only one dimension. Image sizes are measured in pixels, which is a common Web design standard. You can also use the sizing handles on an image to adjust its size. Drag a corner handle to resize proportionately.
- You can adjust the alignment, padding, and margins of an image by creating a CSS in the CSS Designer. You can align it left, right, or centered. And you can specify for text to wrap around the image.

Try It!

1. Open the designers.html page. Position the insertion point to the left of the *All-Natural Gardening* heading.
2. On the Insert panel, click the Image element. Navigate to the data files for this lesson and double-click the **terrace.jpg** file. Save the image in your images folder. Enter **Photo of terrace design** as the alternate text. Change the width to 200 and the height to 140.
3. Insert the **lotus.jpg** image to the left of the paragraph under Garden Pest Expert. Save the image in your images folder. Enter **Photo of water garden** as the alternate text. Change the width to 200 and the height to 140.
4. Follow the instructions above to insert the **butterfly.jpg** image to the left of the third paragraph. Resize it to 200 x 140 and add the alternate text of **Photo of butterfly garden**. Insert the **stonewall.jpg** image to the left of the fourth paragraph, resize to 200 x 140, and enter **Photo of stone wall** as the alternate text.
5. Select the terrace image. Display the CSS Designer. Click the Add CSS Source button and select Create a New CSS File. Click the Browse button and navigate to the styles folder in the Site Root folder. Enter **gardenimages** as the CSS File name and click Save.
6. Click the Add Selector button and type **.floatleft**. In the Properties section, click the Layout button if necessary, scroll down to the float option, and click the Left button.
7. Click Window > Properties to display the Properties panel. Click the Class down arrow and select floatleft. This wraps the text to the right of the image.

   Now, you need to add some space between the image and the text.
8. Make sure the image is still selected. In the Properties section of the CSS Designer, scroll to the margin option. Click the right margin setting and increase the size to 10px.
9. Select the image in the Garden Pest Expert section. In the Properties panel, click the Class arrow and select floatleft. Do the same for the remaining two images.
10. Add line spaces as needed to position the rules and text. Or, if time permits, experiment with CSS styles to make these adjustments. Your page should look similar to the following figure.

11. Close all pages and click Yes to save changes. Leave the site open for the next exercise.

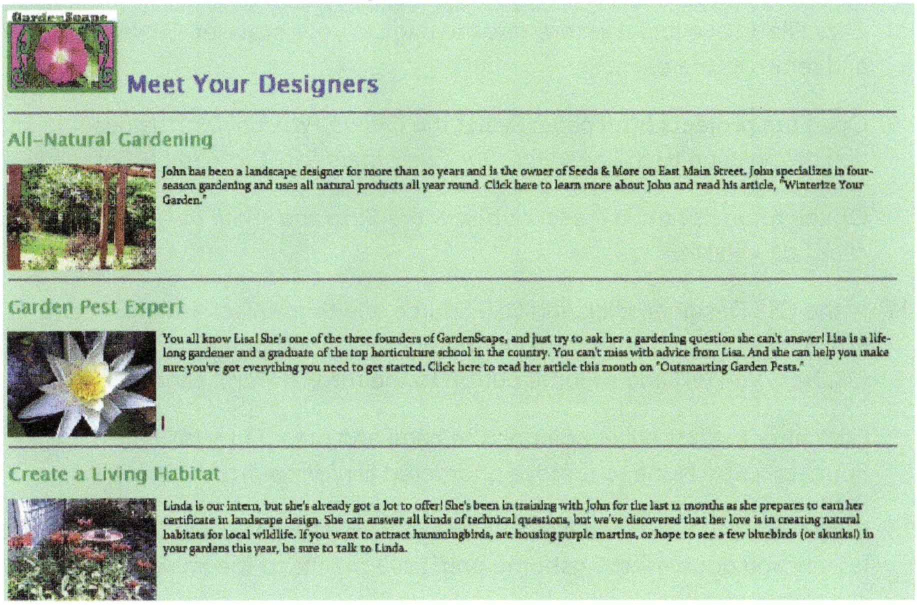

Inserting Animation on a Web Page

You learned how to create simple animations in Chapter 5 of this text. You can easily add Flash animations, symbols, and movies to a Web page to add new levels of impact, creativity, and interest. Remember as you're designing your site that a little animation goes a long way—so choose the best movies and use them sparingly.

When you insert a Flash file, Dreamweaver uses two sets of HTML tags to provide support for multiple browsers. The <object> tags are supplied for Microsoft browsers and the <embed> tags are supplied for browsers such as Netscape, Opera, and Mozilla. Flash movies (identified by the .swf extension) can be added to a Web document using menu commands or the Flash option on the Insert panel.

Try It!

1. Click File > Open. Navigate to the data files for this lesson and double-click **tutorials.html**. Save it in the gardenscape site root folder. Click Yes to update links, if necessary. In the Properties panel, enter the Document Title of **Tutorials**.

2. Close the original **tutorials.html** data file by clicking the Close button on its tab in the Document window.

3. Position the insertion point in the blank paragraph below the main head. On the Insert panel, click Flash SWF.

4. In the Select SWF dialog box, navigate to the data files for this lesson and double-click the **garden.swf** Flash file. Save the file in your images folder and enter the title **garden movie**. Click OK.

5. Change the size to W 325 and H 250. If necessary, click the Loop check box to select it.

6. Change the view to Live mode. The animation will automatically start playing.
7. Switch back to Design view.
8. Click File > Save and then preview the page in your browser. Close your browser and return to the page.
9. Open the **projects.html** page. Select the *Online Project Tutorials* heading and the text below it, up to the heading, *Our Customers Say*. Click Edit > Cut.
10. On the tutorials.html page, click below the *Stop and smell the roses* text, and click Edit > Paste.
11. In the CSS Designer, click Add CSS Source and then select Attach Existing CSS File. Browse to the styles folder in the site root, and double-click **main.css**. Click OK. Now you will add a Home button to the tutorials.html page.
12. Click after the last bullet point on the page and press Enter or Return. Click Format > List > None to remove unordered list format from the line.
13. Click the Insert panel and click the Image item. Navigate to the data files for this lesson, and double-click **gshome.png**. Save the file to the **images** folder in your site root folder.
14. Open the Properties panel if necessary. In the Link box, enter **index.html**. Click File > Save.
15. Open the index.html page. Enter the text **GardenScape Tutorials** after the *Expert Articles* link near the bottom of the page. Create a link between the text and the tutorials.html page.
16. Click File > Save All. Then, preview all your pages in your Web browser and test the links. Close your browser and return to the gardenscape site.

Inserting Rollover Images

You can use rollover images to add interactivity to a Web page. A rollover image is composed of two images. It is designed to replace one image with another. The original image loads with the page; when a site visitor hovers the mouse over the image, the original image is replaced by another.

Rollover images can be used in a number of ways on a Web site. Use them to show two different versions of an image or to display related images. Rollover images can also be used to create navigation buttons.

Try It!

1. Open the **index.html** page. Insert a blank line above the paragraph that begins with *We would love*.

2. On the Insert panel, scroll to and click the Rollover Image element. The Insert Rollover Image dialog box opens.

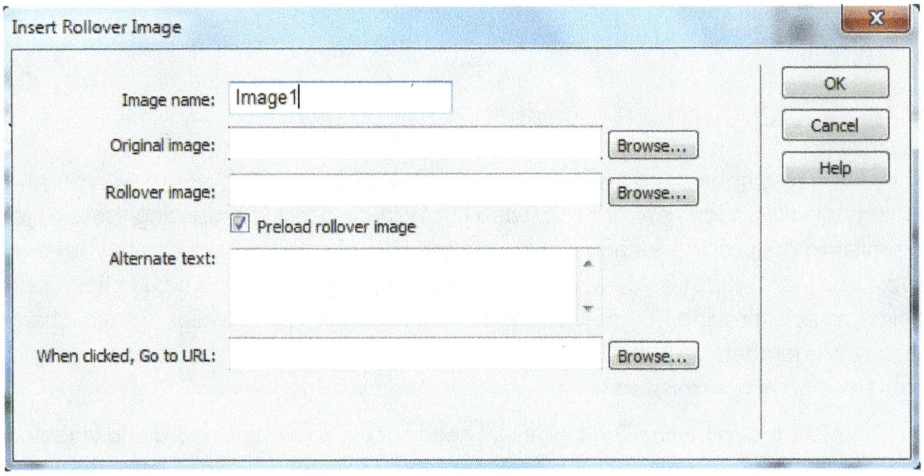

3. Enter Tutorials as the image name. Click the Original image Browse button and navigate to the data files for this lesson. Double-click the **Hyacinths01.jpg** file. Save the file to the **images** folder in the Site Root folder.

4. Click the Rollover image Browse button and navigate to the data files for this lesson. Double-click the **Hyacinths02.jpg** file. Save the file to the **images** folder in the Site Root folder.

5. Enter the Alternate text, **GardenScape's Tutorials**. For the URL, enter **tutorials.html**.

6. In the Properties panel, change the size of the image to 200px W and 140px H.

7. Switch to Live view. Save the page, and then preview the page in your browser. Close the page and return to the Document window.

   You might opt to organize all the page links on the index.html page in a table that can serve as a simple navigation bar.

8. On the index.html page, click at the end of the last paragraph (before the list of page links) and press Enter or Return.

9. Click the Insert panel and then click Table. In the Table dialog box, enter **1** for the Rows, **7** for the Columns, and **945** for the Table width. Click OK.

10. Select the Services link and click Edit > Cut. Click in the first cell of the table and click Edit > Paste. Repeat for the remaining six links.

11. Make sure the table is selected, and then display the Properties panel if necessary.

12. Click the Align down arrow and select Center.

13. Click File > Save, and then preview the page in your browser.

14. Check all the links on all the pages. Return to the Document window and make any modifications you feel are necessary. When you are satisfied with the look and functionality of your Web site, click File > Close All and save changes to all pages. Leave the site open for the next exercise.

Working with Audio and Video

In addition to graphics and animations, you can enhance your Web site with other multimedia files, such as audio and video clips. The process for inserting these objects is similar to the process for adding images and animations. You can create your own audio and video clips (as you learned in Chapter 6) or you can download clips. Some online sources provide free downloads of stock audio and video clips. Others charge a royalty or membership fee. As with all intellectual property, you should check copyrights and obtain permission to use work created by someone else.

To complete the following Try It, you will need access to sample audio and video clips.

Try It!

1. Open the **index.html** page and click before the logo at the top of the page.
2. On the Insert panel, scroll to and click HTML5 Audio.
3. Open the Properties panel, if necessary. In the ID field, enter **audio**, which is a unique identifier used to reference the audio object in the code.
4. Click the Browse button for the Source. In the Select Audio dialog box, navigate to the location where your sample audio file is stored, and double-click it. Click Yes, if you are asked if you want to save the file in the site root folder.
5. In the Title box of the Properties panel, you can enter text for the tooltip that will display in the browser. For the Fallback Text, you can enter text that will appear if the viewer's browser does not support audio. Click the Controls box if you want the audio controls to display on the page; click the Autoplay box if you want the audio to start when the page is opened; Click the Loop box to play the audio continuously; and click the Muted box to turn the track off during playback. The Preload options specify the method used to cache the audio when the page loads. Choosing the auto option will start the audio automatically.
6. Switch to Live view to test the audio. Preview the page in your browser.
7. To insert a movie clip, click the HTML5 Video option on the Insert panel. In the Select Video dialog box, navigate to the location where your sample video file is stored, and double-click it. Click Yes if you are asked if you want to save the file in the site root folder. In the Properties panel, you will set the same basic property options that you set for your audio clip.
8. Preview the page in Live view, and then in your browser.

9. When you are done reviewing, you can keep the audio and video clips on the page or delete them. To delete, simply select the object and press the Delete key. If you want to remove a clip from the site root folder, right-click it in the Files panel, click Edit, and then click Delete.

10. Close all open pages, and then close Dreamweaver.

Although multimedia files add an undeniable punch to Web pages, you must be careful when adding these embellishments. Multimedia files can add substantially to the size of the site, which may result in slow downloads that turn visitors off. Moreover, some multimedia objects, such as audio and video clips, may require a visitor to download a player before the object will display. This can be a time-consuming process that many site visitors will not want to bother with.

Publishing a Site

You may recall that when you start a new site in Dreamweaver, you entered a name for the site and designated a local folder in which to store the site's files. In the Site Setup dialog box, you could also specify the remote server to which you will publish the site. A remote server can be an intranet server within your company or school, a Web hosting company's server, or a server owned by a client or other third party. Some Internet Service Providers (ISPs) also provide free Web space to their customers.

If you did not specify a remote server, you can do so in the Manage Sites dialog box. Select Site > Manage Sites. In the Manage Sites dialog box, click the Edit the currently selected site button.

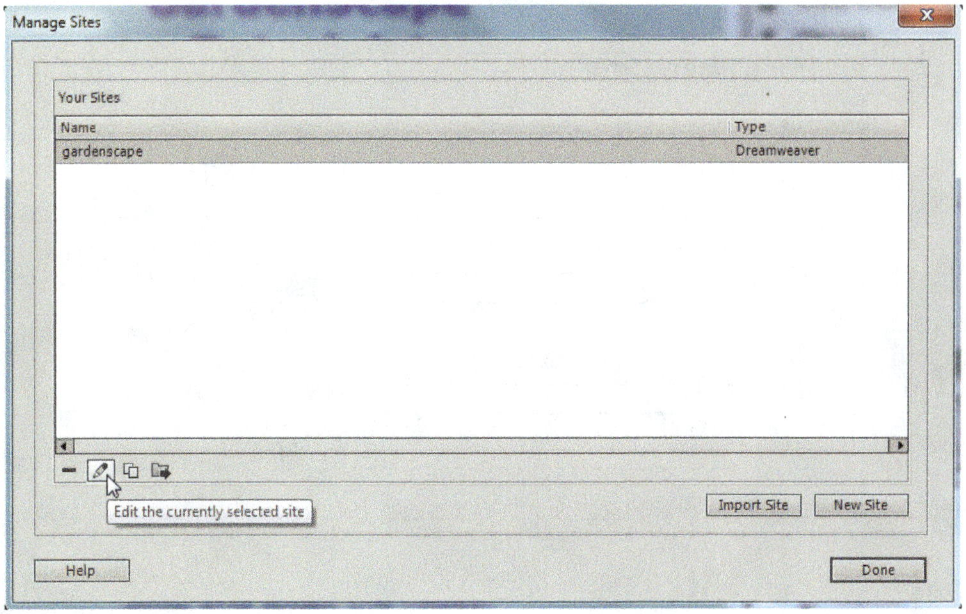

The Site Setup dialog box opens. Click Servers to open the panel where you can designate your server. Click the Add new Server button.

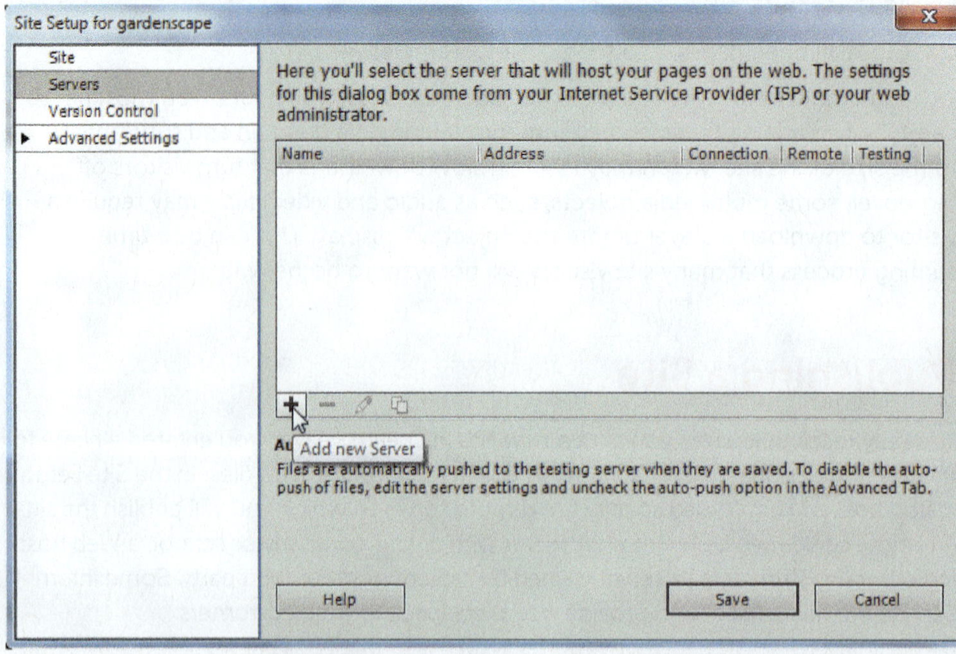

The server definition pane opens.

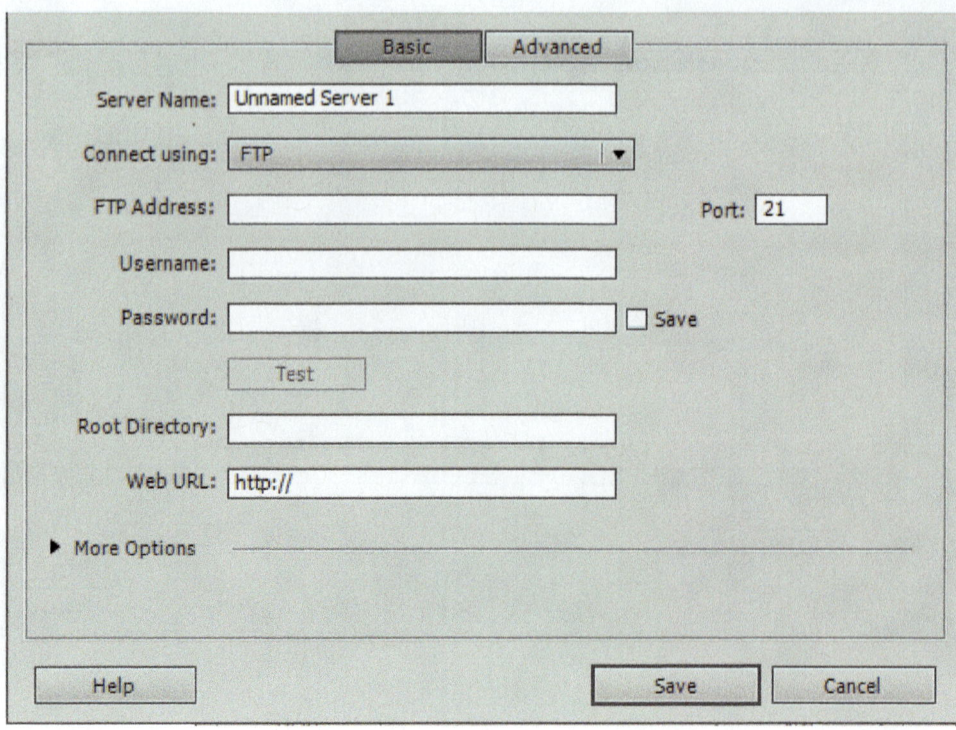

You will need to enter the following information:

- The Server Name is used internally by Dreamweaver, so you can enter a name of your choice.
- Select the method you want to use to connect to the server from the Connect using menu. The most common methods are FTP and SFTP. Enter the server's FTP address, your user name, and password in the appropriate text boxes.
- Click Test to test your connection.
- For the Root Directory, the value you enter will depend on your host server's policies. You will need to verify the path you need to enter after logging into your server to get to the folder when you want to install your index.html page.
- The Web URL text box should contain the URL for the folder that you entered as the Root Directory.
- Click Save to complete your server definition.

You will be returned to the Site Setup dialog box where you click Save to close it. In the Manage Sites dialog box, click Done.

Now you are ready to upload your Web site files from your local folder to the remote server. On the Files panel, select the site's root folder. Click the Put file(s) to "Remote Server" button. A dialog box will open, asking if you want to put up the entire site. Click OK. You can open your site in your remote browser to check that all files uploaded.

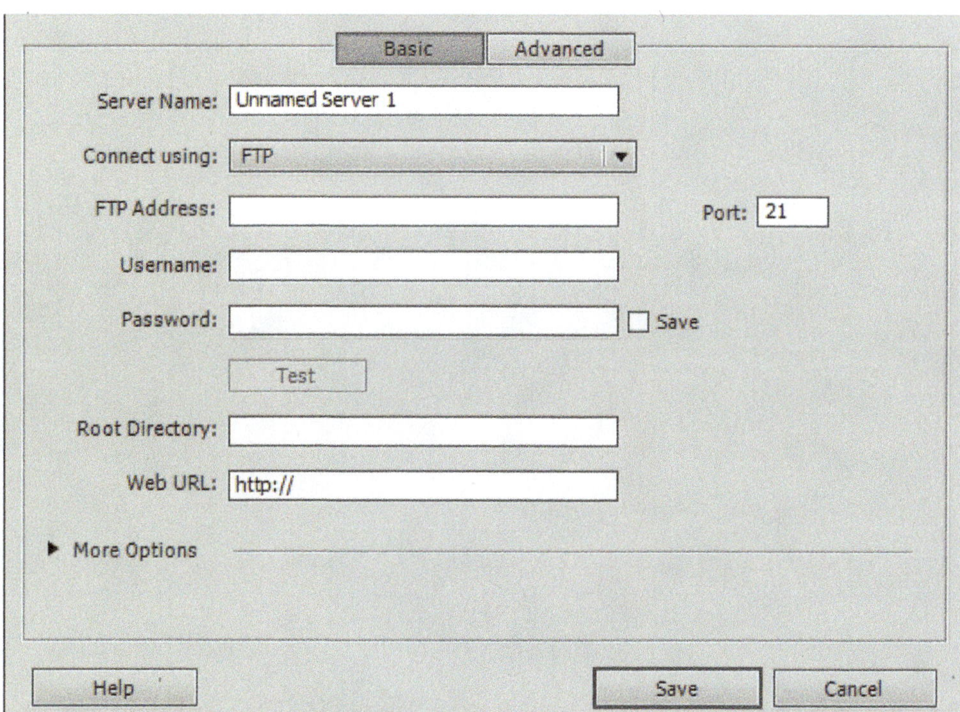

Comprehension Check

1. What are four different types of links you can create on a Web page?
2. What is the difference between a relative link and an absolute link?
3. Why would you specify alternate text for an image?
4. Why would you save files to the Library?
5. What is a rollover image?

Review Project

In the Lesson 28 Review Project, you and your team planned a Web site on a topic of your choice. Make sure each team member has obtained and/or prepared the content for which they were responsible. Using the sketch you created, build a new Web site on your topic. When you are done, preview the site in your browser. With your teacher's permission, publish your site to your school's remote server.

End-of-Chapter Activities

Review Questions

1. Explain the difference between a Web site and a Web page.
2. What is the different between a document's file name and its title?
3. What are keywords and why is it important to select them carefully?
4. What are the two sections that make up the HTML document structure?
5. How do you check spelling on a Web page?
6. What type of link contains the full URL for the page it is to open?
7. Why would you add a horizontal rule to a Web page?
8. Explain the steps for specifying a remote server to which you can publish a Web site.

Chapter 7 – Portfolio Builder

You will write an article on how to use technology to better prepare for college and career pursuits, develop new skills, and stay informed about the changing world around you. You will import the article to a page in a new Web site, build other pages in the site, and then enhance them with other multimedia elements.

DIRECTIONS

1. Open the file **C7_Outline.pdf** from the data files for this chapter. This file is an outline to help you prepare your article. With your teacher's permission, print the outline and then close the file.
2. Use the Internet, library resources, or information from your school's guidance counselor or career center to research the importance of technology to college and career readiness, lifelong learning, and daily living. Search for sites by typing keywords or phrases such as **using technology to prepare for college**. You might also try a Boolean search such as **technology AND "lifelong learning"**.
3. When you find a Web site with relevant information, bookmark it or print the desired pages. Make sure you can legally use the information.
4. Locate any images or photographs related to your research. Again, check copyright or fair use guidelines to make sure you can legally use them. You can also use your own images or photographs, if available.
5. Record your source citation information on a separate sheet of paper, including the sites from which you download images.
6. When you have finished your research, create a new word processing document and use the outline to write your article. The article should be 300-500 words long.
7. When you are finished, save and close the document.
8. Start Dreamweaver and create a new site named **Technology**. Create an index or home page that includes a title and a brief introduction. Use the Properties panel to apply formats to the text. Enter a document title for the page.
9. Enter at least three keywords for the site.
10. Create a new page in the site in which to import your article. Be sure to save it and assign a document title.
11. Add a heading and subheads, if desired. Create a new CSS file and apply styles of your choice to the various text elements on the page.
12. Create a third page in the site that will include a bio of you, the author. Write a paragraph about your education, extracurricular activities, skills, work experience, and interests. Format the text and insert a photo of yourself, if desired.

13. Create links among the pages and to Web sites that you think provide information that's relevant to your topic.
14. Apply rules and a background color or image to the pages, as desired.
15. Consider adding animation, audio, and video clips to enhance the content and provide impact.
16. Preview the pages in your Web browser
17. With your teacher's.permission, publish the Web site to your school's server.

Chapter 7 – Critical Thinking

DIRECTIONS

A Web site can be a powerful platform for communicating information and ideas. For this activity, you will evaluate the design and content of a Web site of your choice. Select a Web site of a local charity, business, academic institution, or other organization with which you are somewhat familiar. Create a word processing document in which you assess the site based on the following Web design guidelines. Provide examples of how the site met the guidelines or failed to meet them. When you are done, share your assessment with the class.

- **Know your audience.** Is the site's content what you expected to see?
- **Name your pages well.** Where did the site fall when you searched for it? Was it in the top list of hits found by your search engine?
- **Be consistent.** Is there consistency in color, graphics, and placement of images, links, and other objects?
- **Make your site easy to navigate.** Are you able to tell from the home page how to get around the site and find the features you need?
- **Pay attention to connection speed.** How long does it take to download the Web site?
- **Keep it simple.** Does the site have clean lines and provide clear, easy-to-read content?
- **Be unique.** Is the site unique and have its own look and feel?
- **Take it easy.** Is the site well-balanced with media objects, or does it have an overload of bells and whistles?
- **Respect your visitors.** Is the site fully functional, where all links work correctly and you can easily find what you are looking for? Is there a way to contact the site's publisher with questions?

A

B

C

E

I

J

K

L

M

N

O

P

Q

R

S

T

U

V

W

X

Z